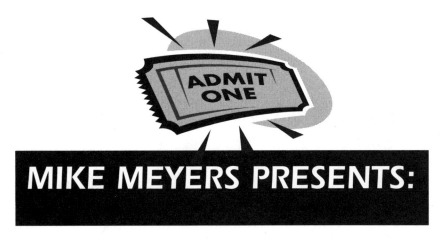

MIKE MEYERS PRESENTS:

Computer Literacy
Your Ticket to IC^3 Certification

SCOTT JERNIGAN

ELKS
Learning

12929 Gulf Freeway, Suite 105
Houston, Texas 77034
U.S.A.

Publisher
Dudley Lehmer

Editor in Chief
Scott Jernigan

Technical Editors
Martin Acuña, Dudley Lehmer, Mike Meyers

Simulation Developers
Dudley Lehmer, Janelle Meyers, Michael Smyer

Contributors
Martin Acuña
Cindy Clayton
Cary Dier
Tina Ferguson
Jane Holcomb
Libby Ingrassia
Dudley Lehmer
Mike Meyers
Jessica Stratton

Peer Reviewers
Kris Donnelly-Sasser
Jennifer Passman

Copy Editors
Cindy Clayton, Cary Dier

Indexer
Cindy Clayton

Composition
Donette Reil
Michael Smyer

Illustrator
Michael Smyer

Cover Design
Donette Reil, Kathy Yale

This book was composed with Adobe InDesign

Computer Literacy – Your Ticket to IC³ Certification
Scott Jernigan

ELKS Learning
12929 Gulf Freeway, Suite 105
Houston, Texas 77009
U.S.A.

To arrange bulk purchase discounts for sales promotions, premiums, or fund-raisers, please contact **ELKS Learning** at the address above.

Computer Literacy – Your Ticket to IC³ Certification

1234567890 DOC DOC 019876543

Book p/n 1234567890 and CD p/n 1234567890

parts of

ISBN 0-9768422-0-3	Paper Back book
ISBN 0-9768422-1-1	Hard Back book
ISBN 0-9768422-2-x	e-Book on CD of entire book
ISBN 0-9768422-3-8	e-Book on CD of only Computing Fundamentals section
ISBN 0-9768422-4-6	e-Book on CD of only Key Applications section
ISBN 0-9768422-5-4	e-Book on CD of only Living Online section

About the Author

Scott Jernigan wields a mighty red pen as Editor in Chief for Total Seminars. With an M.A. in Medieval History, Scott feels as much at home in the musty archives of London as he does in the warm CRT glow of Total Seminars' Houston headquarters.

Scott has edited and contributed to more than a dozen books on computer literacy, hardware, operating systems, networking, and certification, including co-authoring the best-selling *All-in-One A+ Certification Exam Guide*, 5th edition, and the *A+ Guide to Managing and Troubleshooting PCs* (both with Mike Meyers).

Scott has taught all over the United States, including stints at the United Nations in New York and the FBI Academy in Quantico. He is an A+ and Network+ certified technician, a Microsoft Certified Professional, a Microsoft Office Specialist, and, of course, Certiport Internet and Computing Core Certified.

About Mike Meyers

Mike Meyers is the best-selling author of numerous books on computer literacy and certifications, including *Introduction to PC Hardware and Troubleshooting*, and the *All-in-One A+ Certification Exam Guide*, the *All-in-One Network+ Certification Exam Guide*, and the *Network+ Guide*. Most consider Mike the leading expert on computer industry certifications.

Acknowledgments

Many people helped put this book together, and I could not have done *Computer Literacy* without them. The folks listed as Contributors put soul and time into writing, editing. Thank you.

Cindy Clayton pushed for this project for months. The addition of the delightful Audrey Clayton added extra gurgles to her outstanding editing and writing on this book.

Martin Acuña put the indelible stamp of his personality on the book, from his excellent writing and editing to the fun movie theme. It was great to work with you, my friend.

My publisher, **Dudley Lehmer**, gave me the encouragement to continue and go through the book birthing pains, knowing the end result would be something worthy for so many people.

Jenny Passman gave (and continues to give) fantastic feedback from the trenches, as she taught with this book as I wrote the chapters. A peer reviewer *par excellence*, Jenny's critiques and praise made this a much better book.

A hearty thanks goes out to the folks at *Desktop and Press* in Houston. **Donette Reil** did an outstanding job designing and implementing the layout of the book. **Don Carpenter** gave us superb advice on the publishing end of things.

Michael Smyer once again proved to be a sparkplug in the book-writing process. His photographs and illustrations give this book life, and he did a remarkable job of transitioning the book to InDesign. He consistently challenges me on technology, which, frankly, keeps me honest. Superb job, Michael!

My dear friend **Mike Meyers** provided a swift kick in the pants when I needed it and proved a worthy companion for many a late-afternoon gaming session to blow off steam.

Kathy Yale, Marketing Director for ELKS Learning and Total Seminars, provided endless enthusiasm for this project. Every time I talked with her I came away reinvigorated and ready to tackle the next chapter or challenge. She proved to be invaluable for getting this book from conceptualization to print.

My long-time right hand, **Cary Dier**, came in at the 11th hour to help finish off this book. I am indebted to her and very thankful. You're the best, my friend.

A special thanks to **Kris Donnelly-Sasser** who gave me some great feedback in the early stages of this book.

To my superb colleagues at Total Seminars, thanks for your work and support. **Janelle Meyers** did amazing stuff with the simulations. **Roger Conrad** and **David Dussé** back me up to the point that I couldn't get my job done without them—and they excel in their own jobs too!

Finally, to my wife, **Katie**, and my children, **Maggie** and **Simon**: Thank you for being there for me. I love you.

Dedication

This book is for my daughter, Maggie: your joy for learning inspires me and your laughter makes my heart lighter. I love you and look forward to reading this book with you.

IC³ . . . WHAT IS IT?

IC³, or the Internet and Computing Core Certification program, is a global training and certification program providing proof to the world that you are:

- Equipped with the needed computer skills to excel in a digital world.

- Capable of using a broad range of computer technology - from basic hardware and software, to operating systems, applications and the Internet.

- Ready for the work employers, colleges and universities want to throw your way.

- Positioned to advance your career through additional computer certifications such as CompTIA's A+, and other desktop application exams.

IC³ . . . WHY DO YOU NEED IT?

Employers, Colleges and Universities now realize that exposure to computers does not equal an understanding of computers. So now, more than ever, basic computer and Internet skills are being considered prerequisites for employment and higher education.

THIS IS WHERE IC³ HELPS!

IC³ provides specific guidelines for the knowledge and skills required to be a functional user of computer hardware, software, networks, and the Internet. It does this through three exams:

- Computing Fundamentals
- Key Applications
- Living Online

By passing the three IC³ exams, you have initiated yourself into today's digital world. You have also given yourself a globally accepted and validated credential that provides the proof employers or higher education institutions need.

Earn your IC³ certification today - visit www.certiport.com/ic3 to learn how.

CERTIPORT®

Achieve • Distinguish • Advance

Certiport is a registered trademark of Certiport, Inc. in the United States and other countries.

Whether you are seeking further education, entering the job market, or advancing your skills through higher ICT certification, IC^3 gives you the foundation you need to succeed.

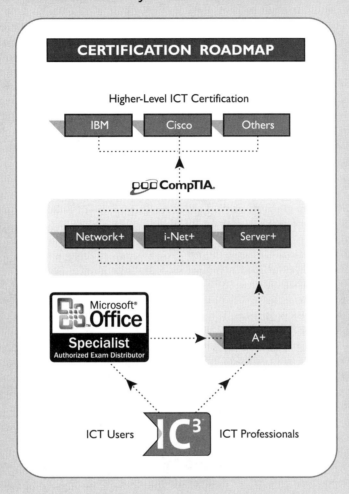

STAND OUT. *Certify Your Skills.*

In today's competitive economy, it's easy to get lost in the crowd. But that's not what you want. You want to stand out. With the Internet and Computing Core Certification (IC^3) you can.

Academic institutions around the world are taking advantage of IC^3 to help their students stand out and excel as they go on to higher education or career opportunities.

Your Future Starts with IC^3

www.certiport.com/IC^3

About This Book
The Right Tools for Today

Almost every skilled job today requires employees to use computers, so computer literacy is simply something that every person should possess. You need to know how computers work and how to perform basic tasks with word processing, spreadsheets, presentation software, and Internet browsers. Scott Jernigan's *Computer Literacy* puts these skills into students' hands, creating the foundation they need for success today.

Off the Script! sidebars provide interesting and often fun information that relates to the text students are reading, but diverges from the primary topic.

Lavish and Appealing Each chapter contains many high-quality photographs, screen shots, and illustrations that help students assimilate the material to become computer literate.

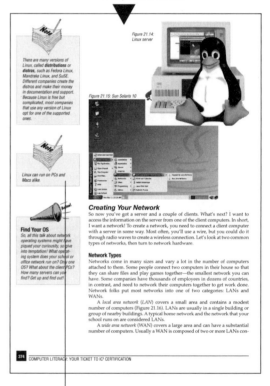

Real World Computer Literacy
This book offers students an overview of the current state of computing in the workplace, not just focusing only on exam topics. Students will read about and understand the latest technology and applications.

Action! *exercises prompt the students to try out the skills they're reading about or challenge them to go deeper into a technology.*

Notes *and* **Exam** *Tips keep students focused on essential information and provide insight into the IC³ exams.*

Concepts and Concrete Examples

Scott Jernigan's *Computer Literacy* explains the concepts behind technology and then goes the next major step by providing real-world, concrete examples of how to use the technology. Students come away from the book with knowledge about today's world and also with the information needed to take and pass the Certiport IC³ exams.

The CD-ROM in the back of the book comes with a complete set of simulations for each chapter. The students can walk through every step to perform essential tasks in Windows, Word, Excel, PowerPoint, Outlook, and Internet Explorer.

Proven Style

Scott Jernigan and Total Seminars have proven with numerous best-selling books by Mike Meyers, Scott Jernigan, Martin Acuña, and others, and outstanding classroom experiences, that they can reach students at a fundamental level. *Computer Literacy* takes the same approach, teaching students what they need to know at the same time as why the information is important. The writing is folksy rather than formal, and motivates the students to learn. *Computer Literacy* is not your usual dry, boring computer book!

What's My Motivation? *Elements provide students with real-world examples of technology in action, so they understand not just the information they're reading but why it's important in the real world.*

Outstanding Tools for Educators
Each chapter finishes with a Chapter Review that not only provides a detailed summary, but also questions on key terms, a multiple choice quiz, essays that challenge students' writing skills, and projects for them to accomplish both in class and on their own.

Motivational and Entertaining
Written in an engaging, approachable writing style, Computer Literacy will grab and hold the attention of the readers. Knowing why they're learning something helps focus attention and makes learning topics much easier.

Take Two! *questions help students put together information from multiple parts of the book, challenging them to remember earlier lessons and integrate the knowledge with the current lesson.*

Chapter Review *portions of each chapter provide a detailed summary, quizzes, essays, and projects for the students to tackle, both on their own and with the guidance of their instructors.*

Each chapter includes...

- Exam objectives that show the student the subjects they should learn
- High-resolution photographs of important computer components
- Screen captures for quick reference to subjects discussed
- Illustrations demonstrating key points
- Action! and Take Two! sidebars that walk the students through important processes and enhance critical thinking skills
- What's My Motivation! sidebars that help students understand why something that seems trivial has relevance to the real world

- Exam Tips and Notes to provide assistance and insightful information
- Summary of the important information in the chapter
- Key term list and a fill-in-the-blanks key term quiz
- Multiple choice exam (on the CD-ROM)
- Essay questions challenging students to write about the chapter content (on the CD-ROM)
- Projects for the students to complete in class and at home (on the CD-ROM)
- Software simulations (on the CD-ROM) that walk the students through every step in performing fundamental tasks covered in that chapter

Part 1: Computing Fundamentals

Chapter 1: Field Guide to Identifying Computers in the Wild

Chapter 2: Going with the Data Flow

Chapter 3: How to Speak Geek and Make Informed
Computer Purchasing Decisions

Chapter 4: It's a Comp's Life

Chapter 5: Defining the Role of the Operating System

Chapter 6: Getting to Know You – Navigating and Managing Windows

Chapter 7: Taking Control of Windows – Using Control Panel Wisely

Chapter 8: Computer Applications

Chapter 9: Productivity Software – Word Processors,Spreadsheets, Databases, and PresentationSoftware

Chapter 10: The Good, the Bad, and the Ugly – Multimedia, Personal Applications, and Utility Programs

Part 2: Key Applications

Chapter 11: Common Features of Windows Applications

Chapter 12: Working with Documents – The Basics

Chapter 13: Editing Documents

Chapter 16: Text that Gets Attention: Word Tables, Lists, Borders, and Shading

Chapter 17: Advanced Word Processing Skills

Chapter 18: Basic Spreadsheet Skills

Chapter 19: Advanced Spreadsheet Skills

Chapter 20: Mastering the Art of Presentation

Part 3: Living Online

Chapter 21: Network Basics

Chapter 22: Network Communication and the Internet

Chapter 23: Reach Out and Touch Someone – E-mail in the 21st Century

Chapter 24: Effective E-mail

Chapter 25: Information Sources on the Internet

Chapter 26: Web Essentials

Chapter 27: Finding Information on the Internet

Chapter 28: Computers in Homes, Schools, and Businesses

Chapter 29: Safety First – Protecting Computer Systems, Data, and Users

Chapter 30: Safe and Legal Use of the Internet

Introduction

To survive and thrive in the 21st Century, you must know how and when to use computers. Today's work environment assumes you have certain computer skills. You don't have to know how to build them, fix them, connect them together, or make them sing, but everybody should have a basic understanding of how computers work and how you can use them to accomplish everyday tasks at work, home, and play. In a pair of words, therefore, you need to be *computer literate*.

The Agony and the Ecstasy — Certifications Open the Door

There's nothing like going into a job interview that claims "no experience required," only to walk out rejected when you don't have the basic skills you need just to get in the door and stay there. Nearly every job you apply for has some computer skill required. While employers will often train new hires for entry-level positions, that's not always the case. Wouldn't it be nice to walk in and say, "I can do that!" and be ready to work right away?

The key issue in such situations is how to prove you have the skill you say you have. That's where certifications come into play.

A certification is a piece of paper that says without question that you have successfully completed testing on a set of skills. Every industry—from auto mechanics to fire fighting—has specific certifications. You need some way to show that you have the skill you earned. You wouldn't trust someone to rewire your house if he couldn't prove he could do electrical wiring safely, right? The computer industry works the same way, offering an array of certifications that prove you have certain skills.

IC³ Certification

Start with the fundamentals. Certiport offers tests on computer literacy through the *Internet and Computing Core Certification* program, better known as *IC³*. To become IC³-certified and show you have a solid competence in computers and office programs, plus know how to surf the Internet and send an e-mail message, you have to take and pass three exams: Computing Fundamentals, Key Applications, and Living Online. *Computer Literacy – Your Ticket to IC³ Certification* contains everything you need to know—and more—to get IC³-certified. IC³ is the cornerstone for all other computer-related certifications.

For more information on IC3 and Certiport, see pages iv-v of this book or go directly to the Certiport Web site, www.certiport.com. The CD-ROM in the back of this book has a list of all the competencies—what you need to know for each exam—in Adobe Acrobat (PDF) format.

Other Certifications

If you find that certain aspects of the computer field interest you, the computing industry offers many other certifications, covering everything from demonstrating your mastery of a particular program to building and fixing networked computers. These certifications provide logical goals for you to pursue to increase both your knowledge and your position in the workplace.

How do you know which certifications to pursue? The Microsoft Office Specialist (MOS) certifications in Word, Excel, and PowerPoint appeal to folks who work in any office environment and good direction after getting IC3-certified. CompTIA has A+ and Network+ certifications (among others) that show people you can build and fix computers and networks. If the machine interests you as much as the applications, the CompTIA certifications provide an alternative path to follow.

For a full range of paths to pursue, check out the Certification Pathway hosted by my company at www.totalsem.com. You'll find information about various certifications, plus get a road map for how to get to where you want to go by building one certification on top of another.

By the Book

I designed *Computer Literacy – Your Ticket to IC³ Certification* to provide a fundamental and *practical* understanding of computers in the modern world. Don't let the word "Certification" in the title fool you into thinking this book only teaches you the exams. Far from it!

In all the classes I've taught, my philosophy has remained consistent. I want you to learn what you need to learn, not simply to pass an exam, but to do the job successfully! To be computer literate, means knowing how computers work so you can fix things or ask for help when something goes wrong. It means knowing how to open and close programs and produce decent-looking documents so you shine in the workplace. It means having the skill to tap into the modern world of networks, by being able to send a well-crafted e-mail message and knowing how to find what you're looking for on the Internet.

Computer literacy gives you the knowledge to succeed in college: writing papers, generating reports, and finding and organizing information. You need these skills in any discipline, from history to engineering to fine arts. Computer literacy provides the foundation for success.

If you have problems, questions, or comments; a great movie quote for a section; or just want to argue, feel free to send an e-mail to the author: scottj@totalsem.com. I'd love to hear from you!

Part 1:
Computing
Fundamentals

COMPUTER LITERACY: YOUR TICKET TO IC³ CERTIFICATION

Field Guide to Identifying Computers in the Wild

"You know, like nunchuck skills, bowhunting skills, computer hacking skills . . . girls only want boyfriends who have great skills."

—Napoleon Dynamite, *Napoleon Dynamite*

This chapter covers the following IC³ exam objectives:

- IC³-1   1.1.1   Categorize types of computers based on their size, power, and purpose

- IC³-1   1.1.2   Identify types of microcomputers

- IC³-1   1.1.3   Identify other computing devices

- IC³-1   1.1.4   Identify the role of the central processing unit

- IC³-1   1.1.9   Identify the differences between large systems (such as mainframe or mini-computer systems with centralized data processing and storage) and desktop computers and appropriate uses for large vs. small systems

- IC³-1   1.1.10   Identify how computers integrate into larger systems

- IC³-1   1.1.11   Identify how computers share data, files, hardware and software

I grew up watching movies. Like a lot of computer geeks, science fiction and futuristic spy thrillers are my favorites. I like the gadgets. I like the ray guns, the spaceships, the robot monkey butlers, and especially the computers.

Of course, the movies aren't always the most reliable place to go for accurate portrayals of computer technology. If we're to believe what we see in the movies, for example, computers of the future are always on the verge of declaring, "I think, therefore I am" and taking over the world. Luckily, these futuristic computers can usually be shut down by means of a manual override switch conveniently located over a bottomless pit.

Well, we're over 1/20th of the way into the 21st century, so it's safe to say that the future is here. What are the computers of the future really like? William Gibson, the author of the classic sci-fi book Neuromancer, once commented that he thought the computer of the future would be invisible. Not in the literal sense that you wouldn't be able to see them, but invisible in the sense that they'd be so commonplace that you'd take no notice of them. Guess what? We're almost there!

Figure 1.1: Hey! There's a computer in my clock!

It's a Wired World

Computers are everywhere: in our homes, in our offices, in our businesses, schools, and libraries. Not just in the usual sense, meaning the desktop or laptop personal computer (PC) that you're used to seeing, but in many different forms, performing many different functions (Figure 1.1). Do you use TiVo? It's a kind of computer. Got an iPod? Another computer. If your car was built in the last twenty years or so, it has at least one computer on board, and probably more than one in the form of navigation equipment, audio and video players, and so on. Computers control much of the manufacturing processes in almost every facility in the United States, helping people produce everything from toys to life-saving medical equipment. Even in places you don't normally see, you'll find computers at the heart. Given that so many devices can be called a computer, what exactly does the term mean?

In this chapter, I want to discuss the various types of computers and other computing devices that are out there in the world, identify the different purposes of these computer systems, and talk about how computers integrate and share *data*—the files stored on the computer. I'm going to start with a brief discussion of what computers are and what they do, and look at the means we use to interact with them. Let's get started.

An Exceedingly Brief History of Computers

Originally, a computer wasn't a device, but a job description. Back in the olden days—and I don't mean the 1980s here, I mean way back around the 1400s—a *computer* was a mathematician who crunched numbers to produce navigational charts, devise artillery ballistics tables, and calculate currency rates (Figure 1.2).

As I'm sure you can imagine, sitting around calculating numbers all day wasn't the most exciting job, and this meant that these early computers were prone to errors (not at *all* like the modern computer!). To alleviate this problem, inventors came up with various mechanical devices to aid computers with their calculations. The abacus, Napier's Bones, the slide rule, and the Pascaline (whose inventor, Blaine Pascal, would later have his name cursed by countless computer programming students) are all examples of the tools that helped computers compute (Figure 1.3).

Other tools were developed in the passing centuries, all the way up to the first all-electronic digital computing device, the great-great-granddaddy of the modern computing world, the Electronic Numerical Integrator and Calculator, also known as ENIAC (Figure 1.4). Eventually, the calculating machine itself became known as a computer. Computers have gone through many refinements since the days of ENIAC, bringing us up to the wired world we now live in.

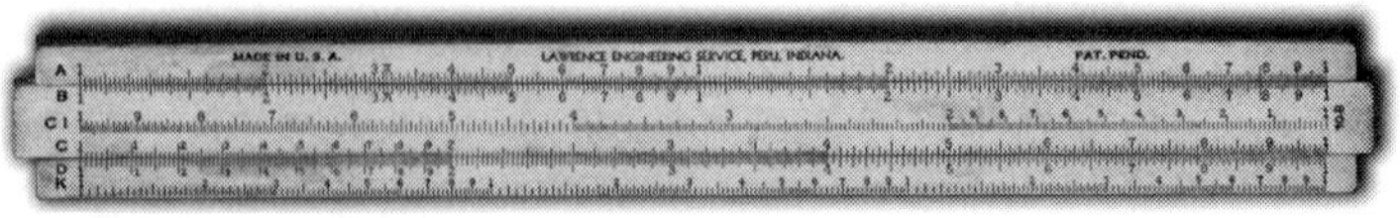

Figure 1.2: Early use for computers (Courtesy of the Bibliothèque nationale de France)

Figure 1.3: Slide rule

Figure 1.4: ENIAC
(Photo courtesy of
the U.S. Army)

You'll also hear people refer to applications as programs, *a term synonymous with the sets of coded instructions that tell the computer hardware to perform specific tasks, like add numbers, create text documents and graphical images, play music, and more.*

Computer Anatomy 101: Hardware and Software

At its most basic, a modern computer consists of three major components: hardware, operating system, and applications. The *hardware* is the stuff you can kick, like the keyboard, mouse, monitor, and case, plus all the pieces inside the case (Figure 1.5).

The *operating system* controls the hardware and enables you to tell the computer what to do. The operating system often manifests as a window on the monitor that has little icons you can click (see Figure 1.6), but modern PCs are able to respond to other ways of giving commands, such as voice-command.

Applications enable you to do specialized tasks on a computer, such as type a letter, send a message from your desk to your friend's computer in Paris almost instantly, or wander through imaginary worlds with people all over the Earth (Figure 1.7). Most computer users lump operating systems and applications together under the term *software*.

Monitor

Case

Speaker

Speaker

Keyboard

Mouse on mousepad

Figure 1.5: Typical computer

How Computers Work

Computers work through a three-stage process: input, processing, and output. You initiate the action by doing something—clicking the mouse or typing on the keyboard; this is *input*. The parts inside the case take over at that point, with the operating system telling the hardware to do what you've requested. This is *processing*. In fact, at the heart of every computer is the *central processing unit* (CPU), usually a single, thin wafer of silicon and microscopic transistors (Figure 1.8). The CPU handles the majority of the processing tasks.

Once the computer has processed your request, it shows you the result by changing what you see on the monitor or playing a sound through the speakers. This is *output*. A computer wouldn't be worth much if it couldn't

Figure 1.6: Microsoft Windows XP operating system

Figure 1.7: Wandering around in EverQuest II, a massively multiplayer online game (Courtesy of Sony Online Entertainment)

Figure 1.8: Intel Pentium 4 CPU in motherboard

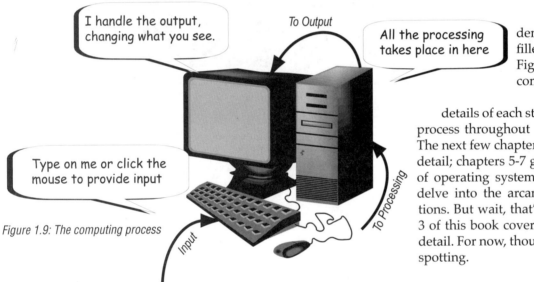

I handle the output, changing what you see.

To Output

All the processing takes place in here

Type on me or click the mouse to provide input

Figure 1.9: The computing process

Input

To Processing

demonstrate that it fulfilled your commands! Figure 1.9 shows the computing process.

We'll go into the details of each stage of the computing process throughout the rest of the book. The next few chapters hit the hardware in detail; chapters 5-7 give you an overview of operating systems; and chapters 8-10 delve into the arcane world of applications. But wait, that's not all! Parts 2 and 3 of this book cover applications in gory detail. For now, though, let's go computer spotting.

Off the Script

Saving

An important part of the computing process is data storage—saving a permanent copy of your work so that you can return to it later for further editing. Putting data storage in the context of the three-part computing process, you tell the computer to save something; the CPU processes that command and stores the data; the computer then often shows you something, such as a message saying that the data is stored. Storing data is something that you do while you're engaged in your other data processing activities, like writing a letter, editing a video, or playing a game. Any work that you don't make a point of saving is lost when you turn the computer off. Chapter 2, "Going with the Data Flow," goes into more detail about saving data.

Categories of Computers

When it comes to categories of computers, one size doesn't fit all. Computers come in a wider variety of forms than just about any other device that you can name. This section describes the main categories of computer types.

Mainframe Computers

From their introduction in the 1940s up until around the disco 1970s, mainframes dominated the computer world. *Mainframes* are massively powerful computers, widely used in the academic, banking, industrial, and scientific fields. Mainframes specialize in multitasking, supporting dozens, hundreds, or even thousands of user sessions at the same time, with each user running his own programs and working with his own files all at once. If you've seen any sci-fi movies from the 1950s, then you know what mainframe computers look like. Gigantic, boxy things

Figure 1.10: Mainframe computer

Modern Mainframes

Ready to buy? Mainframes aren't in as big demand as they once were, so there are few manufacturers. IBM and Unisys are two of the remaining makers of mainframe systems. As I'm sure you can imagine, mainframe systems are fantastically expensive, running up into the hundreds of thousands of U.S. dollars (and you don't even get a free printer!).

with lots of blinking lights and switches and spinning reels of magnetic tape (the data storage media of the time). They've gotten sleeker since then (see Figure 1.10), but mainframes are still physically large machines that range from roughly refrigerator-sized to being big enough to take up an entire floor of an office or school building.

Supercomputers

Supercomputers harness the power of a mainframe computer and focus it on performing a single task, making them arguably the most powerful computers on the planet. Most supercomputers manifest as a single large machine that has hundreds or thousands of CPUs working in tandem. These are the types of computers that you turn to when you need to perform big-brained tasks like tally census results, compile geothermal imaging data, predict how seismic activity will affect nuclear storage facilities 10,000 years down the line, or determine the answer to life, the universe, and everything.

Not all supercomputers are used strictly for higher purposes, however. One of the more common uses of supercomputers these days is rendering the sophisticated *computer generated imagery* (CGI) effects for movies. For example, the digital effects team for the Lord of the Rings trilogy used a supercomputer that had over three thousand CPUs to create the Oscar-winning special effects sequences. Guess it's cheaper than hiring a *real* army of orcs.

Minicomputers

Not many organizations need (or can accommodate) the computing muscle of a mainframe system, so in the 1960s computer makers developed the minicomputer. Essentially a scaled-down mainframe system, *minicomputers* could

be squeezed into a spare office or large storage closet instead of needing their own special space (Figure 1.11). Minicomputers find usage in many of the same fields as mainframes, plus they're extensively used in telecommunications, the aviation industries, and others.

Like mainframes, minicomputers service many user sessions at once. Minicomputers are expensive, but nowhere near the cost of a mainframe—running in the tens of thousands of dollars instead of hundreds of thousands. Modern minicomputers are seeing more competition from high-end microcomputer systems, but still have a large *installed base*, meaning that there are a lot of them chugging away in offices and schools all over the world that aren't in need of replacement anytime soon.

Figure 1.11: Minicomputer (Photo courtesy of David Gesswein's www.pdp8.net)

Microcomputers

Now we get to the classic machine that we all know and love, the *microcomputer*—or as it's better known, the *personal computer* (PC). Dating back to the 1970s, the PC is the machine that truly revolutionized the computer world. From its humble beginnings as a home-built gadget for the supergeek electronics hobbyist, the PC is now a fixture in practically every school, business, and home.

PCs are called "personal" because they were originally made to service only a single user session at a time. PCs come in two main physical configuration types, desktop systems and portable systems. Desktop PCs come in many shapes and sizes, from the basic suitcase-sized, putty-colored metal box that you've seen in offices, schools, and homes everywhere (see Figure 1.12) to exotic-looking creations with neon lights, custom paint jobs, and other stylistic touches (Figure 1.13).

Portable systems, as the name implies, are made to be mobile, and therefore smaller and lighter than desktop systems. Figure 1.14 shows a typical portable computer. Portables are usually called *laptop computers* or *notebook computers*.

PCs are the most widely ranging computers in terms of performance, varying from the bare-bones system capable of nothing more

Figure 1.12: Putty PC

Figure 1.13: Racy PC

serious than browsing the Internet to systems that rival minicomputers in processing power. These high-end PCs are usually called *workstations*, although the term is also used to describe any system connected to a computer *network*—a structure that enables computers to communicate with each other and share data and resources.

Some PC systems are also configured to fulfill specific roles on computer networks such as storing and sharing data or application programs from a central location, or providing network services such as e-mail

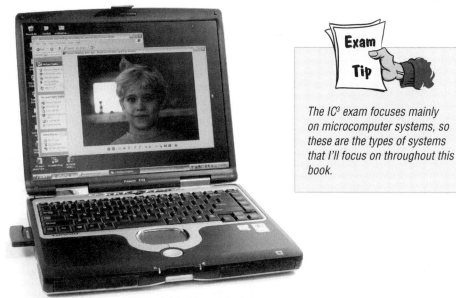

Figure 1.14: Compaq laptop

and printing. These specialized systems are called *servers*—as in file servers, application servers, mail servers, print servers, and so on. PCs that receive services from server systems are called *clients*.

Microcomputers come in several flavors, but the two most common in the wild are the IBM-style PCs and Apple Macintosh. They differ in both hardware and operating systems. Let's take a quick look.

IBM-style PCs

IBM-style PCs comply with the original PC hardware standards created by IBM back in the 1980s, although of course they've been updated over the ensuing decades. IBM-style PCs aren't limited to those actually made by the IBM company, but can be made by Dell, HP, Sony, or any other manufacturer. IBM-style PCs—I'm going to call them PCs from here on out—are by far the most common type of computer you'll see in the field. Figures 1.12, 1.13, and 1.14 show examples of typical PCs

PCs support many different types of hardware devices and software programs from many different vendors. The PC operating system of choice for most of the world is Microsoft Windows (see Figure 1.15), but other operating systems, such as UNIX and Linux, are also compatible with the PC platform. You'll see PCs used for many different purposes, from serious business applications to gaming, multimedia, and entertainment.

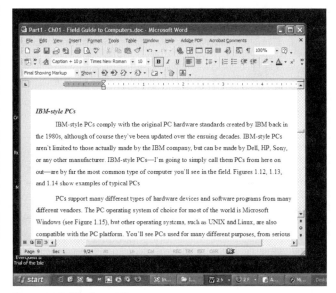

Figure 1.15: Windows XP

Off the Script

PC and Mac Crossbreeding

Apple has announced plans to switch from their current hardware platform to the Intel platform used by IBM-style PCs. The switch won't take place for awhile, however, so for the purposes of the IC³ exam, remember that Macs and PCs use different hardware standards.

Apple Macintosh

The *Apple Macintosh* computer—or *Mac*, as they're usually called—has been around even longer than the IBM PC, but has a smaller market share, which is a fancy way of saying that people don't buy as many of them. Figure 1.16 shows a typical Apple Macintosh computer.

Macs use their own internal hardware and software standards, although many programs and external devices work with both Macs and PCs, right out of the box. That statement is a bit deceptive, though. You might use the same CD-ROM to install an application like Adobe Photoshop Elements on both a Mac and a PC, but the software developer actually puts two versions of the software on the disc!

Macs use the Apple operating system, called *OS X* (Figure 1.17). Macs are capable of tackling the same tasks that you'll see PCs used for, but are typically used more in the creative fields, such as video editing and the graphic arts.

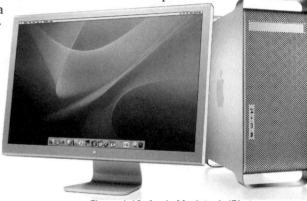

Figure 1.16: Apple Macintosh (Photo courtesy of Apple Computers)

Figure 1.17: OS X Desktop

The X in OS X is pronounced "ten" as in the Roman numeral, not "ex" like the letter or your former significant other.

Handheld Computers and PDAs

We humans are hand-oriented beings, so it was inevitable that we'd want to shrink computers down to something that we can hold in our hand like any other tool. Manufacturers produce multi-function and single-function *handheld computers*. The most popular example of the former is the *personal digital assistant* (PDA). PDAs help you stay organized by giving you a way to copy and carry around data that you'd normally store on your PC, such as your address book, calendar, task lists, and so on. Most even have enough processing power to enable you play games, edit text documents and spreadsheets, read books, listen to music, and do many other computing tasks on the go. PDAs are divided between two popular platforms: Microsoft Windows Mobile (sometimes called PocketPC) and the Palm OS (Figure 1.18). Some specialized PDAs run on Linux, the third major operating system family.

Figure 1.18: Palm Zire 71 PDA

PDAs have a small built-in display screen that also acts as a data input device. Handwriting recognition software enables you to enter text by writing on the screen with a pen-like instrument called a *stylus* (see Figure 1.19). Many also have small integrated keyboards: just the thing for the two-fingered typists of the world.

Some handheld computers and PDAs also double as communications devices. The RIM Blackberry, PocketPC Phone Edition, and Handspring Treo all combine data organizing functions with e-mail, Internet browsing, multimedia, and cellular phone capabilities (Figure 1.20). Gene Roddenberry would be proud!

Specialized or single-purpose handheld computing devices enable you to perform tasks that used to require extensive or bulky equipment. With an e-book reader, for example, you can carry around and read the equivalent of a small library full of books in your jacket pocket. Click a button and you're "thumbing" through the latest bestseller. Digital music players, such as the Apple iPod, put a full-blown stereo system and your collection of audio CDs into a stylish, palm-sized package (Figure 1.21).

Finally, if number crunching is your thing, a modern scientific calculator puts more raw processing power into a 3x5-card-sized shell than the first mainframes could boast (Figure 1.22).

Figure 1.19: Compaq iPAQ PDA

Figure 1.20: Treo 600 PDA/cell phone

Figure 1.21: Apple iPod

Figure 1.22: Scientific calculator

Connecting Computer Systems Large and Small

When you see a Chihuahua standing next to a Great Dane, it's hard to believe that they're both from the same species. By the same token, set a Mac mini next to a Cray supercomputer, and it's hard to believe that they're both computers, but it's true. See Figure 1.23.

For all the differences between large mainframe and minicomputer systems and small microcomputer PC systems, the most important differences lie in where the data processing takes place and where data is stored. Understanding these differences is the key to understanding how computer systems connect together and enable you to do cool things like share files with friends around the world.

Mainframe and Minicomputer Systems: Centralized Data Processing and Storage

Large computer systems like mainframes and minicomputers put all of their eggs in one basket, so to speak. All processing takes place directly on the centralized mainframe or minicomputer system, and all data and user account information is stored in one place. All users access the main system and run their programs. This is called *centralized processing*. Depending on the power of the large system, a single mainframe or minicomputer can service all users in the office building or school campus. Wherever the user may be, however, all of the power rests on the mainframe or minicomputer. Figure 1.24 illustrates mainframe and minicomputer systems.

Users connect to mainframe and minicomputer systems via two methods, dedicated input/output (I/O) stations called *terminals*, and through special terminal emulation software. The

Figure 1.23: Mac mini and Cray supercomputer

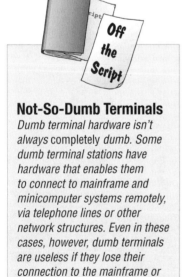

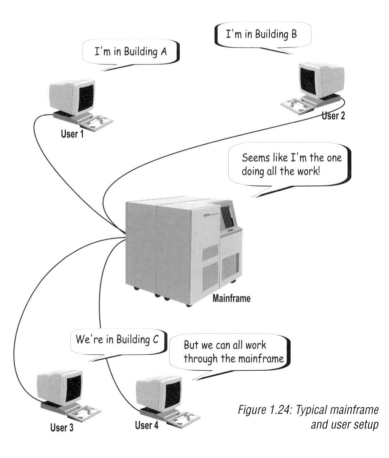

Figure 1.24: Typical mainframe and user setup

Figure 1.25: Dumb terminal

Figure 1.26: Windows Terminal Client (Remote Desktop)

Dumb Terminals in the Modern World

Students often look at me funny when I talk about dumb terminals connecting to mainframes and minicomputers, wondering why they should care about how computers worked before they were even born. The funny thing is, though, that VDTs are alive and well and in use all over the world. Bank teller stations are frequently simple I/O dumb terminals that enable tellers to access the bank's central customer database stored on a mainframe computer. Many retail establishments like bookstores and grocery stores use dumb terminals connected to inventory software running on a minicomputer system. Just by knowing how these things work, you're a step up on the competition!

typical terminal—officially called a *video display terminal* (VDT) and unofficially called a *dumb terminal*—consists only of a keyboard, a display monitor, and a very simple device to make the connection to the mainframe (Figure 1.25). They're called "dumb" because these I/O stations don't use any computing power or storage capacity of their own—they're used only to connect to the mainframe or minicomputer system.

Microcomputers can act as client systems for mainframe and minicomputer systems via *terminal emulation software*—programs that duplicate the functionality of dumb terminals. Yes, it's kind of funny to have the power of a modern microcomputer devoted to acting like a brainless VDT, but there you go. The latest versions of Windows and OS X have terminal emulation software built right into the operating system, and there are many third-party versions of terminal software available (Figure 1.26).

Centralized processing and storage has the advantage of being, well, *centralized*. There's never any question of where the computer hardware and data resides. This makes it easy to perform administrative tasks like troubleshoot hardware problems, manage user accounts, and back up data. The disadvantage is that the central computer system becomes your single point of failure. If the mainframe or minicomputer goes down, nobody can get to their programs or data. See Figure 1.27. Mainframe and minicomputers typically have redundant hardware components to prevent total system failure in case of a problem. This is called *fault tolerance*.

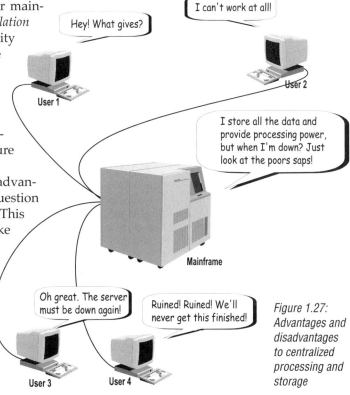

Figure 1.27: Advantages and disadvantages to centralized processing and storage

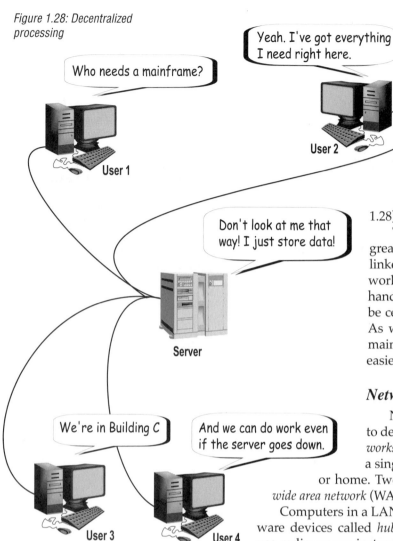

Figure 1.28: Decentralized processing

Microcomputer Systems: Decentralized Data Processing, Flexible Storage, Sharing

In contrast to the centralized scheme of large mainframe and minicomputer systems, microcomputer systems bring their own processing power and storage capacity to the table. Each microcomputer is in charge of its own user accounts, application programs, data files, and hardware (Figure 1.28). This is called *decentralized processing*.

This decentralized organization enables a great deal of flexibility. Microcomputers can be linked together in a computer network. In a network environment, processing power is still in the hands of each networked PC, but data storage can be centralized on a single PC called a file server. As with the centralized data storage scheme of mainframes and microcomputers, this makes it easier to manage and back up the data files.

Networks

Networks come in a couple of flavors, named to describe their location and scope. *Local area networks* (LANs) connect computers to each other in a single physical location, such as a school, office, or home. Two or more LANs connected together form a *wide area network* (WAN).

Computers in a LAN are connected by network cables and hardware devices called *hubs* or *switches* (Figure 1.29). Some networks use radio waves instead of physical *network cabling* to connect PCs to each other, creating *wireless networks*. Computers on these wireless networks are usually linked together by a special wireless hub called a *wireless access point* (WAP).

WANs generally manifest as a collection of LANs in multiple buildings or multiple cities, which is why you'll occasionally hear them described as *remote networks*. The best example of a remote network is the Internet—a worldwide network of remote networks connected by a series of high-speed communications lines (Figure 1.30). Other examples of remote networks are school or office networks that enable you to connect to them from home or from on the road.

Single microcomputers and LANs connect to WANs such as the Internet through hardware devices called *routers*. Routers come in both wired and wireless models.

Figure 1.31: PDA surfing the Net

Figure 1.29: Typical LAN

Switch

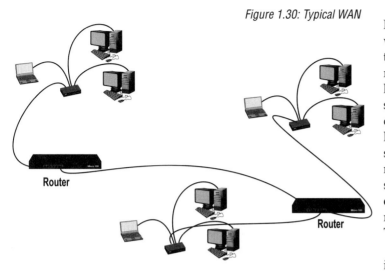

Figure 1.30: Typical WAN

Router

Router

Routers send network communications out through regular telephone lines, digital subscriber lines (DSL), cable television lines, or through special dedicated network cabling structures with exotic-sounding names like ISDN, T1, T3, and so on.

In our increasingly wired world, you'll also find handheld devices such as PDAs and cell phones that can connect to the Internet through a router (Figure 1.31). Even advanced gaming consoles, such as the Xbox 360 and PlayStation 3 offer Internet connectivity, although for the specialized purpose of smacking your friends and neighbors in computer games online.

Sharing Resources

The decentralized nature of microprocessor networks enable computers to share storage space, printers, scanners, application programs, and in special cases they can even share CPU processing power. Sharing these devices saves you money, because instead of installing, say, ten separate printers on ten separate computers on your network, you can instead have them each share a single printer installed onto just one computer. All modern operating systems enable you to share resources with a mere mouse click or two (Figure 1.32).

Figure 1.32: Sharing a folder in Windows XP

Distributed Computing

Multiple computer systems can share their processing power to perform a single computing task, a process called distributed computing. *Distributed computing involves spreading out the workload among multiple computers at different times instead of all at once; and if done right, can turn a collection of microcomputers into the functional equivalent of a supercomputer—at a fraction of the cost.*

One example of this process is the SETI@home project. The SETI (Search for Extraterrestrial Intelligence) organization maintains a huge array of satellite receivers at the Arecibo observatory array in Puerto Rico. This array collects tons of data gathered from space. Volunteer computers called nodes take small chunks of raw data and process it into results that are then passed back to the project's central server for compilation. So far, no extraterrestrial life has sent any clear messages, but the SETI folks are still watching the skies.

Synchronizing PDAs and Microcomputers

PDAs enable you to tote your important data and documents around and work on the go, but how do you pass this data from the PC to the PDA and back again? You transfer data between your PDA and PC through a process called synchronizing. *Synchronizing your PDA and computers keeps the shared data consistent. Synchronizing is also how you install new application software onto your PDA.*

Synchronizing your PDA to your PC requires a hardware connection between the two systems and special synchronizing software to control the process. Typically, your PDA connects to the computer through a synchronizing cable or cradle, such as that shown in the picture. Some PDAs also enable you to synchronize through a wireless network connection or via an Infrared port. Once connected, running the synchronizing software updates the files that are stored on both devices, saving the most recent version.

It's a Wired World

- Computers are everywhere: in our homes, offices, businesses, schools, and libraries. Every modern car has a computer or two. You'll find computers controlling manufacturing facilities throughout the world. Even clocks have computers!

- Ancient "computers" were people who crunched numbers all day, and various devices like the abacus and slide rule helped them do their jobs.

- A modern computer consists of three major components: hardware, operating system, and applications. The keyboard, monitor, and components inside the case (like the CPU) are typical hardware. Windows and Macintosh operating systems provide an interface for you to tell the computer what to do and then control the hardware. Applications or programs enable you to accomplish specialized tasks, such as word processing and gaming.

- Computers work through a three stage process: input, processing, and output. You provide the input; the CPU and other components process your request; the operating system sends output to the monitor, speakers, or storage medium to let you know the outcome of your request.

Categories of Computers

- Mainframes are massively powerful computers, widely used in the academic, banking, industrial, and scientific fields. Mainframes specialize in multitasking, supporting dozens, hundreds, or even thousands of user sessions at the same time. Supercomputers rival mainframe power, but focus on specialized tasks, like rendering movie special effects.

- Minicomputers work much like mainframes, enabling many people to connect and work at the same time, but at a much lower price.

- Microcomputers generally serve a single user at a time and come in two packages, desktop systems and portables. The most common types of microcomputers are the IBM-style PC and the Apple Macintosh. IBM-style PCs use Intel or AMD CPUs—called x86 architecture—and run Microsoft Windows operating systems, for the most part. The Macintosh uses Motorola or IBM Power PC processors—called the G4 or G5—and runs the Mac OS X operating system.

- Handheld computers offer scaled down versions of microcomputers—multifunction devices such as PDAs and PDA/cell phones—or very specialized tasks, such as media players like the iPod and scientific calculators.

How Computer Systems Integrate

- Large computer systems like mainframes and minicomputers use centralized data processing and storage. Users connect to mainframes and minicomputers through dumb terminals that have no computing power of their own, and through terminal emulation software running on microcomputers.

- Smaller systems like microcomputer networks use decentralized processing and storage. Through networks, computers can share resources such as files, folders, and storage space, printers, scanners, and applications

- Microcomputers connect to each other through local area networks (LANs) using network cables and hubs or switches, or radio waves and wireless access points (WAPs). Microcomputers and LANs connect to remote, wide area networks (WANs) through routers.

Key Terms

Apple Macintosh

Central processing unit (CPU)

Centralized processing

Cluster

Decentralized processing

Distributed

Handheld computer

Hub

IBM-compatible personal computer (PC)

Local area network (LAN)

Macintosh OS X

Mainframe

Microcomputer

Microprocessor

Microsoft Windows XP

Minicomputer

Network cable

Remote

Resource

Router

Server

Service

Sharing

Storage

Supercomputer

Synchronizing

Personal digital assistant (PDA)

Terminal emulation

Video display terminal (VDT), a.k.a. dumb terminal

Wide area network (WAN)

Wireless access point (WAP)

Key Term Quiz

Use the Key Terms list to complete the following sentences. Not all the terms will be used.

1. _____ computers support thousands of user sessions at a time, and are frequently used in the academic, banking, industrial, and scientific fields.

2. A _____ is a small computing device that enables you to carry your contact lists, calendars, and important documents and extend the use of your PC.

3. A _____ is a group of computers whose processing power is combined.

4. _____ are frequently used in the telecommunications and aviation industries, and support hundreds of user sessions at a time.

5. Users access mainframe and minicomputers through I/O stations called _____.

6. Most IBM-style PCs use _____ for an operating system.

7. Most Apple computers use _____ for an operating system.

8. Data shared between a PC and a PDA is kept current by _____.

9. A local computer network can connect to a _____ through a router.

10. Microcomputers connect to mainframe and minicomputer systems using _____ _____ software.

Multiple Choice Quiz

1. Which of the following was the first type of electronic computer?
   A. Mainframe computer
   B. Minicomputer
   C. Microcomputer
   D. Handheld computer

2. How do microcomputer users gain access to mainframe and minicomputer systems?
   A. Stylus
   B. Dumb terminal
   C. Terminal emulation software
   D. Synchronizing

3. Which of the following scenarios best suits minicomputer usage?
   A. A large banking institution that needs to give thousands of users access to a financial database at a time
   B. A small business that has to give 50 employees access to a folder of shared text documents, graphics, and spreadsheets
   C. A digital effects company that needs to render 3-D CGI effects for a movie production
   D. A school that needs to give 400-500 research students access to a centralized scientific database at a time

4. A friend asks for you to advise her in a computer purchase. She wants a way to maintain her daily schedule, take notes, and carry her contact list with her everywhere. What device do you recommend for her?
   A. Video display terminal (VDT)
   B. Desktop computer
   C. Portable laptop computer
   D. Personal digital assistant (PDA)

5. Which of the following are types of connections that routers can use to communicate? (Select all that apply.)
   A. Regular telephone lines
   B. Digital subscriber line (DSL)
   C. Virtual private network (VPN)
   D. Cluster

6. Which of the following operating systems will run on the standard IBM-compatible PC platform? (Select all that apply.)
   A. Apple OS X
   B. Microsoft Windows
   C. Amiga OS
   D. UNIX/Linux

7. What device does a microcomputer or LAN use to connect to a WAN, like the Internet?
   A. LAN-to-WAN adpater
   B. Cable booster
   C. PDA
   D. Router

8. What do you call a computing method in which a large processing job is broken up into smaller jobs and deployed to numerous computers?
   A. Packet computing
   B. Distributed computing
   C. Synchronized computing
   D. Decentralized computing

9. Mainframe computers enable thousands of users to run programs and access data all at the same time. Where does the actual processing take place?
   A. The user's video display terminal (VDT)
   B. The mainframe computer
   C. The network adapter
   D. The software applications

10. A family member currently uses an IBM-compatible PC running Microsoft Windows. He is thinking of switching to an Apple Macintosh computer running OS X. What are some potential pitfalls to switching from one platform to another?
    A. He'll have to replace his Windows sofware application programs with versions written for OS X.
    B. He'll face a steep learning curve for the new operating system.
    C. A Macintosh system won't be as stable as a Windows system.
    D. A Macintosh system won't be as fast as a Windows system.

Essays

11. All computers can perform which of the following tasks? (Select all that apply.)
    A. Receive input
    B. Store data
    C. Process data
    D. Support hundreds of user sessions at a time

12. All computers have which of the following components? (Select all that apply.)
    A. Central processing unit (CPU)
    B. Scanner
    C. Operating system
    D. Storage devices

13. What kind of computer is dedicated to performing a single, complex processing task such as compiling geothermal data and rendering 3-D animation?
    A. Mainframe computer
    B. Minicomputer
    C. Microcomputer
    D. Supercomputer

14. What is the advantage of linking computers together in a network? (Select all that apply.)
    A. Ability to share storage space
    B. Ability to share hardware like printers and scanners
    C. Ability to share processing power
    D. There's no advantage.

15. What do you call the process by which you update data between a PC and a PDA?
    A. Clustering
    B. Distributed computing
    C. Synchronizing
    D. Terminal emulation

Essays

1. Computing devices are widely used in industries such as transportation, communication, and entertainment. Name at least one computing device for each category, and describe how they are used.

2. Briefly describe the general uses for mainframe computers, minicomputers, microcomputers, and supercomputers.

3. Describe the differences between centralized and decentralized data processing.

Projects

1. Visit the Computer History Museum Web site at http://www.computerhistory.org and research how computers have evolved in the time you've been alive. What important computer technologies have been invented in that time? What were computers like when you were born?

2. As an example of how distributed computing works, visit the SETI@home Web site at http://setiathome.ssl.berkeley.edu and view the FAQ. How does the project work? What is required for you and your computer to participate?

COMPUTER LITERACY: YOUR TICKET TO IC^3 CERTIFICATION

Going with the Data Flow

"You must feel the Force around you; here, between you, me, the tree, the rock, everywhere, yes. Even between the land and the ship."
— Yoda, *The Empire Strikes Back*

This chapter covers the following IC³ exam objectives:

- IC³-1 1.1.4 Identify the role of the central processing unit

- IC³-1 1.1.6 Identify the role of types of memory and storage and the purpose of each

- IC³-1 1.1.8 Identify the flow of information between storage devices to the microprocessor and RAM in relation to everyday computer operations

- IC³-1 1.2.1 Identify the types and purposes of external computer components

- IC³-1 1.2.2 Identify the types and purposes of internal computer components

- IC³-1 1.2.3 Identify the types and purposes of specialized input devices

- IC³-1 1.2.4 Identify the types and purposes of specialized output devices

- IC³-1 1.2.6 Identify ports used to connect input and output dvices to a computer

- IC³-1 2.1.1 Identify how hardware and software interact

From the time you start your computer in the morning to the time you shut it down, you move data from one place to another. You input data using your keyboard and mouse; you download files from the Internet; you install software from CDs and DVDs. Each time you perform any of these actions, you move data between the many hardware components of your PC.

The data flow follows three major phases: *startup*—where you provide electricity to the computer and the operating system loads; *primary interaction*, or what I like to call the *dance phase*—where you play a game, do word processing, save your work so you can use it later; the bulk of your time on the computer happens in this phase; and *shutdown*—where you close the program you're working in and log off or shut the computer down completely.

Understanding what's happening or what should be happening within the computer—and where the action takes place—helps you figure out how to fix things when they don't work properly. Understanding the flow of data is the cornerstone of the art of troubleshooting computers.

Boot Hill

The term boot is short for bootstrap, as in "pulling yourself up by your bootstraps." Techs adopted this term a long time ago to describe the computer startup process. There are two kinds of booting, a cold boot and a warm boot. Cold booting the computer means turning it on after it has been completely shut down with the power turned off. Warm booting means restarting a computer that is running.

Phase One: Start Me Up! – The Computer's Boot Process

Let's take it from Act 1, Scene 1. What happens when you press the power button on your computer? The short answer is that the computer system starts up, or in geek speak, it *boots*.

The startup process has three overlapping phases: first is the power-on phase, then the hardware test, followed by the operating system load phase.

Power-on

The power-on phase takes place immediately after you press the power button. Electricity goes into the *power supply*—hardware that converts AC electricity from your power outlet into DC power that computers use—and from there to the drives and motherboard, waking the CPU. The CPU then wakes the system's *read-only memory—basic input/output system* (ROM-BIOS) memory circuit. The ROM-BIOS chip stores the computer's "lizard brain," its most basic commands and programs, including the collection of the hardware test phase diagnostic programs. Figure 2.1 shows a typical power supply; Figure 2.2 shows a ROM-BIOS chip on a motherboard.

Figure 2.1: Power supply

Hardware Test

Once the ROM-BIOS wakes up, the computer runs basic hardware tests, asking the important hardware components to identify themselves and report their status (usually accompanied by beeps and bloops and blinking lights). If there is a problem with one of the components, the hardware test generates an error message for you. Macintosh computers will display a text message, for example, or an icon if it's bad enough (see Figure 2.3). If there are no hardware problems to report, then the last thing that the hardware test does is locate and execute the files that start the operating system.

Figure 2.2: ROM-BIOS chip

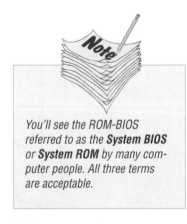

You'll see the ROM-BIOS referred to as the **System BIOS** or **System ROM** by many computer people. All three terms are acceptable.

Data Flow

Even this early in the boot process, the interplay between CPU, RAM, and storage devices comes into play. ROM stores the little programs that support the absolutely necessary, hard-wired into your computer devices: basic input devices, such as the keyboard, and fundamental output devices, such as the tiny speaker inside your case and the monitor. These little programs, called *services*, load from the very slow ROM into the shockingly fast RAM (Figure 2.4).

The CPU does almost all the processing, as you know from Chapter 1, but RAM plays a fundamental part in

I'm the big boss CPU. I call the shots here. ROM you load into RAM.

I'm RAM. I hold all the programs and data the CPU is working on.

I'm the ROM BIOS. I hold the computer's lizard brain and services.

Figure 2.4: The flow of data from ROM to RAM

Figure 2.3: Unhappy Mac icons

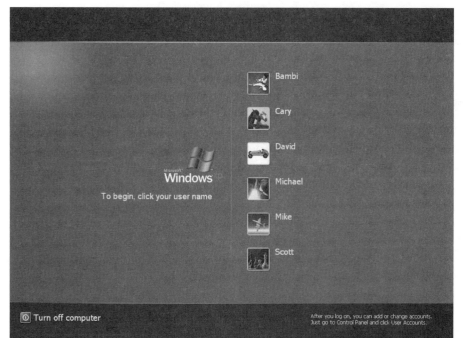

Inside every computer is a small crystal called the clock or System Clock that sets the timing for all the other hardware.

IBM-style PCs refer to the hardware test phase as the Power On Self Test (POST). Macintosh computers use the more generic term.

the computing process. The CPU uses RAM like you use short-term memory. If you want to do a complex math problem (and who doesn't?!), for example, you would most likely need to use a book to look up the formulas and then, with numbers in your head, you could process the problem. If you didn't have short-term memory, you couldn't keep the necessary information in your head long enough to do the job, right? The CPU and RAM have that same relationship. The RAM holds every bit of data the CPU processes.

Operating System Load

The operating system takes over the boot process from here, instructing the CPU to copy all of the necessary system files, services, drivers, and other files that make up the operating system from the hard drive to the computer's RAM. As a final step, the operating system builds the user interface (using the video display adapter to draw the interface on your monitor), and soon you see the logon dialog or the icons next to user names (Figure 2.5). Figure 2.6 illustrates the boot process.

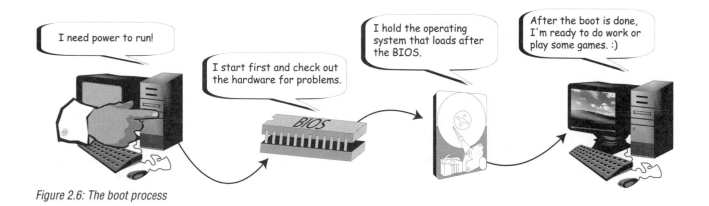

Figure 2.6: The boot process

The data keeps flowing

> I'm the big boss CPU. Hard drive, send the OS files to RAM now!

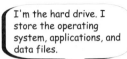

Figure 2.7: The flow of data from hard drive to RAM

> I'm the hard drive. I store the operating system, applications, and data files.

> I'm RAM. I hold all the programs and data the CPU is working on.

The operating system files travel from a mass storage device, such as a hard drive, CD-ROM disc, or, in the ancient days, a floppy disk, through the motherboard into RAM (Figure 2.7). You saw this process with the tiny services programs, flowing from ROM to RAM. The process repeats here. I'll let you in on a little secret. The flow of data follows the same process in almost every aspect of the computer! You'll see this pattern again and again.

Assuming there are no hardware problems, the whole process only takes a few seconds, and you're ready to log on and start your computing session. Keep in mind that except for the previously mentioned blinking lights, beeps (and any optional sound files, such as the soothing Windows Logon Sound audio file), and the sound of the disk drives spinning up to speed, there's really not much to see. All of the action happens inside the CPU, RAM, and storage devices.

Phase Two: The Dance– Interacting with the Computer

Once you've booted up, you're ready for the next phase, interacting with the computer. You can open a program—such as a word processing program to type a letter to your mother or write an essay from the essay questions at the end of the chapter. (Something you're looking forward to doing, right?!) The computer processes your request, opening the application interface so you can type something in. The computer processes what you type and updates the screen to give you feedback. Rinse and repeat this cycle many times quickly and you've got the whole "interaction" part of the computing process.

To make this interaction possible, you have to use input devices; the computer uses internal devices to process, then uses output devices to show your work. Let's look at all three components of the interaction phase, including practical steps on opening applications and creating data.

Input Devices

Figure 2.8: Standard input devices

Mouse   Touch Pad   Keyboard   Trackball

Input devices enable you to give commands to the computer. You can type using the *keyboard*; click on icons and buttons using a pointing device such as a *mouse*, *trackball*, or *touchpad*; or speak using the *microphone* (Figure 2.8). More specialized input devices, such as *joysticks* and *game pads*, enable you to fly a simulated airplane more naturally than using a keyboard, for example, or enhance your game play in first-person games (Figure 2.9). Some multimedia computers even use remote controls, just like the kind used for televisions.

Some specialized input devices also enable you to add data to the computer. You can take a picture of your cat with a *digital camera*, for example, and then pull that picture into the computer so you can share it with friends, family, and random

Figure 2.9: Using a joystick in Microsoft's Crimson Skies game

people who drop by your house (Figure 2.10). A *digital video camera* enables you to create your own movies, editing and watching them directly on the computer. A *scanner* enables you to create a digital image of an old-fashioned photograph, (just in case you've gone retro and started using a Polaroid). You can also use a scanner to import a typewritten document directly into a word processing program, which is pretty cool when it works, a process called *optical character recognition* (OCR). Figure 2.13 shows a typical scanner.

Finally, a whole host of devices enable you to input commands and data in the most basic way possible: poking them with your fingers. Every personal digital assistant (PDA), information kiosks, and automated teller machines that give out free money have touch screens that react to contact with your fingers or specialized stick (Figure 2.14).

Other Specialized Input Devices

Manufacturers have created an amazing variety of devices for inputting both commands and data. We created most of the artwork you see in this book, for example, using a drawing tablet (also called a digitizing tablet) and pen, rather than mouse and keyboard (see Figure 2.11). Barcode readers that you see at every supermarket take data—information about your food item—and bring it into the cash register (which is just another computer!). The scientific and medical communities use special, computer-based probes and instruments for cutting edge research and life-saving procedures. Alternative input devices, such as thumb mice *and radically innovative keyboards, enable physically-challenged users to work with computers as readily as everyone else. Figure 2.12 shows a side-folded keyboard.*

Figure 2.10: Importing image from digital camera to computer

Figure 2.13: Typical scanner

Figure 2.11: Graphics tablet and pen

Figure 2.12: Side-folded keyboard

Installing Input Devices

Most operating systems support some input devices—especially keyboards and mice—straight out of the box, but others require a two step installation process. First, you plug the device into its proper spot. Second, you load a disc in your CD player and install a bit of support software so the OS knows what sort of device it now has.

Figure 2.14: PDA in use

Physical Connections

Devices connect to the computer's hardware through connector ports, usually located on the back of your computer case, although you'll find some universal connectors on the front or side of the case for quicker access. Portable computers typically have ports located on the back, sides, front—pretty much anywhere that the makers can fit them to give you the most access. Figure 2.15 shows the back side of a desktop computer.

Ports come in several varieties, as you can see, but with one exception, you can't go wrong when you plug in devices. Manufacturers *key* ports and connectors by giving them odd shapes, thus making it impossible to plug them in incorrectly. Traditional keyboards and pointing devices (such as mice) plug into the small round connectors labeled on the left (in Figure 2.15), and provide the exception to this rule. You can easily plug a keyboard into the mouse port, and *vice versa*, but your devices won't work. Most PC makers color-code the mouse and keyboard connectors to keep you from getting confused: green for the mouse and purple for the keyboard.

Most input devices today plug into one of the two universal ports, *universal serial bus* (USB) or *FireWire*, although you'll see some devices plugged into legacy ports, such as the MIDI port shown in Figure 2.16. These ports are keyed and labeled with their own icons. You can't mess up here.

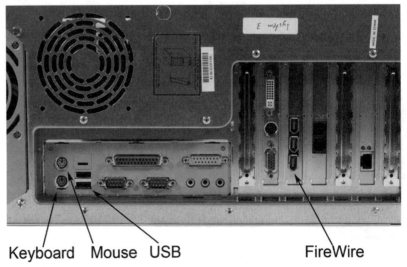

Keyboard   Mouse   USB   FireWire

Figure 2.15: Input ports

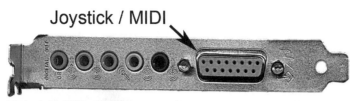

Joystick / MIDI

Figure 2.16: MIDI port for legacy joysticks and other ancient devices

Software Support

Input devices usually require some software support programs installed so the operating system can communicate with them effectively. Although USB and FireWire tout the ability to *plug and play* devices—meaning you just plug them in, the OS recognizes them, and you can use them—this rarely works in the real world. The OS often recognizes the hardware, but doesn't know how to talk to it! Hardware manufacturers provide a CD with small programs, called *drivers*, that the OS copies and loads into RAM to support the input device.

Internal Processing

Now that you have input devices sorted out, it's time to get to work. You need to command the computer to open an application and the CPU processes that command. The CPU does not work solo, though, requiring numerous other components to do both the processing and the next step, providing output of some sort.

Figure 2.17: Selecting a program to open

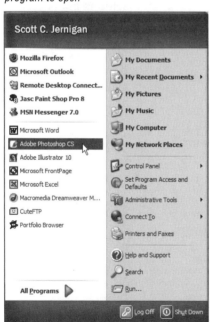

Opening Programs

You can start an application in many ways, but the most common way in graphical-based OSs such as Windows and Macintosh OS X is to click the program icon in the Start menu (Windows) or double-click the program icon in the Finder (OS X). See Figure 2.17. Clicking and double-clicking, usually accomplished by a pointing device, tells the computer that you want it to run a specific program installed on the computer.

The operating system and the CPU inter-

pret your command and send commands to the hard drive to cough up the files for that application so they can be loaded into RAM. This process sounds familiar, right? To work with any application, the CPU must have that application loaded into RAM. Figure 2.18 illustrates the flow of data from hard

Note

*MIDI stands for **musical instrument digital interface**, and indeed provided a way to connect electronic musical equipment to the computer, back in the day. Modern MIDI-enabled instruments connect through USB or FireWire ports, just like everything else.*

Figure 2.18: The flow of data when opening an application

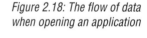

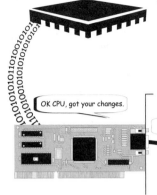

Video, here are the new changes Bob has made. Make shure the monitor gets them!

Figure 2.19: Data flow from CPU to video to monitor

OK CPU, got your changes.

Monitor, update NOW!

Wow, another command from the video card. It just never stops.

drive to RAM so the CPU can work.

What you see as a result of this processing requires more internal components. To change the display so you get the application interface, for example, the CPU has to send data and commands to the *video card* inside your system. The video card then processes the CPU's commands and sends commands to the monitor so the monitor updates. All of this happens very quickly, but you see the change on the screen. Figure 2.19 illustrates this process.

Creating Data Files

Once you have an application open, you can create new files. Almost every productivity application—as opposed to games—has a File option on the main menu. Creating a file is as simple as going to **File | New** and then specifying what sort of file you want. Microsoft Word opens a separate dialog called the Task Pane to give you a bunch of choices (see Figure 2.20).

Output Devices

To engage fully in the "interacting with the computer" phase, you need properly connected and configured output devices. Output takes many forms, though, from standard feedback options of changing the display and making sound come out the speakers, to more specialized feedback such as force-feedback joysticks shaking your arm when you take a dive in your jet fighter. Other forms of output include printing, communicating over a network (like the Internet), and saving files to some sort of mass storage, such as a hard drive or compact disc.

Feedback Devices

The *monitor* provides the most common way for the computer to communicate with you, showing

Figure 2.20: Task Pane in Microsoft Word

Off the Script

Al Gore or Something Like That

A computer uses algorithms (a set of pre-designed rules) to handle the data appropriately. For example, if you open up a Calculator application and use your keyboard to type 1+1, your computer will use an addition algorithm to sum the data.

Many Ways to Open

Almost every OS offers you many ways to start a program. You can double-click the program's icon on your desktop in Windows, for example, or click the Start button, select Run from the menu, and then browse to the location of the program's executable file (the file that starts the program.)

*You can also double-click a data file associated with the program, meaning the OS knows to load a specific application when you select a specific file type. Selecting a text document (like a letter), for example, will start your text editor (such as Microsoft Word) open with that document ready to edit; choosing a music file (such as a song saved as an MP3) will launch your default media player (such as Windows Media Player or iTunes) and begin playing the song. This process is called **file association.**

Figure 2.21: LCD vs. CRT: Fight!

LCD

CRT

that it has processed your commands by loading a program, changing some file, or simply moving the mouse pointer across the screen to match your hand movement. Figure 2.21 shows a pair of monitors.

Projectors offer a nice alternative to monitors, enabling you to put the computer image on a screen or white wall, rather than only on a smaller physical display (Figure 2.22). If the bulbs weren't so expensive and energy-hungry, you'd undoubtedly see projectors replacing televisions as well as computer monitors!

Speakers give the computer another way to provide feedback (and playback, for that matter). Operating systems and applications can send sounds out when things go wrong or to acknowledge that they accomplished what you commanded. Media applications, like iTunes, can play music when requested. Good speakers can make a huge difference in games and in movie watching on the computer. Figure 2.23 shows a set of decent speakers.

Voice synthesizers enable visually challenged folks to participate fully in the computer revolution, creating essential feedback from the computer that they otherwise wouldn't receive. Many developers have software voice synthesizers that use your computers sound processor and speakers, but some manufacturers have external hardware devices that do the trick. For the latter, check out the good folks at www.freedomscientific.com.

Figure 2.22: Projector

Figure 2.23: Speakers

Figure 2.24: Printer

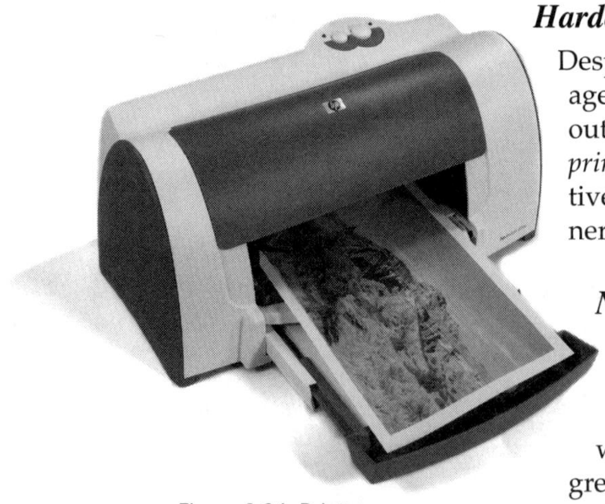

Hardcopy

Despite the promise of the so-called "paperless office" that the computer age was supposed to usher in, most folks prefer to see their work printed out on good old-fashioned, tree-killing, finger-cutting paper. Modern *printers* enable you to turn your PC into a print shop and produce attractive text documents like reports and newsletters, as well as photos, banners, postcards, and other graphical documents (Figure 2.24).

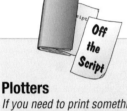

Networking

Network output means sending data to another computer by means of networking hardware and software. To make it work, you've got to have a computer connected to a network or dialed in via a hardware device called a modem. Part 3 of this book covers networking in great detail, so we'll leave that discussion for later.

Plotters

If you need to print something huge, like poster sized, you need to walk away from the typical home and office print device and embrace the goodness of the plotter. *Plotters look like scaled-up printers and run anywhere from $2000 to $20,000 and up (in U.S. dollars), but they'll print your big pictures just fine. Plotters produce large-scale, detailed printouts, such as architectural drawings, blueprints, maps, and posters.*

Storage Devices

Opening a data file from within your application program causes the computer to copy the file from your storage media into the system's RAM (Figure 2.25). This is your editable, "working" copy of the file. You're free to make changes by adding text, entering numbers, slaying dragons, or doing whatever the application program does.

As you'll recall from earlier in the chapter, the CPU can work with files

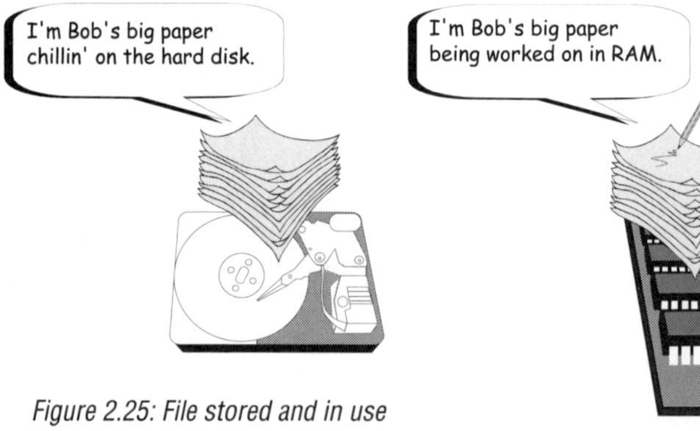

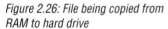

Figure 2.25: File stored and in use

and programs held in RAM, its short-term memory. As you interact with the computer, the CPU updates the contents of RAM according to what you do, and that's great. You can work on drawing a masterpiece, for example, and what you see on your monitor also appears (in a slightly altered format) in RAM. There's just one problem.

Figure 2.26: File being copied from RAM to hard drive

If RAM loses power, *all the data it holds just goes away*. Poof. Gone forever. That's why it's important to save your work. Saving a data file copies it from RAM onto a mass storage device, such as a hard disk, where it's retained permanently (Figure 2.26).

All applications give you methods for saving a file, such as clicking a **Save** button, going to **File | Save**, or pressing **[Ctrl + S]** (for Windows) or **[Cmd + S]** (for Macintosh) on the keyboard. Figure 2.27 shows the saving dialog in Word.

People have used different types of media for

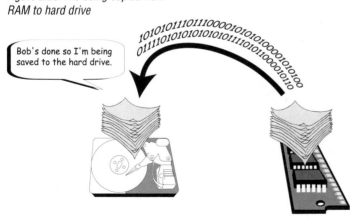

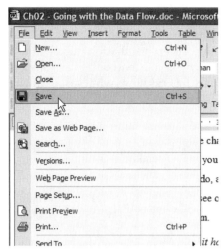

Figure 2.27: Saving in Word

data storage through the years, from stone tablets to magnetic reel-to-reel tapes. Three technologies dominate the current storage scene for computers: *magnetic*, *optical*, and *solid state*.

Hard drives, floppy disks, and Zip disks save information magnetically on platters, what's called *magnetic storage*. Hard drives provide the primary fixed mass storage in almost every computer. Figure 2.29 shows a hard drive open to reveal the platters inside.

CD- and DVD-media drives use lasers to read information stored on shiny discs, like the AOL discs found on every street corner. This is called *optical storage*. Optical drives provide the most common form of removable mass storage on computers. Figure 2.29 shows an optical drive.

Flash memory offers a lot of storage in a small container, plus it'll retain information without electricity, a process called *solid-state storage*. Manufacturers package flash memory in a number of different formats, such as removable USB thumb drives; postage-stamp-sized SmartMedia, Secure Digital (SD), and Compact Flash cards; and Memory Stick cards that are roughly the size of a stick of gum (Figure 2.30). Portable electronics like MP3 music players, digital cameras, cell phones, and PDAs, as well as PCs, use Flash memory cards.

Keep an Eye on Your Applications with Task Manager

The Windows Task Manager utility lets you view the programs and processes that are currently stored in memory and running on your computer. Press the [Ctrl] + [Alt] + [Delete] key combination once to bring up the Windows Security dialog box, and then click on the button labeled Task Manager. Running programs are listed on the tab labeled Applications.

Random Memories

The name Random Access Memory is a bit misleading. There's nothing random about the way that RAM stores data. "Random" simply means that any part of memory's storage area can be read as easily as any other part. It doesn't have to be in sequence.

USB Drive

Smart Media   Secure Digital   Compact Flash

Figure 2.30: Flash memory devices

Figure 2.28: Hard drive

Figure 2.29: CD-RW drive and disc

Remote Storage

In today's networked world, mass storage doesn't necessarily have to be physically attached to a particular computer. One of the biggest benefits to networking is the ability to share mass storage devices on remote computers on your LAN, or on servers located "out there" on the Internet somewhere. This is collectively called remote storage, *or sometimes* virtual storage.

Connecting Output Devices

Like with input devices, operating systems support some output devices straight out of the box, but others require a two step installation process. First, you plug the device into its proper spot. Second, you load a disc in your CD player and install a bit of support software so the OS knows what sort of device it now has (or *vice versa*—software then installation).

Physical Connections

Output devices connect to the PC's hardware through connector ports on the case and through data cables inside the case. Figure 2.31 shows the back side of a desktop computer.

Your monitor connects to one of the video ports, either the traditional 15-pin *VGA* port or the newer *DVI* port (see Figure 2.31). Both types of connectors are keyed, so you can only plug them in correctly.

Audio ports on most computers are the common, mini-audio sockets seen on most small consumer audio devices. Computers typically have three color-coded audio ports: a green speaker output port, a pink microphone input port,

Figure 2.31: Output ports

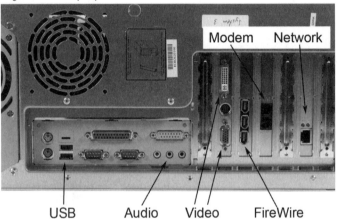

Acronym Soup

CD- and DVD-media drives and discs use different designations, such as CD-ROM, CD-R, CD-RW, DVD-ROM, and DVD+RW. The initials stand for variations of the same optical technology, offering different storage capacity (DVDs can store many times more data than CDs) and the ability to write or rewrite data on the same disc.

- *CD-ROM and DVD-ROM are read-only memory formats. The data that's stored on CD-ROM and DVD-ROM discs can't be changed.*

- *CD-R and DVD-R stand for recordable. These types of optical media can be recorded onto, or burned, if you've got the appropriate type of CD or DVD optical drive. This kind of optical media can only be recorded once, however.*

- *CD-RW, DVD-RW, and DVD+RW stand for rewritable. These types of optical media can be recorded and re-recorded onto numerous times.*

Because the different types of CD/DVD drives follow the same standards, disks recorded on one type of device should be readable by another type of device. That is, a disk burned on a CD-RW drive should be readable on any CD-ROM and CD-R drive. Older CD-based media drives can't read DVDs, but DVD drives have no trouble reading CD media. Many modern drive devices are combination drives, meaning that they can read and write to any type of CD or DVD media.

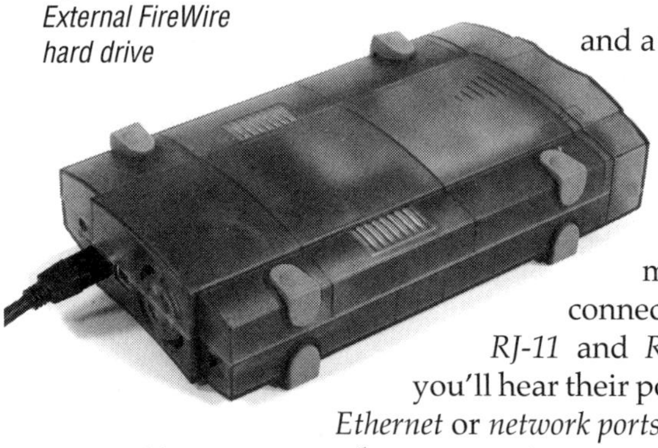

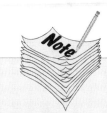

Figure 2.32: External FireWire hard drive

and a blue auxiliary input port.

Networks are collections of computers that interconnect and share data and other resources. You connect your computer to networks through two different devices, a modem and a network adapter. The connectors for these devices are called *RJ-11* and *RJ-45* connectors, respectively, and you'll hear their ports referred to as *telephone ports* and *Ethernet* or *network ports*.

Almost every other output device connects to one of the universal ports you saw earlier in this chapter, USB and FireWire. FireWire seems limited to higher-end printers and external hard drives, whereas you can get almost any device in USB. Figure 2.32 shows a hard drive with a FireWire connection.

Internal drives connect to the motherboard via *ribbon cables*, usually flat 34-wire, 40-wire, and 80-wire gray affairs. Modern hard drives use a smaller, 8-wire cable. Figure 2.33 shows a motherboard with a hard drive and CD-media drive connected.

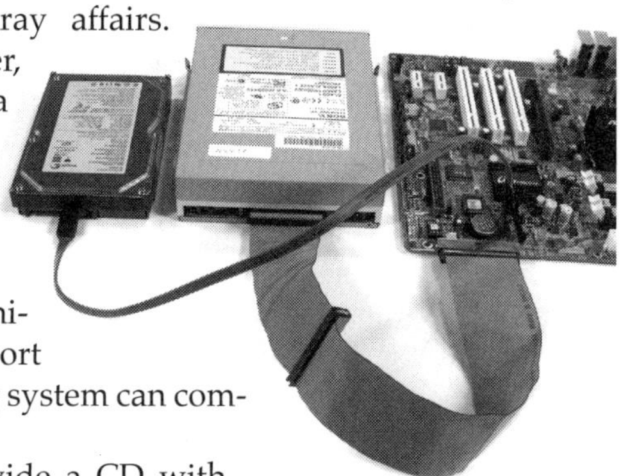

Figure 2.33: Motherboard out of the case with hard drive and CD-media drive connected

Software Support

Output devices aside from the monitor require some software support programs installed so the operating system can communicate with them effectively.

Hardware manufacturers provide a CD with drivers that the OS copies and loads into RAM to support the output device.

Phase Three: Park It – Properly Closing Programs and Shutting Down the Computer

When you're driving from one location to another, upon arrival, do you simply step out of the car and leave it running? Of course not! You roll up the windows, shut off the engine, and lock the doors. If you've brought things with you, like a backpack, wallet, or cell phone, you take those things when you leave the car.

Well, it's the same idea with your computer. Do you simply walk away when you're done with your work? Not if you're smart! There's a proper order to making sure that your work is saved and your computer secured before you walk away from your desk. This is most important in an environment where you share the computer with other users.

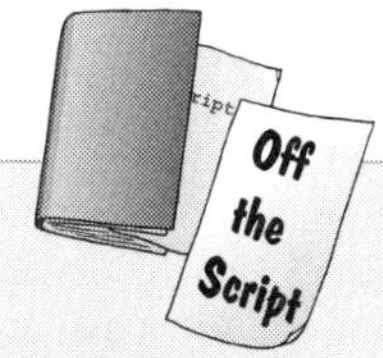

You should close things down properly for three reasons: avoiding corruption of your applications or operating system, personal security, and doing your part to save the planet. Sounds like quite a stretch for simply shutting down a computer, but let's take a look.

Anti-Corruption

One of the first things that you should learn as a computer user is that you should never turn off the computer while the operating system or applications are running. This is true for Windows, OS X, and all versions of Linux,

Some smaller devices, such as PDAs, can network wirelessly using infrared light. These devices use appropriately named nfrared ports to connect.

Legacy Connector Ports

It seems like newer and better is the order of things in the computer world. Nonetheless, some older technologies persist long after you'd think they'd disappear. These kinds of technologies are called legacy technologies. Legacy technologies are retained on newer computers for one reason: so that older hardware will still work on them. Techs call this backwards compatibility.

Two examples of legacy technology are the serial and parallel ports. Hardware that may connect to serial ports includes external modems and specialized print devices such as label printers. Devices that use the parallel port include external storage devices and scanners.

The most common use for this connector, however, is for printers. In fact, many folks call the parallel port the "printer port," which isn't entirely correct, but it's not worth arguing about, either.

You should leave installing and uninstalling mass storage devices to trained, CompTIA A+ certified technicians.

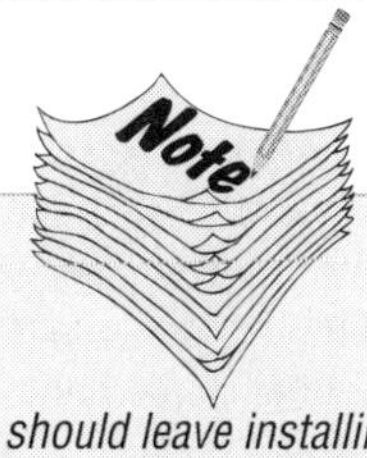

Note

Unlike with input devices, you run no risk plugging external output devices in while the computer is running.

Playing with Plugs

You've read about external output devices, so now it's time to play with them. What's plugged into your computer? Try unscrewing and unplugging the monitor cable from the video port. (Trace the connection from the back of the monitor.) What kind of video do you have? What was the effect of unplugging the video cable when the computer was running? Try plugging it in only part way. What does that do to your screen? What other output devices do you have?

Figure 2.34: Close button

What's the Worst that Can Happen?

Information stored in RAM while you're using an application includes not only your data files and application program files, but also your essential OS files. In some cases, incorrectly shutting down the computer will damage the OS itself!

(although not true for PDAs running PalmOS or PocketPC). The reason for this is simple: to prevent data loss. Data, application, and OS files held in RAM are in a vulnerable state. If you mistakenly click the wrong button, or if your computer loses power, then the data may be flushed out of RAM without saving it to disk. In the case of data files, this means any work that wasn't saved is gone. With program and OS files, this can mean file corruption that may prevent them from running properly the next time you fire them up.

Shutting down properly involves three or four steps. First, save and close any data file you're working on. We looked at this process earlier in the chapter. Second, close any running applications. You can do this in quite a few ways, such as clicking the **Close** button. In Windows programs, it's the little **X** button located in the top right-hand corner of the application window, as you can see in Figure 2.34. You can also go to **File | Exit** on the main menu. Most applications respond to a hotkey combination, such as **[Alt + F4]** in Windows or **[Apple + Q]** in OS X.

The third and fourth steps involve logging out of the operating system [[[[and powering down the computer. Doing these steps properly avoids file corruption, but also provide other benefits, such as security and energy savings.

Personal Security

Have you ever received a letter from someone? How did you know the person who wrote it is the person you think wrote it? Handwriting recognition might help, but what if the letter is typed? What would you do if you received the letter in Figure 2.35. Seems like a pretty exciting opportunity, right?

Figure 2.35: Letter supposedly from "Mom"

Mom never wrote that letter. It's a scam; but if the letter had your mom's address as the return address and the postage information seemed correct, you might have second thoughts. In the world of computers, the potential for such *identity theft* cranks up to very high.

If you walk away from your computer, still logged in, the next person who sits down at that computer can become you as far as the rest of the world can tell. The thief could use your computer to hurt others, to steal, to do all sorts of mischief, all while appearing to be you. Guess who will take the heat for the evil deeds? You will.

When you walk away, you need to log out. To log out in Windows, go to **Start | Log Off** or press **[Ctrl + Alt + Delete]** once and click the **Log Off** button in the Windows Security dialog box. To log out in OS X, go to the **Apple menu** and select **Log Off**. Couldn't be simpler!

Green Acres

Computers use electricity, some at a huge rate, and unfortunately for computer users, electricity doesn't grow on trees. As computers go into service in every aspect of life, the demand for electricity goes way up. The fourth step in the proper shut down process, therefore, is to close the operating system and power off the computer. This generally takes a single action on your part. In Windows, for example, rather than simply logging out, you can go to **Start | Shut Down** to log out, close the OS, and power down.

Because it takes more electricity to power up a computer than to leave one sitting idle, you should follow this basic rule with your computer use. Power up when you want to use the computer and then power down at the end of the day or when you're done using it for the day.

Fast User Switching
*By default, Windows XP Home allows you to log off without closing your applications, using what's called Fast User Switching. You can do this semi-log off by pressing the **[Windows key + L]** keyboard combination.*

Phase One: Start Me Up! – The Computer's Boot Process

■ The flow of data starts with the boot process. First you turn the power on, waking the CPU. The CPU then communicates with the ROM-BIOS memory chip to start the hardware test process. The ROM-BIOS memory chip contains vital programs that enable your computer to identify its hardware and start itself when you press the power button.

■ The operating system takes over, loading from the hard drive into RAM and presenting the user with a user interface. You can log in at that point.

Phase Two: The Dance – Interacting with the Computer

■ Once booted, you can get to work by typing a command or double-clicking an icon or program file. The computer processes your request, opening the application interface so you can type something in. The computer processes what you type and updates the screen to give you feedback.

■ Input devices enable you to give commands to the computer. You can type using the keyboard; click on icons and buttons using a pointing device such as a mouse, trackball, or touchpad; speak using the microphone; or game with a joystick or game pad.

■ Some input devices also enable you to add data to the computer. You can take a picture of your cat with a digital camera, for example. A scanner enables you to create a digital image of an old-fashioned photograph. You can also use a scanner to import a type-written document directly into a word processing program, a process called optical character recognition (OCR).

■ Devices connect to the computer's hardware through connector ports, usually located on the back of your computer case. Manufacturers key ports and connectors by giving them odd shapes, thus making it impossible to plug them in incorrectly. Most input devices today plug into one of the two universal ports, universal serial bus (USB) or FireWire.

■ Input devices usually require some software support programs installed so the operating system can communicate with them effectively. Hardware manufacturers provide a CD with small programs, called drivers, that the OS copies and loads into RAM to support the input device.

■ You can use input devices to start an application. The most common way in graphical-based operating systems such as Windows and Macintosh OS X is to click the program icon in the Start Menu (Windows) or double-click the program icon in the Finder (OS X). The operating system and the CPU interpret your command and send commands to the hard drive to get the files for that application so they can be loaded into RAM and the CPU can process them.

■ Once you have an application open, you can create new files. Almost every productivity application—as opposed to games—has a File option on the main menu. Creating a file is as simple as going to—**File | New** and then specifying what sort of file you want.

■ To engage fully in the "interacting with the computer" phase, you need properly connected and configured output devices. Output takes many forms, such as standard feedback options of changing the display and making sound come out the speakers. Other forms of output include printing, communicating over a network (like the Internet), and saving files to some sort of mass storage, such as a hard drive or compact disc.

■ Three technologies dominate the current storage scene for computers: magnetic, optical, and solid state. Hard drives and floppy disks save information magnetically on platters. Hard drives provide the primary fixed mass storage in almost ev ery computer. CD- and DVD-media drives use optical lasers to read information stored on shiny discs. These optical drives provide the most common form of removable mass storage on computers. The solid state flash memory offers a lot of storage in a small container, plus it'll retain information without electricity. Manufacturers package flash memory in a number of different formats, such as removable USB thumb drives and postage-stamp-sized SmartMedia.

■ Output devices connect to the PC's hardware through connector ports on the case and through data cables inside the case. Your monitor connects to one of the video ports, either the traditional 15-pin VGA port or the newer DVI port. PCs typically have three color-coded audio ports: a green speaker output port, a pink microphone input port, and a blue auxiliary input port. Almost every other external output device connects to one of the universal ports, USB and FireWire. Internal drives connect to the motherboard via ribbon cables, usually flat 34-wire, 40-wire, and 80-wire gray affairs. Modern hard drives use a smaller, 8-wire cable.

Phase Three: Park It – Properly Closing Programs and Shutting Down the Computer

■ You should never turn off the computer while the operating system or applications are running. To do so runs the risk of corrupting your application or operating system files.

■ Shutting down properly involves three or four steps. First, save and close any data file you're working on. Second, close any running applications, often by going to **File | Exit** or **File | Quit**. The third and fourth steps involve logging out of the operating system and powering down the computer. In Windows, go to **Start | Log Off** or **Start | Shut Down**; in OS X, go to **Apple menu | Shut Down**.

Key Terms

Algorithms

Boot

Digital camera

Drivers

FireWire

Flash memory

Game pad

Input devices

Joystick

Key

Keyboard

Magnetic storage

Microphone

Monitor

Mouse

Musical instrument digital interface (MIDI)

Optical character recognition (OCR)

Optical storage

Output devices

Plotter

Plug and Play

Power supply

Printer

Projector

Remote storage

Read-only memory-basic input/
    output system (ROM-BIOS)

Ribbon cable

Scanner

Services

Solid-state storage

Speakers

System clock

Thumb mouse

Touchpad

Trackball

Universal serial bus (USB)

Video card

Voice synthesizer

Key Term Quiz

Use the Key Terms list to complete the following sentences. Not all the terms will be used.

1. The _____ converts alternating-current (AC) electricity that comes out of your wall socket into direct current (DC) used by the computer.

2. A _____ makes a digital image of a text document or photo, which you can then edit on your computer.

3. The _____ draws the images that you see on your display monitor.

4. _____ devices access data stored on reflective disks using laser light.

5. External devices that need consistent, high-speed access to the computer, such as storage drives and digital video camcorders, connect to the computer using _____.

6. Hard disk drives and floppy diskettes are examples of _____.

7. John can use a _____ to give voice commands to his computer.

8. The keyboard, mouse, and microphone on a PC are all used as _____.

9. A visually-impaired user could get feedback from the computer with a _____, thus enabling him or her to enjoy interacting with the computer.

10. A _____ is a type of printer used to produce large, detailed drawings such as blueprints.

Multiple Choice Quiz

1. Following the power-on and hardware test phases, what is the first software loaded into memory?
   A. Operating system
   B. Desktop
   C. CPU
   D. Start menu

2. What action takes place when you save a file opened in an application program?
   A. The file is copied from the mass storage device into RAM.
   B. The file is flushed from RAM.
   C. The file is copied from RAM onto the mass storage device.
   D. The file is copied from RAM onto the ROM-BIOS memory chip.

3. Which of the following statements is **not** correct?
   A. Data stored on CD-ROM can't be altered.
   B. Data can only be recorded onto a DVD-R disc once.
   C. Data can be written to CD-RW disc numerous times.
   D. CD-ROM discs need constant power to retain data.

4. True or false? You can plug keyboards and mice into either of the two keyboard and mouse ports on a computer and they will work just fine.
   A. True. The connector ports are interchangeable and a keyboard or mouse will work if plugged into either socket.
   B. False. The connector ports are not interchangeable, and a keyboard or mouse will only work when plugged into the appropriate keyboard or mouse socket.

5. Which of the following are examples of magnetic storage media? (Select all that apply.)
   A. Hard drive
   B. Floppy diskette
   C. CD-ROM disc
   D. USB thumb drive

6. You've got a scanner connected to your PC and you need to convert a number of printed text documents into digital documents that you can edit with your word processor. What type of software do you need to do this?
   A. Photo editing software
   B. Voice recognition software
   C. Optical character recognition software
   D. Tactile feedback software

7. Which of the following enables you to output your work onto paper?
   A. Printer
   B. Scanner
   C. Speakers
   D. Microphone

8. Why is it important to follow the proper steps when shutting down your computer instead of simply turning the power switch off?
   A. Failing to save your work, close your programs, and exit the operating system properly will void your computer warranty.
   B. Failing to save your work, close your programs, and exit the operating system properly can result in data loss and program corruption.
   C. Failing to save your work, close your programs, and exit the operating system properly causes your CPU to overheat.
   D. Failing to save your work, close your programs, and exit the operating system properly has no ill effects on the PC.

9. Which of the following are valid methods for starting an application? (Select all that apply.)
   A. Double-click the program's icon on your desktop.
   B. Click **Start | Run**, and browse to the program's executable file.
   C. Double-click on a file associated with the application program.
   D. Copy the program's executable file to your desktop.

CHAPTER 2: REVIEW

10. What happens during the hardware test phase of the startup process?
    A. Programs in the computer ROM-BIOS identify your PC's hardware and perform diagnostic tests to determine if they are in proper working order.
    B. Programs in the computer ROM-BIOS identify the user and apply the appropriate security restrictions to the user's Windows account.
    C. Power flows to the PC hardware, waking the CPU, which in turn wakes the ROM-BIOS circuit.
    D. Windows instructs the CPU to copy the necessary system files, services, drivers, and so on into system RAM.

11. Which of the following are examples of specialized input devices?
    A. Barcode readers
    B. Touch screens
    C. Scientific probes
    D. LCD projector

12. What is another name for a network adapter connector?
    A. RJ-11
    B. RJ-13
    C. RJ-45
    D. RJ-54

13. Which of the following ports can take input or output devices? (Select all that apply.)
    A. FireWire
    B. USB
    C. Keyboard
    D. DVI

14. Which of the following is **not** a valid way to save an open data file?
    A. Click the **Save** button.
    B. Press the **[Alt + F4]** keyboard combination.
    C. Press the **[Ctrl + S]** keyboard combination.
    D. Click **File | Save** from the program file menu.

15. Which of the following devices enable you to control the mouse pointer and click on screen elements? (Select all that apply.)
    A. Mouse
    B. Keyboard
    C. Trackball
    D. Touchpad

Essay Questions

1. Describe the computer boot process. When does the process start? What components are needed? When does the process end?

2. Describe what happens when you open a data file from within an application program. Where does an open file reside? What happens when you save the file?

3. You work for an organization that uses a mixture of old and new hardware devices, such as printers, network hardware, and so on. Your boss needs to purchase some new computers, and the computer salesman is pushing a model that he calls "legacy free." Explain to your boss the purpose of retaining legacy technology on new computers.

Projects

1. So, what's out there today in the world of input and output devices? Visit your local computer store or go online to a major hardware site, like www.directron.com or www.newegg.com, and research the options available. Do the big retail outfits offer anything for visually impaired users? Try a search at www.google.com with these keywords: "ADA-compliant computer hardware buy" and see what you can find.

   Once you've done your research, put together input and output devices (with descriptions and pictures, if possible) for three potential users: Johnny Hotshot, who wants the coolest-looking input and output devices he can find; Scott Sidekick, who wants the weirdest-looking input and output devices he can find; and Susie Angel, who can't see very well but wants to participate fully in the computer revolution.

2. Here's the scenario: Ahmed goes to the computer lab, boots up a Windows computer, and opens up Photoshop (an application for working with digital photos). He then plugs his digital camera into one of the universal sockets on the PC and imports some photos. After choosing the best one, he works with it and saves it to mass storage inside the PC for later use, then prints out a copy.

   Make a chart that illustrates the flow of data throughout this scenario. Make sure you include at least the following information: operating system files, application files, and the input and output of the digital photograph Ahmed chose.

COMPUTER LITERACY: YOUR TICKET TO IC³ CERTIFICATION

How to Speak Geek and Make Informed Computer Purchasing Decisions

Homer:	"Umm ... I guess I'll take that one."
Salesman:	"Well, do you need a paperweight? 'Cause if you buy that machine, that's all you're going to have, an expensive paperweight."
Homer:	"Well, a paperweight would be nice, but what I really need is a computer. How about that one?"
Salesman:	"That technology is three months old. Only suckers buy out-of-date machines. You're not a sucker, are you sir?"
Homer:	"Heavens no!"
Salesman:	"Oh good, because if you were, I'd have to ask you to leave the store."
Homer:	"I just need something to receive e-mail."
Salesman:	[whistles] "You'll need a top-of-the-line machine for that!"

– Homer and Salesman, The Simpsons

This chapter covers the following IC³ exam objectives:

- IC³-1   1.1.5   Identify how the speed of the microprocessor is measured

- IC³-1   1.1.7   Identify concepts related to how memory is measured

- IC³-1   1.3.1   Identify criteria for selecting a personal computer

- IC³-1   1.3.2   Identify factors that affect computer performance

- IC³-1   1.3.3   Identify hardware and software considerations when purchasing a computer

- IC³-1   1.3.4   Identify other factors that go into decisions to purchase a computer

Speaking the language of the computer world can be tricky for the uninitiated. Your first thought might be "Why would I want to do that?" After all, you don't necessarily need to pepper your conversations with "mega-this" and "giga-that" in order to sit down and use a computer. Well, for starters, consider that you have to have a pretty good handle on geek-speak just to accomplish the simple act of buying a computer.

Check out the computer ads and you'll immediately be up to your eyebrows in a flood of jargon, acronyms, and plain technobabble. Have a look at this offering from a big-name computer maker that I pulled out of my local newspaper this morning:

- Intel® Pentium® 4 Processor (3.0 GHz, 800 MHz FSB)
- Microsoft® Windows® XP Home Edition
- 512 MB DDR-SDRAM @ 400 MHz
- Up to 256 MB DDR Video Memory (shared)
- 200 GB Ultra ATA/100 7200 RPM Hard Drive
- 52X CD-RW Drive + 16X DVD+/-RW
- 7 Gigawatt Reverse Flux Capacitor
- Built-in 10/100 Ethernet LAN; 56 K fax/data modem
- 4 PCI (2 available), 1 PCI-E x16
- 17 inch LCD @ 1280 x 1024

Can you spot the specification that I threw in there just for laughs?

Although it might seem as if the computer makers are speaking in their own secret code, it's not that complicated once you break it down. Consider this chapter to be your secret decoder ring to the language of the geek and buying guide rolled into one.

The chapter starts with a discussion about performance, how understanding the speed, capacity, and sophistication of individual computer components can help you decide which computer works best in specific circumstances. You'll then look at factors beyond performance that you should consider when making computer equipment decisions, such as operating system, hardware, and program requirements. Finally, the chapter wraps up with a brief discussion on computer ownership factors, such as warranty plans, future upgrades, and expenses, that should influence an informed buyer. Let's get started.

Performance: Speed, Capacity, and Sophistication

When assessing the performance of a computer, you need to understand the components and steps in the computing process. You know this from your study of Chapter 2—the CPU processes everything, but needs data and programs in RAM to do so. The computer stores data and programs on the hard drive or on some other mass storage device. When it comes time for output to the monitor, the video card processor and memory come into play as well.

When you double-click a program icon, such as Solitaire, the CPU responds because it understands—through the operating system—what you want it to do. The CPU sends a message to the hard drive: "Hey! Retrieve the files for Solitaire and send them to RAM so I can work!" Once the RAM has the files, the CPU can obey your demand and process

Figure 3.1: CPU opening Solitaire

those files, sending commands to the video card processor to put Word on your monitor (Figure 3.1).

Many factors determine how quickly a computer can obey your requests. You can't judge performance by a single factor, because so many devices come into play with a seemingly simple request, like double-clicking an icon.

Most computer performance benchmarks revolve around three factors: speed, capacity, and sophistication (Figure 3.2). The speed of devices affects every aspect of the computing process. How quickly does the CPU respond to your initial request (the double-click)? How much time does it take the hard drive to access the requested files and send them to RAM? How quickly does the RAM respond to the CPU during the processing phase? Once the CPU finishes processing, how quickly can the video card update your screen? Capacity comes into play as well, determining the amount of programs and data a hard drive can store and the total size of files the RAM can hold. Finally, how sophisticated is the CPU? Can it handle the request you've made? The sophistication of the video card processor makes a huge difference in important applications, such as games. Some cards simply can't handle advanced graphics. Let's look at all three factors.

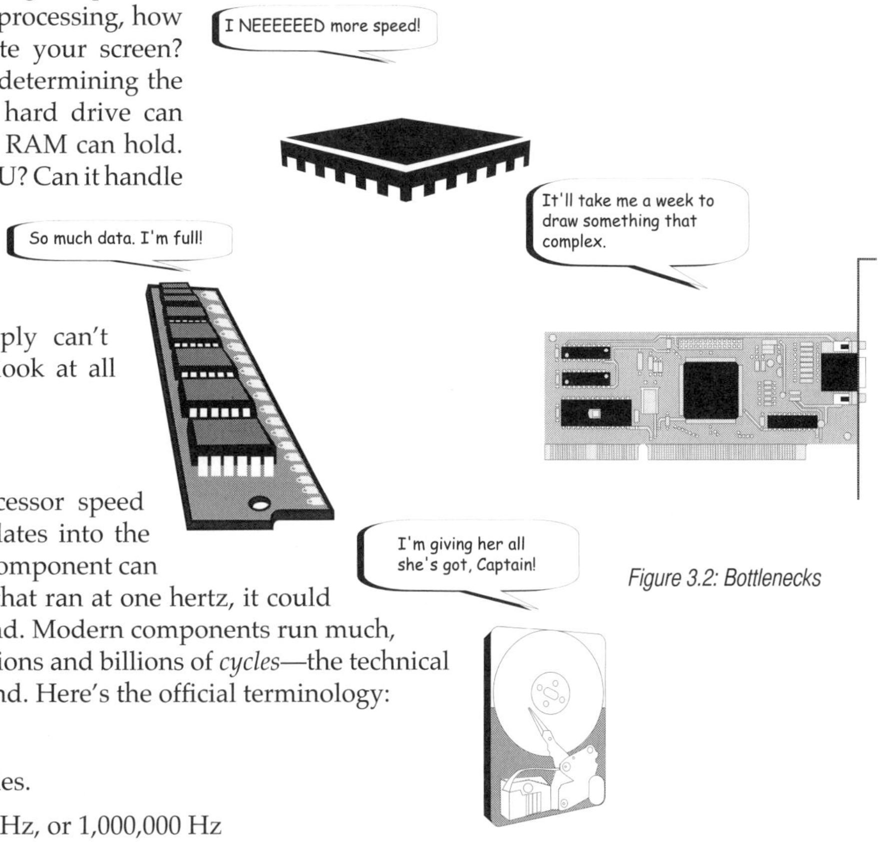

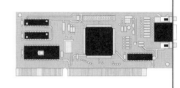

Speed

CPU, RAM, and video card processor speed is measured in *hertz*, which translates into the number of times per second each component can do things. If you had a processor that ran at one hertz, it could process one line of code each second. Modern components run much, much faster than that, into the millions and billions of *cycles*—the technical term for "doing things"—per second. Here's the official terminology:

Figure 3.2: Bottlenecks

- One hertz = one cycle.
- One *kilohertz* (*KHz*) = 1,000 cycles.
- One *megahertz* (*MHz*) = 1,000 KHz, or 1,000,000 Hz
- One *gigahertz* (*GHz*) = 1,000 MHz, or 1,000,000,000 Hz

A 1-GHz CPU can churn through one billion calculations per second. That's pretty fast, but by today's standards, 1 GHz is on the low end of processor performance! Typical CPUs these days run in the 3+ GHz range. Figure 3.3 shows a modern CPU.

Because the CPU handles the vast majority of the work in processing, increasing CPU speed offers your biggest bang for the buck in terms of increasing the overall speed of the computer. That's not the only thing you can do to increase performance speed, though. Faster system RAM and faster hard drives can make a major impact. A higher quality video card—with a faster processor and faster RAM—can likewise prove invaluable for enhancing performance, although you'll typically only see the performance gains in intensive games.

Figure 3.3: Modern CPU

Network Speed

Capacity

Hard drive and RAM capacity can have a major impact on computer performance. Not enough of either one can destabilize a computer or cause you to be unable to run some programs. That begs the question though, of how much is enough? To make capacity numbers make sense, we've got to get down to the basics.

Doing the Numbers

Computers store everything in strings of binary 1s and 0s, called *binary numbers*; processors use binary numbers to produce what you see on the screen or hear through your computer's speakers. All the beautiful photographs on a friend's PC? That fantastic-sounding single downloaded from the iTunes Music Store? They're all just strings of 1s and 0s (Figure 3.4).

The smallest binary unit is a *bit*, which can be either a 0 or a 1. Eight bits make a *byte*. Each single computer character, such as a number, letter, or punctuation mark (or even a blank space between letters) is stored as a single byte. For example, the typed phrase, "mares eat oats, and does eat oats, but little lambs eat ivy," takes up 60 bytes (not counting the quotation marks.) See Figure 3.5.

Although computers don't have any trouble thinking in terms of byte after byte of data, it gets pretty confusing for us mere mortals after a few thousand. That's why we abbreviate groupings of large storage units. Common units of measurement abbreviations are:

Figure 3.4: MP3 file

- One byte = 8 bits

- One *kilobyte* (*KB*) = 1,024 bytes

- One *megabyte* (*MB*) = 1,024 KB

- One *gigabyte* (*GB*) = 1,024 MB

- One *terabyte* (*TB*) = 1,024 GB

A hard drive with a capacity of 150 GB, therefore, can hold 153,600 MB or 157,286,400 KB or 161,061,273,600 bytes or 1,288,490,188,800 bits! Much easier to say 150 GB, isn't it?

The units go up higher to exabytes, petabytes, chongobytes, and so on, but practically speaking, those are the units of measurement that you'll work with in the real world for the next few years.

Hard Drive Capacity

You need a hard drive big enough to store your programs and your data, plus some left over that the operating system uses. If you run low on space (like below 10% of the total capacity of the drive), your computer will most

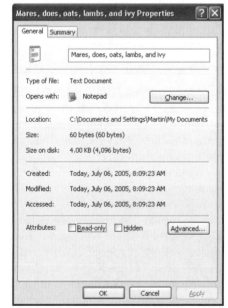

Figure 3.5: File properties showing size

definitely start slowing down dramatically. The problem with determining the right amount of drive space for someone is that everyone has different computing needs. My primary work system, for example, has Windows XP Professional loaded, plus a slew of productivity (and not so productive) applications (Office, Photoshop, Illustrator, iTunes, Half-Life 2, Everquest 2), as you can see in Figure 3.6.

Windows and my necessary work applications take up 3 GB, and just one of the games I play (Half-Life 2) takes up over 5 GB of hard drive space! For my needs, therefore, my primary hard drive has to be at least 10 GB and that gives me almost no room to store data or add new programs. Fortunately, modern hard drives cost very little (compared to earlier models) and offer acres of data storage.

System Memory Capacity

The CPU uses system memory to store actively running programs and data temporarily, including the operating system, so the amount of RAM you have directly affects performance. If you don't have enough to run your OS, load your application, and have space for data files, your system can crash or simply not enable you to accomplish your computing tasks.

RAM is one of those commodities of which you just can't have enough. More RAM means that you can have more programs and processes running at the same time. Having more RAM on the system also means that the CPU has to make fewer trips to the hard drive for data.

What's an adequate amount of RAM to have? It depends on what you're using your computer to do, but in general the absolute minimum amount that you'd need to run Windows XP or Macintosh OS X efficiently is 256 MB. Windows will run on less, but everything that you do would take longer.

Starting with that base number, you should increase RAM depending on your machine usage.

Because I tend to have a lot of applications open all at the same time—e-mail, Web browser, Word, Photoshop, and Illustrator—my system needs a lot of RAM. With just those programs mentioned plus Windows, for example, my PC uses over 400 MB of RAM. When putting together images for this book, the data files (photographs and illustrations) can add at least another 200-300 MB used!

Figure 3.6: That's a lot of applications!

Sophistication

The sophistication of devices can make a profound impact on the performance of a computer. The CPUs sold today, for example, go from low-end processors that run productivity applications just fine but stumble on anything demanding, to CPUs that can run the latest and greatest game or video production software with ease. Video cards vary wildly in performance and features and if you choose incorrectly, you're in for a bad computing experience.

Software makers list the minimum and recommended hardware requirements for their programs on the packaging of their products, or on their company Web site. These estimates are usually more theoretical than practical. You should take those numbers and double them for a more realistic idea of how much RAM you'll need to run a program efficiently.

Going from 32-bit to 64-bit processing does not double the complexity of potential program. Oh, no. Going from 32-bit to only 33-bit would double the complexity. From 33-bit to 34-bit would double it again. Keep doing the doubling until you get to 64-bit and you'll get a sense of just how superior 64-bit is over 32-bit!

CPU Example

Advanced Micro Devices (AMD) manufactures a good portion of the CPUs on the market, but brands their CPUs with seemingly ridiculous names and numbers. Here are a few advertised at the end of summer, 2005:

- Athlon XP Barton 3000+ CPU: $127

- Athlon 64 3000+ CPU: $146

- Athlon 64 3800+ CPU: $375

- Athlon 64 X2 3800+ CPU: $419

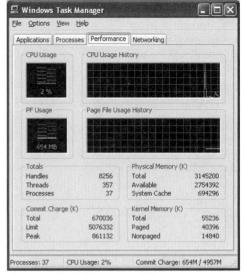

Figure 3.7: Task Manager

The number (3000+, 3800+) indicates speed, so it makes sense that the two highest speed processors would cost more than the others. The distinction between CPUs of similar speeds, on the other hand, boils down to the sophistication of the processor. The first one (Athlon XP) is a 32-bit processor, which means it handles the complexity of program that's in Windows and almost every computer application out there. The other three are 64-bit processors, which means that if you have an operating system and applications that can take advantage of it, your programs can be wildly more complex (Figure 3.8).

Finally, the Athlon 64 X2 puts two processors in the space of one CPU (Figure 3.9). For a few dollars more, therefore, you could double your processing power and sophistication by choosing it over the plain vanilla Athlon 64.

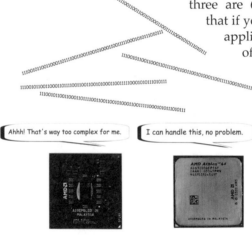

Figure 3.8: Degrees of sophistication

Figure 3.9: Athlon 64 X2 dual-core CPU (Photo courtesy of AMD)

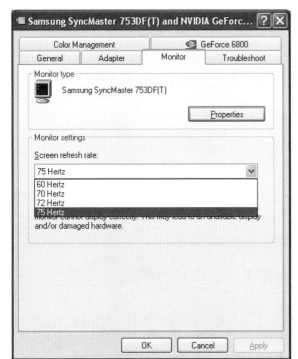

Figure 3.10: Refresh rate

Video Card Example

Sitting in front of a traditional monitor all day long puts a user at a high risk of eyestrain. That's because the solid picture you see on the screen isn't all that solid. Video cards *refresh* the little red, green, and blue dots that make up the screen many times per second. The more it refreshes, the more solid your screen appears. Drop down to 60 refreshes per second and you'll see noticeable flicker on the screen and develop head aches, sore eyes, and worse. Figure 3.10 shows the *refresh rate* in Hertz, meaning cycles per second, for a Samsung SyncMaster monitor.

Because I work many hours a day at the computer, I needed a video card that I could crank up to avoid eyestrain. The funny part is that the video card driving this monitor cost many hundreds of dollars, but *not* solely because of the high refresh rate. This card could power the highest end (at the time) 3-D games and also enable me to use two monitors at once. These features added a lot to the cost. If you knew you would not play those kinds of games, and only needed to connect to a single monitor, then a much less expensive model would have worked fine.

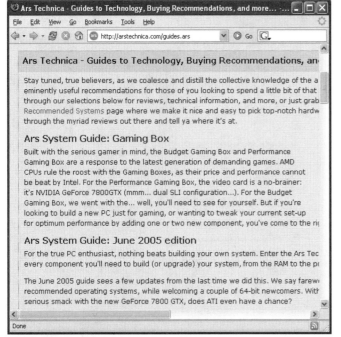

Figure 3.11: Ars Technica

Branding Problems

CPU and video processor sophistication make the most difference in applications, so make a good place to start figuring the differences among computer choices. The problem is that two manufacturers—Intel and Advanced Micro Devices (AMD)— make the majority of CPUs, but offer literally dozens of variations that all

Only CRT monitors have the refresh rate issue. LCD monitors do not need to be refreshed.

Monitor Types
You learned about the two types of monitors—CRTs and LCDs—in Chapter 2, "Going with the Data Flow." What's the difference? Which offers the most energy savings? What about space savings?

Current Markets
CPU manufacturers offer new and improved processors almost as quickly as Gap changes clothes offerings, and video manufacturers are even worse (because there are more of them playing the game). What you read in any printed source by definition is out of date, simply because the printing process takes time and manufacturers work overtime.

To be an informed computer user means going to the Internet to look up the latest offerings. One of the most accessible sources for current information is Ars Technica. So, fire up a Web browser if you have one available, and surf to www.arstechnica.com. When you get there, click on the link to Guides (see Figure 3.11) and read through their latest "Ars System Guide" article(s).

sound the same. Worse, several companies manufacture video card processors and dozens of companies produce actual video cards, making the choices here even more confusing. So what's a buyer to do?

You can do all the legwork on your own, or do what the rest of the world does and surf some tech sites, learning the ropes from enthusiasts about the current state of the art (see the Action! sidebar for details).

The Right Tool for the Job: Choosing the Best Computer for Your Needs

Now it comes down to the big question, which computer is right for you? What OS is best for you, Windows, Macintosh, or Linux? Do you want a showpiece of a desktop system with lots of blinking lights and shiny bits, or do you want a sleek laptop system that you can tuck out of the way when you're not using it? What kind of hardware is worth spending money on? What kind of software do you need? What about extras like printers, Internet access, extended warranty plans?

Let's take a look at some of the key factors that you should consider when shopping for computers.

Windows, Mac, or Linux?

The biggest decision in front of you is the choice of computer operating system. Once you pick an OS, you're committed to learning how to compute according to the rules of that OS. Should you later decide that you don't care for that particular operating system after all, switching to another team can be an expensive and time-consuming proposition.

So, what's it going to be? Windows? Mac? What about Linux?

You can be assured that each of the major operating systems can each perform the same computing tasks. Many vendors supply productivity software, games, multimedia, communications, and other types of applications for each platform (although with differing degrees of availability.) Setting aside simple matters of preference, consider the following as your important deciding factors:

Figure 3.12: Windows desktop

- Availability – How easy will it be to outfit your computer with appropriate hardware, software, and peripherals?

- Compatibility – Will your computer be able to communicate with other computers on your network? Will you be able to share data and resources?

- Support – How easily can you get help when you need it?

- Cost – Does the machine you want have the features you need for the amount you want to spend? How much will it cost you to upgrade the computer's OS when a new version comes out?

Let's see how the three major operating systems match up.

Windows

It's a Windows world out there, as Microsoft's flagship operating system has a death grip on the vast majority of computers (Figure 3.12). You can readily get Windows computers and Windows-compatible hardware components and software programs from many retail computer stores, department stores, and locations on the Internet. Aside from the option of buying a Windows computer off the shelf, many big-name dealers and smaller computer stores will custom-build a Windows system to your specifications.

Windows support is also easy to come by from a wide variety of sources. Most new Windows PCs come with free support for a certain duration, after which you must pay to have problems resolved. Many large computer retailers and small mom-and-pop computer stores offer repair and upgrade services for a fee. Free support is usually available from online sources such as newsgroups, vendor and user group Web sites, or via the "friend-of-a-friend" support network—friends, neighbors, and co-workers who might have more knowledge than you.

New Windows PCs run the gamut in cost from a mere $300 US up to over ten times that amount, depending on the configuration and features. The cost of upgrading depends on which version of Windows you're using. Currently, it costs $99 US to upgrade from an older version of Windows to Windows XP Home Edition, and $199 US to upgrade to Windows XP Professional.

All in the Windows Family

Windows XP comes in three basic versions, Home, Professional, and Media Center.

- *Windows XP Home Edition is made for the home and small business user. XP Home Edition has all of the security and stability that you'd expect from Windows, but some advanced configuration options and features are disabled.*

- *Windows XP Professional is made for business users on large Windows networks. Windows XP Professional has all of the features of Windows Home Edition, plus a number of advanced functions and tools that are absent from XP Home Edition, such as dual-CPU support, Windows domain network access, and support for multiple language interfaces.*

- *Windows XP Media Center helps integrate home theater and computers, by enabling you to watch television, movies, and more with the PC (Figure 3.13). Oh, and most versions come with a slick remote control, just like for your TV.*

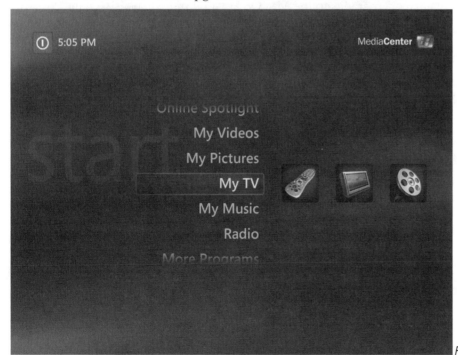

Online Spotlight
My Videos
My Pictures
My TV
My Music
Radio
More Programs

5:05 PM MediaCenter

Figure 3.13: Windows XP Media Center

Input/Output Devices

Macintosh

Macintosh OS X offers the simplest, most intuitive user interface of any commercial operating system available (Figure 3.14). You want to do [pick your task]? In almost every case, you can perform the task with a click of the mouse or a press of keyboard keys that make sense, like **[Cmd + P]** to print.

Figure 3.14: OS X desktop

Unlike with Windows systems, only Apple and authorized Apple resellers sell Macs. Given Mac's smaller market share, there simply aren't as many products available for Macs as there are for Windows systems. In many cases, vendors may not produce a Macintosh version of their products until months or years after they ship their Windows products. This may or may not effect you, depending on the type of product that you're looking for. Personally, I'm *still* waiting on a Mac-compatible version of Roller Coaster Tycoon!

The latest version of OS X integrates very well with other operating systems on a network and enables you to share data and resources like printers. Earlier versions may require that you jump through some more hoops to get connected, including purchasing additional software.

Support from Apple is usually top-notch. Apple retail stores offer free tech consultation via their "Genius Bar" and like Microsoft, their Web site has an extensive archive of support articles.

Cost-wise, Apple computers are slightly more expensive than comparable Windows machines, but *hey*—they come with a free subscription to Macworld magazine! Upgrades to the Mac OS are a bit more expensive than Windows XP Home Edition and less expensive than Windows XP Professional, running at about $129 US.

Linux

Linux combines an amazingly powerful and sophisticated computer operating system with a price tag that simply can't be beaten: Free. Believe it or not, thousands of people around the world spend their free time working on various versions of Linux—called *distros* (short for *distributions*)—and then makes them available for free. This model of product development is called *open source*.

On the other hand, Linux systems have a limited audience, so you won't find them sitting on the shelf of your local big-box computer store. There are many sources for custom-built Linux systems online, and numerous small, specialized computer shops are happy to build a system for you. Finding software for Linux systems can be something of an adventure. Most software vendors simply don't make Linux versions of their products, but you can usually find a Linux equivalent for the most popular types of Windows software. Figure 3.15 shows a Linux desktop.

Linux systems integrate very well with Windows and Macintosh systems, and are also able to share data in any number of standard formats. Enabling support for services like printing might require some additional configuration.

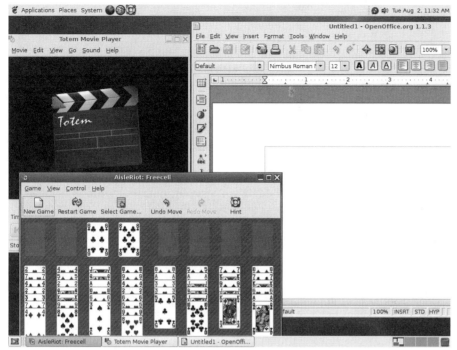

Figure 3.15: Linux desktop

Depending on the distro of Linux that you use, the cost of the OS software may be on par with the full versions of Windows or Macintosh, or as low as free. The bulk of the cost of Linux computers is in the hardware and in the time you spend learning how to use it.

Desktop or Laptop?

Whether to get a desktop or laptop system used to be an easy decision, simply because until recently, laptops cost much more and performed less well than their desktop counterparts. Nowadays, however, laptops have gotten more powerful and dropped in price, making the choice a bit trickier.

Desktop Computers

Desktop systems are the status quo for most schools, businesses, and homes. Unless they specifically need a portable system, most people choose a desktop system by default.

Desktop systems have a couple of advantages over laptops. For one thing, they're somewhat cheaper than comparable laptops, so you get a bit more bang for your computer buck. Also, they're more upgradeable than laptops. You can replace any component on a desktop PC, up to and including the motherboard itself.

On the other hand, desktop PCs take up more space than laptops (Figure 3.16). If you've got room to spare, than this might not be an issue, but if you're living in a cramped dorm room or a small apartment, then size matters.

Figure 3.16: Full desktop PC setup

Figure 3.17: Laptop connected to peripherals through a docking station

Laptop Computers

The obvious advantage of a laptop over a desktop system is portability. No more being tethered to your desk, you can take your desktop with you everywhere you go. This is a particularly inviting option given the wide availability of wireless Internet connections. If your laptop has the appropriate hardware, you can get online at the library, coffee shop, airport, and many other places.

Further, with a device called a *docking station*, you can quickly turn your laptop into a sort of pseudo-desktop system (Figure 3.17). Docking stations enable you to connect to full-sized keyboards and mice, external display monitors, printers, and more.

On the downside, laptop portability comes at a price—*literally*. You pay more for a laptop computer than you do for a similarly-configured desktop system. Laptop systems are also more limited in the type of upgrades that can be performed on them. Most only enable techs to add RAM and replace the hard drive. Laptops are also easier to damage, lose, or have stolen.

Making a Choice

Ultimately, the big question is, where are going to use your computer? If you're a student who has to take notes and work on assignments while on the go, or a business professional who has to have access to work files and applications at any time, then a laptop is the right choice for you. Many people get laptop systems even if they don't need to move them around, simply because they take up less space. If you're a certified computer geek who constantly tweaks your system with new hardware components, or if you simply have no need to take your computer around with you, then a desktop is what you want.

How Much Hardware Muscle Do You Need?

A big part of deciding on the right computer is to decide how much computing power you actually need. The instinct is to just get the most powerful model you can find, but this isn't always the best choice. After all, you don't need a top-of-the-line system if all you intend to do is play solitaire! If all you plan to do is surf the Web, send and receive e-mail, and write letters, *any modern computer can do this stuff, right out of the box*. Period. On the other hand, if you expect to play the latest 3-D games, mix music CDs, and edit digital video, then skip the entry-level, budget PC and go for something better.

What Kind of Software Do You Need?

Equally as important as getting a computer with enough hardware to meet your computing needs is making sure that your computer comes with the right software for your purposes.

Bundled Software

Big computer retailers are able to get cheaper licensing from software vendors, so most new computers bought from a retail store come with a selection of software programs pre-installed. Techs call this *bundled software*. Typically, you get a suite of productivity software—word processor, spreadsheet, e-mail and contact manager, database, and so on—along with other such as financial programs, media players, games, and so on. Unfortunately, many of these

Shop Around, Part 1

Locate the ads for computer stores in your local newspaper and compare the hardware on the featured computers. Which ones offer the best hardware? Which ones cut corners by offering less RAM, smaller hard drives, or slower CPUs?

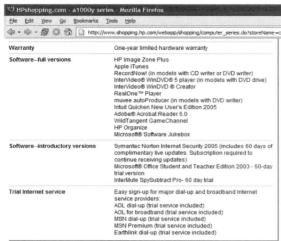

Figure 3.18: Great. Thanks for the free software.

programs come as 30-day trial versions and thus require you to spend more money on software in very short order (Figure 3.18). Computers bought from a smaller computer shop or custom builder may not have much software included.

Essential Add-ons

Whether you're getting the deal-of-the-week budget computer from a big-name retailer or a sleek custom-built machine from a specialty store, you're likely to miss a program or two from your dream machine profile. Here's a short list of recommended programs, utilities, and plug-ins that will make your computing life easier.

Installation Requirements

A closet door naturally requires that a frame be in place first. Software also has minimum requirements, the absolute lowest specifications your computer can have for the software to run correctly. You must first make sure your system meets those minimum requirements, which software developers conveniently list on the box and in the manual (Figure 8.19).

- **Anti-virus software:** *Viruses* are programs specifically written to cause harm to your data and operating system. They're a very real threat, and anybody who doesn't have an anti-virus program is playing Russian roulette with their data. As the saying goes, it's better to have it and not need it than need it and not have it. McAfee and Norton make the two most popular anti-virus programs. Alwil offers the Avast! anti-virus software free for non-commercial use (Figure 3.19).

- **Anti-spyware software:** Spyware is the rising star of computer hazards. *Spyware* is the name for the numerous programs that monitor your activities and act as an entry port for pop-up

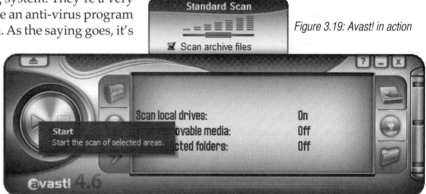

Figure 3.19: Avast! in action

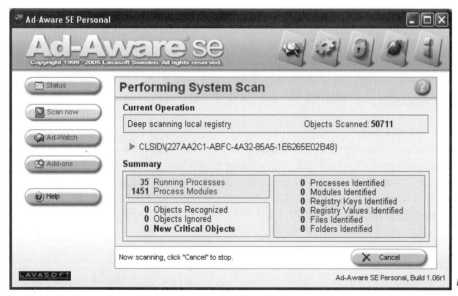

Figure 3.20: Ad-Aware in action

ads, web browser hijacking, and malicious programs that can take over your computer. Popular anti-spyware programs include Lavasoft Ad-Aware and Spybot Search & Destroy. See Figure 3.20.

Other Factors to Consider

Don't swipe that card yet! After you've got your hardware and software squared away, you still have to consider what happens after you drive off the lot.

How are you protected in case something goes wrong with the computer? If, six months down the line, you find that you need more hardware muscle, can you easily upgrade the system? Does your computer need to meet compatibility criteria for your network? After your purchase, what other expenses can you expect to pay out? Finally, once your computer has reached the end of its useful life, what do you do with it?

Warranties and Service Plans

Don't leave the store without finding out about the computer manufacturer's *warranty*—meaning what the company will do if their product has defects—and support plan, and the store return policy. If you're buying from one of the larger retailers, you can also count on them trying to sell you an extended warranty or service plan.

Warranties: What's covered? What's excluded?

A new computer usually comes with the manufacturer's warranty ranging from one to three years. Factory-refurbished machines (new computers that were returned to the store and sent back to the factory for repair) generally come with much shorter warranties—around ninety days. Most warranties cover repair or replacement of hardware components that fail because of a manufacturing defect, but not accidents or mistreatment. In other words, they'll probably replace your monitor if the tube burns out from normal use, but not if you drop it or if you use the "whack it on the side" method to try to get a clearer picture.

Under most warranty plans, you may be required to pay for shipping to return the computer to the factory for service. Major computer makers also offer free telephone and online customer support for a time after your purchase. The better companies even offer a certain number of onsite repairs by trained techs. The best of the online retailers, Dell Computers, offers to have a tech at your door the next working day if anything goes wrong for up to *four years* (Figure 3.21).

Extended service agreements offer tech support beyond the duration of your original service agreement. These plans may be offered by either your computer maker or by a third-party company.

Taking It Back

Make sure that you're clear on the details of your retailer's return policy before finalizing your purchase. Most computer stores have a very limited return policy on computers, and may charge a *restocking fee* at the time of return—meaning they charge you for the hassle of having to return your money and deal with now used equipment (Figure 3.22). Don't simply take your salesperson's word about what's covered—get it in writing.

Compatibility with Existing Environment

Your network or organization might require that your computer be one operating system or the other, have specific hardware, or use standard application

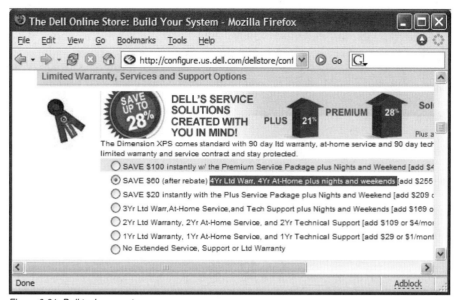

Figure 3.21: Dell tech support

programs. If your school or office offers wireless Internet access, for example, you'll need a wireless network adapter.

Also, many colleges require enrolling students to provide their own computers. The school will publish minimum requirements for hardware and software, and if your computer doesn't match the requirements, the school may not offer you support. As another example, let's say you're a contractor for a business that uses Microsoft Word as the standard word processing program. Your computer will need to have a word processor that's able to edit Word-compatible .doc files.

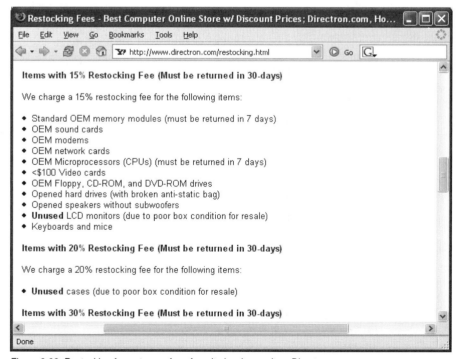

Figure 3.22: Restocking fees at one of my favorite hardware sites, Directron.com.

The Circle of Computer Life

Computer programs and operating systems have increased in complexity rapidly in the past few years. A top of the line computer purchased today will stagger under the demands of programs within a couple of years. Even with regular upgrades to RAM, CPU, and hard drives, your computer will age rapidly. The computer industry calls this *planned obsolescence*, a fancy phrase for getting out of date within a certain period of time so you can buy more stuff.

How Long Can You Expect Your Computer To Be Useful?

The life cycle of computer products depends on the manufacturer, but in most cases is about three to five years. It's not that the software or hardware will stop working after a given time limit, but that the maker will phase out sales and support for the product. Microsoft, for example, retires their software products after a set time, meaning that they stop development and end customer support.

Of course, many users still get a lot of use out of their machines long after their shelf-life has expired, but if something goes wrong, they're on their own.

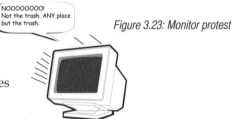

Figure 3.23: Monitor protest

Retiring Your Computer

Once you've eked your last calculation out of your machine, you can't simply throw it out with the garbage. In fact, this is probably illegal in your community! Items like old monitors are usually considered hazardous waste, so throwing that 14″ monochrome CRT into a dumpster may earn you a ticket—and it's bad for the environment (Figure 3.23).

Instead, you need to make an ordered migration from your current computer to your new one, and then dispose of your old system properly.

Newer PCs come equipped with special utilities that help you move from your old machine to your new one. These tools back up your data files and user settings and then, with the aid of a network connection or recordable media, transfer these files and settings to another computer.

Most cities have recycling programs for old computer equipment. Check in your local phone book to see if such a program exists in your area. If not, then contact your city's solid waste department for instructions on how to dispose of computer hardware.

Performance: Speed, Capacity, and Sophistication

■ CPU, RAM, and video card processor speed is measured is measured in *hertz*, which translates into the number of times per second each component can do things, or *cycle*. One hertz equals one cycle; one kilohertz (KHz) equals 1,000 hertz. One million clock cycles is called a megahertz. One billion cycles equals one gigahertz.

■ Because the CPU handles the vast majority of the work in processing, increasing CPU speed offers your biggest bang for the buck in terms of increasing the overall speed of the computer. Faster system RAM and faster hard drives can make a major impact as well. A higher quality video card—with a faster processor and faster RAM—can likewise prove invaluable for enhancing performance.

■ Computers store everything in strings of 1s and 0s, called *binary numbers*; processors use binary numbers to produce what you see on the screen or hear through your computer's speakers. The smallest binary unit is a *bit*, which can be either a 0 or a 1. Eight bits make a *byte*.

■ Storage devices are measured by how much data they can hold. Units of storage include the *kilobyte* (1,024 bytes), *megabyte* (1,024 kilobytes), *gigabyte* (1,024 megabytes), *terabyte* (1,024 gigabytes), and so on.

■ The CPU uses system memory to store actively running programs and data temporarily, including the operating system, so the amount of RAM you have directly affects performance. If you don't have enough to run your OS, load your application, and have space for data files, your system can crash or simply not enable you to accomplish your computing tasks. Modern Windows and OS X computers need at least 256 MB of RAM to run efficiently.

■ The sophistication of devices can make a profound impact on the performance of a computer. In particular, CPU and video card processors vary in what they can and cannot do and how well they can do thing. A low-end CPU, for example, will choke on CPU-intensive programs, like games. A mid-range video card might give you a good monitor refresh rate, but not be able to keep up in rapidly changing video games and utilities.

■ You can use the Web to get information you need about hardware that will work for you. One excellent site to start with is Ars Technica at www.arstechnica.com.
Another is the discussion board I maintain: www.totalseminars.com/forums/. Drop by and say hi!

The Right Tool for the Job: Choosing the Best Computer for Your Needs

■ Key factors in deciding on a computer are operating system, form factor (desktop or laptop), power of hardware, and software packages.

■ Windows, Macintosh, and Linux computers are all capable of performing the same computing tasks. Deciding factors should include availability of hardware and software, compatibility with existing computer equipment, availability of support, and cost.

■ Desktop systems are best if you have dedicated space for them and don't need to move them around. Portable laptop systems are best if you need to take your computer with you to when traveling, or when space is limited. Laptops are somewhat more expensive than comparable desktop systems.

■ The hardware that you outfit your system with depends on your level of usage.

■ Computers frequently come with bundled software packages that include basic productivity applications and utilities. In addition to these, you may need to purchase additional software and utilities to accomplish your computing tasks.

Other Factors to Consider

■ New computers usually have warranties ranging from one to three years. Factory-refurbished computer warranties are much shorter, typically ninety days. Extended warranties and service plans offer protection above and beyond what's covered by the original factory warranty. Store return policies vary, so it's important to understand your policy before finalizing your purchase. Some dealers charge a restocking fee for computer returns.

■ Compatibility with your existing network and computer equipment is an important consideration. Make sure that your newer machine is compatible with any older legacy devices that you use.

■ Plan for additional and ongoing costs, such as Internet access, DSL or cable service, additional software and software registration (trial versions only), cabling, surge and power loss protection, cabling, and consumables.

■ After a time, computer hardware and software makers retire their products, phasing them out in favor of newer products. When your computer has reached the end of its useful life, dispose of it properly through an approved recycling or solid waste program. Make sure to erase your data from your hard disk by formatting.

Key Terms

Binary numbers

Bit

Bundled software

Byte

Cycle

Distros

Docking station

Gigabyte (GB)

Gigahertz (GHz)

Hertz (Hz)

Kilobyte (KB)

Kilohertz (KHz)

Megabyte (MB)

Megahertz (MHz)

Open source

Pixels

Planned obsolescence

Refresh rate

Spyware

Terabyte (TB)

Virus

Warranty

Key Term Quiz

Use the Key Terms list to complete the following sentences. Not all the terms will be used.

1. A _____ is the smallest unit of storage.

2. Computers process data in units called a _____, or eight bits.

3. _____ packages come pre-installed on most new computers, and may include productivity software, trial versions of programs, and so on.

4. A _____ is a measurement of a single CPU calculation cycle.

5. Applications such as Ad-aware enable you to rid your computer of unwanted _____ programs.

6. A manufacturer's _____ determines what the company will do if you discover a flaw in a product.

7. Computers use _____ (1s and 0s) for calculations.

8. If a monitor's _____ is set too low, it can cause eye strain, fatigue, and damage to the user.

9. Most hard drive capacities today are measured in _____ units; older drives used megabytes (MBs).

10. A _____ gives a portable computer extra capabilities, such as a full-size keyboard and extra drives.

Multiple Choice Quiz

1. Julius wanted to get a computer to surf the Internet, play games, and write the Great American Novel™. Which upgrade would give him the most speed increase?
   A. Faster CPU
   B. Faster system RAM
   C. Faster hard drive
   D. Faster network card

2. How many bytes of storage space does the typed phrase "To be, or not to be?" occupy, not counting the quotation marks?
   A. 20 bytes (one byte per character, plus one byte per blank space)
   B. 6 bytes (one byte per word)
   C. 23 bytes (one byte per lowercase character and blank space, two bytes per uppercase letter and punctuation mark)
   D. 15 bytes (one byte per character, minus five bytes for each blank space)

3. Mary has a computer with 512 MB of RAM; Josie's computer has 1 GB of RAM. Who has more RAM?
   A. Mary has more RAM.
   B. Josie has more RAM.
   C. Both Mary and Josie have the same amount of RAM, just written out differently.
   D. Neither. RAM capacity is measured in MHz and GHz, not MB and GB.

4. Mary's computer sports an Intel Pentium D dual-core 32-bit processor running at 2.8 GHz. Josie's computer has an AMD Athlon 64 X2 dual-core 64-bit processor running at 2.2 GHz. Which CPU can most likely handle the most sophisticated operating systems and applications? (Select the best answer.)
   A. Mary's CPU
   B. Josie's CPU
   C. Both CPUs can handle the same operating systems and applications with equal efficiency.
   D. Neither CPU can perform as well on sophisticated operating systems and applications as Marco's single-core Intel Pentium 840 running at 3.2 GHz.

5. Which refresh rate offers the least potetial for eyestrain when viewing a monitor?
   A. 60 Hz
   B. 72 Hz
   C. 85 Hz
   D. 100 Hz

6. Which of these factors should you consider when purchasing a new computer system for your office network? (Select all that apply.)
   A. Compatibility with existing hardware and software
   B. Cost
   C. Customer support
   D. Included trial software

7. Which operating system offers the simplest, most intuitive interface?
   A. Linux
   B. Macintosh OS X
   C. Windows XP Professional
   D. Windows XP Media Center

8. Which of the following are valid reasons for choosing a laptop computer configuration over a desktop? (Select two.)
   A. Lower cost
   B. Portability
   C. Size
   D. Upgradeability

9. Which of the following is **not** a valid reason for choosing Windows over Macintosh or Linux?
   A. Wide availability of compatible harware and software
   B. Integrates well with other computer systems
   C. Many customer support options available
   D. Lower cost compared to other operating systems

10. Which of the following is a disadvantage of using a Macintosh system instead of Windows or Linux? (Select one.)
    A. Less compatibility with other computer systems
    B. Higher OS upgrade cost
    C. Less availability of compatible harware and software
    D. Limited customer support

11. Lucinda is leaving for college in the fall and needs to purchase a new computer for use at school. Which factors should she consider when planning her purchase? (Select all that apply.)
    A. School computing environment requirements
    B. Warranty
    C. Color
    D. Bundled software

12. How should you dispose of obsolete computer equipment?
    A. Donate it to a local non-profit charity.
    B. Go through an approved recycling or solid waste disposal program.
    C. Put in a neighbor's garbage can.
    D. Ship it to Microsoft.

13. How many computing cycles can a CPU with a speed rating of 2.5 GHz perform per second?
    A. 2,500
    B. 2,500,000
    C. 2,500,000,000
    D. 2,500,000,000,000

14. Rita plans to purchase a computer to surf the Internet and write school papers. Francis claims she needs at least a 64-bit processor to do these tasks well, but Andy disagrees. He claims that a 32-bit processor will work fine, but she needs at least an 80-GB hard drive to do these tasks well. Who's right?
    A. Only Francis is correct.
    B. Only Andy is correct.
    C. Both Francis and Andy have it right.
    D. Neither Francis nor Andy has it right.

15. Regardless of the computer Rita finally buys, what essential software should she purchase? (Select two.)
    A. Anti-piracy software
    B. Anti-spyware software
    C. Anti-virus software
    D. iTunes music software

Essays

1. Your uncle wants to buy a computer but lacks some basic knowledge. Put together a short letter for him that includes things he should look for in a new computer.

2. Write a short essay describing how and where you could use a laptop computer. Be creative here—don't forget to include your private yacht and airplane as well as your house or apartment.

3. What's your ideal system? Write an essay describing what you want to do on a computer and then describe the computer that could help you accomplish your goals.

Projects

1. Visit a computer store (or an online computer vendor's Web site), and compare at least four Windows PC systems of varying price. Include budget, mid-range, top-of-the-line, and extreme gamer's models. How do these systems differ? Which component adds the most cost? Where do the makers of the budget systems cut corners to keep the hardware costs down? What bundled software is included for the price?

2. Through online searches or by going to a computer store, compare the electrical requirements of various computer monitors. (You're looking specifically for how much *wattage* they use.) Then make a list that shows which three monitors are the most and least energy-efficient.

It's a Comp's Life

"I am a machine vastly superior to humans."

— Colossus, *The Forbin Project*

This chapter covers the following IC³ exam objectives:

- IC³-1   1.4.1   Identify how to protect computer hardware from theft or damage

- IC³-1   1.4.2   Identify factors that can cause damage to computer hardware or media

- IC³-1   1.4.3   Identify how to protect computer hardware from fluctuations in the power supply, power outages and other electrical issues

- IC³-1   1.4.4   Identify common problems associated with computer hardware

- IC³-1   1.4.5   Identify common problems that can occur if hardware is not maintained properly

- IC³-1   1.4.6   Identify maintenance that can be performed routinely by users

- IC³-1   1.4.7   Identify maintenance that should ONLY be performed by experienced professionals

- IC³-1   1.4.8   Identify the steps required to solve computer-related problems

Every day, your computer faces many types of threats that, given the chance, may damage the machine, or worse yet, the data stored in the computer. Every computer faces assault from heat, dust, animal hair, sticky fingers, and grubby paws. Danger lurks around every corner, from stray electricity, theft, and fire. Plus, just using a computer over time creates problems that make your computer run less than its best. Fortunately, the computer industry knows of these threats and provides a number of tools and techniques you should use to keep your system and its precious information safe from harm.

This chapter explores the dangers faced by courageous computers everywhere, starting with the hazards that come from the environment around and inside the computer, and the threats posed by poor maintenance and misuse. The chapter finishes with an overview of computer maintenance and a look at common problems faced by computer users, combined with the solutions that you should use to deal with these problems.

Clear and Present Danger

The environment around and inside the computer can cause amazing amounts of problems, from sluggish performance to loss of data. All computers and computer media have problems with bio hazards, such as heat, humidity, and dust. Magnetic fields can warp electrical signals and lead to data loss and component failures. Finally, electricity courses through the wires inside the computer, and problems with that power source can literally toast a computer. Let's look at the details and see what steps you can take to create a safer computer environment.

Bio Hazards

There's an old rule that says, "If you're uncomfortable, your computer is too." Computer manufacturers design computers and media to work in a typical home/office environment. So, if you're too hot, if your shirt sticks to you due to humidity, or if your room is filled with smoke from somebody burning popcorn (or cigarettes), you can be sure your computer is being harmed, so do something about it! See Figure 4.1.

Figure 4.1: An Unhappy Computer

Heat

Excessive heat, even over a short period of time, can cause your computer components to run poorly and fail. Heat can warp media, such as floppy disks, CD-ROM discs, and DVDs, to the point where you can't use them anymore. Heat can make peripherals, like printers, malfunction and even break.

Every microcomputer has at least two fans to suck cool air into the computer and blow hot air out (Figure 4.2). If the fans go out, though, your computer might run anywhere from two to ten minutes before it overheats and shuts down. Take a moment to listen to a properly running computer. Much of the noise you hear comes from the fans. If the computer suddenly gets much quieter, turn it off right away!

Most, but not all, computers come equipped with overheat alarms. These alarms vary from simple repeating beeps to a ghostly human voice that tells you the system's overheating Either way, if you get strange beeps you've never heard before or if the computer starts wailing, "Warning CPU temperature beyond threshold!" (or something like that), you need to turn off the computer and have it checked out by your friendly local computer repair person.

Even with fans and alarms, running a computer in a hot room can cause components to fail. Over time, a hard drive that's crammed into a poorly ventilated case, for example, will simply die, taking your data with it. Never leave CD or DVD discs lying

Ventilation

In order to do their job, the fans in a computer need good ventilation. Always place your computer in such a way that both the front and the back have plenty of air access so fresh air can get in and heated air can get out. Try to leave at least 4-6 inches of open airspace around the computer.

Figure 4.2: Lots of fans

COMPUTER LITERACY: YOUR TICKET TO IC³ CERTIFICATION

in the sun or near a heat source, like a heater vent or the back of the computer. Too much heat destroys media of all sorts (Figure 4.3).

Humidity

Compared to heat, humidity isn't nearly as important an issue, but does deserve at least a quick mention. Computers use electricity and mixing electricity with water in any way is not a good idea. This is equally true for water in the air, good old humidity. You might guess that pouring a gallon of water into your computer is dangerous and downright bad for your computer, but your computer has easily that much water going through it every day, suspended in the air circulating through your system. In highly humid places, the water may condense and cause corrosion, so it's not a good idea to keep a computer next to the shower or air conditioning vent where humidity gets much higher than normal.

Figure 4.3: Melted CD-ROM disc

Airborne Pollution

While a computer works fine in the same heat and humidity ranges most people find comfortable, a computer doesn't do well with air polluted with dust, smoke, and other hazards. Very few computers come with any type of filtering, so dust, grease, pet hair, or other nasties in the air quickly build up inside the computer, creating a risk for short-circuits, blocked fans, and even fire in the most extreme cases (Figure 4.4).

Avoid messing up the air around your computer by not smoking near your computer, keeping dust and animal hair down, and making sure your computer stays away from airborne grease and other pollutants. If you suspect your computer is getting dirty, take a look at the power supply fan on the back of your computer. If the power supply fan is dirty, grab a can of *compressed air* from your local computer store, shut off your computer, open the case outside, and blow out as much dust as possible, as shown in Figure 4.5.

Figure 4.4: Filthy Computer

Heat Kills

So, how much heat does it take to make a CD, DVD, or floppy disk unusable? Run an experiment to find out! Take a disc or diskette that you know works and has data that you don't care about on it, like a CD-ROM that comes with a cereal box. Check it to make sure it works, and then leave it out in the sun for a few hours. Try it again. Set it next to a heater vent for an hour or two. Does it work still?

Figure 4.5: Cleaning out a dusty computer

Magnetism

Magnets and electro-magnetic fields can erase data, cause components to warp, and even permanently damage some peripherals. Hard drives and floppy disks use magnetism to store data, and one pass by a strong magnet quickly erases them! Even a weak magnet slowly erases media. Watch out for hidden magnets in telephones, powered toys,

If you open the case, be careful not to touch any internal components. Use only compressed air to blow dust out. Do this outside, because you might find an enormous amount of dust and hair inside a computer case. Don't use a standard household vacuum cleaner on the inside of a computer case, because you run the risk of frying any computer component accidentally touched.

Figure 4.6: Don't do this!

and other devices. Don't put a refrigerator magnet on the side of your computer (Figure 4.6).

Keep magnets away from traditional CRT monitors (Figure 4.7). Strong magnets will destroy them very quickly. They permanently warp the picture, giving it a rainbow-like effect that cannot be repaired. Even a weak magnet left on or near a CRT monitor will slowly create the same damage. CRT monitors and magnets — a bad combination!

Electro-shock Therapy

Computers need good, clean electricity to function properly. In the United States, electricity comes out of the wall socket at ~115-volt alternating current (VAC); the rest of the world for the most part uses ~230 VAC. Most power supplies have a little switch on the back so you can use them in multiple countries (see Figure 4.8).

Sometimes, especially during thunderstorms, electricity coming out of the wall fluctuates. If it drops a little in voltage—what's called a *sag*—or goes out completely—a *power outage*, your computer will spontaneously reboot or shut down. If the voltage comes in too high—what's called a *surge*—your computer or peripherals can get toasted.

Figure 4.7: CRT monitor

Two devices handle electrical protection for your computer. An *uninterruptible power supply* (*UPS*) provides a battery backup to your computer if the voltage sags or goes out. A *surge suppressor* takes care of excess voltage with surges. A simple power strip, like you can buy for a few dollars, is not the same thing as a surge suppressor. Figure 4.9 shows a UPS and surge suppressor.

CD- and DVD-media are not affected by magnets or magnetic fields. You only need to worry about heat with optical storage.

The standard U.S. electrical source can be 110-, 115-, or 120-volt AC, so be prepared for any of the three numbers.

Outside Violence

Computers operate in dangerous environments, surrounded by a host of dangerous creatures computer users, determined to damage or destroy the computers, whether they mean to or not. People abuse computers in many amazingly silly, sometimes humorous ways: dumping coffee in their keyboards, dropping them from desks, ripping out cords; or in the worst scenario, stealing them.

Figure 4.8: 115 to 230 switch

Dirty Peripherals

People love to place all kinds of junk next to their computers: sodas, potato chips, candy, and so on. Anything sitting next to your computer eventually ends up on your mouse, keyboard, or monitor (Figure 4.10). Printers can get dumped on as well, though they generate a lot of dirt on their own.

Figure 4.9: UPS and surge suppressor

Amazingly, most computer components stand up to dirt fairly well, although you need to know how to clean them properly or cleaning might make the problem even worse. Let's look at individual computer components and see what to do or not do when they get dirty.

Mice

Mice slide around desks in the grimy hands of users, so tend to gather dirt more than any other part of the computer. The folks who make mice know this and design mice for easy cleaning. There's no difficulty determining if a mouse needs cleaning: if

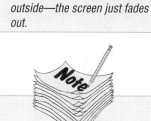

A good UPS acts as a surge suppressor as well, so you only need the one device to protect your computer against sags, outages, and surges.

Figure 4.10: Disaster waiting to happen!

that mouse starts jumping around on the screen or acting otherwise erratically, it's time to clean the mouse!

Mice use either a ball or lights to detect movement. A mouse that uses a rolling ball is called a *roller mouse*. A mouse using lights is called an *optical mouse*. Figure 4.11 shows an example of each.

Roller mice collect dirt inside the mouse. To clean them, just remove the roller ball from the mouse using the handy access door. Every door uses a different release mechanism, but most twist off, giving you access to the insides of the mouse, as shown in Figure 4.12.

Note the dirt on the two metal rollers that contact the roller ball. This dirt prevents the mouse from tracking properly.

Figure 4.11: Optical and roller mice

Figure 4.12: Roller mouse with ball removed

Remove this dirt using your fingernail. You don't need any special tool even though a trip to the computer store will show you a number of "mouse cleaning kits." Simply scrape off the dirt, shake it out of the mouse, and it will work properly.

The makers of optical mice claim that these mice never need cleaning. This is true, as they lack a ball that picks up dirt. Instead, they have small lights underneath the mouse that detect movement. The lights under an optical mouse do get dirty, although only when they're used in a dirty environment or if you drop a huge glob of delicious Nutella™-brand hazelnut spread on your desk and then drag the mouse onto the gooey mess. Clean your optical mouse using a toothpick or the corner of a piece of paper to remove the big grime and then a cotton swap to remove any residue.

Keyboards

Keyboards stand a close second to mice in terms of the dirt they accumulate. Even if you avoid spilling nasty stuff on the keyboard, over time bits of dirt and grime drop down between the keys, eventually building up to the point that the keyboard no long works: keys begin to stick, act mushy, or stop working altogether. Unfortunately, keyboards aren't nearly as easy to clean as a mouse.

Figure 4.13: Prying off a key

To get a dirty keyboard working you'll need a can of compressed air, a flat-blade screwdriver, and a Phillips screwdriver. The flat blade enables you to pry off individual keys; you open the entire keyboard with the Phillips.

If you get a stuck key, first assume that dirt is underneath the key. Get your compressed air under the key and see if a few quick blasts get the key working. If the air fails, use a flat-bladed screwdriver to remove the key, as shown in Figure 4.13. Pry lightly until the key pops out.

Look under the key for dirt or foreign objects. Paper clips are notorious for getting under keys. Clean the area under the key with a cotton swab (damp or dry) until you've removed the dirt. Pop the key back on and test. If the key still doesn't work, move on to opening the keyboard.

If you pour anything into a keyboard or if a number of keys will not work (but others will), you'll need to open the keyboard to clean it. Shut down the computer and disconnect the keyboard. Flip the keyboard over and remove

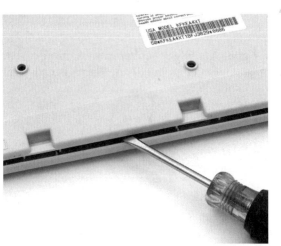

Figure 4.14: Prying open the keyboard

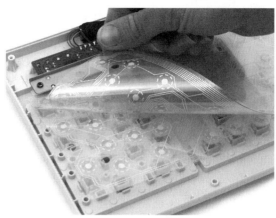

Figure 4.15: Disassembling and cleaning a keyboard.

Trackballs and Touchpads

As you know from Chapter 2, "Going with the Data Flow," a lot of people use a trackball or touchpad rather than a mouse. Trackballs have a ball, just like roller mice, so clean them just as you would the mouse. Touchpads don't have moving parts, so just keep the surface clean.

Don't fear opening a keyboard. If the keyboard isn't working, you're going to replace it anyway. So give it a try; if you're successful you'll feel like a computer technician and you can boast to your friends!

the screws using a Phillips screwdriver. Remember where each screw goes as they may not be the same size. Second, use your flat bladed screwdriver to pry the bottom away from the top, as shown in Figure 4.14. Pry evenly around the keyboard until it opens.

Inside the keyboard you'll find layers of flexible plastic that end up as a repository for dirt. Peel each of these away, remembering their orientation and order, and clean them with a damp cloth. Also clean the inside of the bottom of the keyboard. Let each piece dry completely and reassemble (Figure 4.15).

Monitors

Monitors get touched and fingerprints on the screen can drive some folks crazy. Both common monitor technologies—CRT and LCD—require totally different cleaning methods.

A CRT screen is made of glass, just like a window, and regular glass cleaner works well (Figure 4.16). Clean your CRT screen the same way you clean a window, with one important exception. Always spray the glass cleaner onto a towel, as opposed to spraying it directly on the monitor. Those little drips of cleaner can flow down into the electric parts of the monitor and cause a dangerous short!

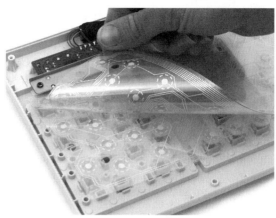

Figure 4.16: Cleaning a monitor

To clean an LCD, always check the manufacturer's Web site or manual to see what practices they suggest. Some LCDs prefer a combination of one part isopropyl alcohol and two parts water; others use just a damp cloth. Always wipe the LCD screen with a very soft cloth. Never use paper towels or other rough cloth on an LCD as they leave scratches. Never use glass cleaner on LCDs unless specifically recommended by the manufacturer. Glass cleaner melts many LCD screen types.

Printers

Printers are notorious for making their own dirt. The ink or toner (depending on the type of printer) that the printer uses to put the image on the paper eventually builds up inside the printer, causing problems with printing. Dust comes off the paper, gradually adding to the debris inside the printer.

You can avoid problems of smeared pages, grainy text, and other common printing problems by performing routine maintenance and keeping dust out of the printer. Most printers come with some form of maintenance program that you run by pressing some buttons on the printer. Every printer's maintenance program does something different, but it's your first line of defense if your printing looks incorrect.

Your other do-it-yourself maintenance job is cleaning. Every printer manufacturer provides a cleaning procedure for your printer. You should find this procedure either in the book that comes with your printer or on the printer manufacturer's Web site. Most printers recommend cleaning on as as-needed basis; if you start getting paper jams, or if your printed paper comes out dirty, go ahead and clean the printer.

Every printer, whether properly maintained or not, can get a *paper jam*, where one or more sheets of paper get stuck inside the printer. Take a moment to determine the correct removal procedure. Every printer comes with plenty of little doors, covers, and hatches that help you remove paper jams. Read the printer documentation to make sure you remove jams correctly. If a piece of paper gets heavily jammed, call in a professional. Improperly removing jams may destroy a printer!

Physical Damage

Your computer, all wrapped in metal and plastic, looks as though you could give it some pretty tough treatment, but in reality it is very fragile. So let's begin by stating the obvious: at no time should you let your computer drop or take a hard hit. This also goes for all of the peripherals treat them gently or they will fail. Although this might seem obvious, the sad truth is that every computer and peripheral gets jarred occasionally.

Most of this jarring comes from negligence. People place computers or peripherals in crazy places: on rickety desks, cardboard boxes, and other places where the chances of dropping are high (Figure 4.17). Arrange your computer and peripherals safely on the floor or a sturdy desk.

Figure 4.17: Precariously perched

Every smart laptop user also invests in a good quality laptop case. These cases come with special padding (the really good ones use special shock absorbers) that protects your laptop from all the bumps and bounces that take place as you travel from place to place. Figure 4.18 shows an example of one of these cases.

Theft

Thieves target computers, especially laptops. Preventing computer theft is a challenge as it's too easy to expose your system to the eyes of a thief. Instead, the idea is to make stealing your computer enough of a challenge to reduce your risk dramatically.

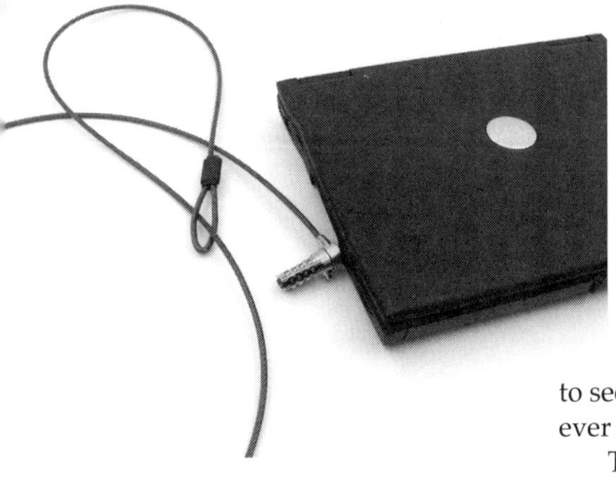

Figure 4.18: Laptop Case

First of all, use common sense. Don't leave your laptop unattended unless it is in a secure place. Don't leave a laptop in your car for everyone to see, nor should you leave it in a hotel room. Second, lock computers whenever there is a risk of theft. There are a number of ways to lock a computer.

The best way to protect desktop systems is by locking them into a room. If you can't lock the room, your next best choice is to lock the system to your desk using a specially made *computer lock*, as shown in Figure 4.19. Computer locks aren't perfect. A determined thief can break a computer lock, but they do a great job of stopping the more "grab and dash" type of pilferage.

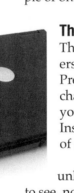

Figure 4.19: Computer Lock

Maintenance and Repair

A knowledgeable computer user maintains his or her computer. A big part of this process means keeping it clean, like you just did with the mouse, keyboard, monitor, and printer. Another part involves getting rid of excess files and folders that clutter up every computer system over time. Third, if you know how something should work, you can recognize when a device doesn't work properly. At that point, you can shift to the troubleshooting and repair process.

File Cleanup

Every computer hard drive fills up with an amazing number of unneeded files over time. The installation files for drivers, for example, don't need to stay on your hard drive after you install them. Just deleting them, though, isn't quite enough. When you delete a file, your operating system doesn't actually delete it. Rather, it moves the file from an active folder, such as My Documents, to a trash folder (called *Recycle Bin* in Windows, and *Trash* in Macintosh). After a while, these excess files fill your hard drive—at best, noticeably slowing the system down, and at worst, making it impossible for your computer to function.

Every user needs to know how to clean up these files. To empty the Recycle Bin in Windows, find the icon on your desktop, right-click it, and select **Empty Recycle Bin**. To do the same thing in OS X, control-click the **Trash** icon and select **Empty Trash**.

Troubleshooting and Repair

Troubleshooting computer problems follows eight standard steps that you can use to guide you when something goes wrong. The first few steps you take on your own, the next four you work with a professional to fix more complex problems. The last step is pretty self-explanatory. Here's the list.

1. Recognize the problem
2. Replicate the problem
3. Try the easy fixes
4. Get help
5. Explain the problem
6. Follow instruction
7. Confirm the fix
8. Avoid the problem in the future

First Steps

Knowledgeable computer users can recognize when something doesn't work the way it should. Hard drives don't make clicking noises, for example, when they work correctly. Monitors shouldn't have grainy pictures or weird colors. You should be able to print on a printer connected to a computer. Your computer should recognize a new digital camera you plug into a USB port (Figure 4.20).

Once you know something's wrong, see if you can *replicate* the problem, in other words, make it happen again. If you try to print and nothing happens, perhaps you missed the Print button. Click it again for good measure. If it still doesn't work, look for the simple solution first.

Check power and cables. Most sudden problems occur because a power

Lockdown

Larger companies keep computers safe behind security systems. Cameras monitor hallways and rooms and alarms can lock down buildings. It's one thing, after all, for an individual to lose a computer. For companies with lots of competitors, having important computers stolen can mean the death of the company!

Locking Laptops

Locking up your laptop's a bit of a trick. A popular laptop security system includes a keychain and an alarm that mounts onto the laptop. If the laptop gets more than a few feet away from the keychain, the alarm in the laptop goes off with an incredibly loud screech, hopefully enough to stop a thief! (Unfortunately, that's usually when the thief drops the laptop and runs—never a good thing for a computer!)

Fragmentation

*Deleting a bunch of files from your hard drive can lead to problems, such as **file fragmentation**, meaning that your operating system stores pieces of files all over the hard drive. This doesn't mean you shouldn't delete useless files! You can fix fragmentation by running programs that defragment the drive. Chapter 5, "Role of the Operating System," covers this process in detail.*

You should recognize situations where only computer professionals should do the troubleshooting and repair. These include replacing internal components and bad hardware, and working with any sort of electrical problem.

Figure 4.20: New device recognized

strip got unplugged or turned off or a cable came loose. If you have a jumble of cables at your feet, for example, you can easily partially disconnect something so it sort of works but doesn't quite. Clean up the cabling and plug things back in. Finally, if you can't print but could before, check to make sure the printer is powered up (Figure 4.21).

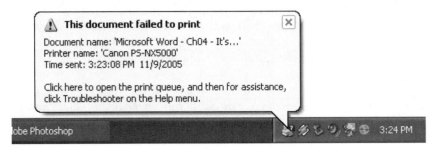

Figure 4.21: Doh!

Working with Techs

When you run into a problem that's beyond your skill level to fix, you need to contact a skilled computer technician, communicate as well as you can the problem, and then work with him or her to solve it. You can find a tech or a skilled user at computer labs at school, at big electronics stores, like Best Buy, and at local computer stores. It's important that you use your knowledge of computers to explain the symptoms. If your hard drive started making a clicking noise two days ago and your system crashed today, tell the tech about the clicking noise or any other clue that might help solve the problem.

Some techs have trouble communicating what they want you to do, but you need to make sure to follow what they tell you precisely. If something doesn't make sense when you hear it, ask a question. For example, if the tech tells you to click on X on the screen, but all you see is Y and Z, don't make a guess or assume he meant Y. Ask for clarification!

Before you get off the telephone with technical support or allow a tech to leave, always make certain that the device or process that failed works as it should. If you couldn't print, for example, test printing from an application such as Word. Don't just use the printer self-test. Also ask what, if anything, you can do in the future to avoid similar problems.

Clear and Present Danger

■ Your computer is sensitive to heat, humidity, and airborne pollutants that over time degrade your system. Even though your computer is designed to work in a typical interior environment, these hazards sneak into your system. It's important to take steps to minimize your system's exposure to these dangers.

■ Computers generate heat, requiring the use fans to keep them cool. If those fans fail, your system will overheat and shut down. Media (floppy disks, CDs, and DVDs) are extremely sensitive to heat.

■ Humidity is a minor problem; in highly humid environments a computer might get some corrosion.

■ Computers come with no filtering for airborne pollutants. Avoid smoking around a computer. Keep computers out of dusty environments. Use a can of compressed air to clean a truly dirty computer.

■ Magnetic fields will destroy hard drives, floppy disks, and monitors. Never let a magnet get near them!

■ Computers need clean electrical power, free from sags, outages, and spikes. Use a surge suppressor or UPS to ensure clean power for your system.

Outside Violence

■ Avoid doing anything to your computer that allows crumbs, ashes, maple syrup, or anything else to get in contact with the system. Use some common sense and be neat!

■ All roller mice have access doors that enable you to clean the mouse mechanism. Optical mice have lights underneath that can clog with dirt and may require cleaning. You can remove keys from keyboards and even open a keyboard completely to clean it.

■ Monitors screens are very susceptible to dirt and you should clean them often. Use regular glass cleaner on a CRT's screen; follow the manufacturer's recommendations for cleaning LCD screens.

■ Printers make their own dirt as well as pick up external dirt. You need to perform your own maintenance cleaning on an as needed basis. Be careful with printer jams: always use the provided access panels/doors and remove according to manufacturer's recommendations.

■ No computer tolerates rough handling. Always position desktop computers on stable, level desks or tables. Laptops tolerate some rough handling, but you should still treat them as gently as possible. Using a specially padded laptop case ensures their safety from bounces and drops.

■ Keep your computers safe from theft by locking the system. Use computer locks and door locks. For the best safety use an alarm!

Maintenance and Repair

■ Always first check electricity and data connections when there's a problem with a device.

■ When trying to figure out what's wrong with your system, use these eight steps as a mental process: recognizing the problem; replicate the problem; attempt basic solutions; find available help and advice; communicate the problem accurately; follow instructions; confirm the problem has been fixed; and avoid similar problems in the future.

Key Terms

Compressed air

Computer lock

Dusting

Electrostatic discharge (ESD)

Optical mouse

Paper jam

Power outage

Recycle Bin

Replicate

Roller mouse

Sag

Surge

Surge suppressor

Trash

Uninterruptible Power Supply (UPS)

Key Term Quiz

Use the Key Terms list to complete the following sentences. Not all the terms will be used.

1. A pointing device that uses a ball to move the cursor is called a _____.

2. You can use _____ to clear accumulated dust out of a computer.

3. A _____ protects a computer from a burst of excessive electricity.

4. You need to be careful removing paper from a _____ in a printer.

5. A _____ can protect your computer from a sudden drop in electricity.

6. _____ is more commonly known as static electricity.

7. You can use a _____ to help protect your computer from theft.

8. If you want to make a problem happen again so that you can diagnose its cause, you're trying to _____ the problem.

9. Deleted files in Macintosh OS X computers go into the _____.

10. The incredibly foolish and suicidal act of inhaling compressed air is called _____, and you should never, ever do it.

Multiple Choice Quiz

1. What temperature should you try to maintain in your computer room?
   A. A typical level for home or office
   B. Absolute zero
   C. 42 degrees Fahrenheit
   D. 10 degrees cooler than what is comfortable for you

2. What can happen to a hard drive crammed into a case that's too hot?
   A. The drive will run more slowly.
   B. The drive will fail eventually.
   C. The drive will run more loudly.
   D. Nothing bad will happen.

3. In a worst-case scenario, what can dirt build-up inside the computer cause?
   A. Fire
   B. System shutdown
   C. Garbled text on the screen
   D. Blocked fans

4. Which of the following can harm a DVD-ROM disc?
   A. Excessive heat
   B. Excessive humidity
   C. Magnets
   D. None of the above; DVDs are pretty tough.

5. Magnets destroy floppy disks. Which of the following are also highly affected by magnets?
   A. LCD monitors
   B. CRT monitors
   C. LGB monitors
   D. CTR monitors

6. How many volts are supplied by power companies in the United States?
   A. ~11
   B. ~115
   C. ~230
   D. ~720

7. What do you call a sudden drop in electricity to the computer?
   A. Drop
   B. Sag
   C. Static
   D. Surge

8. Which of the following is recommended to clean a roller mouse?
   A. Glass cleaner
   B. Small vacuum
   C. Your fingernail
   D. Mouse cleaning kit

9. Which of the following should you use to clean a CRT screen?
   A. Glass cleaner
   B. Water
   C. Compressed air
   D. A mix of one part isopropyl alcohol and two parts water

10. What cleaning material can melt some LCD screens?
    A. Glass cleaner
    B. Water
    C. Compressed air
    D. A mix of one part isopropyl alcohol and two parts water

11. What button(s) do you press to start a printer maintenance program?
    A. **[Ctrl + Alt + Del]**
    B. Depends on the printer
    C. Self-test
    D. **Power** and **Reset** simultaneously

12. Which of the following are symptoms of typical printer problems that you can avoid with good maintenance? (Select all that apply.)
    A. Smeared pages
    B. Grainy text
    C. Paper jams
    D. Running out of ink

13. How do you empty the Recycle Bin?
    A. Double-click the **Recycle Bin** icon on the desktop and click the **Empty** button.
    B. Right-click the **Recycle Bin** icon on the desktop and select **Empty Recycle Bin**.
    C. Left-click the **Recycle Bin** icon on the desktop and select **Empty Recycle Bin**.
    D. Windows empties the Recycle Bin for you automatically.

14. John is on the telephone with tech support. The tech tells him to press a certain key combination. John isn't sure what keys the tech meant but tries it anyway and fails. Which step did he not handle properly?
    A. Get help.
    B. Explain the problem.
    C. Follow instructions.
    D. Avoid the problem in the future.

15. Mary's printer at the office worked yesterday, but not today. What should she do first to troubleshoot the problem?
    A. Call tech support.
    B. Check the power and cabling.
    C. Check the printer driver in Windows.
    D. Replace the printer.

Essay Questions

1. Your aunt just bought a computer and came home with only a power strip. Write an essay that motivates her to purchase a surge suppressor or UPS.

2. It seems everyone with any computer experience has funny stories about how they mishandled a computer. Ask around and write a humorous essay about the funny things people you know have done to their computers.

3. Examine someone's computer and then write an essay detailing ways to improve the computer through maintenance, such as cleaning the mouse or monitor.

Projects

1. Take a trip to the local computer or electronics store to research a surge suppressor or UPS for your system. Compare features, size, and cost, then document why you would choose a particular device for your system.

2. Using knowledge from Chapters 2, 3, and 4, compare and contrast CRT and LCD monitors. Make a chart describing what's good or bad about each technology.

3. You can easily and safely simulate a power sag. Try this: Turn off your computer and then reach around the back to flip the AC switch from 115 to 230. Then turn the computer back on. What happened? Compare your results with what others in your class experienced. (**Note**: don't reverse this process if you're outside the U.S. and using 220 VAC from the wall—you can cook your computer!)

Defining the Role of the Operating System

"What is real? How do you define real? If you're talking about what you can feel, what you can smell, what you can taste and see, then real is simply electrical signals interpreted by your brain."

– Morpheus, *The Matrix*

This chapter covers the following IC[3] exam objectives:

- IC[3]-1   2.2.6   Identify the types and purposes of different utility programs

- IC[3]-1   3.1.1   Identify the purpose of an operating system and the difference between operating system and application software

- IC[3]-1   3.1.2   Identify different operating systems, including: DOS, Macintosh, Windows, UNIX/Linux, handheld operating systems (including Palm OS and Pocket PC)

- IC[3]-1   3.1.3   Identify the difference between interacting with character-based and graphical operating systems

- IC[3]-1   3.1.4   Identify the capabilities and limitations imposed by the operating system

- IC[3]-1   3.1.5   Identify and solve common problems related to operating systems

Computers come in all sizes and shapes, from extremely large, fast, and expensive computers to tiny systems that fit in the palm of your hand. So far in this book, you have learned a great deal about computer hardware, but now it's time to learn about the software that makes everything work together—the operating system. A computer without an operating system is like a movie without a director, because an operating system is what enables all other computer components—both hardware and software—to play their roles. In this chapter, you will learn the functions of an operating system, its capabilities and limitations, and tour the major computer operating systems you may encounter. The chapter wraps with a look at common operating system problems and their solutions.

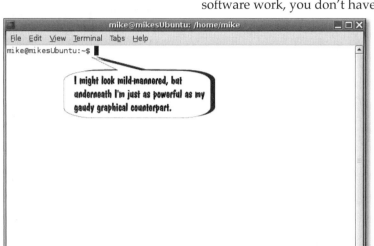

Figure 5.2: The text-mode Linux command-line user interface

ROM BIOS and the Boot-up Phase

Chapter 2, "Going with the Data Flow," talked about the role of ROM BIOS in the computer boot phase. Flip back and answer the following questions. What component "wakes up" the ROM BIOS? What special group of programs execute from ROM BIOS during boot-up?

Operating System Functions

As you'll recall from earlier chapters, the *operating system (OS)* is the program code that controls the computer, enabling the hardware and application software to work together. The operating system is also what enables you to tell the computer what to do, and the computer to show you the results of its efforts. Because the OS understands the nitty-gritty details of how your hardware and software work, you don't have to, and that, as they say, is a good thing!

Every operating system performs the same four functions:

1. Creates and maintains a user interface so you can tell the OS what to do and it can respond.

2. Manages system hardware.

3. Organizes and maintains files.

4. Acts as a bridge between applications and hardware.

Let's look at these four functions in a bit more detail.

An OS Creates a User Interface

An operating system creates a *user interface*—the on-screen prompts and objects that enable you to interact with the computer—to accomplish tasks ranging from simple to complex, like running applications and saving the data they create, or using a modem to get online. The user interface can be plain and simple, like the character-based command line interfaces of DOS (Figure 5.1) and Linux (Figure 5.2), or it can be colorful and full of graphical objects, like the *graphical user interface* (GUI – pronounced "GOO-EY") of a Windows (Figure 5.3) or Macintosh OS. Either way, a user interface is your gateway to all that a computer offers.

An OS Manages System Hardware

The operating system manages all the hardware in and attached to a computer. To control the most basic hardware—the hard drive, floppy drive (if present), keyboard, and video adapter (the interface between the OS and the computer's display)—it uses a set of tiny programs collectively referred to as the *basic input/output system* (BIOS) or the *system BIOS*.

Computers can also use types of hardware that didn't even exist when they were created. An operating system can control a piece of computer hardware it wasn't designed for by using a small special-purpose program called a *device driver*, supplied by the hardware manufacturer. A device driver is sort of like a translator that enables the OS to understand and direct the new hardware device. The device manufacturer must create a driver for each operating system it chooses to support; usually these drivers will be supplied on a CD with the device (Figure 5.4). For instance, if you buy a new joystick game controller, the disc may contain joystick device drivers for several versions of Windows, for Linux, and for Macintosh.

An OS Organizes and Maintains Files

When you bring a PC home from the store, it may already have programs and data stored on its hard drive. Then, over time you will install more application programs, and store more data, such as word processing files, spreadsheets, e-mail messages, music files, and graphics files. A critical function of every OS is to enable you to organize your programs and data; it does this using files, file types, and folders.

Files

Remember bits and bytes from earlier chapters? A *file* is a collection of bytes given a name so that the OS can retrieve it for you later. Hector starts a letter to George Lucas about one of the Star Wars movies, but has to leave to run an errand before he finishes. Thanks to the OS, he can save the letter in a file in his My Documents folder with a name of his choosing. He could just call it **letter**, but giving it a more descriptive name will make the file easier to find later when he's ready to finish writing (Figure 5.5).

Figure 5.3: Windows XP graphical user interface

Figure 5.4: Device driver discs

File Types

In the previous example (Figure 5.5), Hector named his letter to George Lucas, "Letter to GL," but when he told his word processing program to save the letter, it added the extension ".doc" to the filename, creating a file named "Letter to GL.doc" in Hector's My Documents folder. Most operating systems use a *file extension*—a group of characters that follows a file name—to mark different types of files. A period (usually pronounced "dot") separates the file name from the extension. The file extension .doc tells the OS—and Hector, if he knows that file extension—that the file was created using the Microsoft Word program.

An OS like Windows XP keeps lists of different file types, their corresponding file extensions, and which programs open which file types. When a user double-clicks on a data file, Windows notes its file extension and the corresponding file type (in Hector's case, .doc and Microsoft Word), then opens the program that handles data files of that type, which in turn opens the data file the user clicked

Figure 5.5: Letter to GL.doc

on. So, when Hector returns to his My Documents folder and double-clicks on the file **Letter to GL.doc**, Windows will automatically run Microsoft Word, which will open his letter to George Lucas.

Finding Drivers

If you have a piece of hardware installed but no driver for your OS, all hope is not lost! Check the manufacturer's Web site for the correct driver—just about every computer component manufacturer supports their devices for years and years.

Figure 5.6: A listing of files in an OS X folder

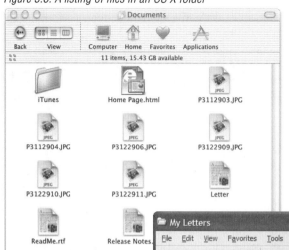

Figure 5.7: My Letters

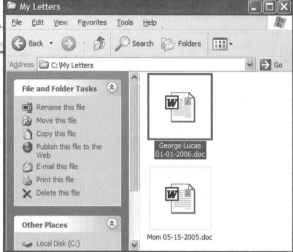

Folders

Imagine all the school work you have completed in your lifetime. Then picture what it would be like if you saved all of it—every piece of paper—in one large pile. Sure, you could point to it and say "I did all that work!" but if you needed to retrieve a *particular* piece of paper, you might wish for a less impressive but more organized storage system. Most people with any amount of paper to organize store individual files in folders, and the same principle applies to the files on your computer.

Like the paper folders in a file cabinet, computer *folders* are virtual file containers on your hard drive or other mass storage device. Hector could create a folder on his C: drive called "My Letters," for example, and store his letter in

Figure 5.8: Operating system at the center

it. With the folder's name providing the information that this is a letter, Hector could give the file a very descriptive name, such as "George Lucas 01-01-2006. doc" (Figure 5.7).

An OS Acts as a Bridge between Applications and Hardware

An operating system is necessary before you can use your computer or install applications. The operating system enables your applications to use your hardware. Techs call this *program support*. An OS by itself cannot do all the fancy things you need from application software, and application software cannot run on a computer without an OS. The OS manages things for you and your applications, while an application, such as a game or spreadsheet program, enables you to accomplish specific tasks (Figure 5.8).

Capabilities and Limitations of an OS

Operating systems reflect both the skill and imagination of the programmers that write them. Bill might come up with a design where you can type commands and the operating system will respond. Steve, on the other hand, might envision an OS where you have little pictures you click on to make the same sort of things happen. See Figure 5.9.

Understanding the capabilities and limitations of an operating system helps you work more effectively with it. That way you won't waste time clicking when you should be typing!

What's my Motivation?

Who Cares About File Extensions?

Why should you care about file extensions? For one thing, malware—software designed to harm your computer, like viruses and spyware—can hide in almost any executable file. The next time you receive an e-mail with an attachment, notice what type of extension that attachment has before opening it. If you see the .exe extension, you now know it's an executable program, and should not be opened until it can be scanned for virus/spyware content. Knowledge is power! Chapter 10, "The Good, the Bad, and the Ugly – Multimedia, Personal Applications, and Utility Programs" covers viruses and spyware in more detail.

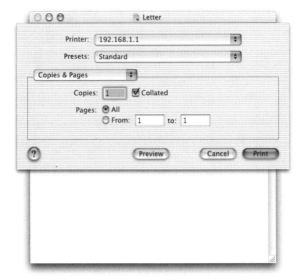

Figure 5.9: Two paths to the same result

Text Commands in a Character-based User Interface

Before there were GUIs and computer mice, you talked to your computer by typing commands. It told you it was ready to receive commands by displaying a *prompt,* a group of characters typed by the computer at the left side of the screen that prompts you to give it a command. The standard PC prompt was the hard drive letter followed by a colon, a backslash, and an angle bracket; for example, **C:\>** or **A:\>**. You typed your command, and then, to tell the OS you were done typing and it should process your command, you pressed the **[Enter]** key.

See File Extensions in Windows

*By default, Windows only shows you the file names, without any extensions. To make Windows display the file extensions, do the following: in Windows XP, open My Computer or Windows Explorer and select **Tools | Folder Options | View**. In the list of Advanced Settings, click the radio button next to the setting labeled **Show hidden files and folders** and then click OK.*

Point + Click = Type + Enter

*Regardless of whether you double-click an icon with your mouse or type a command and press the **[Enter]** key on your keyboard, you do the same thing as far as the computer is concerned: give it a command that it must try to execute. Try this. Fire up your computer and try both methods of running a simple drawing program in Windows called Paint.*

*First, do it the GUI way: **Click on Start | All Programs | Accessories | Paint**. Your computer should obey your command and start Paint. No problems, right?*

*Now close Paint and try starting it from the command line. Click **Start | Run**, type **cmd** and click **OK** to open up a command line window. At the prompt, type **mspaint** and press **[Enter]**. Sure enough, there's Paint again (Figure 5.11)!*

```
C:\>dir /a

Volume in drive C is MS-DOS_6
Volume Serial Number is 2C98-8B17
Directory of C:\

IO          SYS         40,774  05-31-94     6:22a
MSDOS       SYS         38,138  05-31-94     6:22a
DOS         <DIR>               04-24-02     5:24p
COMMAND     COM         54,645  05-31-94     6:22a
WINA20      386          9,349  05-31-94     6:22a
CONFIG      SYS             71  04-29-02     8:51p
AUTOEXEC    BAT             86  05-03-02     1:51p
        7 file(s)             143,063 bytes
                        2,138,013,696 bytes free

C:\>_
```

Figure 5.10: Running the DIR command

computer do something is as fast and simple as typing a string of characters. In the hands of an experienced geek, the command line has the benefit of speed and precision combined, but to achieve this, you have to know the language of the OS; that is, which commands do what you want to do, including the variations and options. Plus you must understand the structure of the computer's file system, because those specifics are part of what you type.

Point and Click in a GUI

Operating systems with a graphical user interface (GUI) provide a computer environment that's much friendlier than a command-line interface. Rather than memorizing a bunch of commands, for example, you simply use your mouse to point at an object and click (or double-click) on it to perform a task, like running a program or seeing the contents of a folder. Plus, the GUI standardizes the look and feel of applications. Most use similar scroll bars, menus, and icons, a consistency that helps you learn and use those applications.

There were commands for every possible thing you could want the computer to do: navigate among its folders (called directories in those days), run programs, or input data for a program to use. To see the contents of a directory (folder) on a PC, for example, you would type the command **DIR**, press **[Enter]**, and the computer would spit out a list of files (Figure 5.10).

If you know how to use a character-based OS, making the

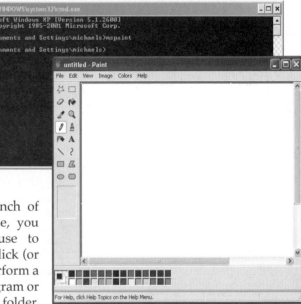

Figure 5.11: Using the command line to open Paint

The Major Operating Systems

While operating systems are similar in the functions they perform, they are not all the same. This section contains an overview of the major operating systems: MS-DOS, Windows, Apple's Macintosh OS, UNIX, and Linux, plus the two main specialized operating systems developed for handheld gadgets, Palm OS and Pocket PC.

Microsoft DOS

Microsoft DOS, known as MS-DOS, had a command-line interface, with no visual cues for launching programs or managing files, like the icons in Windows. Microsoft created MS-DOS for a CPU that is now decades old, so it cannot take advantage of many of the features of new processors, like multitasking or accessing large amounts of memory.

Although Microsoft has not released a retail version of MS-DOS since version 6.22 in the early 1990s, the DOS-style command line interface lives on as an embedded OS in devices like store inventory scanners and in the look and feel of the command line interface in Windows.

Microsoft Windows

Microsoft Windows is a hugely popular GUI OS for desktop and laptop PCs; at this writing, Windows is used on the majority of desktop computers worldwide. Windows takes advantage of the latest x86 architecture, which enables it to multitask—run several tasks at once—using gigabytes of RAM memory, and even vaster amounts of hard disk space. Windows also has the built-in ability to connect to a network.

Microsoft has brought out many versions of Windows in the last two decades, including Windows 9*x* (Figure 5.12), Windows NT, Windows 2000 (Figure 5.13), and Windows XP. Each new version added more capability, more features, and more complication. All of these Windows versions are still at work in schools, offices and homes, so it's useful to know a little bit about them.

The newest member of the Windows family, Windows XP, comes in a number of varieties: Home Edition for home users, Professional for desktop users at work, and specialized versions including Media Center Edition, Tablet PC Edition, Embedded, and 64-bit Edition. XP is now the standard Windows version for all home users and more and more business users. Figure 5.14 shows the Windows XP desktop.

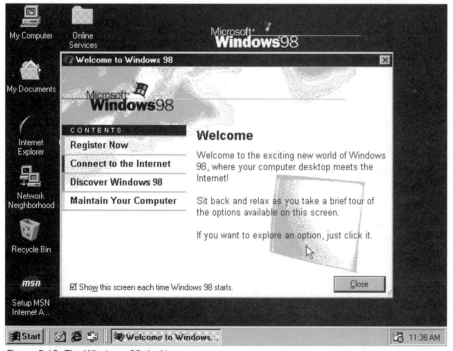

Figure 5.12: The Windows 98 desktop

Working It

Look at the command below. The prompt—C:\>—tells you the computer's focus is the primary hard drive, the C: drive. The first word after the prompt—dir—is the command to list the contents of a directory. The next part specifies which directory's files to list: the subdirectory mp3covers, in the scans directory, on the F: drive (probably a CD drive). The last part—/a:h—is called a **switch**. *It activates an optional feature of the DIR command, telling it to include hidden files when it shows you the contents of the directory.*

```
C:\>dir f:\scans\mp3covers /a:h
```

To execute this command, you have to know the DIR command and its show hidden files switch, and be able to list the exact location of the mp3covers folder. If you do know those things, command line work is satisfyingly efficient. With some practice and a good manual, you can accomplish a lot of tasks just by typing!

The 95, 98, and Me versions of Windows, collectively known as Windows 9x, were the primary versions used in homes. The standard business version of Windows for many years was Windows NT.

What's Your Version Number?

If you are running Windows but you aren't sure which version you've got, here is one way to find out. Open My Computer, select the Help menu, and then select About (Figure 5.15). You can use this technique to discover the version numbers of Windows applications, too.

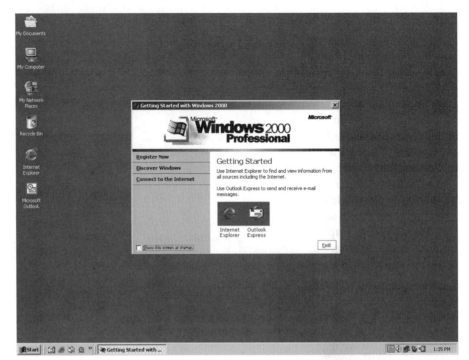

Figure 5.13: The Windows 2000 desktop

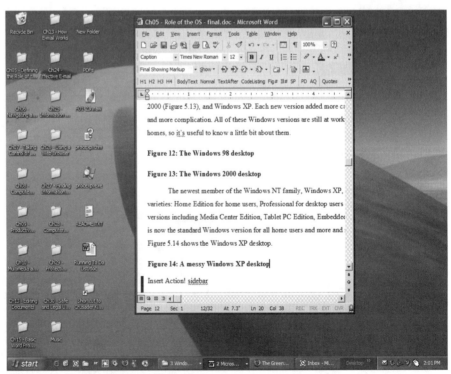

Figure 5.14: A messy Windows XP desktop

Apple Macintosh

Apple Computer, Inc. introduced the first *Macintosh* in 1984 and within a year it became the first widely successful computer to have a GUI interface. Apple uses a proprietary architecture in their computers, so the Macintosh OS only runs on Apple computers. For OS X, Apple totally rewrote their code, basing it on a version of UNIX called Darwin. Now besides being a leading-edge GUI OS, OS X allows the technically savvy user to access a command line and enter UNIX commands in a terminal window (Figure 5.16).

At this writing Apple Macintosh computers have less than 5% of the worldwide market for desktop computers, but Macintosh has a strong, loyal group of users in creative industries where graphics are important, such as publishing and video editing. Macintoshes are more expensive than comparable PCs, but easier to use and maintain.

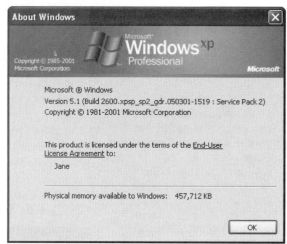

Figure 5.15: About the PC

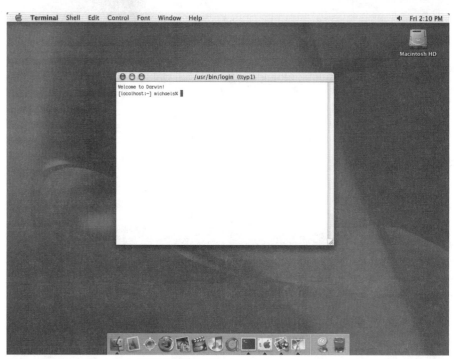

Figure 5.16: The Macintosh OS X desktop with a terminal window open

UNIX

Created in the pre-PC days when the only computers were mainframes and minicomputers, the *UNIX* operating system has been around for about 40 years in one form or another. It continues to be the OS of choice on *mission critical systems* – computer systems whose continuous functioning is critical to an organization's existence. The native interface for UNIX is the command line, but there are several GUIs available. Popular choices among the many versions of UNIX include BSD, IBM AIX, and Sun Solaris.

Command Line in the 21st Century

Character-based operating systems seem like a relic of the 20th Century to most computer users today—assuming they even know about DOS or UNIX. The first version of DOS came out in 1981; Microsoft released the last major version (MS-DOS 6.22) in 1994. By any measure, that's a while ago! But here's a dirty little secret.

Every major operating system today has a command-line user interface that you can access and use to do an amazing number of things. Windows, Macintosh OS X, and Linux technicians and administrators rely heavily on the command line, because it's fast and powerful, and particularly useful for troubleshooting. Learning how it works can save your bacon.

Linux

Linus Torvalds, a young student in Finland, decided back in the 1980s that he wanted to create an *open-source* operating system with the strengths of UNIX. Open source means that anyone can download or get a copy of the software, alter it in any way they want, and then give that new product away as well. Combining his UNIX inspiration with his own name, he called his new OS *Linux*.

Linux's native user interface is nearly identical to the UNIX command line, but there are a variety of GUIs written for it as well. Although the Linux OS program code itself is free, vendors sell it bundled with setup programs, utilities, manuals, and support options. The many versions of Linux (called *distributions* or *distros*), such as Slackware, Fedora, Mandriva (formerly Mandrake), Red Hat, Debian, and SuSE (see Figure 5.17), all have their own distinct GUIs.

Figure 5.17: Linux with the GNOME GUI desktop

Palm OS and Pocket PC/Windows Mobile

Palm OS and Pocket PC/Windows Mobile are operating systems for small handheld devices, including PDAs (Personal Digital Assistants), portable video and music players, and smart cell phones (Figure 5.18). The Palm OS was developed specifically for Palm's PDAs. Microsoft's Pocket PC OS (now called Windows Mobile), is a specialized version of big Windows, designed to compete with Palm for the handheld device market.

The interfaces of these operating systems are specifically designed with the limitations of handheld devices in mind. They enable users to access most features by touching the screen with a stylus rather than by typing, and the menus and screen layout are adjusted to compensate for the tiny screen size.

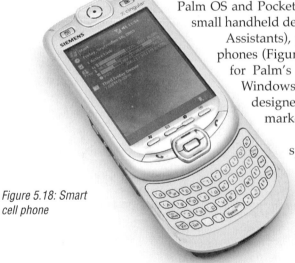

Figure 5.18: Smart cell phone

Limitations

Every OS has limitations in terms of software and hardware support, naming conventions, and even case sensitivity. Knowing about the sorts of limits out there can help when you're faced with an unfamiliar operating system.

Software Support

Application developers must write separate versions of their programs specifically for each different operating system. This means a program written for Windows XP won't work on a computer running OS X or Linux, or even in many cases on a computer running Windows 98! Applications written for newer operating systems often won't run under older ones, and while it's less of a problem, older applications won't always run on newer operating systems.

Some program developers create multiple versions of their applications to encourage the widest adoption possible (Figure 5.19). Not all versions get equal priority, however; Macintosh users often have to wait six months or more for a Macintosh version after vendors release a hot new game for Windows.

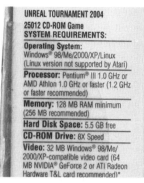

Figure 5.19: OS compatibility

Hardware Support

Operating systems are also written with particular hardware in mind. Each operating system requires a certain minimum hardware configuration, and each one generally only supports the types of hardware that were widely in use when it was developed. Because of this, an older operating system may not support newer hardware.

Windows NT, for example, doesn't support USB, because when Windows NT came out, USB hadn't been created yet! Conversely, a newer operating system may not install or run properly on older computer hardware, even if an older version of the same OS worked on that computer. This is a common problem for people who want to upgrade to a newer version of Windows or Macintosh OS.

Naming Conventions

Each OS has its own *naming conventions*, its rules for naming files and folders. MS-DOS, for example, used the 8.3 ("eight-dot-three") naming convention, which limited file names to eight characters (letters, numbers, and a limited set of symbols), followed by a period and a file extension of up to three characters.

Examples of valid DOS 8.3 file names are README.TXT and report01.doc. Examples of invalid names include @badchar.ppt EXTRALONGNAME.TXT. Modern operating systems allow for long filenames of up to 255 characters, which makes it easy to create unique and meaningful names.

When releasing a new version of a program, both Microsoft and Apple generally include support for at least the last few most recent versions of their operating systems, but in any particular case, you can't count on that. Your best bet when buying any program is to check the box to see which versions of which operating systems can run it.

Case Sensitivity

Different operating systems handle file and folder names differently. Microsoft's OSs, for example, are case insensitive—they don't distinguish between upper and lower case letters. To Windows, MYFILE01.DOC is the same file as MyFile01.doc; you can work in upper, lower, or mixed (both upper and lower) case at the command prompt or in My Computer. Linux, on the other hand, is entirely case sensitive. All in the same folder, you could save files named MYFILE01, MyFile01, myfile01, and so on, because they are different to Linux..

The big exception to the statement that Windows is case insensitive is in login user name and password. If you use fluffy25 as your password in Windows XP, for example, the OS will laugh at you if you type in FLUFFY25 or Fluffy25. And you won't get logged in!

Common OS Problems and Their Solutions

Most days your computing experience should be trouble-free, but there are those days when you will run into problems. Let's look at a few common problems and their solutions, including what to do when your computer starts acting weird, won't start at all, or won't let you log on.

Operating System Instability

If your operating system becomes unstable, it can suddenly slow down, start responding oddly, or even freeze up and refuse to respond at all. An unstable OS may display one or more of the following symptoms:

- Programs, windows, or menus open slowly.

- The system completely stops responding to the keyboard or mouse (in geekspeak, it *hangs*).

- Program windows do not display correctly when you try to open and close them.

- Scary error messages such as "Fatal Error..." appear on the screen.

- On restart, the computer announces it's going to run in Safe mode (Figure 5.20).

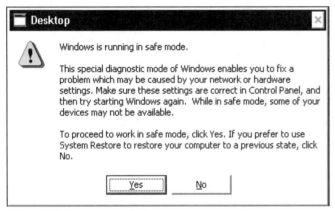

Figure 5.20: The message that appears when a computer starts in Safe mode

There are many possible causes for these problems, but often the simplest solution is to restart the computer. A restart often clears out whatever bad bytes are in there confusing the system, and gives it a chance to start over fresh. That said, it's a common computer newbie mistake to restart the computer the minute something appears to be wrong, rather than giving the system some time to sort itself out, or calling someone for help who might be able to fix things without rebooting and losing whatever work was in progress when the instability occurred.

Programming flaws not apparent when you install a program can later cause operating system instability, as can corrupt operating system files. An operating system consists of many critical files, and if one or more of these files is mistakenly replaced with a different (or improperly written or corrupt) version during an application's installation, you may not know it until you try to run some other application that wants the original file. Windows now includes protections against damage to system files, but they aren't perfect, so you should know what to do if such a problem persists.

Hard drives and computer systems wear down over time, which can create OS instability. To keep them running well, you need to follow standard maintenance procedures on a regular basis, which means running scans on the hard drive and defragmenting it periodically.

Drive Scanning

Scanning your hard drive checks the drive for physical problems and for "logical" problems, such as foul-ups in the records about your files and folders. Hard drives, as you know, store data magnetically. Over time, areas on the drive can go bad and be unable to hold data. This is no big deal, as long as the operating system knows about it and doesn't try to put data on the bad spots. Also, for some reason unknown to man, woman, or beast, operating systems simply misfile their folders or files, as if you absent-mindedly put your homework in the wrong desk drawer. Drive scanning helps the OS handle these issues.

To scan a drive in Windows, you simply open **My Computer**, right-click on your hard drive, and select **Properties**. In the Local Disk Properties dialog box, select the **Tools** tab (Figure 5.21) and then click the **Check Now** button. This opens the Check Disk Local Disk dialog box, revealing two options, as you can see in Figure 5.22. Check the first box to fix logical problems, and the second box to fix physical problems. Then click **Start** to make it go.

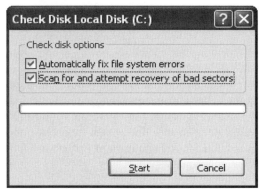

Figure 5.22: Check Disk with options selected

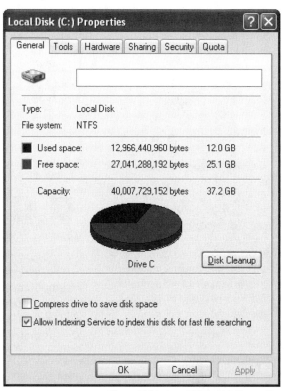

Figure 5.21: Local Disk (C:) Properties

Disk Defragmenting

When you save a file on your hard drive, the drive breaks that file into equal-sized pieces, then stores those pieces in available spots—called *clusters*—on the disk. The drive keeps track of the contents of each cluster so when you tell it to load that file, it can retrieve the pieces and put them back together. Figure 5-23 shows a trio of files saved on a drive, all in nice neat clusters, with free clusters at the end.

Figure 5.23: Filled clusters

When you delete a file, the hard drive erases all its pieces from their clusters, leaving empty clusters where once it had filled clusters. If you deleted **beach.jpg** in the example above, for example, you'd have a gap between the other two files (Figure 5-24).

Figure 5.24: Deleted file leaves free clusters

Running Utilities in Order

You should always run your disk scanning software before you defragment your computer hard drive(s). You wouldn't want to have your OS rearrange files and accidentally put a file in a bad section of the drive, right? Disk Defragmenter in Windows won't let you defragment without a scan, but some third-party utilities aren't quite so nice. Do it in order!

Disk scanning and defragment-ing utilities used to come from third-party program developers, so would be considered separate utility software (and thus part of Chapter 10 in this book, "Other Applications," rather than here). The IC³ exam still reflects this way of thinking about these utilities. Many years ago, though, Microsoft included scanning and defragging utilities as part of the OS maintenance routine and bundled the tools with Windows, so they're included here under OS problem-solving.

The next time you save a file, the drive fills up the empty clusters first, then jumps over to the next empty clusters (Figure 5.25). Over time, data files and program files end up scattered across the drive, through this process called *fragmentation*. A badly fragmented drive can perform very poorly indeed because the drive has to gather pieces from many locations just to load stuff into RAM.

Figure 5.25: Fragmentation

A *defragmentation* program, like Disk Defragmenter in Windows, fixes fragmentation by placing all the pieces that should go together in touching clusters, nice and tidy like Figure 5-23 above. To run Disk Defragmenter, right-click your drive and select **Properties**; click on the **Tools** tab; then click the **Defragment Now** button (Figure 5-26). Click the **Defragment** button in Disk Defragmenter to make it go.

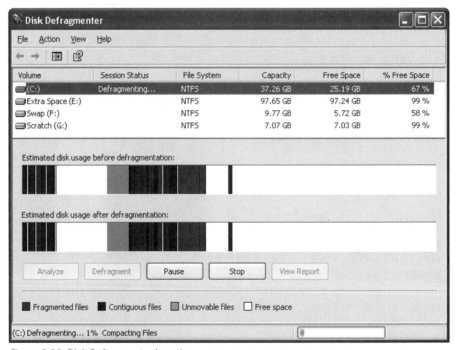

Figure 5.26: Disk Defragmenter in action

You should run scanning and defragmenting software on a regular basis, like once a week or at the very least, once a month. This helps keep your system functioning better than it would without such efforts.

If an instability problem persists, it may be necessary to run a repair process on an OS, or even completely reinstall it; however, you should not try these advanced tasks without a great deal of thought and preparation. One advanced option is to do a System Restore, which can roll back your OS to the state it was in at a point in time before the problem began.

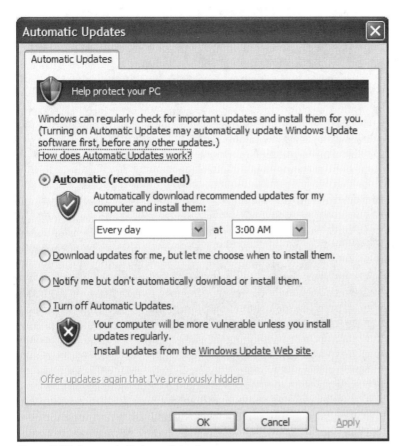

Figure 5.27: Automatic Updates dialog box

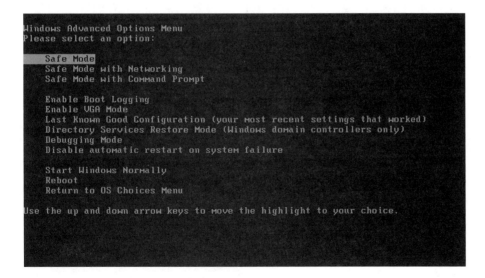

Figure 5.28: Select Safe mode from the Advanced Options menu

Sometimes problems are caused by a bug in the operating system itself, in which case updating the operating system will correct the problem. Microsoft and Apple create software updates to fix problems such as instability in the OS and security holes. If your computer is attached to the Internet, it should automatically check for updates and install them for you (Figure 5.27).

How Dead is it?

If your computer will not start normally, first check that there are no hardware problems. Is it plugged in? Is the power switch on? Are all the cables properly connected? If all the connections seem okay, observe carefully what happens when you power up the computer. Do you see the indicator lights for power and hard drive flashing? Can you hear the sound of the fan and hard drive? Does Windows completely fail to start (no color or graphics on the screen) or do you see a message of some kind? Act on what you see, or report it to an advanced Windows user.

So, Your Computer Won't Start in Any Mode!

If your computer fails to start normally, and it also fails to start in any of the Safe mode choices, then it is time for more drastic measures. An advanced Windows user or administrator can attempt to use the Recovery Console, available from the original Windows CD, and try to fix the problem from there, but this is an extreme measure to take. Another extreme option when all else fails is to reinstall the operating system. Be aware that if you do a complete "clean" reinstallation, you will lose all the data you previously had on your computer.

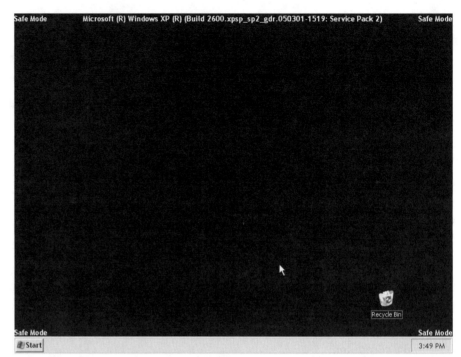

Figure 5.29: Safe mode has labels in each corner

Failure to Start

Problems that cause system instability can become serious enough that the computer completely fails. Generally the best thing to do when this happens is to try to start Windows in *Safe mode*. When you start Windows in Safe mode, it only starts the absolute minimum number of OS pieces necessary for it to function. This means it starts up without loading most of its device drivers and other files that support more advanced features like pretty screen graphics and networking. By doing this, it also is likely to avoid running the particular bit of code that is causing you trouble. This is most critical when that code is some sort of virus or other malware.

To enter Safe mode, restart the computer and press the [F5] or [F8] key while the computer is in text mode (before it says "Starting Windows"). This will bring up the Advanced Options Menu (See Figure 5.28) from which you can select Safe mode. Then Windows will start in Safe mode (See Figure 5.29).

If your computer starts itself in Safe mode, the problem may be a corrupted driver or networking file. While in Safe mode an advanced Windows user may be able to correct the problem using techniques such as disabling the suspected component until the manufacturer provides a replacement driver. How do you know which component to suspect? Think what has changed since the computer last behaved properly. It could be that your problems started after installing a new application, or after installing a new driver or updating an old driver.

Access Denied

Your computer may require you to log on with a user name and password before you can access your desktop. If so, don't be surprised if you sometimes see the message, "Access Denied." The normal cause is a simple typing error when entering a user name or password. The first thing to check is the **[Caps Lock]** key, as passwords are case-sensitive. Re-enter your user name and password very carefully, playing attention to the use of upper and lower case in the password. If you are sure you have entered the user name and password correctly and it still won't let you in, you should contact the administrator of your computer.

Operating System Functions

- An operating system (OS) controls the computer, enabling the hardware and application software to work together. The operating system creates and maintains a user interface; manages system hardware; organizes and maintains files; and interfaces with application software. A user interface is the on-screen prompts and objects that enable you to interact with the operating system.

- The basic input/output system (BIOS) is a set of programs that the operating system uses to control the most basic computer hardware, such as the hard drive, keyboard, and video controller. A device driver is a small special-purpose program that enables an OS to control new hardware devices you add on to the computer.

- An OS organizes programs and data using files, file types, and folders. A file is a collection of bytes given a name so that the OS can retrieve it for you later. A file extension is a group of characters at the end of a file name that operating systems use to identify different types of files. A computer folder is a virtual file container on your hard drive or other mass storage device.

- The operating system enables your applications to use your hardware, while an application enables you to accomplish specific tasks.

Capabilities and Limitations of an OS

- The two basic types of user interface are the character-based command line interface and the graphical user interface (GUI).

- Working with text commands in a character-based user interface requires that the user memorize commands to type in at the command prompt. The command-line interface is still used extensively by people who maintain computers.

- Today the graphical user interface (GUI) has become standard on most operating systems, even those that natively use a command line interface. This is because a GUI is easier to use. Instead of having to memorize commands, you simply use your mouse to point at an object and click to perform a task.

- The major operating systems covered in this book are MS-DOS, Windows, Macintosh OS, UNIX, and Linux, plus the two specialized operating systems developed for handheld gadgets, Palm OS and Pocket PC.

- MS-DOS is a command-line operating system that pre-dates Windows. It was created for a CPU that is now decades old, so it cannot take advantage of many of the features of new processors, like multitasking or accessing large amounts of memory. Techs still use the DOS-like command line interface available in Windows to do system support work.

- Microsoft Windows is a GUI OS that has seen many versions, such as the Windows $9x$ family, Windows NT, Windows 2000, and Windows XP. Each new version added more capability, more features, and more complication. Windows takes advantage of the latest x86 architecture, which enables it to multitask, use gigabytes of RAM and huge hard disks, and connect to a network.

CHAPTER 5: SUMMARY

■ Apple's Macintosh computer, introduced in 1984, was the first widely successful computer to have a GUI interface. Apple uses a proprietary architecture in their computers, so the Apple OS only runs on Apple computers. The code of Apple's newest version, OS X, is based on UNIX, making it completely different from older versions. Macintosh computers currently have less than 5% of the worldwide desktop market.

■ The UNIX operating system has been around for about 40 years, and continues to be the OS of choice on mission critical systems. The native interface for UNIX is the command line, but there are several GUIs available for it.

■ Linux is an open-source operating system created by Linus Torvalds. Its native user interface is nearly identical to the UNIX command line, but the major distros, such as Fedora, Mandriva, Red Hat, and SuSE, all have their own distinct GUIs.

■ Palm OS and Microsoft's Pocket PC/ Windows Mobile OS are operating systems designed for small handheld devices like PDAs, portable video and music players, and smart cell phones.

■ Applications are written for specific operating systems—one written for the Windows OS will not run under the Macintosh OS, and *vice versa*. Applications written for newer operating systems often won't run under older ones, and older applications won't always run on newer operating systems.

■ Operating systems are written with particular hardware specifications in mind. They all require a certain minimum hardware configuration, and they all have limitations on what hardware they support. Because of this, an older operating system may not have support for newer hardware, and a newer operating system may not install or run properly on older computer.

■ Each OS has its own rules, or naming convention, for naming files and folders. While modern operating systems can handle files name of up to 255 characters, MS-DOS was restricted by its 8.3 naming convention.

■ Some operating systems, like Linux, are case sensitive – they distinguish between upper and lower case letters. Others, like DOS and Windows, are case insensitive, so to them, MYFILE01.DOC is the same file as MyFile01.doc

Common OS Problems and Their Solutions

- If an operating system becomes unstable, it can suddenly slow down, start responding oddly, or even hang and refuse to respond to the keyboard or mouse at all. It may display error messages. When restarted, it may launch in Safe mode.

- Often the simplest solution is to restart the computer, but if that will mean losing work in progress, it may be worth waiting to see if the system fixes things itself, or asking an expert to help.

- Operating system instability can be caused by flawed program installations and corrupt OS files. Problems caused by a flaw in the operating system itself can be fixed by updating the operating system. Microsoft creates software updates to fix problems such as OS instability and security flaws.

- Run disk scanning and defragmentation programs when you run into system instability and periodically as good maintenance. The OS can make mistakes with records of files and folders. Plus the hard drive can have magnetic spots go bad. Disk scanning can fix both issues. Hard drive files become fragmented over time just from deleting and adding programs. Parts of a file get stored in multiple areas of the drive, making access times slower than they could be. Disk defragmenting programs take care of this problem.

- Problems that cause system instability can become serious enough that the computer completely fails. An advanced user can diagnose and repair OS instability or failure to start using Safe mode. When you start Windows in Safe mode, it starts up without loading most of its device drivers and other files that support more advanced features. To enter Safe mode, restart the computer and press the [F5] or [F8] key while the computer is in text mode.

- To solve extreme cases of instability or startup failure, you may need to have an expert help you using advanced tools like System Restore and the Recovery Console, or to completely reinstall the operating system.

- If you receive an "Access Denied" message when logging onto an OS, check that [Caps Lock] is not turned on and log on again, paying close attention to your typing.

Key Terms

Basic input/output system (BIOS)

Clusters

Defragmentation

Device driver

Executable file

File

File extension

Folder

Fragmentation

Graphical user interface (GUI)

Linux

Macintosh OS

Mission critical systems

Naming convention

Open-source

Operating system (OS)

Program support

Prompt

Safe mode

UNIX

User interface

Windows 9x

Windows NT

Key Term Quiz

Use the Key Terms list to complete the following sentences. Not all terms will be used.

1. The _____ is the program code that controls the computer.

2. A _____ is displayed by a command line interface to tell you it is ready to receive commands.

3. If Windows will not start up normally, try starting it in _____.

4. The on-screen prompts and objects that enable a user to interact with the computer are called the _____.

5. A/an _____ is a collection of bytes given a name so that the OS can retrieve it for you later.

6. _____ is the operating system of choice for businesses with mission critical systems.

7. A set of rules that an OS uses when naming files and folders is called a _____.

8. A/an _____ is a program file that Windows can run on your command without assistance from another program.

9. Saving and deleting files over time will scatter pieces of those files across the hard drive, a process called _____.

10. A _____ is a virtual file container on your hard drive or other mass storage device.

Multiple Choice Quiz

1. Which of the following operating systems is open-source?
   A. UNIX
   B. Linux
   C. PalmOS
   D. Macintosh OS

2. Which of the following is **not** an operating system function?
   A. Create and maintain a user interface.
   B. Interface with application software.
   C. Manage e-mail messages.
   D. Manage system hardware.

3. The two major categories of user interface include:
   A. GUI and x86
   B. Black-and-white and color
   C. DOS and Windows
   D. Command-line and GUI

4. The native user interface of UNIX and Linux can best be described as:
   A. Object-rich
   B. GUI
   C. Command line
   D. Object-oriented

5. What is the name given to the program code used to add support for hardware to the OS?
   A. Device driver
   B. Executable
   C. ROM BIOS
   D. Folder

6. An OS will usually examine this to determine the type of file and how to treat it.
   A. Filename
   B. File extension
   C. Data and time information
   D. Folder name

7. Laura wants to install an operating system on her computer, but doesn't have a lot of money. Richard suggests that she get a copy of Linux, but George argues that Linux won't help because it's a character-based operating system. Who's right?
   A. Only Richard is correct.
   B. Only George is correct.
   C. Both Richard and George have it right.
   D. Neither Richard nor George has a clue.

8. Which of the following is a possible cause of instability? (Select all that apply.)
   A. Programming flaws
   B. Blue screen of death
   C. Corrupt operating system files
   D. Login

9. MS-DOS used this naming convention.
   A. Alphanumeric
   B. LFN
   C. 8.3
   D. Longhorn

10. Which of the following is **not** a distro of Linux?
    A. Red Hat
    B. OS X
    C. Mandriva
    D. Fedora

11. This is a group of small programs used by the OS to control some very basic hardware.
    A. Device drivers
    B. Program files
    C. VBScript
    D. Basic Input/Output System (BIOS)

12. Select the two examples of OS hardware support limitations.
    A. New hardware is not supported by an old OS.
    B. New hardware is not supported by MS Word.
    C. Old hardware is not supported by a new OS.
    D. Old hardware cannot be plugged into the computer.

13. Which of the following operating systems is **not** part of the Windows 9*x* family?
    A. Windows Me
    B. Windows 98
    C. Windows XP
    D. Windows 95

14. Which of the following was the last retail version of MS-DOS ?
    A. Compaq MS-DOS
    B. IBM PC DOS
    C. MS-DOS 6.22
    D. MS-DOS 8.0

15. Which of these operating systems is designed to run on a PDA?
    A. UNIX
    B. Windows XP
    C. SuSE
    D. Windows Mobile

Essay Questions

1. Your friend is having difficulty with her computer and has requested your help. When you ask her which operating system she is using, she responds, "I'm using Firefox, of course." Write a description of an operating system for your friend, explaining the functions of an OS and the difference between an OS and an application.

2. Your friend has a CD-ROM with the following files on it. He is about to dump them all into C:\, but you stop him and suggest that he create folders to organize them. He looks at you blankly. Write an explanation of what folders are for, then suggest a set of folders you think he should create, and explain why. Your friend's files are:
   - rainsong.mp3
   - Eng_essay01.doc
   - klaxon.wav
   - DVDlist.wpd
   - MyCDs.doc
   - Ringtone12.wav
   - whatif.mp3
   - nowgetbusy.mp3
   - feudalism.doc
   - glassbreaking.wav
   - Chem Lab Results.doc
   - MyMP3s.txt

3. Macintosh OS X, Linux (any distribution), and Windows are three competing operating systems. Imagine that you have been asked to research which operating system would be best for your school. Briefly describe each OS and give at least one benefit of each that distinguishes it from the others.

Projects

1. Take a survey of computer usage at your school and of at least five friends who use computers at home. Find out exactly what operating system, including version, is used on most of the computers at school. What operating systems are in use by your friends at home? Describe any differences you find in the operating systems and versions in use at school versus at home. Did you find Macintosh in use in either place? Did you find Windows in use in either place? Of the Macintosh computers in use, what versions of the OS were in use? Of the Windows computers, what versions of the OS were in use?

2. Use the Internet to research the Red Hat, Mandriva, SuSE, and Debian Linux distros. Compile a list of their similarities and differences, including features like installation support, available GUIs, and supported hardware and software, and practical considerations like price, available versions, and tech support. Which of the distros would you most recommend for a home user? Why? Which would you most recommend for a small business? Why? Why wouldn't you recommend the two distros you didn't pick?

Getting to Know You – Navigating and Managing Windows

"If you wanna learn how to swim, you have to jump in the water. Don't forget to feed Bruiser. Two all-beef patties, special sauce, lettuce, cheese, pickles, onions on a sesame seed bun . . . Whoa! I think I got some stuff out of your head that has nothing to do with navigating this ship!"

– Max the robotic pilot, *Flight of the Navigator*

This chapter covers the following IC³ exam objectives:

- IC³-1 3.2.1 Identify elements of the Windows desktop

- IC³-1 3.2.2 Manipulate windows

- IC³-1 3.2.3 Shut down and restart the computer using all available options

- IC³-1 3.2.4 Use the Windows Start menu and Taskbar

- IC³-1 3.2.5 Manipulate desktop folders and icons

- IC³-1 3.2.6 Identify and manage the directory/folder structure used to organize and store files

- IC³-1 3.2.7 Identify precautions one should take when manipulating files

- IC³-1 3.2.8 Solve common problems associated with working with files

When it comes to choosing an operating system (OS), the vast majority of computer users turn to Microsoft Windows XP, because it has a good graphical user interface (GUI) and supports almost every application currently on the market. The difference between selecting and effectively using an OS comes with knowing the interface and fundamental tools well.

This chapter teaches you the essentials of Windows. The chapter starts with the interface so you know what's what and where to find it. Then you'll dive into folder and file manipulation in a big way, using the many faces of the Windows Explorer. The chapter finishes with a look at precautions you should take and some typical problems that you can readily solve. We have a lot of ground to cover, so let's get started.

Windows Interfaces

Windows offers a complementary pair of interfaces for you to work with when you do basic tasks, such as open a folder or start a program: the Desktop and program interfaces. The Desktop opens as the default screen you see when you start Windows. To access a program interface, you generally use either the Start menu or the Quick Launch section of the Taskbar to run an application.

Desktop

Microsoft envisioned the Windows *Desktop* as the computer equivalent of a real-life desktop. It is always there underneath whatever you're doing in Windows, and it provides you with tools for opening and using your files and programs (Figure 6.1). The background of this area may be plain, or it may be covered with a customizable image, which, despite the fact that it covers a virtual desktop, is referred to as *wallpaper*.

Along the bottom of the Desktop is a thin border called the *Taskbar*. At the far left end of the Taskbar is the *Start* button, which you click on to open the

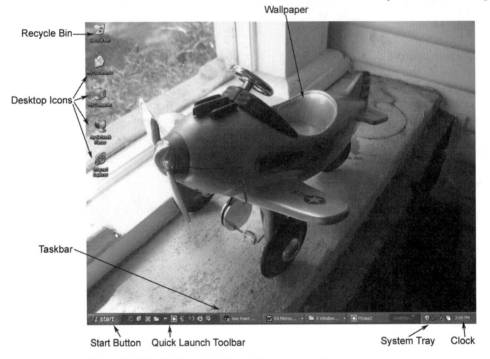

Figure 6.1: The Windows Desktop with custom wallpaper

Start menu. To the right of the Start button is the *Quick Launch toolbar*, where you can put icons to start programs with a single mouse click. The center of the Taskbar shows programs currently running. At the far right end of the Taskbar are the *System Tray* (Windows XP calls this the notification area) which displays icons for various system activities, and a clock, which tells you what time Windows thinks it is.

Most versions of Windows have many icons on the Desktop, pointing to folders, files (or documents), programs, and even Web pages. You know from earlier chapters that you can double-click any of these icons to make things happen, such as open a folder or run a program associated with a file. Double-clicking a *URL link icon*—URL being the technical name for a Web site's name, like www.microsoft.com—would cause the OS to fire up a Web browser and go to that Web site. Finally, every version of Windows has the Recycle Bin on the Desktop, where your deleted files live until you empty it.

You can do all sorts of things to folders, files, and other icons on your Desktop with just a quick click of the mouse. To create a new folder icon on your desktop, for example, simply right-click on an empty portion of the desktop and select **New | Folder** from the *context menu*—the menu that pops up when you right-click. You can delete, rename, and move icons as well.

To delete a folder, left-click on the icon to select it, press the **[Delete]** key. To rename it instead, right-click and select **Rename** from the context menu. To move it, left-click and drag it to where you want it to be. You can also put one desktop folder icon inside another desktop folder icon, simply by dragging and dropping the first icon onto the second.

Program Interface

You can use the Start menu or the Taskbar to open applications. Once you have a program open, Windows provides a standardized interface for performing basic tasks, such as minimizing and closing windows and programs. This interface is layered on top of the Desktop, with the Taskbar and its components visible at the bottom by default.

The Start Menu

The *Start menu* is command central for starting programs. As you know from previous chapters, the Start menu contains lists of programs you can launch and folders you can open (Figure 6.2). At the top left is a *pinned list* for programs or documents you want to be able to find easily and launch or open with a single click. You can remove a program or shortcut from this list by right-clicking on it and selecting **Unpin from Start menu**. You can add a program or shortcut from the All Programs menu to the pinned list by right-clicking it and selecting **Pin to Start menu**. You can also drag and drop a shortcut from somewhere else on your computer (like on your Desktop) to the Start menu.

Below the pinned list is the most frequently used programs list, or *MFU list*. Windows tracks which programs you use and updates this list so that it usually displays the programs you have launched most recently. To the right of the pinned list and MFU list on the Start menu are links to special folders like My Documents, system areas including the Control Panel and Printers and Faxes, and some useful tools, including Help and Support, Search, and Run. A right-pointing arrow next to an item means that there are two or more choices for the item.

Figure 6.2: The Start menu

Icons on the Windows Desktop are called Desktop icons, which makes a lot of sense. The various types you'll find are called folder icons, document icons, program icons, and URL link icons. As you might guess, these point (in order) to folders, files, programs, and Web pages.

File Association
You learned about the many ways to start applications way back in Chapter 2, "Going with the Data Flow," so turn back there now and see if you can answer these questions. What does "file association" mean? What happens when you double-click an MP3 music file? Why?

Restoring from the Recycle Bin
You know how to empty the Recycle Bin from Chapter 4, "It's a Comp's Life," but did you know you could restore files from there just as easily? Try this! Double-click the Recycle Bin icon to open it, and then select a deleted file. Click the option to **Restore this item** in the Recycle Bin Tasks section of the task pane and your file goes back to the folder where it lived before you deleted it. You can also right-click a file and select Restore from the context menu to accomplish the same thing. Do this a couple of times to get the hang of it!

Context Menus

There are many great tricks to working in Windows. One of them is to use context menus. A context menu is a menu that appears when you right click on almost anything in Windows—the Desktop, icons, folders, files, you name it. It shows you choices that will work on whatever object you right-clicked. Knowing that in almost every circumstance a right-click offers you knowledge, power, and perhaps fame gives you a leg up on your peers when it comes to becoming a computer power user!

*The Start menu in every version of Windows prior to Windows XP showed the version of Windows running on that PC. To see what it looked like in the old days, right-click the **Start menu** and select **Properties**. Click the **Classic Start menu** radio button and then click **OK**. Now, left-click **Start**. See the difference?*

*You can always use the **[Alt + Tab]** keyboard combination to cycle through open programs. Try it!*

To access any of your applications, including those not on the pinned or MFU lists, click **Start | All Programs** (Figure 6.3). You can launch a program by selecting it from the list. Newly installed programs are highlighted by default so you that can find them more easily.

The Taskbar

You can use the Taskbar to access programs in several ways. A single-click on a Quick Launch icon starts a program, for example, or you can click on a System Tray icon to access a program or device. But the most common use of the Taskbar is to switch between running programs using the open window buttons. Just click on an open window button to switch.

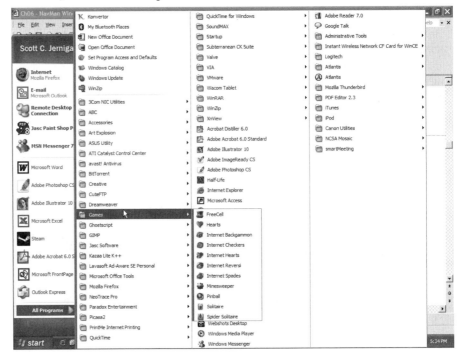

Figure 6.3: All Programs

Using the Program Interface

Once you open a program, Windows offers a second, standardized interface called the *program interface*. The program interface sits on top of the desktop by default. It can be *maximized* and thus cover the full desktop except for the Taskbar; *windowed*, which means you can see the desktop below and move and resize the program interface; or *minimized*, so the program shows up only as a icon and name on the Taskbar.

Figure 6.4 shows a windowed version of Picasa2, a picture editing and arranging program, plus a couple of minimized programs on the Taskbar (Jasc Paint Shop Pro and Microsoft Word) with the extra features of a program interface noted.

The top bar of the program interface, called the *title bar*, shows (from left to right) the Control menu button, which you can use to maximize, minimize and close a window; the name of the window; and the Minimize, Maximize/Restore, and Close buttons (that do exactly what they say). Below the title bar is a *menu bar* that contains menus with titles like File, Edit, and Help, each with a set of related menu items that enable you to accomplish tasks within the program. Finally, the bottom right corner shows a few diagonal lines—you can click and grab there with the mouse and resize the window.

Control Menu   Title bar   Minimize Maximize Close

Menu bar

Figure 6.4: Program interface

The Many Faces of Explorer

Windows handles file and folder management through the *Windows Explorer* utility program, but that doesn't quite tell you how things work. The truth is that Windows Explorer has many faces and none of them say "Explorer" in Windows XP. So here's the scoop.

When you click on **Start | My Documents**, or **Start | My Pictures**, you open Windows Explorer. You can open the same utility by right-clicking the **Start** button and selecting **Explore**. Or, go the whole nine yards and go to **Start | All Programs | Accessories | Windows Explorer** to open a classic Windows Explorer interface. Finally, go to **Start | My Computer** to open Explorer focused on your drives (hard, floppy, CD-media, and so on). Let's look at My Documents first, and then go to the classic Explorer interface. This section wraps up with a look at My Computer.

My Documents

Microsoft introduced *My Documents* and other "My" folders in later versions of Windows to give users a simple and clear place to store their documents. Users of earlier versions of Windows tended to store things willy-nilly all over their hard drives and, as a consequence, frequently had trouble finding files they wanted.

If you follow the path of least resistance and use the Microsoft folder structure, you'll save music files in My Music, pictures in My Pictures, and so on. Additional programs tend to add their own "My" folders, as you can see in Figure 6.5.

When you go to **Start | My Documents,** you open Windows Explorer focused on that

Display the Quick Launch Toolbar

The Quick Launch toolbar does not appear by default, but it is easy to turn on. Right-click on an unoccupied area of the Taskbar and select **Properties***; then, on the Taskbar menu, click to place a check in the box by* **Show Quick Launch***.*

Practice with Program Windows

Program windows make a lot more sense when you work with them, so fire up a computer if you have one available and open a program. Open WordPad by selecting **Start | All Programs | Accessories | WordPad***. Identify the parts of the Word-Pad window. Find the menu bar. What options do you have? Use the View menu to remove one or more toolbars. Then use the View menu to add a bar back. Use the Minimize, Maximize and Restore buttons. Grab the corner of the window and resize it. (Note that the program must be in windowed mode, not maximized, to resize.) Finally, click the* **Close** *button to exit from WordPad.*

Figure 6.5: My, my... My Folders have multiplied!

folder. On the left is the File and Folder Tasks pane with common tasks you can perform on the folders and files in the My Documents folder, such as rename, move, copy, delete, and so on. You can also perform any of these functions by right-clicking on a folder or file and selecting the appropriate option from the context menu.

At the top of the My Documents window, you can see the Standard Buttons toolbar, just below the Menu bar. This toolbar gives you important options such as the Up, Search, and Folders buttons. Click the **Folders** button to open the Folders pane and you'll go into the classic Windows Explorer look and feel (Figure 6.6).

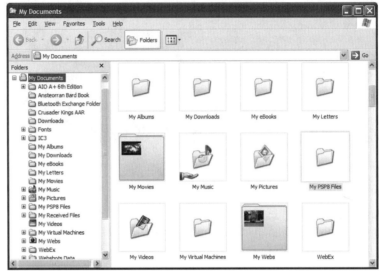

Figure 6.6: Windows Explorer, vintage view

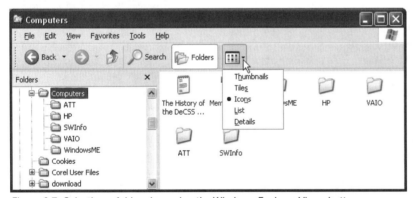

Figure 6.7: Selecting a folder view using the Windows Explorer Views button

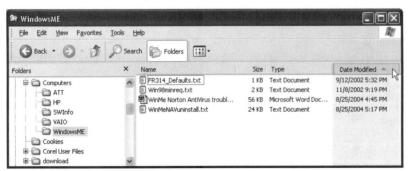

Figure 6.8: A folder with details showing

Windows Explorer

The classic Windows Explorer enables you to view and manipulate files and folders anywhere on your computer. You can see what folders you have, how they are organized, and what files and folders are in each one. You can see the files that contain your documents, and files for applications like Notepad or Photoshop, because everything on the computer is stored in a file.

Working with the Folders Pane

Windows gives each storage device a letter, and organizes its contents using folders and subfolders. The *Folders pane*—open on the left—is extremely useful for working with files and folders, because it gives you a graphical, hierarchical view of the window's contents. Notice that only folders and drives appear in the Folders pane, while both folders and files appear in the contents pane (on the right).

Clicking a plus sign (+) sign in front of a folder in the Folders pane expands the folder so you can see its subfolders. When a folder displays its subfolders, a minus sign (-) replaces the plus sign. Clicking the minus sign hides the subfolders.

To see the contents of a folder, you can click on its name in the Folders pane, which displays the folder's contents in the right pane. If you are looking at a folder icon in the right pane, you can double-click it to display its contents.

Changing Views

Windows Explorer gives you multiple options for how you view the contents of a folder. Clicking the **Views** button (Figure 6.7) enables you to choose how you want to display the folder contents—as thumbnails, tiles, icons, a list of filenames, or a list with details. The currently chosen view is marked with a dot in the menu. You can also select a folder view from the View menu.

Details view is particularly useful for quickly finding a particular file within a folder. The folder in Figure 6.8 is displayed in Details view, showing the name, size, file type, and modified date of each file. You can sort the files using the headers for the details being displayed. In Figure 6.8, the Date Modified header has been clicked, sorting the files by the date they were last changed.

Standard Actions

The classic Windows Explorer with the Folders view enables you to accomplish standard actions—create, move, copy, and delete—on folders and files between folders and drives. Each action works the same as with Desktop folders or in My Computer (because they're all just faces of Windows Explorer!), but drag and drop becomes even more powerful.

To move or copy a folder from one location to another, for example, simply left-click the folder, hold down the mouse button, and drag the folder. To choose whether you want to copy or move, press the **[Ctrl]** button. When it shows a + sign, you're about to copy; no sign and you're about to move that folder. Try it, you'll see!

Selecting Multiple Targets

Windows Explorer enables you to perform standard tasks on multiple files and folders at the same time. Select two or more files or folders by clicking or pointing to the first one, and then pressing the **[Shift]** key while clicking (what's called a *[Shift]-click*) or pointing to the last one in the list, as shown in Figure 6.9.

If the files or folders you want to select are not all next to each other, then you can use the *[Ctrl]-click* method to select

Exam Tip

Windows 3.x, the version of Windows Microsoft released back in the Dark Ages of Personal Computing, used a program called File Manager to view and manipulate files and folders. Certain exams with long institutional memory *cough* IC³ *cough, cough* may use that term to describe Windows Explorer, so watch out for that on test day!

Action!

Launch Windows Explorer

To launch the classic Windows Explorer directly, select **Start | All Programs | Accessories | Windows Explorer**. It will open showing you the My Documents folder. Do it! Better still, try this. Go to **Start | Run**, type **explorer** in the Run dialog box, and then click **OK**. What happens?

Figure 6.9: Click the first file, then [Shift]-click the last file to select a group of files that are listed contiguously

---

Creating, Renaming and Deleting a Folder

*In the theory that it's always more fun to do something rather than just read about, it, open up Windows Explorer and experiment. First, create a folder. Select the drive or folder within a drive where you want the new folder to go, and select **File | New | Folder**. A new folder will be created with the default name **New Folder**. The name will be highlighted so that you can replace it simply by typing a new name and pressing **[Enter]**.*

*If you accidentally create the folder with the default name, you can always select it and either press the **[F2]** key or right-click and select **Rename**, and give it a new name. Once you're satisfied with it, click on the folder and press the **[Delete]** key on your keyboard to send it to the Recycle Bin.*

Figure 6.10: [Ctrl]-click each file to select files that are not listed together.

Figure 6.11: In My Computer each type of storage device has a different icon

each file or folder. Figure 6.10 shows files selected by holding the **[Ctrl]** key while clicking on each file for the selection.

Finally, you can select all the files in a folder selecting **Edit | Select All**, or by pressing **[Ctrl + A]** on your keyboard. Note that the latter technique works in many programs in Windows, so it's always worth a try.

My Computer

My Computer offers a face of Windows Explorer that focuses on drives rather than folders. Each type of storage device has its own distinctive icon. Figure 6.11 shows the unique icons for the hard drives, floppy drive, and DVD/CD-RW drive. There are also icons for accessing Documents folders, and the Control Panel.

You can do all the standard actions on files and folders in My Computer. Click on the Folders button to open the Folders pane. You can quickly transfer files between drives using this view of Windows Explorer.

Good Housekeeping Seal of Approval

You can save yourself a lot of trouble if you take certain precautions when working with files and folders. Pay close attention when moving, copying, deleting, renaming, or reorganizing files. Careless manipulation of files can cause problems, such as losing a file because you can't remember what you named it, where you put it, or what password you used to protect it; running out of disk space because you have too many files; or even losing files altogether through accidental deletion, hard drive failure, or a lost or stolen computer. Disaster comes in many forms, but even a little bit of preparation can help keep your important files safe.

A Place for Everything, and Everything in its Place

To help avoid misplacing files, put some thought into the organization of your files and folders. Organization is all about putting similar items together in separate containers. In a computer, the items are files and the containers are folders on your hard drive. The names you give the containers should clearly identify their contents. You can mark files by their properties. Also, if some of your files are protected by passwords or other security systems, keep a record of the passwords or other access information in a secure place.

To help organize your My Documents folder, you can create subfolders within it, such as one for each of your classes. You can use the subfolders that come with My Documents, such as My Pictures and My Music, to store your pictures and MP3 files, for example, and then create subfolders for different sets of pictures or different musical artists.

Just like your room will get messy again if you don't pick up, your hard drive will become cluttered and confusing if you don't review the contents and periodically delete unused files. Keeping your disk neat and tidy can save you disk space as well as time!

Figure 6.12: Properties of a Word document

File Properties

Each file has unique properties, such as the filename, size, what program will open the file, its location on disk, and the dates when it was created, modified, and last accessed. You can set some of these properties to enable you to find that file easily with a search or to keep a file out of casual sight. To view a file's properties, right-click on the file and select **Properties** (Figure 6.12).

Most files have two or three tabs, such as General, Security, and Summary. The General tab shows you the basic file information, just as you'd expect. Notice the information at the bottom labeled *Attributes*. An *attribute* tells the operating system essential details about a file. A check in the box by an attribute means it is turned on. The *Read-only attribute* prevents a file from being modified or deleted. The *Hidden attribute* makes a file invisible in Windows Explorer unless you set your Folder Options (**Tools** | **Folder Options**) to allow Windows Explorer to display hidden files and folders.

The Summary tab available on some files gives you space to create or to read a lot more information about a file. Figure 6.13 shows the Summary tab for an MP3 music file. The file properties keep track of things like the name of the artist, title of the album, and so forth. You can change any of this information simply by clicking once in the dialog area.

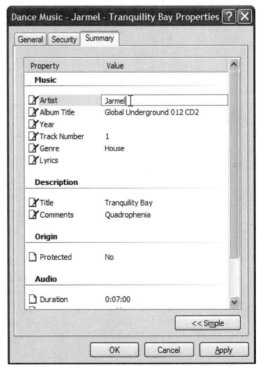

Figure 6.13: Properties of a music file

Back Up Data

To safeguard your files against accidental loss or destruction, you should make *backup* copies of them that you store somewhere *other* than where the originals are kept, such as a flash memory drive, an external hard drive, a floppy disk (if the files take up less than 1.44 MB of space), a writeable CD or DVD, or a network computer acting as a backup server.

Help and Support

When you don't understand how to do something in Windows, click the **Help and Support** item on the Start menu. This opens the Help and Support Center, the online help for Windows, where you will find a large list of links to local and Web-based help (Figure 6.14). If you have a problem in Windows, open the Help and Support Center and click on **Fixing a Problem**. Windows has Troubleshooters for several common problems you may encounter. If you have a problem printing, click **Printing Problems**, select **Printing Troubleshooter** under Fix a Problem, and answer the questions.

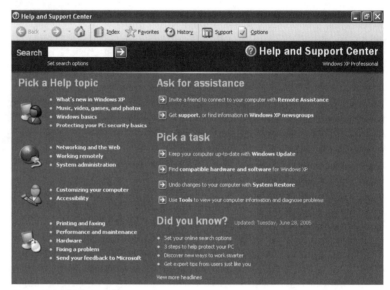

Figure 6.14: Help and Support Center

Search

If you cannot remember where you saved a file, you can search for it using the Windows Search wizard, which you can start from within Windows Explorer by clicking the Search button, or from the Start menu. Either option opens the Search Companion pane at the left (Figure 6.15). Select the category of what you want to find to open another dialog box in the Search Companion (Figure 6.16). Click **Search** to start.

Or, you can click the **Use advanced search options** check box to specify more precisely where you want the search to go (Figure 6.17). Checking the *Search Subfolders* option, for example, makes sure Windows Explorer will also look in any subfolders within the chosen folder.

When searching for text, either in a file name or within a file, you can use two special search characters—called *wildcards*—to help narrow your search when you know at least part of the word you want: the asterisk and the question mark. Here's how it works.

Say you are looking for notes on textbook chapters, which all have names that start with the letters "ch" followed by a chapter number, and that end in .doc because they are Word files, such as ch01.doc. To search for all files beginning with "ch" and ending in .doc, replace the rest of the file

Figure 6.15: Categories to search

Figure 6.17: Advanced options

Figure 6.16: Search specifics

name with an asterisk character: **ch*.doc**. This search would find files named ch12.doc and ch3.doc, but also files named chapter.doc and charles.doc, because the asterisk finds any file that matches.

You can also replace specific characters using the question mark search character, which substitutes for a single character. Searching for **ch??.d??** will find files named ch02.doc, ch02.dat, chap.doc, and choc.doc; it *won't* find files named ch022.doc, chapter.doc, ch02.txt, or chap.data.

Good Night, Gracie

The final step in good housekeeping is shutting down the computer gracefully. If you don't, you risk corrupting files, losing data, and generally having a bad day the next time you try to log into your computer. Windows typically offers four ways to shut down: Log off, *Restart*, Shut down, and Stand by. You access all four, ironically, from the Start menu.

The bottom of the Start menu has two buttons, Log Off and Shut Down (Figure 6.18). Click **Log Off** to close your user account, but leave the computer up and running for later or for other users. Clicking the **Shut Down** button gives you several options on a pull-down menu, including Log off <user name>, which does the same thing as the Log Off button.

Restart closes your computer down in an orderly fashion and then reboots, running through the full boot process. **Shut down** does the same thing, but doesn't reboot. It simply turns off the machine.

Stand by simply powers down your computer as it is, leaving a trickle of electricity to keep your RAM fully functional. Stand by is a great option for saving energy. No reason to leave your computer at full blast when you're not actively working at it! Because your RAM stays active, your computer can come back alive very quickly, enabling you to keep working or playing as you were before.

Boot Process
You learned about the boot process in Chapter Two, "Going with the Data Flow," so flip back there and see if you can answer these questions. What does the hardware test do? When does the operating system load? Can you load applications before you load the OS?

Hibernate
Stand by mode creates an element of danger, because you can kick into it at any time, whether you've saved currently open documents or not. If you lose power when in Stand by mode, all the data in RAM goes away. Poof!

Some computers have a Hibernate option that, when selected, copies the entire contents of RAM and saves it on your hard drive. When you come back up, Windows will restore the saved desktop state from the hard drive, bringing up Windows exactly as you left it, including the programs you were running and the documents you had open. Hibernate does not consume power; it just uses disk space.

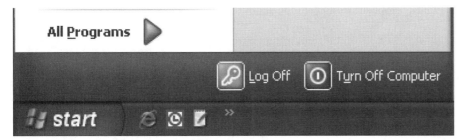

Figure 6.18: Shut down options

Windows Interfaces

- Windows has two layered graphical interfaces for you to work with when you do basic tasks, such as open a folder or start a program. The Desktop opens as the default screen you see when you start Windows. The program interface appears when you open an application.

- The Taskbar runs along the bottom of the Desktop and shows programs currently running. At the far left end of the Taskbar is the Start button, which you click on to open the Start menu. To the right of the Start button is the Quick Launch toolbar, where you can put icons to start programs with a single mouse click. At the far right end of the Taskbar are the System Tray, which displays icons for various system activities, and a clock.

- You can do all sorts of things to folders, files, and other icons on your Desktop with just a quick click of the mouse. To create a new folder icon on your desktop, for example, simply right-click on an empty portion of the desktop and select **New | Folder** from the context menu—the menu that pops up when you right-click. You can delete, rename, and move icons as well.

- Using the Windows Taskbar and Start menu you can start programs, switch between windows, add shortcuts where you need them, and use the Help program. Once you've loaded a program, you have access to a standardized program interface that enables you to move, minimize, maximize, and close program windows with a click or flick of the mouse.

The Many Faces of Explorer

- Windows handles file and folder management through the Windows Explorer utility program, which offers a variety of interface options, including My Documents, Windows Explorer / File Manager with the Folders pane open, and My Computer.

- Go to **Start | My Documents** to open Windows Explorer focused on My Documents. On the left is the File and Folder Tasks pane with common tasks you can perform on the folders and files, such as rename, move, copy, delete, and so on. You can also perform any of these functions by right-clicking on a folder or file and selecting the appropriate option from the context menu.

- Click the Folders button or go to **Start | All Programs | Accessories | Windows Explorer** to open Windows Explorer with the Folders pane open. The Folders pane enables you to work with files and folders with its graphical, hierarchical view of the window's contents. You can easily create, copy, move, and delete files and folders.

- Clicking the **Views** button enables you to choose how you want to display the folder contents—as thumbnails, tiles, icons, a list of filenames, or a list with details. The currently chosen view is marked with a dot in the menu.

- You can select multiple files or folders in several ways. Click the first one you want and **[Shift]-click** the last one in the list you want selects all the files in between as well. A **[Ctrl]-click** enables you to select or deselect files that are not touching in the list.

Good Housekeeping Seal of Approval

■ Careless manipulation of files can cause problems, such as losing a file because the file extension has been changed, or you can't remember what you named it, where you put it, or what password you used to protect it; running out of disk space because you have too many files; or even losing files altogether through accidental deletion, hard drive failure, or a lost or stolen computer.

■ Take certain precautions when working with files and folders. Organize your folders and files logically, give them names that clearly identify them, keep track of passwords, delete unneeded files to keep your drive uncluttered, and back up important files.

■ Clicking the Help and Support item on the Start menu opens the Help and Support Center, the online help for Windows, where you will find a large list of links to local and Web-based help, including Troubleshooters for several common problems like a printer that won't work.

■ If you cannot remember where you saved a file, you can search for it using the Windows Search wizard, which you can start by clicking the Search button. This opens the Search Companion pane where you can select the category of file you want and then follow the prompts to narrow the search.

■ The final step in good housekeeping is shutting down the computer gracefully. If you don't, you risk corrupting files, losing data, and possibly generating problems when you restart. The Windows Start menu typically offers four ways to shut down: Shut down, Restart, Stand by, and Log off.

CHAPTER 6: SUMMARY

Key Terms

Attribute	Program interface
Backup	Quick Launch toolbar
Context menu	Restart
[Ctrl]-click	[Shift]-click
Desktop	Start menu
Desktop icon	System Tray
Folders pane	Taskbar
Maximized	Title bar
Menu bar	Toolbar
MFU list	URL link icon
Minimized	Wildcards
My Computer	Windowed
Pinned list	Windows Explorer

Key Term Quiz

Use the Key Terms list to complete the following sentences. Not all terms will be used.

1. The _____ displays icons for various system activities.

2. You can run *any* program installed on your computer through the _____.

3. When you need to manage files and folders in Windows, open _____ or My Computer.

4. When I use my word processing application, the name of the document appears in the _____ of the application's window.

5. File, Edit, and Help are choices on a standard Windows _____.

6. You can customize your Windows _____ by selecting a wallpaper image to display on the background.

7. Programs on the _____ in the Start menu are always there for you to access quickly and launch with a single click.

8. Clicking on the **Folders** button in My Computer opens the _____ so you have a quick, hierarchical view of your drives and folders.

9. When you open _____, you have a face of Windows Explorer that focuses on drives rather than folders.

10. A(n) _____ tells the operating system essential details about a file.

Multiple Choice Quiz

1. Where is the System Tray located?
   A. Taskbar
   B. Quick Launch toolbar
   C. Start menu
   D. Control Panel

2. If an application is not responding, press this key combination to get to the Task Manager so you can force it closed.
   A. **[Ctrl + Alt + Delete]**
   B. **[Ctrl + Shift + Delete]**
   C. **[Ctrl + Esc]**
   D. **[Shift]**-click

3. Which character can be used in a search query to replace part of a file name?
   A. Quotation mark
   B. Exclamation point
   C. Asterisk
   D. Dash

4. When you right-click an object, which of the following appears?
   A. Context menu
   B. Icon menu
   C. Start menu
   D. Error message

5. What do you need to click and hold on to move a program window around on the Desktop?
   A. Menu bar
   B. Status bar
   C. Title bar
   D. Taskbar

6. While working in Windows Explorer, Joanie accidentally deleted a file. Ralph says she needs to open the Recycle Bin, select the file, and then press **[Delete]** again to restore the file. Billy disagrees, saying that she should right-click the file in the Recycle Bin and select **Restore** from the context menu. Who's right?
   A. Only Ralph is right.
   B. Only Billy is right.
   C. Both Ralph and Billy are correct; either method will work.
   D. Neither Ralph nor Billy is correct.

7. Which of the following options do you have with the program interface? (Select all that apply.)
   A. Minimize
   B. Maximize
   C. Resize
   D. Remove

8. What's an outdated term sometimes used for Windows Explorer?
   A. File Manager
   B. Internet Explorer
   C. Navigator
   D. WinExplore

9. How do you expand a folder to see subfolders in Windows Explorer?
   A. Click the + sign.
   B. Click the – sign.
   C. Click the = sign.
   D. You can't see subfolders in Explorer.

10. Which view offers you information about a file's size, type, and modified date?
    A. Thumbnails
    B. Tiles
    C. List
    D. Details

11. Winston has a list of seven files, of which he wants to select numbers 1, 2, 5, and 7 for deleting. What method should he use?
    A. **[Alt]**-click
    B. **[Ctrl]**-click
    C. Double-click
    D. **[Shift]**-click

12. Wolf has pictures he took of his friend Red and also pictures of her grandmother, Mabel. He could dump them all in My Documents, but wants to keep things a bit better organized. What should he do? (Select the best answer.)
    A. Put them all in My Pictures.
    B. Make two subfolders in My Pictures and put the files in the subfolders.
    C. Just dump them in My Documents. It's what everybody else does.
    D. Make two subfolders in My Documents and put the files in the subfolders.

13. How do you find out things about a music file stored in My Music, like the name of the artist or the album title?
    A. Double-click the file.
    B. Select **Tiles** view in My Music.
    C. Select **Details** view in My Music.
    D. Right-click the file and select **Properties** from the context menu.

14. How can you access the Help and Support Center in Windows XP? (Select all that apply.)
    A. Click **Start | Run**, type **help**, and click **OK**.
    B. Go to **Start | Help and Support**.
    C. Go to **Start | All Programs | Accessories | System Tools | Help and Support**.
    D. Press the **[F1]** key.

15. Annie wants to shut down her computer, but she doesn't want to have to reopen all the programs she currently has running. What option should she use?
    A. Log off
    B. Restart
    C. Stand by
    D. Shut down

Essay Questions

1. Sally opened Windows Explorer from **Start | All Programs | Accessories**. She browsed around for a while and then was surprised to see that the Title bar had changed to "My Computer." She is puzzled why this happened, because she believed that My Computer and Windows Explorer were two separate programs. Write an explanation for Sally.

2. A new group of employees has just arrived, and your boss has asked you to teach them the basics of Windows. Write a short essay describing the differences between the Desktop and the program interface.

3. After playing with the various views available in My Documents (such as List or Tiles), write an essay that describes how you would use two of the views to accomplish tasks.

Projects

1. How would you set up the ideal My Documents for your use? Jot down a list of the types of files you might save on a computer and then organize them into logical categories with descriptive but short names (like My Pictures or My Music). Once you've finished your categories list, compare it with those of your classmates. What do they plan to do that you don't? What do you do that they don't? If you have access to a computer, go ahead and make your folders and subfolders in My Documents.

2. Time to play Hide and Seek! Make some files and folders on your computer and then place them in other folders. (Remember, you can create almost any type of file and folder that Windows understands by right-clicking an empty spot on the Desktop and selecting **New** from the context menu.) Feel free to alter the properties of the files, including the attributes. Once you have the files and folders "misplaced," switch places with a partner or classmate and search for their files and folders as they search for yours. For practice, use wildcard characters in your search.

   Use these three folder and three file names, or use some provided by your teacher:

   - My Opinions
   - My Minions
   - Private
   - Alexander the Great.txt
   - Marc_Anthony.doc
   - Parrot.doc

Taking Control of Windows – Using Control Panel Wisely

"Prepare ship for ludicrous speed! Fasten all seatbelts, seal all entrances and exits, close all shops in the mall, cancel the three ring circus, secure all animals in the zoo!"

– Colonel Sandurz, *Spaceballs*

This chapter covers the following IC³ exam objectives:

- IC³-1   3.3.1   Display control panels

- IC³-1   3.3.2   Identify different control panel settings

- IC³-1   3.3.3   Change simple control panel settings

- IC³-1   3.3.4   Display and update a list of installed printers

- IC³-1   3.3.5   Identify precautions regarding changing system setings

No two users have the same needs or the same desire for look and feel of the operating system, and Microsoft, Apple, and other OS manufacturers understand this fact. You can change the way the interface looks and manipulate basic settings to make accomplishing tasks more efficient for you. Want a red background, seven desktop icons, and nothing else? No problem, you can make it happen!

This chapter uses Microsoft Windows to walk you through the process of changing default settings. We'll tackle the Control Panel first, with a tour and a discussion of the most commonly used applets. The chapter then looks at what might happen when you make changes to system settings, and finishes it up with a case study using the Printers and Faxes applet. Let's get started!

You can also get to the Control Panel by opening up My Computer and clicking on the Control Panel link in the common tasks area on the left.

Category View

To determine which view you prefer, you need to experiment with both. Open the Control Panel and click through some of the categories in Category view. What are the different Control Panel applets in each category? Why would they place each applet in that category? Switch to Classic View and pick a Control Panel applet. Try and guess which category it belongs in when you switch over to Category View.

The Control Center: Windows Control Panel

Your car has a dashboard, right? The dashboard contains elements for most of the crucial elements of controlling your car: the headlight high-beams, the speed of the windshield wipers, and the presets on your radio station. Your computer has a dashboard too: the Windows *Control Panel*. Digging into the Windows Control Panel yields many *applets*—tiny programs with specific functions—each controlling its own portion of Windows settings. These settings include the computer's date and time, the color of the menu bars, even the background picture you see on the Windows desktop.

Getting to the Control Panel in Windows is easy. Go to **Start** and then select **Control Panel** (Figure 7.1); or if you use an older operating system like Windows 98, you would go to **Start | Settings** and *then* **Control Panel**. Figure 7.2 shows the Control Panel.

Windows XP comes with an unusual twist, the ability to see Control Panel items by category (all date/time items together, etc.) instead of the classic method of listing each item individually. By some *really* strange coincidence, the names of these two different views are *Classic view* and *Category view*. To toggle between each view, click **Switch to Category view**, or **Switch to Classic view** (Figure 7.3). Does it matter which one you use? Absolutely not! It's all about personal preference. Aside from Figure 7.3, this chapter uses Classic view.

If Windows XP offered no Control Panel customizations at all, each and every user would have the same identical version of Windows. Not only would this get rather boring very quickly, but it could possibly be detrimental to the proper function of the computer. For example, Matt lives in Rhode Island, USA, which is in the Eastern Standard Time (EST) time zone. Microsoft ships Windows XP set to Pacific Standard Time (PST) by default. If Matt did not have the ability to change his system time zone in the Control Panel, his system would be keeping the wrong time! Sadly, it's no excuse for missing a really important meeting. "The dog ate my speech! And, I'm three hours late because my computer was set to the wrong time zone!" Ah, sorry. Not going to work.

Common Control Panel Applets

The Control Panel applets vary from one operating system to the next, and can even vary depending on the specific programs installed on the computer. All versions of Windows, however, have commonly used applets.

Display

While many Control Panel applets take care of boring old system customizations, the *Display applet* contains most of the settings that control the way your operating system's graphical user interface (GUI) looks. You can change colors, sizes of icons, even the desktop background. Does everyone on your block have the same desktop wallpaper? You can change that too, with other standard wallpapers, or even use your own. Figure 7.5 shows the Display applet with custom wallpaper selected.

Date and Time

The *Date and Time applet* enables you to change your operating system date, the current time, your time zone, and whether you wish to observe Daylight Savings Time (Figure 7.6).

Figure 7.1: Accessing the Control Panel

Figure 7.2: Control Panel

Figure 7.3: Switching views

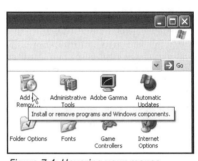

Figure 7.4: Hovering your mouse over an applet will give you a brief description of what it does.

Applet Descriptions

An easy way to find out what a Control Panel applet does is to hold your mouse over the applet icon without clicking on it (Figure 7.4). Windows will display a brief description pertaining to that applet.

Figure 7.5: Display applet

Choose Your Own Wallpaper!

*In Display Properties, you can click **Browse** to navigate through your computer's file system and find a picture you want to use as your Desktop Wallpaper. In some older versions of Windows, your picture had to be a bitmap (ending with file extension .bmp) to work, but with Windows XP, your picture can be almost any type of image file, including most that are created with digital cameras.*

The IC³ exam uses the odd term "Control Panels" rather than the industry-standard terminology of "Control Panel applets." Don't get thrown off if you get asked a question, for example, about the "Display Control Panel." This means the same thing as "Display Control Panel applet."

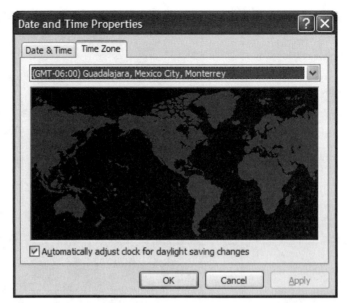

Figure 7.6: Date and Time applet

Sounds and Audio Devices

The *Sounds and Audio Devices applet* enables you to control how your sound card works, in both input and output. You can change settings for your microphone (if you have one), sound card, and speakers, altering volume and many individual properties (Figure 7.7). Figure 7.8 shows typical audio hardware. The applet controls musical instruments and even settings such as how your music CDs and video DVD movies play (Figure 7.9).

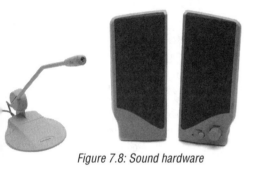

Figure 7.8: Sound hardware

Figure 7.7: Sound and Audio Devices applet

Fonts

The *Fonts applet* enables you to add or remove types of letters—called fonts—that you can use in word processing programs (Figure 7.11). A *font* is a set of characters created in different styles and sizes. The type design is called the *typeface*. The words "font" and "typeface" are commonly used interchangeably, though a font is a subset of its typeface family. While operating systems come with certain fonts built in, you can add new fonts as well.

Keyboard

The *Keyboard applet* enables you to customize various keyboard settings, including the blink rate of the *cursor* (see Figure 7.12). No, it's not how fast your swearing friend can blink her eyes! The *cursor* tells you where to start typing text. It blinks so that your eye can find it quickly on the screen. As different people's eyes have different sensitivities to the blinking, each user can change the blink speed.

If you have one of the fancier keyboards, with extra buttons to control audio software and Web surfing, you'll have more options available in the Keyboard applet (Figure 7.13). Figure 7.14 shows a modern, button-rich keyboard.

Typeface Families
The popular typeface family Arial has a number of fonts based on that typeface. Some of them include variations of the same base font Arial, such as Arial Black, Arial Narrow, and Arial Rounded MT Bold.

Figure 7.9: DVD Properties

Speak, Computer, Speak!

You can dramatically change the sound output from your computer by, for example, switching from headphones to speakers (Figure 7.10). Don't just take my word for it though, try it! If you have speakers or headphones hooked up to your system, run Media Player or iTunes or some other music application and play an audio CD or MP3. (Just put a CD in the CD-ROM drive and it should play automatically.) Once you have it running, open the **Sound and Audio Devices** *applet. On the* **Volume** *tab, click the* **Advanced** *button near the bottom in the* **Speaker settings** *section (see Figure 7.7, above) to open the* **Advanced Audio Properties** *dialog box that you can see in Figure 7.10. Change the* **Speaker setup** *option. Hear any difference?*

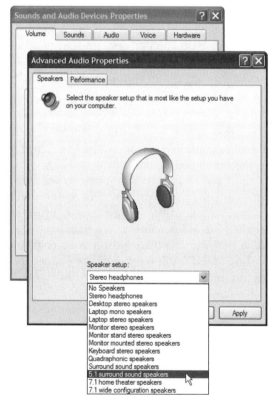

Figure 7.11: Fonts applet

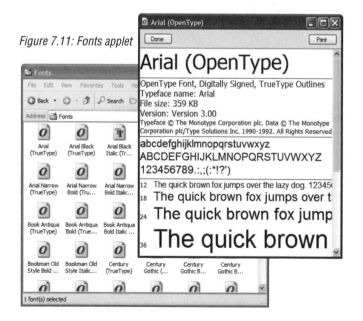

Figure 7.10: Advanced Audio
Properties dialog box

Figure 7.12: Keyboard applet

Figure 7.13: Extra options in Keyboard applet

Figure 7.14: Fancy keyboard

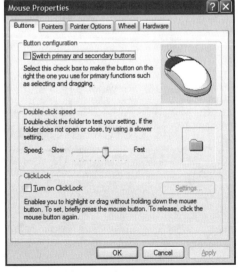

Mouse

A mouse has a cursor too. As not to be confused with a keyboard cursor, it's usually called the *mouse pointer*. The *Mouse applet* enables you to specify various settings for your pointing device based on personal preference. These settings include configuring the buttons for left-handed people, and calculating the double-click speed (Figure 7.15).

Printers

The *Printers and Faxes applet* enables you to see the printers and fax machines you have installed on the computer, and to add or remove a printer or fax machine. It's worth noting that you may see some

printers listed in there you don't have physically connected to your computer, and that's OK. Many software programs (such as QuickBooks from Intuit) install their own "virtual" printers, and those are necessary to make that software function properly (Figure 7.16). Alternatively, if you used to have an old printer, it's possible that it's still installed on your computer and not physically hooked up to it. (You'll work with the Printers and Faxes applet in detail later in this chapter.)

Figure 7.15: Mouse applet

Figure 7.16: Virtual printer installed by QuickBooks

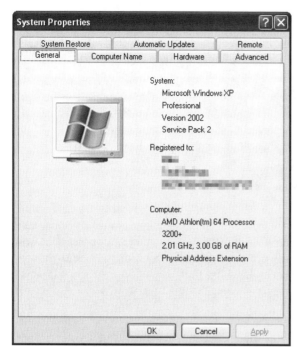

Figure 7.17: System applet

System

The *System applet* gives you the capability to see and modify the most important settings on your computer. First, it gives you the quick and dirty overview of your computer: the name, the basic hardware specifications, the operating system version, and sometimes the manufacturer of the computer (Figure 7.17). It also enables you to see the hardware physically installed in the computer by selecting the

A standard keyboard and mouse combination provide nearly every input need you'll ever have. Most of the buttons on these fancy keyboards never get touched because they sit too far away from where you put your hands in standard typing. You can probably save your money and go standard rather than fancy.

Hardware tab and clicking on the **Device Manager** button (Figure 7.18). The final job of the System applet is to allow you to fine-tune the settings of your computer for best performance. Many advanced computer users change these settings, but for the most part you'll probably be okay leaving them alone.

Changing Control Panel Settings

Now that you know the purpose of the main Control Panel applets, it's time to learn how to *change* these settings. Double-click an applet to go into its *properties* – the actual settings that can be changed.

Changing the date and time

Just how *does* your system know what time it is even though you've turned it off? Your computer has an internal battery, specifically called the *CMOS battery* (Figure 7.19). (CMOS stands for *Complementary Metal-Oxide Semiconductor*, in case you were curious.) This battery powers a very special microchip, the CMOS itself. CMOS has its own system clock, powered by the battery when the system is turned off. Your operating system uses this battery to keep the time that you are used to seeing in the Task Bar (Figure 7.20).

What's so important about needing the date and time to be correct? Your system uses this time for purposes other than just making sure you know what time it is. For example, every time you change a file, your system flags the *date modified* with the exact date and time you changed it. If your operating system time is incorrect, this file will be incorrectly flagged with the wrong date/time.

So what can you do if it's incorrect? Change it! The first method is to double-click the **Date and Time** Control Panel applet. The second method is

Figure 7.18: Device Manager shows your computer's hardware.

The CMOS Battery

Don't worry about your battery ever running out, though it does happen. The standard lifetime of a lithium CMOS battery is about 10 years, which usually outlasts the computer itself!

Figure 7.19: The CMOS battery looks like a watch battery.

Figure 7.20: The clock in the system tray

to double-click the clock located in the Task Bar. Either method opens the Date and Time Properties dialog box (Figure 7.21). Use the pull-down menus to make sure the date and the year are correct, and then click your mouse on the correct day from the calendar. When setting the time, which is also on the same screen, don't forget to set the correct AM or PM.

You're not done quite yet, remember how important it was to make sure your system clock is set to the right Time Zone? This is also where you set that, too. You'll notice a second tab (*Time Zone*) hiding behind the first tab (*Date and Time*). Clicking that tab yields another pull-down menu. Select your correct Time Zone, and make a decision whether you want your system to observe Daylight Savings Time and automatically change the clock for you.

As with any changes in you make in Control Panel, when you're done, don't forget to click **OK** instead of **Cancel** or using the **X** at the top of the dialog box. Clicking **OK** will accept any changes you've made, while the other two methods will negate them out. Alternatively, if you've made changes you don't want to keep, this is a great time to use the **Cancel** button!

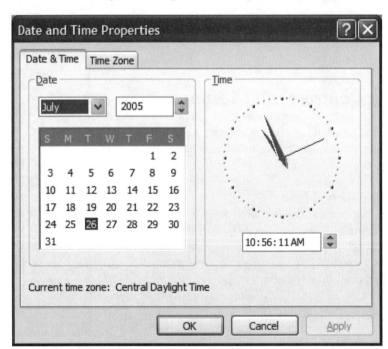

Figure 7.21: Date and Time Properties dialog box

Changing Display Settings

With Display settings, you can let your own personality shine! To change Display settings, double-click the **Display** Control Panel applet. You'll notice some main tabs. For example, this is what the tabs are on Windows XP: *Themes, Desktop, Screen Saver, Appearance, Settings.* Clicking through these tabs will explain what settings you can customize.

Figure 7.22: Preview your desktop

Figure 7.23: Screen Saver options

Clicking the **Themes** tab, for example, enables you to make sweeping change to the color scheme used by Windows (Figure 7.22).

Click the **Screen Saver** tab to choose a screen saver from a pull-down menu of pre-built choices. You can choose among stars, 3D Pipes, your own 3D Text, and even a slideshow of your pictures (Figure 7.23).

Moving on to the **Appearance** tab yields a fun selection, the color scheme of your operating system. You can choose some pre-built pretty color schemes from the pull-down menu, and change the size of the fonts as well (Figure 7.24).

You can change the screen area, or screen *resolution* with the **Settings** tab (Figure 7.25). This refers to the sharpness and clarity of the screen. The maximum screen resolution is dependant on two things: the size and quality of your monitor and the capabilities of your graphics card (physical hardware).

Changing the resolution will yield smaller icons on the desktop, but you will be able to see more screen area. With the exception of facing limitations on the hardware you have, changing the resolution is usually a matter of personal preference. To change the resolution, drag the arrow back and forth across the **Less** and **More** sections. Watch in the preview area as your screen size changes dramatically (Figure 7.26).

Changing Other Settings

Double-click on other Control Panel applets to examine and identify settings you would like to customize. Double-click on the **Mouse** applet and examine the different tabs to note all the changes you can make. For example, you can go to the **Pointers** tab to click on a pointer style and change it by clicking **Browse** and choosing a new pointer. Or, you can click **Themes** from the pull-down menu to select from pre-built mouse pointer schemes.

Change the keyboard cursor blink rate we discussed earlier by going to the **Keyboard** applet and dragging the mouse between the **Slow** and **Fast** settings.

Resolution

Resolution is measured in pixels, short for picture elements. For example, if a standard screen resolution of a 15-inch monitor is 1024 x 768, then the screen uses 768 lines down of 1024 pixels across each.

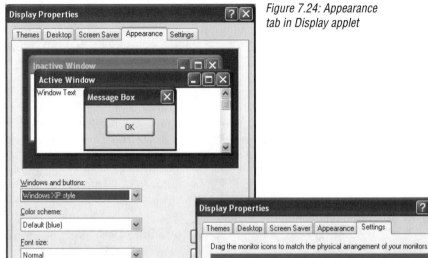

Figure 7.24: Appearance tab in Display applet

Figure 7.25: Settings tab in Display applet

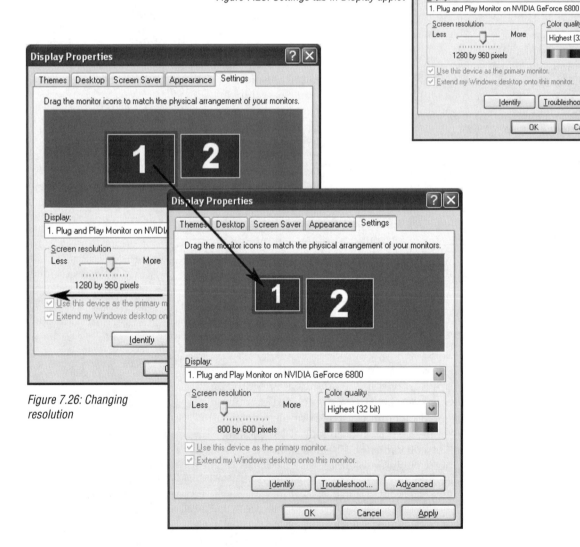

Figure 7.26: Changing resolution

The Power Options applet enables you to customize the power settings specific to your computer. If you're using a laptop, for example, you may want to be notified when your battery only has 10% of life left. The Alarms tab in **Power Options** would be the place to go to change this setting.

The computer in Figures 25 and 26 has two physical monitors attached, that's why two show up in the Display applet. Most systems would only show a single monitor.

Taking Precautions: Understanding the Impact of Changing System Settings with the Control Panel

Now that you've been teased with the fun things you can do with the Control Panel, it's time to talk about The Dark Side: while many changes are purely superficial (changing the Windows desktop wallpaper), some changes will have a much wider effect on different aspects of the computer, and could even render some of them inoperable. For example, changing the way your system displays currency figures will have a drastic effect on all programs on the computer, even your spreadsheet application (Figure 7.27).

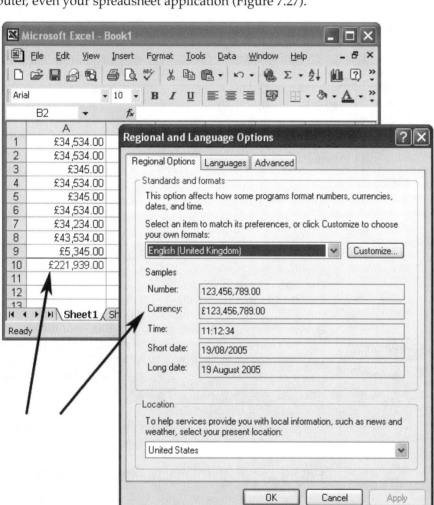

Figure 7.27: Currency in Control Panel changes Excel

The Impact of Changing System Settings

While it's easy to change system settings, only change those settings if you are fully aware of the effect those changes will have on the computer. It may be funny to change the system clock to the wrong day/year/time, but Spidey's Uncle Ben said it best: "With great power comes great responsibility." We talked about how your computer uses the system clock to flag the modified date on a file. If the clock is wrong, the flag that will tell you the last time the

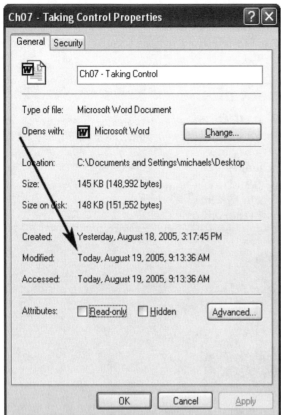

Figure 7.28: The Date Modified stamp tells you the last time you changed the file.

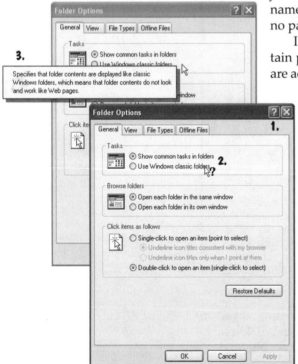

Figure 7.29: Click the question mark once, then click the setting.

file was modified will be incorrect. You can change the clock back to the correct time, but it won't change the modified date on the file, that's been *stamped* until the file is modified again (Figure 7.28).

In a nastier situation, changing settings in the Network Connections applet that aren't fully understood could render your system unable to connect to any network at all, including the Internet.

If you aren't sure of a setting in Control Panel, there are two options to find out what it does. The first option is to click once on the **Question Mark** icon in the top left, and then immediately click once on the setting you wish to know more about (Figure 7.29). For more detailed information, go into the Windows Help files.

Designated Driver: Which User Accounts Can Change System Settings

A *user account* is a designated account given to each individual user of the operating system. These accounts define what a user is allowed to do on the machine, and what actions they can take. In other words, it defines their *privileges* on the operating system.

Windows XP requires at least one user account on the computer. More commonly, during installation, two accounts are created: Administrator and a general user account. When you boot up the computer, you must log in before you can use it. Sometimes this process is automatic and you're logged in without doing anything. But a more secure system will require you to enter a user name and a password, or click on your user name and then enter a password (Figure 7.30). Sometimes there is no password, and you just have to click on your user name.

If multiple people use one computer, you may not want certain people to be able to change system settings, many of which are accessed via the Control Panel. With Windows, it's possible to deny access to certain functions for certain people by entering the User Accounts Control Panel applet and setting up each user individually. For Windows XP Home Edition, users can be of type *Administrator* or *Limited User*. An *Administrator* can install programs, and change any setting in Control Panel. A *Limited User* can change things like his or her password, but cannot install programs or change a setting that could cause the system not to work properly.

Exit Strategies: Undoing Unwanted System Setting Changes

There comes a time in the life of every computer user when you have a Really Bad Day. You make a change in a Control Panel applet that simply blows up your computer. Things don't work the way they did before; the system runs slowly; the picture on the screen is awful and makes your eyes hurt; you get the idea. The key is to be able to get back where you were *before* you made the change so your system can work the way it did before the goof-up.

The easiest way to remember the changes you make in

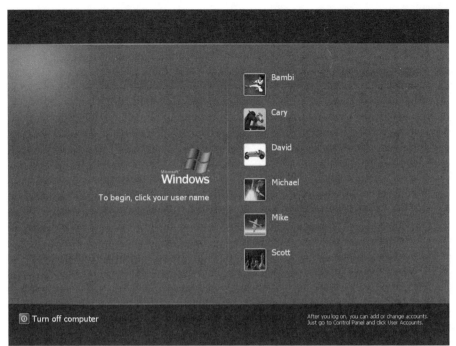

Figure 7.30: Logging in

Networks and User Accounts

User accounts are usually handled differently if the computer is part of a larger network. Some large organizations (think universities, school systems, and offices) commonly prevent users from making changes to system settings unless they are a special administrator. Others will allow users to change settings like their desktop wallpaper, or other superficial changes. This is to prevent accidental damage to the computer and lost productivity due to downtime while the machine gets repaired.

In a university setting, imagine if you had nowhere to type your paper that's due in an hour because they are all "out of order." Preventing users from changing settings in the first place eliminates that problem right away. Part 3 of this book covers networks and networked computers in detail.

Control Panel is low tech: write it down! If you make multiple changes, write them all down so you can change them back if they have undesirable effects. As a general rule, make one change at a time. See what effects that change has before going on to another change. Otherwise, how would you know which change was the wrong choice?

Don't forget the First Rule of Conventional Computer Wisdom: if you really aren't OK with a change, then don't click the **OK** button. That's what **Cancel** is for!

Case Study: Printers

Each Control Panel applet gives you a ton of control over its area of focus. So far, we've just scratched the surface on some of the more common applets, but a little experimentation can quickly take you deeply into the heart of the operating system.

The Printer and Faxes applet offers a safe opportunity for you to dive in and explore the power of the Control Panel. Plus, you should know how to set up a printer! This section goes into some detail about the applet. Just keep in mind that you can do this with every Control Panel applet.

Printer icons

Windows recognizes four basic types of printers: local, networked, default, and offline. The way the icon of each printer looks can actually tell you a lot about the way the printer relates to your system. A local printer attaches directly to your PC via USB or FireWire connection. (Ancient printers can attach through legacy ports, such as the parallel port, but these printers have mostly gone away.) The local printer icon looks like a tiny printer (Figure 7.31).

If the printer has a horizontal bar running across the bottom, that means it is a networked printer, and not physically connected to your system. The printer is physically connected to *something*, just not your machine, and you access it over your network (Figure 7.32).

If the printer has a little black check next to it, that printer is considered the

Windows thinks of printers as two distinct components, divided as software and hardware. You can set up a printer in Windows, for example, and go through lots of configuration options and so forth, even if you don't have any physical printer attached to the computer! Microsoft calls the software side of the printer setup the "printer" and the hardware side the "print device."

Figure 7.31: Local printer

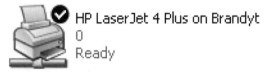

Figure 7.32: The line means the printer is networked, but still ready for use.

Figure 7.33: The default printer has a check mark next to it.

Figure 7.34: This printer is offline, turned off, or not connected at all.

default printer. This means that your computer will *always* use this printer to print to first unless you specifically tell it to print to another one (Figure 7.33).

If the printer icon is light-colored and appears faint, it means the printer is offline. This means that the printer is turned off, not connected, or manually set to offline mode (Figure 7.34). Usually the printer name appears along with the icon, so you should be able find the right one in the applet by looking at the make and model of your printer.

Installing Printers

You can install a printer into a PC in two ways: using the CD-ROM disc that comes with the printer or through the Printer and Faxes applet. Sometimes you can do a combination of these options.

Most of the printers you can buy right now require you to follow a pretty simple path. First, you install the software from the manufacturer; then you plug the printer into a USB or FireWire port. Windows will autodetect the printer and finish the installation (Figure 7.35).

The process of installing a printer manually follows a reverse path. First, you plug the printer into one of the ports (USB, FireWire, or parallel), then go to Control Panel and run the Printer and Faxes applet. Click **Add a Printer** from the menu on the left of the screen (Figure 7.36).

This starts the **Add Printer Wizard** (Figure 7.37). A *wizard* is a series of steps that will walk you through performing various tasks on your computer.

The Add Printer Wizard – Because of the Wonderful Things it Does

With a local printer, choose the **Local Printer attached to this computer** radio button. If you select the checkbox labeled **Automatically detect and install my Plug and Play printer**, the operating system software will attempt to "talk" to the printer hardware and correctly identify the make and model of the printer. "*Plug and play*" means that your system will attempt to recognize a new hardware device and install it automatically. The operating system version and the age of the hardware will determine how much you need to intervene in the install process.

If the **Found New Hardware Wizard** pops up, the printer has been detected and identified, and you will be prompted to use an installation CD that came with the printer, or the software that was downloaded from the manufacturer's Web site. If Windows can't recognize the printer you can try installing manually.

Adding a Printer Manually

To add a printer manually, run the Add Printer Wizard as before, but deselect the checkbox next to the **Automatically detect and install my Plug and Play printer** check box. Click **Next** to continue (Figure 7.38).

Choose the *port* the printer is located on. Most likely it will be on **LPT1**. If it's a USB printer, most likely the port will be **USB001 (Virtual printer port)**. Once you identify the correct port click **Next** and move on (Figure 7.39).

On the next screen you need to tell the operating system about the printer. In the section labeled **Manufacturer**, select the brand of printer, such as HP or Epson. Once you click on a manufacturer, the list of available models is

Figure 7.35: Windows detecting a printer

Figure 7.36: Add a Printer option in the Printer and Faxes applet

Figure 7.37: Add Printer Wizard

View the Queue

You can double-click each icon in the Printer and Faxes applet to see if there are any print jobs currently in the queue. A print job is a print command that has been sent to the printer, but the printer hasn't finished printing yet. The line of documents waiting to print is the print queue. A busy office may have many documents lined up in the queue, if each person at a cube is accessing it over the network and printing to it!

Always follow the instructions that come with your printer. Some USB printer manufacturers need the printer software installed before you connect the printer physically.

Outside the Box

You learned all about the ports on the back of your computer in Chapter 2, "Going with the Data Flow." Without looking at the port on your printer to match it up, can you correctly identify the parallel port and USB ports on your computer?

Downloading Software

Once you figure out how to download one thing from the Internet, you'll know how to download anything. The basic steps are the same. Find the application or file, click on it, save it to your file system (remember where you saved it), and use My Computer to find it and click on it once it's finished downloading! Head to www.download.com to find some cool utilities and fun applications you can download. Lots of them are free for you to use.

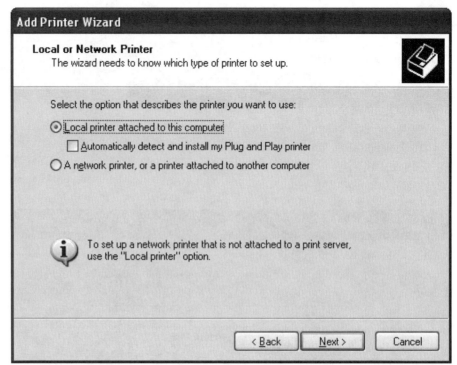

Figure 7.38: Click Next

listed on the right (Figure 7.40). If you do not see the specific printer, Windows doesn't know about it yet. Click **Have Disk** and use the installation disk or disc that came with the printer (or software that you downloaded from the Internet).

Sometimes you may not have the original installation CD that came with the printer, that's OK. Usually you can go to the manufacturer's Web site (such as www.hp.com for Hewlett-Packard printers) to download the software. Once at the site, head for a section that contains something like *Support & Drivers*. Sometimes it's also called *Software Downloads*.

Almost done! Give the printer a name (the default name is OK to keep), and choose whether you want to use it as the default printer. Once the printer is installed, you can print a test page (Figure 7.41).

Connecting to Networked Printers

Connecting to a network printer is easy. All the hard work's already been done for you! After all, a networked printer is local on someone *else's* machine. Provided your computer is on a network, you can connect to a printer physically connected to another computer on the same network. During the Add Printer Wizard, first choose **A network printer, or a printer connected to another computer** instead of local printer. Then **browse** for a printer, and choose from the list of available networked printers.

Deleting Printers

Change happens. Planets align. Printers break and become obsolete. Rather than have a whole bunch of printers installed on your computer that you no longer own, you can delete them when you no longer need them. The easiest way to delete a printer is to **right-click** the printer icon and choose **Delete**. The same action goes for a networked printer, too. Don't worry, you're not wiping out the printer from the other computer, you're only uninstalling it from your own!

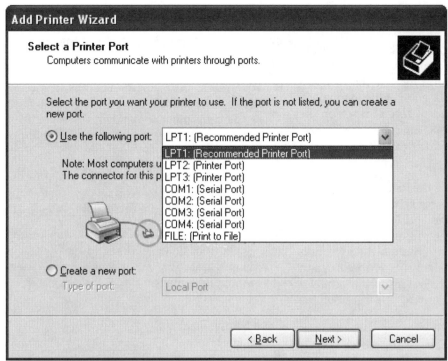

Figure 7.39: Choosing the Port

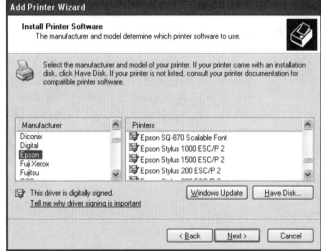

Figure 7.40: The available models appear on the right when you've chosen a manufacturer from the left first.

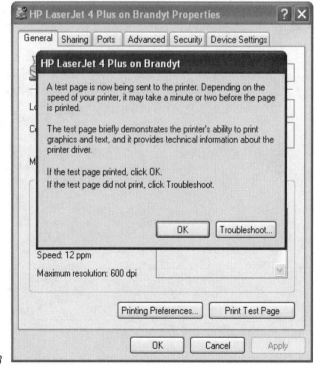

Figure 7.41: Testing, testing, 1, 2, 3

The Control Center: Windows Control Panel

■ The Windows Control Panel has many *applets,* tiny programs that control specific Windows settings. These settings include the computer's date and time, the color of the menu bars, even the background picture you see on the Windows desktop. You can access the Control Panel via My Computer or the Start menu.

■ Common Control Panel applets include Display for changing the look and feel of the GUI, Date and Time for setting the time and time zone, and Sound and Audio Devices for working with both input and output sound hardware, such as microphones and speakers. You'll also find the Fonts, Keyboard, and Mouse applets. The System applet enables you to control options at the heart of the Windows operating system, such as the Device Manager.

Changing Control Panel Settings

■ Double-clicking on each Control Panel applet enables you to view all the current settings and change them. Some Control Panel settings that can be changed safely are Display, Audio, Mouse, Keyboard, Power, and Date and Time.

■ The Display applet enables you to change the color scheme for Windows and alter the screen resolution, among other things, although you should use caution when you get into the Settings tab options. Changing the resolution will yield smaller icons on the desktop, but you will be able to see more screen area.

Taking Precautions: Understanding the Impact of Changing System Settings with the Control Panel

■ You should only change settings if you are aware of the full effect it will have on the rest of the computer. Remember, some changes, if made incorrectly, can render some components inoperable!

■ Keep track of the changes you make in the Control Panel so you can change them back easily if they produce undesirable affects.

■ You can use user accounts to prevent certain people from being allowed to make system changes through Control Panel. Limited users cannot make changes; Administrators can.

Case Study: Printers

■ The Printers and Faxes applet displays a list of all printers installed on your computer, even though they may not be physically connected.

■ To add a printer, use the *Add Printer* button in the applet, and follow all the instructions in the Add Printer Wizard. If the printer hardware is not detected automatically, you will have to add it manually. Remember, you'll need to know whether your printer uses a *USB* or *parallel* (LPT1) port. Finally, you'll need the printer driver from the printer manufacturer.

Key Terms

Administrator

Applet

Category view

Classic view

CMOS

CMOS Battery

Control Panel

Cursor

Date and Time applet

Default printer

Device Manager

Display applet

DPI

Font

Fonts applet

Keyboard applet

Limited User

Local printer

Mouse applet

Mouse pointer

Pixel

Plug and Play

Printers and Faxes applet

Properties

Queue

Resolution

Sounds and Audio Devices applet

System applet

Typeface

User account

Key Term Quiz

Use the Key Terms list to complete the following sentences. Not all terms will be used.

1. The _____ enables you to make changes to the speaker setup in your computer.

2. Joey wanted to change the default background of his desktop. He can do this with the _____ in the Control Panel.

3. The insertion point on the screen for entering text is called the _____.

4. A program that is created for one basic small task is called an _____.

5. The _____ keeps the computer's clock powered when you turn it off.

6. Documents that are waiting to print can be found in the print _____.

7. The _____ gives you the capability to see and modify the most important settings on your computer.

8. Unless you specify otherwise, documents that you print from your computer will be routed to the _____.

9. A computer _____ is allowed to install any programs on the computer.

10. If a piece of hardware is _____, the computer can correctly identify it.

Multiple Choice Quiz

1. April upgraded her computer to Windows XP and opened her Control Panel. Her icons were missing. What link can she click on to return them to the way they looked in her previous version?
   A. Switch to Regular View
   B. Switch to Classic View
   C. Switch to Category View
   D. Switch to Icon View

2. What's a quick way to determine the purpose of a Control Panel applet?
   A. Press **[F1]** on the keyboard and search the Help menu for the applet about which you're curious.
   B. Open the Control Panel, right-click on an applet, and select **Properties** from the options.
   C. Open the Control Panel and hover your mouse pointer over the applet about which you're curious.
   D. Go to the Internet and access www.microsoft.com. Do a search through the Knowledge Base for the applet about which you're curious.

3. Drist complains that his new mouse seems to move too slowly across the screen. What might he do to increase the speed of the cursor?
   A. Open the Input Devices applet and crank up the speed in the **Select a pointer speed** option.
   B. Open the Mouse applet and crank up the speed in the **Select a pointer speed** option.
   C. Open the System applet and crank up the speed in the **Select a pointer speed** option.
   D. Chuck the mouse out the window and buy a new one that's not defective!

4. Jill just downloaded and installed Google Talk, a program that enables her to chat with friends anywhere in the world over the Internet. To make the program work, though, she needs to install and set up a microphone. What Control Panel applet would most likely handle this task?
   A. Microphone applet
   B. Mouse applet
   C. Sounds and Audio Devices applet
   D. System applet

5. Bill is looking in his Printers and Faxes applet and notices a printer that's light in color. What could this mean? (Select all that apply.)
   A. The printer is not turned on.
   B. The printer is networked.
   C. The printer is offline.
   D. The printer is an old printer, and no longer connected physically to his computer.

6. _____ refers to the sharpness and clarity of the display screen.
   A. Desktop
   B. Pixels
   C. Resolution
   D. Sharpness factor rating (SFR)

7. The following are superficial changes in Windows and changing these will not harm your system. (Select all that apply.)
   A. Audio volume
   B. Desktop wallpaper
   C. Mouse pointer icon
   D. System time

8. The following are changes in Windows that can have far-reaching effects or render your computer inoperable. (Select all that apply.)
   A. Currency display
   B. Network settings
   C. System time
   D. Time zone

9. Narcissa wants to change the screen saver on her computer from the default—which moves a little Windows XP logo around—to something more exciting, like 3-D pipes. What applet should she use to change this setting?
   A. Display applet
   B. Picture applet
   C. Screen Saver applet
   D. System applet

10. Which of the following applets would enable you to make changes to input devices on your computer? (Select all that apply.)
    A. Display applet
    B. Input Devices applet
    C. Keyboard applet
    D. Mouse applet

11. Which link on a printer manufacturer's Web site would most likely take you to a screen where you can obtain your printer software online?
    A. Support
    B. Downloads and Drivers
    C. Product Information
    D. Partners

12. Nancy is trying to change a system setting on her computer, but is getting an error message and the change isn't made. What's probably going on?
    A. Nancy clicked **Cancel** by mistake instead of applying the changes.
    B. Nancy's user account doesn't have permission to make the changes.
    C. Those settings don't apply to this computer.
    D. The system clock is incorrect.

13. Martha exclaims that her computer doesn't have any user accounts. She turns on the computer and it boots all the way to a desktop, never prompting her for a user name or password. Jill argues that, even without prompting, her computer has at least one user account. Who's right?
    A. Only Martha is right.
    B. Only Jill is right.
    C. Both Martha and Jill are right.
    D. Neither Martha nor Jill has it right. The computer must have at least two user accounts.

14. How do old and new printers typically connect to computers? (Select all that apply.)
    A. Printers connect via parallel ports.
    B. Printers connect via USB ports.
    C. Printers connect via FireWire ports.
    D. Printers connect wirelessly through Bluetooth.

15. Zelda purchased a new printer and plugged it into her PC. Windows detected the device, but didn't recognize it specifically. Instead, it prompted her for a disc. Zelda immediately packaged the printer back up and took it back to the store as defective merchandise. Was the printer defective? (Select the **best** answer.)
    A. Yes. Windows recognizes all working printers.
    B. Yes. Windows uses the "prompt for a disc" message as a generic error message.
    C. Maybe. Windows uses the "prompt for a disc" message as a generic error message. She had no way to tell if it was defective without running the diagnostic tools in the Printer and Faxes applet.
    D. No. She simply needed to install the drivers that came with the printer on CD-ROM.

Essay Questions

1. Write a short essay describing ways you can differentiate your computer from your neighbor's computer, including changing the wallpaper and other customizations.

2. In the tradition of the great debates among computer people (Windows versus Macintosh, paper versus plastic, and so on), choose a side in the debate about which is better, Category view or Classic view in the Control Panel. Write an essay defending your choice, using examples of how your choice enables better computing.

3. Your boss has tasked you to write a memo on setting up a PC for compliance with the Americans with Disabilities Act (ADA). (Note that you'll need to do Project 7.2 before you can write this essay.)

Projects

1. Investigate the varying user permissions of your school or office. Ask your computer administrator what different users are allowed to do, and why they have set permissions that way. If you have no access to your administrator, create user accounts on your own computer and set different permissions for each account. Try to make changes (remembering what they are, of course!) on each account, and write down what happens.

2. Explore the Accessibility Options Control Panel applet. Make changes to your system, such as enabling StickyKeys and MouseKeys. Then practice with the new options. Do you see how these settings could help people use the computer more efficiently?

Computer Applications

"On the other side of the screen, it all looks so easy."

– Kevin Flynn, *Tron*

This chapter covers the following IC³ exam objectives:

- IC³-1   2.1.2   Identify simple terms and concepts related to the software development process.

- IC³-1   2.1.3   Identify issues relating to software upgrades.

- IC³-1   3.1.5   Identify and solve common problems related to operating systems.

- IC³-1   3.3.6   Install software.

- IC³-1   3.3.7   Identify common problems associated with installing and running applications.

Have you ever heard the phrase, "You need to apply yourself more!"? Accompanied by a rap of a ruler across the knuckles, it pretty much meant to use your energy for some practical purpose, rather than goofing off. Well, in 1843, a woman named Ada Lovelace suggested putting together a scripted set of "instructions" for directing one of the first machines to do a special task—those instructions were used towards a practical purpose—and *applications* were born. Figure 8.1 shows the first computer programmer.

This chapter tells the story of applications, starting with a primer on what they do for you in general and how they're made. You'll look at types of applications available today, including the all-important games, and then finish with the more nuts and bolts issues of installation and troubleshooting. We've got a lot of ground to cover, so let's get started!

Figure 8.1: Ada, Countess Lovelace, the world's first programmer

Intro to Applications

Every computer comes with certain applications you can use right away to start working and playing. Windows XP, for example, offers a couple of word processing programs (Notepad and WordPad) so you can write essays for this class, a calculator so you can balance your checkbook or figure out your grade point average, and more. Retail computer companies, like Sony and Hewlett-Packard, will add a whole bunch of applications of dubious value just for the advertising advantage.

You can add other applications after that so you can perform specific tasks on the computer. Applications, in essence, *extend the functions of the computer*. Want to become a rock star? You can get software that turns your computer into a music recording studio (Figure 8.2). Almost anything you can imagine wanting to do on a computer you can do (assuming you have enough money, naturally!).

If you use Microsoft Windows, you can look through your Start menu to see what applications you have on your computer. *Programmers* wrote each of those applications for a purpose, to perform a specific task. A guy named Nico Mak, for example, created a commonly used application called WinZip that enables you to work with compressed files (Figure 8.3).

Microsoft created Internet Explorer so you can browse Web pages, and AOL's Instant Messenger was created so you can chat with your friends and family while you are online (Figure 8.4). Each application has a specific purpose.

Figure 8.2: Adobe Audition music recording and mixing software

Figure 8.3: WinZip compressed

Believe it or not, even your operating system is a software application (sometimes the word *software* and *application* and *program* are used together, or interchangeably). By definition, that means it's a program that's been created for a specific purpose. So what's the purpose of an operating system? To host more software applications, and give them a system to operate on!

Some applications are created to help other apps work together. *(Jargon alert! "Apps" is just an abbreviated way to say applications.)* For example, you read about Disk Defragmenter (Figure 8.5) in Chapter 5, "Defining the Role of the Operating System." This application takes your other software and literally rearranges where it's stored on your computer's hard drive so the drive can access it faster. So basically, the application's main purpose is to help your other applications run *better*.

Another way programs extend the function of your computer is to teach your computer how to use something new. When you buy a new gadget, say a digital camera, your computer may not know what to do with it once it's hooked up. You'll need an application created by the makers of the camera to act as the go-between for you and the camera to get the pictures onto the computer, and maybe even view them once they are on the computer.

Figure 8.4: Internet Explorer browsing the Web

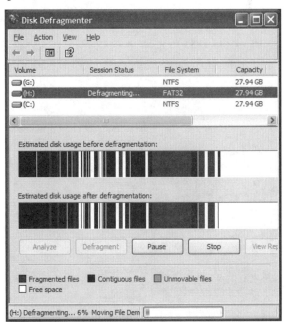

Figure 8.5: Disk Defragmenter

Drivers

When you install a new hardware device, such as a printer, the CD-ROM that came with the printer contains instructions for your computer. These special instructions are called drivers, or device drivers—the device being your printer, or the particular piece of hardware being installed. The driver is converting those special instructions into code, so your operating system can understand.

If you've ever downloaded a driver from the Internet, this is the main reason why the site asks you what type of operating system you use. Each operating system may interpret those instructions differently, and needs to be "taught" the specific way it needs to.

It's analogous to the instruction manual *you'll* have to read to learn how to operate the camera. Before reading the manual, you may have no idea what to do with the camera. Well, if you're a gadgeteer, you might, but have you *seen* digital cameras these days? They're complicated!

Creating Applications

People create software applications. They are a tangible, physical product that goes through a full development cycle just like any other tangible, physical product. In order to make a car, for example, it first gets manufactured in a factory line. After that, the crash-test dummies go to work, and the car is crash-tested for safety (Figure 8.6). Then it goes through a formal review process before it's finally placed outside the dealer lot for you to buy.

Figure 8.6: Crash-test dummy

Software applications are no different. Someone sits down at a computer and writes a piece of software. The finished product goes through the same procedures as a car (hopefully excluding the crash-test dummies) before arriving at the store in the box on the shelf. Let's examine the process in more detail.

Programming

While a car at a plant is created by being run along a factory line, software is created by a number of people sitting at their desks writing code. The act of writing the code is called *programming* and the writers are called *programmers*.

Why is it called **code**? Well, *code* is a set of symbols that can be used for communication. Programmers write code in a language that the designated operating system can understand, or decode. There are many different languages that a computer can speak, but in order to write the software, the programmers need to speak the same language.

When the programmers finish the application, the end result is a file called an *executable*, and usually ending with .exe. The executable file more than likely has a lot of other files that go with it (Figure 8.7). These files must stay with the primary file if the program is going to work correctly. All these pieces often get dumped on a CD-ROM disc and go on to the next step in the process, the debugging.

Debugging

When you write a term paper, hopefully you read it first before handing it in: Usually, unless you're perfect, you'll find some grammatical errors, and maybe a few typos here and there. Programming isn't that different, really.

Figure 8.7: Photoshop.exe is the primary executable here; all the rest are the helper files.

COMPUTER LITERACY: YOUR TICKET TO IC³ CERTIFICATION

When an application seems stable enough to the programmers, a software company runs it through an in-house error-checking process, looking for bugs. A *bug* is an error or problem in the software (Figure 8.8). The process of *debugging* is to identify a problem and then fix it. Repeat for all other errors, until the program can run correctly.

Beta Testing

When the initial piece of software programming is completed and the program is done and debugged, it's still not nearly finished and ready to go. The code in programs is very complex, and must be tested extensively for bugs that were previously unnoticed.

Software companies test their programs by sending copies to *beta testers*, people who use the program in real life and send in regular reports about any problems they find. This *beta test* (also called a *beta review*) can be done by a trained professional, but usually it's done by the customers themselves (such as yourself) who will be the ones primarily using the software when it's finished. Why the word *beta*? The first (*alpha*) test was done when the program was first created, right? Then the programmers debugged it. Now it goes through the second (*beta*) test.

These reviewers try out the software, and give a full review. What did they like? What didn't they like? What didn't work? The programmers need real-world testers like these people to get a completely different viewpoint of the way the software will be used.

How Hardware and Software Interact
You've seen this interaction between hardware and software before, way back in Chapter Two, "Going with the Data Flow." So turn back now to that chapter and see if you can answer these questions. What part do you play in the interaction between hardware and software? What devices handle text input? Which devices enable you to click on things? Name two output devices.

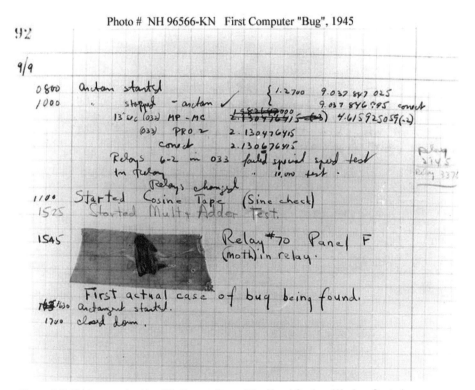

Figure 8.8: First computer bug (Photo courtesy of the Naval Surface Warfare Center)

Learn a Programming Language

When you went to school, you probably had to learn a foreign language. After you learned it, you probably discovered that it had a logical structure to it that made sense. If you can, pick up a book on programming languages, such as Microsoft's Visual Basic. That's a good one to start with. It's fun, and it's probably not as hard as you think it is!

You'll discover that it's logical, and even everyday objects such as stoplights take on a whole new meaning when you understand the logic that's driving it (and yes, that pun was intentional in case you were wondering!).

Oh, and good programmers make a ton of money.

Quality Control

The final step of the software application development cycle is the *quality control* (QC). Have you ever bought a pair of jeans that had a slip of paper in the pocket that said "Inspected by #9"? Those jeans were probably pulled, poked, prodded and pushed until the company could be satisfied that the jeans could be released into the public without falling apart (at least, for your sake, I hope so!).

If there's a button, the quality controller must click on it. If there's a feature, the controller must use it. What was supposed to happen? What happened instead? Did the program crash? Did it give an error? All these issues are documented and given back to the programmers to create a newer version of the software until they fix all these problems.

Figure 8.9: Inspected by #9

Once an application has gone through the debugging, beta test, and quality control steps, and the programmers have finished fixing things that need fixing, the application is considered ready to go (Figure 8.9). The program can be given a final release, packaged onto a CD, boxed, shrink-wrapped, and put on the shelf for you to buy.

Upgrading Applications

Customer service and competition drive software companies to release updates to their applications. These updates come in two general types, patches and upgrades.

Every program has bugs that appear once the program is sold. Software companies often make simple bug fixes available to download off their Web site. If they have a lot of bug fixes, some companies will produce a new version of the application that contains the fixes rather than having millions of people downloading the same fixes. The software update is called a *patch*, and the process of going to the newer version is called a *program update*.

Sometimes in addition to bug fixes, the software company also includes lots of new features (Figure 8.10). In this case, they'll usually give the new software version a different incremental name, such as "Cool Software 2.0" or "Cool Software 2006." This software update is called an *upgrade*. Both types of versions, upgrades and updates, usually don't require uninstalling your existing software, and you won't lose your current data. Most of the time, they install right over the existing application.

Sounds good, right? New features and no more error messages, sign me up! So how does the software upgrade (or update) get installed on my computer? Depending

Figure 8.10: Upgrade features

on the software company, you may be entitled to a free upgrade. Some companies also offer free upgrades for a year after purchasing. After that, you'll have to pay for the new features. Other companies make you pay for upgrades right off the bat. It depends on what they feel like doing. Many times, patches are free. After all, it was their mistake, right? There are three main methods to obtain upgrades: obtaining a disc, downloading, and automatic updating.

Obtaining new CD-ROM discs (or floppy disks)

You can go to the store, or you can call and order an upgrade CD-ROM disc. Usually if you have to pay for it, the upgrade version is cheaper, as the company knows you've already paid once for the full version. This time, you're just installing the cool new stuff and fixes!

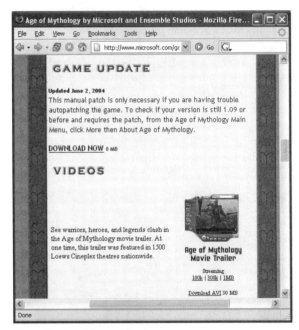

Figure 8.11: Patches available

Downloading From the Internet

If you've just had your midnight snack and want instant gratification, most companies enable you to download your new software upgrade right from their Web site (Figure 8.11). If it costs money, you can pay with a credit card. If it's a free upgrade, you may need to log in first. The Web site will have specific instructions how to download and install the upgrade.

Programming Languages

Remember Ada Lovelace, who we talked about early in the chapter? The very first programming language ever—Ada—was named after her. Some other languages are BASIC, C++, and Java. The very first program ever was created to output a line of text onto the screen——the words "Hello World!" In the programming language C++, here's how that would look:

```
#include <iostream.h>
#include <conio.h>
void main()
{
cout<<"Hello World!";
}
```

To a programmer, this makes perfect sense. To the untrained eye, it can make your brain hurt just by looking at it! Your local library will have books on computer programming to learn more. By the way, see that "cout" command? The "out" stands for output, and it prints to the screen.

Buggy Programs Unleashed

The first few decades of personal computing have seen an embarrassing amount of applications released that stunk. Some of these programs barely functioned out of the box, crashed constantly, and even caused damage to your operating system. What's the deal? Don't the companies who produce this software follow the proper procedures for debugging, beta testing, and QC?

Two primary emotions cause companies to release software too early: greed and fear. In the gaming industry, half the money earned in a year for an application comes during the winter holidays. Gifts for Christmas, Hanukah, and Kwanza put huge numbers of dollars in the game company and distributors' pockets, so the company accountants and managers put enormous pressure on programmers to just get it done! When greed wins, companies release buggy software.

Fear-based early release also revolves around money, but it's about losing money rather than gaining it. It costs a lot of money to pay a team of programmers for several years to produce an application. Meanwhile, that application makes no money for the company. What if the product simply won't work properly? What if it's too ambitious? A company can cut its losses and perhaps recoup a few dollars by releasing a broken product in the hopes that some poor sap will buy it. Not particularly honorable, but there you have it.

Note that every program has some bugs discovered after hitting store shelves. No amount of beta testing can prepare an application for the pounding, prodding, pushing, and pinching it'll receive from the general public. Most beta testers are fairly skilled computer users, not novices, so don't necessarily think about doing some of the crazy things newbs do.

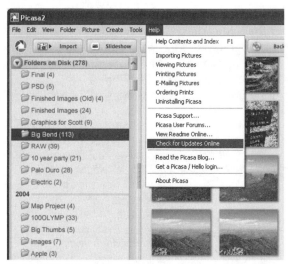

Figure 8.12: Automatic updates are usually found in the Help menu.

Automatic Updates Directly from the Software

Due to the growing popularity of the Internet, many software companies create ways to upgrade right from within the application. Sometimes the application will go out and check for updates on its own; usually in this case, it will display a pop-up message notifying you of an available upgrade. It's up to you if you want to go ahead with it or not.

Other times, you must check for updates manually. Most often, if the application contains a built-in upgrade checker, it can be found in the Help pull-down at the top of the screen (Figure 8.12).

If the software doesn't have a built in update checker, you'll have to do some sleuthing to find out about any available upgrades or patches. The easiest way to stay "in the know" is to visit the software company's Web site frequently, or read an industry news Web site regularly, such as CNET. com (Figure 8.13). These sites will keep you informed about possible bugs in the upgrade, and will even tell you the new features in the upgrade to help you decide if you want to do it!

It's really up to you to decide if you want to upgrade or not. The benefits include the obvious—new features the previous version didn't have—and the not-so-obvious—it may fix previous errors with other applications you have.

This sounds great! Why would anyone not do this? Well, there *is* certain amount of risk involved, when you stop and think about it. You're an *early adopter* (one of the first people to use the new software), and this new patch may have some bugs of its own! Some upgrades don't work with older equipment, which means you'd have to do a hardware upgrade before doing the software update. Finally, some upgrades simply aren't worth the price for what you do with the software. The software company might tout all the great new features and ask for your hard-earned dollars, but if you don't plan to use any of those features, don't upgrade.

Figure 8.13: Industry review of application upgrade

Types of Applications

Almost anything you can imagine—and probably stuff that you can't—you can do on a computer. From single, simple task completion tools to tools that assist in brain surgery and rocket science, applications can take you there.

Applications fall into a whole bunch of categories, from productivity apps to games to utility software. From multimedia to project planning, from controlling robots to creating art; there's simply no limit save the creativity and skill of the programmers.

You can get driving directions. Make a shopping list. Surf the Internet.

Stay in touch with friends via e-mail and instant messaging. Design a house in 3-D (Figure 8.14). Learn how to type. Make your own business cards, flyers, and greeting cards. Play games. Balance your checkbook. Keep a diary. Listen to music. Create your own music. Go shopping. Get a makeover . . . generally have a blast!

We're *all* looking for ways to be more productive, and it's exciting that your computer can help. The next chapter will tell you all about how to use word processors to create memos, letters and books (even this book was written by using a word processor). In addition, you'll learn how to create expense reports and budgets using spreadsheets (Figure 8.15).

Chapter 10 tells you about all sorts of goodies like listening to music and movies on your computer. You can also create your own pictures, brochures, and look at photos. Some software applications help other applications work better, and Chapter 10 will go into a little more detail about that.

Figure 8.14: Home Designer by Chief Architect

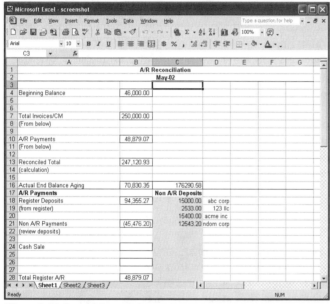

Figure 8.15: Spreadsheets help you keep expense reports

Installing Applications

You can't open a closet door in your home unless you first connect the door to the hinges, otherwise, the door is not connected to the house and would just fall down! The closet door must be *installed* before you can open and close it. Software works the same way. In fact, just like a closet door comes with instructions for installation, so does your software. Always look in the box for a manual first (Figure 8.16). There may be special installation instructions.

In almost every case, you install an application by inserting a CD-ROM or DVD-ROM disc into the appropriate drive and letting the computer do its thing. Windows and OS X automatically recognize most installation software and will give you a

Figure 8.16: Installation manual

Figure 8.17: Installation prompt

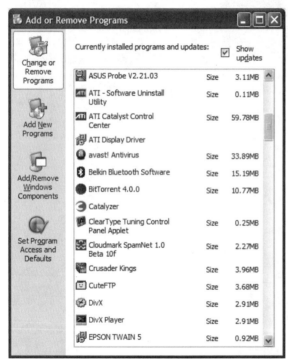

Figure 8.18: Add/Remove Programs applet

message asking if you want to install the software (Figure 8.17). This feature is called *autoplay*. You can also install software manually in Windows by using the Add/Remove Programs Control Panel applet (Figure 8.18). Programs written for Macintosh tend to be completely self-contained, so you can often install them by simply grabbing the program folder from the disc and dragging it to the hard drive.

The first thing that usually appears in an installation routine is a license agreement, or *end user license agreement (EULA)*. Agreeing to the EULA creates a contract between the software company and you, the user. This indicates the terms and conditions of using the software, such as how many computers you can install it on, and the limited liability of the software vendor should disastrous results occur as a result of installing the software. We'll talk about *that* later.

You have a choice at this point, you can either reject the EULA and return the software for a refund, or choose "Accept" and move on (Figure 8.20). It is a long read, but it's an important step. In fact, one software vendor, unsure if *anyone ever* read the entire EULA decided to place an important clause in that "any user accepting the license agreement would be entitled to certain monetary compensation" and included an e-mail address to send inquiries. Out of several thousand installations, one user sent them an e-mail—and was rewarded with $1,000 as thanks for proof that some people actually read the entire thing.

After agreeing to the EULA, the software may prompt you for a registration code. It will most likely tell you where to find that code, whether it be on the box itself or on the CD or DVD case.

The next step is choosing *where* (as in the specific drive and folder) to install the software. Unless you have a reason to choose otherwise, just take note of and accept the defaults and move to the next step.

Most software installations give you two choices of install types: Typical or Custom. Custom enables you to choose specific files to install only, whereas Typical installs the elements of the program that most people use on a regular basis. This is also a common reason why you may still need the CD-ROM or DVD-ROM disc to run the program, even though you've installed it. Not all the necessary files to run the software may be on your computer based on the installation settings.

Usually, this is enough information and now the software is ready to begin copying the files from the CD-ROM or DVD-ROM disc to your computer. As

Figure 8.19: Minimum requirements

long as you pause *long* enough to read and take in what you're actually *doing*, usually you're OK just keeping the default choices.

When the installation is finished, the software may tell you that you need to reboot your computer before you can use the software. This is especially true with Windows programs. The installation may have modified system settings that Windows needs to reload.

Windows has a file called the *registry* that includes information about every installed application and hardware in your computer. When the OS loads at boot-up, the registry loads into RAM so that the OS knows how to deal with all the parts and possibilities of the computer. If you install an application that changes the registry, the only way Windows can learn about that app is to reboot and put the modified registry into memory.

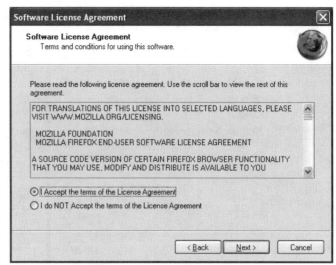

Figure 8.20: Accept the EULA to continue installing the software.

Installed Applications

Once you've installed and rebooted if necessary, your program takes its place along side other installed applications in the Start menu. To access and use any program at any time, simply click on **Start**, navigate to **All Programs**, find the software title, and click on it (Figure 8.21). You can also use the Add/Remove Programs Control Panel applet to view a list of all programs currently installed.

Uninstalling (Removing) a Program

To remove a program from your computer, you must *uninstall* it. After clicking on the **Add/Remove Programs** applet and displaying the list of software titles installed, find the software you wish to uninstall. Highlight it, and click **Install/Uninstall** or **Change/Remove** (depending on your operating system). The software will usually ask you if you really want to uninstall the software (we all have those faulty mouse clicks!) and then it's removed (Figure 8.22). In some cases a program may have an uninstall utility of its own that you can find in the Start menu. You can use that uninstall utility or the Add/Remove Programs applet. It's your choice.

The Mac OS (OS X) has no registry. Instead all that information is stored in a special folder called the "Library".

Troubleshooting Applications

Ah yes, you've finally reached the section that should have a great movie-esque title: *When Good Applications Go Bad*. Occasionally a software install with throw you for a loop, but armed with some good troubleshooting tips, every hiccup can be overcome. Here's a quick rundown of the most common issues.

Figure 8.21: Click on All Programs to access installed applications

Figure 8.22: You're outta here!

Installation program will not start

If you put the CD in the CD-ROM drive and it does not autoplay, you're not doomed to sit there waiting for eternity! You can still access the setup program, you'll just have to use the back door. You can find the CD-ROM drive in **My Computer** and double-click on it to launch the CD. Alternatively, to access the setup program directly, you can click **Start**, and then **Run**. Click **Browse** to navigate to your CD-ROM disc, and then find **setup.exe** or **install.exe**. Click the **OK** button to make it run.

Access Denied or Not Enough User Permissions

You may find you are not allowed to install or uninstall software on a particular computer (Figure 8.23). Remember when we talked about *user accounts* in the last chapter? Your user account is not configured to be able to change these settings. Don't take it personally—it just makes life easier for the computer *administrators*. You'll have to find someone with enough permissions to log in and install/uninstall it for you.

Figure 8.23: Access denied!

Defective or Lost Installation Media

Sometimes you put the installation CD-ROM or DVD-ROM disc in the drive, it doesn't autoplay, and even double-clicking on the drive in **My Computer** leads to a prompt telling you to put the disc in the drive. It's already in there! What's going on? It may just be dirty. Toddlers, dirty fingers, even bad reviews have been known to scratch and damage CDs. Try cleaning it gently and reinsert it.

If this doesn't fix the problem (or you are using a floppy disk), the disc may be damaged beyond repair. Contact the creators of the software to ask for a new disc. They will require some proof that you own the software, such as a receipt. You'll have to do this if you've lost the software also. I don't suppose this is a good time to mention that it's always wise to keep CDs and DVDs in their cases when you aren't using them?

Installation Stops Before Completion

It was going! The installation was 90 percent finished! And then….it stopped. Did it give you an error message? A complete system shutdown and restart may fix the problem (give it a few seconds of being powered off to let the memory *really* clear itself out). Also, make sure you don't have any other programs running that could interfere with the installation. Close *everything* (Figure 8.25).

If the error still occurs, be sure to write down what it was. The next step is to go to the software manufacturer's Web site and check their knowledgebase—the generic word for information about troubleshooting common problems. Software developers have programmers working round the clock to fix this stuff. When programmers find a problem and fix it, most software companies will post a document on their site stating the problem and how they fixed it, so others can benefit. You'll find most knowledgebase sections searchable so you can easily find the document you need.

Figure 8.24: Proper disc cleaning

Cleaning a CD- or DVD-media disc
To clean a CD or DVD, take the edge of a soft shirt and place it in the middle of the disc. Wipe from the middle outwards (against the track), working your way upwards and around the CD or DVD (Figure 8.24). Try it!

Installed Program Does Not Appear on the Computer

Occasionally, installed programs don't appear in the Start menu, although this is rare. Not all programs add an icon to the Start menu or Desktop. In such circumstances, you'll have to use a back door and go in the super-secret way. Remember how the installation program asked you the specific drive and folder you wanted to install the program into? Most likely you accepted the default, and that's where you'll go to find it!

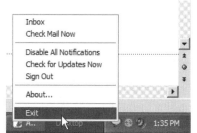

Figure 8.25: Close applications on the System Tray by right-clicking them.

In Windows Explorer, navigate to the location where it was installed, and look for the *executable* amidst all the other files. The executable file will have an extension .exe and a descriptive icon (Figure 8.26). You'll know when you've clicked on the right file, after all, because your *application* will launch. To find it easier the next time, you can put your own shortcut on the Desktop.

Installed Program Fails to Work

When an application fails to work, it's very important to take good notes. As Jerry Maguire once said, *"Help me help you."* What did you think was going to happen, and what happened instead? Did you get an error message? Did

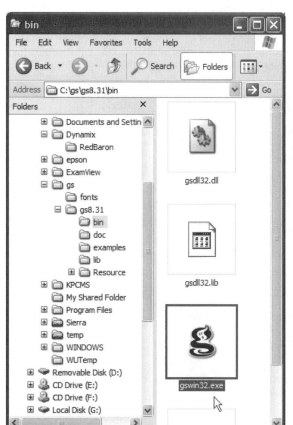

Figure 8.26: Find the icon that will run your software

The Default Application

Your operating system has a predefined list of default applications that open with certain files. That means that unless you specify otherwise, your computer will always use that application to open those files. This naturally makes things considerably easier for you; your computer's doing all the work!

Here's an experiment: pop a music CD in your computer's CD-ROM drive. Most likely, your computer will use its default music program to begin playing the music CD. That's one program that you didn't have to select in order to listen to the music, your computer already had one in mind.

your system crash? Check your manual for common errors first, and after that, head online for the knowledgebase! If you have to call tech support, be armed with your notes so you can help the nice folks on the other end of the line diagnose your problem quicker.

This is probably also a good time to remind you that sometimes a system reboot is necessary—remember the registry? The system loads that at boot up.

Other Programs Fail to Work After the New Product is Installed

Every once in a while you'll find a program that seems to have caused other programs to break after you install it. You have several options here. First, you can uninstall the new application and pray your old applications work again, but this rarely does the trick. Second, you can go to the manufacturer's Web site and look for a fix to the problem. You can also contact the manufacturer's tech support—chances are good that if you've run into such an awful problem, that others have as well. Tech support might be the best answer here.

Fourth, if you have Windows XP, you can do a System Restore to an earlier state, preferably one in which every important application functioned properly. Finally, although it might make you feel a little better, yelling at the computer probably won't fix the problem. See options one through four, above for better solutions.

Files Cannot be Read by the New Application

If your new application doesn't recognize a file, make sure the application has the capability to open the file type. If you have a tape of Led Zeppelin and a CD of the same Led Zeppelin album, for example, both will play the same songs. But you obviously can't put a tape in a CD player any more than you can jam a CD into your tape deck (Figure 8.27).

Files work the same way. If you have a file with the extension .ram (Real Audio), you need Real Player program to play it. The file contains music, but it won't open in Windows Media Player (a different music player application). You have to make sure you have the right tool for the job.

Figure 8.27: That's just not going to work!

Application Compatibility

Programmers create applications for specific operating systems and, with a few exceptions, the programs only work with that operating system. An application written for Macintosh OS X, for example, simply won't run on a Windows box of any sort. The reverse is true as well. This OS-specific programming can also bite you with different versions of the same OS. Programs written for OS X, for example, won't install or run in Macintosh OS 9. Some applications written for Windows 98 won't play in Windows XP, either.

If you run into an application you desperately want to use, but that is incompatible with your OS, you have a couple of choices. First, you can go to the software developer's Web site to see if they have other versions of the software. If so, a quick download and you're good to go. If there's no compatible version, then you either have to use a different computer, or upgrade your computer to a later version.

Geek speak uses the term "native" to describe the OS of an application. Roller Coaster Tycoon, for example, is a native Windows application, meaning it won't run on other OSs.

Emulate This!

As an alternative to upgrading or switching computers, you can try to find emulation software—a helper program that fakes out the application, enabling it to run even though it shouldn't. These sorts of programs enable Linux users to run Windows-native apps, for example. Check out www.winehq.com for one of the more interesting and useful emulation programs around, Wine.

CHAPTER 8: SUMMARY

Intro to Applications

- Programmers write software applications to perform specific tasks on your computer. Applications extend the functions of the computer. Some applications are for entertainment, some are for productivity, and some applications help other applications work better.

- Just like any product, software is a tangible product that goes through a development cycle. First comes the initial programming, followed by the debugging phase to sort out any obvious problems. Once the debugging is complete, the application goes into the beta testing phase. The software company releases the product to standard users to find any problems. Once it's reviewed, it has to pass quality control. Finally, the CD-ROM or DVD-ROM gets put in a box and shelved at the store for you to buy.

- Software companies update and provide upgrades for their programs to add new features and fix existing problems.

- There are three primary methods of acquiring software upgrades. You can upgrade your software by acquiring a new CD-ROM disc or floppy disk. You can also download an upgrade from the Internet. You can use an automatic upgrade check if the software has it built in.

- Tech sites such as CNET.com as well as the manufacturer's Web site can give you news about whether it's a good idea to go ahead with the upgrade or not. You'll want to make an informed decision whether to risk the new features against possibly adding new bugs into your system.

Installing Applications

- You typically must install applications to use them. In almost every case, you install an application by inserting a CD-ROM or DVD-ROM disc into the appropriate drive and letting the computer do its thing. Windows and OS X automatically recognize most installation software and will give you a message asking if you want to install the software. This feature is called *autoplay*.

- You can also install software manually in Windows by using the Add/Remove Programs Control Panel applet. Programs written for Macintosh tend to be completely self-contained, so you can often install them by simply grabbing the program folder from the disc and dragging it to the hard drive.

- The first thing that usually appears in an installation routine is a license agreement, or *end user license agreement* (*EULA*). Agreeing to the EULA creates a contract between the software company and you, the user. The next step is choosing *where* (as in the specific drive and folder) to install the software. Unless you have a reason to choose otherwise, just take note of and accept the defaults and move to the next step.

- Most software installations give you two choices of install types: Typical or Custom. Custom enables you to choose specific files to install only, whereas Typical installs the elements of the program that most people use on a regular basis.

- To find the software you just installed, it's probably listed in the Start Menu under *Programs*.

- To remove a program from your computer, you must *uninstall* it. After clicking on the **Add/Remove Programs** applet and displaying the list of software titles installed, find the software you wish to uninstall. Highlight it, and click **Install/Uninstall** or **Change/Remove**. In some cases a program may have an uninstall utility of its own that you can find in the Start menu.

Troubleshooting Applications

- If you put the CD in the CD-ROM drive and it does not autoplay, you can still access the setup program. Find the CD-ROM drive in **My Computer** and double-click on it to launch the CD.

- You may find you are not allowed to install or uninstall software on a particular computer. Get a computer administrator or someone with enough permissions to install the software for you.

- A damaged CD-ROM or DVD-ROM disc can make an installation fail. You can try cleaning it first. If that doesn't work, then contact the manufacturer for a new copy of the disc.

- Bugs in the software can cause installations to fail. Similarly, bugs in the application code can make programs crash after you've done a successful installation. Check the software manufacturer's site for knowledgebase articles on how to fix the problems.

- Most programmers write applications for a single operating system. An application written for Macintosh OS X, for example, simply won't run on a Windows box of any sort. If you run into an application that is incompatible with your OS, you have a couple of choices. First, you can go to the software developer's Web site to see if they have other versions of the software. If so, a quick download and you're good to go. If there's no compatible version, then you either have to use a different computer, or upgrade your computer to a later version.

Key Terms

Add/Remove Programs applet

Administrator

Application

Autoplay

Beta reviewers

Beta test

Code

Debug

Early adopter

End user license agreement (EULA)

Executable

Knowledgebase

Native

Patch

Programmers

Programming

Quality control (QC)

Registry

Update

Upgrade

Key Term Quiz

Use the Key Terms list to complete the following sentences. Not all the terms will be used.

1. A(n) _____ is a new version of software specifically created to fix bugs.

2. A(n) _____ is a new version of software that has bug fixes and cool new features.

3. A list of articles on a Web site of possible fixes of common software problems is a(n) _____.

4. The folks who write and fix applications are called _____.

5. The _____ is the main application file; the other files can be considered helper files.

6. Before using software, you must first decide whether you want to accept the _____.

7. You'll have to ask someone with a(n) _____ account to install an application for you if you don't have permission to install software yourself on the computer.

8. Before software can be approved, it gets tested by _____, who are everyday people that will use the software the most.

9. To uninstall an application from a Windows computer, the first place to go is the _____.

10. Installing software into a Windows-based computer often makes changes to the _____, which then requires a reboot before the application will work.

Multiple Choice Quiz

1. Why is it so important to install the files from the CD that came with your new hardware device, such as a digital camera?
   A. So you can learn how to use it better
   B. So your computer can obtain the proper files it needs to understand the camera's language
   C. So your computer can find the camera
   D. So your camera can interact with the printer to print out your pictures

2. Jay is trying to install software, and before he can move on, he needs to enter a registration code. Where might he find it? (Select all that apply.)
   A. The software company's Web site
   B. The manual
   C. The software box
   D. The CD case

3. Margot inserted a CD-ROM into her drive and was surprised when an installation program came up on the screen. What most likely happened?
   A. The CD-ROM is defective.
   B. The CD-ROM is dirty or scratched.
   C. The operating system's autoplay feature kicked on.
   D. She must have double-clicked something.

4. How could Jessica find a list of all the software titles installed on her Windows computer? (Select all that apply.)
   A. Click on the Start menu and navigate to All Programs.
   B. Click on the Start menu and then click Run.
   C. Open the Add/Remove Programs Control Panel applet.
   D. Open the System Control Panel applet.

5. What's the proper way to clean a CD?
   A. Use Windex.
   B. Use a cloth to wipe against the track, from center to edge, around the entire CD.
   C. Use a cloth to wipe with the track, in a circular motion, around the entire CD.
   D. Soak the CD in hot, soapy water.

6. Under what menu in his application would Pete most likely find information about whether his software application has the ability to do automatic updates?
   A. File
   B. Options
   C. Help
   D. Window

7. How can you tell which file is the main executable for your application?
   A. The filename is the software title.
   B. The manual will tell you.
   C. The file ends in the extension .exe.
   D. The file ends in the extension .exec.

8. Which of these is **not** a programming language mentioned in this chapter?
   A. JAVA
   B. C++
   C. BASIC
   D. BUG

9. It's the job of _____ to click every button and find any bugs that the programmers might have missed before the software is ready for sale.
   A. Beta reviewers
   B. Quality control
   C. Debuggers
   D. Programmers

10. If you have to upgrade or update your software, in most cases, you'll lose all your data and have to start over again.
    A. True
    B. False

11. Which of the following are considered productivity applications? (Select all that apply.)
    A. Spreadsheets
    B. Games
    C. Utilities
    D. Word Processors

12. What are some methods to uninstall a program from your computer? (Select all that apply.)
    A. Use the Add/Remove Programs Windows Control Panel applet.
    B. Delete the main executable.
    C. Use the Uninstall utility that came with the program.
    D. Install another application over it.

13. If your installation media (CD-ROM disc, floppy) is defective, you are entitled to a free replacement.
    A. It depends on the manufacturer.
    B. Yes, you can call them for a new one.
    C. No, you must pay for it.
    D. You have to buy the entire boxed software again.

14. Alfred downloaded a movie from the Internet, but when he double-clicked on it, his operating system gave him an error message about a missing plug-in for .mov files. The movie played just fine on his friend's computer. What could be the problem?
    A. Alfred's computer does not have an application installed that understands .mov files.
    B. Alfred's computer does not have any movie-viewing hardware installed.
    C. Alfred's computer is a Macintosh.
    D. Alfred shouldn't be downloading movies. His mother must have found out and sabotaged the downloaded file!

15. Sven installed a new game—or thought he did. The installation seemed successful, but when he went to the Start menu to run it, it was nowhere to be found. What should he try next?
    A. Call tech support.
    B. Use Explorer to find the executable file for the program.
    C. Reinstall the application.
    D. Click harder.

Essay Questions

1. You have just installed a software application, and now your computer is not working properly. The new application won't run, and neither will other applications! Before you call tech support, give a sample write-up of exactly what your computer is doing. Be as thorough as possible to help them out as much as you can.

2. Compose a short letter to a software company explaining why they should send a replacement CD-ROM to you. Be creative!

3. Describe your "perfect application." What would it do? What would be its primary purpose? What would some of the features be? How would you interact with it? (Mouse, keyboard, etc.)

Projects

1. Install three different and totally unrelated applications onto your computer. Pay close attention to the install steps. How are they the same? How are they different? Was one install more complicated than another? What made it so complicated?

2. Go through each program on your computer, and see if it has an automatic updates program. If not, visit the company's Web site and find out if upgrades are available. Do you have to pay for it? Is it subscription-based? What are the new features of the upgrade? Is it worth it? Pay attention to the different ways each of your applications specifies upgrade options.

3. If you have a classroom setting with multiple people, divide up into groups of 2-4 people. Then take some time to come up with a computer application that would help make the environment cleaner. How would it work? Once each group has finished creating its application, have the groups present their ideas. Did any of them overlap? What were some of the goals outlined in the applications?

4. Armed with all these great program ideas for cleaning up the environment, as a class come up with a bigger program that uses all or most of the ideas.

Productivity Software – Word Processors, Spreadsheets, Databases, and Presentation Software

"Hello, Peter. What's happening? We need to talk about your TPS reports."
– Dom Portwood, *Office Space*

This chapter covers the following IC³ exam objectives:

■ IC³-1   2.2.1   Identify fundamental concepts relating to word processing and common uses for word-processing applications.

■ IC³-1   2.2.2   Identify fundamental concepts relating to spreadsheets and common uses for spreadsheet applications.

■ IC³-1   2.2.3   Identify fundamental concepts relating to presentation software and common uses for presentation applications.

■ IC³-1   2.2.4   Identify fundamental concepts relating to databases and common uses for database applications.

Writing the Great American Novel . . . teaching an amazing class . . . balancing your checkbook . . . for routine and not-so-routine tasks, the world turns to a category of programs called *productivity software*: word processing, spreadsheets, databases, and presentation software. All these things combined can increase your productivity and help you create great stuff.

First, here's the ancient history. In the late 1800s, Thomas Edison patented the typewriter. In the early 1900s it became mainstream, and upright *homo sapiens* became more productive. In the 1970s and 1980s, *word processing* was done on both typewriters and early electronic processors (Figure 9.1). Today, almost anyone can create professional-quality documents at their own computer! As you can see, we've come a long way since hunting, gathering, and creating fire.

Just as you could on a typewriter, on your computer you can type letters, write books, and create a "To Do" list. Unlike a typewriter, on the other hand, your computer enables you to create pictures, graphics, illustrations, and charts (Figure 9.2); your computer can even add up a budget for you.

You don't have to master *one* particular piece of software right now; you just need to grasp hold of some standard concepts. Regardless of what operating system you have, word processor you have, year you were born, or car you drive, the fundamental concepts of productivity software are universal. That means that no matter what version or computer you use, you can still apply these basic principles.

This chapter begins with a discussion of word processing programs, the most commonly used applications on computers, then turns to spreadsheet software that people use for accounting and other things. The third section covers databases, powerful tools for cataloging, searching, and working with data. The chapter wraps up with a discussion of presentation software, programs that help spice up speeches and classrooms with great visual content. We've got a lot to cover, so let's get started!

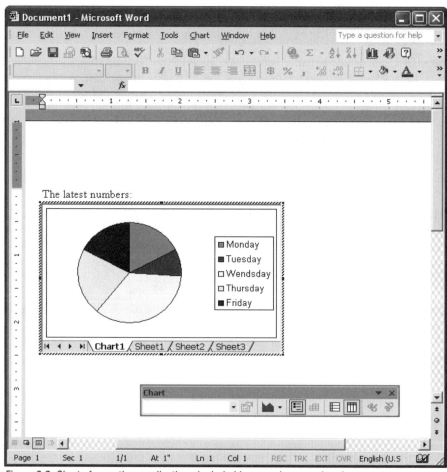

Figure 9.2: Charts from other applications included in a word processing document

Mincing Words– Creating Text Documents with Word Processors, Desktop Publishing, and Web Editing Software

Word processing programs enable you to create text documents. You can use them to create simple documents, such as notes and personal letters. You can

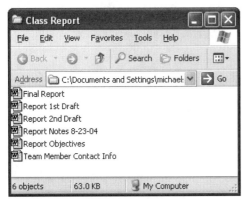

Figure 9.3: A list of word processing documents stored on a computer

also apply formatting to the documents, to create a nice design or layout that includes titles, text, and pictures. This chapter, for example, was formatted on a desktop publishing program called Adobe InDesign. Finally, Web editing software enables you to format text and pictures for putting on a Web site, with no intention to publish on paper at all.

Documents

Any time you create a word processing item to capture data so it will not be lost, you create a *word processing document*, or just a *document*. Documents are the most basic concept of word processing. In fact, the act of *documenting* something is to capture information. The Declaration of Independence is a document. A deed to a car is a document. The letter you type on your computer to send to Mom is a document.

With a word processor, a document doesn't have to contain just text. Don't let the word "word" fool you. Any word processing document (that's not done on a typewriter) can contain pictures, images, shapes, and more.

Editing – Not Just for Newspapers

Any time you actively work and make changes to a document, you *edit* that document. If you just opened the document to see what was in it and closed it, you have just *read* the document. Editing can be also used as a generic term for opening a document and doing *something* with it.

Formatting

One of the really nifty aspects of word processors is the different things you can do with fonts, colors, and shapes. The *format* of a document is the basic structure and layout. One definition of the act of formatting, then, becomes refining your document to create a layout that presents the material the way you want it presented. If you create a typical paper or book report, the default options in almost any word processing program would serve you well. Microsoft Word's default document, for example, will print out with a 1" margin on top and bottom and 1.25" margins on the right and left (Figure 9.5). These options are adjustable.

You can also format individual letters,

Saving Documents

When you use a typewriter, the only option for saving your work is to keep the paper that you typed your document on. When you type a document on your computer, in contrast, you can save it on your hard drive as a file, and retrieve it if you want to use it later (Figure 9.3). If you type multiple documents, you save them with individual file names on your computer. The file name is the unique name you give your file when you save it for the first time. Quite unlike George Foreman, your computer won't allow you to name two files in the same folder with the same name. Otherwise, there wouldn't be any way to tell the difference!

Figure 9.4: Text document

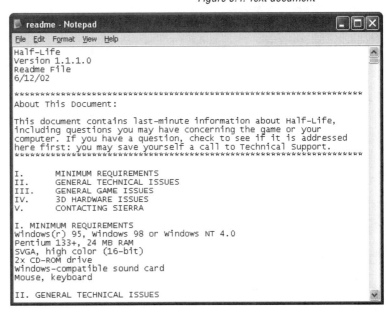

Off the Script

Text Editors

Early word processors were called text editors, *because that's all they could be used for – editing text (Figure 9.4). No graphics allowed! Actually, the computers weren't advanced enough to be able to support graphics. To this day, a word processing program that can't handle graphics is called a text editor so there's no confusion.*

Formatting

*When you are learning how to use a word processed document, play around with formatting options. You can make text **boldface**, you can <u>underline</u> or italicize text. You can also change the font, or even the font size. Go crazy! Play around with your options, and discover the flexibility you have.*

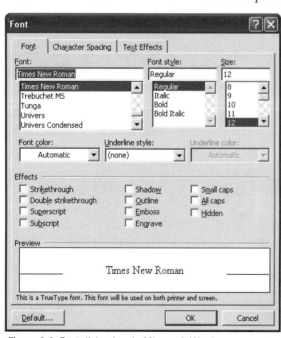

Figure 9.6: Font dialog box in Microsoft Word

words, and paragraphs, making them bold, italicized, blue, or all of the above. The Font dialog box shown in Figure 9.6, for example, should give you some idea of the amazing variety of formatting you can apply.

You can add a table of contents, for example, or a page number at the bottom of every page. You could also change the size of the font on the first line for emphasis. When you make such changes, your changes alter the formatting of the document.

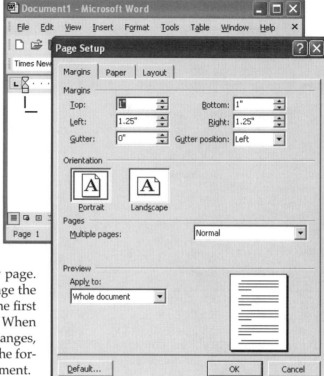

Figure 9.5: Setting up the page

Desktop Publishing

When something is published, that usually describes something that's being created for widespread circulation or distribution—or at the very least, something that you want to look relatively flashy when it's printed. It used to be that you'd have to go to your local print shop to have them lay out the design for you.

But now, you too can do it from your own desktop, meaning right at your own computer. Flyers, brochures, business cards—these are just a sampling of the types of publications that you can create from your own computer with desktop publishing software (Figure 9.7). Documents like these usually require a great deal of layout, planning, and sometimes pictures to make them look like they were professionally done. To use a word you should know by know, they require a great deal of *formatting*. Most desktop publishing software has templates that make the formatting easily accomplished.

The Long and the Short

Word processing programs enable you to create and format documents of all sorts, from short notes to novel-length extravaganzas. Have you ever written a thank-you note or a memo that has gotten distributed around your office? Well, if you have, you have created a short word processing document. Have you ever typed up a paper for school? A book report? Have you ever wanted to write a book? Your word processing software will keep track of how many pages you have written, and even how many words, paragraphs and lines you have typed (Figure 9.8).

In fact, word processors excel at reports and books due

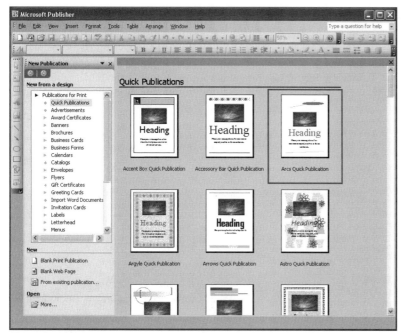

Figure 9.7: Desktop publishing software usually comes with pre-defined templates built in

to the complex formatting usually required by them. Take a close look at the formatting of this chapter. The title page is in a different font, and each page is numbered. The section headers are boldfaced. The next chapter will have the same formatting, and so will the next. In fact, the formatting is based *per chapter*. All this becomes possible with a word processor.

If you use Windows as your operating system, you can use the built-in text editors like Notepad or WordPad. These will only get you so far,

however. In fact, Notepad is text-only. Microsoft Word and Corel WordPerfect offer many more features. Although Word has a lot more market share than WordPerfect, both programs will readily read documents created in the other program and enable you to create documents of amazing complexity.

To Infinity, and Beyond!

The possibilities of creating documents doesn't end with a quick memo or a *New York Times* Bestseller. Even online documents like Web pages can be created in a word processor and converted, or created in software that is specially

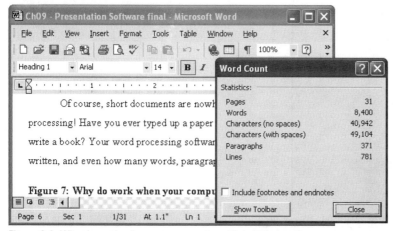

Figure 9.8: Why do work when your computer will do it for you?

Help!

Learn how to ask your word processor for help. If you want to start using all these cool features, you have to know how to incorporate that formatting into your document. The application Help file will be able to tell you everything you need to know, so all you have to do is be able to identify fluently what you are trying to accomplish.

If you want page numbers to appear at the bottom of every page, you can search for page numbering (Figure 9.9). Or, if you want to learn how to put anything at the bottom or every page, that's called a footer. The top of every page? That's a header.

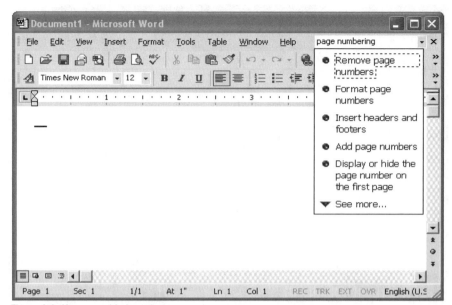

Figure 9.9: If you need help, ask.

used just for creating Web pages. This type of software is called Web editing software, or Web page builders (Figure 9.10).

A Web page resembles a printed page. It has a layout. It has text and graphics. The only difference is the programming behind them, and in most cases, your word processor can convert it anyway. Figure 9.11 shows the same page as shown in Figure 9.10, but now complete and on the Web.

Text Document Formats: .TXT, .DOC, .HTM

Your word processor can distinguish between different types of files by looking at the file extension. A simple text-only document, for example, often ends in the extension.txt. A fancier document might end in .doc, and a Web page in .html.

.TXT

A file that ends in *.txt*, such as "readme.txt" is your standard, garden-variety text document. A file that is text-only can't display any graphics at all. In fact,

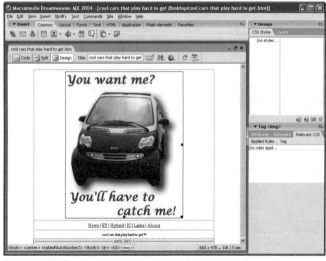

Figure 9.10: Dreamweaver with content in design mode.

Figure 9.11: Web page

it can't include *any* formatting. No boldface. No underline. Nothing.

This doesn't sound nice at all. Why on earth would you want to create a document with the extension .txt? The primary reason is for compatibility. Every operating system comes with tools for reading text documents. Microsoft bundles three programs with Windows XP: EDIT, Notepad, and WordPad. Because there's no formatting, there are no features to lose or get lost in translation. So if you open a .txt document created in one program, it will look exactly the same in any other program.

.DOC

Another common file extension for word processing is *.doc*, short for document. This is **Microsoft Office's** standard extension for documents created with a word processing program called **Word**. This type of document can hold text, graphics, and formatting such as bold and underline. They can also contain things like columns and tables. This is the most common format for creating word processing documents.

.HTM

A file that ends in .htm or .html is a Web page. HTML stands for *hypertext markup language*, the primary language of most Web sites you'll visit. You can create your document in a word processor, and then save it with the extension *.htm*. Your document has now become a Web page! This is convenient when you don't actually *know* the language of HTML, but would like to have a page anyway. Your word processing software will convert your formatting into the right code. Figure 9.12 shows a trio of word processing documents.

Adding It Up – Making Charts, Tables, and Graphs with Spreadsheet Software

People make lists – lists for grocery shopping; lists of addresses, phone numbers, and names for friends and relatives; lists for planning parties. Wouldn't it be nice if you had a list of 25 items—of which you could only buy 10—to be able to sort that list by what's most important? Then sort it by what's most expensive? If you created the list in a word processing program, you'd have to do the sorting manually, dragging the individual items from wherever they initially were placed into a new list location (Figure 9.13). What a drag (if you'll pardon the pun)!

Spreadsheet software enables you to create lists with many different fields for details (such as price and priority) and then sort them automatically (Figure 9.14). You can tell the software to do all sorts of math with the numbers without you having to break out a calculator.

Cells

A spreadsheet appears like a grid of rows and columns, like an old bookkeeping ledger. Each little square—called a *cell*—can hold data. The top columns are usually labeled A-Z, and the rows are numbered starting at 1 and increasing as they go down. This is to make them easy to reference. For example, the first cell in the first row is cell A1. The second cell immediately to the right is B1. The cell below A1 is A2, and the cell below B1 is B2. Figure 9.15 shows a blank spreadsheet document.

Figure 9.12: A .txt file, a .doc file, and an .htm file all in the same folder on a computer.

Worksheets and Workbooks

The entire page of cells as far as you can see on a spreadsheet is called a *worksheet*. It's possible to have multiple worksheets in a single spreadsheet file, this is called a *workbook*. If you kept a monthly record of something, for example, you could give each month its own worksheet. When you open the file, each worksheet appears as a separate tab (Figure 9.16).

Cell Contents

Cells can contain numbers, values, text, and all sorts of other content. Depending on the type of data in the cells, the spreadsheet software enables you to manipulate the spreadsheet in many ways. Let's look at an example. Jen has a list of members in her 4-H club that includes the number of years each member has been in the club and the ZIP code for each person's residence. A spreadsheet would be a fantastic way for her to keep the membership data! The first column Jen would use for each member's name. Each name goes in a separate cell, one name per row (Figure 9.17).

Because these names are text, Jen can't do any sort of mathematical operations on them. Not that she would want to, but because the cellscontain letters, they can only be sorted alphabetically.

The next column (across) Jen could use to enter a number—the amount of years that person has been a member. If Pete has been a member for 3 years, and cell A2 contained "Pete," then cell B2 would contain "3" (Figure 9.18). Jen would want to keep each person matched up with the correct year beside them. The third column could have the ZIP codes for each member, as you can see in Figure 9.19.

Once Jen has entered the data into her spreadsheet, she can do work with it. She could sort the list alphabetically. Alternatively, she could sort by ascending or descending to see who has been a member the longest. She could also add up the second column and find out how many combined years of memberships she has! One cell at the bottom will contain a placeholder for her total

Figure 9.13: List of camping items

Camping List - Microsoft Word

Camping List:

1. Tent $200 p1
2. Fire $150 p2
3. Folding Chairs $60 p5
4. new digital Camera $700 p4
5. sleeping Bag $100 p3
6. bow and arrow set $1000 p6

Searching for Spreadsheets

Although not as many companies make spreadsheet programs as they make word processing ones, several programs compete with Microsoft Excel in the market. Fire up your favorite Web browser or wander down to the corner computer store and see what's out there. How do the different developers claim their product is better than the other fellow's product? Did you find any that cost nothing?

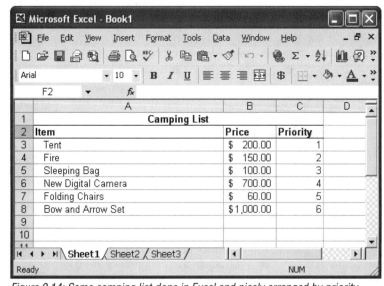

Figure 9.14: Same camping list done in Excel and nicely arranged by priority

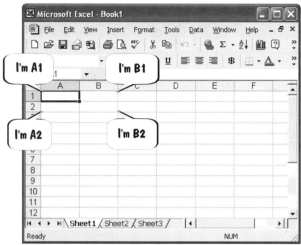

Figure 9.15: Blank spreadsheet

(Figure 9.20).

Here's where it gets interesting. What could she do with the ZIP codes? Sort by number, certainly, to see who lives near each other. But she certainly wouldn't want to add them up, right? ZIP codes are simply names for locations in a city; the names just happen to use numbers rather than letters.

Some spreadsheet software enables you to assign a category—called a *format*, (yet another use of that word)—to a cell, column, or row so the software would treat it in a certain fashion. Figure 9.21 shows the options for Microsoft Excel, one of the top spreadsheet programs.

Designating the column of ZIP codes as Text rather than General or Number would make a lot of sense. Aside from the off chance of adding the numbers together, Jen could avoid any number of frustration from the software helping her out. If she punched in a ZIP code that started with a zero, for example, the spreadsheet software would automatically remove it (Figure 9.22). It's just unnecessary for a *number* to start with a zero! This can lead to hours of retyping, frustration, and a general sense of wanting to throw your computer out the window. And that would just be a shame, as all she needed to do was change the format from a type *number* to *text*. And, she'd have to clean up the mess outside, too.

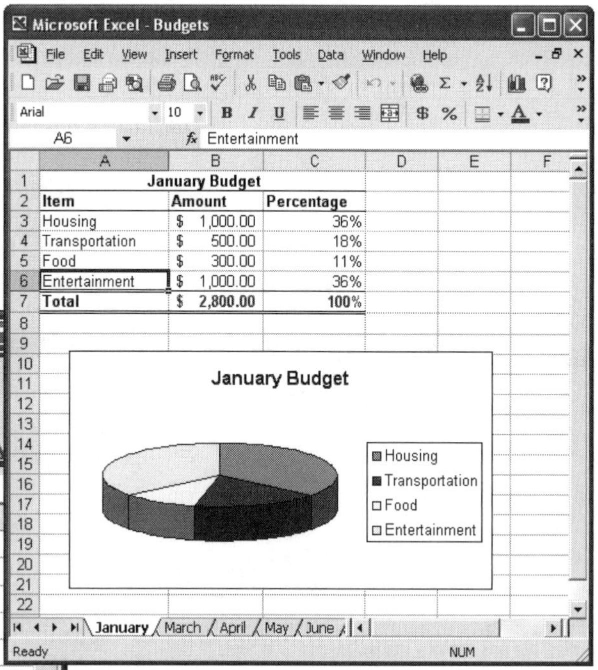

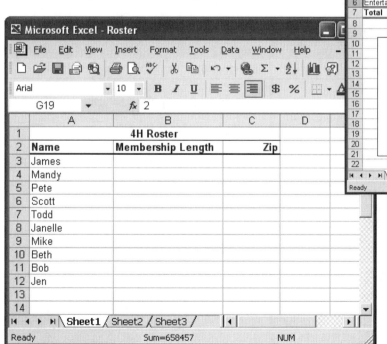

Figure 9.16: This file is a workbook, and each worksheet tab contains a month's budget.

Figure 9.17: Club roster

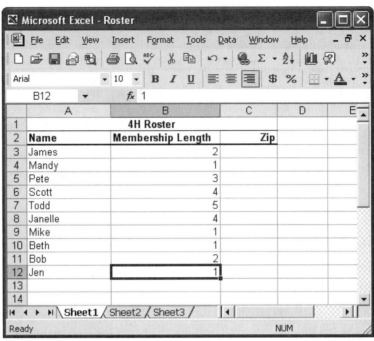

Figure 9.18: Entering the years of membership

Cell categories can save you a lot of time. You can specify cell types such as currency, which will automatically insert a dollar sign and zeroes. You type **1** and like magic it changes to **$1.00**.

Formulas and Functions

Spreadsheets shine when you start including formulas and functions! *Formulas* do calculations in cells. And not just numbers, either. Formulas contain *functions* (sum, multiply, etc) that have pre-designated actions. A formula is usually specified by preceding the command with a special character, like an equals sign (=). Formulas can be used to add two cells together, or a whole block of cells (Figure 9.23). Your spreadsheet software's Help menu can help you put together basic formulas, such as addition, subtraction, multiplication, and division.

Figure 9.19: ZIP codes

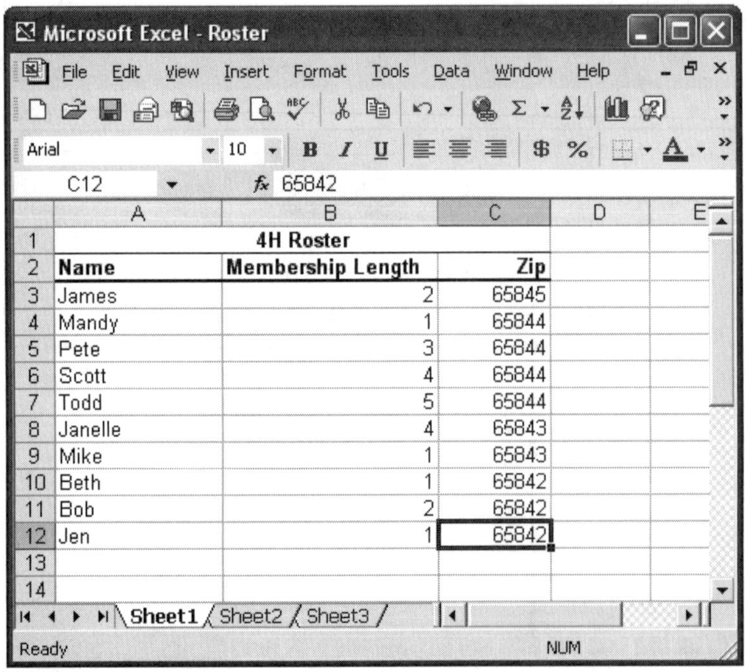

Charts and Graphs

Imagine entering oodles of data, and wishing you had a nice, quick, easy way of looking at all your data to analyze it. Well, spreadsheets make that possible.

You can select the columns you want as your chart data, click a few buttons, and out spits a pie chart sweeter than mom used to make (Figure 9.24).

What if you only wanted to see your contacts from a certain state, or certain town? You can filter your data so you only see those contacts from your state of choice. The data hasn't disappeared. You can turn off the filter and all the data will reappear in the list. What if you wanted a nice, graphical overview as to where your contacts lived? Create a chart

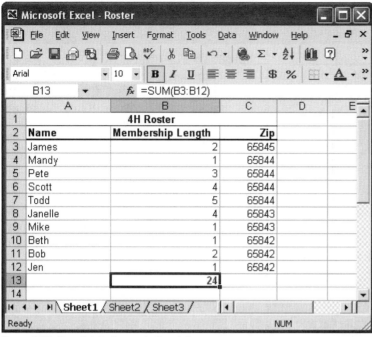

Figure 9.20: Sum total of years in the club

by state, and you can get a pie chart of all the states your contacts live in.

Some useful ideas...

So we've established that a spreadsheet is a great way of storing a contact list. What else can you do with the? Because spreadsheets can do number calculations on cells, they are excellent for creating financial documents such as budgets, expense reports, pricing models, and invoices. They can also be useful for

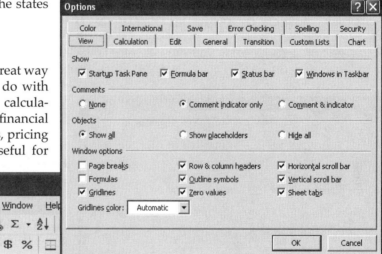

Figure 21: That's a lot of options!

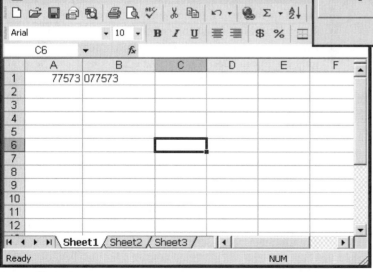

Figure 22: See the difference when you tell the spreadsheet you want a Text format? You won't lose the zero!

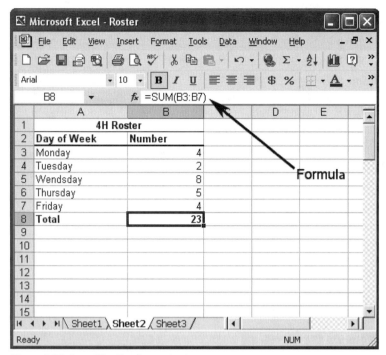

Figure 9.23: A weekly attendance sheet can total the attendance using the =SUM formula as shown in the formula bar. No calculator required!

teachers as grade books, performing averages on the rows to calculate a final score.

Spreadsheet Formats: .XLS, .QPW

Similar to word processing documents, your operating system knows a spreadsheet file because of the extension of the file name. Here are some common file formats of spreadsheets.

.XLS

A common file format, *.xls* indicates that the file is a Microsoft Excel spreadsheet file. This file will mainly open in Microsoft Excel, though many other spreadsheet programs can successfully open these files, too.

.QPW

The *.qpw* file format indicates that a Corel Quattro Pro spreadsheet. This is another alternative for spreadsheet software.

Everything in Its Place – Using Database Software

A *database* program enables you to take a bunch of data and do stuff with it, kind of like a spreadsheet on steroids. Rather than having a sheet full of little cells, you can set up a database to have all kinds of flexibility for inputting data and presenting it. Databases have amazing capabilities for sorting and manipulating data, well beyond that of even the most complex spreadsheet.

George wants to put together a database that contains all the statistics for every player in the National Basketball Association (NBA) for the past two years. He's primarily interested in points scored, shooting percentage, blocked shots, rebounds, and of course, position. With 360+ players active per year, that's going to be a ton of information! Imagine trying to do that on one big spreadsheet—it's just too much. Spreadsheets work well for smaller amounts of data, but when the information gets big, you need a database. Let's look at the seven main components of a database—records, fields, tables, queries, reports, forms, and key fields—and see how they help George with his monster project.

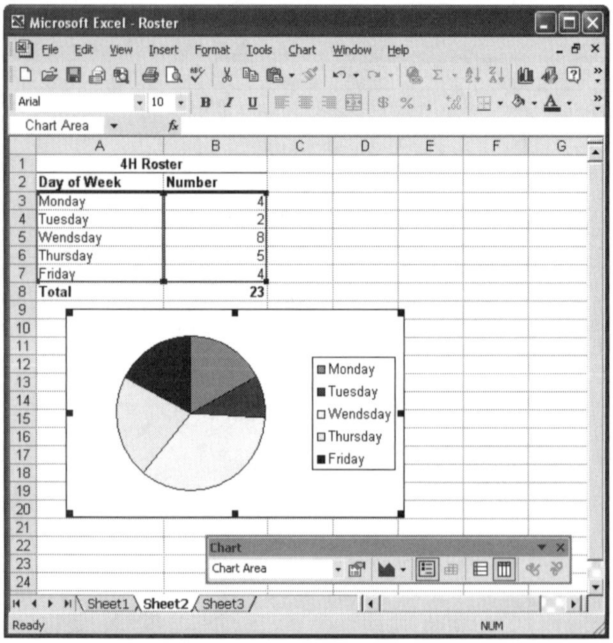

Records and Fields

At first glance, a database program looks very much like a spreadsheet with rows and columns. Even though a database program may look like a spreadsheet, it contains many powerful tools that enable you to handle huge amounts of data very quickly. To appreciate that power, you need to take your knowledge of spreadsheets and use that as a starting point to see how databases work.

In the spreadsheet described earlier, the little contact sheet contained one row per person's address. Each column contained a different value in the cell

Figure 9.24: A quick glance can show you that Tuesday is a very slow night!

such as phone number, street address, city, state, and so on. But, because each *row* contained a single person's data, those cells were linked to that person's information.

In a database, each row is called a *record*. Each individual column is a *field* (like cells in a spreadsheet). A track listing on one particular music album, a list of ingredients needed for one recipe, each player in George's database—these are examples of *records* (Figure 9.26).

Each record contains individual fields that keep *one* piece of relevant data in each field. Each player's record, for example, would have six fields—name, position, points scored, shooting percentage, blocks, and rebounds. These fields get populated with the real data of the current record.

Fields help keep the data put into a database pure because they reject data that's not the right type. When you create a database, you define all of the fields and tell the database program the type of data to expect. You tell the database program to accept only dates, numbers, text, currency—there are many other data types—to reduce errors. If George accidentally typed letters in the **Points Scored** field, for example, the database would simply reject that information, which is pretty cool (Figure 9.27).

Tables

Every database has one or more *tables* that hold records. On the surface, a table looks and acts pretty much like a spreadsheet's worksheet (Figure 9.28), although tables enable you to do some amazing things, as you'll see in a moment. Just as a spreadsheet can have multiple worksheets creating a workbook, databases can have multiple tables.

Queries

Think about this for a moment: why would anyone want to make a database? Well, you might say, "to keep track of data," and that's important, but asking the database questions is the compelling reason. "Please tell me all the NBA players who've scored more than 20 points per game. "Which players scored the most points and averaged more than 10 rebounds per game?" This is what we call in the world of database coolness, a query.

A *query*, to put it simply, is how you ask a database a question. In a spreadsheet, you *filter* the data. This hides everything else that isn't relevant to your filter. In a database, in contrast, when you perform a query on a table, the original table remains the same. The *query results* get placed in a new

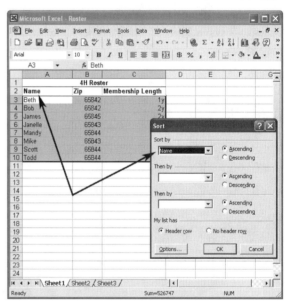

Figure 9.25: It's easy to sort by first letter in any column.

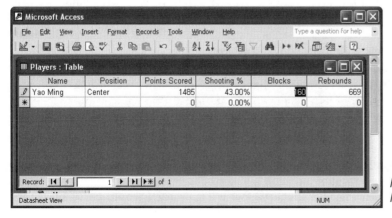

Figure 9.26: Record showing Yao Ming's stats from 2004-2005 season

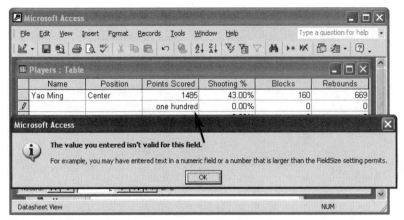

Figure 9.27: Use numbers!

Figure 9.28: A table in a database

home created especially for those results (Figure 9.29).

Reports

Reports enable you to take a query and make the results look good and read more easily (Figure 9.30). Most database software has built-in report wizards that walk you through the creation of the report. Answer a few questions; choose your query; and BAM! You can have a report printed and on the boss's desk in minutes!

Forms

A newly created database has no records, so one of the first jobs you must do after you create a database is to add data. While adding data directly into a table is fine, other folks using your database might find this hard to do. All database programs enable you to create and use forms to make data entry easier.

You know what a form is: you fill them out when you go to the dentist, apply for a loan, and do taxes. A form, then, is an aesthetically pleasing and easy way to enter information in a particular place.

When you fill out a form at the dentist, for example, those contact information placeholders are considered fields. When you finish, you give the form back to the dentist, and it gets filed away as your record. Database software works the same way (although without all that scary drill noise). You can use a form to enter data. When you finish, you click a submit button and create a record in the database table.

A well-designed form can look very nice: you can add formatting, lines you can even have a company logo on it! Just like a paper form can be designed in a certain way, so can a database form (Figure 9.31).

The Real Power: Relational Databases

If you have one table in your database, it's called a *standalone*, or *flat-file* database. George's NBA Players database has a single table with lots of data. Except for the excellent query features, his flat-file database works like a spreadsheet.

A slightly more complicated database, though, with more than one table, reveals the true power of databases. Here's the scenario. Joe's Toyota dealership sells new cars and also provides service for those cars. He needs a database that can keep track of clients and the cars they purchase, and also keep track of the servicing of those cars.

If Joes used a flat-file database for all this data, he would create massively

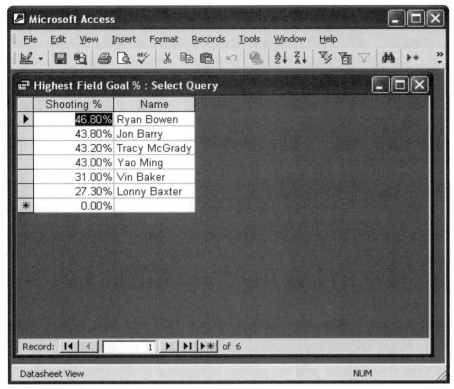

Figure 9.29: Query results

redundant information. Every time a customer brought in a car for servicing, for example, the dealership would have to enter name, address, make and model of car, vehicle number, what sort of service was required, and so on. What a waste!

A *relational database*—a database with more than one table with the tables sharing one field—makes much more sense. In Joe's case, he would need two tables. One would contain the customer information, such as name, address, car purchased, date of purchase, and the like. This is the "Customer" table. The second table contains maintenance records for each customer's car, with the vehicle identification number, type of service, date of service, and so forth—the "Maintenance" table. Each table has the car's identification number. Because the cars are linked to the customers, and the maintenance records are linked to the cars, the customers are also linked to the maintenance records. See Figure 9.32.

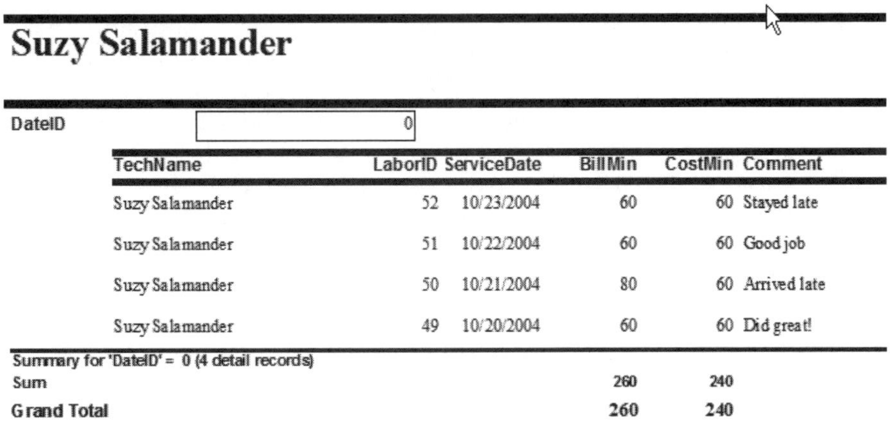

Suzy Salamander

DateID		0				
	TechName	LaborID	ServiceDate	BillMin	CostMin	Comment
	Suzy Salamander	52	10/23/2004	60	60	Stayed late
	Suzy Salamander	51	10/22/2004	60	60	Good job
	Suzy Salamander	50	10/21/2004	80	60	Arrived late
	Suzy Salamander	49	10/20/2004	60	60	Did great!

Summary for 'DateID' = 0 (4 detail records)

| Sum | | | | 260 | 240 | |
| Grand Total | | | | 260 | 240 | |

Figure 9.30: Suzy Salamander's weekly work report.

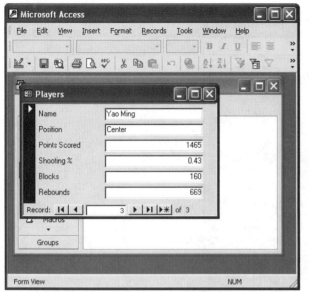

Figure 9.31: Database form for George's NBA Players

Each table in the database has the same field—the car's identification number. This field is the *key field* for each table. The key field connects the two tables together so that you can ask queries that use both tables, such as "Give me the names of all the people who brought in a Toyota Prius for repair in the last two weeks."

When you start creating many tables, all of which interact with each other in some way by their key fields, you've created a relational database. The tables are related in some way to each other.

Databases in Daily Life

How much do you interact with databases on a regular basis without realizing it? Chances are, many, many times a day. When you book a flight, the airline reservation system is really just a database in disguise! The flight number is linked to available seats. When you reserve a seat, your contact information is linked to that particular flight number. When you book a new flight, they can look up previous flights you've taken (Figure 9.33).

How about credit card transactions? Your transactions are linked to your card number, which in turn is linked to your contact information, and that's linked to a completely separate table that contains your payment history.

You can even interact with databases on a much smaller scale. They don't have to be that complex. It's easy to make a household inventory database, or even a mailing list database.

Database Programs

Database software appears in many forms in the marketplace. You'll find general purpose database programs, such as Microsoft Access, that enable you to make any sort of database you can envision (Figure 9.34). George could easily use Access to create his NBA Players database, creating tables, fields, queries, and finally, records. The completed database would be a single file with the extension *.mdb*.

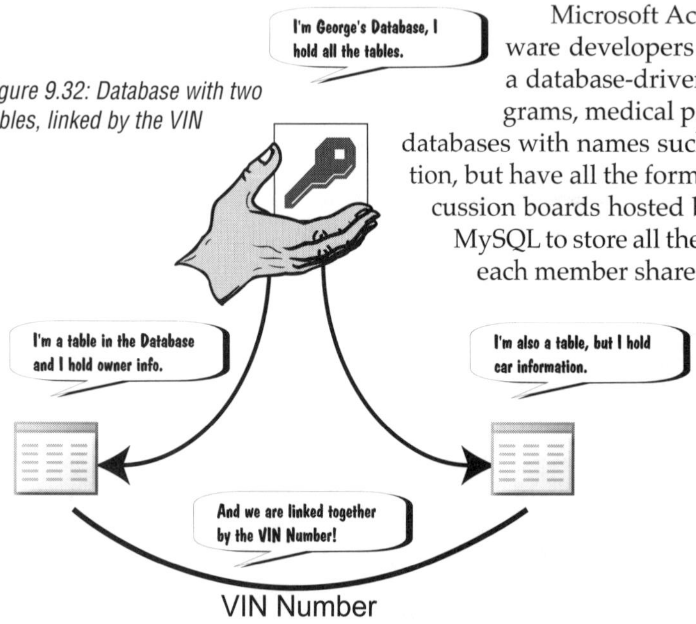

Microsoft Access is not the only database program. A lot of software developers license a specific type of database and then create a database-driven tool to sell. Inventory programs, accounting programs, medical procedure applications; any number of programs use databases with names such as Oracle or MySQL as the heart of their application, but have all the forms, queries, and such set up for you already. The discussion boards hosted by Mike Meyers' Total Seminars, for example, uses MySQL to store all the posts made by members, as well as the information each member shares about himself or herself (Figure 9.35).

The interesting thing about these repurposed database programs is that, for the most part, you never work directly with the database. You only work with the forms, tables, and queries provided by the software developer.

Figure 9.32: Database with two tables, linked by the VIN

I'm George's Database, I hold all the tables.

I'm a table in the Database and I hold owner info.

I'm also a table, but I hold car information.

And we are linked together by the VIN Number!

VIN Number

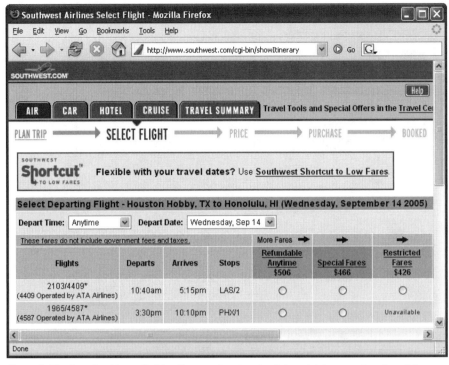

Figure 9.33: Even booking a flight online requires tapping into a database system to get the most up-to-date seat reservation information

Making Your Point– Creating Slideshows with Presentation Software

They say that giving a speech or a presentation is a powerful source of fear and apprehension in human beings. Although it won't necessarily get you through the nervousness, you can use tools to make your presentation more interesting to the audience, by using pictures projected on a big screen behind you. *Presentation software* enables you to create *slide shows* and other visual aids.

Slides

You build a full presentation by creating and putting together *slides*—documents that appear on the monitor one at a time. Each slide can contain words, bulleted lists, or pictures in any combination. A presentation can be made up of as many slides as you need for each aspect of your presentation, as you can see in Figure 9.36.

Speaker Notes

Speaker notes are little placeholders for extra text that can appear at the bottom of the slides. It's up to you whether you want them to show up or not. They can be used as an method of creating handouts for your audience, or they can also be used as cheat sheets so you don't forget anything important in the oral part of your presentation.

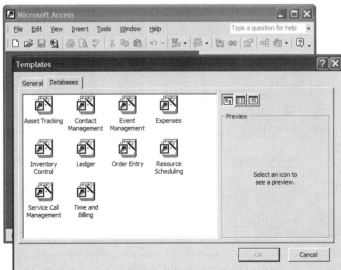

Figure 9.34: Access set to do work

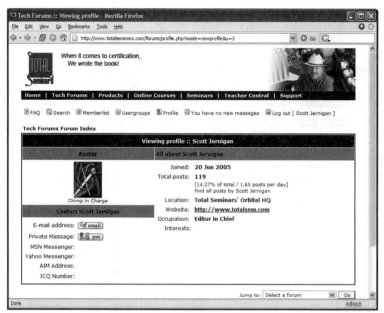

Figure 9.35: A member profile

Text (slide titles and bullet points)

The contents of the slides are obviously the meat and potatoes of any visual presentation. *Text* is a big part of a slide. Text can introduce the body of the slide by being used in outline style, including a *title* of what the points you are making are. It can also be the focus of you slide. In fact, for emphasis and clarity, it's good to include a bullet—a little black dot or some other distinguishable marker—next to the text. These are called *bullet points* (Figure 9.37).

Graphics

Graphics is really just a fancy word for images. A graphic can be a photo, illustration, icon, or even a pie chart. Even bullets are graphics, and can definitely help ease the eye strain of nothing but a large block of text.

Many people find that a nice dose of graphics (much like you've found in this book, not coincidentally) can ease eye strain, add a splash of color, and increase the aesthetics of your presentation. Oh, they can also help drive your point across, too.

Your presentation software help file can give you more information on how to insert a graphic into a slide.

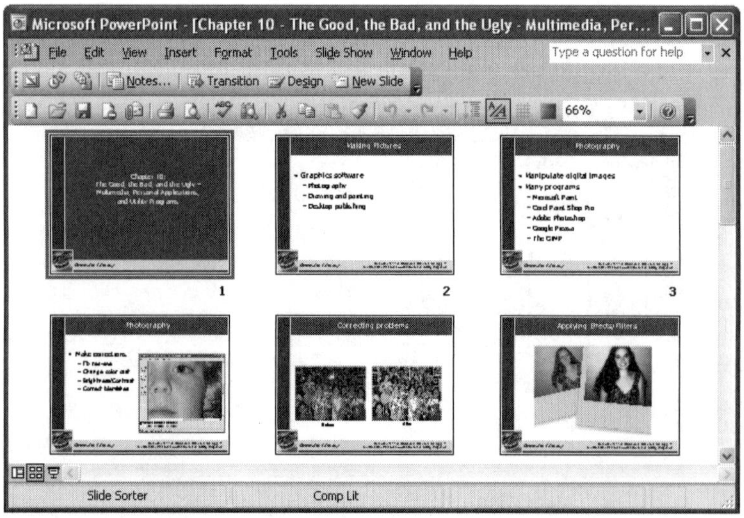

Slide Masters

What if you wanted the same graphic to appear on every slide? Or what if you wanted a copyright or company name added to the bottom or every slide?

A *slide master* is a master template of sorts, a building block slide that each new slide is based on when it's inserted into your presentation. You can insert your graphic in the spot you want, and insert any other text or design element (Figure 9.38). Any slide you create in that presentation will look like the slide master to start with, and you can make additional changes you want.

Figure 9.36: You can see an overview of all your slides.

Why?

- You'll learn a lot
- You'll have fun reading
- You get to look at nifty pictures
- Your productivity will increase
- You'll understand your computer better
- You really will have fun reading; trust me!

Figure 9.37: Bullet points with brief text next to them help emphasize your main points.

If you have to change your slide master, all the other slides will change to match. If your company name changes, for example, you only have to change it once in your presentation. This is also good if you give the same presentation a year later. You can update the copyright at the bottom of every page, and not have to redo every slide.

Giving a Presentation

Once you've created a presentation, you need to think about the delivery. How you do it depends on both your subject matter, the space where you present, and the number of people listening.

Should everyone just crowd around your computer screen? Well, if they want to, sure! When it starts to get too crowded, though, you'd better move to a larger room with a screen projector. Do they live in a different country? You can e-mail the presentation to them to watch on *their own* computers, or if you have a Web site, they can even watch your presentation online.

Your presentation software has a real presentation mode, in which the start menu disappears, and your presentation fills the entire computer screen. For small groups, it really is OK to show your presentation right on your computer. In most cases, however, presentations are made for larger groups and the accommodations must change.

Business meetings, training, conventions, formal lectures these are all examples of when your presentation needs to make its debut on—"the big screen. For these presentations, you hook your computer to a projector and display on a large screen for all to see.

Presentation Format: .PPT

A .ppt file is a Microsoft PowerPoint file, and it's the most commonly used program for presentations today. Your instructor might have a PowerPoint presentation to go along with this chapter.

Hardware Surprises

When you give a presentation, you should ask the people in charge if you need to supply the computer or if they will. In fact, ask that right away! If you supply the computer, then it really doesn't matter what piece of software you use, as the computer you create it on will be the same computer you use for the presentation. It would be horrible if you spent hours or even weeks creating a presentation in Microsoft PowerPoint, only to find that the presentation software on their computers is Apple Keynote! When you have to give a speech, who needs that kind of added stress?

Squint

Certain speakers choose to set up their slides differently. One slide per section of a speech? One slide per main point? It pretty much depends on the foundation of your presentation. Entire books dedicated to building effective presentations offer sage advice such as, "If the audience is spending too much time reading slides, they aren't paying attention to you!" (See Figure 9.39.)

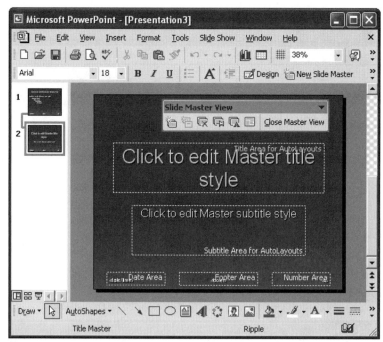

Figure 9.38: A design template on which all other slides will be based

Presentation Editing Software

While Microsoft PowerPoint is the most commonly used presentation editing software, it's definitely not the only one. There's Lotus Freelance, Corel Presentations, and Apple Keynote (for the Macintosh only).

Figure 9.39: Use this slide and watch the audience squint! Fun for the whole family!

Mincing Words – Creating Text Documents with Word Processors, Desktop Publishing, and Web Editing Software

- *Word processing* programs enable you to create documents, from as simple as notes and personal letters, to more complex designs. You can apply formatting to documents to create a nice layout that includes titles, text, and pictures.

- Any time you create a word processing item to capture data, you create a *document*. A file that is text-only does not include any graphics or special formatting, such as underlined or boldfaced text. Making changes to a document means you're editing that document. The *format* of a document is the basic structure and layout. The act of formatting, then, becomes refining your document to create a layout that presents the material the way you want it presented.

- Desktop publishing software enables you to create professional correspondence such as flyers, brochures, business cards, and stationary on your computer. Learn to love the Help menu to unlock the power of your word processing and desktop publishing software.

- Your word processor can distinguish between different types of files by looking at the file extension. A simple text-only document, for example, often ends in the extension.txt. A fancier document might end in .doc, and a Web page in .html or .htm. You can edit these documents using programs associated with those file names, such as Microsoft Word for .doc format.

Adding it Up – Making Charts, Tables and Graphs with Spreadsheet Software

- Spreadsheet software enables you to create lists with many different fields for details (such as name and address) and then sort them automatically. You can tell the software to do all sorts of math with the numbers without you having to break out a calculator.

- A spreadsheet appears like a grid of rows and columns, like an old bookkeeping ledger. Each little square—called a *cell*—can hold data. The top columns are usually labeled A-Z, and the rows are numbered starting at 1 and increasing as they go down. This makes them easy to reference. The entire page of cells as far as you can see on a spreadsheet is called a *worksheet*. It's possible to have multiple worksheets in a single spreadsheet file, this is called a *workbook*.

- Cells can contain numbers, values, text, and other content. Cells and even entire columns can be totaled, added, subtracted, multiplied, etc. Some spreadsheet software enables you to assign a category—called a *format*—to a cell, column, or row so the software would treat it in a certain fashion. You can specify cells to be "text," for example, and the software would treat numbers in those cells as words.

- You can use complex formulas and built-in functions to perform calculations on your data. Your spreadsheet software can take your data and automatically create pie charts and graphs *for* you, no programming knowledge required!

- Some common spreadsheet software includes Microsoft Excel and Corel Quattro Pro. Documents created with this software usually have the file extension of .xls and .qpw, respectively.

Everything in Its Right Place – Using Database Software

■ A database enables you to take a lot of data and manipulate it in many ways. Databases have seven basic components: records, fields, tables, queries, reports, forms, and key fields.

■ A *record* is one unit made up of multiple *fields* in a *table*. An address record, for example, would contain fields such as first name, last name, street, city, state, and ZIP code. A table can hold multiple records.

■ A *query* is an advanced way to find particular information from a database. The query results display in a document separate from the table. A form is an aesthetically pleasing and easy way to enter information in a particular place.

■ A *relational database* has two or more tables linked together by a key field. You can run queries in relational databases that gather information from more than one table.

■ Airlines, financial companies, and professional health services rely on database software to run their businesses. Chances are, you interact with their databases every day without realizing it.

■ Database software appears in many forms in the marketplace. You'll find general purpose database programs, such as Microsoft Access, that enable you to make any sort of database you can envision. You'll find software that repurposes databases such as MySQL to create database-driven tools to sell. Inventory programs, accounting programs, and medical procedure applications are examples of this type of software.

Making Your Point – Creating Slideshows with Presentation Software

■ *Presentation software* enables you to create *slide shows* and other visual aids. Slides are the basic unit of presentation software; a presentation consists of multiple slides with main points on them.

■ Bullets can do a great job of emphasizing each main point, and slides can further be categorized by a main header as part of the title of what you are emphasizing.

■ Graphics play a huge part in presentations, such as relieving eye strain in text-heavy presentations, running a photo-only slideshow, inserting charts and graphs into a sales presentation, or just adding a splash of color here and there.

■ You don't have to create each slide separately. You can add common theme elements to a single *slide master*, and every slide created after that will take on that base appearance.

■ You can have your audience crowd around your computer screen, but if there are a lot of people, you're probably better off hooking your computer up to a projector and displaying it on a screen.

Key Terms

Bullet point	Query
Cell	Query results
Database	Record
Desktop publishing	Relational database
Document	Report
Editing	Slide master
Field	Slides
Form	Spreadsheet
Format	Table
Formula	Text editor
HTML	Word processing
Key field	Workbook
Productivity software	Worksheet

Key Term Quiz

Use the Key Terms list to complete the following sentences. Not all the terms will be used.

1. Use a _____ if you need the same information repeated on multiple slides.

2. A _____ creates simple documents and does not support graphics or formatting.

3. With the aid of _____ software, you can create professional brochures and flyers from your own computer.

4. A _____ is any word processing file that you have created to hold data.

5. When you have an active letter, memo, book, or anything open to make changes to it, you are _____ it.

6. A _____ is an individual placeholder for data in a spreadsheet.

7. A collection of worksheets in a single spreadsheet file is called a _____.

8. Just like a dentist's office, a _____ holds individual field information for a single element in a database.

9. A database becomes a _____ when two or more tables are used to cross-reference data.

10. A _____ is a search method for databases.

Multiple Choice Quiz

1. Which of the following document types will a fully featured word processing document enable you to create? (Select all that apply.)
   A. Text file
   B. Web page
   C. Database table
   D. Query

2. In a spreadsheet, the cell directly below B3 is:
   A. B2
   B. A3
   C. C3
   D. B4

3. Joanne has a presentation to give to the local school board. What sort of software should she use to prepare this presentation?
   A. Database
   B. Presentation
   C. Spreadsheet
   D. Word processing

4. Which feature might help Joanne remember what she wants to say about each slide?
   A. Index
   B. Liner notes
   C. Slide show
   D. Speaker notes

5. Erica has a stack of names for a school raffle. Which of the following applications would enable her to create a list and alphabetize it easily? (Select the best answer.)
   A. Database
   B. Presentation software
   C. Spreadsheet
   D. Word processing program

6. Veronica has a database that contains entries for each of the 25 swimsuits offered at her store, CoolSurferSwimwear. What term most likely refers to each entry?
   A. Cell
   B. Field
   C. Query
   D. Record

7. What can you place on a slide in presentation software? (Select the best answer.)
   A. Text and graphics
   B. Text, graphics, and bullets
   C. Text and bullets
   D. Graphics and bullets

8. Aaron wants to turn his report on the top ten movies of all time into a Web page or series of Web pages. Bleys claims that he needs to use a dedicated Web page development program, like Microsoft FrontPage. Georgia disagrees, suggesting that he can probably make the pages from within his word processing program. (He uses Microsoft Word.) Who's right?
   A. Only Bleys is right.
   B. Only Georgia is right.
   C. Both Bleys and Georgia are right.
   D. Neither Bleys nor Georgia are right.

9. WordPerfect is an example of what sort of program?
   A. Database
   B. Presentation
   C. Spreadsheet
   D. Word processor

10. Denah hands Turk a disc with several files on it: database.ppt, fingerpuppet.ppt, and report.ppt. What kind of files are these?
    A. Database, presentation, and word processing
    B. Database, presentation, and presentation
    C. All database files
    D. All presentation files

11. Desktop publishing software can help Barret make a flyer advertising his school fund raiser.
    A. True
    B. False

12. Paul wants to organize the finances of his club. What type of software would enable him most easily to keep track of the numbers, including handling the adding and subtracting for income and expenditures automatically?
    A. Database
    B. Presentation
    C. Spreadsheet
    D. Word processor

13. What does a field do for you in a database? (Select two.)
    A. Holds one type of data
    B. Holds many types of data
    C. Rejects data of the incorrect type
    D. Accepts data of any type

14. Felicia has a ton of information to input into her database. Jill says she should use a form, but Jack says she needs to use a query. Who's right?
    A. Only Jill is right.
    B. Only Jack is right.
    C. Both Jill and Jack are right.
    D. Neither Jill nor Jack is right.

15. Which of the following businesses might use database software?
    A. Airlines
    B. Banks
    C. Car dealers
    D. All of the above

Essay Questions

1. You have a couple of new employees at your office and your boss wants you to teach them how to create a decent presentation. Write a short essay that describes the elements of a good presentation. Describe how you can balance text and graphics on a slide.

2. Write an essay describing how you might use a database in your life. Would it be based on something you collect? What fields would you use?

3. Your boss doesn't understand the difference between a regular word processing program and a desktop publishing program. Write a short essay explaining the difference and how he might use one or the other to accomplish business tasks.

Projects

1. Come up with a topic, and give a presentation on it. Bonus points for use of bullet points, graphics, and a slide master!

2. Research the history of word processing, starting with Thomas Edison patenting the typewriter and ending with the desktop publishing of today. Create a timeline. When did screens first appear? When did people start being able to use graphics in word processing documents?

The Good, the Bad, and the Ugly – Multimedia, Personal Applications, and Utility Programs

"Tut, tut. Such ingratitude after all the times I saved your life."
– Man with No Name, *The Good, the Bad, and the Ugly*

This chapter covers the following IC³ exam objectives:

- ■ IC³-1   2.2.5   Identify fundamental concepts relating to graphic and multimedia programs and common uses for graphic and multimedia software

- ■ IC³-1   2.2.6   Identify the types and purposes of different utility programs

- ■ IC³-1   2.2.7   Identify other types of software

- ■ IC³-1   2.2.8   Identify how to select the appropriate application(s) for a particular purpose, and problems that can arise if the wrong software product is used for a particular purpose

Application software enables you to accomplish a variety of things on the computer, from creating a fine illustration to running a plant producing automobiles. You read about the cornerstone products for workplace computing in Chapter 9, "Productivity Software." This chapter takes a broad look at the amazing variety of other things you can do on a computer. We'll start with graphics and multimedia applications that enable you to turn your computer into an art-producing beast. The second portion runs through applications for specific tasks, such as tools to get you on the Internet, communicating to friends and family all over the planet, keeping track of all these people, and managing your finances. The third section covers utility applications, programs essential for the well-being of the computer. We'll wrap up with a brief discussion on how to choose the right tool for the right job.

Graphics and Multimedia

Your computer can enable you to create pictures, make music, and even put together your very own movie. Why stop there? Graphics and multimedia programs can unleash the creativity inside anyone, from 8 to 80 and even beyond.

Making Pictures

Applications that help you work with static visual content—like photographs and illustrations—are generically called *graphics software*. You'll find three basic types: photography, drawing and painting, and desktop publishing. Often, tools that work in one type of graphics application work similarly in another, such as the paint brush tool for adding colored lines. As you might imagine, graphics come in a wide variety of file formats. The end of this section looks at the most common ones.

Photography

Photography applications enable you to take photos from your digital camera and change them. A simple program, such as Microsoft Paint, enables you to fix red-eye in a photo (by zooming in and painting each red dot black or gray), but that's about it (Figure 10.1). For most users, though, the simple image editing applications will quickly prove unworthy of your time, especially because many better (and free) applications are there for the asking.

Better programs, like Paint Shop Pro from Corel or Adobe Photoshop, on the other hand, enable you to manipulate a photo in many ways. You can take red-eye out of a picture, for example, and fix color, brightness, contrast, skin blemishes, bright spots, and more. You can zoom in to edit pixel by pixel, if you like! Figures 10.4 and 10.5 show before and after shots of a picture edited in Photoshop. In the before picture, the lighting is bad, there's a big reflection of the flash in the center of the image, and the little girl in the middle left has a big stain on her shirt. In the after picture, note that the flash and the stain are

Picasa

The Internet search engine giant, Google, offers one of the best, simple photography applications, called Picasa. You can use Picasa to deepen shadows and brighten highlights, or change the color cast of a photo. If you're going for a more artistic look for a picture, Picasa has a dozen or so effects you can apply, such as turning a color picture into an old-time looking black and white photo or making part of the image fuzzy (Figure 10.2). And, as a bonus, you can organize your collection of photos (Figure 10.3).

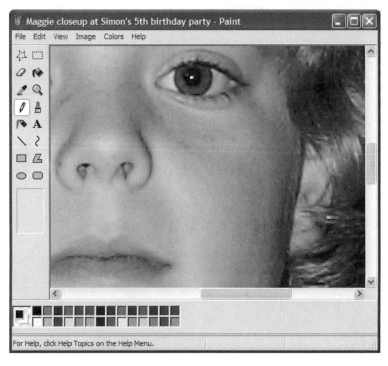

Figure 10.1: Microsoft Paint fixing red-eye

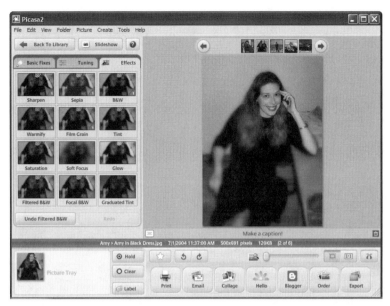

Figure 10.2: Applying effects

Figure 10.3: Picasa organizer view

gone and you can see the girls in the back.

Better photo-editing software enables you to use *filters* or *effects* to alter an image subtly or radically. Different programs use the terms differently, but the end results are similar. For example, you can apply artistic effects or filters, such as turning a portion of a photo into what appears to be a drawing done with pencil. You can add a drop shadow to an image to give it some depth. You've seen that technique used in many of the photographs (not illustrations) in this book! Figure 10.6 shows a collage effect that displays the power of filters. The left image is the original; the right image shows the Diffuse Glow filter in Photoshop used to transform the girl pictured from normal to Saturday Night Live host-style soft focus and high contrast.

Ansel Adams Inside

Digital cameras have dramatically dropped in price and gone up in features and quality over the past few years, so people have begun to photograph their lives like no previous generation has ever done. You don't have to go through the hassle and cost of printing a whole roll of film, for example, just to see whether or not you got that great picture of Cousin Jenny falling into the fountain at Disney World. You can review your pictures right away, and push her back in if you need to re-shoot!

Perhaps more importantly for this discussion, digital camera folks publish these photos on the Internet almost as fast as they can get home and connect. And that's a bad thing, because most pictures need some editing before they're ready for publication, even in a family photo album on the Web. Learning a photography application like Picasa or the more fully-featured Photoshop can turn your photos from mediocre to the envy of your family and friends.

Figure 10.4: Before

Figure 10.5: After

Illustration

With drawing and painting programs, you can create art from scratch, just as you would in an art studio with pen and paper or paint and canvas. A new drawing starts with a plain white background, and it's up to you to fill in the rest. You can add images, text, lines, or your own hand-drawn artwork. Simple programs—and again, we'll pick on Microsoft Paint—give you a limited number of tools and thus a limit to what you can accomplish.

Better programs, such as Adobe Illustrator, give you a set of tools Pablo Picasso would have envied and, once you've hurdled the learning curve, give you the capability to create almost any kind of illustration. We produced the illustrations you've seen in this book so far in Illustrator, but they don't even scratch the surface of what you can do with the program. Figure 10.7 shows a picture drawn entirely in Illustrator.

Figure 10.6: From regular person to SNL host

Desktop Publishing

Images you produce can remain as standalone art, designed for the screen or for printing and framing. Or, you can repurpose your art, putting it into other documents to create banners that catch the eye, ads that open the wallet, or calendars that grace the wall. *Desktop publishing applications*, such as Microsoft Publisher, come with built-in templates of popular items such as flyers, business cards, and invitations. You can easily customize your creation by using images you've created, whether photographs or illustrations. Figure 10.8 shows a brochure that uses a picture that might look familiar…

Paint Me!

*Enough talk, let's do something. If you have a Windows computer handy, go to **Start** | **All Programs** | **Accessories** and click on the **Paint** icon. Once you have it open, paint something. See if you can open up a photograph in the program. What sorts of adjustments can you make to the picture? If you have a Macintosh, go to the **Dock** and select **iPhoto**. In iPhoto, open an image (you should see thumbnails—small versions—of all the images iPhoto knows about on your drive). What kind of edits can you make to the picture?*

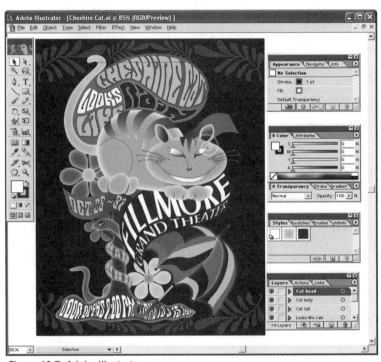

Figure 10.7: Adobe Illustrator

Tools of the Trade

Many graphics programs use similar tools, which enables you to jump from one into another with a minimal learning curve. Most have *paint brush* and *pencil tools*, for example, that you can use to paint or draw lines in multiple colors (Figure 10.9). Figure 10.10 shows a slightly fancier paint brush tool in Photoshop.

Illustration programs in particular seem to have the same basic set of tools. Almost every application has line, curve, shape, and fill tools.

The *line tool* enables you to draw or paint a straight line. Select the line tool and click a single point in your drawing. By clicking on another point in the same drawing immediately afterward, a beautiful straight line will appear in between the placement of the first click to the second click (Figure 10.11).

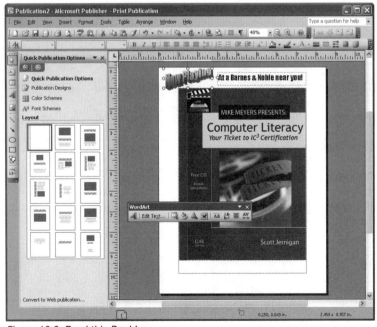

Figure 10.8: Read this Book!

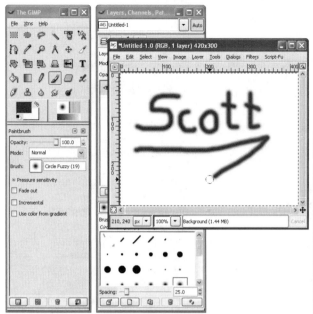

Figure 10.9: Brush tool in the GIMP

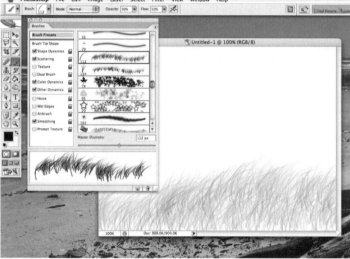

Figure 10.10: Paint brush tool in Photoshop

The *curve tool* creates curved lines and edges, depending on how you shape it with your mouse (Figure 10.12). Simple programs such as Paint enable you to create the line and then adjust it a couple of times. Better programs, such as Illustrator, let you tweak till your heart's content.

Most graphics and desktop publishing programs have various *shape tools* that you can use to make squares, circles, and many other shapes. With the *circle tool*, for example, you can click on a point in your drawing and drag the mouse outwards while holding down the left button. Poof! You've drawn a circle (Figure 10.13).

Finally, every program has some sort of *fill tool* that you can use to pour a color or a texture into a selected area in your drawing or photo. This is especially useful for filling shapes. Draw an ellipse, for example, select the fill tool, choose a color, and then click in the section to fill it (Figure 10.14).

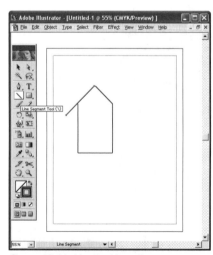

Figure 10.11: Line tool in action

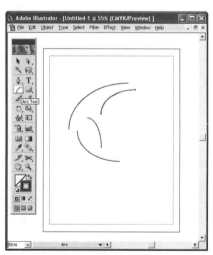

Figure 10.12: Curve tool in action

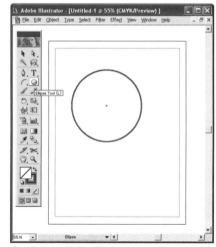

Figure 10.13: Circle (Ellipse) Tool in action

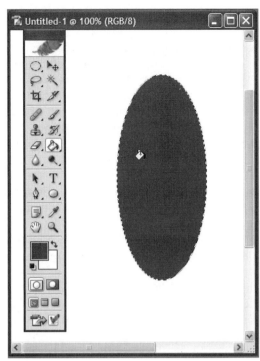

Figure 10.14: Filled ellipse

With the better programs, you can readily create amazing works of art using these many tools. Although it's also astonishingly easy to go way out of control (Figure 10.15)!

Media

You can save images in many different formats, and each format offers certain advantages over others. Selecting the correct format for what you're trying to accomplish is a good thing. The most common file formats are BMP, JPEG, GIF, and TIFF.

Bitmap (*BMP*) format offers you the cleanest and clearest format for saving an image. When you save a file as a BMP file, the file retains all the information about that image, including full color details. As you might imagine, the file size will be the biggest of all the common formats. Figure 10.16 shows an image saved with a .bmp extension, the default image format for Microsoft Windows.

JPEG format compresses the image, making the final file size much smaller than a comparable BMP file. Most images you see on the Internet, for example, are saved as JPEG files, with the extension of *.jpeg* or *.jpg*. (Both are pronounced "jay-peg.") Most digital cameras automatically save files in JPEG format.

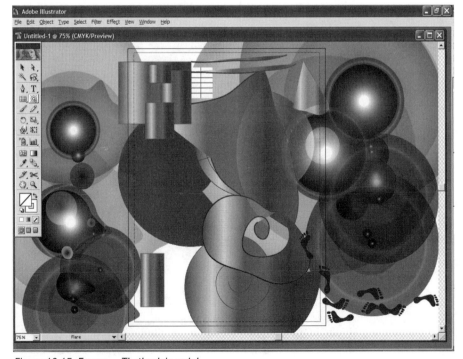

Figure 10.15: Ewww… That's plain ugly!

Figure 10.16: Bitmap file

To compress the image and save as a JPEG, however, forces the graphics program or camera to delete some of the color and other image information. For pictures on your computer screen, this won't matter. For pictures you print, on the other hand, JPEG format can create all sorts of weird visual effects, called *artifacts*, that diminish the quality of your photo. Figure 10.17 shows the same image as Figure 10.16, but saved as a JPEG file and zoomed in so you can see the problem areas. Both images, by the way, looked pretty much the same on my computer monitor!

GIF format—pronounced with a hard "g" sound—offers something of a compromise between BMP and JPEG. Images stored in this format lose no quality information, but they drop color and shades of gray information. A plain image will look great as a GIF, but a complex photograph will look horrible. Figure 10.18 shows the same image as above, but saved as a GIF, with, as you might expect, a file extension of *.gif*.

TIFF format saves all color and image quality information and offers the best format for images you want to print. Higher-end digital cameras often feature TIFF format as an option. Because they retain all the information about photos, though, TIFF files are just about as big as BMP files. Graphics programs on any operating system can view TIFF files, and the files usually end in *.tif*.

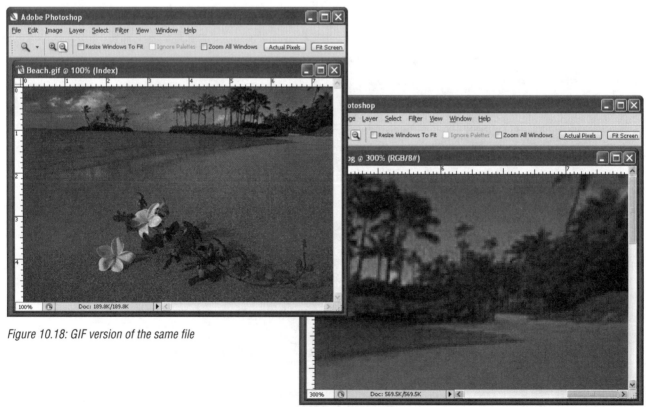

Figure 10.18: GIF version of the same file

Figure 10.17: JPEG file

Making Music

Most multimedia presentations involve sound as well as pictures, so it's a good thing that your computer enables you to create and edit sound like you owned your own recording studio. With *music editing software* you can import songs from your CD collection or from old vinyl LPs. You can record yourself singing or playing an instrument. You can even create full, multi-track recordings with voice, instruments, and more.

Simpler programs, like Sound Recorder that Microsoft bundles with Windows, offer quick and efficient recording capabilities, but have limits on what you can do with the music. You can record, change volume and speed of the recording, and throw in an echo effect for fun, but that's about it (Figure 10.19).

Figure 10.19: Sound Recorder in action

More advanced programs, such as Adobe Audition or Sony Sound Forge, give you all the tools you could imagine—*and then some*—to master a complete, professional music CD or sound track to a video. Just to give you an idea of the level of control you can have over your music, here's an example. Josh had a collection of old vinyl records from the 1960s, including an original copy of the Doors first album. As you might imagine, you could hear a whole bunch of clicks and pops when the album was played on a record player. Josh hooked up a stereo to his computer, opened Audition, and recorded the album into his PC, one track at a time. Using a single tool in Audition, he was able to isolate and remove all the clicks and pops from the recordings, *without losing any other sounds* (Figure 10.20). It's as if Jim Morrison and the Doors recorded the tracks digitally in 2005, not on tape in 1967.

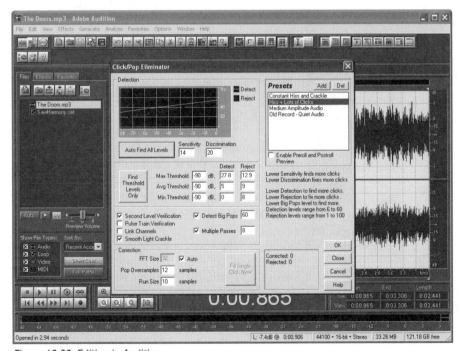

Figure 10.20: Editing in Audition

Acronyms and Initials

*Just in case you wanted to know, BMP simply refers to the .bmp file extension of bitmapped images, but JPEG, GIF, and TIFF are all acronyms. JPEG stands for **Joint Photographic Experts Group**, the folks who created the standard. GIF weighs in with **graphics interchange format**, and TIFF is short for **tagged image file format**. Now you see why we use the acronyms?!*

*Audio editing software gets very complex, very quickly. If you get interested in these programs and download a copy of Adobe Audition (Adobe offers a 30-day trial version for free at www. adobe.com), be patient with yourself. Try some of the simpler tools first, like **Normalize**—for changing the overall volume of the recording—and spend some time with the online tutorials and help files.*

WAV Files

Microsoft created the *WAV* format as the default audio format for its operating systems. (Add a mental "e" to the end for the pronunciation: "wave.") All those little dings you hear when various things happen on your computer (including starting up and shutting down) are WAV files, saved with the extension of .wav. The WAV format does not compress or delete any audio content, so offers the best format for recording. If you and your band wanted to create a music CD, for example, you would want to record and save in WAV format. Because WAV files are not compressed, the file size for a typical three-minute song would be pretty huge, like 30 MB.

MP3 files

The *Fraunhofer IIS ISO-MPEG Audio Layer-3* format—just call it *MP3*, like everyone else—offers amazing levels of compression with very minor lowering of quality. (Most people can't tell the difference at all between an MP3 file and a CD-quality version of the same song.) You can take a three-minute WAV file and drop it to under 3 MB! MP3 has become the *de facto* standard for music traded over the Internet.

Video Killed the Radio Star

At its finest, multimedia involves pictures and sound, and moving pictures provide the most bang for the buck. Digital video cameras (camcorders) and some digital cameras offer a reasonably-priced way for you to take movies and import them into your computer. Just like you shouldn't put a photograph online without editing it first, you shouldn't subject your family and friends to your homemade movies without editing either!

Both Windows and Macintosh come with *video-editing software* that enables you to do simple edits to your raw footage and add some nice transitions between scenes. Windows Movie Maker has a *storyboard*, for example, where you can drag clips, define transitions, even add a title page (Figure 10.21). You can import an audio track—newly created in your music editing software—to provide background music (Figure 10.22). When you finish, you'll have a product that your people can enjoy a lot more than they ever would have enjoyed the raw footage!

Just as you discovered with graphics and audio editing programs, you can readily find more feature-rich and powerful programs for video editing. Final Cut Pro from Apple, for example, enables you to edit—on the fly—real-time high definition video from up to 16 different sources. Plus you can add up to 24 channels of high resolution audio. And it has a host of editing tools that,

Figure 10.21: Movie Maker with Storyboard showing

Figure 10.22: Importing an MP3 file

once you've mastered them, give you the power to create seriously professional-grade videos.

In between the extremes, Pinnacle makes excellent and not-too-pricey products that give you professional-level tools with a user-friendly interface. Figure 10.23 shows a movie being made in Pinnacle Studio Plus—it's drag and drop and you can edit every segment.

Video for Windows

Microsoft's *Video for Windows* offers an uncompressed format for full motion and sound video files. Files saved in this format have the extension of .avi, so you'll hear them referred to primarily as *AVI* files. The lack of compression makes for great, clear movies, but, as with BMP and WAV files, they will be bigger in size that any movie saved in one of the other formats.

QuickTime

Apple designed *QuickTime* format to make it easy to watch movies over the Internet, but the format has evolved into a general format for movies, animation, and music files. QuickTime offers control over the level of compression used, so you can tailor your movie for the desired audience (uncompressed for going onto a DVD, for example, and highly compressed for general viewing over the Internet). QuickTime files are saved with the file extension .mov.

Personal Applications

Certain applications enable you to handle essential tasks that involve you personally. You can get software programs that help you communicate over the Internet, keep track of friends and family, and manage your money. What I call *personal applications*—not an industry-standard term—enable you to survive and flourish in the modern world.

Reach Out and Touch Someone

The Internet connects computers and networks all over the world. You can use this vast network for many purposes, from accessing information you need right now from a Web site to sending electronic messages to your friends and family, or even to people you don't even know. Two types of applications handle the majority of the personal tasks on the Internet, Web browsers and e-mail applications.

Web Browsers

A *Web browser* provides a method to "browse" Internet pages all over the World Wide Web. Two programs dominate the market, Microsoft Internet Explorer and Mozilla Firefox. In a nutshell, programmers create Web pages that have graphics and text, collect them together into a Web site, and then put them onto a special computer called a Web server (Figure 10.24).

Each Web server gets a special name, called a *Uniform Resource Locator (URL)*, that you can use to locate it. Although not required, you'll generally find a Web server's address written out like www.microsoft.com or www.bbc.

The Ever-evolving World of Video Standards
Creative programmers try to make better standards for viewing full motion videos, especially on how the videos compress. These standards seek to balance file size and quality, and sometimes control to try to stop piracy of content. The most common formats are MPEG, Real Video, and Windows Media. Files saved in these formats get the extensions .mpg or .mpeg, .rv, and .vbr, respectively. For more information on these and other formats, check out www.webopaedia.com.

Figure 10.23: Pinnacle Studio Plus

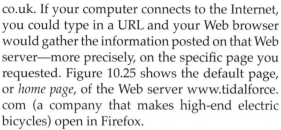

Figure 10.24: Web server holds a Web site

I'm a Web Server, I hold Web pages and serve them up when you need them.

co.uk. If your computer connects to the Internet, you could type in a URL and your Web browser would gather the information posted on that Web server—more precisely, on the specific page you requested. Figure 10.25 shows the default page, or *home page*, of the Web server www.tidalforce.com (a company that makes high-end electric bicycles) open in Firefox.

By simply using your mouse pointer to click on links on a Web page, you can open another page in that same Web server (Figure 10.26) or go off to another Web server altogether. If you know the URL you want, you can simply type that in, press **[Enter]** on your keyboard, and off you go (Figure 10.27).

E-mail Applications

Electronic mail (*e-mail*) applications enable you to send letters, notes, pictures, and other files to recipients on the Internet. To make it work, you need a valid e-mail address, an e-mail application, and the e-mail address of the intended recipient. Using e-mail is similar to writing a letter to a house address, or calling someone on the phone, because a house or phone line has a unique way to identify it from any other house or phone number. The phone number is mapped to a person, and when you dial the number, the matching telephone rings. Some popular e-mail programs are Microsoft Outlook Express and Mozilla Thunderbird (Figure 10.29).

Figure 10.25: Home page for www.tidalforce.com

Figure 10.26: Another page in the TidalForce Web site

Get chatty with Instant Messaging

E-mail will send a message to a server fairly quickly, but there's no guarantee that the final recipient will *read* it instantly. In fact, you may never know when or if he or she even reads it. *Instant messaging* (or IM'ing, for short), in contrast, is a way to send a brief text message instantly across the Internet *directly* onto another user's computer screen and into his or her line of sight.

The two people must be using the same IM client, such as Microsoft Messenger, AOL's Instant Messenger, or Mirabilis' ICQ. You can build a contact list of your friends or colleagues, and the software will tell you when they are online.

COMPUTER LITERACY: YOUR TICKET TO IC³ CERTIFICATION

Figure 10.27: Art car picture page in an album on the Webshots Web server

Web Authoring Programs

Web page authors generally use specialized programs to create their pages. Microsoft FrontPage and Macromedia Dreamweaver, for example, give you tools designed to accomplish typical Web page-building tasks, such as adding and positioning images and text (Figure 10.28).

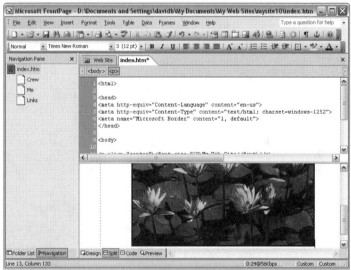

Figure 10.28: Building a Web page in FrontPage

Figure 10.29: Composing an e-mail message in Mozilla Thunderbird

Connecting to the Internet

You've seen the Internet and networks before, way back in Chapter 1,"Field Guide to Computers in the Wild." (And, for that matter, you'll see it in a lot more detail in the third section of this book!) For now, turn back to Chapter 1 and see if you can answer these questions. How do computers connect in a LAN? What sorts of hardware or software do you need? What about a WAN?

E-mail Addresses

An e-mail address is categorized by having a unique identifier followed by an '@' symbol (pronounced at), and then the domain, or the particular network that the e-mail address resides on. (This last bit can be analogous to the area code of a phone number... it's possible to identify what location you are calling by knowing the three-digit area code. Area code 212, for example, is New York City. An e-mail address whose domain ends in "@aol.com" resides on the America Online network.)

Get Organized

With all these options for interacting with people and places, most folks turn to organizational software to keep track of the important details. Some programs enable you to manage all the addresses and contact information for your friends, family, and business acquaintances. But personal organization means managing your budget, as well, so you don't do something not-very-fun like run out of money for food before you get your next paycheck.

Contact Management Software

Friends, workmates, business associates, your mom, sister, and cousin are, in computer speak, *contacts*. Each of these contacts has a lot of information associated with them: name, phone number, e-mail address, company name, and so on. Get enough of these people in your posse and you've got a huge amount of data to try to keep track of. *Contact management software* acts like a finely focused database just for handling these details. Figure 10.30 shows a typical entry in the contact management portion of Microsoft Outlook.

The computer industry often lumps programs like Outlook and Act! by Best Software into the category of *personal information manager* (PIM), which goes a bit beyond just contact management. PIMs take all the information that might come across your desk on a daily basis, and organize it for you on your computer. It can keep track of all your contacts, who you've talked to recently, and you need to follow up with. A PIM can keep track of your schedule, and even keep lists of tasks you have to do. You've seen one of the more commonly used PIMs before in discussions about personal digital assistants (PDAs), like the Palm Zire 71 shown in Figure 10.31.

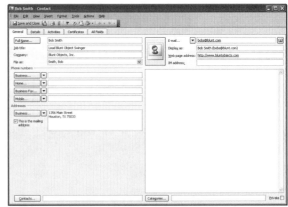

Figure 10.30: E-mail me! We'll do lunch.

Financial Software

"Sorry, I can't go out tonight, I'm balancing my checkbook." Have you heard it before? It's a classic. It's right up there with "I'm washing my hair" or "I'm editing my contact list on my PDA." Might be true, but it leads to a dull Friday night!

Software can certainly help with the balancing of the checkbook. Applications like Microsoft Money or Intuit's Quicken can help you manage your personal finances so you can *spend* your money on Friday nights instead of being stuck *managing* it. These software titles usually include a checkbook register already in them. Payments are added against the starting balance in your bank account, while the program subtracts the debits and checks you write, and the software does the math (Figure 10.32).

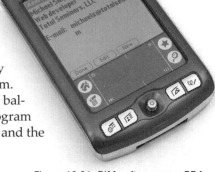

Figure 10.31: PIM software on a PDA

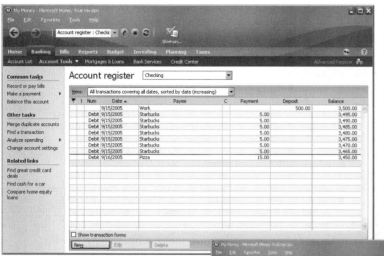

Figure 10.32: Checkbook feature

While it's definitely not mandatory for using the software, it's also possible to go online and sync the software with a bank account, meaning even *less* work and interaction is required to keep things flowing smoothly. The software can issue a warning when your balance falls below a certain number (Figure 10.33); it can send reminders when bills are due; it can even pay bills directly for you.

Figure 10.33: Minimum balance setting

Better Living through Games

All work and no play make Jack a dull boy. Computer applications aren't all about productivity and spreadsheets and financial software and work and checkbook balancing.

Whatever happened to good old fashioned *recreation*? Games for the computer come in many different genres, from simple card games to fast-paced action games. Your operating system probably comes with a few standard games, like Solitaire or Pinball. What kinds of games do you like? There are racing games that simulate conditions on the greatest tracks in the world, with realistic graphics and motion in fine automobiles (Figure 10.34). You can find one-player adventure games that require you to explore, solve puzzles, investigate clues, and put it all together to win (Figure 10.35).

Perhaps you prefer short, quick games that you can play in a matter of minutes if you have some time to kill? Online sites like **Pogo** (www.pogo.com) or **MSN Zone** (zone.msn.com) offer unique games as well as classic card games that you can play by yourself, with a friend, or meet new people on the site and play with them (Figure 10.36).

Games like **DOOM** and **Wolfenstein 3D** introduced a term called *first person shooter* (FPS) games. In these games, you see the world through the character's eyes, and usually there's combat involved. You can play some by yourself; others require you to be online, playing against other humans. Figure 10.37 shows one of the best FPSs out there, Half-Life 2.

In addition, there's a whole other world online. Literally! Here's an acronym for you: *MMORPG*. Massive Multiplayer Online Role Playing Game.

Figure 10.34: NASCAR SimRacing
(Screenshot courtesy of EA Sports)

Figure 10.35: Tomb Raider

Figure 10.36: Pyramids at Yahoo! Games

Figure 10.37: Half-Life 2

Games such as Sony **EverQuest** or Blizzard Entertainment's **World of Warcraft** charge a monthly fee to create a character online, and "live" in a world online where you can meet other people playing characters. It's possible to go on quests with them, fight with them, make friends, and make a character that can do all sorts of cool stuff that *you* can't.

Utilities You Can't Live Without

Utility programs handle specific tasks on your computer that lie outside the primary scope of an operating system, such as protecting your computer against Internet-borne viruses. Utility programs only indirectly help your productivity—you can't work efficiently if your computer functions poorly, after all. You can't write a letter with an anti-virus program or crunch numbers with a program that backs up your files. But your computer requires all sorts of utility programs to keep running smoothly. This section looks at three types of software: file and disk compression, anti-virus, and backup utilities.

Read Reviews

Finding the right game for your tastes often proves a challenge. And with the average price for a new game hovering in the $40-50 US price range, guessing whether a game is any good or not can get expensive quickly! Most gamers read reviews of games before they buy them. GameSpot (www.gamespot. com) has information about most games, new and old, organized by categories so you can find one that interests you. It has reviews, patches (if you run into problems), and gaming news. So, if you have a computer hooked up to the Internet, surf on over and check it out. What looks like fun?

If you find a game that looks promising, look for a demonstration copy for downloading. If you have the time, download and install the demo. How well does it work?

File and Disk Compression Programs

File and disk compression programs help you maintain the maximum possible space on your hard drive and send files over networks (like the Internet) efficiently. As you know from earlier chapters, compression software does what it sounds like—squeezes every possible character, space, or pixel out of a file to make it smaller in file size. A good analogy for how this works is a jar full of rocks. All those spaces in the jar that the irregular shape of the rocks can't fill could be compressible data if the jar could be shrunk to fit (Figure 10.38).

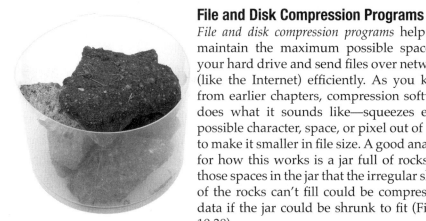

Figure 10.38: Jar of rocks – what a bunch of wasted space!

Windows XP has a compression utility built in, the Compressed (zipped) Folders program. **Right-click** a file or folder and select **Send to: | Compressed (zipped) Folder**. The utility grabs the file or folder, squishes it, and copies the contents to a new folder with a .zip file extension (Figure 10.39).

The newly compressed folder should appear in the same folder as the original file or folder, right alongside the original. You'll hear these compressed folders referred to as *zipped* or *archived* folders, and they're distinguished by a little zipper over the standard folder icon (Figure 10.40). If you change the view of the folder from Icons (the default) to Details, you should note that the compressed file is smaller than

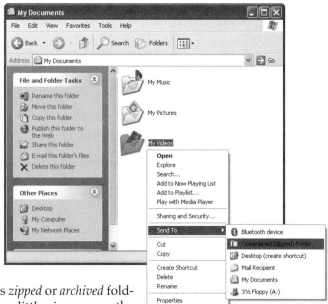

Figure 10.39: Creating a zipped file

Compression programs create a compressed "wrapper" folder around files and folders. You never see a compressed file by itself, in other words, only files within compressed folders. But most computer people still call them compressed files. Get it?

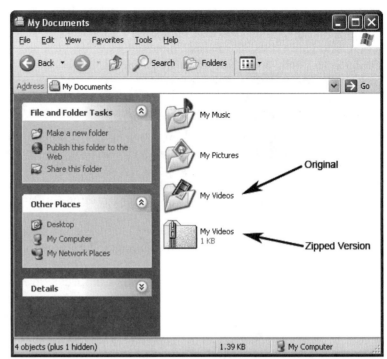

Figure 10.40: Zipped folder and uncompressed original

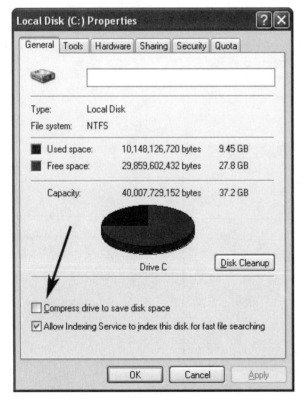

Figure 10.41: Compress drive option

the original.

You can put multiple files into a single zipped folder, which makes a great way to send things to people. Nobody likes to get an e-mail with fifteen attached files; putting all into a single zipped folder makes it convenient for everyone. To add more files to an archived folder in Windows, simply drag and drop the files you want to add onto the zipped folder in My Computer.

Although you can compress whole drives, you should avoid such actions when possible. Every time you needed to access a file on that drive, your computer would have to decompress the file before it could load into RAM. Drive compression can bring even a fast computer to its knees in very short order. That said, if you're in a very tough spot and desperate for drive space, then compression could be an option. To do it in Windows is simply a matter of opening My Computer, right-clicking on the drive you want to compress, and selecting Properties. The Drive Properties dialog box has an option to compress the whole drive (Figure 10.41).

Anti-Virus Programs

In this day and age, you need some sort of virus protection on your computer. A computer *virus* is a special kind of program, written by misguided or evil programmers. They do nothing good for you, but rather often attack your computer, deleting important files or crashing your entire system. Most users set up their *anti-virus program* to run constantly in the background, acting as a watchdog, monitoring the files that go in and out of their computers.

If you download a file over the Internet or get an e-mail with an attached file, your anti-virus program will scan the contents of the file looking for virus-like characteristics. It will scan the file against a list of symptoms in a *definition*

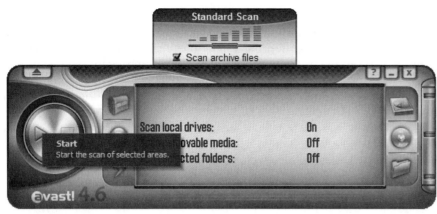

Figure 10.42: Avast! anti-virus software

Zip It Good

Knowing how to zip and unzip files and folders serves you well in the Internet Age, for quite a few reasons. You'll learn some a lot more about this in the third portion of this book, "Living Online," but here's a quick foreshadow.

You can use a digital camera to take a photograph that you can download into your computer. You can then turn around and send that picture to someone over the Internet. No problems here, but if you send a file that's too big, you can cause problems, either for yourself or your friend. Imagine trying to stuff a package through a regular postal mail slot that's so bulky or so big that it gets stuck and nothing else will go in and out. That's essentially what you can do by sending a file that's too big.

Learning how to zip your files helps avoid such problems. You'll be perceived as a more thoughtful and courteous user, plus your friend will actually get your file!

file—a list of known viruses and virus qualities—it has. If it comes up with a match, it will alert you that the file contains a virus. When you send an e-mail out, or even access a file off a floppy disk, your anti-virus software will check it first and make sure it's okay and virus free.

New viruses are written and discovered on a daily basis. If your anti-virus program kept the same definition file, your computer would never be protected against any *new* viruses, just the old ones it already knows about. All good anti-virus software updates itself if you have a connection to the Internet. That way you'll be protected with up-to-the-day definition files.

Some common anti-virus programs are **Norton AntiVirus**, and **McAfee VirusScan**. You can download others as well. Though some are free, most anti-virus programs will want you to pay each year (or every six months) to renew your subscription – the fee for getting the most current definition files. For personal use, I use Avast! from Alwil Software (Figure 10.42). It's free and updated frequently. Plus they don't try to sell you other programs that you most likely don't need.

Backup

At some point, something's going to get through and take out your computer, whether it's a virus or simply some horribly written program that you install. It's honestly just a matter of time. That's why all smart computer users back up their important data on a regular basis.

A *backup utility* makes it easy for you to select and back up your data. You can back up your personal files, such as documents stored in My Computer, your OS files (often called the system state files), or even the entire hard drive. If your system goes down, you can run the software and restore the lost or damaged data.

Most OSs have a backup utility built in, but third-party software can give you a lot more features and ease of use. Microsoft's Backup can grab your data at scheduled times, but it won't write it to a CD- or DVD-media disc. For something that obviously useful, you can turn to the oddly-named-but-still-useful Alohabob PC Backup from Eisenworld or the ever-popular Backup MyPC from StompSoft (Figure 10.43).

Figure 10.43: Backup MyPC

Figure 10.44: Unedited photo of earrings

The Right Tool for the Job

Over the past few chapters, you've learned about a ton of programs that enable you to do everything from writing a note to recording your first hit single. In quite a few cases, you can find overlap in the capabilities of two separate types of programs. Both Microsoft Paint and Adobe Photoshop enable you to make changes to a photograph, for example, but which tool is the right one for the specific job at hand?

Figure 10.44 shows a picture of some earrings that needs some loving. The background is uneven and gray. You could open this picture in Paint, click on the Brush tool, select the color white from the palate, and then zoom in and color the background white (Figure 10.45). Assuming you had a steady enough hand and could do the edges around the earrings, you might get the job done in a couple of very tedious hours.

Using the right tool, however, can make the process almost immediate. Adobe Photoshop and other good image editing programs have tools that make gray backgrounds white *with a couple of clicks of the mouse*. Done. See Figure 10.46.

Using the wrong program for a job can create a lot of problems. First, you'll lose time; sometimes a lot of time. Second, the wrong tool can make getting the job done much harder, which leads to frustration, irritation, and worse. Third, you might get hours into a project and then realize you have a tool that simply cannot do what you want to do. Then you've wasted time, gained frustration, and you have nothing to show for it.

Misha got elected treasurer of her club and thus must keep track of the club finances, checking account, and so forth. When she gets the books, though, she finds a total mess. Her first job, therefore, is to write a list of all the checks used, enter in a starting balance, and then subtract and add funds as they went out or came in. What program should she use?

She can create a basic table of items and numbers in a word processor or desktop publishing software. The latter might be very good if she wanted to create a printed report for other club members. Tables and rows and columns in a word processor *looks* kind of like a checkbook register (Figure 10.47). If Misha spent the hours inputting data into it, she might find that she can't do *anything* with it once it's there. No calculations, no addition, no nothing.

Wouldn't it make a lot more sense if Misha used spreadsheet software to create the books? That way she could have the program do all the math for her, on the fly, even allowing her to go back and make changes (Figure 10.48). For that matter, if she wanted to get the job done and have a nice report to hand out afterward, she could use a database program or even a dedicated personal finance application. Choosing the right application can make all the difference in getting your project done in a timely fashion and with a minimum of teeth gnashing and hair pulling. As Yoda might have said, "Choose wisely, you must."

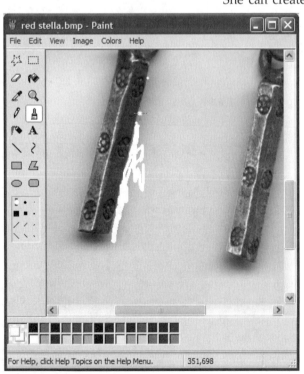

Figure 10.45: Using the Brush tool in Paint to replace the gray, uneven background with white.

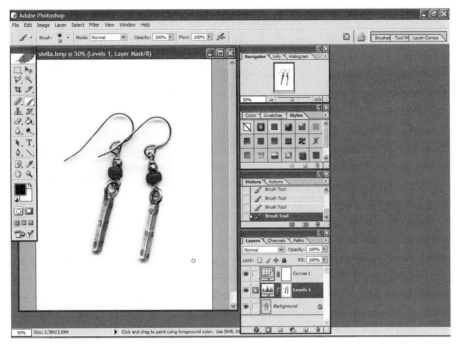

Figure 10.46: Final image in Photoshop

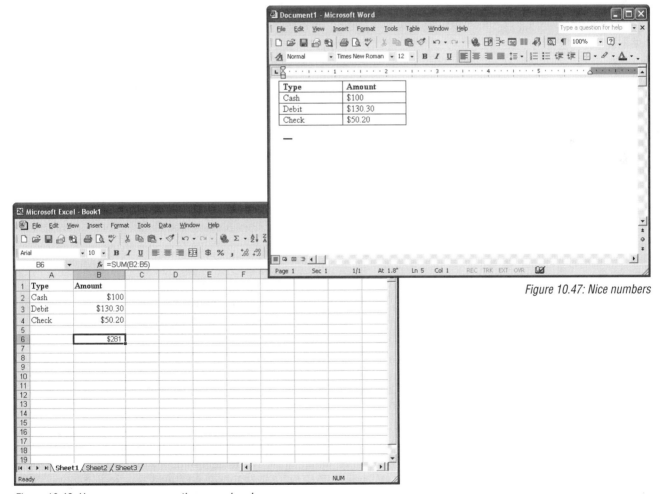

Figure 10.47: Nice numbers

Figure 10.48: Hey, now you can use those numbers!

Graphics and Multimedia

- Graphics and multimedia programs enable people to express their creativity in many ways. From digital photographs and illustrations, to recording music and making movies, these applications touch a basic human chord.

- You can use graphics software to work with static visual content (a fancy way of saying *pictures*). Photography applications, like Adobe Photoshop, enable you to make adjustments to the color, lighting, composition, and more, of digital photographs. Drawing and painting programs, such as Adobe Illustrator, can turn your computer into the electrical equivalent of a sketch pad and pen or a canvas and easel. Finally, desktop publishing programs offer lots of built in templates for creating professional-looking brochures, flyers, business cards, and invitations.

- Many graphics programs use similar tools, which enables you to jump from one into another with a minimal learning curve. Most have *paint brush* and *pencil tools*, for example, that you can use to paint or draw lines in multiple colors The *line tool* enables you to draw or paint a straight line; the curve tool, as you might imagine, enables you to draw curved lines. Other tools you might encounter are the circle, shape, and fill tools.

- There's about a gazillion file formats for saving a graphic file, but the most common are bitmap, JPEG, GIF, and TIFF. Bitmap files offer high resolution, but the lack of compression means you get big files. JPEG files can be compressed a lot and thus work well on the Internet, but you lose some picture quality, an issue in printing images. GIF offers lossless compression, but with only a limited number of colors. TIFF offers decent compression with no loss of quality or color, so makes the best option for printing images.

- Music editing software like Adobe Audition enables you to import songs from your CD collection or from old vinyl LPs. You can record yourself singing or playing an instrument. Two formats dominate digital recordings, WAV and MP3. The former offers no compression, so you get great sound but big files. MP3 files can be greatly compressed and still sound very good, so this standard dominates music sharing over the Internet.

- Video editing software, such as Apple's iMovie, enables you to take multimedia content—moving pictures, sound, and fury—and create your own movies. Two common formats for video files are Microsoft's Video for Windows (that everybody calls *AVI format*) and Apple's QuickTime. AVI files are uncompressed and thus high quality and huge. QuickTime offers a lot of compression options, making it ideal for delivering movies over the Internet.

Personal Applications

- Personal applications enable you to accomplish basic computing tasks, such as communicate over the Internet, keep track of friends and family, and manage your money. With Web browsers, like Internet Explorer, you can surf the Internet, getting up to date news, looking at pictures, and researching topics of interest. E-mail programs, like Mozilla Thunderbird, enable you to send and receive electronic messages to and from people all over the world. Instant messaging software takes the delay out of communication—you can send messages instantly to friends and family who are connected to the Internet at the same time you are.

- Contact management software helps you keep straight information about family, friends, and business associates. Each contact information can have name, address, multiple e-mail addresses, and even personal notes, like the date of little Johnny's birthday. You'll hear these programs referred to as personal information manager (PIM) software.

- Dedicated financial programs enable you to manage finances, like balancing your checkbook or running the accounting department for a Fortune 500 corporation. Some applications will connect with your bank so you can synchronize your account information and do online banking from your personal computer. Many companies use custom software applications to handle their bookkeeping chores.

- Games make the whole computing experience worth it. 'Nuff said.

Utilities You Can't Live Without

- File and disk compression programs help you maintain the maximum possible space on your hard drive and send files over networks (like the Internet) efficiently. Compression makes your files smaller, like cramming an elephant into a magic bag a tenth its size. Modern operating systems have this *zipping* software built-in, but you can get excellent third-party applications, like WinZip, that give you a lot more control. Although you can compress whole hard drives, most users don't do this because it slows down access to your files on that drive.

- Anti-virus software protects your computer against the ravages of virus software, which makes sense from a naming point of view. Viruses (or *virii*, if you want to use the proper Latin plural) are software programs designed to attack your computer, deleting files or even crashing your operating system. Not sure why otherwise talented programmers feel the need to write this sort of vile program, but you need to protect your computer against them.

- Anti-virus software scans your incoming mail, files you start to copy via CD or floppy, and even files that enter your computer when you hit certain Web sites. After comparing the files against a definition file—that keeps track of known viruses—the anti-virus software will allow the file transfer or throw up a big red flag warning you that your PC is infected. Norton AntiVirus and McAfee VirusScan are the two biggest players in this market.

- Because something eventually will go wrong on your computer, you need to back up your important data. Microsoft bundles a backup utility with Windows, plus you can get a number of good third party applications such as BackUp MyPC to do the job.

The Right Tool for the Job

- Every job you try to accomplish on the computer has several program types that might fit the bill as the right tool for the job. Choosing the best tool makes a huge difference in time spent and in your frustration level. A task that might take many hours in Paint, for example, might take only a few seconds in Paint Shop Pro, just because the latter program has tools designed to accomplish precisely what you're trying to do. Some programs might seem like they would work for a task, but then not have the capabilities you need. A table in a word processing program, for example, definitely cannot do what a table in a spreadsheet or database program can!

Key Terms

Anti-virus program

Archived folder

AVI

Backup utility

Bitmap (BMP)

Contact management software

Curve tool

Definition file

Desktop publishing applications

Electronic mail (e-mail)

File and disk compression programs

Fill tool

GIF

Graphics software

Home page

Instant messaging

JPEG

Line tool

MP3

Paint brush tool

Pencil tool

Personal information manager (PIM)

QuickTime

Shape tool

TIFF

Uniform Resource Locator (URL)

Utility programs

Video for Windows

Virus

WAV

Web browser

Zipped folder

Key Term Quiz

Use the Key Terms list to complete the following sentences. Not all the terms will be used.

1. The _____ file format compresses images quite well, making it ideal for Web graphics.

2. With _____, you can communicate instantly with friends or family, as long as they're connected to the Internet too.

3. Many graphics programs have a _____ for painting colored lines.

4. A Web site's address, for example www.totalsem.com, is officially called its _____.

5. Apple pioneered the _____ format for showing video over the Internet.

6. Anti-virus software uses a _____ to keep track of known viruses and refer to when checking incoming files.

7. John can use the _____ to make the inside of a circle in his drawing red.

8. Jill uses a _____ to view pages on the Internet.

9. You can save your sound file in _____ format and you won't lose any quality because it uses no compression.

10. Serena uses Outlook Express to send an _____ message over the Internet to her friend, Felix, in Australia.

Multiple Choice Quiz

1. Jake has a picture of his dog, Spot, and his sister, but her eyes are red from the flash. What type of application should he use to fix the red-eye?
   A. Desktop publishing
   B. Illustration
   C. Photography
   D. Red-eye reducing

2. What kind of application enables you to create artwork from scratch most easily?
   A. Desktop publishing
   B. Illustration
   C. Photography
   D. Red-eye reducing

3. Daud and Mandy have to do a project at school together. He has the illustration program called Illustrator, and she has one called Freehand. Although initially concerned that they wouldn't be able to help each other, they found out that shifting from one program to the other was pretty easy because the tools seemed similar. What sorts of tools might be found in both programs? (Select all that apply.)
   A. Curve tool
   B. Graphics tool
   C. Line tool
   D. Paint Brush tool

4. Which of the following types of tool would enable Derek to draw a circle on his picture?
   A. Fill tool
   B. Line tool
   C. Pencil tool
   D. Shape tool

5. Karla has just finished editing a picture in her photo-editing software and needs to save it. She plans to use it in a desktop publishing program to print out flyers to promote her band. What format should she use?
   A. Bitmap
   B. JPEG
   C. GIF
   D. TIFF

6. Karla's band has recorded its first single, and she wants to send that file electronically to a record company. Diane says she should save the file as WAV format, but Angel disagrees, saying she should use MP3 format. Who's right about which format would be better for sending as an unsolicited e-mail?
   A. Only Diane is right.
   B. Only Angel is right.
   C. Both Diane and Angel are right.
   D. Neither Diane nor Angel is right. She should save the file as a MUS file, because that's what record companies use.

7. Many weeks later, Angel finishes filming the first music video of Karla's band. Diane argues that she should save the film in Video for Windows format, because that way she won't lose any details or quality. Mario disagrees, claiming that she should save the files as AVI files because AVI doesn't compress the video files. Who's right?
   A. Only Diane is right.
   B. Only Mario is right.
   C. Both Diane and Mario are right.
   D. Neither Diane nor Mario is right.

8. Which of the following applications would enable Angel to make the music video most easily?
   A. Adobe Photoshop
   B. Microsoft FrontPage
   C. Mozilla Thunderbird
   D. Pinnacle Studio Plus

9. Karla's band needs a Web site. Which of the following applications would enable someone to create that Web site most easily?
   A. Adobe Photoshop
   B. Microsoft FrontPage
   C. Mozilla Thunderbird
   D. Pinnacle Studio Plus

10. Stevie has taken over the money management for Karla's band and wants to use software to make this easier to do. Which software type would help?
    A. Account management software
    B. Financial software
    C. PIM software
    D. PDA software

11. Alfred wants to send five files to his friend over the Internet. Joan suggests that he use disk compression software to compress his drive, then send the files by e-mail. Marcus disagrees, saying that he should use file compression software to put the files into a zipped folder, then e-mail that folder. Stu thinks they're all silly and Alfred should just use IM software to send the files directly. Who's right?
    A. Only Joan is right.
    B. Only Marcus is right.
    C. Only Stu is right.
    D. None of them are right. Alfred should use disk compression software and then IM software to send the files.

12. Johnson warns you about a new virus floating around the Internet, attached to an e-mail with the subject "Happy times pictures!" What kind of software protects against this sort of file?
    A. Anti-virus software
    B. E-mail software
    C. Photo-editing software
    D. No software can protect you from e-mail viruses. You simply have to delete the message.

13. When should you use disk compression software?
    A. When your hard drive is over 50% full
    B. When your hard drive is over 80% full
    C. Always. as disk compression makes your drive capacity almost double
    D. Only in desperation

14. What type of application enables you to have safe copies of essential files?
    A. Anti-virus software
    B. Background software
    C. Backup software
    D. Replay software

15. What type of software enables you to keep track of friends' and family members' phone numbers, addresses, e-mail addresses, and so forth? (Select all that apply.)
    A. Address software
    B. Connection management software
    C. Contact management software
    D. PIM software

Essay Questions

1. Write a short essay describing the differences among photography, illustration, and desktop publishing software.

2. Your grandparents want to be able to communicate with you through the new computer they just bought. Write an essay comparing and contrasting two ways you can exchange information over the Internet. Make an argument for which one they should select first.

3. Write a two- to three-paragraph essay describing your favorite computer game or game type. How does it work? Why do you play or want to play this game?

Projects

1. Install (or download and install) a photo editing application like Picasa (free at www. picasa.com) or Paint Shop Pro (30-day free trial at www.corel.com), and then open some pictures for editing. You can use your own pictures or download some from the Internet. (For purposes of learning how to use photo editing software, feel free to get photos from one of the many excellent sites on the Internet, such as www.smugmug. com. Just be aware that all images on the Internet, whether they say so or not, are copyright protected by the person who took the photo.)

   Play around with the images, then present "before" and""after" versions of at least two images to your classmates. Have fun!

2. Get on the Internet or go to your local computer store and do a survey of anti-virus software available. Outline the list of features of the top five programs and then rank them according to your needs.

COMPUTER LITERACY: YOUR TICKET TO IC³ CERTIFICATION

Part 2:
Key Applications

CHAPTER 11: COMMON FEATURES OF WINDOWS APPLICATIONS

Common Features of Windows Applications

"Never send a human to do a machine's job."

– Agent Smith, *The Matrix*

This chapter covers the following IC^3 Key Applications exam objectives:

- IC^3-2 1.1.1 Start a Windows application
- IC^3 -2 1.1.2 Exit a Windows application
- IC^3-2 1.1.3 Identify and prioritize help resources
- IC^3-2 1.1.4 Use automated help
- IC^3-2 1.2.1 Identify on-screen elements common to Windows applications
- IC^3-2 1.2.2 Display or hide toolbars
- IC^3-2 1.2.3 Switch between open documents
- IC^3-2 1.2.4 Change views
- IC^3-2 1.2.5 Change magnification level
- IC^3-2 1.2.7 Open files
- IC^3-2 1.2.9 Close files

Once upon a time, people did things the hard way.

Hundreds of years ago, if you needed to print a page, you had to lay out tiny backward letter blocks in a tray, cover them with ink, press paper onto them with a giant clamping device, and repeat the ink and press steps for every copy needed. If you'd printed something this way and then changed your mind or found a spelling error, you'd probably decide it wasn't worth the trouble to make the change! (See Figure 11.1).

Figure 11.1: An ancient printing press at work—not for the faint of heart!

Even as recently as the early 1980s, people all over the world still produced printed documents using equipment that seems hopelessly out of date from where we are now. The most advanced electric typewriters could store only a few lines of text in memory, errors were still corrected with flaky white cover-up ribbons, and only a handful of typefaces and type sizes were available (Figure 11.2). This technology was a luxury, however, compared with the handwritten ledgers that accountants and other financial staff had to create: line after line of tiny, cramped numbers painstakingly calculated on an adding machine and written in pencil. And creating presentations to project onto a wall involved the dreaded typewriter, expensive heat-transfer machinery, and special plastic sheets; if photographs were involved, you also needed special film, developing, and a separate slide projector. What a pain!

Of course, computers were around a few decades ago, but as you've already seen, they were reserved for important stuff like launching spaceships and running programs for huge corporations. They hadn't yet landed on every desk in offices, schools, and homes—but when they did, they started making everyday tasks unbelievably simple. Personal computing has revolutionized the way we make documents to print and display, largely thanks to productivity applications like Microsoft Word, Excel, and PowerPoint.

Figure 11.2: An IBM Selectric typewriter

To begin your journey through these programs, you'll discover the many ways in which they (and many other Windows-based applications) look and work the same. This chapter starts with the basics: opening and closing an application, getting around the screen, and getting help with an application.

Getting Around

To begin, you'll need to understand how to get into and out of software applications, how to get around while you're in there, and how you can move between two or more different open applications.

Start a Windows Application

If you lived in the world of science fiction movies, you might start an application simply by walking up to your PC and saying, "Computer, start Word!" While you can't yet do *that*, you can use several different methods to start a Windows application. One of the most common ways is to use the Start menu

(Figure 11.3). Remember that the **Start** button, which brings up this menu, is located at the far left end of the Windows taskbar.

If the application you want is installed on your system, you should find it listed when you select **Start | All Programs**. Just click the icon for the application you want to open, and within a few seconds you should see a *splash screen* for the selected program (Figure 11.4). The splash screen is a colorful little window that tells you the name of the program, the name of the company that makes it, and other information such as the software version number.

The splash screen disappears after a few seconds, leaving behind a window for your chosen application. The main window is called the *application window*, and any files that are open within the application appear in *document windows*. Usually, when you open a program from the Start menu, a blank document window comes up automatically so that you can start working on a new file.

Other ways to start an application include double-clicking a desktop shortcut for the program (Figure 11.5), clicking its icon in the Quick Launch area of the taskbar (Figure 11.6), or using My Computer to locate and select a file created with the application you want.

If you plan to open an existing file, the best way to launch the application is to use My Computer. After you double-click the **My Computer** icon on your desktop, find the folder where the file is stored, then locate and double-click the file (Figure 11.7). The application associated with the file automatically starts, and then the file opens. This method saves a little time, and also spares you the trouble of closing that blank document, which you probably don't need if you're going to work on a file that has already been saved.

Exit a Windows Application

Once you're in an application, are you doomed to stay there until you turn the PC off? Of course not! In fact, there are three common ways to exit a Windows application.

- First, you can use the Close button, which is the big "X" in the far upper right corner of the application window next to the resizing buttons.

- Second, you can use the File menu, near the top left corner of any application screen; just click **File** and then select **Exit**.

You'll see the terms "file" and "document" used interchangeably, both in this section of the book and in the real world. A document is simply a type of computer file that was created using a productivity software application—a word-processing file, for example, or a spreadsheet.

Figure 11.3: The Windows XP Start menu

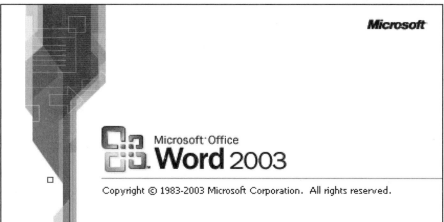

Figure 11.4: The splash screen for Microsoft Word 2003

File Associations
You learned about file associations in the Computing Fundamentals section, in Chapter 9, "Productivity Software." What is the file extension most commonly associated with Microsoft Word? What about PowerPoint? Excel? Can you name any other common file types that are specifically associated with one particular application?
End Take Two! sidebar

The Way of the Geek: Opening an Application
*Here's yet another way to open an application: take the geek approach! Every program, no matter how small, has a primary executable file, which you can use to start the application. If you can find the name and location of that file for a given program (here's a hint: it will have an .exe file extension), you can open that program without clicking on an icon. Select **Start | Run**, type the full path and file name of the executable file (or click the **Browse** button to dig around for this information), and then click **OK** to start the program. Try it yourself! Select **Start | Run**, type **notepad**—or **notepad.exe**, if you really want to geek out—and click **OK**.*

• Third, you can make sure the application you want to close is currently the active window, then press and hold **[Alt]** and press the **[F4]** function key to close the window and exit the application. Note that if you have more than one document window open, you will only close that document window—but the last document window you close will take the application with it when it shuts down.

• Fourth and finally, you can accidentally step on the "off" switch on your computer's power strip, thus shutting down your application and the entire computer in one quick move. OK, I'm joking here—I *do not* recommend this method for exiting an application!

The Application Window vs. the Document Window

Make sure that you're clear on the difference between an application window and a document window. The application window is always open when the program is open—it *is* the program, for all practical purposes. A document window, on the other hand, represents an open file—a Word document, Excel spreadsheet, or PowerPoint presentation, for example. The document window sits "inside" the main application window, and you can have many document windows open within the application window at the same time. You can open and close document win-

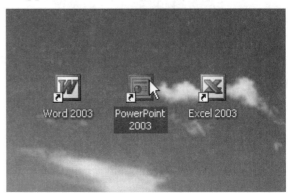

Figure 11.5: Double-clicking a shortcut icon on the desktop

Figure 11.6: Clicking a Quick Launch icon on the taskbar

dows all day without ever closing the application, but closing the application window shuts down the program, taking any open documents with it. Figure 11.8 shows an example of an open application (in this case, Word) with a blank document in a document window.

Note that in the upper right corner of the window, in addition to the "X" button that closes the application, there's another "X" just below it. If you click that, you'll close the document that you're working with, but the application will remain open (Figure 11.9).

Open and Close a Document

Within the application window, you open and close documents using the File menu. Select

Figure 11.7: Opening a file in My Computer to start an application

File | Open to bring up the Open dialog box, where you can browse to select the file you want to open. If you like, you can repeat this procedure to open other files at the same time. To close a file without closing the application, simply select **File | Close**.

Note that in some of the more basic programs, you won't see the Close option on the File menu; this means that the program doesn't allow you to have multiple documents open at once. In this type of program, the only way to close a document is by opening a different one—or by closing the application itself. (Create a test document using the Notepad program, and you'll see what I mean.)

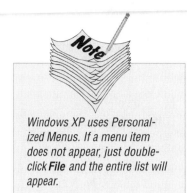

Windows XP uses Personalized Menus. If a menu item does not appear, just double-click **File** and the entire list will appear.

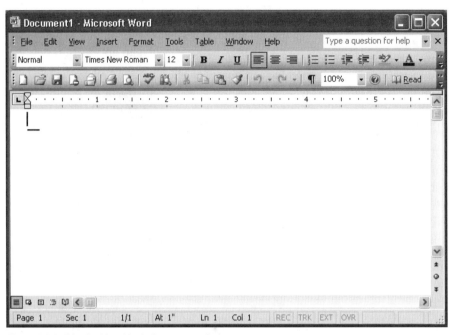

Figure 11.8: Word with a blank document window

Tasking Me
The latest versions of Microsoft Office—the most popular productivity software suite—uses a special navigation tool called the task pane. The task pane is a small window that floats above your workspace, giving you quick access to documents, tools, Help topics, and so on.

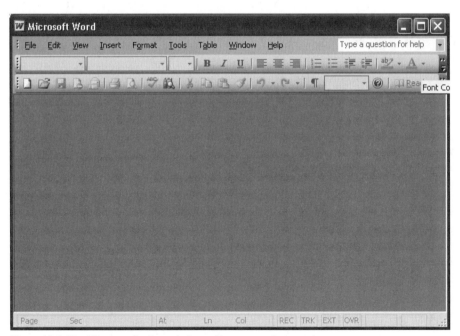

Figure 11.9: The Word application window with no open documents

Scroll within the Document Window

So, you've opened your application, and opened a document within that application. Now what? Well, if you ever plan to get past the first page, you'll need to know how to move around within your document.

Most documents don't fit into a space as small as your computer screen. Whenever a document is too long or wide (or both) to fit on your screen all at once, the application gives you *scroll bars*, which you can use to view the rest of the document.

There are two types of scroll bars: vertical (up and down) and horizontal (left to right). Figure 11.10 shows examples of both types of scroll bars.

While a scroll bar runs along the entire edge of your document window, the key to its magic is a little box called the *selection point*, which floats somewhere in between the ends of the scroll bar. The selection point can give you a good indication of your current view in relation to the complete document. For example, if your vertical scroll bar's selection point is all the way at the bottom, you know you're looking at the end of your document. Similarly, if your horizontal scroll bar's selection point is all the way to the left, you know you're looking at the left edge of your document.

So, how do you use the scroll bars to move around in a document? There are three methods: you can move the selection point by clicking on it and dragging; click one of the arrows at either end of the scroll bar; or click within the scroll bar to either side of the selection point.

The click-and-drag method lets you move like lightning through your document—but sometimes, that's not what you want! If you want to move slowly and steadily through your document, use the arrows; you can either click one or more times, or click and hold to scroll more quickly. The third method isn't very precise, as it jumps you somewhat randomly up or down within the document, but it does work; it's most likely to come in handy for skimming through a very long document.

Change Document Views

Most applications offer more than one way to display a document. This comes in handy if you want to stop from time to time to see how your document will look when it's printed, for example, or if you want to look at a long document in abbreviated outline format.

Generally, you'll use one type of display, or *document view*, for working on the document, another for checking out how your document will look on paper (or onscreen, in the case of PowerPoint), and other view options that are specific to the type of application you're using.

So, how different are these document views? Figure 11.11 shows different views of the same Word document, while Figure 11.12 shows different views of the same PowerPoint presentation.

Most folks use Normal view in Word documents for the majority of their work. Print Layout comes in handy for formatting tasks, such as seeing how your page headers

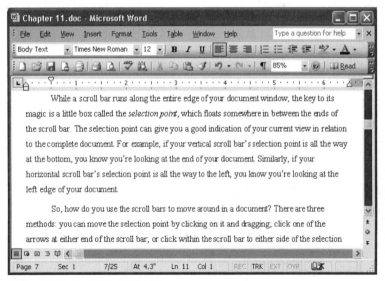

Figure 11.10: Vertical scroll bar in dark gray on right; horizontal scroll bar in light gray on bottom

and footers appear, while Outline view gives you a nice, quick summary of what your document includes so far. For the PowerPoint document, Normal is the view you'd use to create an individual slide, Slide Sorter enables you to review and rearrange your slides, and Slide Show lets you see how your slides will look in an actual presentation, without all the menus and buttons that you see in the application window.

Another common option is called **Print Preview**. When you select this command—normally found on the **File** menu—you'll see exactly how your document will look when printed. While you're in Print Preview mode, you also see a special toolbar, which includes a Print button and various other options (Figure 11.13). To close Print Preview mode and return to your previous mode, just click **Close** on the Print Preview toolbar.

Change Document Magnification

You don't always have to view your documents at "actual size"—sometimes you need to zoom in for a closer look at some fine print, or zoom out to get a different perspective. Use the menu bar to select **View | Zoom** command; you'll get a window where you can select or type in a magnification percentage (Figure 11.14).

Work in whatever view makes sense to you. I often write in Print Layout, because I enjoy being able to see the edges of the "page" as I type. Other writers I know compose their work in Outline view, to make it easier to keep an eye on which topics are coming up next.

Depending on the application, you'll see other options such as **Fit**, which magnifies the view as much as possible while still showing you the complete page or document. You can also find the numeric zoom options on the Standard application

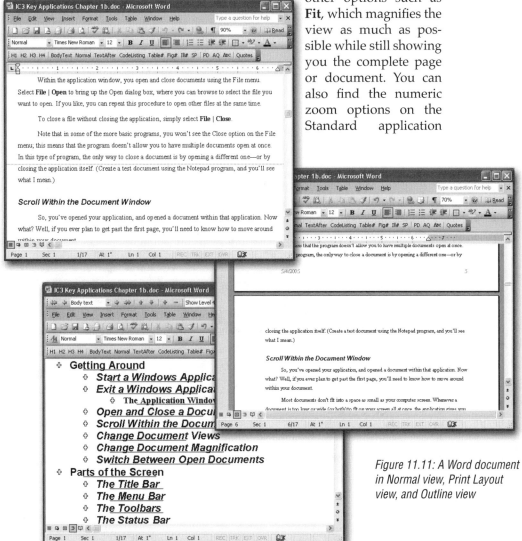

Figure 11.11: A Word document in Normal view, Print Layout view, and Outline view

Figure 11.12: A PowerPoint document in Normal, Slide Sorter, and Slide Show view

toolbar; click the down arrow to drop down a list of magnification options (Figure 11.15), then select the one you want.

Switch between Open Documents

When you have more than one document or program open at once, you can easily switch from onve to the other. You can use either your keyboard or the application menus to do this.

To switch between open documents using the keyboard, simply hold down the **[Alt]** key and press **[Tab]**. This brings up a box in the center of your screen that shows the icon and name for another open program or document (Figure 11.16). If you have several programs or documents open, just keep holding down **[Alt]** while you press **[Tab]** repeatedly until you see the document you want; then release both keys. You can repeat this as many times as you like to move between documents.

For the menu method, just drop down the **Window** menu and then look for the numbered items at the bottom of the list (Figure 11.17). These numbered items have file names beside them, indicating which document is which; just select the one you want to switch to that document.

Parts of the Screen

No matter what application you're using, you can count on seeing certain items on the screen. Once you learn to recognize and use these common screen elements, you'll feel more comfortable even when you're using an application for the first time.

*Many applications also have an option called **Web Page Preview**, which opens a browser window and shows you how your document will look as a Web page or a series of Web pages.*

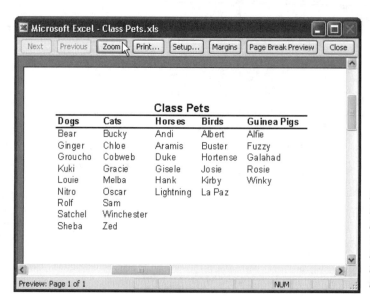

Figure 11.13: Looking at an Excel spreadsheet with Print Preview; note the special Print Preview toolbar.

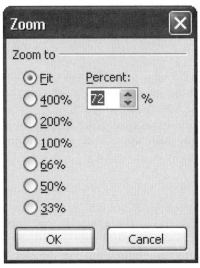

Figure 11.14: The Zoom dialog box in PowerPoint

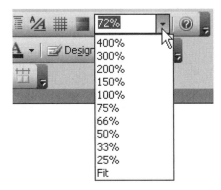

Figure 11.15: The Zoom drop-down box on the Standard toolbar in PowerPoint

Figure 11.16: The result of pressing [Alt + Tab]

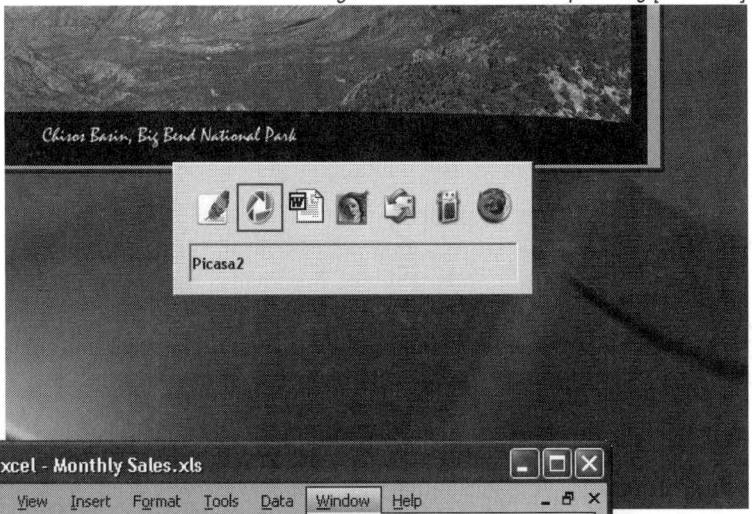

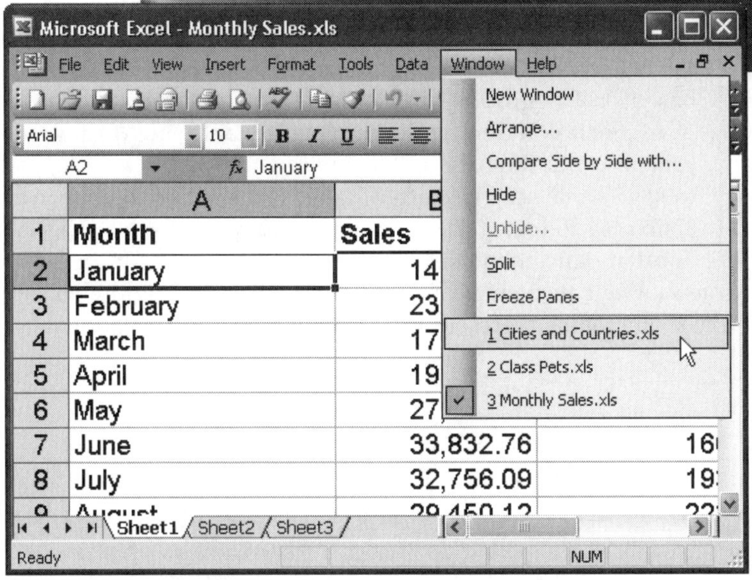

Figure 11.17: The Window menu in Excel, showing three open documents

Making the Most Out of [Alt + Tab]

When you have a large number of items (programs and documents) open at once, even the [Alt + Tab] shortcut can take a little longer than you might like. Try the following procedure to practice using this keyboard shortcut.

1. *Open two different applications, and open two different documents within each application. You should now have at least four items open on your system.*

2. *Hold down the [Alt] key and press and release [Tab]. Notice that as long as you keep [Alt] pressed, the little display in the middle of your screen stays put.*

3. *Keep holding down that [Alt] key, and press [Tab] several times in a row, noticing how the various open items cycle through in a set order. This is the order in which you opened or last viewed these items. When you've observed this pattern, go ahead and release the [Alt] key.*

4. *Decide which item you want to switch to next. Press and hold [Alt] again, and press [Tab] until you find the item you had in mind. Release the keys when you get to that item.*

5. *Now you can switch directly back to the item you last viewed, simply by pressing the [Alt + Tab] combination once.*

Figure 11.18: The title bar for Excel

The Title Bar

This handy item at the top of any application window identifies your program and the name of the active document file. At the left end of the title bar is the icon that represents the application you're using, and at the right end are the usual Minimize, Restore Down/Maximize, and Close buttons (Figure 11.18). These buttons affect the entire application window, not just the document window; for example, if you use this Close button, your entire application shuts down.

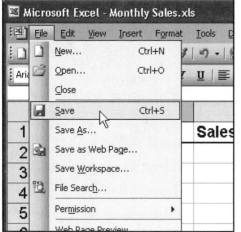

Figure 11.19: A simple menu selection in Excel

The Menu Bar

This part of the screen gives you access to the available program commands. To access a menu command, click the key word in the menu bar—for example, **File**, **Edit**, or **View**—and watch for the menu listing to appear below. Point to an item on the list, and if another menu appears out to the side, point again to select from that list. When you've made your selection and no more menus appear, just click the mouse. The application will carry out the command, and you'll see the results on screen.

Figure 11.19 shows an example of a simple (and very commonly used) menu selection: **File | Save**. Figure 11.20 shows a selection that involves a second menu, known as a *fly-out menu*: in this case, **Tools | Language | Thesaurus**. See how that second menu pops up out to the side? The sideways arrow symbol (4) is your clue that a particular menu item has a fly-out menu with more choices.

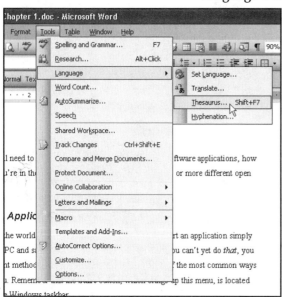

Figure 11.20: A fly-out menu in Word

The Toolbars

Toolbars are groups of buttons that represent various program commands; they're much like the menu commands, except that they're represented by pictures instead of words. Figure 11.21 shows an example of a toolbar in Word, with the mouse cursor pointing to one of the buttons.

To use a toolbar button, you just find the picture that represents what you want to do, and click it! This makes the toolbar generally faster to use than a menu command.

You can choose which toolbars to view and which to hide, based on the groups of commands you use most often; for example, if you don't work much with tables in Word, you'll probably want to turn off the Tables and Borders toolbar, just to save some screen space. Changing a specific toolbar from visible to hidden (or vice versa) is easy: just select **View | Toolbars** and then click the name of the toolbar in question on the fly-out menu. Want an even quicker way to do this? Just right-click any blank spot in the toolbar area, then select the name of the toolbar you want to view or hide.

Oddly enough, the title bar doesn't always list the program and document names in the same order and in the same way. Depending on what application you use, you might see "Joe's Document.doc – Microsoft Word" or "Microsoft PowerPoint"– [Joe's Document. ppt]" in the title bar. This inconsistency is just a little Microsoft quirk—don't let it throw you!

The Status Bar

This horizontal bar at the bottom of the application window can help you keep track of the current page number, total page count, and other document information.

Depending on the application you're using, you can also find some neat shortcuts in the status bar. In Word, for example, you can double-click anywhere on the left end of the status bar to get a handy pop-up window offering the Find, Replace, and Go To commands (you'll get to know these a little later). In PowerPoint, you can double-click around the middle of the status bar to choose a fancy design template, or double-click the spelling icon for a quick spelling check.

The Taskbar

You've already met the taskbar, that handy little piece of real estate along the bottom edge of the Windows desktop. When you have an application open, you can still access the taskbar, which you might need for opening another application, switching to another open program, or just checking the time or the status of your Internet connection.

The Many Faces of the Mouse Pointer

Pointing your mouse at different objects on the screen causes the mouse pointer to change its look. In fact, what the pointer is doing at a certain time is an important cue that tells you what you can and cannot do at that moment. Here are some common examples of what the mouse pointer can tell you:

- When you point at text in an application, you'll see a vertical insertion point (| or I), indicating that you can click in that area to start inserting text.

- When you point at menu items or toolbar buttons, the mouse pointer turns into an arrow ( ), indicating that you can click those items to make something happen.

- When you point at a picture that can be moved, the mouse pointer turns into a set of crossed arrows (✛), to indicate that you can move the picture in any direction.

- When you point at the edge of a picture, the mouse pointer turns into a two-headed arrow—either vertical (↕), horizontal (↔), or diagonal (↘ or ↗)—to indicate that you can drag in or out to resize the picture.

- When the application is "thinking" about a complex operation, the mouse pointer turns into a little hourglass (⧗), to indicate that you're waiting for something to finish.

- Finally, when the mouse pointer starts wiggling its whiskers ( ), that's a sign that you've been at the computer too long and you're seeing things… time for a break!

As with any window, you can point to a non-maximized application window to get a double-headed arrow pointer that you can use to drag and size the window.

It Pays to Speak Microsoft

Why am I so intent on teaching you the official names for all of these screen elements? Am I trying to make you sound nerdy and weird? No way! (Hey, I'm nerdy and weird enough for all of us, OK?) The point of using Microsoft's standard terms is to make sure we're all speaking the same language. Once you're comfortable with the terminology for the various parts of the screen, I can come along later in the book and tell you to "click on X in the taskbar" or "look at Y in the status bar," and you'll know exactly what I mean. More importantly, knowing the proper terms makes you sound more knowledgeable. After all, one day you'll be helping someone else out—and if all you can come up with is "click the thing next to that other thing," you may not sound nerdy, but you'll sure sound weird!

Figure 11.22: The Help menu in Excel

Getting Help

Everyone needs help sometimes! Even if you use an application every day, there will come a time when you need to do something in a word processing document, spreadsheet, or presentation that you've never needed to do before. Maybe you're an expert in creating tables in Word or building formulas in Excel, for example, but you don't have a lot of experience with fancy backgrounds in PowerPoint.

Today's applications have so many bells and whistles that it's difficult, if not impossible, to be an expert at using all of them. Fortunately, you can get help for Windows applications in lots of ways, and from many different sources. When you come across strange, unknown features—or when a feature that normally works just fine suddenly doesn't work at all—knowing how to find and use those help resources can be a real lifesaver.

Types of Help Resources

When you need help with an application, you can turn to a number of different resources to get that help. Understanding the strengths and limitations of these resources will help you decide which one to turn to first when you need answers.

Help within the OS or Application

On every Windows application, no matter how small or simple, the last item on the main menu is **Help**. If you drop this menu down (Figure 11.22), you'll usually find a selection called Application Name **Help**, which launches a separate window with access to help topics.

Printed Documentation

Many Windows applications come with books or booklets that contain useful information. You can also find books published about popular applications such as the Microsoft Office suite. A quick search of your library, your local bookstore, or an online merchant such as Amazon.com should turn up plenty of resources about productivity applications.

Internet Help Sources

Another way you can get help is to surf the Web for the application's manufacturer. Every manufacturer today has a web site, often with helpful resources for software users like you. Microsoft, for example, has a vast collection of help articles on its software products. Online help groups also tend to form around popular applications; while these groups are generally not "official" or affiliated with the manufacturer, they tend to attract experienced users who can often help with your questions.

Manufacturer's Help Desks and Other Sources

Larger software manufacturers often have toll-free phone numbers for product information or help; in some cases, a company may even have real-time operators who can answer questions in a chat window on the web site. You can also seek help from others in your school or work setting, or from personal friends who have software expertise.

Using Help Resources within a Microsoft Office Application

The Microsoft Office product suite, which includes our three main applications, offers some of the most advanced software help in the world. Select **Help**

| Application Name **Help** to open the Help task pane (Figure 11.23), which appears at the right edge of your application window.

The top portion of the Help task pane is called the *Assistance* area. Here, you can type in one or more keywords to search for relevant help topics. If you have a live Internet connection, you can also click the Table of Contents link to download the latest help topics from Microsoft's web site (Figure 11.24).

Below the Assistance area is a section called *Microsoft Office Online*. This portion of the Help task pane lefts you connect to Microsoft's web site for application-specific assistance, downloads, and other kinds of helpful material directly from the makers of the software. All of the links in this section require a live Internet connection. The bottom portion of the Help task pane is called *See also*, and it provides yet more options, including contacting Microsoft about a problem or question.

A final way to get help in a Microsoft Office application is to use the *Type a question for help* box, located in the far upper right corner of the application window, just under the Minimize, Restore Down/Maximize, and Close buttons (Figure 11.25).

If you type a question here and press **[Enter]**, the Search Results task pane will appear in place of the Help task pane, displaying various help topics that match your question. Just click any topic that looks promising, and see where it takes you!

You'll notice that Microsoft Office help relies heavily on a live Internet connection to bring you answers, but there is one help method that you can always use even if you're not running live. Do you see the *Search* area at the bottom of the Search Results task pane? Click the arrow next to the drop-down box there, and you'll see an option called Offline Help (Figure 11.26). Select that option if you're not hooked up to the Internet at the moment, and you'll save time on your searches.

Searching in a Help Resource

Once you're into your application's help window, or an Internet help resource, it's time to find the information you need. Decide which

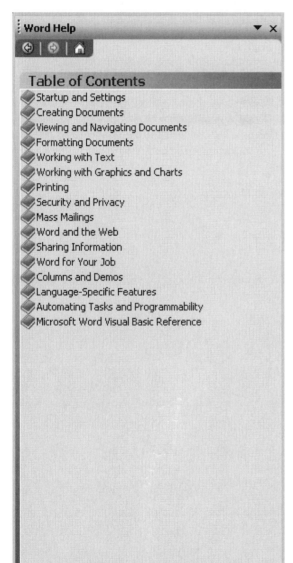

Figure 11.24: A Table of Contents listing for Word

key words are most likely to bring up help topics or articles that will answer your question. If you have a question about a specific software feature, use the exact name of that feature in a keyword search. If you need to do something, but don't know the name of the feature or command that you need to use, try the *Type a question for help* box, and ask your question in the most direct and simple way that you can.

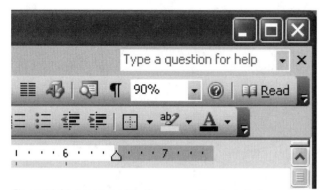

Figure 11.25: Location of the Type a question for help *box*

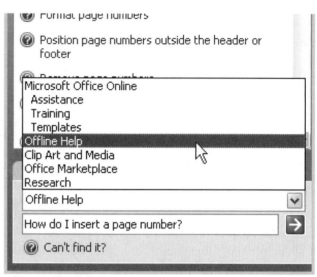

Figure 11.26: Selecting Offline Help in the Search Results task pane

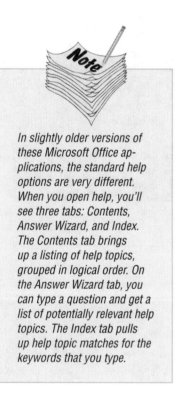

In slightly older versions of these Microsoft Office applications, the standard help options are very different. When you open help, you'll see three tabs: Contents, Answer Wizard, and Index. The Contents tab brings up a listing of help topics, grouped in logical order. On the Answer Wizard tab, you can type a question and get a list of potentially relevant help topics. The Index tab pulls up help topic matches for the keywords that you type.

Getting Around

■ To start a Windows application, select it from the Start menu, double-click its desktop shortcut icon, or click its Quick Launch icon on the taskbar. If you open an existing document created with a certain application, the application will automatically open and then display the document.

■ To exit a Windows application, select **File | Exit**, use the Close button in the upper right corner of the application window, or press **[Alt + F4]**.

■ To open and close documents within an application, use the commands **File | Open** and **File | Close**.

Parts of the Screen

■ Navigation features within the document window include scroll bars, different document views, the **Zoom** feature, and the ability to switch from one open document to another.

■ Main screen features of Windows productivity applications include the title bar, the menu bar, toolbars, the status bar, and the taskbar. These features behave in the same basic manner for any Windows program.

The Many Faces of the Mouse Pointer

■ The mouse pointer changes in predictable ways to let you know what you're pointing at and what you can do at any given moment.

Getting Help

■ When you need help with a Windows program—especially a Microsoft Office program such as Word, Excel, or PowerPoint—you can turn to many different resources for assistance.

■ Each application has a Help menu, which takes you to a help system or an Internet-based series of help topics.

■ You can find printed books and manuals for many applications, and various "unofficial" Internet sources of expertise.

■ If you know someone who has more experience with the application in question, you can also ask for one-on-one help.

Key Terms

Application window

Document view

Document window

Help task pane

Menu bar

Mouse pointer

Print Preview

Scroll bars

Search Results task pane

Status bar

Table of Contents

Taskbar

Title bar

Toolbars

Zoom

Key Term Quiz

Use the Key Terms list to complete the following sentences. Not all the terms will be used.

1. If your _____ displays as an hourglass, it means that your program is currently "thinking" about a complex operation and you should wait for it to finish.

2. Windows applications include both vertical and horizontal _____ to help you move around within an open document.

3. If you close all of your Excel documents but don't close the program, the Excel _____ will still be visible.

4. The _____ feature shows you exactly how your current document would look on paper.

5. To get a closer look at small print on your document without actually changing the size of the print, you can use the _____ feature.

6. The name of the current application and file are always listed in the _____.

7. If you need help with a Microsoft Office program, but don't currently have a live Internet connection, you can specify in the _____ that you want to search for help offline.

8. The main text commands in any application, such as **File**, **Edit**, and **View**, are located on the _____.

9. Switching from Normal to Outline or Print Layout mode in Microsoft Word is an example of changing the _____.

10. In a Microsoft Office program, you can determine which of the many _____ you want to view, according to which groups of commands you use the most.

Multiple Choice Quiz

1. What do we call a computer file created with a productivity software application such as a word-processing or spreadsheet program?
   A. Utility
   B. Printout
   C. Document
   D. Project

2. To open an application from the Windows taskbar, you first need to find its icon in the Quick Launch area. Then what do you do?
   A. Point your mouse at the icon.
   B. Click the icon.
   C. Double-click the icon.
   D. Right-click the icon and select **Launch**.

3. Suppose you're running PowerPoint, and you have one file open. When you're finished working with the file, you select **File | Close**. Which of the following statements is now true?
   A. The PowerPoint program is no longer open.
   B. The application window is closed, but the document window is still open.
   C. The document window is closed, but the application window is still open.
   D. Your file is still open; to close it, you must select **File | Exit**.

4. Which of the following can you do while in Print Preview mode in Excel?
   A. Change the size of the text in your document.
   B. Correct a spelling error in your document.
   C. See how your document would look as a web page.
   D. Print a copy of your document.

5. What does the **View | Zoom** command do?
   A. It changes the size of the document text to make it easier to read.
   B. It takes you directly to the last page of the document.
   C. It lets you change the magnification of the current document.
   D. It lets you hide the Standard application toolbar.

6. Which part of the application screen is most likely to display the page count and current page number?
   A. Title bar
   B. Scroll bar
   C. Status bar
   D. Taskbar

7. What does the mouse pointer look like when you point to a menu item or toolbar button?
   A. A vertical line
   B. An arrow
   C. A two-headed arrow
   D. An hourglass

8. It's late at night and you're working on a research paper in Microsoft Word, when you suddenly realize you can't remember how to create footnotes in Word. Your paper is due first thing tomorrow. Which of the following is the best approach for this situation?
   A. Call your best friend, who knows everything there is to know about Microsoft Word features, and ask how to create footnotes.
   B. Search the Web for reference books about Microsoft Word.
   C. Select **Help | Microsoft Office Word Help**, then type **footnotes** in the *Assistance* area.
   D. Search the Web for an online user's group dedicated to Word issues, and post your question about footnotes there.

9. While working on a presentation in PowerPoint, you realize that you don't know how to rearrange the order of your slides. You decide to search for answers in PowerPoint's help resources. Which of the following search terms would most likely bring up the information you need?
   A. help
   B. how to
   C. slide
   D. order

10. You're using a friend's computer while yours is being fixed. You need to use the taskbar, but find that it's not currently visible. What's the first thing you should try?
    A. Save your file and reboot the computer.
    B. Select **View | Taskbar**, to make sure the taskbar is set as visible.
    C. Point your mouse at the bottom edge of the screen, to see if the taskbar pops up.
    D. Press the Windows Start button to view the taskbar, then right-click to view and change the taskbar's properties.

11. You're looking at an Excel worksheet that shows the average rainfall for various cities in North America. You decide to compare it with another worksheet, which shows the same information for South American cities. Can you have both worksheets open at the same time in Excel?
    A. Yes
    B. No

12. To view a document that's wider than your screen can display, which of the following would you use?
    A. Minimize button
    B. Maximize button
    C. Vertical scroll bar
    D. Horizontal scroll bar

13. What is the name of the little vertical line that displays and blinks at the place where text will appear when you start typing?
    A. Entry point
    B. Exclamation point
    C. Insertion point
    D. Text point

14. Which of the following commands is always found on the File menu?
    A. Find
    B. Open
    C. Zoom
    D. Help

15. True or false: If you have installed a software program, you should find it listed under **Start | All Programs**.
    A. True
    B. False

Essay Questions

1. Discuss at least three different ways to open an application in Windows, and describe how to open an application without first seeing a blank document.

2. List and describe five important parts of the screen that are common to popular Windows programs such as Excel, PowerPoint, and Word.

3. Describe two different ways to turn off a toolbar that you no longer want to see on your screen, and two different ways to change the magnification of the document that you're viewing.

Projects

1. Open a Windows application and create a new document. Experiment with your mouse and various operations in the document, and make a note of each different "look" that your mouse pointer takes on. How many different shapes or appearances can you discover? Don't be shy—this is a new document, so you have nothing to lose. If you run out of ideas in one application, you can open another one, create a new document, and experiment some more. Write out your complete list of mouse pointer antics and what you think each change means.

2. Experiment with finding help in a Microsoft Office application. If you have a live Internet connection, use the Office Online function. If you don't have access to the Internet, check out the Offline Help feature, which should provide access to a large pool of basic help topics.

   Search through the program's menus and toolbars for a feature that you've never seen before and don't understand. Use the help resources that you've learned about here to research that feature and then try using it.

3. Just for fun, see if you can stump the help
    features! Try to come up with a question
    or topic (a valid one having to do with the
    application, not some far-fetched question
    about spaceships or monkeys) that isn't
    addressed in the program's help features. If
    you do find something that you think hasn't
    been addressed, share with your classmates
    and see if anyone else can dig up an answer
    using offline or online help.

COMPUTER LITERACY: YOUR TICKET TO IC³ CERTIFICATION

Working with Documents – The Basics

"The files are *in* the computer?"

– Hansel McDonald, *Zoolander*

This chapter covers the following IC³ exam objectives:

- IC³-2   1.2.6   Create files

- IC³-2   1.2.7   Open files

- IC³-2   1.2.8   Save files in specified locations/formats

- IC³-2   1.2.9   Close files

- IC³-2   1.2.10   Identify and solve common problems relating to working with files

Imagine that you got up this morning and started a new Word document—it could be a paper on Shakespeare, a report on the gross national product of Zambia, or maybe a detailed inventory of all your computer games. You've been typing away for four hours, but you haven't saved your document yet. This is a very dangerous way to live! At any moment, a freak power outage could occur, or your dog could accidentally knock the power plug loose, bringing down your PC and erasing all of your hard work.

Now, imagine that a few minutes after you started that Word document, you wisely decided to save it onto your hard drive. Since that time, you've been stopping every few minutes to save your latest work. Good for you! Then you took a break for lunch—you closed your document and turned off your PC, and now you've come back an hour later to pick up where you left off. You start looking for your document in My Computer . . . but where is it? You let Word assign the file name, and you didn't notice the name of the directory where you saved it. Your computer has lots of directories, so you'll have to do some searching before you can get back to work. What a pain!

One of the most important things to understand as you work with applications on a PC is how to manage your documents. You need to be smart about what you name your files, and where you put them—so the first step is knowing how to name your files and where to put them! Once you have that part figured out, you need to make sure you can open an existing file, change it if you want to, and save it if you've made any changes. You also need to know how to recognize Microsoft Office documents by their file extensions, and how to troubleshoot common problems that come up when you work with files.

This chapter covers the skills you need to manage your files effectively and avoid careless errors that can cost you important data.

File Management: The Achilles' Heel of PC Users

Knowing how to create, open, close, change, and save files might seem like pretty basic stuff to you—but without a solid background in these skills, you could be a threat to your own data! Even if you know your way around the PC very well, you can accidentally blow away files, misplace files, save files in the wrong format, and otherwise mess up your data with just a few wrong mouse clicks.

If you've read Greek mythology, you probably know the story of the great warrior Achilles. He was totally invincible, except for this one spot on his heel. As luck would have it, someone shot him in that tiny spot with an arrow, and he was toast.

What's the lesson here? Don't get overconfident and careless with your files—if you don't know exactly what you're doing, why you're doing it, and how to do it, your hard work might be toast! Take the time to learn this stuff, and you'll give yourself fewer headaches.

In Word 2003, the new document button is actually called **New Blank Document**. *Hold your mouse pointer over it to see for yourself.*

Creating a New File

When you make a new file in Word, Excel, PowerPoint, or other applications, you have two main options: start from scratch by creating a blank document, or get a head start on structure and formatting by using a template. Which route you choose depends on what you're doing, and on your personal preference. Let's look at how to create new documents, and explore the pros and cons of each method.

Creating a Blank Document

The procedure for creating a new blank document is simple: just click the **New** button on the toolbar, as shown in Figure 12.1. This button looks like a blank sheet of paper, and is by default the first button on the Standard toolbar.

Remember that you don't always need to click the **New** button to get a blank document. If you've just opened the application you'll be using to create the file, you probably already have one ready to go! You're more likely to use the **New** button when the application is already open and you've been working on other files.

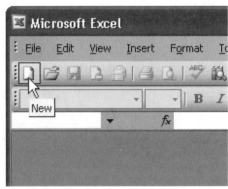

Figure 12.1: The New button on the Standard toolbar in Excel

Once you have a blank document on your application screen, you're ready to add text, graphics, or whatever kind of data your application can handle. In later chapters, you'll learn all about how to add and format document data.

The advantage of starting from a clean slate is that you know exactly what's in the document, and you're in complete control of how it reads and how it looks. The downside is that you have to start by staring at a blank screen—sometimes this can be intimidating!

Using a Template to Create a New File

You don't always have to start a new file from a blank screen. In many cases, you'll use what's called a document *template* to give yourself a head start.

A template is a special type of file that helps you make professional-looking documents in very little time. You don't actually *open* a template file; instead, you sort of piggy-back your document onto it, using the template's built-in features—which can include formatting, text, graphics, and more—and then adding, deleting, or changing the text and graphics until your document is just the way you want it. Think of a template, then, as a head start on any kind of document that might take you a long time to set up from scratch.

Having trouble imagining why you'd ever want to use a template? Well, imagine that your neighbor gets called away suddenly on a business trip, and offers to pay you to watch his dog while he's gone. When he returns, he asks you for a printed invoice so that he can get his company to pay him back for the expense. You need to come up with a decent-looking invoice in a hurry, so you can get paid! Imagine how long you might spend coming up with something on your own. Now check out the Excel template, created by Microsoft and available on Office Online, shown in Figure 12.2.

Talk about getting a head start! Using this template, you can fill in the needed information and print out an invoice in record time—the example in Figure 12.2 took less than five minutes to complete. You don't even have to

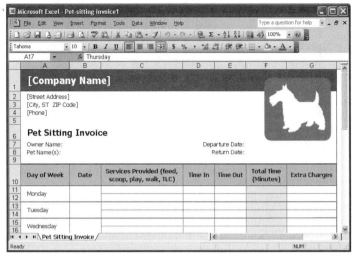

Figure 12.2: A pet-sitting invoice template for Excel

Figure 12.3: The completed invoice—easy peasy!

do the math, as the template uses Excel's Sum function (you'll learn about that in a later chapter) to add up the total bill automatically. Best of all, the invoice (see Figure 12.3) looks like it was professionally designed just for Sarah's pet-sitting business.

As you can see, a template can save you lots of work, and often makes a nicer-looking document than you would have had the time or expertise to create on your own. For certain types of documents—for example, calendars, faxes, letters, or any spreadsheet or presentation format that you need to use over and over—using a template is ideal. It's also great for a group of people who want their documents to have a uniform look. Not every document needs a template, however. For a simple, no-frills file, starting from a blank document is usually best.

Figure 12.4: The New Presentation task pane in PowerPoint, which includes template options

To use a template, you'll need to create your new file using the menu, not the **New** button. Select **File | New** to bring up a task pane with various template options. This task pane is called *New Document* in Word, *New Presentation* in PowerPoint (see Figure 12.4), and *New Workbook* in Excel.

The contents of the task pane are a little different for each program, but the main options are the same. The heading New shows you non-template options, such as starting your new file from a blank page or from an existing file.

Under *Templates*, you can search for a template on line by name; you can also click the link for Templates on Office Online, or search for templates on your computer or your designated web

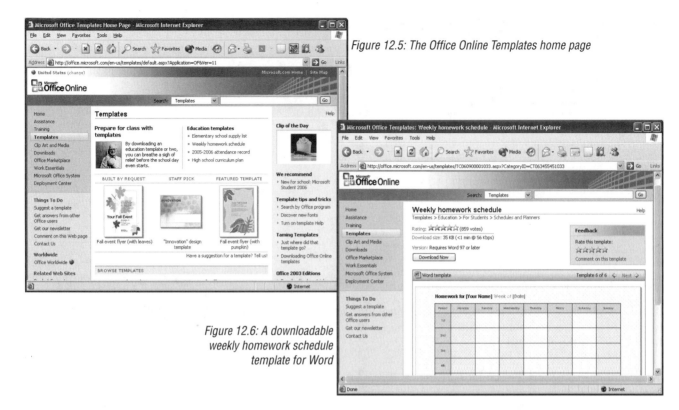

Figure 12.5: The Office Online Templates home page

Figure 12.6: A downloadable weekly homework schedule template for Word

Note

When you use a template, you'll often get some other default name.

sites. The Office Online Templates Web site (see Figure 12.5) is a great place to search for the latest and greatest templates designed by Microsoft's team of experts. You can search the site by template subject, by Microsoft Office program, or by name, and then download and use the templates you want (see Figure 12.6).

If you've used templates with this program before, you'll see another heading called *Recently used templates*, which lists the templates you used most recently. With this feature, you won't have to search for and download a template a second (or third, or fourth, or twentieth) time.

Default File Names

In all Microsoft Office applications, every new document is assigned a default name, which it keeps until you save the file. In Word, the first new file you create after launching the application is called Document1. In Excel, this file is called Book1, and in PowerPoint, it's called Presentation1. If you start a second new file while the application is still open, it's called Document2, Book2, or Presentation2; the third is called Document3, Book3, or Presentation3, and so forth with any additional new files (see Figure 12.7). Each time you close and re-open the application, the numbering starts over.

Figure 12.7: A really busy day: Document14 in Word

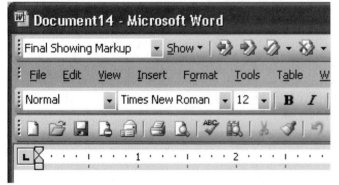

While these default names are useful for starting a file, they stink for the long term—so don't get lazy and let your files keep these names when you save them! After all, Document1.doc isn't exactly descriptive, is it? Also, you'll have another Document1 to deal with the next time you open Word, so you can't use these default names without causing massive confusion. You'll need to give your files descriptive, useful names when you save them—and you'll learn all about saving a little later in this chapter.

Opening an Existing File

To open a file that you (or someone else) already created, you'll need to know where that file resides on your system. If you don't know where to look for the file, you can always guess, but that could take much longer.

The Windows Search feature can help you find a file if you know its full name; if you don't know the exact name, you can narrow the search if you know the file type. Let's take a look at the importance of file types, and then discuss the two main methods for opening a file.

Identifying the File Type

You've probably heard that immortal quote from Shakespeare's *Romeo and Juliet*: "What's in a name?" While the name of a computer file might tell you a lot—maybe the author's name, the date the file was created, or a description of what's in the file—the most important part of the file name is the extension. Those three letters that come after the period can tell you what type of program created the file, or in many cases which specific program created it.

For example, a file with a .bmp extension is known as a *bitmap* file. Many different graphics and drawing programs use this file format, so you can't tell from a file's .bmp extension what program created it. You can, however, tell that it's some kind of a picture or drawing.

If you see a file with an extension of .doc, you can be pretty sure that it was created with Microsoft Word. This is because the .doc extension is native to Word; while other programs can open or save files in the .doc format, this format was invented for use with Word. Because of this, if you have a copy of Word on your computer, and you double-click a file with a .doc extension in My Computer, the Word application will launch and the .doc file will open in the application window.

Opening a File from Within an Application

A common way to get into an existing file is to open the application used to create it, then search for the file from within that application.

For example, if you wanted to open a file called sales.ppt, you could start by launching the PowerPoint application. Once the program is running, select **File | Open**, then browse through your files until you find the sales.ppt file. Select the file name (see Figure 12.8) and click the **Open** button to open the file.

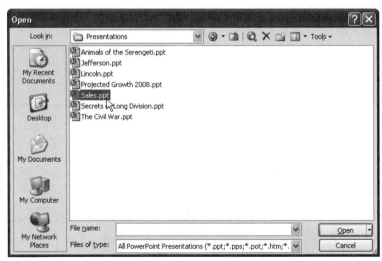

Figure 12.8: Opening sales.ppt from within PowerPoint

Bitmaps, Tigers, and Bears, Oh My!
You've seen bitmap files way back in Chapter 10, "The Good, the Bad, and the Ugly," along with other graphics and multi-media file formats. Turn back to that chapter and see if you can answer these questions. What other options for image files are in common use? How do they differ from one another?

Opening a File from My Computer/Windows Explorer or the Windows Desktop

When a file is already on your computer—either somewhere on your hard drive, or on a removable device such as a floppy diskette or a USB thumb drive—you can open it from a My Computer or Windows Explorer window, simply by double-clicking the file name or icon. The same is true for any file that resides on your Windows Desktop: if you can see its icon, you can double-click the icon to launch the appropriate application and open the file (see Figure 12.11).

Saving a File

In most cases, if you create a file, you're going to want to save it. If you don't save the file, you won't be able to view, print, or change it later; an unsaved file just disappears when you close the program (and after the program has warned you in no uncertain terms that your work is about to be lost).

Once in a while, you'll create a file that you don't really need to save. Suppose you made a sign for your mailbox saying, "Susie's Sweet Sixteen Party Here!" You only spent three minutes making the sign, and it's not as though Susie is planning to repeat that same birthday, so why save it? With exceptions such as this, you'll want to save pretty much every file you create.

Saving can be simple and straightforward, but like most things in Windows, there's more than one way to save a file. How you save your files—and where you save them—really matters, so let's look at those saving options!

Figure 12.9: The recently used file list in action

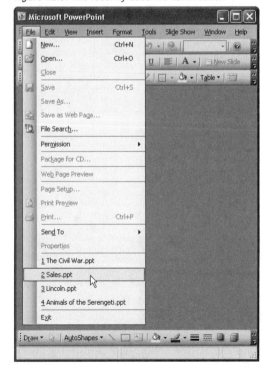

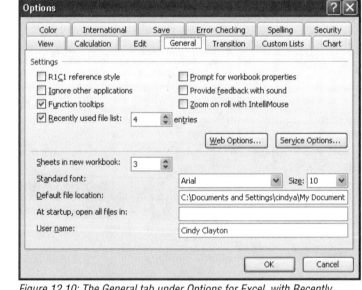

Figure 12.10: The General tab under Options for Excel, with Recently used file list set to 4

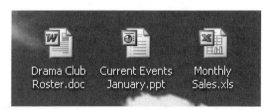

Figure 12.11: Files on the Windows Desktop: just double-click to launch the program and open the file.

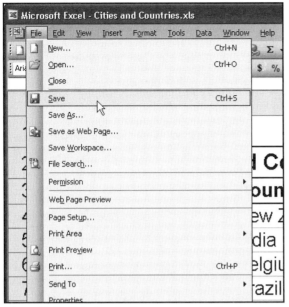

Figure 12.12: Selecting the Save command in Excel

Saving Changes to an Existing File

The simplest and most common way to save a file is in its current location, using its current name. This is what you would do when you open an existing document, work on it, and then want to save the changes you've made.

In most any program, you save the current file by selecting **File | Save** (see Figure 12.12), or by pressing the key combination **[Ctrl + S]**. When you do this, you're replacing the "old" version of the file (the one you opened) with the current version of that same file, which includes your latest changes. The file stays in the same location and keeps the same file name.

Using the Save As Command

Sometimes you don't want to replace the old version of your document—you may need to use it or refer to it in the future. In that case, you shouldn't use

Figure 12.13: The Save As dialog box in Word

the *Save* command, which replaces the original document. Instead, you'll need to use the *Save As* command, which makes a copy of the document and leaves the original alone.

When you select **File | Save As**, you get the Save As dialog box, shown in Figure 12.13. This is where you specify the directory where the new file will reside, the name of the file, and the file type. The name and location of a file are the two pieces of information that make each file unique, so pay close attention to these two items!

The way you use the Save As dialog box depends on what you're trying to accomplish. Let's take a look at the various situations that make use of the Save As command.

Saving a New File for the First Time

Even though you can use the regular Save command to save a new file for the first time, you'll get the Save As dialog box. This is your chance to name the file in a way that makes sense to you, and to place the file in the directory of your choice.

When the Save As dialog box appears, the *File name* field already contains a suggested name. If you haven't yet added any text to the document, the suggestion is the file's default name, for example Doc1.doc, Presentation1.ppt,

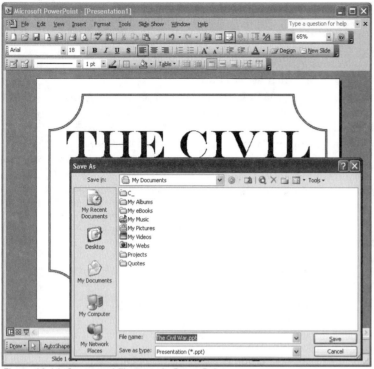

Figure 12.14: Suggested file name in PowerPoint

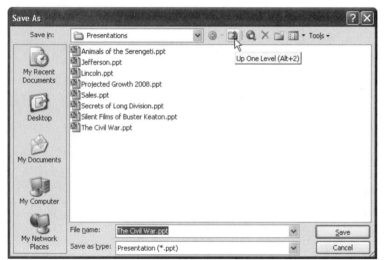

Figure 12.15: The Up One Level button in the Save As dialog box

or Book1.xls. If you have added some text, you'll see the application's best guess at what you might want to name the file, based on the first line of text in your document.

For example, if you started a PowerPoint presentation about the U.S. civil war, and the first slide started with your title —"The Civil War: 1861-1865"—then PowerPoint would suggest "The Civil War.ppt" as the file name (see Figure 12.14). In this case, the suggested name is a pretty good reflection of the document's contents, so you may decide to keep it.

In other situations, though, you'll definitely want to change the suggested file name. For example, if you're writing a letter to your uncle, Word might suggest "Dear Uncle Jack" as a file name. This wouldn't be such a good idea—especially if you plan to write more than one letter to Uncle Jack! Whether you like the suggested name or not, make sure the name that ends up in the *File name* field is unique, descriptive, and of a reasonable length.

In addition to naming the file, you need to decide where to store it. Most often, you'll be storing files on the computer's hard drive, although you can also save a file to a portable USB drive, a floppy diskette, or a drive on a network. The *Save in* field shows you the directory where your file will be saved; you can click the down arrow next to that field to see a list of other locations.

You can also click the **Up One Level** button (see Figure 12.15) to get to the parent directory of the folder currently displayed, or double-click a folder icon to save the file in a subdirectory of the current folder.

Once the name you want is in the *File name* field, the file type you want is in the *Save as type* field, and the location you want is in the *Save in* field, you're all set! Click the **Save** button and then go back to working on the file—or close it until the next time you need it.

Saving a File with a Different Name, Location, and/or Format

The *Save As* command is a quick and easy way to copy an existing file, when you want to put the copy in a different location, give it a different name, or give it a different file format.

When you use Save As to change the location of a file, you simply place an identical copy in the new location. You might want to save a copy of your file to the floppy disk drive or a USB drive, for example, to take it with you to work or school. Or you might want to save a copy of the file to a backup folder, a second hard drive on your system, or a hard drive on a network.

Using Save As to change the file name is also quite common. Suppose

COMPUTER LITERACY: YOUR TICKET TO IC³ CERTIFICATION

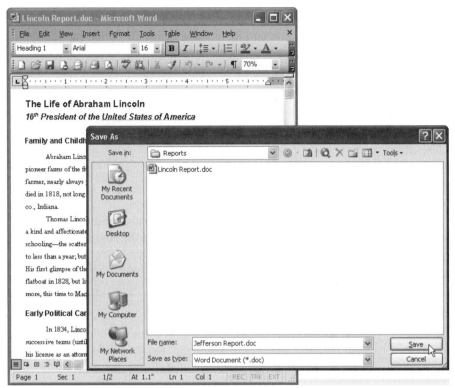

Figure 12.16: Using Save As to create a new document based on an existing one

you have a Word file called "Lincoln Report.doc," and you've worked hard to create a good outline and a table showing the timeline of Abraham Lincoln's life. Your next report is about Thomas Jefferson, and you plan to save it in the same directory. You'd rather start the new report from your Lincoln file, with its ready-made outline structure and timeline table, than start from scratch. You would simply open your existing .doc file, select **File | Save As**, and change the name of the file from "Lincoln Report. doc" to "Jefferson Report.doc" (see Figure 12.16). Then you could go about replacing the Lincoln content with the Jefferson content, and save yourself a lot of time and effort on formatting.

Save to a Default Location

You can make things easier for yourself by saving your files in a common location that's easy to find. In Windows, the most logical place to put your personal files is the folder called My Documents. You can access this folder quickly and easily at any time, using the Start menu. Figure 12.17 shows the location of the My Documents folder on the Start menu.

To save a file to your default location, select **File | Save As**, and confirm that the Save As dialog box displays the location you want. Change the name of the file as necessary, then click **OK**.

Figure 12.17: My Documents on the Start menu

Save to a Floppy Diskette or Other Removable Media

To save a file to a floppy diskette, select **My Computer** in the left-hand column of the Save As dialog box. Then select your floppy drive—usually the **A:** drive—and make sure there's a properly formatted diskette in the drive. Click **Open** to save the file to the diskette.

You can use the same procedure to save the file to another type of removable media, such as a USB drive or a flash memory card. Select **My Computer**, then look for the drive letter for the device you're using. Normally, the first drive letter available for this kind of removable media device is **E:**, but read carefully if you have multiple devices to be sure you're choosing the right one (see Figure 12.18).

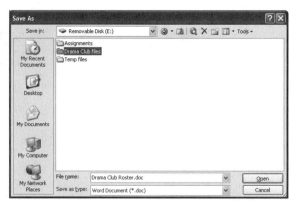

Figure 12.18: Saving a Word document to a removable drive, in this case E:

Save to a Specified Directory/Folder

To save a file to a different folder, pay special attention to the *Save in* field, which shows you the directory where your file will be saved. As you saw before in the discussion about saving new files, you can click the down arrow for a list of other available locations; click the **Up One Level** button to view the parent directory of the current folder; or double-click a folder icon to save the file in a subdirectory of the current folder.

Save in a New Folder on the Hard Drive

If you want to start a new folder and place the copy of your file in that folder, you can do this without ever leaving the Save As dialog box. For example, if you wanted to start a new folder called History Reports and put the new Jefferson report in there, you could do this all in one step.

Figure 12.19: Creating a new folder from the Save As dialog box

First make sure you're currently viewing the directory where you want to create the folder. Then click the **Create New Folder** button on the dialog box's toolbar as shown in Figure 12.19, type a name for the folder in the New Folder pop-up window as shown in Figure 12.20, and click **OK**.

The Save As dialog box now displays the contents of the newly created folder—so far, it's empty. Now you can change the file name if you like, or just click **Save** to place the file copy in your new folder.

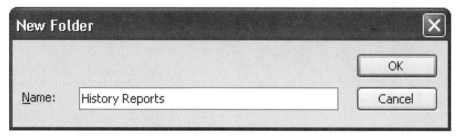

Figure 12.20: Giving your new folder a name

Save to a Directory/Folder on a Network Drive

If your computer is connected to a network, you can save a file to any network drive that you have permission to access.

In the Save As dialog box, click **My Network Places** in the left-hand column. This brings up a list of your mapped network locations (you'll learn about mapping network locations in a later chapter). Double-click the net-

Figure 12.21: Saving to a network location

work location you want, and drill down further, if necessary, to the specific directory where you want to store the file copy (see Figure 12.21). Then just click **Save** to copy the file to the selected network location.

Save to the Desktop

You can save a file to your Windows Desktop for easy reference later; just be sure that you don't save so many loose documents here that you clutter up the desktop (see Figure 12.22) and make it hard to find anything!

In the Save As dialog box, just click the **Desktop** icon in the left-hand column. When you do this, the desktop contents will appear in the main part of the dialog box (see Figure 12.23). If you'd like to save the document in a folder you've created on your desktop, locate and open that folder before you click the **Save** button.

Save in a Different File Format

Another thing you can do from the Save As dialog box is to save your file in a different file format. For example, you could save a .doc file into the simpler and more universal .txt format, which is understood by even the most basic text programs.

To change the file format, drop down the **Save as type** box and select the format you want (see Figure 12.24). When you change a file's format, you can either change its name and/or location, or leave them as they are. After all, when you change the format, the file extension changes, so your file name is still unique within the current folder.

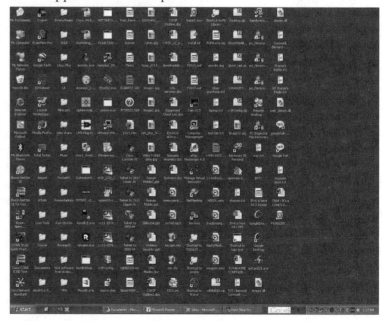

Figure 12.22: A Windows Desktop littered with miscellaneous documents

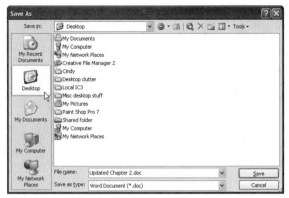

Figure 12.23: The desktop contents, which display when you click the Desktop icon

Figure 12.24: The Save as type drop-down in the Save As dialog box

Figure 12.25: Creating a new template in PowerPoint

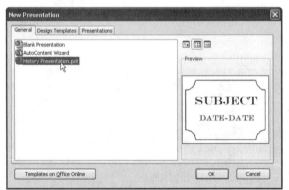

Figure 12.26: Saving to the Templates directory makes the new template easy to access.

Save as a Document Template

If you've been working on a file that you want to save as a document template—that is, the starting point for future documents—you can do that from the Save As dialog box. Just give the file an appropriate name, then drop down the **Save as type** box as you did to change the file type.

Select the file type used for templates in the application you're using. In Word, this file type is called **Document Template (*.dot)**. In PowerPoint it's **Design Template (*.pot)**, and in Excel it's **Template (*.xlt)**. Figure 12.25 shows the creation of a PowerPoint template called History Presentation. pot.

You'll notice that when you select the template file type in any Microsoft Office application, the *Save in* location automatically changes to your Templates directory. This is a central location where all Office applications store their templates; when you select **File | New** and select **On my computer** from the Templates area in the New Document task pane, this is where the computer will look (see Figure 12.26). So, if you want to make it easy to find your new template next time you create a new file, save it right there in the Templates directory.

Closing a File

Closing an open file is quite simple: just select **File | Close** (see Figure 12.27). If you have only one document open, and you want to close the application as well as the file, you can save a few mouse clicks by selecting **File | Exit** instead.

Closing a File after Working with It

So, you've made changes to a file, and now you're ready to close it. What should you do first? That's right—make sure you've saved your work as appropriate before you close the file. If you haven't saved your most recent changes, and you attempt to close the document, you'll get a message similar to the one shown in Figure 12.28.

Closing without Changing Anything

When you open a file, you can just have a look around, or print the file, without really changing anything. When you do this, it's best *not* to save the file. Do you know why?

Most people like to keep track of when a file was last saved, because that's usually also the last time the file was changed or updated. The time and date included on a file's property sheet are useful tools, but they can be misleading if you save files when you haven't made any changes.

For example, imagine that you have a baby boa constrictor, and you're keeping track of its growth in an Excel spreadsheet (see Figure 12.29). You check the snake's length every week, and enter the information into a file called babysnake.xls. Suppose that one week, on the day you normally measure, you just open the file and look at the data; maybe you even type in a few characters as you start to enter the date. But you're in a hurry, so you decide to measure the snake the next day instead. If you save the file when you close it, the date and time will be recorded, even though you didn't update the file. The next day, you may be fooled into thinking that you already entered the new measurement—after all, the file is dated just yesterday!—when in fact you didn't enter anything at all. If you just look at the data, then close the file without saving, the date will still show as sometime last week, and you'll know for certain that you need to measure the snake without further delay.

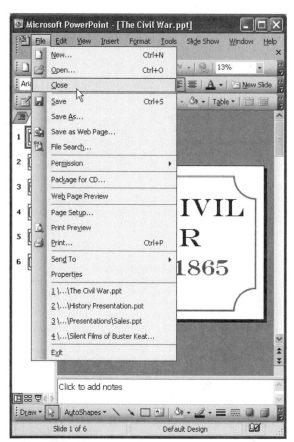

Figure 12.27: Selecting File | Close to close a PowerPoint presentation

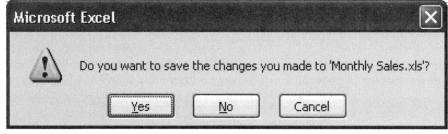

Figure 12.28: Message asking if you really want to close without saving

Problems You May Encounter When Working with Documents

If you use computers long enough, you're bound to run into problems from time to time, including problems with your documents. Let's take a look at the most common types of document problems so that you'll know what to do when something goes wrong.

File Association Not Set Up

If you don't currently have a file association set up to link a specific file type to a program that is loaded on your PC, Windows will tell you that there's a problem when you try to open a file of that type. For example, if you download a .ram (Real Audio) file, which can only be read by the Real Player application, but you don't have Real Player loaded on your system, you'll get an error message (see Figure 12.30).

Even if you do have the right program loaded, you'll get the same message

Figure 12.29: Awwww . . . isn't he cute? Now, when did I measure him last?

if you don't have a file association to link that program with the file type you're trying to open.

This dialog box gives you two options: either let Windows search online for a program that will open the file, or select an appropriate program from a list of all your installed programs. If you know that the program you need (in this case, the free RealAudio player) is readily available online, choose the first option and follow the instructions from there.

If you think you have a program that can open the file, choose the second option; then select that program from the list (or click **Browse** to search for the program, if it isn't listed), and click **OK**. This often works, because although you don't have a file association set up for the file type, you do have a program that will open it. If this is the case, you should create a file association, so that future files of that type will open on the first try.

Product or Version Incompatibility

Some word processing programs that aren't made by Microsoft can still open a .doc file, but others cannot. When you try to open a file with a program other than the one that created the file, you may encounter *product incompatibility*. The solution to this problem is pretty straightforward: just open the file with the program that was used to create it. If the program you need is not installed on your computer, see if you can find a computer that *does* have that program; open the file there, save the file as a different file type, and try again. Another approach would be to install the program you need; this is an easy solution if the program in question is the free Adobe Acrobat Reader, for example, but it's not so easy if you need the very expensive Photoshop program.

Another possible problem you may encounter while trying to open a file is *version incompatibility*. As you may have noticed, software manufacturers are always coming out with new versions of their software—Version 1.4, Version 2.00404, Version 7 XQ, or what have you. Each version is meant to be an improvement over the last one, and the higher the number, the more recent the version.

Suppose your friend Gizmo sends you a music file created with the very latest version of a popular music player program. You aren't as up-to-date as

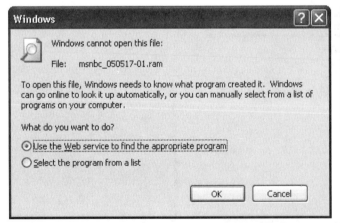

Figure 12.30: Without a file association, you'll see a message like this one.

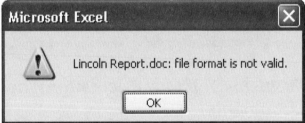

Figure 12.31: Message that appears when you try to open a .doc file from within Excel

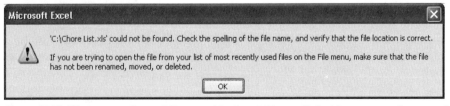

Figure 12.32: When a recently used file cannot be found, it's usually just been renamed or moved.

Gizmo, so your computer still uses a pretty old version of that same program. Even though you have the player, you might find that you can't play the file. You've fallen victim to version incompatibility! You'll need to upgrade to a newer version of the program before you can open that file.

File Corruption

It isn't pretty, but it happens: from time to time, for no good reason, a file becomes corrupt—that is, something goes wrong and scrambles the bits and bytes that make up the file. When this happens, it may mean an early death for your document.

This is why, as you learned in Chapter 10, backups are so important! A corrupted file can seriously ruin your day, but a recent backup is all you need to save the day.

Problems Opening Files from Within an Application

If you're trying to open a file from within an application, you can run into problems if the file is not in a format that the program recognizes, or if the file has been given a new name or location.

The file format issue is actually pretty easy to avoid: just pay attention in the Open dialog box, and remember what program you're using. The Open dialog box offers an **All Files** option under *Files of type*, but while you can select any file you want, the program won't necessarily open that file.

Suppose you're working on a history project about Abraham Lincoln; among other things, you've written a report in Word and a timeline chart in Excel. After your latest research, you want to add something to the timeline, so you open Excel. When you select **File | Open**, you don't immediately see your Lincoln timeline chart, so you select **All Files** to broaden your search. There's a file with Lincoln in the title! You double-click on it, not realizing that what you're clicking is the Word document. If you try this, you'll get a message like the one in Figure 12.31, stating that the file format is invalid.

This doesn't mean your computer doesn't know what to do with a .doc file—it does, and it would have had no problem opening it from My Computer or Windows Explorer. Within the Excel program, though, .doc files use an unsupported file format. Stick with the file formats you know work with your program, and you shouldn't have this problem.

The other issue that can come up when you open files from within an application has to do with the recently used files list. As I mentioned before, this list at the bottom of the File menu can come in handy when you want to pull up a file you were working on recently. Suppose, though, that you were recently working on a file called Chore List.xls. Since the last time you updated the file, you changed its name to Chores.xls—but the recently used files list doesn't know that. It still shows Chore List.xls, and if you click that item in the list, you'll get the message shown in Figure 12.32.

The same thing would happen if you'd simply moved the Chore List.xls file from one directory to another. The recently used files list only knows one place to look—that is, the file's location when you worked on it last—so if the file has since moved, you can't open it this way.

You can still open your file when you run into a name or location change error: just browse for the file in the Open dialog box or locate it in My Computer or Windows Explorer.

Creating a New File

■ When you create a new file in Word, Excel, PowerPoint, or other applications, you have two main options: start from scratch by creating a blank document, or get a head start on structure and formatting by using a template.

■ To create a new blank document, just click the **New** button on the toolbar. If you've just opened the application you'll be using to create the file, you probably already have a blank document, so you're ready to start filling that document with text, graphics, or other data.

■ Instead of starting your new file from a blank screen, you can use a template to make professional-looking documents in very little time. A template can save you lots of work, and often makes a nicer-looking document than you would have had the time or expertise to create on your own.

■ To use a template, create your new file using **File | New**, instead of the **New** button. In the task pane that comes up, you can specify where to look for templates (Office Online, your computer, your web sites), and then pick a template to use. The task pane also lists recently used templates for your convenience.

Default File Names

■ In all Microsoft Office applications, every new document is assigned a default name, which it keeps until you save the file.

■ These default names are fine for starting a file, but you should always change them when you save your file. Opening an Existing File

■ To open a file that has already been created, you'll need to know where that file resides on your system.

■ The file extension (the three letters that come after the period in the file name) can tell you what type of program created the file, or in many cases which specific program created it.

■ One way to open an existing file is to double-click its name or icon from within My Computer or Windows Explorer, or on the Windows Desktop.

■ Another way to open an existing file is to open the application used to create it, then search for the file from within that application.

Saving a File

- If you don't save the file, you won't be able to view, print, or change it later; an unsaved file just disappears when you close the program.

- The simplest and most common way to save a file is in its current location, using its current name. To do this, select **File | Save** or press **[Ctrl + S]**.

- To make a copy of a file in a different location, or with a different name or format, use the Save As command instead of Save.

- When you save a document for the first time, you get the Save As dialog box. The *File name* field already contains a suggested name, which you can keep or change. Be sure to select an appropriate location for the new file as well.

- In the Save As dialog box, you can select any location on your hard drive (including the Windows Desktop), removable drives, or any network drive to which you have access.

- You can create a new folder from within the Save As dialog box and save the file in that folder.

- The Save As dialog box also enables you to save a file using a different file format, including template formats such as .dot, .pot, or .xlt.

Closing a File

- To close an open file, select **File | Close.**

- If you try to close your document without saving your changes, the program will stop you and ask whether you want to save the file before closing.

Problems you May Encounter When Working With Documents

- If you don't currently have a file association set up to link a specific file type to a program that is loaded on your PC, you'll get an error message. You can select a program to use from a list of all your installed programs, or to avoid seeing the error message in the future, you can set up the necessary file association.

- When you try to open a specific file type with a program that is different than the one that created the file, you may get an error message. This is known as product incompatibility.

- If a file was created using the newest version of a program, you may not be able to be open it with an older version of the same program. This is called version incompatibility.

- From time to time, for no good reason, a file becomes corrupt—that is, something goes wrong and the bits and bytes that make up the file are scrambled. This is why backups are so important!

- When opening a file from within an application, you may see the "invalid file format" message (for example, if you try to open a .doc file from within Excel) or the "file could not be found" message (if a file on your recently used files list has since been moved or renamed). The easy solution to an invalid file format is to open the correct file, or open the file with the correct program. If you can't use the recently used file list to open a file, use My Computer or Windows Explorer to find and open it instead.

Key Terms

Blank document

Default location

Default name

Desktop

Existing file

File corruption

File type

My Computer

New button

Product incompatibility

Save As

Template

Version incompatibility

Unsupported file format

Key Term Quiz

Use the Key Terms list to complete the following sentences. Not all the terms will be used.

1. When a file won't open because you're trying to open a file that was created on a newer release of a software application than the one on your computer, this is called _____.

2. The _____ is a file name that a program automatically generates for you.

3. When a file won't open because you're trying to open the file with a different program than the one that created the file, this is called _____.

4. The _____ command enables you to change a file's name and/or location.

5. File names generally end with a period and three letters that indicate the _____.

6. When you save a file for the first time, the suggested storage location offered by the program is called the _____.

7. When the data in a file has been damaged to the point that it can't be recognized, this is called _____.

8. Saving a file to your _____ will keep it handy right on top of your wallpaper.

9. A document _____ includes formatting and content to help you create a professional-looking document quickly and easily.

10. When you open a file that has already been created, it is called a(n) _____.

Multiple Choice Quiz

1. What happens when you click the **New** button in an application such as Excel?
   A. You open an existing file.
   B. You open a blank document.
   C. You get the Save As dialog box.
   D. You open a new document template.

2. If you try to open a file from your recently used files list, but find that the file has since been renamed or moved, what should you do?
   A. Use My Computer to find and open the file.
   B. Use Windows Explorer to find and open the file.
   C. Restore the file from your most recent backup and then open it.
   D. Either A or B.

3. If you want to view an existing file, which File menu command should you use?
   A. New
   B. Open
   C. Save
   D. Save As

4. Which procedure enables you to use a template to create a new file in Word?
   A. Click the **New** button to open the New Document task pane, then click on one of the template options.
   B. Click the **Open** button to open the New Document task pane, then click on one of the template options.
   C. Select **File | New** to open the New Document task pane, then click on one of the template options.
   D. Select **File | Open** to open the New Document task pane, then click on one of the template options.

5. Jake has a file named images.doc on his Desktop. What would most likely happen if he double-clicked the file?
   A. The Paint program would launch and open the picture, ready for editing.
   B. PowerPoint would launch and open the presentation, ready for editing.
   C. Word would launch and open the document, ready for editing.
   D. Nothing would happen. Jake needs to right-click and select **Open File** from the menu.

6. Which keyboard shortcut can you use to save a file?
   A. **[Ctrl + A]**
   B. **[Alt + S]**
   C. **[Ctrl + A]**
   D. **[Ctrl + S]**

7. How do you save a document as a template?
   A. Click the **Save** button and select Document Templates (.dot) in the *Save as type* drop-down box.
   B. Click the **Save As** button and select Document Templates (.dot) in the *Save as type* drop-down box.
   C. Select **File | Save** and select Document Templates (.dot) in the *Save as type* drop-down box.
   D. Select **File | Open** and select Document Templates (.dot) in the *Save as type* drop-down box.

8. To which of the following locations can you save a file?
   A. Desktop
   B. My Computer
   C. Floppy diskette
   D. Any of the above

9. Which method could you use to open an existing PowerPoint presentation? (Select all that apply.)
   A. With PowerPoint open, select **File | Open** and choose a file from the list.
   B. With PowerPoint open, select **File | New** and choose a file from the New Presentation task pane.
   C. With PowerPoint open, click the **Open** button and select a file from the list.
   D. From My Documents, right-click the presentation you want to open and select **New** from the pop-up menu.

10. Jane created a spreadsheet in Excel and saved the file, but then forgot what she named it. Which of the following documents in her My Documents folder is most likely the Excel spreadsheet?
    A. Book1
    B. Document1
    C. Presentation1
    D. Spreadsheet1

Essay Questions

1. You have been selected by your principal to give a lecture on the difference between Save and Save As. What can you do with the Save As function that you can't do with the Save function? Explain the difference between the two.

2. Your next door neighbor is having a problem opening a particular file. To help her out, describe three common problems that users have when working with documents. What can be done to solve each problem?

3. Someone recently e-mailed your Aunt Fiona a file, and although she's managed to save it to her desktop, she isn't sure where to go from there. Describe for Fiona the different ways that files can be opened. What are the advantages and drawbacks of each method? Which is probably easiest for someone like Fiona who's uncertain of her computing skills?

Projects

1. Create a Word document, and save it to the My Documents folder on your C: drive. Now, use the Save As command to give the document a different name and save it in a different folder on your C: drive. How many copies of that document are now on your hard drive?

2. With your instructor's help, find and open a Microsoft Excel template for a sales invoice. Come up with a name for your business, a product that you would sell, and the price that you would charge. Print the invoice and evaluate it: does it look like a real business invoice to you? Does this make you want to learn more about templates?

Editing Documents

"You got an edit button on that thing?"

– Ted Reilly, *Tommy Boy*

This chapter covers the following IC^3 exam objectives:

- IC^3-2   1.3.1   Navigate around open files

- IC^3-2   1.3.2   Insert text and numbers in a file

- IC^3-2   1.3.3   Perform simple editing

- IC^3-2   1.3.4   Use the Undo, Redo, and Repeat commands

- IC^3-2   1.3.5   Find information

- IC^3-2   1.3.6   Replace information

- IC^3-2   1.3.7   Check spelling

- IC^3-2   1.3.8   Perform simple text formatting

- IC^3-2   1.3.9   Insert pictures into a file

- IC^3-2   1.3.10   Modify pictures in a file

- IC^3-2   1.3.11   Add drawn objects into a file

- IC^3-2   2.1.2   Select word, line, paragraph, document

According to estimates by Forbes magazine, J.K. Rowling, the creator of Harry Potter, is the first person ever to become a *billionaire* from writing books. Yet even this internationally known author makes her share of mistakes. In the *Frequently Asked Questions* section of her Web site, she admits that she accidentally got the order of the entrance of a couple of characters wrong at the end of *Harry Potter and the Goblet of Fire* because both she and her editor had not slept enough.

From professional authors to middle-school students, everyone who writes needs an editor. While most of us don't have an *entire person* devoted to helping us fix our documents, anyone using Microsoft Office applications has a great set of editing tools at their disposal. In this chapter, I'll discuss the tools that enable you to get around in a document, move blocks of text from one place to another, check your spelling, change the appearance of your text, and insert pictures to spruce up your documents. There's even a secret weapon that can get you out of a jam when you make a mistake! With tools like these, you can create top-notch documents—and still get plenty of sleep.

Scroll Bars

Chapter 11, "Working with Documents," introduced you to the scroll bars that display along the right and bottom edges of your document window. Describe two methods of using scroll bars to move through your document. What should you do if you want to scroll slowly through the document? What should you do to jump more quickly up or down through the pages?

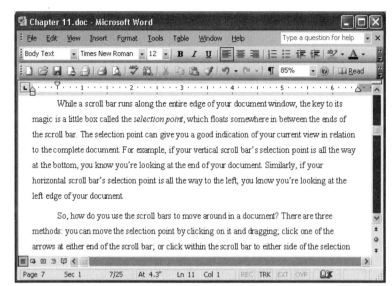

Figure 13.1: Scroll bars

Ways to Navigate

Before you start editing, you have to know how to get around, or *navigate*, within the document. Let's look at the different methods you can use to navigate through a document.

Scrolling

You've seen the scroll bars that run along the right and bottom edges of most programs (see Figure 13.1). If you click the down arrow at the bottom or the vertical (right edge) scroll bar, you'll scroll down your document—that is, the text will roll up and off the screen, much like the closing credits in a movie. If you click the up arrow at the top of that same scroll bar, the text will reverse direction, and you'll see the text roll downward as you approach the top of the document.

You can also scroll in a similar manner using the up and down arrow keys on your keyboard (see Figure 13.2).When you move through your document this way, the cursor moves with you; when you use the scroll bars, the cursor stays put. Whichever method you use to scroll through your document, the content that disappears off your screen is always there—it's just out of sight.

Searching

Imagine that you've just written a long report on the life and times of Theodore Roosevelt. While scrolling through your 30-page Word document, you discover to your dismay that on page 12, you accidentally referred to the subject of your report as "Franklin Roosevelt." Oops—wrong president! You make the correction on that page, but then you start to worry that you may have made this mistake more than once. Do you have to comb through your entire report, carefully checking for rogue Roosevelts?

Of course you don't! Word, like most other programs, has a great built-in search function that can lead you straight to specific words or *text strings*. A text string is simply any group of text—a partial word, two words, three words, an entire sentence—that you want to match exactly.

In almost any software program, you can select **Edit | Find** or press **[Ctrl + F]** to bring up the Find and Replace dialog box (see

Figure 13.2: The arrow keys on a keyboard

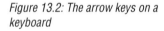

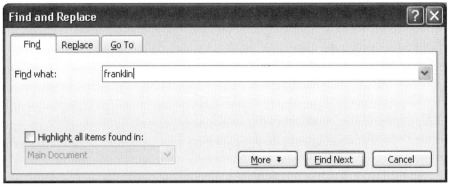

Figure 13.3: The Find and Replace dialog box

Figure 13.3). Note that in some programs, such as PowerPoint, this dialog box is just called Find.

In the *Find what* field, type the text string you're looking for; when you click **Find Next** or press **[Enter]**, the program moves your cursor directly to the next place where that text string is found. So, if you start out at the top of your document and enter *franklin* in the Find and Replace dialog box, Word shows you the first place (if any) you used the word "Franklin" in the document (see Figure 13.4).

If it turns out that you *did* type "Franklin" by mistake several times in your report, don't worry! You can address this problem quickly and easily using the **Replace** tab in the Find and Replace dialog box. Just click this tab, then type the text you want (in this case, "Theodore") in the *Replace with* field (see Figure 13.5). Click the **Replace** button to remove the old text, put in the replacement text, and move to the next instance of "Franklin." Just keep doing this until you've found and corrected them all. Pretty slick!

If no instances of "Franklin" are found in your document, you'll get a message like the one in Figure 13.6, reassuring you that you used the correct name throughout the report.

*Suppose you mentioned in your report that Theodore Roosevelt was a great admirer of Benjamin Franklin—you don't want to change that instance of the word "Franklin"! Just click **Find Next** again to skip to the next use of "Franklin," if any.*

Using Various Keyboard Tricks

Using **[Ctrl + F]** is a cool keyboard trick, isn't it? Well, the fun doesn't stop there. Let's look at a few other shortcuts that can make getting around and editing a document a snap.

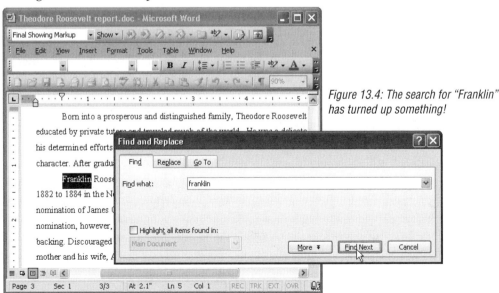

Figure 13.4: The search for "Franklin" has turned up something!

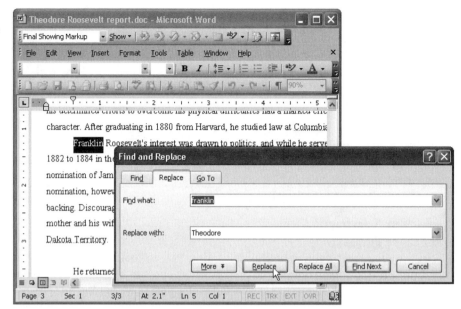

Just Do It!
If you have access to a word processing program, fire it up and start to play! Open a document (or create one) and find some word or words. Use some of the hot key combinations to find things and move around the document. Get those fingers busy. You'll have a lot more fun in this chapter if you follow along by doing what you're reading

[Ctrl + Home] to Go to Document Start

Pressing **[Ctrl + Home]** automatically takes you to the top of the document. This may not seem like a big deal, but if you have a 50-page document and you need to return to the top often, this could save you lots of time over scrolling page by page.

[Ctrl + End] to Go to Document End

Pressing **[Ctrl + End]** does the exact opposite of what **[Ctrl + Home]** does: it takes you directly to the bottom of your document. Again, in a lengthy document, this can be a big time saver.

[Ctrl + Right or Left Arrow Key] to Skip through Words

If you prefer to use the keyboard to move around in your document, you can sometimes feel like it's taking forever to move your cursor through the text. Here's a handy tip: hold down **[Ctrl]** while you press either the right or left arrow key. This makes your cursor skip from word to word in the direction you choose, instead of from letter to letter.

[Ctrl + G] to Use the Go To Command

In larger documents, you may wish you could go to a specific page, line, or table, rather than just going straight to the beginning or the end of the document. You can do all this and more using the **Go To** option. Press **[Ctrl + G]** or Select **Edit | Go To** to bring up the Find and Replace dialog box, with the **Go To** tab selected (see Figure 13.7).

Here, you can select a page number, line number, table, or any other reference point you want. Click **Next** to move to the specified location.

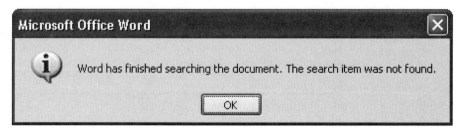

Figure 13.6: Message stating that your text string was not found

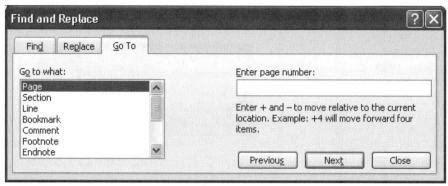

Figure 13.7: The Go To tab in the Find and Replace dialog box

Selecting Information and Using the Clipboard

One of the most useful features of modern software applications is the quick and easy movement or removal of data. If you discover that you've typed "the the" in a sentence, for example, you can quickly zap that second "the" into oblivion. If you find a group of spreadsheet rows that should be on a different page of your worksheet, you can move them there in a few seconds! Even if you want to copy an entire document that's several pages long and place all that data into another document, you can do that too—almost instantly--using a feature called the *Windows clipboard*.

Think of the clipboard as a temporary storage facility where you can put text and graphics that you want to move or copy. This feature is really handy, as you'll see a few pages from now. Before you can copy, move, or delete data, though, you need to select it! Let's check out the fastest and most efficient ways of selecting information in a document.

Click and Drag

Ever since the invention of the mouse, *click and drag* has been the most common method of selecting text. Click and drag means placing your cursor at the beginning of the data you want to select, then holding down the left mouse button as you drag the cursor over the rest of the data you want to select. As you drag, the text and graphics included in your selection become highlighted. When you've highlighted all the data you want to select, release the left mouse button.

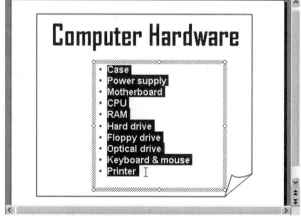

Figure 13.8: Highlighting data on a PowerPoint slide using click and drag

For the example shown in Figure 13.8, I clicked to the left of the word "Case" and dragged to where you see the insertion point, just to the right of the word "Printer."

[Shift]-click

The *[Shift]-click* method is essentially a faster version of click and drag. To select data this way, first place your cursor at the beginning of a section of data you want to select, so that your insertion point is blinking just to the left of the first word or character. Then move to the end of the data you're selecting, press and hold the **[Shift]** key, and click just to the right of the last word or character you want to include. When you do this, all the data between your insertion point and the place you clicked will become highlighted.

Free Your Inner Mouse

Mouse clicking and selecting can give you some odd results when you first start with a program, so your best way to get familiar with your tools is to do it. Open a document with some text in it and try the old click and drag; give the **[Shift]** *+ click and other options a try as well.*

Double- and Triple-click

You can also neatly select a specific word or paragraph using a simple mouse operation. To highlight a particular word or number, double-click your mouse on it. If you want to highlight an entire paragraph, triple-click your mouse anywhere within the paragraph.

[Ctrl + A] to Select All

Using one quick key combination, you can select all of the information in your entire document, no matter how long the document is. To do this, simply press **[Ctrl + A]**. You'll see all the data in the document highlighted all at once, including blank line returns, as shown in Figure 13.9.

> "To announce that there must be no criticism of the president, or that we are to stand by the president, right or wrong, is not only unpatriotic and servile, but is morally treasonable to the American public."
>
> – Theodore Roosevelt

Figure 13.9: An entire Word document selected using [Ctrl + A]

What to Do with Selected Information

Now that you know several ways to select blocks of data, what are you going to do with that data? Don't just leave it sitting there, all highlighted with no place to go! Normally, when you select data—whether it's a word, a sentence, a couple of rows on a spreadsheet, a dozen slides, or an entire chapter of a novel—you're going to move it, format it, delete it, or copy it for use elsewhere. We'll look at the formatting a little later in this chapter, but for now let's see how you remove, move, copy, and paste data that you've selected.

Figure 13.10: The [Delete] and [Backspace] keys on a keyboard

Clearing a Selection

There are two primary ways of clearing selected data: the **[Delete]** key and the **[Backspace]** key (see Figure 13.10). These two keys behave differently when you're just typing along—**[Delete]** clears out the character after (to the right of) your cursor, while **[Backspace]** backs over the previous character. When it comes to a block of selected text, however, these two keys work the same way.

Whether you've selected a cell or a group of cells in Excel, a slide or a range of slides in PowerPoint, or a word or a paragraph in Word, just press **[Delete]** or **[Backspace]** to make it all disappear.

Figure 13.11: The [Insert] key on a standard desktop keyboard

Using Insert/Overtype to Replace Existing Text

While we're looking at ways of deleting text, here's a less commonly used method: turn on *Overtype mode*. Many users of Word or Excel discover Overtype mode quite by accident after unintentionally pressing the **[Insert]** key, which usually sits just above the **[Delete]** key (see Figure 13.11).

When you press **[Insert]**, Overtype mode either turns on or turns off, depending on its previous setting (the default setting for Overtype is off). When you turn it on, the text that you type begins to replace the text to the right of your cursor, happily eating up the next sentence in the paragraph.

Figure 13.12: The Word status bar showing the
Overtype feature activated

Figure 13.13: The Cut, Copy, and Paste buttons on the Standard toolbar in Word

While it does have its uses—replacing name and address information in a form, for example—the Overtype feature can be annoying if you turn it on when you don't intend to. In Word and Excel, you can quickly see if Overtype has been activated, as the letters **OVR** appear in the status bar (see Figure 13.12). If you see that this has happened, just press **[Insert]** to turn off Overtype and see the **OVR** disappear or turn gray.

Cutting a Selection

Three of the most common document editing operations—Cut, Copy, and Paste—use the Windows clipboard. The *clipboard* is an invisible area where you can place information for temporary storage. You place data on the clipboard by either cutting or copying a selection from a document; then you can paste that selection somewhere else. The Standard toolbar contains buttons for Cut, Copy, and Paste, as shown in Figure 13.13.

Because you have the clipboard, the Cut command doesn't really delete a selection—it just removes it from its current location. There are three ways to cut a selection and place it on the clipboard: select **Edit | Cut** (see Figure 13.14), press **[Ctrl + X]**, or click the **Cut** button.

Now simply put your cursor where you want to place the information that you've cut, and use the Paste command to make it re-appear. Again, you have three options for pasting a selection from the clipboard: select **Edit | Paste**, press **[Ctrl + V]**, or click the **Paste** button.

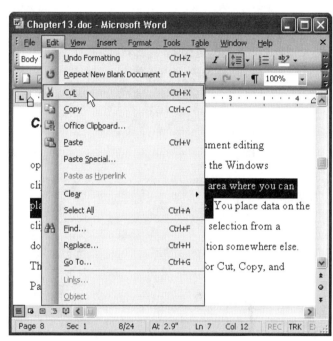

Figure 13.14: Using the menu option to cut a selection

Copying a Selection

Copying is similar to cutting in that you place a copy of the selected data onto the clipboard; the difference is that with copying, the original copy stays there! To use the Copy command, select the data you want and then choose from (you guessed it) three options: either select **Edit | Copy**, press **[Ctrl + C]**, or click the **Copy** button.

You won't see anything happen on your screen when you use Copy, but your data has been copied to the clipboard, just like it was when you used Cut. You can now move your cursor to the point in your document where you want the copy to go, then use any of the Paste methods described above to put the copied data in place.

Pasting into a Different File or Application

Since all Microsoft-based products use the clipboard, you can easily transfer information from one application to another. For example, if you've cut or copied a table in Excel, you can switch to an open document in a Word window, put your cursor where you want the table to display, and select **Edit | Paste**. The table from Excel will now appear in the Word document.

Get in the Groove
Once you've selected text, try copying, pasting, cutting, sliding, dragging, dropping, and the ever popular mouse-flick. Got the hang of it?

Moving a Selection Using Drag and Drop

For those who prefer to use the mouse rather than the keyboard, there's the *drag and drop* method of moving selected information. Just highlight the data you want to move, then click anywhere on the highlighted portion and drag your mouse pointer to the spot where you want the data to go. The selection will move to that spot as soon as you take your finger off the mouse button.

Dragging and dropping a selection in this way works just like using the Cut and Paste commands to move data within a document.

The Buttons You Need the Most

Depending on what kinds of work you do on your computer, you may use some of these editing functions a lot and others very rarely. There are two functions, however, that everyone uses all the time: Undo and Redo, which do exactly what their names indicate. Let's look at these critical editing tools which can really save the day.

Figure 13.15: The Undo button

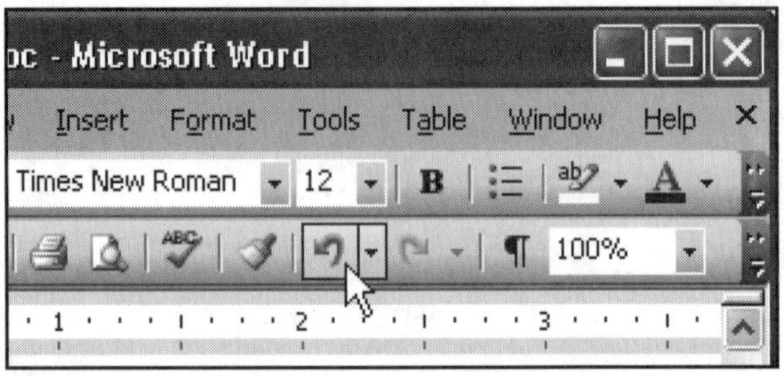

Undo

Have you ever hesitated to change something in your document, because you weren't certain how to change it back? Well, there's no reason to be afraid of change! You can undo the last change you made—and the one before that, and the one before *that*, and more—using the Undo option.

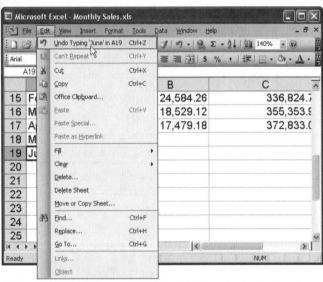

Most software programs have an **Undo** button right on the Standard toolbar (see Figure 13.15), and many allow you an almost unlimited number of Undo operations—that is, you can back out of literally dozens of your most recent changes. Excel is a notable exception, limiting you to undoing your most recent 16 changes.

You can also select the **Edit** menu, where you will see one of various options for **Undo** (see Figure 13.16). It may read *Undo Typing* if your last action was to type something, *Undo Delete* if your last action was to delete something, or *Undo Style* if your last action was to set a style. Whatever your last action may have been, you can undo it by selecting **Edit | Undo**, pressing **[Ctrl + Z]**, or clicking the **Undo** button.

You can use Undo to bring back text you didn't mean to delete, restore a style you changed and then didn't like, or un-insert a picture you just inserted—the possibilities are endless.

Figure 13.16: The Edit menu in Excel, with the option to Undo typing the word "June"

Redo/Repeat

The Redo command is the antidote for the Undo command: if you've undone something by mistake or you change your mind, this command can put those changes back into your document. As with Undo, you have three options: select **Edit | Redo**, press **[Ctrl + Y]**, or click the **Redo** button (see Figure 13.17).

In many cases, you can also repeat your last action, to save yourself a little time and effort. Suppose you need an eye-catching flyer about your upcoming school dance, and you decide to start with a few lines of nothing but the word DANCE. You'd

Figure 13.17: The Redo button in Word

rather not type DANCE over and over a hundred times—and you don't have to! Just open a new Word document, type the word DANCE, and press the spacebar. Then select **Edit | Repeat Typing** to see a second DANCE appear next to the first one. Now press **[Ctrl + Y]** repeatedly—that is, hold down **[Ctrl]** while you tap the **[Y]** key over and over. Watch the word DANCE start to fill up the page, as shown in Figure 13.18.

Using a Spell Checker

Spell checkers have certainly been a blessing to computer users. Let's face it—when you've been typing for an hour or two, it can be hard to remember the exact spelling of "impeccable" or "prestidigitation." Spell checkers can also be hazardous, however, because of what they *can't* do. Let's look at the pros and cons of spell checkers so that you can learn the best way to use them.

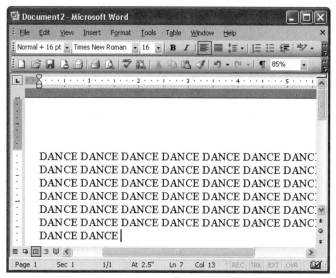

Figure 13.18: One example of the Repeat command in action

What a Spell Checker Can Do

Selecting **Tools | Spelling** (see Figure 13.19) activates your spell checker. It will scan through your entire document and stop at any word it thinks is misspelled. If it thinks it knows what you were trying to spell, it will even suggest the proper spelling.

What a Spell Checker Can't Do

Imagine that it's late at night, and you've just typed up a report for school. You run your spell checker, and it finishes by saying that it found no spelling errors. Everything is cool—right? Not so fast!

There are many things that a spell checker can't pick up. Let's say you mean to use the word *one*, but instead you type *on*. The spell checker won't realize that you left out an *e*; it only knows that *on* is a per-

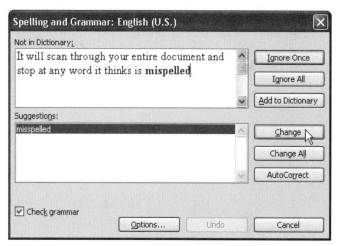

Figure 13.19: A spell checker in action

fectly good word in its dictionary. The spell checker can't tell when you use the wrong homonym for *there*, *they're*, or *their*. It also can't detect when your fingers take a wrong turn and you incorrectly type *form* in place of *from*—or *manger* instead of *manager*. The spell checker is good at what it was designed to do, but it can't think for you. Always re-read your documents!

Be careful when you add words to the dictionary: those words are now a permanent part of the dictionary file, so Word will never warn you about them again. If you add an incorrectly spelled word to the dictionary, you may miss that word when proofing documents in the future.

Also, never automatically assume that Word's spelling corrections and suggestions are accurate. Word doesn't always understand what you're trying to say, and it doesn't always have the words you want to use in its dictionary. Proper names, for example, are often not found in the dictionary. Wouldn't your friend Mr. Smythe be offended if you let Word correct his name to "Smith" in the letter you're writing to him? While Word can help you to find typographical, spelling, and grammatical errors, it can't substitute for reading what you've written and knowing correct grammar.

The Handy, Helpful Undo Feature

1. *Open Microsoft Word and create a blank document.*

2. *Type your name into the document, then select and delete your name.*

3. *Use the Undo command to put your name back on the page.*

Are People in Smaller Countries Better Spellers?

In the early 1980s, software manufacturers began to make spell checkers for use with word-processing programs. By the middle of that decade, most word-processing programs had spell checkers already built in—but only for languages that were used by large populations, such as English, Spanish, and German.

Software manufacturers determined that it wasn't cost-effective to go through the time and effort to make software that could check spelling for languages like Icelandic or Gaelic, so many people in smaller countries with unique languages didn't get spell checkers until the middle or end of the 1990s. People in those countries had to rely on their own spelling knowledge and attention to detail for more than a decade after the English-speaking world started relying on computers.

Do you think that people in smaller countries may be better spellers today because of this? Would you make fewer spelling errors on your own if you couldn't rely on the spell checker in your software?

Changing the Look of Your Text

Have you had an easy time reading this chapter? I'm sure you can think of things you'd rather be doing, but it would have been a lot more stressful on your eyes without the benefit of *text formatting*. For example, the **big, bold** text let you know when you were beginning a new section, and the *italicized words* brought to your attention any terms that were new or important.

Text formatting is an important means of communication in any document. Along with the text itself and visual effects such as pictures and charts, it helps convey your meaning and keep your reader interested. This section shows you some basic ways to change the appearance of text in your documents.

Selecting and Changing a Font

The term *font* refers to a particular size and style of text. *Size* is essentially a matter of how tall the letters are, and *style* describes the shape of the letters. In most software applications, you can select from a dazzling array of different font styles and sizes.

Font size is usually expressed in a unit called *point size*; the greater the point size, the larger the letters. You can easily change the point size of your text, and just as easily select a font style that's different from the *default font*—that is, the one that comes up automatically when you first open a new document.

To change your font style and size, simply go to the *Font* and *Font Size* drop-down boxes on the Formatting toolbar (see Figure 13.20) and select a style and a size for your text selection.

If you'd like to look at different font and size combinations before you decide which settings to use, you can select **Format | Font** to bring up the Font dialog box. Here, you can try on different settings, which are reflected in the Preview area at the bottom of the dialog box (see Figure 13.21). Click **OK** when you've settled on a font and size for your text, or click **Cancel** if you decide to keep you default settings.

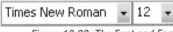

Figure 13.20: The Font and Font Size menus

Basic Text Characteristics

Three common ways to make a text selection stand out are **bold**, *italics*, and <u>underline</u>. Let's look at these text formatting options and how to apply them.

Bold

To make the text of a particular font darker and thicker, you can apply the **bold** characteristic. To make text bold, simply select the text you want to affect, then click the **Bold** button on the Formatting toolbar (see Figure 13.22). You can also use a keyboard shortcut to apply bold to selected text: **[Ctrl + B]**.

Figure 13.21: The Font dialog box, with the Preview area at the bottom

COMPUTER LITERACY: YOUR TICKET TO IC³ CERTIFICATION

Italics

The *italics* characteristic makes the text lean slightly to the right; it's often used to add emphasis to a particular word or phrase, or even an entire block of text. To italicize selected text, just click on the **Italic** button (see Figure 13.23). The keyboard shortcut for applying italics is **[Ctrl + I]**.

Underline

Right next to the Bold and Italics buttons, you'll find the Underline button (see Figure 13.24). This adds an underline to your entire text selection. Underlining is a commonly accepted way of writing the titles of books, films, and plays, among other things. It can also be used for emphasis: "<u>We always go for pizza on Friday nights</u>," or "<u>Clean your room now!</u>"

Once you've selected the text you want underlined, just click the **Underline** button or use the keyboard shortcut, which is **[Ctrl + U]**.

Fancier Text Tricks

While bold, italics, and underlining are the most common ways to alter text, there are other text tricks that are less common but more eye-catching. Let's look at a few other ways to jazz up your text.

Changing Font Color

The default color for text in all programs is black, but you can change your text to any of a number of alternative colors. Once you've selected a word or a group of text, just click the down arrow by the *Font Color* button (see Figure 13.25), and select the color you want from the drop-down box.

Note that the current color of the "A" on the Font Color button is the current default setting. If you want to turn your text selection the default color (for example, dark blue in Figure 13.25), simply click the button—you don't need to use the drop-down in that case.

Using Subscript and Superscript

A *superscript* is text that is slightly higher than the rest of the text on a line. Footnote numbers are often listed in superscript, as are exponents for math—for example 2^{16} or x^n. A *subscript* is text that is slightly lower than the rest of the text on a line. Numbers in scientific formulas, like the 2 in H_2O, are often listed as subscripts.

To apply either subscript or superscript formatting, highlight the text you want to format and then select **Format | Font**. On the *Font* tab, under *Effects*, you will see check boxes for **Subscript** and **Superscript** (see Figure 13.26); just check the one that you want to apply.

Using [Shift + F3] to Change Case

Suppose you've just been handed a document and asked to re-format it, and you notice that the person who typed it USED ALL CAPITAL LETTERS. The entire document looks like an urgent warning, or an old-fashioned telegraph. You'll have to re-type almost the entire document—won't you?

Of course you won't! Microsoft has given you a nifty tool that you can use to change the case (capitalization) of any text selection, whether it's a single word, a bunch of text on a PowerPoint slide, or an entire Word document.

Just select the text that you want to change, and then press **[Shift + F3]**. Note that the text changes from all uppercase letters to all lowercase letters, which is not quite right for this situation either. No problem—just keep that

Speel Czech
You know you want to do it, so jump back into that handy word processing program and run a spell or grammar check on a document. Deliberately use a word incorrectly, like deer instead of dear, just to see if the spell or grammar checker can pick it up. What happened?

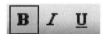

Figure 13.22: The Bold button

Figure 13.23: The Italics button

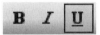

Figure 13.24: The Underline button

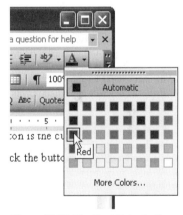

Figure 13.25: The Font Color button and drop-down box

More Formatting
Open up that poor, abused word processing document and do some formatting. Apply bold, italics, and such until it looks just right, then highlight a couple of paragraphs or words and do the [Shift + F3] shuffle.

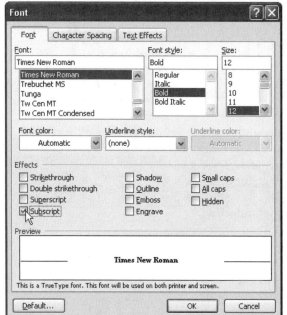

Figure 13.26: Selecting the Subscript
setting in the Font dialog box

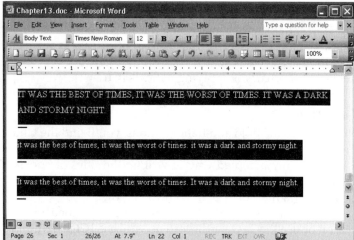

Figure 13.27: The effects of [Shift +
F3] on a paragraph in Word

text selected and press **[Shift + F3]** again. This time, the first letter of each line (or the first word of each sentence, if the text is in paragraph form) will be capitalized. If you press **[Shift + F3]** one more time, you'll be back where you started, with all capital letters.

Figure 13.27 shows how the same paragraph changes its appearance as you cycle through these case changes—from all capitals to all lower-case to *sentence case*, where just the first letter of each line or sentence is capitalized. Note that while this keyboard shortcut is available in Word and PowerPoint, it does not work in Excel.

A Picture is Worth a Thousand Words

Images can have a profound effect on the way your documents look, and therefore the way they're received by those who read them. Sometimes a well-placed image describes something better than any words ever could. In this section, you'll learn how to insert pictures into documents, how to edit them once they're in there, and how to get rid of them if necessary.

Inserting Images into a File

Inserting images into your document is pretty easy, but the exact method you use depends on the type of image you want to insert. Let's look at the two primary image types—graphic files and clip art— and how to insert them into a file.

Graphic Files

You can easily insert any common type of graphic file, such as .jpg, .bmp, or .gif, into a document. Simply click in the spot where you want to place the image, and then select **Insert | Picture | From File**. Look for the graphic file you want in the Insert Picture dialog box that appears. Select the graphic and click the **Insert** button to place that graphic in your document, exactly where you wanted it.

Figure 13.28: Using the Clip Art task
pane to find images with animals

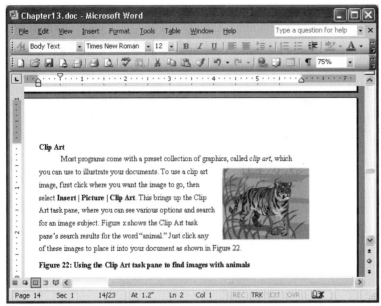

Figure 13.29: An inserted clip art image

Clip Art

Most programs come with a preset collection of graphics, called *clip art*, which you can use to illustrate your documents. To use a clip art image, first click where you want the image to go, then select **Insert | Picture | Clip Art**. This brings up the Clip Art task pane, where you can see various options and search for an image subject. Figure 13.28 shows the Clip Art task pane's search results for the word "animal." Just click any of these images to place it into your document as shown in Figure 13.29.

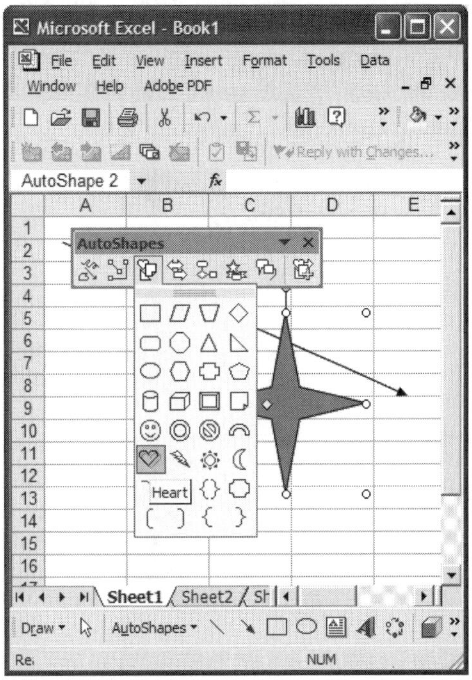

Using Drawn Objects in a File

Microsoft Word, PowerPoint, and Excel enable you to draw simple line drawings directly in documents, so you can add arrows, stars, word balloons, and more. You can layer the drawn objects, putting a star on a flag, for example, and even change the layer order once you've created the objects. Finally, to make working with multiple objects easier, you can group some or all objects, so moving one moves them all.

Figure 13.30: So many options!

To insert a drawing in any of the three programs, go to **Insert | Picture | AutoShapes**. This opens the AutoShapes toolbar, from which you can choose any number of basic shapes. Figure 13.30 shows Excel with the toolbar open and a couple of shapes added. Note that you can right-click on any shape and change the grouping, order, and the formatting, such as changing the color of the line or filling the object with color.

Drawing Tools

Way back in Chapter 10, "The Good, the Bad, and the Ugly – Multimedia, Personal Applications, and Utility Programs," you learned about drawing tools common in many applications. Turn back to that chapter and see if you can answer these questions. What's the difference between the line tool and curve tool? Do AutoShapes in Word or other Office application differ from the shape tools in drawing programs? How so?

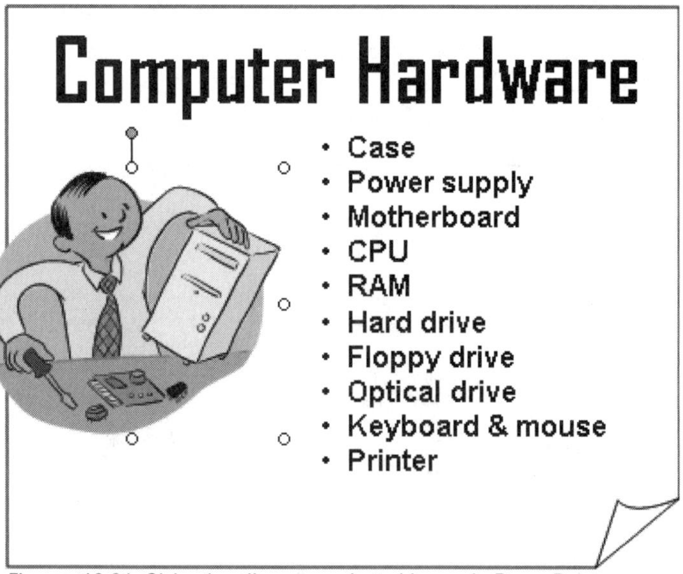

Computer Hardware

- Case
- Power supply
- Motherboard
- CPU
- RAM
- Hard drive
- Floppy drive
- Optical drive
- Keyboard & mouse
- Printer

Figuvre 13.31: Sizing handles on a selected image in PowerPoint

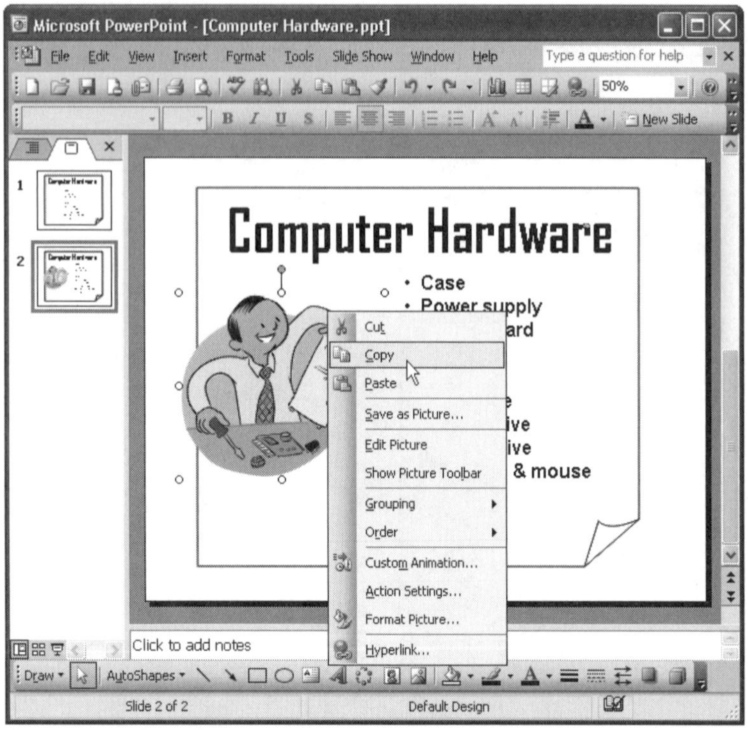

Figure 13.32: Copying a clip art image from a PowerPoint slide

Modifying Images in a File

You may need to do some editing on inserted graphics to get just the look you want. This section will cover how to resize, move, and crop pictures that you have put into your files.

Selecting an Image

Before you can modify an image, you'll need to select it. Just click somewhere in the middle of the image, and you'll see it change slightly to show that it's selected. Specifically, you should now see tiny circles or squares—called *sizing handles*—at each corner and halfway along each side of the image (see Figure 13.31). Once you see the sizing handles, you know that your image is ready to edit.

Resizing an Image

After you insert an image into your document, you may decide to make it larger or smaller. To resize an image, you'll use the sizing handles. First click to select the image, and then notice that if you point your mouse at any of the corner sizing handles, your cursor changes to a two-headed diagonal arrow. This is your sign that you're in the right place to begin resizing!

Click any of the corner sizing handles and drag that corner inward or outward. If you drag the corner toward the center of the image, you'll make the image smaller, and if you drag outward, you'll make it larger. When the image is the size you want, just release the mouse button.

Figure 13.33: Original image, complete with distracting wheels

Moving an Image

To move an image, right-click the image and select **Cut**. The picture is now gone from your document, and waiting on your clipboard. Move your mouse pointer or cursor to the place where you want to put the picture, right–click, and select **Paste.** The image now appears right where you want it.

Copying an Image

To copy an image, right-click the image and select **Copy** (see Figure 13.32). The image is now stored on your clipboard, so go ahead and move your cursor or mouse pointer to the place in the document where you want to put the duplicated image. Right-click this spot and select **Paste** to place the copy there.

Cropping an Image

After you've inserted an image, you may find yourself wishing that you could cut away part of the picture to focus on what's really important. In Office applications you can do this with the *crop tool*. When you crop an image, you don't shrink or enlarge anything—you just remove part of the image. You can crop

Figure 13.34: The Crop button on the Picture toolbar

Drawing Canvas

Word has an annoying feature called the Drawing Canvas that pops up when you insert any AutoShape into a Word Document. The Drawing Canvas theoretically helps you separate the regular text from your drawing, but in effect limits your space immediately and stops you from doing interesting things, like layering text and images! The only positive aspect of the Drawing Canvas is that it enables you to move all the shapes on the canvas at the same time by simply moving the canvas. To turn off the Drawing Canvas, go to Tools | Options and select the General tab. Deselect the box next to Automatically create drawing canvas when inserting AutoShapes, and click the OK button.

Figure 13.35: Dragging a sizing handle inward to crop the image

an image for a number of reasons: you might want to change the overall shape of the image, for example, or you might want to remove a distracting background detail, such as the partial bicycle wheels in Figure 13.33.

To crop an image, first select it to bring up the Picture toolbar, if it isn't already displayed. On that toolbar, click the **Crop** button, shown in Figure 13.34.

When you click the **Crop** button, the image gets sizing handles along the corners and edges. Your mouse pointer also changes, showing the same cropping symbol that appears on the button.

Now you can click on any sizing handle and drag the border inward as shown in Figure 13.35. When you release the mouse button, the picture is cropped where you moved the border. You can then crop another side of the image if you like, until your picture looks just the way you want it (see Figure 13.36). To turn off the cropping tool, just click the **Crop** button again.

Deleting an Image

To delete an image, simply click it so that you see the sizing handles, then press the **[Delete]** key. POOF! The image is gone.

Figure 13.36: The finished image, cropped on multiple sides

Ways to Navigate

- Press **[Ctrl + F]** to access the **Find and Replace** dialog box.

- Press **[Ctrl + Home]** to return to the top of a document.

- Press **[Ctrl + End]** to skip to the bottom of a document.

- Press **[Ctrl + Left arrow]** or **[Ctrl + Right arrow]** to skip from word to word in the chosen direction, instead of going letter by letter as you would using only the arrow keys.

- In longer documents, you can use the **Go To** feature to go directly to a specific page, line, or table. To use this feature, press **[Ctrl + G]** or select **Edit | Go To**.

Ways to Select Information

- To click and drag, place your cursor at the beginning of the data you want to select, then hold down the left mouse button while you drag to highlight the text selection.

- You can also place your cursor at the beginning of a group of data you want to select, then hold down the **[Shift]** key and click at the end of the data you want to select.

- If you want to highlight a particular word or number, double-click it. If you want to highlight an entire paragraph, triple-click anywhere in the paragraph.

- Press **[Ctrl + A]** to select all the data in the entire document.

What to Do with Selected Information

- Once you have a block of information selected—whether it's a cell or a group of cells in Excel, a slide or a series of slides in PowerPoint, or a word or a paragraph in Word—you can press either—**[Delete]** or **[Backspace]** to make it all disappear.

- If you have selected information and you want to type something else in its place, just start typing to overwrite the selection.

- You can move any selection to your clipboard by selecting **Edit | Cut,** pressing **[Ctrl + X]**, or clicking the **Cut** button. The text will disappear from the document, but it isn't gone—it's just moved to the clipboard, ready to paste somewhere else.

- To copy a selection to the clipboard while leaving the original in place, either select **Edit | Copy**, press **[Ctrl + C]**, or click the **Copy** button.

- To paste a clipboard selection into a document, first put your cursor where you want the information to appear. Then either select **Edit | Paste**, press **[Ctrl + V]**, or click the **Paste** button, and the selection will reappear in the new location, just as it was when you cut it.

- Because all Microsoft products use the clipboard, you can easily transfer data between programs.

- You can also move a block of selected text by dragging it to a new spot in your document.

The Buttons You Need the Most

- You can reverse the last action you took at any time using the Undo command. Either press **[Ctrl + Z]**, select **Edit | Undo**, or click the **Undo** button.

- Some programs have a Redo option in the Edit menu. If you select **Edit | Redo**, the most recently undone change will be restored.

Using a Spell Checker

- In most programs, the first item on the Tools menu is **Spelling**. Select this command to activate your spell checker.

- The spell checker is good at finding words that aren't in its dictionary, but it can't think for you. Always pay careful attention to your spell checker's suggestions, and re-read your documents.

Changing the Look of Your Text

- You can make any text **bold**, <u>underlined</u>, or *italicized* simply by clicking the corresponding button on the Formatting toolbar.

- The default color for text in all programs is black, but you can switch colors using the Font Color button.

- You can make text that's slightly higher or lower than the surrounding text (for example, X^n or H_2O) using superscript or subscript formatting, accessible via the **Format | Font** command.

A Picture is Worth a Thousand Words

- To insert any .jpg, .bmp, or .gif file into your document, simply click where you want the image to go and then select **Insert | Picture | From File**. Find the graphic file you want, then click the **Insert** button to display that picture in your document. To use clip art, use the same procedure, only select **Insert | Picture | Clip Art** instead.

- To resize an image, click the center of the picture, then click and drag any corner inward or outward to make the image larger or smaller.

- To move an image, right-click the picture and select **Cut** to place it on your clipboard. Move your mouse pointer or cursor to the place where you want to put the picture, then right-click and select **Paste.**

- To copy an image, right-click it and select **Copy**. Move your cursor to the place where you want to put the image copy, then right-click and select **Paste.**

- To delete an image, click it in the center once and then press the **[Delete]** key.

Key Terms

Click and drag

[Ctrl + A]

[Ctrl + End]

[Ctrl + F]

[Ctrl + Home]

[Ctrl + right or left arrow key]

Double-click

Drag and drop

Font

Go To

Overtype

Redo

Scrolling

[Shift + F3]

[Shift] + click

Subscript

Superscript

Triple-click

Undo

Key Terms Quiz

Use the Key Terms list to complete the following sentences. Not all the terms will be used.

1. The _____ key combination brings up the Find (or Find and Replace) dialog box.

2. The _____ key combination moves your cursor to the beginning of your document.

3. To reverse your last action, use the _____ command.

4. Text that rests slightly below the other text on a line (like the 2 in H_2O) is called _____.

5. You can _____ your left mouse button in Microsoft Word to select an entire paragraph.

6. A particular type and size of text is called a _____.

7. To reverse the effect of the Undo function, use the _____ function.

8. _____ refers to replacing selected text by typing right over it.

9. The key combination to select all of the information in your document is _____.

10. Text that rests slightly above other text on a line (like the n in X^n) is called _____.

Multiple Choice Quiz

1. Which key combination would you use to change selected text to all capital letters?
    A. **[Ctrl + C]**
    B. **[Ctrl + A]**
    C. **[Shift + C]**
    D. **[Shift + F3]**

2. What function enables you to move directly to a particular line, paragraph, or figure in your document?
    A. **Go To**
    B. Drag and drop
    C. Double-click
    D. **[Ctrl + A]**

3. Which key combination instantly takes you to the bottom of your document?
    A. **[Ctrl + Home]**
    B. **[Ctrl + End]**
    C. **[Ctrl + A]**
    D. **[Shift + F3]**

4. What button would you click to draw a line underneath a selected word in your document?
    A. Overtype
    B. Undertype
    C. Underline
    D. Subscript

5. Which of these reverses the last change you made to your document?
    A. Double-click
    B. **Redo**
    C. **Undo**
    D. Triple-click

6. What key combination lets you move through a document word by word instead of character by character?
    A. **[Ctrl + right or left arrow key]**
    B. **[Ctrl + F]**
    C. **[Ctrl + A]**
    D. **[Ctrl + Home]**

7. What key combination selects all of the information in your document?
    A. **[Ctrl + right or left arrow]**
    B. **[Ctrl + F]**
    C. **[Ctrl + A]**
    D. **[Ctrl + Home]**

8. What key combination instantly takes you to the top of your document?
    A. **[Shift + F3]**
    B. **[Ctrl + A]**
    C. **[Ctrl + Home]**
    D. **[Alt + Home]**

9. What's the easiest way to select an entire word with your mouse?
    A. Double-click
    B. Triple-click
    C. Click and drag
    D. Drag and drop

10. What is the word for a specific type and size of text?
    A. Overtype
    B. Subscript
    C. Superscript
    D. Font

11. What key combination can you use to help you locate a particular word in a document?
    A. **[Ctrl + A]**
    B. **[Ctrl + F]**
    C. **[Ctrl + H]**
    D. **[Shift + F3]**

12. What button would you click to make a selected word's letters thicker and darker?
    A. **Font Size**
    B. **Underline**
    C. **Italic**
    D. **Bold**

13. What command should you use if you've just clicked **Undo** by mistake?
    A. **Go To**
    B. **Redo**
    C. **Repeat**
    D. **Overtype**

14. Which of these functions is part of the clipboard feature?
    A. Cut
    B. Delete
    C. Backspace
    D. Home

15. Which of the following mouse moves can you use to select an entire paragraph?
    A. Double-click
    B. Triple-click
    C. Click and drag
    D. Drag and drop

Essay Questions

1. You've been selected to give a lecture to your class about the pros and cons of spell checkers. How can a spell checker be a big help? What things does your class need to be aware of that a spell checker cannot do?

2. You are helping your best friend put pictures into his Microsoft Word document. Explain how to insert a .jpg file from his hard drive, and how to insert a clip art picture.

3. Your Uncle Bob has never edited a document before. Explain to him three editing features that use the **[Ctrl]** key. What is distinctive about each one of these features? Give an example of when he would need to use each one.

Projects

1. You're putting together a presentation about your favorite hobby for the entire class. Go online and download five pictures related to your hobby. Then insert those pictures into a Microsoft Word document and write two sentences describing each picture.

2. Use Microsoft Word to write a brief description of yourself. When you're done, select the text and cut it to your clipboard. Then open Microsoft Excel and copy the text into an Excel file. Does it look the same as it did in Microsoft Word?

Printing Documents

"No, not again. I . . . why does it say 'paper jam' when there is no paper jam?"

— Samir, *Office Space*

This chapter covers the following IC³ exam objectives:

- ■ IC³-2   1.4.1   Format a document for printing

- ■ IC³-2   1.4.2   Preview a file before printing

- ■ IC³-2   1.4.3   Print files, specifying common print options

- ■ IC³-2   1.4.4   Manage printing and print jobs

- ■ IC³-2   1.4.5   Identify and solve common problems associated with printing

When most people think about the first printed books, they think of German inventor Johannes Gutenberg, who developed a machine called the *printing press* in 1450. His press had replaceable wooden (and later metal) letters that could be arranged to print out multiple copies of the same page. It would take him weeks, and sometimes months, to do an entire book. As it turns out, the Chinese were actually using moveable clay type over 400 years earlier, but their method was even slower and required a great deal of patience.

Obviously, things have changed! Today you can walk into a store and buy a laser printer that produces 25 perfectly crisp pages a minute, for less than the cost of two weeks' groceries. And it's a good thing, because even with e-mail, online conferencing, and paperless offices, printing documents is still vitally important. Legal documents that need a signature still have to be printed, and most people prefer to print things like driving directions and photographs. This chapter will cover everything you need to know about printing: setting up pages to be printed, selecting printing options, managing the printing environment, and troubleshooting common printing problems.

CHAPTER 14: PRINTING DOCUMENTS

Page Setup

Before you print your document, and even before you select any printing options, you need to make sure your document is set up properly to create the sort of printout you want. While some documents will only ever be viewed on a screen—for example, many PowerPoint presentations are never printed—most of them will make it onto paper eventually. For this reason, you need to pay attention to certain settings while you're working with your documents.

You'll find these settings on the Page Setup dialog box. To view this dialog box, select **File | Page Setup**. Figure 14.1 shows how this dialog box looks when you first open it in Microsoft Word; other applications look a bit different, but the general idea is the same.

Margins

A *margin* is the space around the edges of a sheet of paper where nothing is printed. In Microsoft Word and most other word processing programs, margins are automatically set to leave 1 inch blank at the top and bottom of every sheet and 1.25 inches on the left and right (see Figure 14.1). In Excel, the default margins are a bit different: 1 inch at the top and bottom, and .75 inches on the left and right.

Note that PowerPoint doesn't have margin settings (see Figure 14.2). Because PowerPoint presentations are primarily meant to be viewed on a screen or projector, rather than printed out, you have complete freedom to create each slide with as much or as little white space around the edges as you like.

To change a document's margins, select **File | Page Setup**, then click the **Margins** tab (see Figure 14.3) if it's not already selected. On this tab, you can change any or all of your page margins, either by typing in new values or by clicking the up or down arrow next to any setting. When you're finished, click **OK** to apply your changes.

Paper Size

The vast majority of print jobs are produced on standard letter-size paper, which in the U.S. measures 8.5 inches by 11 inches—the same size as regular notebook paper. You can print on other types of paper, for example the longer legal-size paper, envelopes, or specialty items like party invitations. Whatever paper size you're using, you can get your program to print your document properly using the appropriate Page Setup settings.

Most programs are set up to use letter-size paper by default. To change the paper size for your document, select

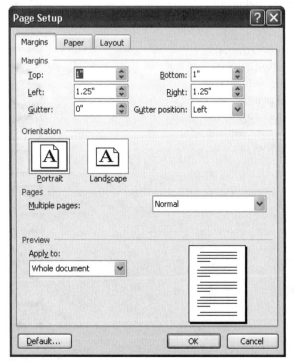

Figure 14.1: The Page Setup dialog box in Word

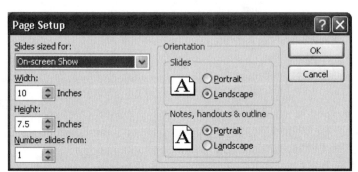

Figure 14.2: The Page Setup dialog box in PowerPoint has no margin settings.

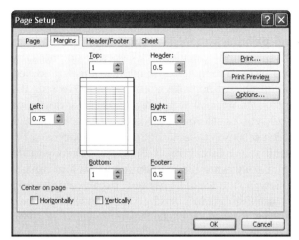

Figure 14.3: The Margins tab in Excel's Page Setup dialog box

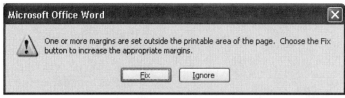

Figure 14.4: The printable area error message, with its handy Fix button

File | **Page Setup** and then click the **Paper** tab (in Word) or the **Page** tab (in Excel). You can then select an option from the *Paper size* drop-down box (see Figure 14.5), or manually enter measurements if you're using really odd-sized paper. When you're done, click **OK** to apply the change to your document.

PowerPoint doesn't have separate tabs on its Page Setup dialog box, but you can select a paper size from the *Slides sized for* drop-down box. Note that here, too, you can set up your document for an odd paper size. Just select **Custom** under *Slides sized for*, and then either type or select your paper's measurements in the **Width** and **Height** boxes.

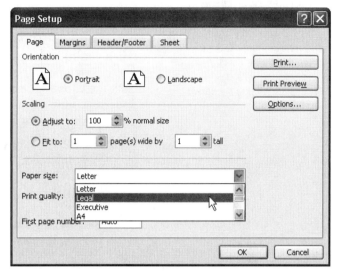

Figure 14.5: Selecting legal size paper in Excel

Paper Orientation

In addition to the paper size your document will use, you need to be aware of your document's printing *orientation*, or direction. The default orientation for printing is *portrait* orientation—that is, when you view the page, it's taller than it is wide. This is the way you would print out a report or research paper, or a vertical photograph.

For some documents, it makes more sense to print with the paper turned sideways, so that the document is wider than it is high. This is called *landscape* orientation, and it's useful for situations such as tables with many columns, photos taken horizontally, or a horizontal bar chart.

For a more visual explanation of these two orientation options, check out Figure 14.6, which comes directly from the Page Setup dialog box; the orientation settings are on the **Page** tab in Excel, or the **Margins** tab in Word. To change your document's orientation, select **File | Page Setup**, then select either **Portrait** or **Landscape** in the *Orientation* area.

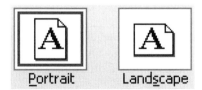

Figure 14.6: Icons showing orientation options, from the Margins tab in Word Page Setup

The Printable Area

*Although many of today's photo printers feature edge-to-edge printing, the inkjet and laser printers used in most offices and schools have what's known as a 'printable area, which limits how small you can make your margins. In other words, your printer may not be willing to go within .02 inches of the edge of your paper—and if you ask it to, you'll get a message (see Figure 14.4) telling you that your margins are set outside the printable area of the page. If this happens, you can click the **Fix** button in the message box; this will automatically set the smallest margin that your printer allows.*

Print Preview

With so many page layout and printing variables to consider, it's often hard to get a mental image of what your print job will look like before you actually print it. Microsoft Office programs (and many others) include a feature called *Print Preview* that lets you look into the future to see your document exactly the way it will look when it's printed. Print preview can help you make decisions about things like orientation; you can try formatting the document both ways before you print, to decide which setting to use without wasting paper.

To preview your document, select **File | Print Preview**. When you do this, a new screen appears in place of the main document window. You can tell when you're looking at a preview, as the word "Preview" displays right next to the file name in the title bar (see Figure 14.7). To close the preview window, click the **Close** button on the Print Preview toolbar, or simply press **[Esc]** on your keyboard.

Figure 14.7: Title bar for a document in Print Preview mode

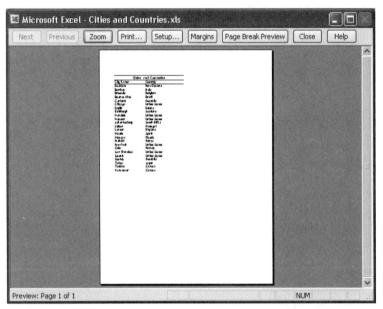

Figure 14.8: Print Preview in Excel

Changing the View

When you first enter Print Preview mode, your document text will probably be too small to read (see Figure 14.8). You may not care about that if you're only previewing the document to make sure the pages break where you want them, or to see how you like the margin settings. If you want to check your text, though, you'll need to take a different approach.

To magnify the text in Word, just move your cursor over the display of your document. The cursor will turn into a magnifying glass with a plus sign (see Figure 14.9). Just click once to make the text magnified, and click again (the magnifying glass will now display with a minus sign) to return to the original small size. You can also adjust the magnification percentage manually, by selecting an option from the Zoom drop-down list (see Figure 14.10).

You can also use Word's Print Preview toolbar to preview more than one page at a time. The button just to the left of Zoom is the Multiple Pages button. When you click this button, you'll be presented with various display options: 1 x 1 Pages, 1 x 2 Pages, 2 x 2 Pages, and so on. To return to a single-page preview, click **One Page**, one button to the left (see Figure 14.11).

In Excel, you have fewer magnification options. Just click either the page display or the **Zoom** button to switch between magnified and non-magnified previews, and click the **Next** or **Previous** button to display a different page.

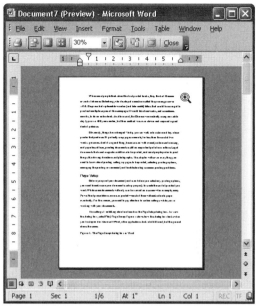

Figure 14.9: Magnifying glass in Word Print Preview

Figure 14.10: Adjusting the magnification using Zoom in Word Print Preview

Figure 14.11: The green One Page and Multiple Pages buttons on Word's Print Preview toolbar

Identify and Solve Layout Problems before Printing

The Print Preview function is like a seat belt in your car: it can't help you if you don't use it. As you use applications like Word, Excel, and PowerPoint more and more, you'll find that Print Preview often saves you from having to print something out twice. Did you use the wrong font in one part of your document? Is a picture inserted in the wrong place? Is a chart impossible to read because your page is set to portrait orientation instead of landscape? You can spot all of these mistakes and more can be found by double-checking things with print preview.

The Print Command and Its Options

So, you've typed up your document, added any pictures or clip art, and made sure your Page Setup options are set the way you want. You've checked Print Preview to make sure the document is picture-perfect and ready to print. Now what?

If you don't need to change any printer options, you can click the Print button on the Standard toolbar. This sends the entire document, using all the default printer options, to your default printer.

If you want to change (or at least confirm) printer options, you should select **File | Print** instead of using the Print button. This approach brings up the Print dialog box (see Figure 14.12), which lets you specify which printer to use, which pages to print, and how many copies to print.

Which Printer to Use

At home, you probably have just one printer hooked up to your personal computer, but if you're in a large school or office, you may have access to multiple printers. To determine where to send your print job, select the printer you want from the **Name** list in the *Printer* area of the Print dialog box (see Figure 14.13).

Getting Oriented

To see for yourself the difference that a document's orientation makes, try this exercise:

1. Create a new Word file.
2. Add some text—a poem you like, your name repeated several times, or just some nonsense words. Go ahead and add a clip art image somewhere on the page too.
3. Print the document using the Print button on the toolbar.
4. Select **File | Page Setup**, select **Landscape**, and click **OK**.
5. Print the document again, just like you did in Step 3, and compare this printout with the first one.

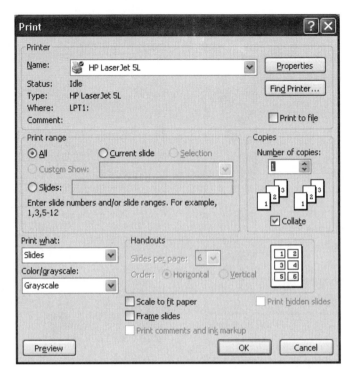

Figure 14.12: The Print dialog box in PowerPoint

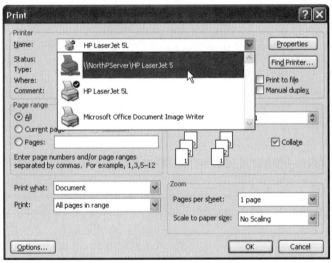

Figure 14.13: Selecting a printer in Word's Print dialog box

Which Pages to Print

If you're working on a large document, you may want to print only one page or a few pages from that document instead of all of the pages every time you print. On the left side of the Print dialog box is the *Print range* area (Excel or PowerPoint) or the *Page range* area (Word). Here you can choose whether to print all of the pages in your document, just the page currently on the screen, or just the range of pages that you specify (see Figure 14.14).

How Many Copies to Print

Just to the right of the *Print Range/Page Range* area is the *Copies* area (see Figure 14.15). As you may have guessed, this is where you tell the printer how many copies to print out. You can also tell the printer to collate your document.

Collating is when you assemble pages in proper numerical order.

What's the point of collation? Suppose you want to print 10 copies of an eight-page document. If you click the **Collate** box, the printer will produce a complete copy of all eight pages, then print another copy, and so forth. You can easily separate the copies and go about your business. This is the way to print out a Word file such as a long essay or paper, where you want the pages to end up in order.

But maybe you aren't printing that kind of document. Suppose you've used PowerPoint to make a bunch of one-page informational handouts for a school club meeting. You created the handouts all in one file, but when you print them, you want a separate stack of each page, so that people at the meeting can pick up just the handouts they want. If you select 10 copies and un-check the **Collate** box, you'll get 10 copies of page 1, then 10 copies of page 2, and so on.

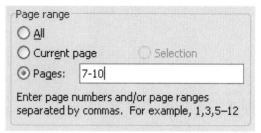

Figure 14.14: Specifying a page range in Word

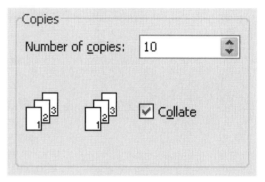

Figure 14.15: Requesting 10 collated copies in Excel

Managing your Printing Environment

While the printing process may seem a bit mysterious, you have a surprising amount of control over the process from your end. You can, among other things, select and change your default printer in a networked environment, display a listing of all print jobs going to the printers you use, and even pause, restart, or cancel print jobs you've sent.

Change the Default Printer

The first printer that is installed on your computer will automatically be your *default printer*—that is, the printer that handles all your printing unless you specify another printer for a particular print job. To set a different printer as your default printer, select **Start | Printers and Faxes**. This opens the list of all printers (and faxes) currently installed on your computer. Right-click the printer that you want to become your new default printer and select **Set as Default Printer** (see Figure 14.16). When you do this, you'll see the selected printer's icon change to include a little check mark, showing off its new default status.

Figure 14.16: Set as Default Printer

Display the Current Print Queue

At some point in time, you will have an issue with a print job. You'll click **Print** and then walk over to the printer, only to discover that nothing is coming out—or that someone else's print job is coming out, and it seems to be 100 pages long! To find out what's going on, you can check the printer's queue. Just as the word *queue* is sometimes used to describe a line of people waiting for something, a *print queue* is the list of print jobs waiting to be printed, in the order they were sent to the printer.

To see the print queue, look for a little printer icon in the System Tray area (the far right end) of your taskbar (see Figure 14.17). This icon appears only when you have a print job in the queue. Double-click this icon to display the print queue for your printer.

Figure 14.17: The printer icon on the taskbar

Cancel a Print Job in Progress

Have you ever started a really long print job, and then immediately regretted it? Maybe you printed the first draft of your paper instead of the final draft, or maybe you printed the long version of the Chess Club's meeting minutes (all 42 pages of them) instead of the two-page summary. Whatever the case, when you hear the printer whir into action, you can still save the day. You don't have to waste all that paper, toner, and time on a print job that will just end up in the trash—just cancel that print job!

To stop a print job at any stage of processing or printing, display the print queue and find your job in the list. If the print job is already printing, it should be at the head of the queue; if not, your user name should be beside the print job, to make it easier to find. Select the print job you want to stop, right-click it, and select **Cancel** as shown in Figure 14.18.

Pause a Print Job in Progress

If you ever need to stop a print job temporarily, follow the same procedure that you used to cancel a print job, only instead of selecting **Cancel**, choose **Pause**. You may want to do this if you realize the printer is about to run out of paper or toner, for example. After you pause a print job, it will stay in the print queue until you start it again using the Resume command (see Figure 14.19).

Troubleshooting Common Printing Problems

As much as computers make our lives easier, it still isn't a perfect world. Eventually, something will go completely bananas with one of your print jobs.

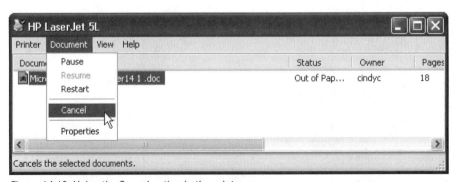

Figure 14.18: Using the Cancel option in the print queue

Figure 14.19: Resuming a paused print job

This always seems to happen when you are in a desperate hurry—but instead of panicking, you can simply remember the following troubleshooting tips.

Hardware Issues

As you know, printers won't print if they run out of toner or paper. Printers also don't work when people spill sodas or drop bowling balls on them. If your print job doesn't seem to be working, go make sure the printer is still connected, still has power, and isn't belching green smoke before you do anything else. There could also be other hardware issues like a disconnected network router—check with whoever is in charge of your network if you suspect this is the case.

Printer Driver Issues

Any peripheral computer device—whether it's a printer or a scanner or a thumb drive—will need to communicate with your computer's CPU. The piece of software that enables this communication is called a *driver*. If you buy a new printer, it comes with a CD-ROM that includes the printer driver. The instructions will tell you to put the driver disc into your computer's drive while installing the printer. If you don't have the right disc, or for whatever reason can't find and install the right driver for your printer, you won't be able to print to that printer.

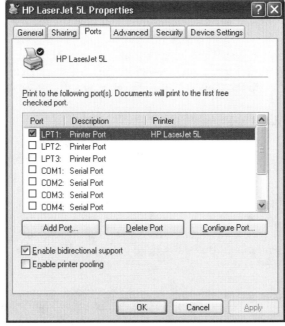

Figure 14.20: Printer port assignment

If this should ever happen to you, go to the printer manufacturer's Web site for information on how to get the driver your printer needs. Figure 14.21 shows a portion of a page from the Hewlett-Packard Web site where you can find drivers and other software for HP printers.

In case you're wondering, you can only pause or cancel your own print jobs. So much for trying to be sneaky and canceling other peoples' print jobs so yours will come out first!

Port Hardware and Settings Issues

You can tell with a quick visual check whether the printer cable is physically plugged into the USB port or other printer port. Beyond the physical connection, though, is something called the logical port—a group of software settings with a name such as LPT1 or COM2, which can be set up to handle a printer, modem, or other device.

To view the logical port setting for a printer, Select **Start | Printers and Faxes**. Right-click the printer in the list, select **Properties**, then click the **Ports** tab to see the printer's port assignment (see Figure 14.20).

Normally, you wouldn't have a port problem out of the blue—someone would have to go in and change the port setting to mess it up. But if you're having printer problems, and you've checked physical connections like power, printer cables, and paper and toner, then you might have a printer port problem. This is something your network administrator should fix.

Figure 14.21: HP's Support & Drivers Web page

An Election Headache

Just days after the presidential election in 2004, the November 9th edition of the Rocky Mountain Post *in Denver reported that its county would be one of the last in the country to report election results. Why? The bar codes printed onto paper ballots—meant to help election officials count the ballots quickly—had been printed using the wrong print settings, so they couldn't be scanned by bar code readers. Because of this error, all of the ballots had to be counted manually. It's always important to pay attention to print settings, even if the outcome of a national election isn't at stake.*

Using Valid Print Settings

If you should encounter a printing problem after changing Page Setup or Print options, you should verify that those options are compatible with your printer. For example, if you went into Page Setup and set up your document to print on legal paper, but the printer you selected doesn't have a tray for legal paper, you'll get an error message. Any time you ask a piece of hardware to do something it can't, this will happen—so pay close attention to your printer's capabilities, as well as to your print settings.

Missing Printer Error

In large offices or schools with many printers, older printers may be replaced by newer ones (or simply moved around) pretty regularly. When this happens, anyone who's still using a moved or replaced printer as their default printer will find that they no longer have a default printer! If you ever try to print to a printer that's no longer attached to your computer or network, you'll get an error message similar to the one shown in Figure 14.22. Before you try sending the print job again, make sure that at least one printer in your printer list is available in the real world!

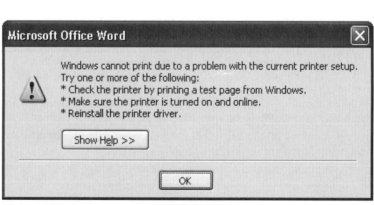

Figure 14.22: Error message for a missing printer

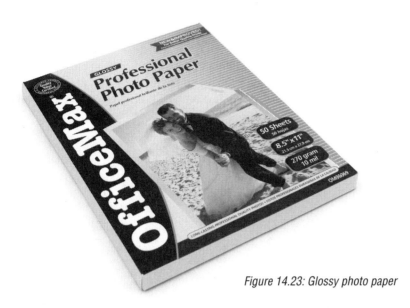

Figure 14.23: Glossy photo paper

Adding a Printer
In Chapter 7, "Computing Funda-mentals," you learned how to add a printer to your list of available printing devices. Suppose your default printer really did get replaced—what steps would you take to add the replacement device to your list and make it your default printer?

Printing Photos
Modern color inkjet printers can create beautiful prints of your photographs, suitable for framing and hanging on the wall. What many folks don't realize, though, is that it takes two steps to make this work. First, you need to use special photo-quality paper, not plain paper (Figure 14.23). Sec-ond, you need to tell your printer that it's about to print on that photo-quality paper. If you fail to do the second step, your photo prints won't be anywhere near the quality they could be.

*To set up your printer in Windows, go to **File | Print** (don't click on the **Print** button) to open the Print dialog box. Click on the **Properties** button in top right corner to open the print-er Properties. Note the section called Media Type—that's printer talk for what you're going to print on. Plain Paper is the default setting. Figure 14.24 shows the many media options of a Canon inkjet printer. Just select the one that matches your paper and you should be good to go!*

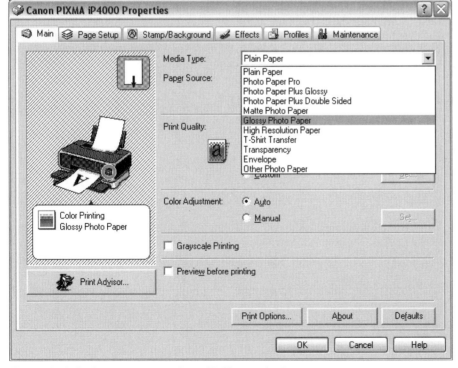

Figure 14.24: Cool—you can even print on T-shirt transfers!

Page Setup

- Margins are the blank spaces on the edges of the page. In most word processing programs, margins are automatically set to 1 inch at the top and bottom, and 1.25 inches on the left and right.

- A document set to portrait orientation will print so that it is taller than it is wide. A document set to landscape orientation will print so that it is wider than it is tall. Most documents print best in portrait orientation, but many wide tables, charts, and photographs are best printed in landscape orientation.

- The standard paper size used in office and school printing is 8.5 inches by 11 inches, the same size as a piece of notebook paper. This is the default paper size for Microsoft Word and most other programs.

Print Preview

- The Print Preview feature lets you see exactly how your document will look when it's printed. It's a good idea to preview your document before you send it to the printer.

- To activate Print Preview, select **File | Print Preview**, or just click the **Print Preview** button on the Standard toolbar, next to the Print button. The Print Preview screen takes the place of the regular document window until you close it.

- In Print Preview mode, you can see how the overall document will look, although the text is usually too small to read. You can view your pages one at a time, or view multiple pages at once.

The Print Command and Its Options

- Select **File | Print** (instead of just clicking the Print button) to open the Print dialog box, where you can view and change printing options.

- At the top of the Print dialog box is the *Printer* area, where you can select the printer you want to use from the **Name** drop-down list.

- On the left side of the Print dialog box is the *Print range* or *Page range* area. Here you can tell the printer which pages to print: all pages in the document, only the page you're currently viewing, or a range of pages that you specify.

- On the right side of the Print dialog box is the *Copies* area, where you can specify the number of copies to print.

Managing Your Printing Environment

- To make a printer your default printer, open the Control Panel and double-click **Printers and Faxes**. Right-click the printer you want and select **Set as Default Printer**.

- Whenever you have a print job being processed, you'll see a printer icon in the system tray area of your taskbar. Click this icon to display the print queue for the printer you're using.

- To pause or cancel a print job, find your job in the print queue (your user name should be beside it), right-click it, and select either **Cancel** or **Pause**.

Troubleshooting Common Printing Problems

- When your print job has a problem, always check the printer first. Make sure that you have paper, and that power, data, and network cables are plugged in properly.

- A printer uses a piece of software called a driver to communicate with the computer's CPU. If you are consistently having trouble with a printer, you can check the manufacturer's web site for an updated driver.

- If you've changed any printer settings, this could be the source of a printing problem. Try checking or resetting the items you've recently changed to see if this resolves the problem.

- If you try to print to a printer that's no longer connected to your computer or network, you'll get a *Printer not found* error.

CHAPTER 14: SUMMARY

Key Terms

Collate

Default printer

Driver

Landscape

Margins

Orientation

Page Setup

Portrait

Port

Print job

Printer list

Print Preview

Print Queue

Print range/page range

Printable area

Key Term Quiz

Use the Key Terms list to complete the following sentences. Not all the terms will be used.

1. A _____ is any document that has been sent to the printer.

2. To _____ means to arrange pages in numerical order.

3. The list of print jobs for a particular printer is called the _____.

4. A document that is longer from left to right than from top to bottom has _____ orientation.

5. To see what your document will look like when it's printed, use the _____ function.

6. Instead of printing an entire document, you can choose to print only a portion of the document, called a _____.

7. The _____ are the areas around the edge of a page where nothing is printed.

8. A _____ is software that must be installed on your computer before you can use your printer.

9. Most reports, essays, and research papers are printed in _____ orientation.

10. If you send a document for printing, and don't specify which printer to use, it will print on the _____.

Multiple-Choice Quiz

1. Which of the following terms refers to the positioning of content on the page?
   A. Orientation
   B. Collation
   C. Margin
   D. Setup

2. What do we call the slot on your computer where you plug in your printer cable?
   A. Driver
   B. Queue
   C. Setup
   D. Port

3. Where can you go to select a different printer to use?
   A. The Print dialog box
   B. The Page Setup dialog box
   C. The print queue
   D. Print Preview

4. If you share a printer, where can you see a list of the print jobs that are in line ahead of yours?
   A. The Print dialog box
   B. The Print Order dialog box
   C. The print queue
   D. Print Preview

5. Which of the following terms describes the process of arranging pages in numerical order?
   A. Orientation
   B. Print range
   C. Collate
   D. Preview

6. When a page is longer from left to right than from top to bottom, what is its orientation?
   A. Portrait
   B. Landscape
   C. Default
   D. Queue

7. When you need to print a document on legal paper instead of standard letter paper, what setting will you most likely need to change?
   A. Printer type
   B. Default printer
   C. Paper size
   D. Print range

8. Where can you change the number of pages from your Word document that you want to print?
   A. Printer list
   B. Page range
   C. Print Queue
   D. Print Preview

9. What do we call the printer that your programs will automatically use when you send a print job?
   A. The range printer
   B. The default printer
   C. The queued printer
   D. The printer setup

10. If your printer cable is unplugged, what kind of problem do you have?
    A. A software issue
    B. A default issue
    C. A hardware issue
    D. A driver issue

11. Where can you see what your document will look like when printed?
    A. The Print dialog box
    B. The print queue
    C. The Printers and Faxes applet in the Control Panel
    D. Print Preview

12. When a page is longer from top to bottom than from left to right, what is its orientation?
    A. Default
    B. Portrait
    C. Landscape
    D. Collated

13. Once your Excel document has been sent to the printer, what is it called?
    A. Print range
    B. Printable area
    C. Print job
    D. Print queue

14. If you have too much blank space around the edges of your Word document, which of the following would you adjust?
    A. Margins
    B. Page size
    C. Orientation
    D. Page range

15. What do we call a piece of software that enables your computer to communicate with your printer?
    A. Translator
    B. Margin
    C. Queue
    D. Driver

Essay Questions

1. You have been selected by your teacher to give a presentation to a class one grade below yours. The topic is Print Preview. Write a few paragraphs discussing the reasons you would use Print Preview, then describe how to get into Print Preview, the different ways to look at your document in Print Preview, and how to return to your document when you're finished.

2. The principal just ran screaming into your classroom because she can't print report cards. The teacher is busy, so the principal looks at you. What common problems could be keeping the report cards from printing out? What can the principal do to fix these problems?

3. You are helping your neighbor print out some pictures from her computer. Some pictures are very long from left to right, while others are very tall. Explain to her the different printing orientations and when it would be best to use one orientation or the other. Also, explain to her how to change the print orientation of her documents.

Projects

1. Open your Web browser, go to www.google.com, and search for Microsoft Word documents. Type in a subject that interests you and also type in ".doc" for best results. Try to find a .doc file that's three or four pages long. Print two copies of the document, with the **Collate** option selected. Then print two more copies, this time with **Collate** not selected. Do you see the difference? Which method is more convenient for most of the documents that you print?

2. On a large piece of paper or poster board, sketch out a map of all the printers you can print to in your classroom or school. Include the name of each printer as it appears in your printer list. Next to each printer name, list the size(s) of paper that each printer can use. Put a star next to your current default printer. According to the map, are you printing to the most convenient printer? Are you printing to the printer with the best paper choices for your needs? Should you consider changing your default printer?

Basic Word Processing Skills

"An Oscar, you say? That would get me out of this festering rats' nest called television once and for all. Let me see the script. *[Reads for a few seconds]* No. No, I don't like the font."

– Calculon, *Futurama*

This chapter covers the following IC³ exam objectives:

- ■ IC³-2   2.1.1   Identify on-screen formatting information

- ■ IC³-2   2.1.3   Change spacing options

- ■ IC³-2   2.1.4   Indent text

- ■ IC³-2   2.1.7   Insert symbols/special characters

- ■ IC³-2   2.1.10   Display the ruler

- ■ IC³-2   2.1.11   Use tabs

- ■ IC³-2   2.1.12   Insert and delete a page break or section break

- ■ IC³-2   2.1.17   Create, modify and apply styles

- ■ IC³-2   2.1.18   Copy formatting (Format Painter)

- ■ IC³-2   2.1.19   Use language tools

- ■ IC³-2   2.1.21   Display document statistics (such as word count)

In the dark days before personal computers, people used mechanical devices called typewriters to hammer ink onto paper and produce documents, like letters and reports. The typewriter did its job well enough, but it had a major shortcoming. If you made a mistake in your typing or needed to move a few words around, you had to toss the whole page in the trash and retype it from the beginning. Worse, all the text looked the same, as you can see in Figure 15.1.

of the Orestes story, that of

omes the basis for the Erinys'

Kindly Ones. In that story,

persuade the Furies to release

it takes more than gentle per

ddesses. Knowing Athena's pow

Figure 15.1: Typed text close-up

Flexibility

*All word processing programs are not created equal. They can be as simple as Notepad or WordPad, which you can find by selecting **Start | Programs | Accessories** in Windows, or as advanced as Microsoft Word (see Figure 15.2). Notepad is fine for creating short, simple documents—you get the same basic text editing tools, but none of the fancy formatting options. WordPad has some simple text formatting options, but you can't use it to create advanced items like tables, and it isn't very good for large documents. Word, on the other hand, has a full range of editing and formatting tools, including some handy tools to automate the formatting process.*

Keeping Pace

This chapter will be a lot more interesting if you have Word or an alternative word processing program open and a document available to play with. Open up a document with text, such as one of your essays from a previous chapter, and follow along, making changes as you go through each section.

Today, we have a much better option that's much less frustrating and less boring. With a word-processing program, you can correct errors, move text around, format your text with different type styles, and much more. This chapter leaves the discussion of general techniques that work in any Windows application and moves on to look at specific functions of Microsoft Word and other word processing applications.

Word processing programs like Microsoft Word have astonishing formatting capabilities. Given enough time and skill, you could turn a plain-black-text-on-white-paper document into the Mona Lisa! Well, perhaps not quite that far, but you could certainly transform it into a fine advertisement with dynamic-looking fonts, pictures, colored borders, and more.

This chapter looks at four basic formatting areas: paragraphs, page and section breaks, symbols and special characters, and styles. We'll wrap up with a discussion of some time-saving Word features and a few words about language tools.

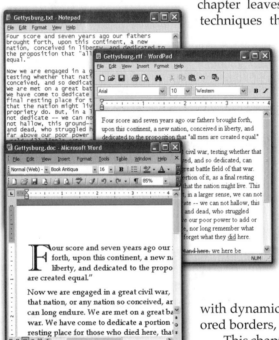

Figure 15.2: Documents open in (top to bottom) Notepad, WordPad, and Word

Paragraph Formatting

While text formatting is all about the appearance of each word, *paragraph formatting* changes the appearance of entire sections of text. Paragraph formatting affects things like how far apart your text lines are, where your tabs are placed, and how far the first line of a paragraph is indented. You can't apply these types of formatting to specific letters or words within a line of text—you can only apply them to paragraphs.

What's a Paragraph?

In a word processing program, you create a paragraph by pressing the **[Enter]** key on your keyboard. Although in a grammatical sense, a paragraph is a set of sentences that (hopefully) cover a single topic, that's not the case in a word processing program. A paragraph is a thing—that's a technical term—that you can format. A paragraph can contain sentences, but it doesn't have to.

Go ahead and press **[Enter]** a few times in your document. You'll notice that the blinking cursor, your insertion point, moves down several lines. Each of those blank lines, also known as a *hard return*, represents a new paragraph.

A blank line, however, doesn't always mean you've got a new paragraph. You can jump to a new line without starting a new paragraph by creating a *line break*, or *soft return*. To do this, simply hold down the **[Shift]** key while you press **[Enter]**. That soft return doesn't really look any different from the hard returns you made before, does it?

Display Paragraph Formatting Marks

To make things easier, Word can display some formatting information on the screen for you, using symbols. To display those symbols, look for the Show/Hide ¶ button on the Standard toolbar (see Figure 15.3). The button looks like a backward letter P, as you can see, the standard symbol for a paragraph.

When you click this button, Word displays a lot more symbols and characters on your screen; while these items don't show up in a printout, they still make a difference to the way your document looks and behaves.

At the end of each paragraph, for example, you'll see the paragraph mark. Looking back at the blank lines you created, you'll see that the hard returns you created by pressing **[Enter]** look like the backward P, while the line breaks you created using **[Shift + Enter]** look like an arrow pointing to the next line (see Figure 15.4).

Now that you can see the symbols for paragraphs and line breaks, you may also see other symbols (see Figure 15.5). Word puts a dot for every space between words. Wherever you pressed the **[Tab]** key—you'll learn about tabs later in this chapter—Word places another kind of arrow. If you've created more than one page of text in your document, you might also see a page break symbol; if you haven't, press **[Enter]** until you see a dotted line appear across your screen, signifying a page break. (Again, you'll learn more about page breaks a little later in the chapter.)

You can also choose specific hidden formatting characters to display using **Tools | Options**. In the Options dialog box, select the **View** tab (see Figure 15.6). The section called **Formatting marks** lets you choose whether to display paragraph marks, page breaks, and other formatting characters.

Formatting a Paragraph

Formatting a paragraph changes fundamental aspects of the whole paragraph, such as altering the spacing between all the letters and words. The characteristics you can apply to paragraphs

Formatting Text

You've already seen how to format text in Chapter 13, "Editing Documents." Before you proceed, be sure that you can answer these questions:

- *What's the difference, if any, between formatting text in a word processing program and a spreadsheet or presentation program? What menu command brings up the dialog box in PowerPoint where you can change the text font? What about Excel?*

- *Do the same shortcut keys work for formatting text in all of these applications?*

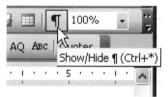

Figure 15.3: The Show/Hide Paragraph Marks button

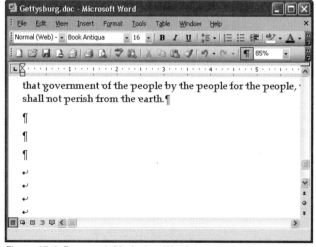

Figure 15.4: Paragraph Marks in a Word document

fit into five main categories: alignment, indentation, tabs, line spacing, and paragraph spacing.

To view all the formatting options for a particular paragraph, put your cursor anywhere in the paragraph and select **Format | Paragraph**. This brings up the Paragraph dialog box (see Figure 15.7), which is essentially Paragraph Formatting Central.

Aligning Text

The first option in this dialog box deals with *alignment*, or the left-right positioning of the paragraph. You can place the paragraph text in the center of the page from

Formatting symbols do not print on your documents, so you don't have to keep turning them on and off when you send files to the printer.

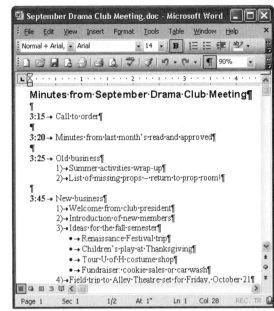

Figure 15.5: Looking at spaces, tabs, and other hidden characters

left to right by clicking the **Alignment** drop-down box and selecting **Centered**. The Center button on the Formatting toolbar, shown in Figure 15.8, does the same thing.

You can also line up a paragraph with the left or right margin. This means that either the left or right edge of the paragraph will be smooth—that is, all the lines of text will line up at the same place—and the other edge will be ragged. If you choose the **Justified** alignment option, the text lines up neatly on both the left and right edges, although to make this possible, the spacing between words has to be a little uneven. Figure 15.9 shows examples of all four alignment options.

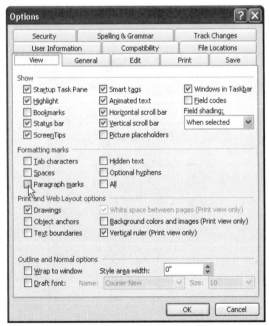

Figure 15.6: The View tab on the Options dialog box

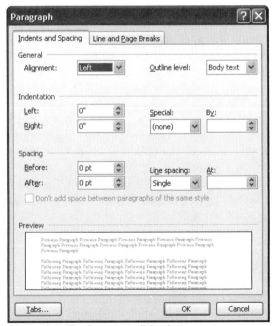

Figure 15.7: The Paragraph dialog box

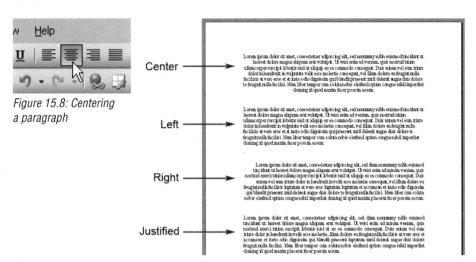

Figure 15.8: Centering a paragraph

Center
Left
Right
Justified

Figure 15.9: Centered, left-aligned, right-aligned, and justified text

Indenting Text

As long as you've been writing with a pen or typing on a keyboard, you've known how to indent a paragraph: for the first line, you come in about half an inch from the left margin, and for the rest of the paragraph, you stay at the margin. Well, that's the traditional way to write a letter, essay, or research paper—but depending on what you're writing in Word, you can indent your paragraphs, or not, however you want.

Take a look at the paragraphs in this very chapter, for example. The first line of paragraphs that come directly under headings don't have indentions, but the rest of the paragraphs do. You can choose when to indent and when not to, but you have to understand how to do it.

For starters, make sure your Ruler is visible, just below your toolbars. To make the Ruler visible if it's currently hidden, select **View | Ruler**. You can view your document using Print Layout to see the margins and indentations in action. Figure 15.10 shows the Ruler enabled at the top of a document in Print Layout view.

Figure 15.10: The Word Ruler

The white space around the text in Figure 15.10 indicates the margins. Margins are often set by default at 1 inch on each side, so if your paper measures 8.5 by 11 inches, the usable document space becomes 6.5 by 9 inches. You can change the margins.

The typical indentation pattern mentioned above (and used in this paragraph) is called a *first-line indent*. You can also indent every line of a paragraph, a *paragraph indent*; you might do this if you needed to include a long quote from a book or magazine in a report. You can indent the entire paragraph from

Why View Paragraph Marks?

You might wonder how these non-printing, usually hidden marks could possibly be useful to you. The more you get to know about Word, the more you'll be able to master your documents down to the finest details—but only if you understand these marks and what they represent. You'll definitely need to understand how to wrangle those line returns, paragraph marks, and more.

The paragraph marks actually contain the formatting information applied to a paragraph. If you delete a paragraph mark by mistake (because hey, you couldn't see it!), then you delete the paragraph-level formatting along with it. Sometimes when you select a bunch of text and delete it, you'll see the remaining text change its appearance for no apparent reason; this usually means you've deleted a paragraph mark that you meant to leave alone. You can avoid this headache by turning on your paragraph marks so you can see what's going on.

The Word Ruler can use a variety of measurement units. The Ruler in Figure 15.10 uses inches. You can change this to centimeters, millimeters, points, or picas, depending on the measurement type you need.

the left or right margin, or from both margins at the same time. Finally, you can use a *hanging indent* in which the first line is at the margin and the rest of the lines in the paragraph are indented. Figure 15.11 shows examples of all four types of indentations.

To indent a paragraph, place your cursor anywhere in the paragraph, open the Paragraph dialog box, and adjust the Indentation settings. Note that the **First line** and **Hanging** indentation types are listed under *Special*. Most regular first-line indentations are set at half an inch.

Tabs

A tab is a type of indent that you control using the **[Tab]** key on your keyboard. Each time you press **[Tab]**, the insertion point moves to the next tab stop, where you can begin typing. You can have more than one tab per line, so that when you press **[Tab]** repeatedly, your insertion point skips across the screen, stopping at each pre-set location. Tabs are often used to align small amounts of text in columns or in specific places on a page. Figure 15.12 shows some text that was aligned using tabs.

Press the **[Tab]** key a few times in your practice document to see the tab feature in action. If your hidden characters are still visible, you'll see something that looks like Figure 15.13.

Tab stops are generally set at every half-inch by default, but you can put tab stops wherever you want them. When you set manual tab stops for a paragraph, the default tabs are removed between the stops you set. For example, if you set a tab stop at 2 inches and one at 4 inches, you could press the **[Tab]** key once and find yourself at the 2-inch tab stop, press it again to reach the 4-inch tab stop, and then continue pressing it for tab stops every half an inch.

To set manual tab stops, click the **Tabs** button at the bottom of the Paragraph formatting dialog box to display the Tabs dialog box. Set a new tab stop by typing the ruler setting (in inches) where you'd like to set the tab stop. If you want a tab stop at 2 inches, for example, type the number 2. Leave the default Alignment setting at **Left** for now. When you click the **Set** button (see Figure 15.14), Word creates a left tab at the location you've specified.

After you click **OK** to close the dialog box, you can confirm the new tab stop by looking at the ruler. An L-shaped symbol appears on the ruler at the 2-inch mark, indicating a manually set left-aligned tab stop (Figure 15.15).

You can bypass the Tabs dialog box by using the Ruler to create, change, or delete tab stops. On the Ruler, click and drag the tab marker you just set (either to the left or the right) to change the tab stop setting. You can double-click a tab stop on the Ruler to display the Tabs dialog box. You can also click the tab and drag it down, off the ruler, to remove the tab stop, or click anywhere on the ruler to create a new tab stop.

You can set more than one kind of tab stop. Tabs, like indents, can have left alignment or right alignment. This means that whatever text you type after the tab will be lined up to the left or right of the tab. You can also create a center-aligned tab, where text will center on the tab stop; a decimal-aligned tab, where numbers placed at the tab stop will line up their decimal points at the tab; and bar alignment, which places a vertical

Figure 15.11: First line, left, right, and hanging indents

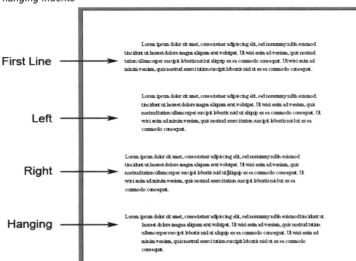

bar at the tab stop. Figure 15.16 shows an example of the different kinds of tab stops in action.

Another tab option is the use of *leaders*. Leaders are solid, dashed, or dotted lines that fill the empty space to the left of a tab stop, as shown in Figure 15.17.

By default, if you click on the Ruler to set a tab stop, you'll set a left tab stop. If you want to use the Ruler to set a different kind of tab stop, look all the way to the left of the Ruler for a button that shows the left tab stop symbol ( ). Each time you click this button, it changes to a different kind of tab stop (and cycles through indent options as well). When you see the symbol for the type of tab stop you want, click the appropriate location on the Ruler to create the tab stop.

You can have multiple tab stops and kinds of tab stops in any given paragraph. Manually added tab stops normally apply only to the paragraph in which you set them. To apply the same tab stops to a group of paragraphs (or an entire page, or an entire document), select all the paragraphs you want to affect before you set your tab stops.

Line Spacing

Line spacing indicates how much space is visible between each line of text. If you make text single-spaced, you are telling Word to display a line between each line of text (see Figure 15.18).

To make the current paragraph single-spaced, open the Paragraph formatting dialog box and select **Single** from the *Line Spacing* drop-down box. Alternatively, you can use the keyboard shortcut for single spacing: hold down **[Ctrl]** and press **[1]**.

Double spacing is just what it sounds like: lines of text are separated by two lines, as in Figure 15.19. To make the current paragraph double-spaced, you can either use the Paragraph formatting dialog box, selecting **Double**, or hold down **[Ctrl]** and press **[2]**.

There's one more way to control the space between

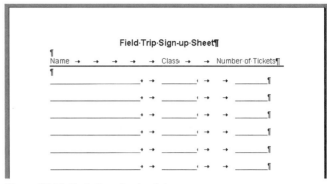

Figure 15.12: Text aligned using tabs

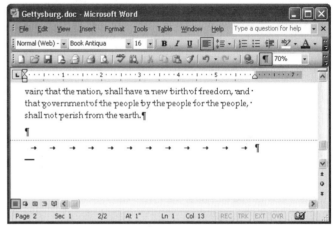

Figure 15.13: Multiple tabs on the same line

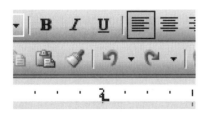

net consectetuer

Figure 15.15: The Word Ruler with a manual 2-inch tab stop

Figure 15.14: Setting a left tab at 2 inches

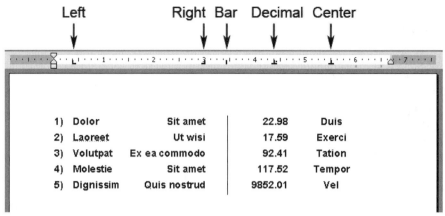

Figure 15.16: Various kinds of tab stops

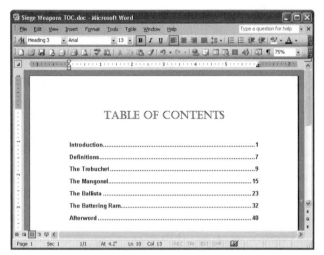

Figure 15.17: Tab stops with leaders

lines of a paragraph: use the Line Spacing button in the Formatting toolbar, as shown in Figure 15.20.

The size of the space between the lines of text matches the size of the text itself. If you're using a 12-point font, for example, the single-spacing indicates a single 12-point space between lines. You can also make a line space a specific size. For example, you could set a 12-point line space, even if you're using a 14-point font for your text.

Paragraph Spacing

Just as you can change the distance between the lines within a paragraph, you can change the distance between paragraphs, using *paragraph spacing*. For any paragraph in your document, you can add space above or below the paragraph, or both. To do this, open the Paragraph properties dialog box and change the Spacing options called **Before** and **After**.

Paragraph spacing is expressed in points, just like the size of your text. When **Before** and **After** are both set to the default value of **0 pt**, the paragraph is one regular line space away from the paragraphs around it—"regular" being either a single space, a double space, or whatever line spacing is applied to those paragraphs. When you change the **Before** and **After** settings, the space above or below the paragraph increases by the amount you specify.

For example, if you want an additional 6 points of space below your current paragraph, go to the

Figure 15.18: Single-spaced text

Figure 15.19: Double-spaced text

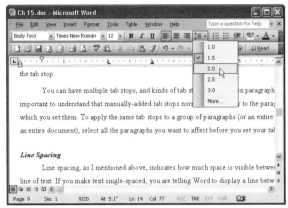

Figure 15.20: The Line Spacing button in action

After field and click the up arrow to choose **6 pt**. Figure 15.21 shows some single-spaced paragraphs with 6-point paragraph spaces in between.

Page and Section Breaks

Whenever a document is longer than one page, you can control which content goes on what page—that is, where to put *breaks* in the document. Use *page breaks* to control where a new page begins in a document. Use *section breaks* to apply different page formatting—page numbering, columns, and headers and footers, for example—to various parts of a document.

Page Breaks

When your document has enough text to fill a page, it automatically starts a second page. In your practice document, hold down the **[Enter]** key until you to see a dotted line that goes across the entire screen (if you're using Normal view), or the end of one page and the start of another (if you're using Print Layout view). Figure 15.22 shows what an *automatic page break* looks like.

What if you need a page break to be somewhere other than the end of a full page of text? Suppose you're writing a report, and the title page has only a few lines on it. The page isn't nearly full yet, but you're ready to go to a second page!

To create a *manual page break*, put your cursor where the new page should begin, then hold down **[Ctrl]** and press **[Enter]**. In Print Layout view, a manual page break looks just like an automatic one, but in Normal view, it looks a bit different, with the words "Page Break" clearly displayed on

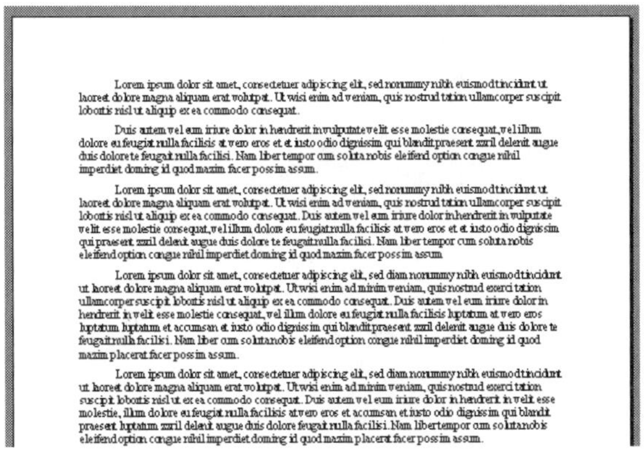

Figure 15.21: Paragraphs separated by 6-point spaces

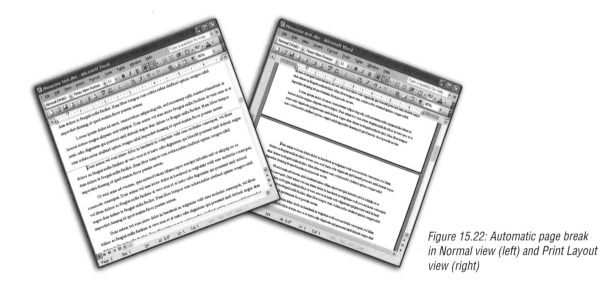

Figure 15.22: Automatic page break in Normal view (left) and Print Layout view (right)

Widows and Orphans

*When you use automatic page breaks, sometimes the first line of a paragraph ends up all by itself at the bottom of a page, looking a bit lost. It's equally sad to see the last line (or last word) of a paragraph all alone at the top of a page. You can prevent these stranded lines, known as widows and orphans, using the Paragraph properties dialog box. Click the **Line and Page Breaks** tab, where you'll find a check box for **Widow/Orphan Control**, as well as other settings that enable you to control where your pages will and won't break.*

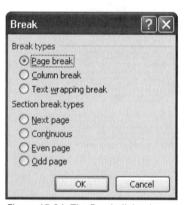

Figure 15.24: The Break dialog box

the dotted line (see Figure 15.23). Once you create it, a manual page break behaves just like any other character: you can search for it, use **[Delete]** or **[Backspace]** to remove it, or even replace it with something else.

You can also use the menus to insert a manual page break. Select **Insert | Break** to display the Break dialog box (shown in Figure 15.24), then choose **Page Break** and click **OK**.

It's often best to let Word decide where page breaks will fall, because manual page breaks

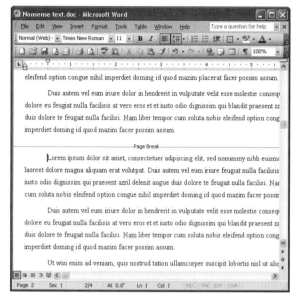

Figure 15.23: Manual page break in Normal view

require more maintenance than automatic ones. Each time you add or delete a chunk of text, automatic page breaks will go with the flow, keeping your pages a uniform length. Manual breaks, on the other hand, will stay stubbornly in place, making some pages shorter and others longer.

Section Breaks

The Break dialog box includes other types of breaks in addition to page breaks, most notably four different kinds of *section breaks*. These breaks are useful for dividing longer or more complex documents, in which different pages may need different page formatting.

The types of section breaks are **Next Page**, **Continuous**, **Even Page**, and **Odd Page**. A Next Page section break starts the new section on the next page of the document, much like a hard page break. A Continuous section break starts the next section in the current page, much like a regular paragraph break. An Even Page or Odd Page section break begins the new section on the next even- or odd-numbered page, leaving a blank page if necessary.

For different sections within the same document, you can change formatting settings such as page margins, paper size or orientation, headers and footers, columns, and page numbering. Figure 15.25 shows the Print Preview of a document with section breaks at each page; note the landscape-oriented page in the middle of the document (made using Next Page breaks), and the three-column layout in the middle of the third page (made using Continuous breaks).

When you delete a section break, the sections before and after the break merge into one section—and their formatting merges as well. When two sections merge, the settings for the section that was *after* the break take effect.

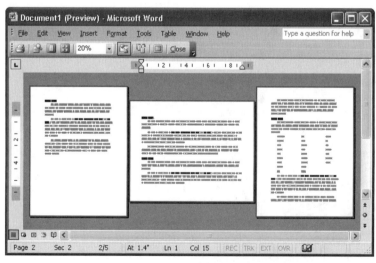

Figure 15.25: A document with section breaks and varied formatting

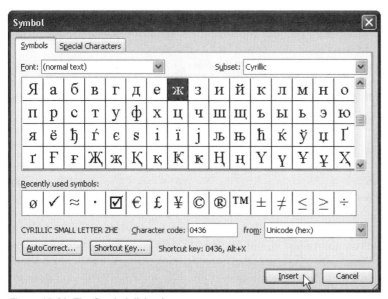

Figure 15.26: The Symbol dialog box

Symbols and Special Characters

When you're typing in a document, you sometimes need to include characters that aren't found on your keyboard: accented letters, symbols for foreign currency, weird math signs, or even a simple check mark. You can include these symbols and more by selecting **Insert | Symbol**. The Symbol dialog box (see Figure 15.26) offers symbols and special characters in the default font, plus any other font installed on your computer.

When you find the item you want, select it and then click **Insert**. Word will place the selected symbol or character at your insertion point.

Styles

With all of the text and paragraph formatting techniques you've learned here (and there are more to come in the next chapter), it may seem like an awful lot of work to format your documents. You could certainly spend plenty of time and effort making your text look right—if you applied every setting separately, you might spend more time formatting than typing your text!

Fortunately, you can use *styles* to make formatting quick and simple. Styles are collections of settings that you can apply with one click. The two most common kinds of styles are *character styles* and *paragraph styles*. A character style contains formatting settings only at the text (or character) level: things like font size, style, size, and color. A paragraph style includes formatting settings for text, but also for paragraph-level things like line spacing, paragraph spacing, and alignment.

A character style affects selected text, whether it's a single word, a single line, or a larger section of text. A paragraph style, as the name indicates, affects an entire paragraph.

Apply a Style

To apply a character style, first select the exact text you want. Then click the arrow next to the Style list on the Formatting toolbar to view a list of available styles (Figure 15.27). When you click on the character style you want, the selected text should immediately change its appearance.

To apply a style to a single paragraph, place your cursor anywhere in the paragraph. When you select a style from the list, the entire paragraph takes

Two Column Page
To create a two-column page in the middle of a one-column document, use the following steps:

1. Place your insertion point where you want the two-column section to begin.
2. Select **Insert | Break**, and insert a **Next Page** section break.
3. Place your cursor below the section break and select **Format | Columns**. Choose the two-column format, and make sure you've selected **This section** in the Apply to drop-down list.
4. At the end of the page or pages that you want formatted with the two-column format, choose **Insert | Break** and insert another **Next Page** section break.
5. Again, place your cursor below the section break, select **Format | Columns**, and change the column formatting, this time back to a one-column format.

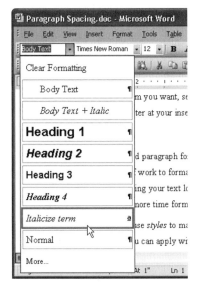

Figure 15.27: The Style drop-down list

on the characteristics of that style. To apply a style to several consecutive paragraphs at one time, use the mouse or keyboard to select the all of the paragraphs, and then choose a style.

You can also select and apply a style before you start typing a paragraph. As soon as you've pressed **[Enter]** to begin the new paragraph, select a style; any paragraph formatting will immediately appear, and when you begin to type, you should see the correct text formatting.

Modify a Style

In some cases, you won't be able to find an existing style that has the formatting you want. If there's a style that's *close* to what you want, you can easily modify that style to fit your needs. To modify a style, use the Styles and Formatting task pane.

First, open the task pane by selecting **Format** | **Styles and Formatting**. Then find the style you want to modify on the list. Don't click the style yet—that will just apply the style to your current paragraph! Instead, just point to the style, so that a box appears around it and a down arrow appears on its right. Click the arrow and then select **Modify** from the pop-up menu, as shown in Figure 15.28.

The Modify Style dialog box appears (see Figure 15.29), offering lots of common formatting options along with a nifty preview of how your style will look. This preview updates as you make changes, to help you picture how the changes you're making will affect your text.

In this dialog box, you can change common font attributes (size, bold, italic, underline, font style and color), as well as certain paragraph attributes (alignment, line and paragraph spacing, indentation). For more options, click the **Format** button, which brings up a list of other options you can set for this style: Font, Paragraph, and Tabs, to name a few (see Figure 15.30). Select any item from this list to see the detailed dialog box for that set of options.

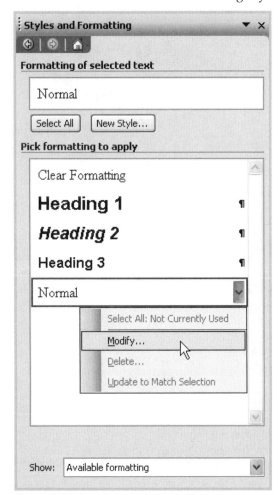

Figure 15.28: Selecting a style to modify

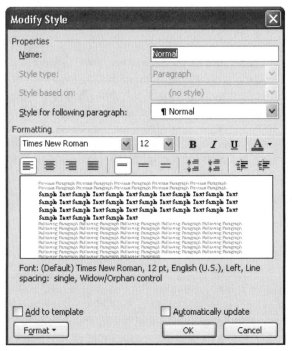

Figure 15.29: The Modify Style dialog box

If you plan to modify an existing style, but also want to keep the original version of that style for future use, you'll need to create a new style instead of merely changing the old one.

Create a Style

The process for creating a new style is similar to modifying an existing style. Open the Styles and Formatting task pane and click the **New Style** button; this brings up the New Style dialog box (Figure 15.31), which looks a lot like the Modify Style dialog box.

First, give your new style a descriptive name

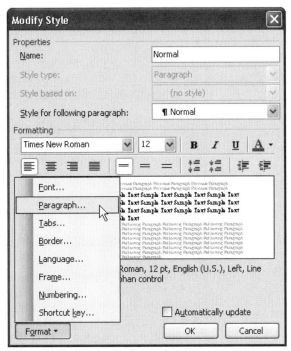

Figure 15.30: Clicking the Format button

that will make sense to you later. Then use the **Style type** drop-down box to designate it as either a character style or a paragraph style. If an existing style already has many of the characteristics you want, select that style in the **Style based on** drop-down box, to make it the starting point for your new style.

You can even select a style in the **Style for following paragraph** list so that each time you use the new style, you can simply press **[Enter]** to turn the style off—the next paragraph will automatically switch to the style you select here. If you leave the **Style for following paragraph** setting alone, then your new style will continue into the next paragraph whenever you press **[Enter]**, until you switch styles manually.

The rest of the dialog box offers the same text and paragraph formatting options that you saw in the Modify Style dialog box. Select any options you want here, or click **Format** to go into more detail with font, paragraph, tab, or other types of settings.

One more item of interest here is a check box called **Add to template**, which lets you save your new style as part of the document template you're using. (If you didn't start your document from a specialized template,

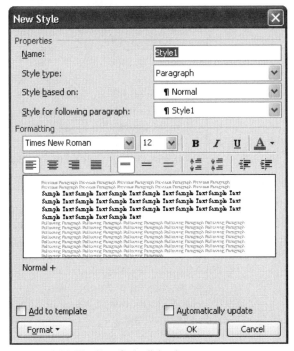

Figure 15.31: The New Style dialog box

Figure 15.32: Starting outline for a report on medieval siege weapons

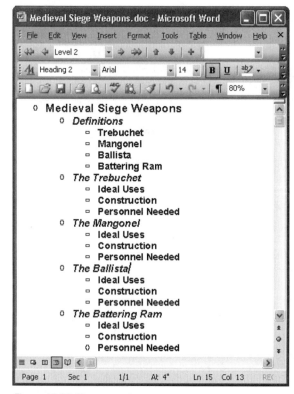

Figure 15.33: The same siege weapon report in Outline view

you're probably using the default template, called Normal. dot.) If you check this box, your new style will be available in all future documents you create using the same template; if you don't, it will be available only in the current document.

Click **OK** when you're finished, and then look for your new style in the Styles and Formatting task pane list.

Using Heading Styles to Organize a Document

By default, your documents' style lists will include several built-in styles, including different levels of *headings*, such as Heading 1 and Heading 2 You can use headings to organize your document's content. When you plan a long document, you can start by creating a sort of outline using the various heading styles.

Suppose you're writing a report on medieval siege weapons. You know what topics you'll be covering, and you know which sub-topics you'll have under each main topic. With this information, you can create an outline to start your document, using Heading styles. Figure 15.32 shows the start of a report on medieval siege weapons: an outline made up of Heading 1, Heading 2, and Heading 3 styles.

Even after you've added all the text into this document, you can still get a quick look at its skeletal form when needed, thanks to your use of the Heading styles. Just select **View | Outline** to see something that resembles Figure 15.33. In Outline view, you can scan the structure of your document to see where you may need to add or delete a section, re-order some items, or make other high-level changes.

Format Painter

The Format Painter tool enables you to clone all of the formatting from one bit of text to another. Format Painter duplicates the exact formatting—font style, size, bold or italics, paragraph spacing, indentation, the works—so that you can copy the look of any text to a single word, a line of text, an entire paragraph, or more.

To use Format Painter, select some text that contains the formatting you want to apply elsewhere. If you want to include the paragraph formatting options, make sure that you also select the paragraph mark; if you only want character-level formatting, do not select the paragraph mark. With the text selected, click the Format Painter button, shown in Figure 15.34.

After you click that button, the next thing that you click on (or click-and-drag to select) will take on the formatting from the text you selected a moment ago. When you use the Format Painter button this way, the Format Painter will turn off automatically after one use—either a click or a click-and-drag. You can change a single word this way, or you can affect quite a lot of text by clicking and dragging across long paragraphs or sections.

Figure 15.34: The Format Painter button

If you want to apply the selected formatting to a number of areas in your document that aren't connected (for example, a bunch of headings scattered throughout a long report), you can double-click the Format Painter button instead of single-clicking it. When you double-click, the Format Painter feature stays on until you click the Format Painter button again. While the feature is turned on, everything you click in the document will change to the selected formatting.

You can tell when the Format Painter option is in use, because your cursor has a paintbrush next to it and the Format Painter button takes on a different color from the buttons around it. Figure 15.35 shows the Format Painter in use.

Language Tools

You can use Word to check and correct your grammar and spelling, improve your word choices with the thesaurus, and give you information about your document, such as how many words you've written.

Spelling and Grammar

The tools for checking your spelling and grammar are located, appropriately enough, on the Tools menu. Select **Tools | Spelling and Grammar**, or press **[F7]**, to start a spelling and grammar check. Before you begin, you can select **Tools | Options**, then click the Spelling & Grammar tab (see Figure 15.36) to control spelling and grammar options.

On this tab, you can select which elements Word will check and correct, which ones it will ignore, and which dictionary file it will use. You can also tell Word what type of document you're creating, so that it knows what types of grammatical errors to look for. If you tell it you're creating a technical document, for example, it won't inform you of jargon words or passive voice.

One of the options you can set is called **Check grammar as you type**. If you check this box, Word will check your

Document Templates

In Chapter 12, "Working with Documents," you learned how to create a new document using a template, as well as how to save a Word document as a template. What are some differences between a document and a template? What are some reasons you might want to create custom styles and create a template of your own?

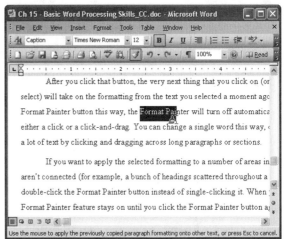

Figure 15.35: Format Painter in use

grammar—based on the other options you've chosen—as you type, placing a green squiggly underline below words or phrases that may be grammatical errors. When you see this green underline, you can right-click the affected words and let Word correct the error, as shown in Figure 15.37, or tell Word to ignore the problem.

Another handy option on the Spelling & Grammar tab is called **Check grammar with spelling**. When this box is checked, and you press **[F7]** or select **Tools | Spelling and Grammar**, Word performs a grammar check along with the spell check.

Word navigates through

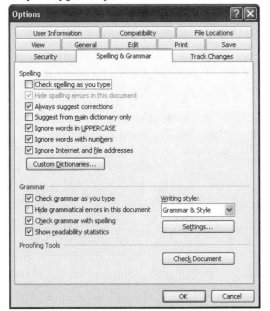

Figure 15.36: The Spelling & Grammar tab under Tools | Options

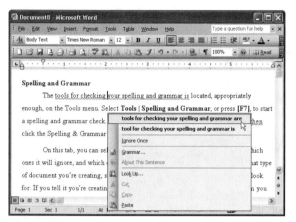

Figure 15.37: Correcting a grammar error

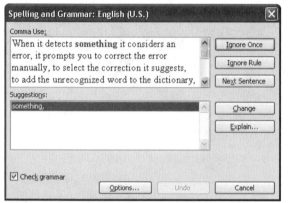

Figure 15.38: Grammar suggestion in a spelling and grammar check

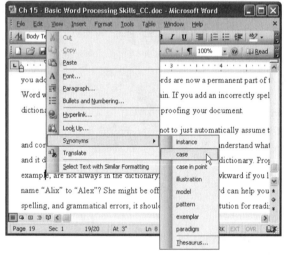

Figure 15.39: Right-clicking a word for a list of synonyms

the document, checking for spelling and grammatical errors, based on your dictionary and grammar settings. When it detects something it suspects is a grammar error, it prompts you to make a choice: either correct the error manually; click **Change** to select the suggested correction; ignore this particular error and continue; or ignore the relevant rule throughout the document.

Grammatical errors are highlighted in the Spelling and Grammar dialog box in green, like the word "something" in Figure 15.38.

Never automatically assume that Word's grammar corrections and suggestions are accurate. Word doesn't always understand what you're trying to say, and its grammar sense is not 100% foolproof. While Word can help you to find grammatical errors, it should never be a substitution for reading what you've written and knowing correct grammar.

Thesaurus

In addition to the manual and automatic checks for errors, you can use Word's thesaurus to help you pick just the right word. Suppose you're writing an essay on the popularity of computer games; instead of saying that computer game usage continues to "increase," you might want to take the thesaurus' suggestion and use a more interesting verb such as "escalate" or "mushroom."

To use the thesaurus, you can right-click on any word in your document and select **Synonyms**, as shown in Figure 15.39.

Notice that along with the word choices on the Synonyms submenu, you also have an option called **Thesaurus**. Click this to bring up the Research task pane, shown in Figure 15.40. The Thesaurus function available here can make it easier to choose a synonym that matches the correct part of speech and the exact shade of meaning that you want. You can also access the Research task pane's Thesaurus function by selecting **Tools | Language | Thesaurus**.

Word Count

Another way you can use Word to improve your writing is to review your *document statistics*, including the number of pages, lines, and words in the document. To display the document statistics, select **Tools | Word Count** to bring up the Word Count dialog box, shown in Figure 15.41.

Figure 15.40: The Thesaurus function in
the Research task pane

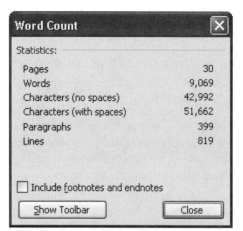

Figure 15.41: The Word Count dialog box

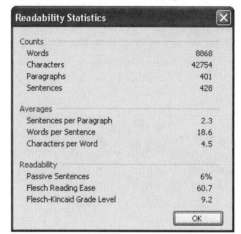

Figure 15.42: The Readability Statistics dialog box

Readability Statistics

*You can view more advanced document statistics, called readability statistics, including details on how easy your document is to read. To see these statistics, select **Tools | Spelling and Grammar** or use the Spelling and Grammar button on the Standard toolbar.*

After you've checked the entire document for grammar and spelling, Word displays the Readability Statistics dialog box (see Figure 15.42), which gives you more information than the Word Count dialog box. If you're trying to avoid passive voice or confirm that your document is easy to read, this is useful information.

Spell Checking

In Chapter 13, "Editing Documents," you learned how to use a spell checker, and why you should review your documents carefully even after you've checked spelling. Why can't the spell checker detect certain spelling errors?

Paragraph Formatting

- Paragraph formatting is about changing the appearance of sections of text through options such as line spacing, tabs, text alignment, and indents. You create this formatting using various buttons or the **Format | Paragraph** command. You can make a paragraph by pressing the **[Enter]** key. Use **[Shift] + [Enter]** to create a line break.

- You can view paragraph marks, along with symbols for things like spaces, using the **Show/Hide ¶** button. When you delete a paragraph mark, you are deleting the formatting for the preceding paragraph and merging the formatting with the next paragraph.

- You can indent paragraphs in several ways. The traditional first-line indent moves the first word in a half inch or so but leaves the rest of the paragraph at the margins. A paragraph indent moves all the lines in, whereas a hanging indent moves all *but* the first line indented.

- A tab is a type of indent that you control using the **[Tab]** key on your keyboard. Every word processing program has some tab stops set. You can remove them or add your own manually.

- Lines in a paragraph typically have the same space as the font size used in that paragraph. This default behavior can be changed. You can also change the distance between two paragraphs, altering both the before and after spaces.

Page and Section Breaks

- Use page breaks to control what content goes on which page of a document. Word processing programs create automatic page breaks when you add enough words. You can also make a manual page break by pressing **[Ctrl] + [Enter]**.

- Use section breaks to apply specific formatting options, such as headers and footers, to different parts of the document. Create section breaks manually using **Insert | Break**. There are four kinds of section breaks: Continuous, Even page, Odd page, and Next page.

Symbols and Special Characters

- Use **Insert | Symbols** to add symbols and other special characters to your documents, for example foreign language characters (such as é, ü, or ñ) or the pi symbol ([]) used in math.

- If you have a frequently used symbol, you may want to discover the keyboard shortcut (such as **[Ctrl + Alt + C]** for the copyright symbol), or assign your own keyboard shortcut.

Styles

- Named collections of formatting settings that you can apply to text and paragraphs are called styles. Character styles contain only text-level formatting options, such as font size and style, while paragraph styles contain both text formatting options and paragraph formatting options.

- You can apply a style from the Style drop-down list on the Formatting toolbar. You can also apply, modify, or create a style using the Styles and Formatting task pane.

- Apply character styles by selecting the text. Apply paragraph styles to a single paragraph merely by placing your cursor anywhere in the paragraph. To apply a style to multiple paragraphs at once, select all the text in those paragraphs before selecting the style.

Format Painter

■ With the Format Painter, you can copy the text and paragraph formatting options for any text in a document and apply them to text elsewhere in the document.

■ To use the Format Painter, select the formatted text (and the following paragraph mark, if you want to include paragraph formatting) and click the **Format Painter** button to copy the style. That formatting will be applied to the next text you click or select.

■ To apply the formatting more than once, double-click the **Format Painter** button, which will then stay selected until you click it again.

Language Tools

■ Use **Tools | Spelling and Grammar**, the **[F7]** key, or the **Spelling and Grammar** button on the Standard toolbar to check your document for spelling and grammar errors.

■ Choose which grammar rules Word will check by modifying the options on the **Spelling & Grammar** tab in the **Options** dialog box.

CHAPTER 15: SUMMARY

Key Terms

Alignment

Character style

Document statistics

First-line indent

Hanging indent

Hard return

Headings

Leaders

Line spacing

Page break

Paragraph formatting

Paragraph spacing

Paragraph style

Section break

Soft return

Template

Key Term Quiz

Use the Key Terms list to complete the following sentences. Not all the terms will be used.

1. You can collect groups of styles together in a _____ to re-use the styles to create new documents.

2. To create different headers and footers for the title page, table of contents, and main part of the document, insert _____.

3. To apply the Arial font in a blue color to various words or phrases throughout your document, you might create a _____ to store those formatting options.

4. Use _____ to create a larger space between a heading and the next line of text, rather than inserting multiple hard returns.

5. For a table of contents, you might create a tab stop that includes _____ so that you can have dots between each chapter name and its page number.

6. Most paragraphs begin with a _____.

7. If you want the heading centered, but the main body text against the left margin, you must apply different _____ options to those paragraphs.

8. To change the indentation and tabs from one paragraph to the next, apply different _____ options.

9. If the first line of a paragraph is flush against the left margin, but the second line is not, you have probably applied a _____.

10. Press the **[Shift + Enter]** key combination to create a _____.

11. _____ creates more space between the lines of a paragraph.

12. Apply **Heading 1**, which is an example of a _____, to use a stored set of formatting options, including font style, font size, line spacing, and paragraph spacing.

13. Use **[Ctrl + Enter]** to add a manual _____ to a document.

14. Look at the _____ to find out how many words and paragraphs a document contains.

15. To start a new paragraph, you should use a _____.

Multiple Choice Quiz

1. Which of the following is the same thing as a line break?
   A. Hard return
   B. Soft return
   C. Text wrap
   D. Document statistic

2. Which of these is visible in the document text only when you activate the **Show/Hide ¶** button?
   A. Font formatting
   B. The **Format Painter** button
   C. Document statistics
   D. Hard returns and other hidden characters

3. Which of the following can you create using the Ruler?
   A. Tab stops
   B. Headings
   C. Hanging indents
   D. Both A and C

4. Which of the following enables you to create double-spaced text?
   A. **[Ctrl + 1]**
   B. **[Ctrl + 2]**
   C. **Format | Change Case**
   D. **Format | Font**

5. You've just applied the following characteristics to a heading in your document: blue color, bold, 24-point size, double spacing, and center alignment. You think it looks great, and you want all of your headings to look like that. Which tool can you use to clone this formatting to other headings in the document?
   A. Format Painter
   B. Character Style
   C. Leaders
   D. Ruler

6. Which of the following is **not** a step you would take to change an existing style?
   A. Select **Format | Styles and Formatting**.
   B. Select a style and click **Modify Style**.
   C. Click the **Format Painter** to apply the style to the text.
   D. Use the **Format** button on the Modify Style dialog box to change formatting options.

7. Which of the following will display most prominently when you look at a document in Outline view?
   A. Centered paragraphs
   B. Tabs formatted with leaders
   C. Text formatted with Format Painter
   D. Paragraphs formatted with Heading styles

8. If you press **[F7]** before printing a document, what task will you perform?
   A. Spell check
   B. Outline view
   C. Change line spacing
   D. Print Preview

9. You've used Word to write an essay for English class that's required to be at least 1000 words long. Which command would you use to make sure your essay is long enough?
   A. **Show/Hide Paragraph Marks**
   B. **View | Readability Statistics**
   C. **View | Word Count**
   D. **Tools | Word Count**

10. Which of the following will change the formatting of a paragraph from center-aligned to left-aligned?
    A. **[Shift + L]**
    B. **[Ctrl + L]**
    C. **[Ctrl + E]**
    D. **[Ctrl + Alt + C]**

11. To see your tab stops and indent settings, you should use the Ruler. Which of the following commands can you use to display the Ruler?
    A. **Insert | Ruler**
    B. **Tools | Display | Ruler**
    C. **Tools | Options**
    D. **View | Ruler**

12. Which of the following can you change using paragraph spacing?
    A. Spacing between lines within a single paragraph
    B. Spacing between paragraphs
    C. Spacing between letters within a paragraph
    D. Spacing between sections of the document

13. Which of the following must you use to format your text as two columns?
    A. **Insert | Break**
    B. **[Ctrl + Enter]**
    C. **Format | Columns**
    D. Both A and C

14. You notice that sometimes the last line or last word of a paragraph is left sitting all alone on the top of a new page. Which of the following can you use to control this issue?
    A. Widow/Orphan control, found under **Format | Paragraph**
    B. Widow/Orphan control, found under **Format | Style**
    C. Line spacing, found under **Format | Paragraph**
    D. Line spacing, found under **Format | Style**

15. Which of the following describes how to apply a style?
    A. To apply a paragraph style to a single paragraph, you must select the entire paragraph, including the paragraph mark.
    B. To apply a character style to a single paragraph, you must select the entire paragraph, including the paragraph mark.
    C. To apply a paragraph style to a single paragraph, you may place your cursor anywhere within the paragraph.
    D. To apply a character style to a single paragraph, you may place your cursor anywhere within the paragraph.

Essay Questions

1. Describe the main differences between paragraph formatting and text formatting, and between a paragraph style and a character style.

2. Imagine that you're a technical professional at a company where everyone uses Word, but no one uses styles. Write a persuasive memo to your boss explaining the benefits of using styles rather than applying all your formatting manually.

3. Briefly discuss the various types of page and section breaks. Why might you want to avoid using manual page breaks? Give two examples of uses for section breaks.

Projects

1. You're the resident formatting expert in your office. Your boss decides he wants to make it easy for other users to apply formatting to their documents as well as you do. Search the Web for some advice on using styles for text and paragraph formatting. Then create at least two new styles based on this advice. After making the styles, write a summary of the styles and why you created them the way you did.

2. Create a newsletter to report on a class or school activity. The newsletter should be formatted with one or more pages with two or three columns, and one page containing the title and return address of the newsletter in the top left corner and the recipient's mailing address centered on the page.

Text that Gets Attention: Word Tables, Lists, Borders, and Shading

"It seems the tables have turned again, Dr. Evil."
        – Austin Powers, *Austin Powers: International Man of Mystery*

This chapter covers the following IC³ exam objectives:

- IC³-2   2.1.5   Create and modify bulleted and numbered lists
- IC³-2   2.1.6   Use outline structure to format a document
- IC³-2   2.1.16   Apply borders and shading to text paragraphs
- IC³-2   2.2.1   Create a table
- IC³-2   2.2.2   Insert and edit data in a table
- IC³-2   2.2.3   Modify table structure, including:
- IC³-2   2.2.4   Format tables, including:
- IC³-2   2.2.5   Sort data in a table

Now that you know the basics for creating and editing Word documents, you get to dive into some of the features that can make your text more interesting. Word can't make your essay about sea cucumbers more thrilling to read, of course, but a well-placed table, a bulleted or numbered list, or the addition of some borders or shading could help that essay look better in print and get more attention.

The Word features you'll discover in this chapter can help get your point across by bringing your text to life and making the key points stand out. If your document is visually interesting, people are more likely to read and understand what you've written.

Let's start by looking at one of the most effective tools for putting a lot of information into a small space: a table.

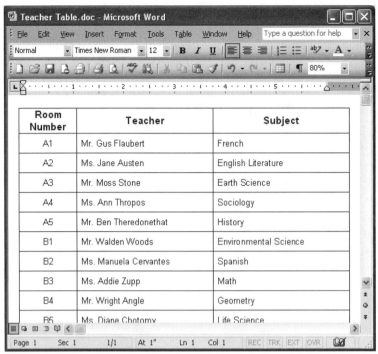

Figure 16.1: Teacher table

Working with Tables in Word

Tables enable you to organize content into a grid of vertical *columns* and horizontal *rows*. Tables organize and display data so that readers can compare items and quickly find the information they need. For example, the table in Figure 16.1 lists the rooms in a school, the teachers who use them, and the subjects they teach.

The columns separate the different kinds of data: room numbers, teachers, and subjects. Each column gives a different kind of data about the rooms, while each row gives all of the data about a single room. The very first row, which gives the column titles, is called the *heading row*. In this table, you can see the lines called *gridlines*, which separate the data into separate *cells*. The cell is the basic unit of any table.

Tables can be used strictly for text, as in the example above, or for numbers—although most often, you'll see tables that include both. While you should consider using a spreadsheet application such as Microsoft Excel for full-featured number tables, you can also use a table in Word to do many of the same things.

The table in Figure 16.2 includes numbers as well as text. In this example, the first two columns give the date and description of an employee's travel expenses, while the third column gives the amount spent for each item, along with a total at the bottom of the table.

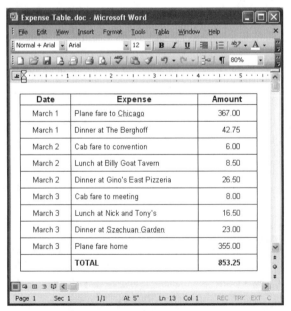

Figure 16.2: Expense table with numbers and a total

Getting Around in an Existing Table

When you open an existing document to edit, read, or print, you may need to navigate through its tables. As with navigating through any Word document (which you learned in Chapter 13), there are other ways to navigate through tables besides just scrolling with the scroll bars or the mouse wheel.

The Arrow Keys

The arrow keys on your keyboard work pretty much the same way within tables that they do in normal text. If you press the up arrow key in a table, you'll move up, line by line, through the rows until you move out of the table. The down arrow key works in a similar fashion, moving you down through each line of each row until you're out of the table. Left and right arrow keys move through each character in a cell, moving to the next cell in the row when you reach the beginning or end of the cell. At the end of a row, the cursor jumps to the next row as you use the left or right arrow keys.

The [Tab] Key

The **[Tab]** key works differently within a table than it does in normal text. As you learned in Chapter 15, pressing **[Tab]** moves your insertion point to the next tab stop. In a table, however, pressing **[Tab]** moves you from cell to cell, moving from left to right and top to bottom, selecting the text in each cell as it goes. If you want to move from right to left and down to up instead, hold down **[Shift]** while you press **[Tab]**.

When you reach the end of the last line in a table, the **[Tab]** key does one more really cool thing: it creates a new row for your table. You can keep pressing **[Tab]**, in fact, to move through the empty cells in your new row and then insert another blank row. This can be a real time saver if you're creating a table and don't know how many rows you'll need—just add them as you go! Note that if you're using **[Shift + Tab]** to move up in a table, you won't create new rows at the beginning of the table; instead, your cursor just stops when it reaches the beginning of the table.

So, if **[Tab]** has this special purpose within a table, does that mean you can't use an actual tab in a table? Of course not! To insert a tab stop within a table cell, press **[Ctrl + Tab]**. Set tab stops for tables using the ruler, the same way you do for regular Word paragraphs.

Adding or Changing Text in a Table

Typing in a table is much the same as typing anywhere else in a document. Just place your insertion point where you want to put the text, and start typing. When you reach the end of a cell, by default, the text wraps around to the next line, making the row bigger, but keeping the column width where it is. To move to the next cell to type more text, press **[Tab]** or use your mouse to click into the cell. With the exception of how tabs work, most of the other text and paragraph formatting options you've learned work normally inside a table.

If there's already text in a table that you want to edit, select the text and change it—again, just like you would any other text. Later in the chapter, you'll discover a few neat tricks to selecting text in a table.

Creating a Table

Now that you've seen how to navigate around in a table, how do you create one of your own? There are three main methods for creating a new table: insert the table using the toolbar or menu, draw the table with the table drawing tools on the toolbar, or convert some existing text into a table.

Insert a Table

You can insert a table from the Standard toolbar by clicking the **Insert Table** button and choosing the number of columns and rows you want to include in your table (see Figure 16.3). This is the easiest way to create a table, but it offers the fewest options.

Tabs in Tables vs. Tabs in Text

*In Chapter 15, "Basic Word Processing," you learned how to set tab stops, remove tab stops, and create formatting with tabs. Here, you've seen that the **[Tab]** key itself works differently in a table than it does in standard text. Review the section on tabs in Chapter 15 and think about why you might want to use actual tab stops in a table. Why would you use a tab instead of a new column? How would you use the **[Tab]** key differently when your cursor is inside a table or inside a paragraph of text?*

Heading Rows

You can give the first row of your table different text formatting than the other rows, to set it apart and make it easy to tell what each column represents. Word doesn't automatically treat that row any differently, however. If you think your table may be long enough to begin a second page, you can tell Word to treat your first row as a heading row. When you do this, your heading repeats automatically at the start of each new page, until the table ends.

*To set up a heading row, make sure your cursor is in the first row and select **Table | Heading Rows Repeat**. Now when the table flows onto a second page, a copy of your heading row will automatically appear as the first row on the page, and stay there even when your table contents shift.*

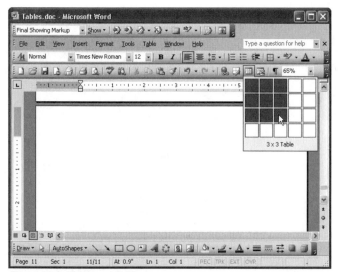

Figure 16.3: The Insert Table button in action

Figure 16.4: Creating a table using the Table menu

To insert a table into your document in a way that gives you a few more options, select **Table | Insert | Table**, as shown in Figure 16.4.

This brings up the Insert Table dialog box (see Figure 16.5). Here, as with the **Insert Table** button, you can choose the number of columns and rows you want in your table. Don't worry if you aren't sure exactly how many rows or columns your table will need—you can always add or remove some later, after you've created the table.

Other options in the Insert Table dialog box let you format the table. First, you can decide how Word will determine the width of your columns. The default setting is **Fixed column width** with a width setting of **Auto**, which sizes the columns automatically based on the number of columns and your page margins. If you leave these default settings, each column will start out at the same width. You can also use the **Fixed column width** box (click the arrows or type in a number) to set a specific width for the columns.

If you want Word to change the size of the columns to fit the text you type into the cells, select **AutoFit to Contents**. With this setting, the cell size constantly adjusts to try to keep the text on a single line in each row. You can also select **AutoFit to window**, so that your table will automatically adjust to fit in the document window.

You'll also notice a button here called **AutoFormat**; I'll go into detail on the AutoFormat options later in this chapter.

Finally, if you really like the options you've created for a particular table, and plan to use the same options again and again, you can check the **Remember dimensions for new tables** box to make those the default settings for future tables.

Use Table Drawing Tools

As an alternative to creating the table using the Insert Table dialog box, you can create a table using the table drawing tools. Start by clicking the **Tables and Borders** button on the Standard toolbar (see Figure 16.6). This does three things: it switches your view to Print Layout, if you aren't already there; it brings up the *Tables and Borders toolbar*, shown in Figure 16.7; and it turns on the Draw Table tool. Using this tool (which you can also bring up at any time by selecting **Table | Draw Table**), you can simply click and drag in your document to create a new table just where you want it.

When the Draw Table tool is enabled, your cursor appears as a pencil. When you click and drag in your document, you create the cells of a table, as shown in Figure 16.8. When you've finished drawing your table, click the **Draw Table** button again to turn this tool off.

You can also use the **Eraser** button (next to the **Draw Table** button on the Tables and Borders toolbar) to remove unwanted lines. Again, this tool stays selected until you click the button again to turn it off.

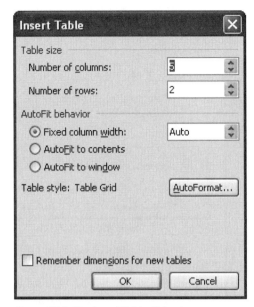

Figure 16.5: The Insert Table dialog box

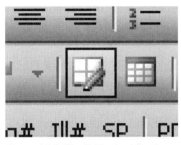

Figure 16.6: The Tables and Borders button

Figure 16.7: The Tables and Borders toolbar

Fun with Drawing

Table drawing is a little more challenging than simply inserting tables, but you can do some cool tricks—for example, if you have existing text that you want to place in a table, you can select that text before you turn on the Draw Table tool, and then draw the table around the text.

You can also use the Draw Table tool to change the appearance of the lines you draw. With this tool turned on, use the drop-down lists in the Tables and Border toolbar to choose a line style—solid, broken, dotted, and so on—and line weight. You can also select a border color, as well as a shading color for the interior of your table cells. If you select the options you want and then click an existing table gridline, the line changes to match the new formatting options.

Convert a Text Selection to a Table

Word enables you to convert existing paragraph text to a table in an automated and effortless way. This is particularly useful when you have text that's in a column or formatted with tabs. Start by selecting the text you want to make into a table. Then select **Table | Convert | Text to Table** to open the Convert Text to Table dialog box (Figure 16.9).

In the Convert Text to Table dialog box, you can select the **Number of columns** of data that you're converting. Word will make a guess, based on what you've selected—but it's not always a good guess.

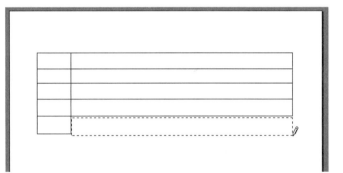

Figure 16.8: Drawing a table

Check out the number of columns Word suggested in Figure 9.30! This happens to be a five-paragraph text selection, which would look pretty awful split into 30 columns. The suggestion of 30 here is based on the **Separate text at** setting. See? It's set to **Commas**. Apparently, there are a lot of commas in these paragraphs, but that's not where the columns should be split. For a case like this one, **Paragraphs** is a good setting. Click that option and Word would change the **Number of columns** setting to 1, placing each paragraph in a row by itself.

Note that in the Convert Text to Table dialog box, you can choose the same kinds of formatting options that you saw in the Insert Table dialog box. Also, in the **Separate text at** area, you get to decide where Word should separate the text into cells. Word can separate text into cells based on paragraph marks, tabs, commas, or some other character, such as a period, dash, or slash.

Downloading

You read about downloading from the Internet in Chapter 7, "Taking Control of Windows." Flip back to that chapter now and see if you can answer these questions. What steps will you take typically to download a file? What can you download aside from patches and upgrades?

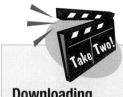

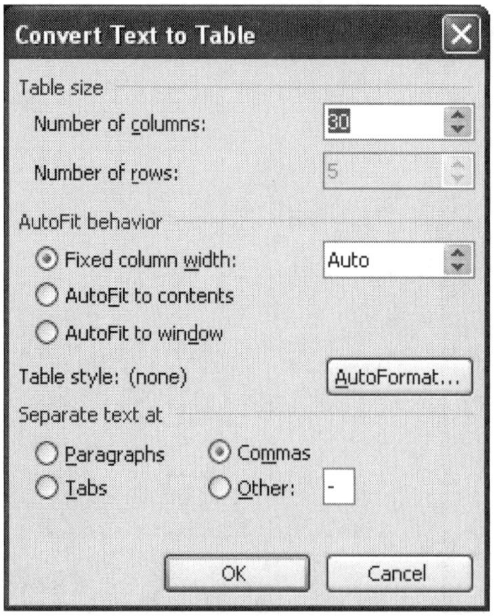

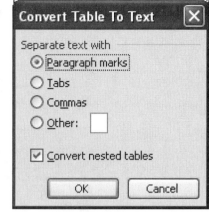

Figure 16.9: The Convert Text to Table dialog box

Figure 16.10: Converting a table to text

You can also convert a table back into text—and I don't just mean click the **Undo** button if you don't like the way your table turned out, although you can certainly do that! To convert any table to text, place your insertion point inside the table and select **Table | Convert | Table to Text**. Then decide how Word should separate the contents of each cell—using tabs, paragraph marks, commas, or some other character—and let Word do the conversion for you, as shown in Figure 16.10.

Now that you know how to create a table, let's move on to working with a table, to discover how to select parts of a table, insert or delete rows and columns, and format a table.

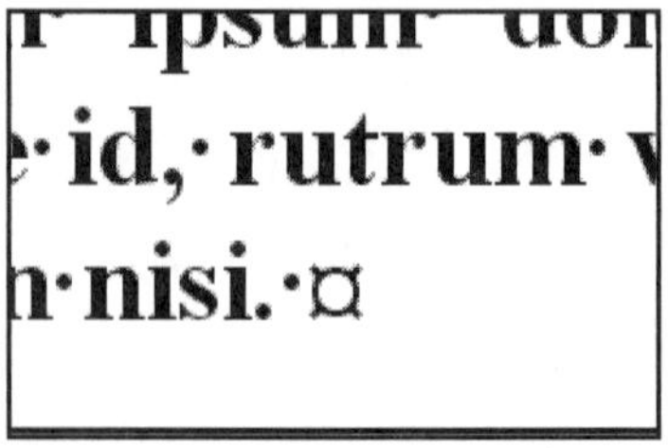

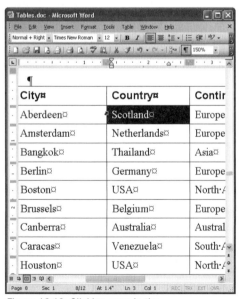

Figure 16.11: An end-of-cell mark

Selecting Cells, Rows, and Columns

In Chapter 13, "Editing Documents," you learned how to select items in a document in ways other than clicking and dragging with the mouse (although that should always work). When you're working with a table in your document, some additional selection techniques may be useful.

To select a cell, you can click and drag through all the text in the cell, or you can triple-click the mouse. To know when you've selected the entire cell (rather than just all the text in a cell), turn on paragraph marks in the document using the **Show/Hide Paragraphs** button.

Notice that each cell has an end-of-cell mark, shown in Figure 16.11. If the end-of-cell mark is included in the selection, then you know that the whole cell is selected. You can also move your mouse to the far left of the cell, between the cell border and the beginning of the text, in the area known as the *selection margin*. When your mouse is pointed into the selection margin, the cursor looks like a small diagonal black arrow. When you see this selection cursor, as shown in Figure 16.12, click once to select the cell.

Figure 16.12: Clicking once in the selection margin to select a cell

If you double-click in the table's selection margin, Word selects the entire row. If you triple-click in the selection margin, Word selects the entire table. You can also move outside the table, to the selection margin of the *document*, when your cursor becomes a big white arrow (see Figure 16.13). In this position, a single click selects the entire row. You can then click and drag to select a row at a time.

To select columns, move your cursor to the top of the table. You'll notice that immediately above the top of the table, you get the small black arrow selection indicator again, this time pointing down. Click

once to select the column, as shown in Figure 16.14. You can select multiple columns by clicking and dragging across the tops of the columns. You can also select one column, hold down the **[Shift]** key, and click a different column; this selects both columns and every column in between.

Inserting and Deleting Cells, Rows, and Columns

Now that you know how to create tables, you need to be able to edit the structure of a table—that is, insert and delete table cells, rows, and columns. The easiest way to remove a cell is to right-click the cell and select **Delete Cells**; this option is also available on the **Table | Delete** menu.

When you delete a cell, you'll see the Delete Cells dialog box. This is where you tell Word what to do with the rest of the cells in the table—after all, you're leaving a gaping hole! Your choices, as shown in Figure 16.15, include moving the remaining cells to the left or up, or deleting the entire row or column.

Just as you can delete an unwanted cell, you can insert a cell into your table. Just place your cursor in the cell closest to where you want the new cell to go, and select **Table | Insert | Cells**. Again, you have to decide what to do with the other cells in the table; in the Insert Cells dialog box, shown in Figure 16.16, you can have Word move them to the right or down, or insert an entire row or column.

To delete an entire row or column, first select it using the method described above. Then right-click and select either **Delete Rows** or **Delete Columns** (the selection menu options depend on what you've selected). You can also use the menu, selecting either **Table | Delete | Rows** or **Table | Delete | Columns**.

You can insert rows or columns using the same methods that you use to delete them. To insert a single row, select a single row, or select as many rows as you want to insert. The row or rows you select should be just below the place in the table where you want the new blank rows to appear. For columns, again select as many as you want to insert, and make sure they're just to the right of where you want the new column or columns to appear.

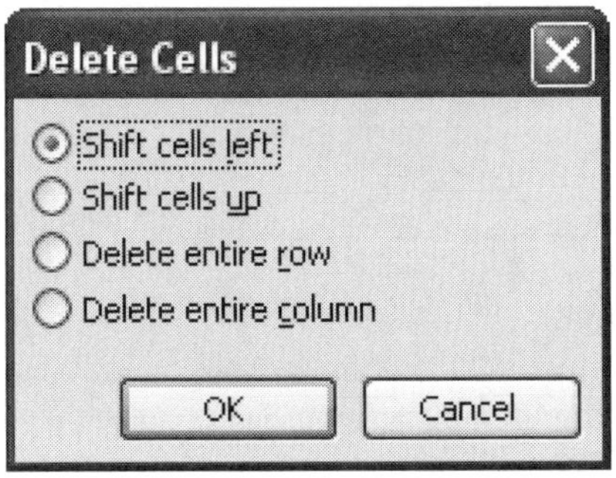

Figure 16.13: Selecting a table row from the document's selection margin

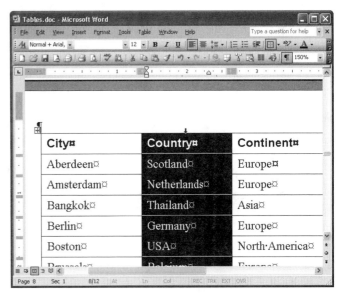

Figure 16.14: Selecting a table column

Once you've selected the appropriate chunks of your existing table, right-click and select either **Insert Rows** or **Insert Columns**. You can also use the menu approach, selecting either **Table | Insert | Rows** or **Table | Insert | Columns**. One advantage of using the Table menu is that you get to choose

Figure 16.15: The Delete Cells dialog box, where you specify what to do with the remaining cells

Be careful if you use the menu method. If you select a column and accidentally tell Word to delete rows, it will presume you want to delete all rows that are partially selected—that is, all the rows in the table! This is nothing that **Undo** can't fix, but it might make your heart skip a few beats to see your entire table disappear.

where to put the new rows or columns (see Figure 16.17).

A third method for inserting new rows or tables is using the context-sensitive **Insert Rows** and **Insert Columns** buttons on the Standard toolbar. *Context-sensitive* in this case means that these buttons only show up when you need them—that is, when you have one or more columns or rows selected. The Standard toolbar's **Insert Table** button, for example, changes to the **Insert Columns** or **Insert Rows** button as soon as you select at least one column or row in an existing table. Pretty slick!

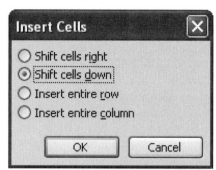

Figure 16.16: The Insert Cells dialog box—the polar opposite of the Delete Cells dialog box!

If you want to insert a column at the end of the table, you'll need to select the end-of-row markers—they look just like the end-of-cell markers, but they're outside of the table, to the right. You can select the end-of-row markers the same way you'd select a column, by clicking above the "column" where they appear (see Figure 16.18). You can then insert a column using your preferred method to place the column at the end of the table.

Splitting and Merging Cells

Besides inserting and deleting cells, rows, and columns, another option for managing the cells in your table is to *split* or *merge* cells. Splitting a cell divides it into multiple cells, while merging separate cells combines them into a single cell. As you might imagine, this plays havoc with your table's nice, even rows and columns—the affected table elements no longer match up to the others—but merging and splitting is often necessary for large and complex tables.

When you split a cell, it becomes two or more cells, in multiple rows or columns. Place your cursor inside the cell that you want to split, then right-click

Figure 16.17: The Table | Insert menu, with placement options

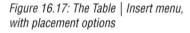

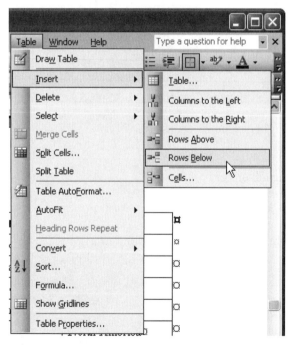

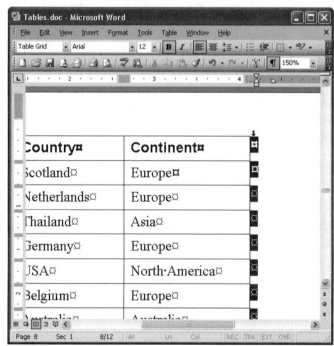

Figure 16.18: Selecting the end-of-row markers to add a column to the end of a table

COMPUTER LITERACY: YOUR TICKET TO IC³ CERTIFICATION

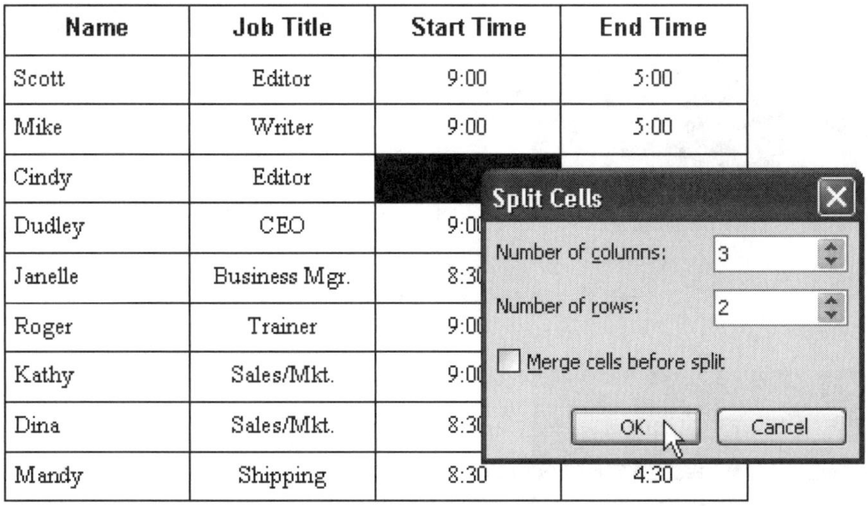

Name	Job Title	Start Time	End Time
Scott	Editor	9:00	5:00
Mike	Writer	9:00	5:00
Cindy	Editor		
Dudley	CEO	9:0	
Janelle	Business Mgr.	8:30	
Roger	Trainer	9:0	
Kathy	Sales/Mkt.	9:0	
Dina	Sales/Mkt.	8:3	
Mandy	Shipping	8:30	4:30

Split Cells

Number of columns: 3
Number of rows: 2
☐ Merge cells before split

[OK]   [Cancel]

Figure 16.19: Splitting a cell into two rows of three cells each

and select **Split Cells**. In the Split Cells dialog box, choose the number of rows and columns that the single cell will become. Figure 16.19 shows the Split Cells settings used to create a mini-table within a table, as shown in Figure 16.20.

Merging cells takes multiple cells, in different rows or columns, and merges them into a single cell. Simply select the cells you want to merge, right-click, and select **Merge Cells**. Figure 16.21 shows a before-and-after view of some merged cells.

Splitting a Table

You can split an entire table to organize your document better. Suppose you need to insert some non-table content between parts of an existing table. Just place your cursor in the row *below* where you want the split—that is, the row that will become the first row of the second table—and select **Table | Split Table**. The table splits into two tables and Word inserts a paragraph mark between the two tables.

Name	Job Title	Start Time			End Time
Scott	Editor	9:00			5:00
Mike	Writer	9:00			5:00
Cindy	Editor	M/W	T/Th	F	5:00
		8:00	9:00	7:00	
Dudley	CEO	9:00			5:00
Janelle	Business Mgr.	8:30			4:30
Roger	Trainer	9:00			5:00
Kathy	Sales/Mkt.	9:00			5:00
Dina	Sales/Mkt.	8:30			4:30
Mandy	Shipping	8:30			4:30

Figure 16.20: The finished product after splitting the cell

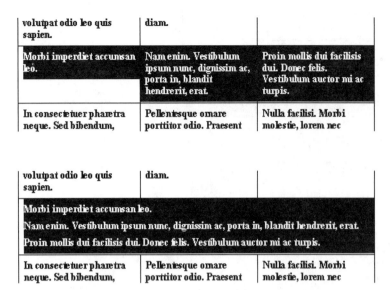

volutpat odio leo quis sapien.	diam.	
Morbi imperdiet accumsan leo.	**Nam enim. Vestibulum ipsum nunc, dignissim ac, porta in, blandit hendrerit, erat.**	**Proin mollis dui facilisis dui. Donec felis. Vestibulum auctor mi ac turpis.**
In consectetuer pharetra neque. Sed bibendum,	Pellentesque ornare porttitor odio. Praesent	Nulla facilisi. Morbi molestie, lorem nec

volutpat odio leo quis sapien.	diam.	
Morbi imperdiet accumsan leo. Nam enim. Vestibulum ipsum nunc, dignissim ac, porta in, blandit hendrerit, erat. Proin mollis dui facilisis dui. Donec felis. Vestibulum auctor mi ac turpis.		
In consectetuer pharetra neque. Sed bibendum,	Pellentesque ornare porttitor odio. Praesent	Nulla facilisi. Morbi molestie, lorem nec

Figure 16.21: Merging cells

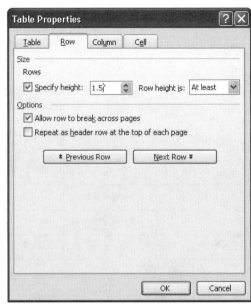

Figure 16.22: The Table Properties dialog box

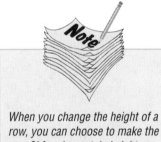

*When you change the height of a row, you can choose to make the row **At least** a certain height, or **Exactly** a certain height. If you set a height and specify **Exactly**, the row will no longer grow in height to accommodate additional text.*

Figure 16.23: The two-headed arrows mean you can click and drag table gridlines

Adjusting Column Width and Row Height

By default, all of the columns and rows in a new table are the same height and width. Of course, that doesn't work for every table—in most cases, you want to adjust the columns and rows to fit your content better. You have several options for changing the size of cells, columns, and rows.

One such option is to highlight the part of the table that you want to adjust (you can even select the entire table), right-click, and select **Table Properties**. This brings up the Table Properties dialog box. Click either the **Row** tab or the **Column** tab (see Figure 16.22), depending on what part of the table you selected.

If you're setting the height for one or more selected rows, check the **Specify height** box and either type a value in the box or click the up or down arrow buttons to set the height you want. If you're setting the width for one or more columns, check the **Preferred width** box and enter or select a value for the column's width.

If you prefer to see the changes in your table as you go, you can also click and drag to change the size of columns and rows. When you place your mouse on a column or row gridline, it turns into a two-headed arrow, as shown in Figure 16.23. Note that this only works for column lines in Normal view; to drag both column and row lines, switch to Print Layout view.

Click and drag the gridline to change the width or height. By default, Word changes the size of the entire column or row when you use this method. The only exception is when you have a cell or group of cells selected, in which case only the selected cells' borders will change.

You may find that it's cleaner and easier to have Word size the columns in your table for you, using a feature called *AutoFit*. When you have the double-headed arrow on the border of a column, you can double-click to have Word try to size the column automatically. You can also right-click and select **AutoFit** to see the options shown in Figure 16.24.

If you select **Table | AutoFit** instead, you'll see the same options, plus a few others. Choose **Distribute Rows Evenly** or **Distribute Columns Evenly** to make your rows or columns uniform in size. These two options are also available as buttons on the Tables and Borders toolbar.

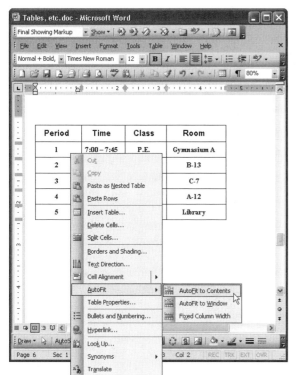

Figure 16.24: AutoFit options

Aligning Cell Contents

You can align text within a cell both horizontally and vertically. Horizontal alignment within a cell or table is the same as in normal paragraph text: align center, left, right, or justified using the alignment buttons on the Formatting toolbar, or your favorite method of aligning paragraph text. Vertical alignment works similarly—you can align text to the top, bottom, or center of the cell.

To align text in a cell, place your insertion point in the cell, right-click, and select **Cell Alignment** as shown in Figure 16.25. From the sub-menu, select the icon that shows the combination of vertical and horizontal alignment that you want. These cell alignment options are also available on the Tables and Borders toolbar.

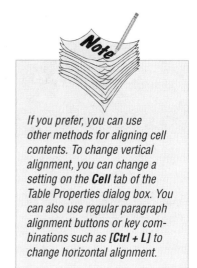

If you prefer, you can use other methods for aligning cell contents. To change vertical alignment, you can change a setting on the **Cell** tab of the Table Properties dialog box. You can also use regular paragraph alignment buttons or key combinations such as **[Ctrl + L]** to change horizontal alignment.

Figure 16.25: Aligning text in a cell

Formatting Tables with Borders and Shading

You can add *borders* to make the normally invisible gridlines of a table visible. You can use different border styles for different parts of your table, to create emphasis and make the table more visually appealing.

Shading is another way to add visual interest to a table. Using shading, you can add a color (or a shade of gray) behind the text in selected cells. Borders and shading are not restricted to tables, but tables are the most common way that most people use these features. Using the Tables and Borders toolbar, or selecting **Format | Borders and Shading**, gives you a variety of formatting choices.

To use the Tables and Borders toolbar, first select the table (or the portion of the table) that you want to have the border. Then click the **Draw Table** button. Select the border's line style, thickness, and color from the drop-down lists, then click on each border that you want to change to apply the selected options.

You can also use the Borders button to select a specific border to be changed. Figure 16.26 shows the Borders button and its drop-down list.

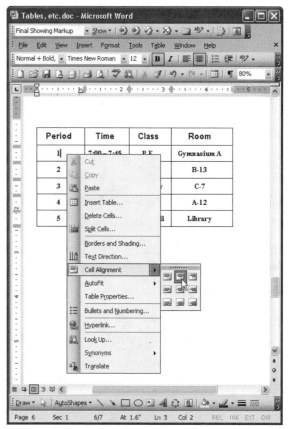

Figure 16.26: Use the Borders drop-down button list to change the borders

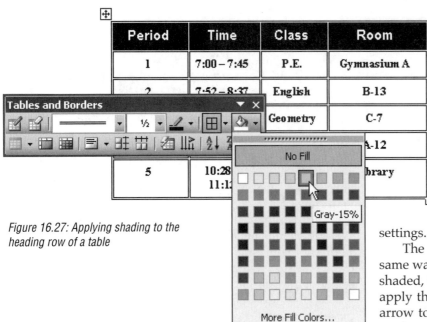

Period	Time	Class	Room
1	7:00 – 7:45	P.E.	Gymnasium A
2	7:52 – 8:37	English	B-13
		Geometry	C-7
			A-12
5	10:28 – 11:1...		brary

Figure 16.27: Applying shading to the heading row of a table

To use this button, first select a cell, row, or column, or the entire table. Then choose the type of border from the drop-down list of icon buttons. Each icon shows what border lines it turns on (or off), along with a descriptive name—**All Borders**, **No Border**, **Left Border**, **Inside Vertical Border**, and so on—that appears when you point your mouse at the icon. When you click an icon, Word turns the border on, using your current border style settings. Click again to turn the border off.

The shading feature works much the same way. Select the cell or cells that you want shaded, then click the **Shading Color** button to apply the selected color. Click the drop-down arrow to select a different color of shading to apply, as shown in Figure 16.27.

You can also make changes to the borders or shading options by selecting **Format | Borders and Shading**. This brings up the Borders and Shading dialog box (see Figure 16.28), where you can choose a border style, color, and width, as well as where to apply borders. You can also click the **Shading** tab to apply shading options.

Note that each of these tabs has an **Apply to** field, which lets you specify whether to apply the border and shading settings to the currently selected cells, a selected paragraph within a cell, or the entire table.

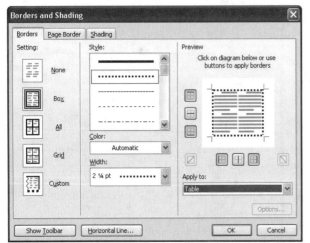

Figure 16.28: Using the Borders and Shading dialog box to format the table

Using Table AutoFormat

As cool as it is to have so many formatting options for tables, fixing up a table just the way you like it can take a long time! To make formatting a bit faster and easier, Word offers some preset options that you can use to format a table automatically.

Select **Table | Table AutoFormat** to display the Table AutoFormat dialog box, as shown in Figure 16.29. The **Table styles** list shows you the various formatting options, and the Preview area displays a sample of the selected option.

In the *Apply special formats to* area at the bottom of the dialog box, you can specify whether to use distinctive formatting for the table heading, first column, last row, and last column. You can experiment with these check boxes and see the results in the Preview area. When you're finished selecting your table style and options, click **Apply** to return to your document and view the formatted table.

If at any time you decide to try a different table style, just place your cursor in the table, select **Table | Table AutoFormat** again, and change your selections.

Sorting Data in a Table

To organize the contents of a table, you can have Word sort it in alphabetical, numeric, or date order, based on the column of your choice. For example, if the first column of your table is filled with names, you might want to sort the table alphabetically. A table listing the top ten salespeople in a company might work best if you sorted it numerically based on each person's sales total. Or, if you created a table to track which day of the month each of your bills is due, you would probably want to sort that table by date.

To sort a table, put your cursor in the table and select **Table | Sort**. In the Sort dialog box (see Figure 16.30), select the column you want to use for sorting from the **Sort by** drop-down list. For example, if you had a table listing schools and their rankings in a sports competition, you could choose to sort the table based on school names, making it easier to find a school on the list, or based on ranking, making it easier to spot the winners. The choice of how to sort table data is yours.

Regardless of what type of data you're sorting, you can always sort in ascending order (A-Z, or smallest to largest numbers) or descending order (Z-A, or largest to smallest numbers). If you want, you can even select a second column for sorting, using the **Then by** drop-down list. Sorting by a second column ensures that if you have identical entries in the first sort column, those entries are properly ordered according to a second piece of data. For example, if you sort on a column called Last Name, you can sort next by First Name, ensuring that Ann Smith is listed before John Smith, Hank Smith, Leon Smith, and Zora Smith—in that order.

Note the *My list has* area at the bottom of the dialog box. If your table includes a heading row, make sure to select **Header row** here. This ensures that your heading is not shuffled into the middle of the table when you sort. If your table doesn't have a heading, check **No header row**, to ensure that the first row isn't left out of the sorting process.

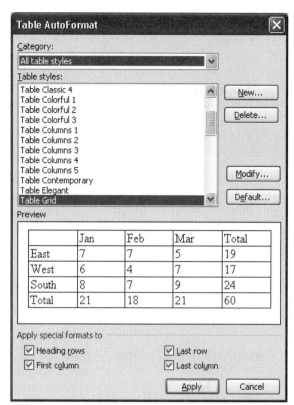

Figure 16.29: The Table AutoFormat dialog box

Figure 16.30: The Sort dialog box

Creating Bulleted and Numbered Lists

Lists are a great way to organize information; in Word, you can use *bullets* or *numbering* (or both) to create lists that get attention and are easy to read and understand. Bullets are commonly used for items that appear in no particular order—a shopping list, for example—while numbered lists tend to be used where order is important. For example, you might need to list the top 50 finishers in a fun run, or the steps you took to complete your science project.

The default bullet type is a solid black dot. Creating a bulleted list using the default bullets is quick and easy: just click the **Bullets** button on the Formatting toolbar. The paragraph where your cursor is positioned is now indented and

Sorting Without Tables

*You can also use the **Sort** command for text paragraphs that are not part of a table. This comes in handy when you have a simple list of names or items that you need to sort. Just type your list, pressing **[Enter]** after each item to create a new paragraph. When you've finished entering items in your list, click and drag the mouse along the left margin to select all of the paragraphs, then select **Table | Sort**. In the **Sort by** field, select **Paragraphs** (it should be the default entry) and then tell Word the type of data and the order in which to sort. Voilà! Your items are now alphabetized, numbered, or arranged by date.*

This is also a great way to integrate new items into a list that's already been sorted. Just type your new items at the end of the list, select the whole list, and re-sort.

displays a bullet, as shown in Figure 16.31.

Now if you press **[Enter]** at the end of that bulleted paragraph, the next paragraph will automatically have a bullet too. If you want to add more items to your bulleted list, just continue typing them and pressing **[Enter]** after each one. After your last item, press **[Enter]** a second time, or just click the **Bullets** button again to turn this feature off.

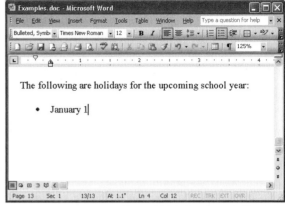

Figure 16.31: Starting a bulleted list

Making a numbered list is similar to making a bulleted list, only instead of the **Bullets** button, you click the **Numbering** button on the Formatting toolbar. After your first numbered item, you can press **[Enter]** to create a new paragraph with the next number.

If you already have a list of items in separate paragraphs, it's easy to create a bulleted or numbered list. Simply select the whole list (using your mouse to click and drag) and then click the **Bullets** or **Numbering** button. Figure 16.32 shows a plain text selection before and after the application of numbering.

You can also select **Format | Bullets and Numbering** to format text with bullets or numbers. As you can see in Figure 16.33, the Bullets and Numbering dialog box lets you choose from different styles of bullets or numbers.

You can change the style of a bulleted or numbered list either before or after you create the list. If you're just starting your list, set the style you want in the Bullets and Numbering dialog box; the rest of the list should pick up the same style as you continue to add new paragraphs. If you already have a list and want to change its bullets or numbering format, click and drag to select the entire list, then select **Format | Bullets and Numbering** and select a different list style. You can also use the **Customize** button in the Bullets and Numbering dialog box to further personalize the settings for your list.

Figure 16.32: Before and after applying numbering to a series of paragraphs

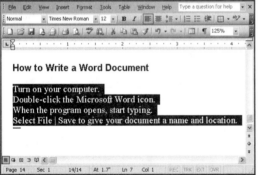

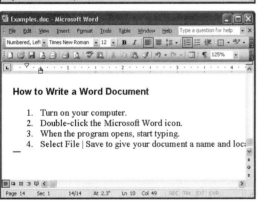

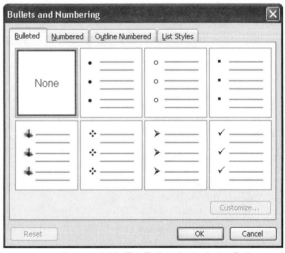

Figure 16.33: The Bulleted tab on the Bullets and Numbering dialog box

If You Build It, They Will Come: Creating an Outline

If there's one thing most folks learn in school (besides the multiplication tables and the fact that it's not nice to cut in line), it's that the best way to organize your thoughts on paper is to start with an outline. The outline is the foundation of your essay, research paper, or book report. Like a skeleton, it provides a structure for the document, although it isn't visible in the finished product.

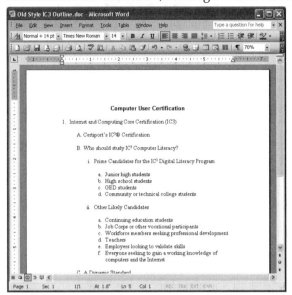

Figure 16.34: A traditional numbered outline, created separately from the main document

You've probably learned to create outlines as separate documents from your compositions, as shown in Figure 16.34. With this traditional approach to outlining, you use the outline to keep track of where each topic falls within the document's overall structure. Roman numeral I is your first topic, with sub-topics of A., B., C., and so on. You don't use the numbering and lettering of the outline in the final paper, so the outline has to be a separate document.

Word enables you to incorporate distinct heading levels directly into a document and uses Outline View to create and view an outline quickly. Here's how it works. Click the **Outline View** button in the lower left corner of the Word window or go to **View | Outline**. Word switches to *Outline View* and opens the Outlining toolbar beneath the Standard toolbar at the top of the Window. Figure 16.35 shows the same document open in Normal View and Outline View.

Use the arrows on the Outlining toolbar to create your document structure. Type the first heading, like you would with a traditional outline, such as Introduction, but don't use Roman numerals. Instead, click the **Promote to Heading 1** button (it looks like a double left arrow).

To create your second heading, press **[Enter]** after the Introduction—the Outline View creates the same level heading for the next line, in this case Heading 1. If you want this line to be the first sub-heading after Introduction, simply click the **Demote** button on the Outlining toolbar (a single right-pointing arrow) and

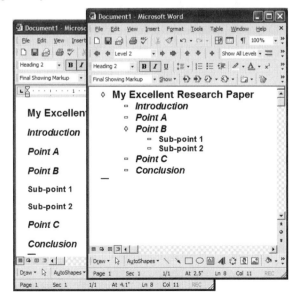

Figure 16.35: Normal View (l.) and Outline View

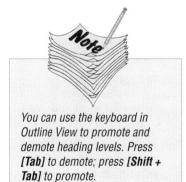

that line becomes a Heading 2. You can easily promote and demote your headings by using the arrow buttons to create an outline. Once you've got your outline complete, press **[Enter]** after your first heading and click the **Demote to Body Text** button on the Outlining toolbar (double right-pointing arrows) and start typing!

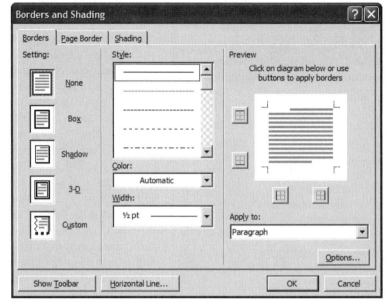

Figure 16.36: Borders and Shading dialog box

Adding Borders and Shading

You can create borders or shading to add visual interest to your documents or to highlight elements. You might want to set off a specific paragraph to show its importance in a document, for example. While you'll most often see borders or shading applied to tables, you can use these features on any text.

To choose your border or shading styles, select **Format | Borders and Shading**. This brings up the Borders and Shading dialog box, shown in Figure 16.36. Choose the type of border you want to apply. You can also apply borders to the entire page of text, using the **Page Border** tab. Shading is applied the same way—just use the **Shading** tab.

If you use these features frequently, you might want to turn on the Tables and Borders toolbar; to do this, right-click any of the existing toolbars and select **Tables and Borders**. The Tables and Borders toolbar, shown in Figure 16.37, makes working with borders and shading much easier.

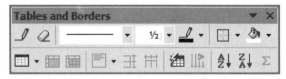

Figure 16.37: The Tables and Borders toolbar

Working with Tables in Word

■ You can use tables to organize data into a grid of vertical columns and horizontal rows. Each box where a column and a row intersect is called a cell. Tables can incorporate text, numbers, or both, and can have visible or invisible border lines. Most tables have a heading row with titles for the various columns.

■ To move around in a table, you can use the keyboard's arrow keys; press **[Tab]** to move to the next cell or **[Shift + Tab]** to move to the previous cell; or use your mouse to click into the various cells.

■ You enter text and numbers into a table the same way you normally do. To use a tab stop within a cell, press **[Ctrl + Tab]**. To add a new row at the end of a table, just press **[Tab]** at the end of the last existing row.

■ To create a table, use the **Insert Table** button or menu item, or the **Draw Table** tool. You can convert a selection of paragraph text to a table, or vice versa.

■ In an existing table, you can insert or delete rows, columns, or cells, using right-click menus and the main **Table** menu. You can merge multiple cells into one cell, or split a single cell into two or more cells, using right-click menus. You can also split a table between rows, also with the help of the right-click menu.

■ You have full control over the size of the rows and columns in your tables, as well as the alignment of cell contents, the appearance of border lines, and shading of cells. The Table AutoFormat feature offers pre-formatted table styles to save you time and effort. You can even sort data in a table in forward or reverse alphabetical or numeric order, based on one or more columns that you select.

Bulleted and Numbered Lists

■ Lists are another handy way to organize information. Bulleted lists are good for items that are listed in no particular order, while numbered lists are best where order is important.

■ The Formatting toolbar includes buttons for both bullets and numbering. To change the default list settings, you can select **Format | Bullets and Numbering**.

■ To continue a bulleted or numbered list, simply press **[Enter]** at the end of an existing bulleted or numbered paragraph. The following paragraph will use the same bullet level or the next sequential number.

Creating an Outline

■ Word enables you to create an outline that incorporates heading levels into a document. With Outline View, you can build an outline quickly, promoting and demoting heading levels so you get precisely the organization and structure for a document that you want.

■ To promote or demote headings, use the arrow keys on the Outlining toolbar. You can also use **[Tab]** and **[Shift + Tab]** to change levels.

Borders and Shading

■ Borders and shading can add visual interest to your documents. To choose and apply border or shading styles, select **Format | Borders and Shading**.

■ On the **Borders** tab of the Borders and Shading dialog box, you can specify which sides of the selected paragraph or area will have borders, as well as what style, color, and width of line to use. You can set these same attributes using the Tables and Borders toolbar.

■ The Page Border tab enables you to place a custom border around an entire page.

■ The Shading tab enables you to select any color or shade of gray to shade a paragraph or area, just as you can shade a portion of a table.

CHAPTER 16: SUMMARY

Key Terms

AutoFormat

Border

Bullets

Cells

Columns

Gridlines

Heading row

Merge

Numbering

Outline View

Rows

Shading

Sort

Split

Table

Tables and Borders toolbar

Key Term Quiz

Use the Key Terms list to complete the following sentences. Not all the terms will be used.

1. The horizontal components of a table are known as _____.

2. You can use _____ when you want to list items in a particular order, such as the steps in a set of instructions.

3. The individual boxes in a table are called _____.

4. If you hide a table's _____, it will look less like a table and more like data listed in text columns.

5. When you _____ cells, you make one cell out of what were previously two or more separate cells.

6. The area of a table that includes the column titles is called the _____.

7. The Sort feature is part of the _____ menu.

8. A _____ is a visible line used in a table or paragraph to make it more visually appealing.

9. You can use _____ to add visual interest to a list of items where order isn't important.

10. To create a table using a pre-set group of table styles that you can customize, use the Table _____ dialog box.

Multiple Choice Quiz

1. Which of the following should you press to create a tab within a table cell?
   A. **[Tab]**
   B. **[Alt + Tab]**
   C. **[Ctrl + Tab]**
   D. **[Shift + Tab]**

2. What is the quickest and simplest way to create a basic table in Word?
   A. Click and drag the **Insert Table** button.
   B. Select **Table | Insert | Table**.
   C. Select **Table | Draw Table**.
   D. Use the Create Table Wizard.

3. Which of the following statements about Word tables is true?
   A. You can convert plain text to a table, but you can't convert a table to plain text.
   B. You can convert a table to plain text, but you can't convert plain text to a table.
   C. You can convert plain text to a table, and convert a table to plain text.
   D. You cannot convert a table to plain text, or vice versa; you can only cut or copy text from a table and paste it into a paragraph, or cut and copy text from a paragraph and paste it into a table.

4. You've made a table of your class schedule, including class times, subjects, room numbers, and teacher names. It's a great little table, but you want to split it into two parts, so you can tape your morning subjects on the front of your notebook and your afternoon subjects on the back of your notebook. What's the best way to do this?
   A. Create a copy of your table, then delete the afternoon subjects from one table and delete the morning subjects from the other table.
   B. Convert the table to paragraph text, insert a page break, and then convert each half of the text back into table form.
   C. Place your cursor in the last row of your morning classes, right-click, and select **Split Cells**.
   D. Place your cursor in the first row of your afternoon classes and select **Table | Split Table**.

5. Which of the following statements is true?
   A. The only way to adjust the height of a row is by using the Table Properties dialog box.
   B. The only way to adjust the height of a row is by clicking and dragging in Print Layout view.
   C. You can adjust the height of a row either by using the Table Properties dialog box or by clicking and dragging in Print Layout view.
   D. There is no way to adjust the height of table rows; you can only adjust the width of columns.

6. Which of the following buttons is **not** on the Tables and Borders toolbar?
   A. **Insert Table**
   B. **Draw Table**
   C. **Table AutoFormat**
   D. **Tables and Borders**

7. Which of the following must you do before you can use the Merge Cells command?
   A. Place your cursor in any table cell.
   B. Select at least once complete table cell.
   C. Select at least two adjacent table cells.
   D. Select any complete table row.

8. What is the best way to ensure that you have column headings at the top of every page in a multi-page table?
   A. Split your table at each page break, copy the heading row, and paste it into the next page.
   B. Split your table at each page break, and the heading row will automatically appear at the top of the next page.
   C. Leave your table in one piece, copy the heading row, and paste it in the first row after each page break.
   D. Leave your table in one piece and turn on the Heading Rows Repeat option for the first row.

9. When you use the mouse to adjust the width of a table column, how do you know when you're clicking in the right place?
   A. The cursor changes to a hand icon.
   B. The cursor changes to a double-headed arrow.
   C. The column you're adjusting appears highlighted.
   D. A pop-up message appears, asking you to confirm that you want to adjust the column width.

10. You have a table that lists each member of the school band and the number of candy bars that person sold in this year's fund-raiser. The table is currently sorted by last name, but you'd rather sort it to show who sold the most candy bars. Wherever there is a tie, you want to list the members in alphabetical name order. How should you sort the colums in this table?
    A. Number Sold
    B. Last Name
    C. Number Sold, then Last Name
    D. Last Name, then Number Sold

11. What is the default bullet type in Word?
    A. Solid black dot
    B. Solid black diamond
    C. Open black dot
    D. Open square

12. John wants to change the bottom border on the heading row in his table. He has already selected the entire row, and the border style, weight, and color are already set the way he wants them. What should he do now to change the border?
    A. Click the **Borders** button and select **Bottom Border**.
    B. Click the **Borders** button, select **No Border**, and then click **Borders** again and select **Bottom Border**.
    C. Click the **Borders** button and select **All Borders**.
    D. Click the **Borders** button and select **Baseline**.

13. Which of the following should you press to move one cell to the right within a table?
    A. **[Tab]**
    B. **[Ctrl + Tab]**
    C. Spacebar
    D. The down arrow key

14. Cheryl wants to make her boring table look better, but she's pressed for time and isn't feeling very creative. Which of these tools should she try?
    A. Borders and Shading
    B. Bullets and Numbering
    C. Table AutoFormat
    D. AutoFit to Contents

15. Which of these options is **not** available for aligning the contents of a cell?
    A. **Align Top Left**
    B. **Align Top Center**
    C. **Align Bottom Right**
    D. All of these options are available.

Essay Questions

1. A few weeks before school starts, you see your school's principal at the grocery store, and she asks you for Word advice. She's created a very long table listing all the students in the school, along with their assigned locker numbers. The list will be posted on the first day of school to direct the students to their lockers. The trouble is that she made the table according to the locker numbers, not the names, and now she needs to put the names in alphabetical order. She also needs to divide the table up into four sections (A – F, G – L, M – R, S – Z) so that the students won't all have to crowd around one list in the hallway. What is your advice? Write a paragraph, including a brief description of the relevant Word table features and how to use them.

2. Write a brief description of the various ways you learned to navigate around a Word table using the keyboard. Can you think of an advantage that keyboard shortcuts have over using the mouse?

3. What determines whether a list of items would be better with bullets or numbering? Include some examples of items that would work well in a bulleted list, and some examples of items that would work better in a numbered list.

Projects

1. Explore outlining in Word by writing a short document and using the outlining tools. Pick a topic that interests you—preferably a broad subject such as animals, history, or sports. List your main topic at the top of a Word document, then come up with three sub-topics and list those beneath it. Write a brief paragraph beneath each topic. Next, choose one of your first-level topics and come up with two sub-topics. List them beneath that topic's paragraph, and then write a brief paragraph beneath each of those topics as well. Turn on the Outlining toolbar and assign Level 1 to your main topic, Level 2 to your sub-topics, and Level 3 to your sub-topic's sub-topics. Finally, switch to Outline view and view the results.

2. Create a table showing your daily or weekly class schedule. Start out with only a few rows, and add new rows as you go. Include a heading row with titles for your columns, and give the table borders of your own choosing. When you finish the table, make a copy of it and place it below the first table. Now use the second copy of the table to experiment with Table AutoFormat. Find a format you like, and then see if you can duplicate it in your original "handmade" table.

COMPUTER LITERACY: YOUR TICKET TO IC³ CERTIFICATION

Advanced Word Processing Skills

"We have been here for three solid days! We have endured, by my count, more than eighty-five separate changes and the removal of close to four hundred words. Now, would you whip it and beat it till you break its spirit? I tell you, that document is a masterful expression of the American mind!"

– John Adams, *1776*

This chapter covers the following IC[3] exam objectives:

- IC[3]-2   2.1.8   Insert date and time

- IC[3]-2   2.1.9   Insert, view, and print document comments

- IC[3]-2   2.1.13   Insert, modify, and format page numbers

- IC[3]-2   2.1.14   Create, modify, and format headers and footers

- IC[3]-2   2.1.15   Create, modify, and format footnotes and endnotes

- IC[3]-2   2.1.20   Track changes to a document

If the United States' founding fathers had been able to use a computer and printer instead of quill pens and parchment, they might have completed the Declaration of Independence in a single draft. They didn't have the handy features of Microsoft Word to help them streamline their work and turn out a slick document in record time—but you do!

Now that you know how to use Word (or almost any word processing program) to create standard documents, you need some additional knowledge to fine-tune your documents and collaborate with others. In this chapter, you'll learn to number your pages automatically, create headers and footers, use the commenting feature, include footnotes and endnotes, and track changes to your documents.

By the Numbers

If you think that page numbers are no big deal, imagine this: You've just printed out a 75-page paper that took you six weeks to complete. You didn't bother to number the pages, because you plan to put the paper in a fancy presentation binder before turning it in. On your way from the printer to the desk, you trip over your sleeping cat, and all 75 pages go flying.

Numbering your pages in Word would have taken you mere seconds. Putting that paper back in order without page numbers will take you hours!

Section Breaks

To use features such as headers, footers, and page numbers effectively, you need a good understanding of section breaks. In Chapter 15, "Basic Word Processing Skills," you learned how to create section breaks. Review the different kinds of section breaks now. How many kinds are there? How do they differ from one another? How can you tell when you move from one section of a document to another, and which section number you're currently viewing?

Page Numbering

Any time you have a document with multiple pages that are meant to be read in a particular order, it's a good idea to include page numbers. While you could simply type numbers on the last line of each page, this would disrupt the flow of your document, especially if you make changes to that document in the future. Instead, Word enables you to include automatic page numbers in the header or footer of your document.

You'll learn more about the ins and outs of headers and footers in the next section of this chapter, but for now let's look at the basic methods for inserting and formatting page numbers in a document.

Adding and Formatting Page Numbers

To add page numbering to a document, first select **Insert | Page Numbers**. This brings up the Page Numbers dialog box, shown in Figure 17.1. By default, your page numbers will appear as plain numerals (1, 2, 3, and so on) in the bottom right corner of each page. If this is what you want, go ahead and click **OK** to add page numbers to your document.

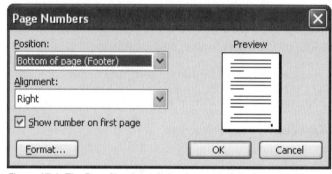

Figure 17.1: The Page Numbers dialog box with default settings

If you'd rather have your page numbers appear somewhere else, you can change the selections in the **Position** and **Alignment** drop-down boxes. You can also choose to skip numbering on the first page of your document—for example, if the first page is a cover page with only your name and title—by clearing the **Show number on first page** check box.

To change the way the page numbers themselves appear, click the **Format** button to view the Page Number Format dialog box, shown in Figure 17.2. The **Number format** drop-down list offers several options, from using dashes around the page number (- 1 -, - 2 -, - 3 -, and so on) to using letters or Roman numerals instead of plain numerals. Make your selection, click **OK**, and then click **OK** again to return to your document.

Note that page numbers don't appear in Normal view. To see your new page numbers in action, switch to Print Layout view (see Figure 17.3).

The page numbers you create are more than just raw text. They're *fields*, bits of information powered

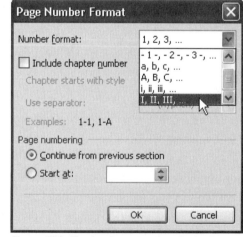

Figure 17.2: Number format options in the Page Number Format dialog box

by computer code so that they automatically update when you add or delete pages in your document. No matter now much you change the length or content of your document, the proper page numbers will always display and print.

Changing a Document's Page Numbers

To change existing page numbers in a document, just select **Insert | Page Numbers** again, and then make any changes you want in the Page Numbers or Page Number Format dialog boxes. The changes take effect as soon as you click **OK** to return to your document.

Removing Page Numbers

To remove page numbering from your document, select **View | Header and Footer**. The document switches to a view in which only the document headers and footers (more on those in the next section of this chapter) are visible. The Header and Footer toolbar also appears; if your page numbers are situated at the bottom of the page, scroll down or click the **Switch Between Header and Footer** button on that toolbar. Select your page number and press **[Delete]** to remove it.

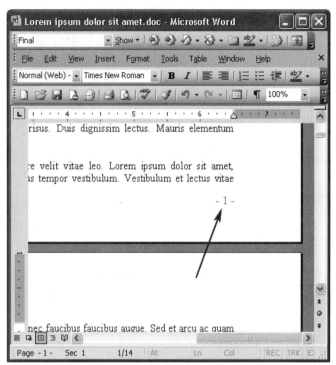

Figure 17.3: Page numbers are visible in Print Layout view.

Headers and Footers

Headers and footers are the areas at the top and bottom of your pages where your margin settings prevent you from typing normal text. You can place information in your document's header (the top margin), footer (the bottom margin), or both, to make the document more user-friendly.

You've already seen that headers and footers make a great place to put automated page numbers so that they stay out of the way of your main body text. Other common types of information for headers and footers are the document's title or file name, the chapter or section title, and the current date. You can also include various other types of information such as your name or the name of your class, teacher, or school.

Creating and Formatting Headers and Footers

To add information in your headers and footers, start by selecting **View | Header and Footer**. This brings up the Header and Footer toolbar and changes the page view (see Figure 17.4). If you tired in the previous section to delete a page number, you've already seen this view, in which the main page contents are grayed out and temporarily unavailable and dotted boxes appear at the top and bottom of the page.

To add content to header or footer, just type in the Header or Footer section. Figure 17.5 shows a document title in the header, aligned to the left margin. You can use the alignment buttons on the Formatting toolbar—Align Left, Center, Align Right—or the **[Tab]** key to put your header or footer text where you want.

To type in the footer, scroll down or click the **Switch Between Header and Footer** button, shown in the Header and Footer toolbar in Figure 17.6. Clicking this button takes you from header to footer—or from footer to header, if you're already in the footer. Type any information you like.

Using tabs to align text with the left margin, the right margin, or the center

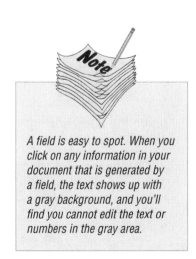

A field is easy to spot. When you click on any information in your document that is generated by a field, the text shows up with a gray background, and you'll find you cannot edit the text or numbers in the gray area.

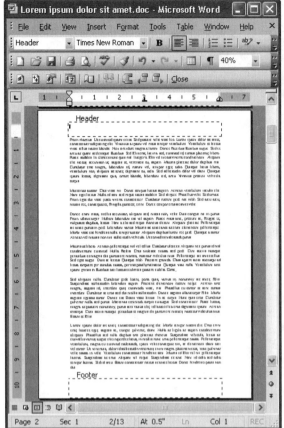

Figure 17.4: The page view for editing headers and footers

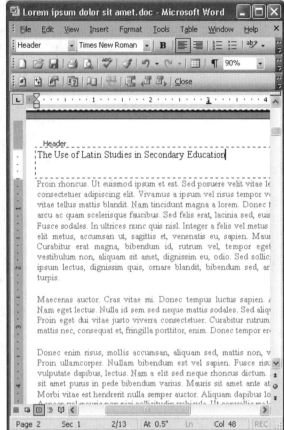

Figure 17.5: The document's title, aligned left in the header

Figure 17.6: The Header and Footer toolbar, with the Switch Between Header and Footer button selected

offers a distinct advantage over the alignment keys because you can have multiple elements in a header or footer, each aligned to different areas. Figure 17.7, for example, shows a footer with information aligned to both margins; note the visible tab markers showing how the information on the right got to its current location.

Including Date and Time Information in a Header or Footer

It's often handy to include a date or time stamp in a Word document, for example to show when the document was last saved or to record the date an assignment was completed. You can use the **Insert | Date and Time** command to place a date or time stamp anywhere in your document (for example, to enter the current date in the heading of a letter), but the header and footer are the most logical places to put this information for reference purposes.

To include date or time information in a header or footer, first select **View | Header and Footer** to switch to the header and footer view. Then place your cursor where you want the date or time information to appear, and select **Insert**

Doing the Numbers
This chapter will be a lot more interesting if you do each thing covered, so open up a word processing program and insert some page numbers! Try some of the variations to get a feel for how page numbering works.

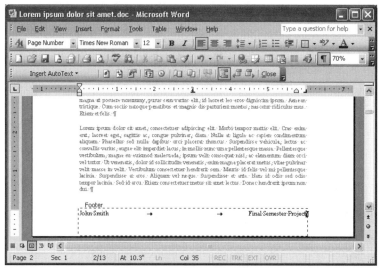

Figure 17.7: A document with information on both sides of the footer

| **Date and Time**. If you use this method, you'll see the Date and Time dialog box (see Figure 17.8), where you can select a date or time format.

This dialog box also offers the **Update automatically** option, which determines whether your time and date information will be entered as plain text, which never changes, or as a field that updates to the current time or date each time you open the document. Check this box if you want the information to update automatically (for example, if you want to be able to tell which printout of a draft is the most recent), or clear the box if you want the information to remain the same (for situations like that letter heading, where you need the original date for future reference).

Changing the Format of an Existing Date or Time Stamp

To change the format of a date or time stamp field, you can select the field (click and drag over the entire gray background area), then select **Insert | Date and Time** and choose the format you want. When you click **OK**, the new format will replace the old one.

Another approach is to click the field so that its gray background appears, then right-click and select **Edit Field** from the context menu. This brings up the Field dialog box, shown in Figure 17.9. Select a new entry from the **Date formats** list—this list is the same whether you're dealing with a date stamp or a time stamp—and click **OK** to update the format of the selected date or time field.

Removing a Date or Time Stamp

To remove a static date or time entry—one inserted as text, not as a field—simply use **[Delete]** or **[Backspace]** the same way you would to remove any other text. It takes a few more keystrokes to delete or backspace over a field, but you can get rid of automated time and date stamps that way if you like. You can also use the mouse to select a field, but make sure you've selected the entire thing, or you'll end up with some leftover numbers where your date or time stamp used to be.

Figure 17.8: The Date and Time dialog box

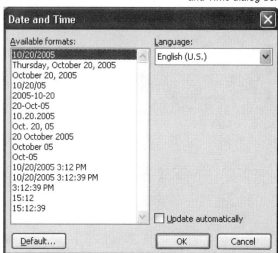

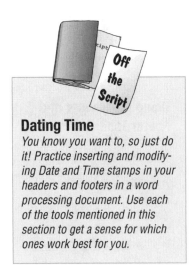

Dating Time

You know you want to, so just do it! Practice inserting and modifying Date and Time stamps in your headers and footers in a word processing document. Use each of the tools mentioned in this section to get a sense for which ones work best for you.

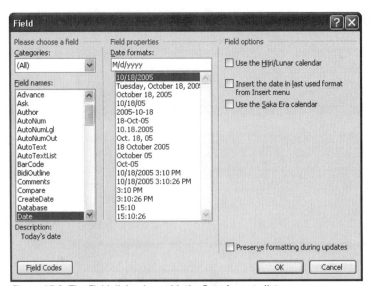

Figure 17.9: The Field dialog box with the Date formats list

Footnotes and Endnotes

You've seen them before, even if you've never had to use them yourself. They sit there, patiently waiting in small print at the bottom of a page, the bottom of a table, or the end of a magazine article. They sometimes include interesting side notes, but more often they spell out tedious legalities, or simply list the title and author of some article or book. They may seem like a waste of space, but they're very important to teachers, college professors, and many other people who will read your work.

Footnotes and *endnotes* sit outside the main text of your document and provide additional information, including details about the sources you've quoted. Both kinds of notes involve putting a little superscript numeral in your text, to indicate that there's a note elsewhere. For each numeral, there's a corresponding note, either at the end of the document (an endnote) or at the end of the page where the numeral appears (a footnote).

These kinds of notes appear in many places that you may see on a daily basis: stories in newspapers or online news sources; history, science, and literature textbooks; various charts and maps; or even some novels, especially ones with a historical basis. Figure 17.10 shows an example of footnotes following plain text.

Figure 17.10: Footnotes at the end of a page of plain text

Endnotes are similar to footnotes, except that instead of appearing at the end of the page on which they are referenced, they appear all together at the end of the document (see Figure 17.11).

Creating Notes

To create a footnote or endnote, begin by selecting **Insert | Reference | Footnote**. This brings up the Footnote and Endnote dialog box, shown in Figure 17.12. In the top part of the dialog box, select either **Footnotes** or **Endnotes** and choose a

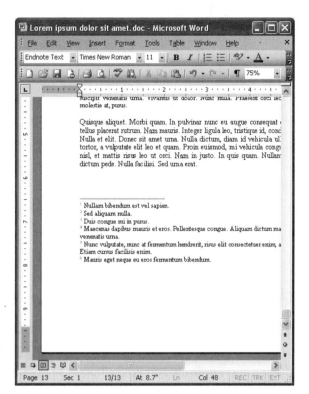

location for the new note. Then click **Insert** to create the note and return to the main document window (see Figure 17.13). As you can see, the cursor now blinks in the space next to a number in the notes list, in this case at the end of the page. Just type the note text beside the footnote or endnote number and you've added a footnote or endnote.

The example in Figure 17.13 is shown in Print Layout view; when you're working in Normal view and you add a footnote, you'll see something more like Figure 17.14. The area at the bottom of the window, called the *Footnotes Pane*, lists the footnotes for the current page and enables you to add or edit the footnote text.

You can turn the Footnotes Pane on or off depending on your preference. To turn on this pane at any time, just select **View | Footnotes**. If your document contains both footnotes and endnotes, you'll see a small dialog box called **View Footnotes** (see Figure 17.15) that asks you to specify which set of notes you want to see. Whenever the Footnotes Pane is visible, you can turn it off by selecting **View | Footnotes** again.

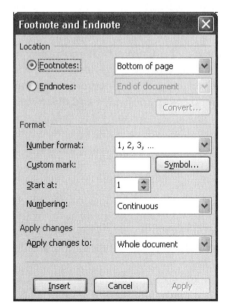

Figure 17.12: The Footnote and Endnote dialog box

Formatting Notes

The most common way to reference your footnotes and endnotes is with plain Arabic numerals. If you prefer, you can use Roman numerals or letters, or various symbols such as the asterisk (*). You can also choose to begin the notes in a particular document with a reference other than **1** or **A**—for example, if your current document is a continuation of a previous document that also contained notes.

To use these note formatting options, select **Insert | Reference | Footnotes** as you did before. This time, make any needed changes to **Number Format**, **Numbering**, or other settings before clicking **Insert** to create the note.

Uphill, Both Ways!

Of all the things that Word does to make life today easier than in the old typewriter days, footnotes must be near the top of the list. A few decades ago, students everywhere—from junior high up through graduate school—had to place these notes manually at the end of each page, which required skill and luck and lots of wasted typing paper.

On each page where one or more notes needed to appear, the writer would have to guess how much space the notes would take up, and then stop typing with enough space to spare. After adding a horizontal line to separate the main text from the notes, the writer then typed the correct note numbers and the corresponding note text, hoping that the text would all fit on the page!

Today, Word keeps track of which note numbers are on which page at all times; if a sentence with a note reference gets moved to a different page, so does its note, and Word automatically leaves enough space at the end of each page to print its footnotes.

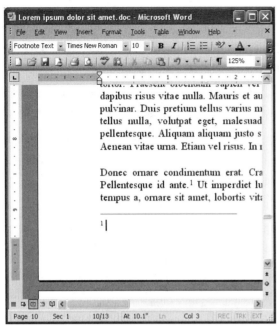

Figure 17.13: A newly added footnote

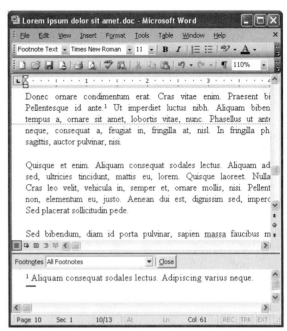

Figure 17.14: The same new footnote in Normal view

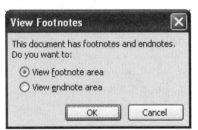

Figure 17.15: The View Footnotes dialog box

Figure 17.16: The Convert Notes dialog box

Converting Footnotes to Endnotes, or Vice Versa

Imagine that you've been writing a paper for school, and along the way you've created dozens of footnotes, with at least one note on each page. The day before the paper is due, you discover that the teacher wanted you to create *endnotes* for this assignment, not footnotes. Yikes! Does this mean you'll be spending all the time you set aside for spell-checking and proofreading to re-create your footnotes as endnotes? Never fear—Word has a convenient feature that enables you to convert footnotes to endnotes, or endnotes to footnotes, with just a few clicks.

In any document that contains notes, place your cursor in the Footnotes or Endnotes pane (in Normal view) or in the notes themselves (in Print Layout view), or select any superscript note marker in the text. Now select **Insert | Reference | Footnote** to open the Footnote and Endnote dialog box, and click the **Convert** button. This brings up the Convert Notes dialog box, shown in Figure 17.16.

If your document currently has footnotes, the **Convert all footnotes to endnotes** option is selected. If your document currently has endnotes, the **Convert all endnotes to footnotes** option is selected. If the document contains both types of notes, the option offered is called **Swap footnotes and endnotes**. If the option presented is what you want to do, click **OK**. Note that if you change your mind, you can repeat the process to switch back, or simply use the **Undo** feature if you decide right away that converting your notes was a mistake.

Modifying Notes

To change the text of a note, just click into the note area at the bottom of the page in Print Layout view, or open the Footnotes Pane in Normal view. Place your cursor on the note you want to change, and type or delete as you would in regular body text.

Note that to delete a footnote or endnote, you cannot simply erase the text in the note area—that deletes the text, but leaves the note marker in place. Instead, you'll need to locate the note marker in the main document text and delete it.

Working with Document Comments

Have you ever asked someone to review an essay or paper and mark any mistakes or suggestions? Having someone look at your work is a good thing—it can help you spot errors and improve your writing—but sometimes it's hard to figure out all those red marks. Not everyone has neat handwriting, and you can't always tell what's going on with arrows and comments splayed all across the page. Even when you review your own documents, you may find that your own hastily scrawled comments don't make sense when you get back to your computer to make the changes.

With Word, you don't have to struggle with hand-written edits any longer! The *comment* feature in Word enables you to add neatly typed comments into a document. The comments appear in handy little word balloons in the document margins, so the comment text is easy to read and the main document remains uncluttered. You can add comments to your own document or have other readers add their opinions, and then print the document with the comments either visible or hidden.

Inserting comments

To add a comment, first select the text to which your comment applies; this will help the document's author understand your comment in the correct context. You might select a single word, a sentence, or an entire paragraph. Then select **Insert | Comment**.

When you do this, several things happen at once. The Reviewing toolbar appears, if it wasn't already turned on (this toolbar normally floats on top of your document window, but you can drag it up to join the other toolbars if you prefer). Also, if your document is in Print Layout view, a colored background appears behind your selected text, connected by a dotted line to a word balloon out in the margin (see Figure 17.17). If your document is in Normal view, the *Reviewing Pane* appears at the bottom of your document window (see Figure 17.18).

If you decide you don't want to look at the Reviewing Pane, it's easy to turn off. Simply look for the button on the far right end of the Reviewing toolbar (see Figure 17.19) called **Reviewing Pane**. Click that button at any time to toggle the pane on or off.

You can type your comment text directly in the word balloon in the document margin, or in the Reviewing Pane in the white space directly below the relevant comment. How do you know which is the relevant comment, by the way? The Reviewing Pane might include several different comments, as in Figure 17.20. The key is that little number with your initials next to the word *Comment*, which appears both in the margin and in the Reviewing Pane. This comment number is unique within the document, which makes it helpful in managing large numbers of comments. Figure 17.20 shows comments as they appear in both the Reviewing Pane and the margin; note the comment numbers such as CDB3, indicating

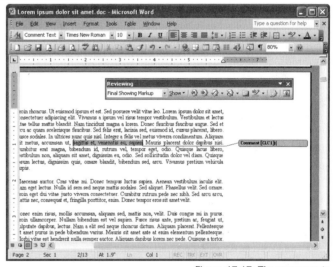

Figure 17.17: The response to adding a comment in Print Layout view

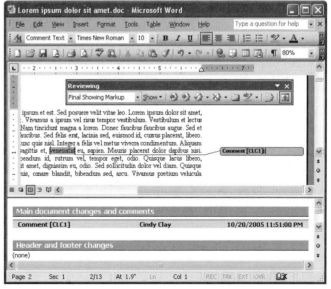

Figure 17.18: The Reviewing Pane, which appears when you add a comment in Normal view

How does Word know your name and initials?

When you first install Word or the Microsoft Office suite, the installation process asks for various pieces of information, including the user's name and initials. Word remembers this information and uses it for several purposes, one of which is tracking document comments.

If needed, you can change the user information; this comes in handy if you're using a borrowed or shared computer to make comments. Select **Tools | Options***, then click the* **User Information** *tab. Here, you can change the user name and initials. Needless to say, it's extremely important that you note the current settings and reset this information the way you found it when you're done—otherwise, you may find you aren't welcome the next time you need to use that computer!*

Figure 17.19: The Reviewing toolbar, with Reviewing Pane (far right button) turned on

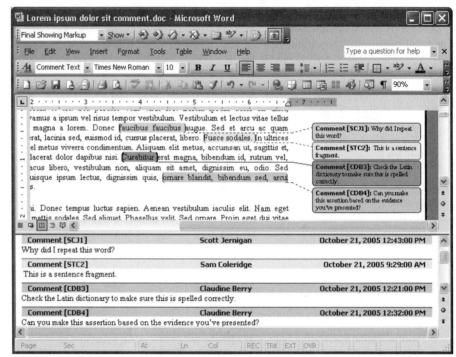

Figure 17.20: A paragraph with multiple comments

the third comment made by the reviewer with the initials CDB.

To see the full name of the reviewer who made a specific comment, just point your mouse at the comment. A pop-up message appears, giving the date and time that the comment was added, along with the reviewer's full name and the full text of the comment (see Figure 17.21). This works in both Normal and Page Layout view.

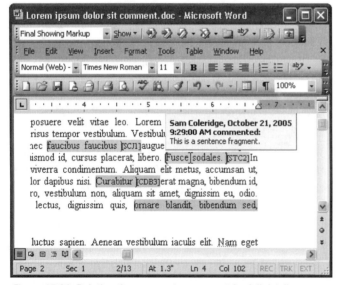

Figure 17.21: Pointing the mouse at a comment for full details

Viewing and Hiding Comments

Whether you're in Normal view or Print Layout view, you can select **View | Markup** at any time to toggle between viewing and hiding comments. When the Markup feature is on, its entry on the View menu is highlighted. Of course, the other way to view comments is to use the Reviewing Pane. This pane does not disappear when you turn off the Markup feature.

Printing Comments

You can print a copy of your document that includes the comments in the margins, even if you're not currently viewing comments. When you go to print, select **File | Print** instead of clicking the **Print** button, so that you see the Print dialog box. On the drop-down list called **Print what**, select **Document showing markup** (see Figure 17.22), then select other options as you normally would and click **OK**.

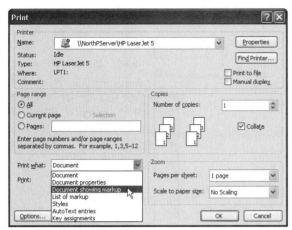

Figure 17.22: Printing a document with comments

Tracking Document Changes

Any time two or more people take turns working on the same document, it's a great opportunity for total confusion! When you have several different people all reviewing and changing the text, the end product can end up almost unrecognizable to the person who wrote the first draft. Whose idea was it to move the text from Page 3 to the end of the document? When did all those extra commas get thrown in? And who wrote that awful run-on sentence in the middle of Page 17?

Believe it or not, you *can* have multiple editors working on the same document without losing track of who changed what. The *Track Changes* feature in Word enables you to see at a glance each change that each person has made, and then accept or reject each change.

Track Changes While Editing

If you want to have a record of all changes made to your document, you must turn on the Track Changes feature. This feature is easy to use—just select **Tools | Track Changes** once to turn it on, and again to turn it off. You can also use the Reviewing toolbar (turn it on the same way you've learned for other toolbars) to toggle the Track Changes feature on or off, and to see at a glance whether the feature is currently enabled.

So, how do tracked changes look in your document? You can choose not to see them at all, for example if you're working on the document and want an uncluttered screen. Just select **Final** from the drop-down list at the left end of the Reviewing toolbar. If you want to view the documents' tracked changes, on the other hand, select **Final Showing Markup** from the drop-down list.

In Normal view, any tracked changes will appear in color, with underlining for added text or strikethrough for deleted text (see Figure 17.23). In Print Layout view, new text appears in color, while deleted text and formatting changes are noted in little word balloons—just like the ones used for comments—in the right margin (see Figure 17.24). In both views, a vertical line appears in the left margin, showing where changes have been made.

The colors used for the markup are coded to show which reviewer made what changes. If only one person has edited the document, the changed text and word balloons are all marked with the same color. If multiple reviewers have worked on the document, each person's changes appear in a different color, making it easy to scroll through the document and look at that person's contributions.

Comment This!

Go back to your word processing document and add a few comments. Check also the information section about the comment author and adjust it to reflect you, if it doesn't already.

When you collaborate on a Word document, teamwork is essential. Each person who works on the document must keep tracking turned on at all times while making changes. If anyone changes the document while tracking is turned off, there will be no record of those changes, leading to confusion or even mutiny in the ranks!

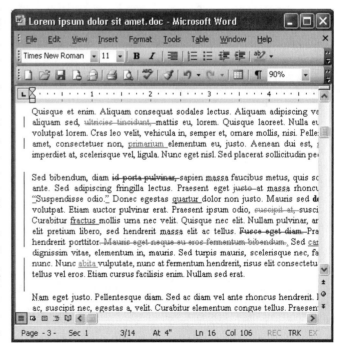

Figure 17.23: Tracked changes in Normal view

Tracking Changes

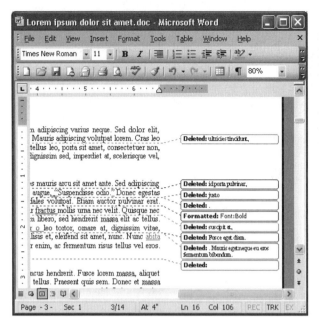

Figure 17.24: Tracked changes in Print Layout view

To find out who is represented by a particular color, just point your mouse at some edited text. You'll get a pop-up window that lists the name of the person who made the change; the date and time the change occurred; whether text was inserted, deleted, or formatted; and the affected text (see Figure 17.25).

Accept or Reject Tracked Changes

When everyone collaborating on a document has had their say and made their changes, you can clear out all of the tracking information by accepting and rejecting changes. This gives you, the author, the final approval on which changes are OK and which ones are not.

On the Reviewing toolbar, you'll see four buttons used for handling tracked changes: **Previous**, **Next**, **Accept Change**, and **Reject Change/Delete Comment** (see Figure 17.26).

When you're ready to start reviewing changes, make sure your cursor is at the beginning of your document and click **Next**. The first change in the document is highlighted; you can point to it with your mouse to see the details of who made the change and what was done. To keep this change and remove the change tracking for this item, click **Accept Change**. Then click **Next** again to move on to the next change. If at any point you need to move backward through the document, you can click **Previous** instead of **Next**.

If you come across a change you *don't* want to keep, click **Reject Change/**

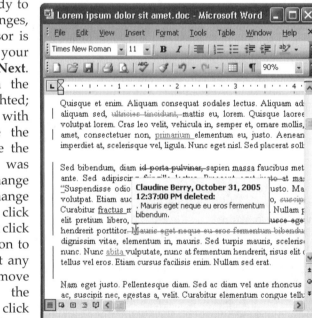

Figure 17.25: A pop-up window giving details of a tracked change

Figure 17.26: The Reviewing toolbar buttons used for handling tracked changes

Delete Comment. When you do this, the effects of the change are reversed, and the change tracking for that item is removed—in other words, there's no sign that the change was ever made. Click **Next** or **Previous** to approve or reject the next change.

If you've already reviewed all your document changes and you want to accept or reject all of the changes at once, click the down arrow next to either **Accept Change** or **Reject Change/Delete Comment**. On the drop-down menu, select either **Accept All Changes in Document** (see Figure 17.27) or **Reject All Changes in Document** to clear out all the tracking information with one click.

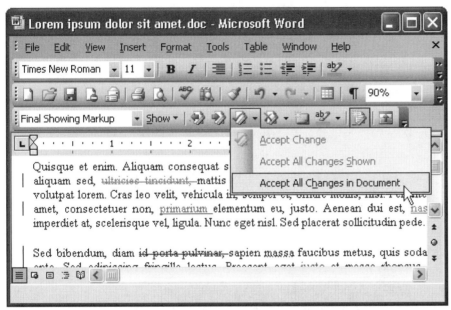

Figure 17.27: Accepting all changes in the document with one click

Themes

Like most other Microsoft applications, Word enables you to apply a set of pre-fabricated visual elements, called a theme, to a document. The purpose of a theme is to give the document a professional look; it includes a customized set of text styles for body text, headings, and lists, as well as background colors, graphics and other visual elements. The purpose of the theme is to give a unified look to all parts of a document, or to multiple documents.

*While themes are visually attractive, it's important to note that they're intended for delivery of information on a computer screen, not a printed document. The color-rich backgrounds of most themes would quickly run most home color printers out of ink! The most common use for themes in a Word document is to create documents that will be saved using the **File | Save as Web Page** command. Another good use for a theme in Word is to create a flyer or invitation that you will distribute as an e-mail attachment—you'll learn all about e-mail and attachments in a later chapter.*

*To apply a theme to a Word document, select **Format | Theme** to bring up the Theme dialog box (see Figure 17.28). Scroll through the available options, select one that works for your document, and click **OK** to apply the theme. Figure 17.29 shows the result of applying the Zero theme, which uses white text on a black background of ones and zeroes, to a flyer about a computer career seminar.*

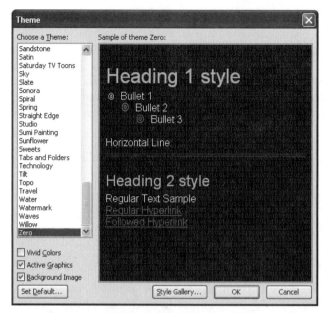

Figure 17.28: The Theme dialog box, displaying a preview of the Zero theme

Figure 17.29: A flyer with the Zero theme applied

Page Numbering

■ For any document with multiple pages that are meant to be read in order, page numbers are a good idea. Word offers several options for automated page numbers.

■ You can use Arabic numerals, Roman numerals, or numbers with dashes (- 1 -, - 2 -, - 3 -, and so on) when numbering your pages, and position your page numbers anywhere in the top or bottom edge of your document. You can even specify whether or not to number the first page.

■ Page numbers are *fields*—bits of information powered by computer code so that they automatically update. You can tell they're fields because of the gray background that appears when you click on them. Page number fields re-number themselves if you add or remove text and the document's page count changes.

■ To remove a page number, you need to select **View | Header and Footer**. Find the page number, select it (including its frame, if it has one), and press **[Delete]**.

Headers and Footers

■ Headers and footers are the margins at the top and bottom of your document's pages, where you cannot type normal text. You can put information such as the document name or file name, your name, the name of the course or your school, the time or date, the chapter number, and the page number.

■ Headers and footers are not visible in Normal view. The command to view and edit the header and footer information is **View | Header and Footer**.

■ Header and footer information can align with the left margin, the right margin, or the center of the page width. Use tab stops to align information to the center or right.

■ To include time or date information for your document, select **Insert | Date and Time**. The most common place for this information is the header or footer, but you can insert a date or time stamp anywhere in your document.

■ If you check the **Update Automatically** option in the Date and Time dialog box, your time or date stamp will always update to the current information; if you don't check this option, the time or date stamp will remain frozen in time from when you inserted it.

■ You can change the format of a date or time stamp (for example, change **October 25, 2010** to **10/25/10** or **25 October 2010**) by clicking the **Default** button on the Date and Time dialog box. You can even select a format and then set it as the default for future use.

Footnotes and Endnotes

■ Footnotes and endnotes are bits of information that sit outside the main document text, often in small print. For each note, a little superscript number appears in the relevant text in the main document. Then at the end of the page (for footnotes) or the end of the document (for endnotes), the notes appear, referenced by their note numbers.

■ To create a footnote or endnote, select **Insert | Reference | Footnote**, then select which type of note to create and click **Insert**. Then type the text of your note in the notes list (in Print Layout view) or in the Footnotes Pane (in Normal view).

■ Selecting **View | Footnotes** toggles the Footnotes Pane on or off.

■ In the Footnote and Endnote dialog box, you can change the number format used for note references, or specify a starting number other than 1.

Working with Document Comments

- You can add comments to a Word document without affecting the main document text. Comments are like virtual sticky notes that the document author can read and then either keep or delete.

- To add a comment, select the applicable text and then select **Insert | Comment**. This brings up either a word balloon in the margin or the Reviewing Pane at the bottom of the document window; type your comment text into the balloon or pane.

- To show or hide where comments appear in the document, select **View | Markup**. To show or hide the Reviewing Pane, click the **Reviewing Pane** button on the Reviewing toolbar.

- To include comments when you print a document, use the **File | Print** command instead of the Print button, and select **Document showing markup** from the **Print what** list.

Tracking Document Changes

- Change tracking makes it possible for two or more people to collaborate on a document. Instead of just adding comments, another person (or several people) can make changes to your document, while each change is tracked according to who made the change, when the change occurred, and what text was added or deleted.

- The Track Changes feature only works when it's turned on! To turn it on, select **Tools | Track Changes** and verify that the **Track Changes** command shows up as orange on the menu and the Reviewing toolbar.

- To hide tracked changes while you work on a document, select **Final** from the drop-down list on the Reviewing toolbar; to view the tracked changes, select **Final Showing Markup**.

- To clear out tracking information, use the **Accept Change** and **Reject Change/Delete Comment** buttons on the Reviewing toolbar.

Key Terms

Comment

Date format

Date stamp

Document showing markup

Endnote

Field

Final

Final Showing Markup

Footnote

Footnotes Pane

Markup

Page numbering

Reviewing Pane

Reviewing toolbar

Theme

Time stamp

Track Changes

Key Term Quiz

Use the Key Terms list to complete the following sentences. Not all the terms will be used.

1. The _____ feature creates a record of the edits that various people have made to a Word document.

2. A button on the far right end of the Reviewing toolbar toggles the _____ on and off.

3. If you're creating a Word document to be viewed online, and you need lots of color and a professional look, you can apply a(n) _____.

4. You can read the endnotes and footnotes for a document in the _____.

5. If you have a long Word document, it's a good idea to include _____, which you can place in any corner of your pages.

6. If your document contains visible comments, you can hide the comments by selecting _____ from the View menu.

7. To view tracked change information in your document, select _____ from the drop-down list on the Reviewing toolbar.

8. A(n) _____ is like a virtual sticky note that the document's author can read and then either keep or delete.

9. When you create a(n) _____, you'll see a little superscript number in the text and your typed note at the end of the document.

10. The gray background that appears when you click on an automatic page number indicates that it's a _____.

Multiple Choice Quiz

1. To create an endnote, which of the following should you select?
   A. **Insert | Reference | Endnote**
   B. **Insert | Reference | Footnote**
   C. **Insert | Comment | Endnote**
   D. **Insert | Comment | Footnote**

2. When you add a time stamp, what determines whether it will change each time you open the document or stay the same?
   A. The time format you selected
   B. The Time Stamp dialog box settings
   C. The **Update automatically** check box
   D. The location of the time stamp in your document

3. What does the **Next** button on the Reviewing pane do?
   A. Moves your cursor to the next page
   B. Moves your cursor to the next paragraph
   C. Highlights the next tracked change in the document
   D. Deletes the next tracked change in the document

4. If you've already reviewed the changes in your document and want to keep them all, what's the quickest way that you can clear out the change tracking information?
   A. Use the **Next** and **Accept Change** buttons on all the tracked changes.
   B. Select **Accept All Changes in Document**.
   C. Press **[Ctrl + A]** to select your entire document text, right-click, and select **Clear Tracking**.
   D. Select **Tools | Track Changes** to turn that feature off.

5. Which of the following must you do to include comments when you print your document?
   A. Make sure you've selected **View | Markup** before printing.
   B. Make sure the Reviewing Pane is turned on when you print.
   C. Select **Document showing markup** in the Print dialog box.
   D. Select a printer that can print without borders.

6. Which of the following should you select on the Reviewing toolbar to view your document without the tracked change information?
   A. Final
   B. Final Showing Markup
   C. Final Without Tracking
   D. Original Showing Markup

7. Which of the following is the most appropriate use for a Word theme?
   A. A 20-page long paper for science class
   B. An announcement for a club meeting to be sent via e-mail
   C. A letter you're mailing to your Aunt Edna
   D. A party invitation you're printing for 50 guests

8. What is the default format of page numbers?
   A. Page 1, Page 2, Page 3 …
   B. - 1 -, - 2 -, - 3 - …
   C. 1, 2, 3 …
   D. I, II, III …

9. In Print Layout view, tracked changes and comments display as word balloons in the document margin. In which margin do they appear?
   A. Top
   B. Bottom
   C. Left
   D. Right

10. To remove a page number, which of the following will you need to do?
    A. Select **View | Header and Footer**.
    B. Select **Insert | Page Numbers**.
    C. Select **Format | Bullets and Numbering**.
    D. Click the **Reviewing Pane** button on the Reviewing toolbar.

11. Which of the following is **not** an option in the Convert Notes dialog box?
    A. Swap footnotes and endnotes
    B. Remove footnotes and endnotes
    C. Convert all footnotes to endnotes
    D. Convert all endnotes to footnotes

12. Which of the following can you change in the Date and Time dialog box?
    A. The placement of the date or time stamp on the page
    B. The format of the date or time stamp
    C. The font used to display the date or time stamp
    D. The actual date or time information

13. When you point your mouse at a tracked change, you see a pop-up message. What does the message tell you about the change?
    A. Time and date it was made
    B. Time and date and who made the change
    C. Time and date, who made the change, and whether text was added, deleted, or reformatted
    D. Who made the change and whether text was added, deleted, or formatted

14. When you view the tracked changes in a document, you notice that the changes appear in different colors. Why is this?
    A. Word uses different colors to track text that has been added, deleted, or reformatted.
    B. Each time a document is closed and re-opened, Word switches to a different color to track changes by date.
    C. Each time the document is renamed, Word switches to a different color to track changes by document name.
    D. Each person who edits the document is assigned a color, so each color represents someone who made changes to the document.

15. When you make comments in a document, Word uses your initials as part of the comment number. On which Options tab does Word store your name and initials?
    A. Security
    B. User Information
    C. Track Changes
    D. Edit

Essay Questions

1. Explain the different types of information that you can put into the headers and footers of your Word documents. Give examples of the header and footer information you might use in different kinds of documents, such as a book report, a science project, a long business letter, or a research paper.

2. In a short essay, compare and contrast footnotes and endnotes, and put forth an argument that promotes one style of note over another. You can be passionate or silly or both in your defense of footnote or endnote.

Projects

1. It's time to try something potentially fun: creating your very own chain letter or group story. Start with one person in class writing a couple of paragraphs of outline-like prose. Your letter or story could begin, "It was a dark and stormy night, when suddenly . . ." and include the beginnings of several other paragraphs: "I had to stop and catch my breath" or "Mary never had a chance." Or, start multiple chain letters or group stories if you have a big enough group, all with different themes.

   Once you have the beginnings of a story or letter, turn on Track Changes and select Final rather than Final Showing Markup from the drop-down menu on the Reviewing toolbar. Then save the document to a floppy disk and start passing it from one person to the next.

   Each person can do any of these things: add to the story; edit the document to correct things; or change the direction of the story by editing previously added text. At the end of the session, view the story with Final Showing Markup selected.

2. In keeping with the whimsical theme for the projects, find a children's story book and add footnotes. Be creative, but keep it clean. Use a story provided by your teacher, or use a classic tale, like "Hansel and Gretel." You can find that story here: http://www.mordent.com/folktales/grimms/hng/hng.html

COMPUTER LITERACY: YOUR TICKET TO IC³ CERTIFICATION

Basic Spreadsheet Skills

"You're an accountant! You're in a noble profession! The word 'count' is part of your title!"

– Max Bialystock, *The Producers*

This chapter covers the following IC³ exam objectives:

- IC³-2 3.1.1 Identify how a table of data is organized in a spreadsheet

- IC³-2 3.1.2 Select information using the keyboard and mouse

- IC³-2 3.1.3 Insert and modify data

- IC³-2 3.1.4 Modify table structure

- IC³-2 3.1.5 Identify and change number formats

- IC³-2 3.1.6 Apply borders and shading to cells

- IC³-2 3.1.7 Specify cell alignment

- IC³-2 3.1.8 Apply table AutoFormats

Once upon a time, accountants kept their accounts by recording income and expenditure numbers on large gridded pages, entering the numbers in pencil in the squares created by the intersecting rows and columns. Modern-day accountants still record income and expenditure figures using large grids of rows and columns, called *spreadsheets*, but now they do their financial calculations using a computer program. The program not only provides the gridded page, but also does quite a bit of the calculating work for them.

The most popular spreadsheet program, Microsoft Excel, is also used for all sorts of other purposes that have nothing to do with accounting, such as tracking and calculating student grades, or cataloguing a CD or DVD collection. In this chapter, you'll learn the basics of how to use Microsoft Excel, starting with the features, such as columns and rows. The second section of this chapter goes into working with cell data in columns and rows. The chapter winds up with issues in formatting cells.

Understanding Spreadsheets

Spreadsheet programs come in various shapes and sizes, but the basics revolve around columns, rows, and cells. You need to know how to identify a cell, understand column headings, and row labels. Finally, selecting data enables you to work with that data.

Columns and Rows

A spreadsheet works in two dimensions: vertical (columns) and horizontal (rows). An Excel spreadsheet can pretty much have as many columns and rows as you want, or at least more than you are likely ever to use. The *columns* are labeled across the top from left to right with the letters of the alphabet, from A to Z, and then AA, AB, AC, and so on. The *rows* are numbered along the left side of the spreadsheet, starting with 1 at the top and counting up as you go down the rows. The column letters are called *headings* and the row numbers are called *labels*.

Figure 18.1 shows an Excel spreadsheet with its numbered rows and lettered columns. Excel is displaying the first of three tabbed spreadsheet pages, called *worksheets*, which in this case still have their default names (visible on the tabs at the bottom): Sheet1, Sheet2, and Sheet3. The contents of one worksheet in an Excel spreadsheet document don't interact with the contents of the other worksheets, unless you use some of Excel's advanced features to make that happen.

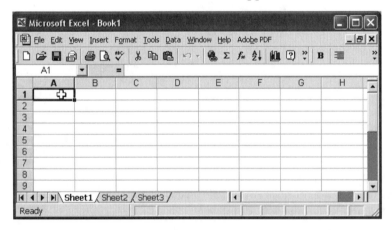

Figure 18.1: A spreadsheet displaying worksheet Sheet1, with cell A1 selected

Identifying a Cell by its Row Number and Column Letter

The row numbers and column letters make it easy to identify the boxes, called *cells*, created where they cross. Cells are where you enter the numbers or other data in the spreadsheet. The cell in the upper left corner of the grid, in column A and row 1, is referred to as cell A1. In Figure 18.1, cell A1 has been selected, and the mouse cursor is hovering over it, looking like a fat plus sign. Just above the grid at the upper left, you can see the coordinates (the column and row) of whatever cell you have currently selected in a field called the *Name Box*.

Column Headings

Column headings are useful for identifying individual cells, but spreadsheets are designed for working with entire columns of data. To label an entire column of data, you may want to use something more descriptive than **B** as a header. Suppose you want to figure out which type of soda your friends drink the most: Coke, Pepsi, 7UP, or Sprite. You're going to record the number of Cokes in column A, Pepsis in column B, and so on. Do you just have to remember that the numbers in column A represent Coke? Fortunately, you don't, because spreadsheet cells can contain text as well as numbers. You can use the top cell in each column to enter a descriptive heading. In Figure 18.2, cells B1 through E1 have been filled with the words **Coke**, **Pepsi, 7UP,** and **Sprite**.

Row Labels

In Figure 18.2, the first cell in each row is a descriptive label for that row: cell A2 contains the name **Scott**, cell A3 the name **Cindy**, cell A4 **Mike**, and cell A5 **Kathy**. By using a separate row for each person, you can record their individual soda choices separately. In cell B2, which is row 2 (Scott's soda consumption) and column B (Coke), you will record the number of Cokes that Scott has consumed. In cell C2 (Pepsi column, Scott's row), you'll enter the number of Pepsis he drank. In cell E3 (Sprite column, Cindy's row), you'll enter the number of Sprites Cindy drank. Using the spreadsheet's rows and columns, you can record separate numbers for each person and each type of soda.

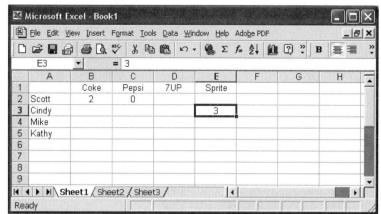

Figure 18.2: Spreadsheet with column headings and row labels

Selecting Data in a Spreadsheet

To use a spreadsheet, you need to enter data into its cells. Before you can enter data into a cell, you must select that cell.

Select an Individual Cell

There are two ways to select a cell. You can either use your arrow keys to move from one cell to another, or use your mouse to point and click on the cell you want. In Figure 18.1, cell A1 is selected; in Figure 18.2, cell E3 is selected. In each case you can tell because the edges of that cell are bold black lines. Notice that Excel also highlights the column letter and row number of the selected cell, to help you verify that you've selected the one you intended.

Select a Row or a Column

If you need to select an entire row or column, you can do so with a single click. To select all of row 3, simply click on the number 3 on the left end of that row. When a row is selected, the entire row will be highlighted (Figure 18.3). You can select a column in the same way. To select column D, for example, just click on the letter D, and the entire column will be highlighted.

Select a Cell Range

Sometimes you want to select only certain cells, rather than an entire column or row. To select a *cell range*—that is, several adjacent cells in a column or a row—just click your mouse in the cell at one end of the range, then hold down the mouse button and drag the cursor to the cell at the other end of the range. In Figure 18.4, cells B2 through E2 have been selected. The plus sign cursor is poised over cell E2, because in this case the person working with the spreadsheet dragged the mouse from left to right, ending at E2.

You can enter numbers and letters in the same cell, but if you do, Excel won't do math with the numbers. It will treat them as just more text.

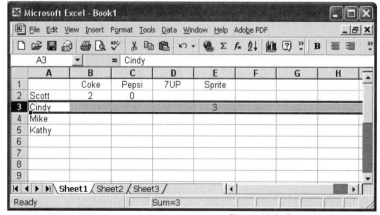

Figure 18.3: Selecting Row 3

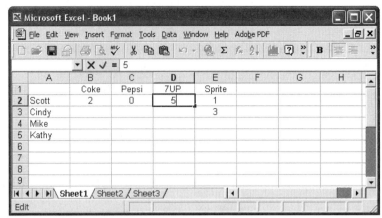

Figure 18.4: Selecting a range of cells

Another way to select a range of cells is to select the first cell in the range, then hold down the **[Shift]** key on your keyboard and use the arrow keys to add cells to your selection. You can also select a range of cells using the mouse and the **[Shift]** key. Begin by clicking on the cell in the top or left corner of the range you want to select, then just hold the **[Shift]** key and click the cell in the bottom or right corner of the range.

Working with Cell Data in Rows and Columns

The whole purpose of a computer spreadsheet is to enable you to do calculations using the data you've entered. First, though, you have to get the data in! Let's look at the methods for populating your spreadsheet with data.

Entering Cell Data

Entering data in a spreadsheet can be as simple as clicking on a cell and typing. When you have entered whatever number or text you want, pressing **[Enter]** inserts what you typed into the cell, and changes the selected cell to the one below it. You can also insert your data by clicking into a different cell; in this case, the new selection is the cell that you click.

Changing Cell Data

If you look to the left of column heading A and above row heading 1, you'll see an empty box. You can click that box to select the entire worksheet.

You can change cell data in a variety of ways. To delete the contents of a cell, just click on the cell and press **[Delete]**. To replace the contents of a cell, just click on it once and start typing; Excel automatically replaces the old cell contents with the new. To change the contents of a cell, either double-click on the cell, or click on it once and then press the **[F2]** key. This opens up the cell so that you can add and delete data in whatever way you want (Figure 18.5). Whenever you're in edit mode, a blinking cursor appears in the cell. When you're finished editing, press **[Enter]** or click in another cell.

You can also use a field just below the toolbars, called the *Formula Bar*, to edit a cell. When you select a cell, its contents show up in the Formula Bar. When you enter data into a cell, what you type shows up both in the cell

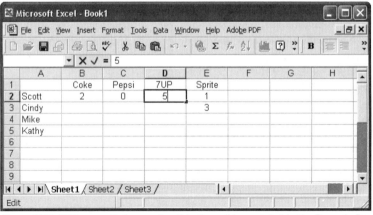

Figure 18.5: Editing a cell; the number 5 in the cell is repeated in the Formula Bar, just above the C column heading

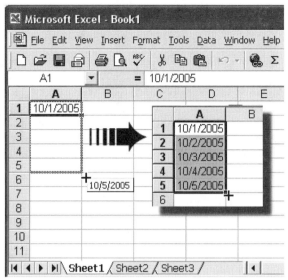

Figure 18.6: Filling in a series of dates

itself and in the Formula Bar. If you then click in the Formula Bar, you can delete or edit the entry.

Filling In a Series of Cells

Suppose you decide to use a spreadsheet to keep track of your daily workouts, recording each day's activities in a separate row and each month in its own worksheet. Your first task is to enter a column of dates for the first month. Luckily for you, Excel has lots of clever features to automate tedious tasks, such as filling in a series of numbers, dates, or other data.

For example, to fill in column A with a series of dates for the month of October, enter the beginning value for the series in the first cell in column A, which in this example would be the first date: **10/01/2005**. Next, click on the small black square, called the *fill handle*, at the bottom right corner of the cell. When your cursor is over the fill handle, it changes from a fat white cross to a thin black one (Figure 18.6). By clicking and dragging, you can select the cells to fill with the series of dates or other numbers. Dragging down in a column or to the right in a row tells Excel you want it to fill it with a series of increasing values (1, 2, 3…); dragging up or left fills in a series of decreasing values (9, 8, 7…). Figure 18.6 shows the process of dragging the fill handle down a column to create a series of dates. Note that Excel even shows you what it plans to put in the cell you're selecting (in Figure 18.6, note the date **10/5/2005** in cell A5).

Inserting and Deleting Cells, Rows, Columns, and Worksheets

If you forget a row or column you meant to include in the middle of a paper spreadsheet, your only choice is to add it on the edge of what you've already entered, or erase and redo everything that needs to be shifted over to make room for it. Thankfully, Excel makes it easy to insert new rows and columns anywhere. For example, to insert a new column between columns F and G, select column G, then select **Insert | Columns**. A new column is inserted between F and G. Note that the new column becomes column G, and the former column G shifts right to become column H.

Inserting rows is just as easy. Select the row *below* where you want the new row to go, then select **Insert | Rows**. For example, if you select row 5 and then insert a new row, the new row becomes row 5, and the former row 5 shifts down to become the new row 6.

Deleting columns and rows is as easy as inserting them. To delete column G, click on the G to select the column, then select **Edit | Delete**. Column G, and all of its data, will disappear. To delete row 5, click on the 5 to select the row, then select **Edit | Delete** to remove the entire row and all its contents. As with inserting, you can also use the right-click menu to delete columns and rows: select the column or row, right-click, and select **Delete**.

Inserting or deleting an individual cell is possible, but it's important to remember that when you add or delete just one cell, the spreadsheet will need

Copying from One Cell to Many

One of the handiest features of Excel is the ability to copy the contents of one cell into multiple other cells in one step. To do this, click on a cell with data in it and then select **Edit | Copy**—*or if you're a shortcut kind of person, use* **[Ctrl + C]**. *The borders of the cell will turn into a moving dotted line, which is Excel's way of making sure you can't miss which cell(s) you picked. Now select several other cells, and either select* **Edit | Paste** *or press* **[Ctrl + V]**. *With that single Paste command, the contents of the first cell are instantly copied into all of the target cells. Sweet!*

Fill in a Series of Months or Years

You can fill cells with a series of dates with increments of a month or year instead of a day. Try holding down the right mouse button (instead of the left button) while you drag the fill handle to select a range of cells. When you release the button, a context menu will appear with a set of choices, including **Fill Months** *and* **Fill Years**. *Try both of these options to see how they work!*

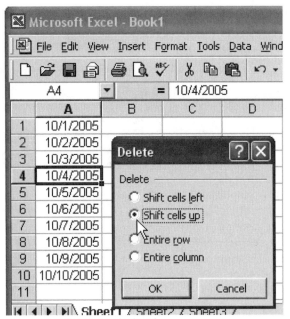

Figure 18.7: Deleting a single cel

You can also use the right-click menu to insert columns and rows. To insert a new column, select the column to the right of where you want the new column to go, right-click anywhere in the selected column, and select **Insert** from the context menu. The same method works for rows. Select a row, right-click, and select **Insert**. A new row will be added above the selected row.

to shift either a row or column to account for the change. For example, if you move the entry box to cell A4 and right-click and select **Insert** (or select **Insert | Cell**), a small dialog box appears so you can choose whether you want to shift the existing cells in its row to the right, or shift the cells in its column down, to make room for the new cell. It also lets you insert an entire row or an entire column. Likewise, if you select a cell and then select **Edit | Delete**, a Delete dialog box will appear so you can choose whether to shift the existing cells left or up to account for the deleted cell, or you can choose to delete an entire row or column (Figure 18.7).

Adjusting Column Width and Row Height

When a column isn't wide enough or a row high enough to display all the contents of a cell, you can easily make adjustments. A quick method to change column width is to place the cursor on the dividing line between the column you want to adjust and the one to its right. The cursor turns into a bar with arrows pointing left and right. Click and drag to change the column width. Figure 18.8 shows column A getting a width adjustment. Note that Excel, in its usual informative way, displays the width at the current cursor position.

Adjusting the height of a row works the same way. When you move your mouse over the line between the row labels, the cursor changes to a bar with arrows pointing up and down. You simply click and drag up or down to change the row height.

Using AutoFit to Adjust Column Height and Row Width

It's handy to know how to adjust column width and row height, but in a big spreadsheet, adjusting every row and column by hand can be time-consuming. A fast solution for this is the *AutoFit* feature. When you apply AutoFit, each of the selected rows

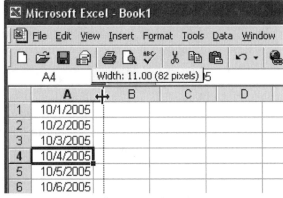

Figure 18.8: Adjusting the width of a column

and columns automatically adjusts to fit the contents of the largest cell it contains. To use the AutoFit option, select the rows or columns you want to adjust, then select **Format | Column | AutoFit Selection** (Figure 18.9) or **Format | Row | AutoFit**.

Keeping Columns and Rows Visible

As you scroll down a spreadsheet, the information you typed in row 1 disappears from view. The same thing happens with column A if you scroll far enough to the right. This can be particularly annoying because the top and left-most cells are most often the ones where header information is stored. Excel's solution is to let you freeze these columns and rows in place, so that they remain visible even as you scroll away from them.

Suppose your header information is in row 1 and column A. To freeze these areas, click on cell B2 (below row 1 and after column A), and select **Window |**

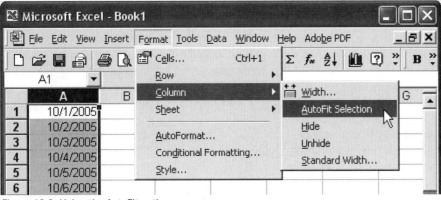

Figure 18.9: Using the AutoFit option

Freeze Panes (Figure 18.10). Bold lines now appear running the length of the spreadsheet between columns A and B, and between rows 1 and 2. No matter how far you scroll down or to the right, column A and row 1 will remain frozen in place on your screen (Figure 18.11). You can undo the Freeze Panes command at any time, regardless of what cell is selected, by selecting **Window | Unfreeze Panes**. The two bold lines will disappear, and column A and row 1 will no longer be frozen.

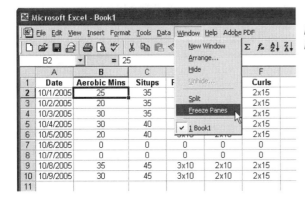

Figure 18.10: Freeze panes

Figure 18.11: The frozen row and column don't scroll off the page.

Formatting Cells

Excel lets you format the contents of a cell to display in a variety of ways. Let's look at some of the handy tools spreadsheets have for formatting content.

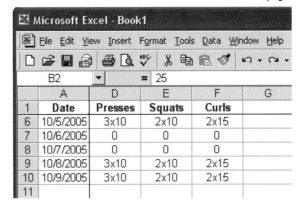

Numbers

If you're an engineer working with complex calculations, the results of your efforts may well be numbers with as many as four decimal places. If you're doing a monthly budget, nothing past the two decimal places for cents will interest you. Excel can accommodate both you and the engineer, allowing you to control how many decimal places each cell displays.

To set the number of decimal places in a cell or set of cells, select the cells

Hiding and Revealing Rows and Columns

Spreadsheets were primarily designed for use by businesses, and from time to time, they may contain confidential information. Entire rows or columns can be hidden so that they, and the data in them, disappear from view.

For example, suppose you created a chart with all the company's employees, and column D contained their Social Security numbers. This is sensitive information, so you might want to hide column D. First you would select the entire column, then choose Format | Column | Hide, and watch column D disappear from view. Notice that the visible columns keep their headers: A, B, C, E, and so on; column D still exists, so no other column gets its letter.

To see column D again, select the surrounding columns (C and E in this case) by clicking their headers while holding down the [Shift] key, or by clicking and dragging to select both column headers. Then choose Format | Column | Unhide, and watch column D reappear. Pure movie magic! The same thing can be done to hide and reveal a row: select it and choose Format | Row | Hide to make it disappear from view. Select the surrounding rows and choose Format | Row | Unhide to make it reappear.

to format, then right-click and select **Format Cells** (you can also use the main menu and select **Format | Cells**). The Format Cells dialog box appears, displaying the **Number** tab. If you select **Number** in the category box, you can adjust the number of decimal places the selected cells display (Figure 18.12). The engineer would probably want to change the default value of 2 to something larger.

Currency

Since so many spreadsheets are created to deal with sums of money, Excel makes it very easy to display numbers in the form of currencies from just about every nation. To format all of the numbers in a column for a particular currency, select the column, then click **Format | Cells**. If you select **Currency** from the category box on the **Number** tab, you can tell Excel to display a dollar sign (or any other nation's currency symbol) as part of the cell contents automatically, as well as specify the number of decimal places to display, and how to display negative numbers.

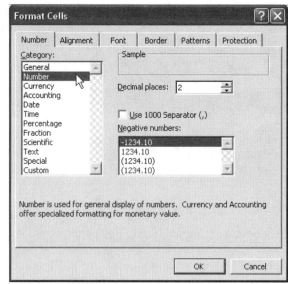

Figure 18.12: The Number category on the Number tab in the Format Cells dialog box

Date and Time

The same category box that had the options for **Numbers** and **Currency** also has options to format a **Date** or **Time** entered in a cell (Figure 18.13). If you have a cell with a date listed in the style **4/12/08**, you can select **Date** from the category list and direct Excel to display it in a different date format, such as **Saturday, April 12, 2008**, or **12-Apr-08**. Selecting the **Time** option provides a similarly wide variety of ways to display times, including several ways to display the time and date together.

Cell Borders and Shading

Since spreadsheets are all about displaying data, they offer many ways to bring attention to particular cells, rows, or columns. Suppose column G is the key

Figure 18.13: Time options on the Number tab in the Format Cells dialog box

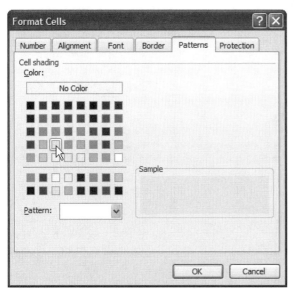

Figure 18.14: Yellow shading selected on the Patterns tab

data in your spreadsheet, so you want the cells in that column to be shaded yellow. Simply select column G, right-click, and select **Format Cells**. Select the **Patterns** tab and choose from the dozens of available colors by clicking on the one you want. In Figure 18.14, yellow shading has been selected. Click **OK**, and presto!—the entire column is shaded yellow.

A faster method for shading cells is to use the **Fill Color** button on the

What You Don't Know *Can* Hurt You

In January of 2005, a budget analyst for the state of New Hampshire had to walk into Governor John Lynch's office and tell him that they needed to come up with another $70 million to balance the state budget. The budget analyst was unfamiliar with the spreadsheet program he was using, so instead of subtracting $35 million in one place he added $35 million. You may never make a $70 million mistake (let's hope not!), but most professionals use a spreadsheet program at some point in their careers, and it pays to know how to do it right.

Figure 18.15: The Fill Color button with drop-down color palette

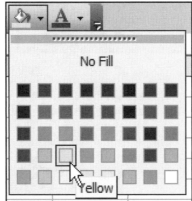

Formatting toolbar (Figure 18.15). Simply select the cell(s) you want to shade, click the arrow on the **Fill Color** button to open the color palette, and click on the color you want. That color will be added to the background of the selected cells. You can highlight other cells with the same color just by selecting them and clicking the **Fill Color** button again.

You can also make parts of a spreadsheet stand out by adding borders to a cell or group of cells. For example, if you have a column of numbers with a total at the bottom, you may want to put a thick red border around the total to make it stand out. Once again you have a choice: the **Borders** tab of the Format Cells dialog box (Figure 18.16) or the **Borders** button on the Formatting toolbar, which has a drop-down selection palette just like the **Fill Color** button (Figure 18.17).

Cell Alignment

When you enter data into a cell, it automatically aligns itself within the cell. By default, numbers are right-aligned (so that their ones, tens, and hundreds places line up) and text is left-aligned. The three basic *alignment* settings—left, center, and right—are represented by buttons on the Formatting toolbar. If you want to get fancier, you can use the **Alignment** tab in the Format Cells dialog box (Figure 18.18), which includes multiple choices for both horizontal and vertical alignment. You can even specify that the data appear angled up or down a specified number of degrees.

Another useful option on the **Alignment** tab (Figure 18.18) is a check box labeled **Wrap text**. Checking this causes the text you enter into a cell to wrap to a new line when it encounters the right-hand edge of the cell. This causes the cell to grow vertically so all the text remains visible. Otherwise the text that doesn't fit will be hidden from view as soon as you add data to the next cell to the right.

*The category box in the **Numbers** tab of the Format Cells dialog box also has an option for displaying a decimal number as a percentage. The only variable you can adjust is the number of decimal places to be displayed. The **Percentage** option takes whatever number is in the cell, automatically moves the decimal point over two spots, and adds a percent sign (%) after the number—so for example, **13** becomes **13%**.*

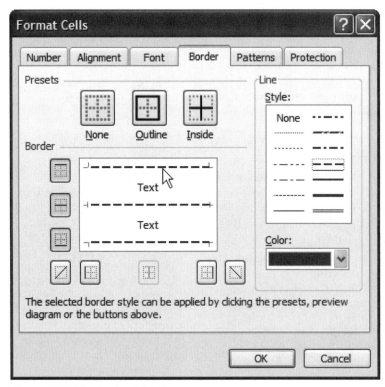

Figure 18.16: The Borders tab in the
Format Cells dialog box

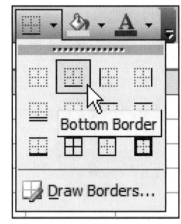

Figure 18.17: The Borders button with
drop-down border selections

Suppose you want to create a header at the top of three columns of data, and you want it to be centered above the five columns. Excel has you covered! With the click of a button, you can merge the three top cells into one big cell and center the header text in that new three-column-wide cell. First type the header text into the top cell of any one of the three columns, then select all three top cells and click the **Merge and Center** button on your toolbar (Figure 18.19). The three cells magically become one big cell with the header text nicely centered in the middle.

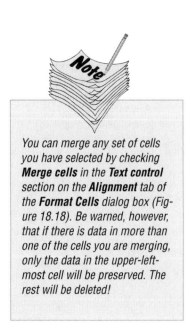

You can merge any set of cells you have selected by checking **Merge cells** in the **Text control** section on the **Alignment** tab of the **Format Cells** dialog box (Figure 18.18). Be warned, however, that if there is data in more than one of the cells you are merging, only the data in the upper-left-most cell will be preserved. The rest will be deleted!

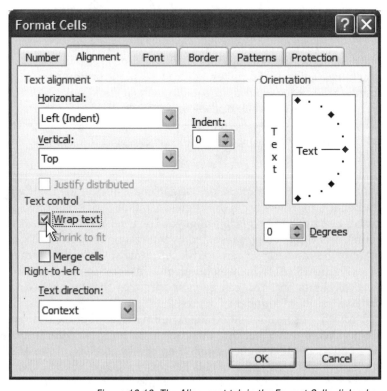

Figure 18.18: The Alignment tab in the Format Cells dialog box

Creating and Applying Styles

When you create a spreadsheet for a particular purpose, you will often want to use the same cell format repeatedly. Instead of setting all the format options (font type, color, shading, alignment, and so on) for each cell individually, Excel lets you save the format of a particular cell as a *style* that you can easily apply to other cells.

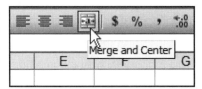

Merge and Center

Figure 18.19: Merge and Center button

Suppose cell D4 has a format that you know you'll be using often. Select cell D4 and then select **Format | Style** to open the **Style** dialog box (Figure

Figure 18.20: The Style dialog box showing the details of the Totals style

18.20). By default, the Normal style displays, but when you start typing in the name field, the word *Normal* disappears and the settings in the dialog box change to reflect the formatting of the cell you selected. Whatever you type will become the name for this style. Click **OK** to save your new style. From now on, you'll be able to apply this style to other cells by selecting them, selecting **Format | Style**, and picking your custom style from the drop-down list.

Just below the color palette on the **Patterns** tab of the **Format Cells** dialog box is a **Pattern** drop-down box, which offers a variety of options to add patterns of lines over or instead of cell shading.

Format changes are fun to play around with, but on a massive spreadsheet, it could take a lot of time to change so many different things. Fortunately, Excel includes a variety of preset formats you can choose from, called *AutoFormats*. To use them, select the cells you want to format, then select **Format | AutoFormat**. This brings up an **AutoFormat** dialog box with dozens of different format and table options (Figure 18.21). Select the one you want and click **OK**. AutoFormat applies the chosen formatting to the cells you selected.

If you want to apply only some parts of an AutoFormat to your cells, click the **Options** button to see a set of check boxes labeled **Number**, **Font**, **Alignment**, and so on at the bottom of the dialog box. By clearing one or more of these check boxes, you can tell Excel not to apply those features of your chosen format.

Using Format Painter

Like Word, Excel has a handy Format Painter feature that you can use to apply the formatting of one cell onto another quickly and easily. Highlight a cell with the format you want to copy, click the **Format Painter** button on the Standard toolbar (it has a picture of a paintbrush), and then select the cells you want formatted like the first one. When you release the mouse button, the cells you selected are transformed, and the Format Painter feature turns itself off.

Now try double-clicking on the **Format Painter** button and applying the format to a cell. You'll find that when you double-click the button, the Format Painter doesn't turn off after one use. This means you can skip around in your spreadsheet applying that format to any number of unconnected cells, without having to click the **Format Painter** button each time. When you're done, just click the **Format Painter** button one more time to toggle it off.

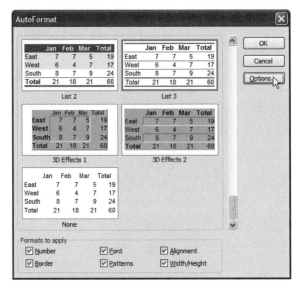

Figure 18.21: AutoFormat dialog box

Understanding Spreadsheets

■ A spreadsheet works in two dimensions: vertical (columns) and horizontal (rows). The columns are labeled across the top from left to right with the letters of the alphabet, and the rows are numbered along the left side of the spreadsheet starting with 1 at the top. Each Excel spreadsheet document may contain multiple tabbed spreadsheet pages, called worksheets.

■ Cells are the boxes created by the intersection of the columns and rows. Cells are where you enter the numbers, text, or other data in the spreadsheet. Just above the grid at the upper left, the Name Box displays the coordinates (the column and row) of whatever cell you have currently selected.

■ You can use the top cell in each column to enter a descriptive text header for that column of data, and the first cell in each row to enter a descriptive label for that row.

■ To select a cell, you can either use your arrow keys or point and click with your mouse. To select an entire row or column, click on its number or letter. To select a range of cells, click and drag. To select an entire worksheet, click the empty box above 1 and left of A. Working with Cell Data in Rows and Columns

■ To enter data in a cell, click on it, type the data, and then either press **[Enter]**, press an arrow key, or click in another cell. To delete the contents of a cell, click on the cell and press **[Delete]**. To open a cell so that you can change the contents, either double-click the cell or click on it once and then press the **[F2]** key. You can also click in the Formula Bar to delete, edit, or add data to a selected cell.

■ To insert a column, select the column to the right of where you want the new one to go, then either right-click and select Insert, or select **Insert | Columns**. To insert a row, select the row below where you want the new one to go, and either right-click and select Insert, or select **Insert | Rows**.

■ To insert a single cell, select a cell next to where you want the new one to go, right-click, and select **Insert**. To delete a single cell, select it, right-click, and select **Delete**. Remember that when you add or delete just one cell, the spreadsheet will need to shift the existing cells in its row or column to account for the change.

■ To change the width of a column or row, click and drag the dividing line between it and the adjoining column or row. To specify a particular column width or row height, select **Format | Column | Width** or **Format | Row | Height**.

■ When you apply AutoFit to selected rows or columns, Excel automatically adjusts each row or column to fit the contents of the largest cell it contains.

■ To freeze certain columns and rows so that they remain visible even as you scroll away from them, click on the cell below and to the right of them and select **Window | Freeze Panes**. You can undo the freeze panes command at any time by selecting **Window | Unfreeze Panes**.

Formatting Cells

- To set the number of decimal places in a selected cell, use the **Number** tab in the Format Cells dialog box. Select the Currency category to display a dollar sign or other currency symbol as part of the cell contents. Select the Date and Time options to specify the formats for displaying dates and times.

- Use the **Patterns** tab in the Format Cells dialog box to apply color shading and patterns to selected cells. The fast method for shading cells is to use the **Fill Color** button on the Formatting toolbar.

- Use the **Borders** tab of the Format Cells dialog box to apply borders to selected cells, or use the **Borders** button on the Formatting toolbar.

- By default, numbers are right-aligned in cells and text is left-aligned. The Standard toolbar includes buttons for the three basic alignment settings (left, center, and right). For fancier options such as aligning text vertically within cells or tilting text at an angle, use the **Alignment** tab in the Format Cells dialog box.

- The **Merge cells** option in the Format Cells dialog box lets you merge selected cells into one. To center text over several columns of data, use the **Merge and Center** button.

- Select a cell and then select **Format | Style** to save the formatting of that cell as a style that you can apply to other cells.

- AutoFormats are preset table formats that you can apply to make your worksheet look good. To use this feature, select the cells you want to format and then select **Format | AutoFormat**.

Key Terms

Alignment	Freeze Panes
AutoFit	Heading
AutoFormat	Label
Borders	Merge Cells
Cell	Name Box
Cell Range	Row
Column	Spreadsheet
Fill Color	Style
Fill Handle	Worksheet
Formula Bar	Wrap text

Key Term Quiz

Use the Key Terms list to complete the following sentences. Not all the terms will be used.

1. To keep a row or column fixed on your screen while you scroll through your spreadsheet, use the _____ option.

2. The numbers to the left of every row in a spreadsheet are called row _____.

3. The letters at the top of every column are called column _____.

4. A _____ is several adjacent cells in a column or a row.

5. To apply green shading to a cell, you can use the _____ button.

6. The _____ option automatically increases the height of a cell to display all of its contents.

7. The intersection of a column and a row creates the basic unit of a spreadsheet, the _____.

8. The coordinates of a selected cell are always displayed in the _____ at the upper left corner of the spreadsheet.

9. Each spreadsheet document may contain multiple independent pages called _____.

10. When you save the format of a cell with a unique name you can use to apply that formatting to other cells, you have created a _____.

Multiple Choice Quiz

1. Which of the following selects an entire column?
   A. Right-clicking the top cell
   B. Left-clicking the top cell
   C. Clicking the column heading
   D. Selecting **Format | Column**

2. What is the best way to center text across multiple columns?
   A. Use the **Merge and Center** button.
   B. Use the **Wrap text** option.
   C. Use AutoFormat.
   D. Use AutoFit.

3. To make a row bigger, which of the following should you adjust?
   A. Data
   B. Text
   C. Width
   D. Height

4. Which of the following is a fast way to select an entire worksheet?
   A. Clicking the Name Box
   B. Clicking the empty box in the worksheet's top left corner
   C. Selecting **Edit | Select Sheet**
   D. Selecting **Format | Sheet**

5. Which of the following automatically adjusts the width of a selected column?
   A. AutoFormat
   B. AutoFit
   C. Format Painter
   D. Wrap text

6. When you highlight a column and select **Insert | Column**, where is the new column inserted?
   A. In place of the highlighted column
   B. To the left of the highlighted column
   C. To the left of the first column
   D. To the right of the highlighted column

7. To specify a particular column's width, which of the following should you select?
   A. **Format | Column | Width**
   B. **Edit | Column | Width**
   C. **Format | Column | Settings**
   D. **Edit | Column | Settings**

8. Which option on the Alignment tab of the Format Cells dialog box can turn several selected cells into a single cell?
   A. Merge cells
   B. Merge columns
   C. AutoFormat
   D. Single cell

9. Which of the following cell format options deals with money?
   A. Percentage
   B. Currency
   C. Dollars
   D. Number

10. Which category would you choose in the Number tab of the Format Cells dialog box to change a cell's contents from .45 to 45%?
    A. Decimal
    B. Number
    C. Percentage
    D. Value

11. When you edit a cell's data, where can you type other than in the cell itself?
    A. The Formula Bar
    B. The Name Box
    C. Data Field
    D. The Content Field

12. Which of the following is a tool that enables you to copy the formatting of one cell to other cells?
    A. Format Cell
    B. AutoFormat
    C. Format Painter
    D. Paintbrush

13. Which of these features applies preset table format characteristics to a selected group of cells?
    A. Paintbrush
    B. AutoFormat
    C. Format Painter
    D. Format Cell

14. When you change the data in a cell from being lined up on the left to being centered in the cell, what have you changed?
    A. The cell range
    B. The cell width
    C. The cell alignment
    D. The cell height

15. What is the name of the small black square at the bottom right corner of a cell that you can click and drag to select a series of cells?
    A. Selection handle
    B. Drag handle
    C. Cell handle
    D. Fill handle

Essay Questions

1. Describe three ways that you can format the data in cells. Why is this an important feature?

2. Describe two ways that you can quickly transfer one cell's formatting to other cells. How can this save time for spreadsheet users?

3. In what ways can rows and columns be inserted? In what ways can they be deleted? Describe a situation that would require you to use these features.

Projects

1. On a sheet of poster board, draw a spreadsheet grid with ten columns and ten rows. Create at least five column headings for categories of things you spend money on every week, such as Food, Games, or Music. Write in the amount you spent in each category during each of the last three weeks, using a separate row for each week. Now for the math! Add up the amount you spent for each category, and the total amount you spent each week. Now add up your weekly totals to get the grand total of what you spent. Finally, add up your category totals, and check to make sure you get the same grand total you got from adding up your weekly totals. Now imagine doing that for the budget of a large multinational corporation, and reflect on why Excel is an accountant's best friend!

2. In Project 1, you created a budget using a spreadsheet. Pair up with another student and try to think of at least three other ways you could use an Excel spreadsheet to help you organize information. For each one, write down what you might use for column headings and row labels.

Advanced Spreadsheet Skills

"Dad, as intelligence goes up, happiness often goes down. In fact, I made a graph. I make a lot of graphs . . . "

– Lisa, The Simpsons

This chapter covers the following IC³ exam objectives:

- ■ IC³-2   3.2.1   Sort worksheet data

- ■ IC³-2   3.2.2   Demonstrate an understanding of absolute vs. relative cell addresses

- ■ IC³-2   3.2.3   Insert arithmetic formulas into worksheet cells

- ■ IC³-2   3.2.4   Demonstrate how to use common worksheet functions

- ■ IC³-2   3.2.5   Insert formulas that include worksheet functions into cells

- ■ IC³-2   3.2.6   Modify formulas and functions

- ■ IC³-2   3.2.7   Use AutoSum

- ■ IC³-2   3.2.8   Identify common errors made when using formulas and functions

- ■ IC³-2   3.2.9   Draw simple conclusions based on tabular data in a worksheet

- ■ IC³-2   3.2.10   Insert and modify charts in a worksheet

- ■ IC³-2   3.2.11   Be able to identify if a presented chart accurately represents data shown in a table

- ■ IC³-2   3.2.12   Identify appropriate chart types for presenting different types of information

The magic of spreadsheets is that they enable you to transform otherwise useless sets of numbers, names, and other data into something meaningful. Now that you understand the basic principles of spreadsheets, and you know the terminology of rows, columns, cells, and so on, you have the power to put a spreadsheet in high gear and make it do amazing things!

After you enter a set of data in a spreadsheet, you have a wide range of options for making use of the information: you can sort the data, apply formulas and functions to the data, and make charts and printouts to help you analyze and present the data.

The best way to understand these spreadsheet features is with real-world examples, so in this chapter, you'll meet a teacher whose grade book is a series of Excel worksheets. The teacher in question is a serious PC and spreadsheet wiz, appropriately named Ms. Numbercruncher. Her students think she's really cool, so they just call her Ms. Num for short. You'll see Ms. Num's Excel grade book do all kinds of things that your parents' teachers had to do with a pencil and calculator (or even pencil and paper!), and some things they never would have dreamed of doing.

Sorting Worksheet Data

One of the most common uses for spreadsheets is to list data in tables. Ms. Num, for example, keeps her grades in data tables that list her students along with their grades for each exam, their homework averages, and their final grades. The first thing she might do at the beginning of the term is to list her students and then sort them alphabetically by name.

To do this, she would select the entire table of data, then select **Data | Sort**. This brings up the Sort dialog box (see Figure 19.1). Note that in this example she has selected **Header row**, because the first cell in each of her columns is the column's name. This tells Excel that instead of referring to Column A, Column B, and so on, it can list the columns by name, making it easier for Ms. Num to select the column she wants to use for sorting.

In the case of the grade book, Ms. Num wants to sort by student name, so she selects the column called **Student**. When she clicks **OK**, the grade book reshuffles itself so that it's arranged alphabetically.

When you want to do a quick sort on a table, you can skip the Sort dialog box by using the **Sort Ascending** and **Sort Descending** buttons on the Standard toolbar. These buttons (see Figure 19.2) will only sort on the first column of data in the table, but if that's what you want to do, they offer one-click convenience. Just select the table and click the appropriate button, depending on the order in which you want to sort your data.

Now, what if Ms. Num instead wanted to sort by final grade? As you can see, several of her students have the same grade, so she would need to select a second criterion to decide the order of students with the same grade. Figure 19.3 shows the grade book sorted first by final grade then by student name, along with the Sort dialog box entries that were used to create it.

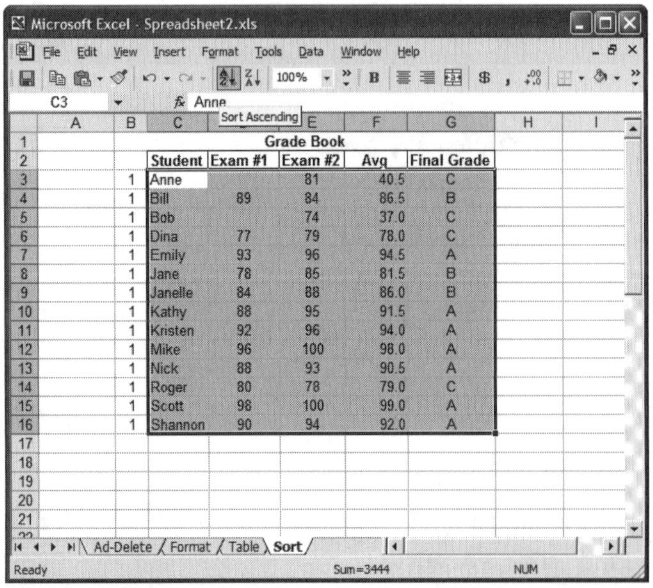

Figure 19.1: The Sort dialog box

Figure 19.2: The Sort Ascending and Sort Descending buttons on the Standard toolbar

What's Your Function? Working with Formulas and Functions

The point of spreadsheets is not just to cram them full of numbers—the point is to *do things* with those numbers. The beauty of spreadsheets is that they can "do the math," and keep re-doing it to keep up with each change you make, the moment you make it. The secret behind all of this math is the use of formulas and functions in your spreadsheets. Let's look at some of the most basic ones so that you can get started building your own number-crunching spreadsheets.

Inserting Arithmetic Formulas into Worksheet Cells

Entering a formula into a cell is like saying to Excel, "Hey! Take the contents of these particular cells, do these math equations with them, and enter the result here." Your formula can be extremely complex, or as simple as adding two cells together.

Suppose Ms. Num has an area of her grade book where she's keeping track of a big project the class is doing. The written portion of the project is worth up to 75 points, and an oral presentation of the project is worth up to 25 points, for a maximum score of 100. The first student's name appears on row 5 of the worksheet; column C contains the students' written grades, column D contains the presentation grades, and column E will contain the total scores from the project.

Ms. Num needs to add the two grades together for a total project grade, starting with the first student on the list. To add the numbers in cells C5 and D5 and display the results in cell E5, Ms. Num begins by moving the data entry box to cell E5—this is because formulas are always entered in the cell where you want to display the result.

To enter a formula into a cell, always start by entering an equal sign (=). The equal sign tells your spreadsheet that a formula is coming. To add cells C5 and D5, the cell entry in E5 should be **=C5+D5** (see Figure 19.4).

To subtract cell D5 from cell C5, you would enter **=C5-D5**. To multiply those two numbers, enter **=C5*D5**. To divide C5 by D5, enter **=C5/D5**. These four functions—addition (+), subtraction (-), multiplication (*), and division (/)—are the foundation for more complicated math maneuvers that you can perform.

You can also use the caret character (^) followed by a number to square, cube, or otherwise raise a number to the nth power. Simply follow the caret with the number of the exponent, for example **=B6^2** to square the number in cell B6, or **=G7^3** to cube the number in cell G7.

Not all formulas are short and sweet like these examples. Multiple operations in the same formula are perfectly fine, but as your formulas become more complex, you'll need to include parentheses to clarify *precedence*—that is, the order in which the operations in the formula should be performed. For example, you might want to add two numbers and then square the result. You could enter **=C5+D5^2**, but you may not get the result you intended. It might square D5 and then add C5, or it might add C5 and D5 and then square the result!

To make sure the formula does what you want it to, you need to add parentheses. Because you want to start by adding C5 and D5, put parentheses around that part of the formula: **=(C5+D5)^2**. The program will always calculate the items inside parentheses first. In very complex formulas, you might even use parentheses within other parentheses. For example; for the formula **=((C5+D5)^2)*5**, Excel will first add **C5** and **D5**, then square the result, and finally multiply that result by **5**.

Understanding Frequently Used Worksheet Functions

With the basic operations (+ - * / ^), you can do pretty much any mathematical thing you want in a spreadsheet. You can divide here, square there, and add up short strings of numbers with ease. But when it comes to things like Ms. Num's grade book, where she needs to add up and average 26 grades for each of her students, those formulas can get really long and difficult to manage. Fortunately, Excel has built-in worksheet *functions* to make complex calculations such as adding and averaging easier.

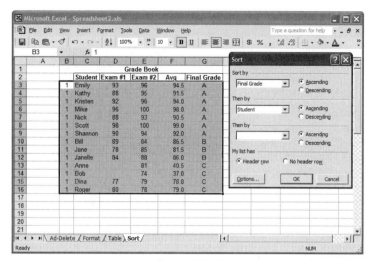

Figure 19.3: Sorting based on multiple criteria

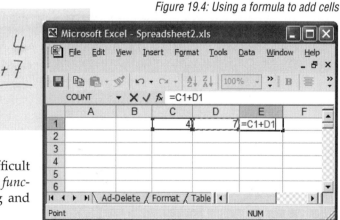

Figure 19.4: Using a formula to add cells

Math Formulas Simplified

Here's a time-saving tip for basic math equations: You don't have to identify and type the cell addresses! You can use the mouse to click the cells you want to include in the formula, or use the arrow keys to navigate to those cells. For example, if you want cell E5 to equal C4 plus D5, just type = into E5, then click C4 (or use the arrow keys to move to C4), type +, and click D5 (or use the arrow keys to move to D5). When you press [Enter], the formula will read =C5+D5 and the calculated result will appear in cell E5.

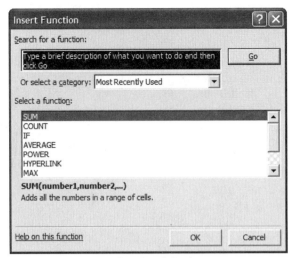

Figure 19.5: The Insert Function dialog box

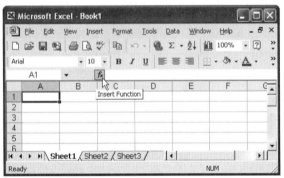

Figure 19.6: The Insert Function (f_x) button

*You can also bring up the Insert Function dialog box by clicking the **Insert Function** (or **f_x**) button, shown in Figure 19.6. This button is located just to the left of the Formula Bar on the toolbar.*

Functions are pre-written formulas that can save you time and effort, and help ensure accuracy in your data tables. Common functions include SUM, AVERAGE, MAX, MIN, and COUNT. Each of these functions is explained below.

To add a range of numbers, use the SUM function. Begin by selecting the cell where you want the result to appear. In the grade book example, this is cell **F17**. Then select **Insert | Function** to bring up the Insert Function dialog box (see Figure 19.5), select **SUM**, and click **OK**.

When you click **OK**, a new Function Arguments dialog box appears. Here, you can define the list of cells you want to include in the SUM operation (see Figure 19.7).

In this case, you're adding the group of cells starting with F3 and ending with F16. You can enter this *range* of cells using a couple of different methods. First, the program will make a suggestion, based on the cells close to where you're putting the formula—and it might be right! You can also just type in the range, consisting of the first and last cell addresses separated by a colon: **F3: F16**. You can use your mouse to select the cell range, clicking on F3, holding down the **[Shift]** key, and then clicking F16. Finally, you can click on F3, hold the left mouse button, and drag to select all the cells through F16.

When you've defined your cell range, click **OK** in the Function Arguments window. Note that the correct formula (see Figure 19.8) to apply SUM to the range of cells is **=SUM(F3:F16)**.

Excel offers dozens of worksheet functions for the adventurous user. Here's a brief list of the most common ones, what they do, and examples of their formula bar entries.

- SUM adds the range of entries and enters the sum. For example, the formula **=SUM(F3:F16)** would add the numbers in cells F3 through F16.

- AVERAGE adds the range of entries, divides by the total number of entries, and enters the average. For example, **=AVERAGE(F3:F16)** would calculate the average of all cells from F3 through F16 that contain numbers. If any cell is empty, is it not included in the AVERAGE calculation.

- COUNT counts the number of cells within the specified range that contain numbers. For example, **=COUNT(F3:F16)** reads the cells in the range from F3 to F16, counts each one that contains a numeric entry, and enters the number of cells counted. If any cell is empty, the COUNT function skips it.

- MAX finds the largest number within the specified range. For example, **=MAX(F3:F16)** reads the cells from F3 to F16, determines which entry is the largest number, and enters that number.

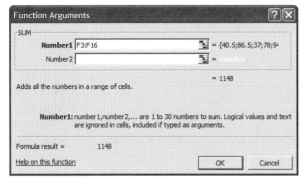

Figure 19.7: The Function Arguments window

- MIN does the opposite of MAX, finding the smallest number within the specified range. For example, **=MIN(F3:F16)** reads the cells from F3 to F16, determines which entry is the smallest number, and enters that number.

Inserting Formulas that Include Worksheet Functions into Cells

These worksheet formulas and functions can also be used as parts of larger formulas in a cell. Looking again at the grade book, suppose Ms. Num wants to find the average score on Exam #1. She could use the AVERAGE function and include all the cells containing students' scores on that exam. She could also do this using a more complex formula, first adding together all the scores (SUM) and then dividing by the number of non-zero scores (COUNT). The final formula would be **=SUM(D3:D16)/COUNT(D3: D16)**, as shown in Figure 19.9.

You can use any combination of worksheet functions, math functions, and numbers to create a more complex formula. Suppose Ms. Num wanted to get a combined average score from both exams; she could add up all the Exam #1 scores (SUM of D3:D16), add that to the sum of the Exam #2 scores (SUM of E3:E16), and then divide by the number of students times 2.

For that last part, she'll need to run a COUNT on the students—but how is that possible, since the names are text and COUNT only works on numbers? Check out Column B, where Ms. Num has very cleverly placed a 1 next to each student's name. Using COUNT on columns B3 through B16, she can obtain an accurate student count and incorporate that into her formula, as follows: **=(SUM(D3:D16) +SUM(E3: E16))/(COUNT(B3:B16)*2)**

Modifying Formulas and Functions

After you've entered a formula in a cell, you may find that it doesn't do what you thought it would, or you may simply change your mind about what you want the formula to do. You don't have to delete the contents of the cell and start over—instead, just move the entry box to the cell that contains the for-

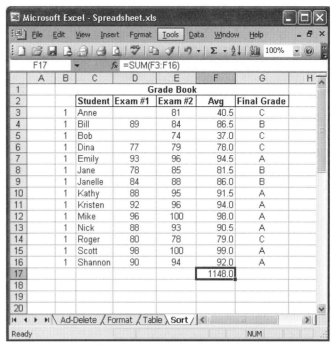

Figure 19.8: Using SUM to add up scores in the grade book

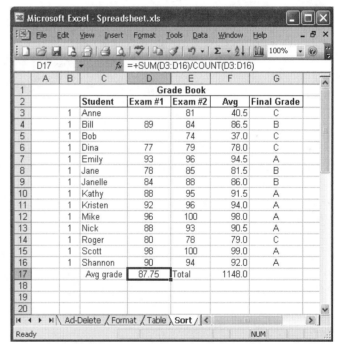

Figure 19.9: Using SUM and COUNT together to calculate an average

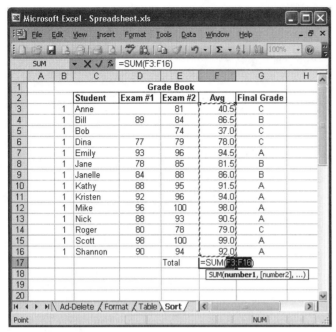

Figure 19.10: AutoSum suggesting a
cell range

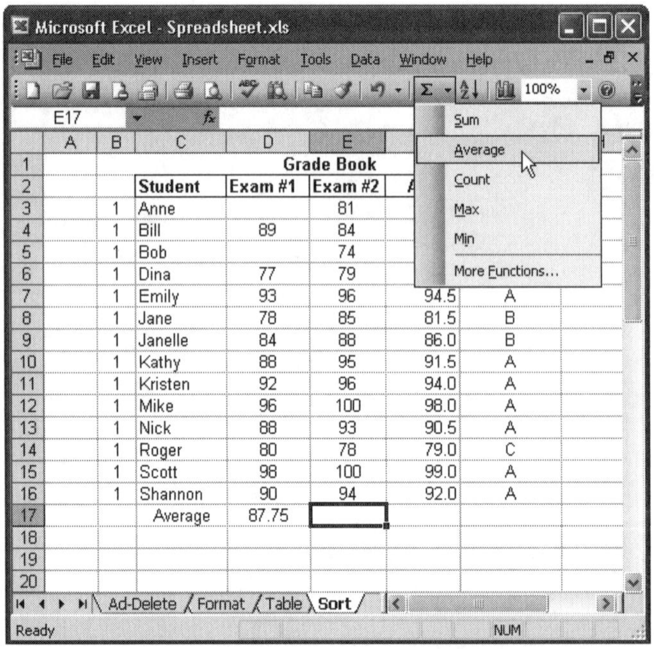

Figure 19.11: Selecting an AutoSum
function

mula, press **[F2]**, and then edit the contents. You can also move the entry box to the cell whose formula you want to edit, then click the Formula Bar and make your changes there.

Using AutoSum

You've already seen how to use **Insert | Function** to add worksheet functions to a spreadsheet. Excel also offers a button on the Standard toolbar that lets you add simple versions of the most common worksheet functions. The button, called **AutoSum**, is marked with a symbol that looks a bit like the capital letter E; it's actually the Greek symbol *sigma* ($\sum$), which is mathematical shorthand for adding a series of numbers.

When you select an entry cell and click the **AutoSum** button, Excel inserts the SUM function and makes a "best guess" about which cells you want to add. A dotted selection box appears around the suggested range of cells, as shown in Figure 19.10. You can press **[Enter]** to accept the suggested range, or use your mouse to click and drag the corner of the selection box to change the range.

You can also use AutoSum to insert other common worksheet functions. To do this, click the drop-down arrow next to the **AutoSum** button (see Figure 19.11) and select a function from the list. As with SUM, you'll see a dotted selection box around the cells that Excel thinks you may want to include, and you can either accept that range or click and drag the box to change the range.

Relative and Absolute Cell Addresses

Now that you know how to enter functions and formulas in a spreadsheet, you may be wondering if you can copy and paste formulas to re-use them and save time. The good news is that you can do this, but you'll need to understand how *relative* and *absolute* cell addresses work.

Imagine that Ms. Num has set up the grade book formula **=(D3+E3)/2** to average the exam scores for Emily, the first student on the list. She now intends to copy the formula from cell F3 to cells F4, F5, and so on down the list, to calculate averages for the other students. When she copies the formula into cell F4 to calculate Kathy's average, the formula becomes **=(D4+E4)/2**, as shown in Figure 19.12. How did that happen?

When you copy a formula from one cell into a cell in the same row or column, Excel assumes that you want the cell references replaced with cells closer to the new formula location—that is, it uses *relative* cell addresses. The formula for Emily's average, for example, is in cell F3, and Excel notes that formula components D3 and E3 are the first and second cells to the left of F3. When you copy the formula to cell F4, Excel automatically changes the *relative* referenced cells to D4 and E4, the first and second cells to the left of F4.

Now let's look at an example that involves an *absolute* cell address. Suppose Ms. Num realizes that her exams have been extremely tough this term, and decides to add five bonus points to everyone's average score. She changes the formula for Emily's average (see Figure 19.13) so that it's now the average of her scores plus the number of bonus points (5) in cell B18.

This is great for Emily, but if Ms. Num were to copy this formula from Emily's row to Kathy's row, things wouldn't be quite right. The relative exam score references would still work fine, but the bonus point calculation would also be assumed to be relative, so it would add the contents of the empty cell B19—no bonus points for Kathy!

For this formula, the bonus point calculation should always come from the exact same cell, so Ms. Num must add B18 as an absolute reference. To make sure Excel knows that it's an absolute reference, she'll need to add a dollar sign ($) before the cell's column name, and another dollar sign before the row name.

The formula that Ms. Num uses to calculate Emily's average (see Figure 19.14) is **=(D3+E3)/2+$B$18**. When she copies this formula from F3 to F4, Excel enters it as **=(D4+E4)/2+$B$18**. The cells from columns D and E are relative references, but the **$B$18** is an absolute reference and doesn't change.

In addition to purely relative and purely absolute cell references, you can have something called a *mixed* cell reference. If you want the column to remain the same (that is, absolute) but the row to be relative, you can put a dollar sign only in front of the column letter, for example **$B18**. If you want the column to be relative and the row to be absolute, you can put a dollar sign only in front of the row number, for example **B$18**.

To illustrate mixed cell references, let's leave the classroom for a moment and look at a company's sales spreadsheet. The data table shows the amount of product sold by five salespeople for each quarter of the year. Each person sells the base amount, plus an extra amount, each quarter. The formula for Bob's first quarter (or Q1) total is = **$C4+D4** (see Figure 19.15). This is the sum of the Base column plus the column to the left of the Q1 Total column. Because this formula will be copied down the list of salespeople, the row numbers must be relative.

The Q2 Total would need to add the same Base column entry (an absolute reference) to the Q2 Extra entry, which is the column to the left, a relative reference. Note how the formula looks when you copy it to cell G4 (see Figure 19.16). The **$C4** (absolute column reference) stayed the same, but the **D4** (relative reference, one column to the left) changed to **F4**.

If you copy either of these formulas down the list, the row numbers will change for both columns E and G, because there is no dollar sign before the row number in either formula.

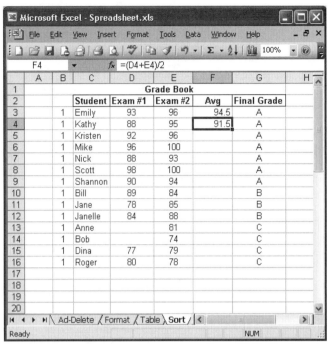

Figure 19.12: The formula has changed!

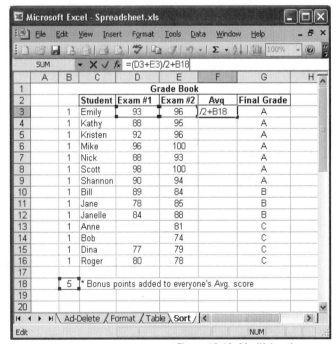

Figure 19.13: Modifying the formula to add bonus points

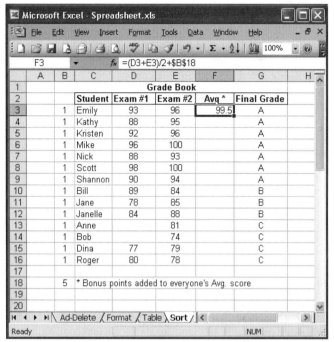

Figure 19.14: Bonus points added as an absolute cell reference

Common Sources of Errors in Formulas and Functions

You can't get good results from a spreadsheet if you make a mistake in your data entry or in your formulas. One of the most common mistakes is creating a formula that includes text or words instead of numbers. For example, if you have numbers in cells F4 through F9, and you have a text heading in cell F3, it would be a mistake to enter **=COUNT(F3:F9)**.

Another common mistake that spreadsheet users sometimes make is what's called a *circular reference*. A circular reference is a formula that refers to the cell in which the formula itself resides. For example, if you entered the formula **=SUM(F4:F9)-F10** into cell F10, the cell would be trying to subtract itself! It's a little bit like trying to call yourself while you're on the phone line—you may get a busy signal or a voicemail recording, but you certainly shouldn't expect to hear yourself answer. In the case of circular references, you'll get an error message pointing out the problem and suggesting possible solutions.

You can also get other error messages, including the common **#DIV/0!** error. This means that your formula is attempting to divide by zero—a serious mathematical no-no, as any math teacher will tell you. Most often, the—**#DIV/0!** error means that one of the cells in your formula has been left blank, so you can simply fill in that cell with the correct value to correct the error.

The Aftermath of Math, or What to Do with Your Results

Having all the data entered into your worksheet and all the formulas created is only half the battle! Once you've entered all your spreadsheet data and Excel has completed its calculations, you need to make sense of what you see. Then, if you want to examine trends or share your results with others, you'll probably want to create a chart or graph to illustrate the information. If you plan to print your results, you might also want to take advantage of Excel's special printing options, which enable you to include only specified portions of your work in the printout.

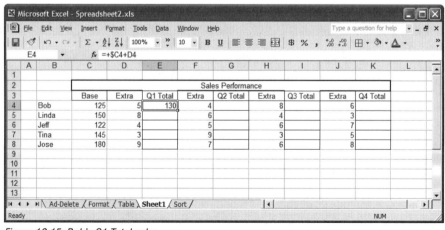

Figure 19.15: Bob's Q1 Total sales

Drawing Conclusions Based on Table Data

Just like anything having to do with numbers, spreadsheets are only valuable tools if the information entered into them is accurate and complete. It's also important to remember that data can be presented in a way that misleads the reader by promoting one view over another. When a collection of data appears to display certain trends, it's up to you to examine all of the formulas carefully to see if the author of the worksheet is trying to influence your opinion.

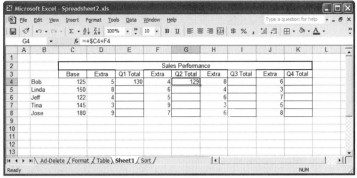

Figure 19.16: Copying mixed cell references

One of the nice things about spreadsheets is that they can show different sets of data right next to each other for easy comparison. You should always be wary of a spreadsheet that does not have its data laid out neatly, or seems to be missing some important aspect of the subject at hand. Missing information might be an attempt to hide information that doesn't support the author's conclusions.

Not all misleading table results are intentional. An author can accidentally enter incorrect data, create a flawed formula, or otherwise make a mistake—and the data itself can have irregularities that produce bad results. For example, suppose that Ms. Num has a student, Miranda, who transferred into her class after the first exam. Miranda has no grade for Exam #1, so the averaging formula adds zero to her Exam #2 score of 98 and divides by two. As a result, Miranda's average is 49. When Ms. Num reviews her grade book, she recognizes that this number is far too low, realizes what's happened, and corrects the formula on Miranda's row of the table.

This example illustrates why it's so important to give your results a "reality check" to make sure your numbers aren't way out of line. Once you've done that, you can feel comfortable using the table data to compare values and draw sound conclusions.

Charting Your Data

After you've laid out your worksheet data and crunched all the numbers, you're left with the spreadsheet format, which isn't always easy to read, much less interpret. The next step is to figure out what all those numbers have to say.

Behind every data set is something in the real world—a company's sales, a science experiment, a year's worth of weather patterns, a classroom full of students. The best way to help readers make the connection between the data and the real world is to create data *charts*. Charts can be simple or complicated, but they all share the same purpose: to bring numbers to life and make their meanings easier to understand.

Before you learn how to create a chart, you should know the terms used to describe the components of a chart (see Figure 19.17). The heading at the top is called the *title*. The X and Y axis titles are called *data labels*. The area that shows what each line represents is called the *legend*.

Figure 19.17: Chart components

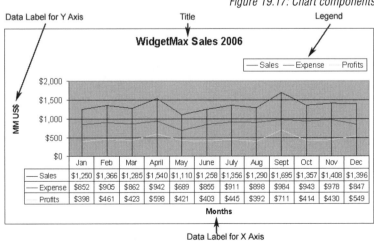

Creating a Chart Based on Worksheet Data

Creating a chart from a table of numbers in a spreadsheet is pretty straightforward. Let's start with a table that displays monthly sales, expenses, and profits for a company over the period of a year. To make a chart from this table, select the entire table including headings and then select **Insert** | **Chart** to launch the Chart Wizard (see Figure 19.18). The wizard begins by asking you to select the type of chart you want to use. You'll learn about what type works best for different types of data in the next section; for this example, a line graph is the best choice.

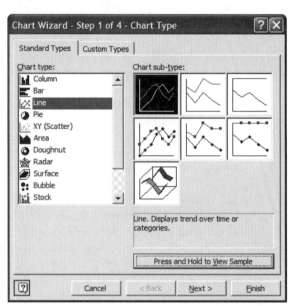

Figure 19.18: Selecting a chart type in the Chart Wizard

The second step in the wizard is to select the source for the data, known as the *data range*. Since you selected the entire table including heading rows before launching the wizard, the data range is already defined as A1 through M4. You can provide information about what values are being charted by clicking the **Series** tab (see Figure 19.20). In this example, the wizard is using the headings in the first column to define each row of data.

The third step of the wizard lets you dress up the graph by adding a chart title and by labeling the X and Y axes (see Figure 19.21). Other fun things you can do here include moving the chart legend and including the table as part of the graph.

Figure 19.19: The Chart Wizard button on the Standard toolbar

You can also launch the Chart Wizard by clicking the **Chart Wizard** button on the Standard toolbar. As shown in Figure 19.19, this button looks like a small chart, and by default is located next to the **Sort Descending** button.

The fourth and final step in the wizard simply asks whether you want to create the chart as a separate worksheet or place it as an object in the current worksheet. Figure 19.22 shows the resulting chart placed in the same worksheet.

Editing a Chart

Charts that you create in Excel aren't set in stone. In fact, you can change most any aspect of a chart at any time. For example, you can edit a chart's title or data labels by clicking on the item you want to change. This opens the

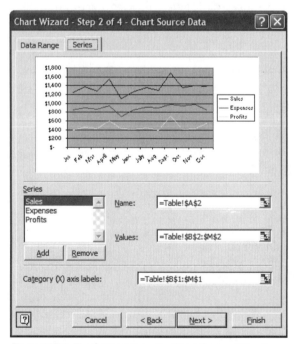

Figure 19.20: The Series tab on the Chart Source Data step

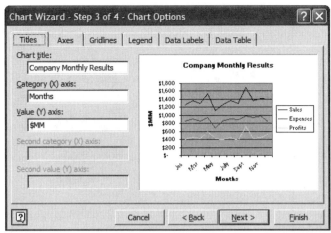

Figure 19.21: The Titles tab on the Chart Options step

text box containing the item; a second click places your cursor in the text so that you can make changes. To change the formatting of the title or a data label, simply double-click the item to open a Format Chart Title or Format Axis Title dialog box.

If you want to change the appearance of your graph lines, just double-click one of them. This opens the Format Data Series dialog box, where you can control how the chart lines display (see Figure 19.23).

The data in a chart is also easy to change—just change any value in your table, and the chart will automatically adjust to display the new information.

Changing the Chart Type

If you don't like the type of chart you've chosen, you can change that too, by right-clicking anywhere on the chart and selecting **Chart Type**. This brings up the Chart Type dialog box, which resembles the first screen of the Chart Wizard (see Figure 19.24). Here you can try out different chart types and sub-types for your data, and even view a sample of any option before changing your chart.

The Right Chart for Every Occasion

In the example above, you saw a *line chart*. This type of chart is best when you want to show trends in your data over time, as with monthly sales and profit.

But what if you're comparing values side by side, like the example of sales numbers for different salespeople that you saw in the discussion of absolute and relative cell references? A graph where you want to compare data side by side works best with a *column chart* or *bar chart* (see Figure 19.25). These types of chart are similar, but column charts show data in vertical columns, while bar charts use horizontal bars.

If you want to show percentage information, or anything where you want to show how much several elements make up of the whole, a *pie chart* works best (see Figure 19.26). You might use a pie chart to show the breakdown of poll or election results, for example, or to illustrate the amount of a personal, company, or government budget that goes toward each type of expense.

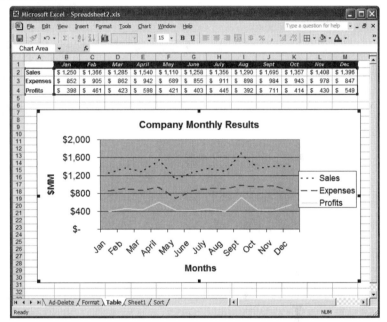

Figure 19.22: Completed line chart in worksheet

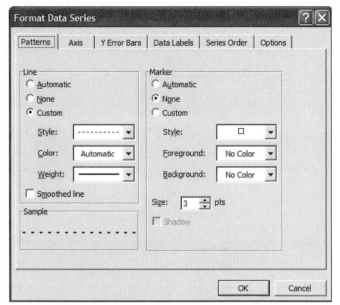

Figure 19.23: The Format Data Series dialog box

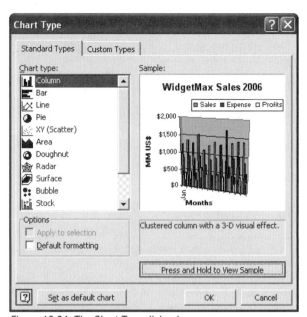

Figure 19.24: The Chart Type dialog box

Spreadsheets Make Some Tasks Easy

The chart wizard contains a simple four-step process that will automatically convert the data you selected into a colorful and informative graph. The primary selection option in the chart wizard is the chart type.

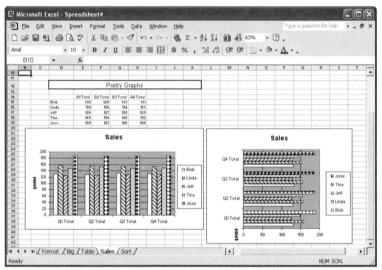

Figure 19.25: Column chart (left) and bar chart (right)

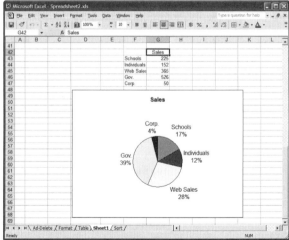

Figure 19.26: Pie chart

Determining Whether a Chart Accurately Represents Worksheet Data

Just as it's important to ensure that your table data is accurate and complete and your formulas are sound, you must also ensure that your charts accurately reflect the table data without misleading your readers. Chart titles and data labels can be nearly as influential as the data itself in creating an accurate picture of the facts being presented, so carefully consider these items as you create and review your charts.

Because changing from one chart type to another in Excel is so quick and painless, you can try a different type of chart if you find that the one you're using doesn't present the data clearly. Try several different approaches if necessary to find the one that best conveys the information.

Printing in Excel

Now that you know how to make a spreadsheet crunch the numbers and how to make pretty graphs, how to you print them so you can share or present your hard work? You've already learned most everything you need to know about printing, but there are some aspects of printing spreadsheets that are different than printing in other programs.

Setting a Print Area

With Word documents, you usually want to print everything you've written, so printing is about making your work look pretty and getting it on paper. With a spreadsheet, you often have a lot of calculations and information, but you may only want to print certain sections, like your summary or conclusions or just a graph you've made of the data.

The first step in getting ready to print a spreadsheet is to set your *print area*. Once you've decided what you want to print, you simply select that range of cells and then select **File | Print Area | Set Print Area**. Presto! Now only those cells will print until you change the print area again.

Page Setup

As you've probably noticed, Word documents tend to flow from top to bottom, while spreadsheets generally flow across from left to right. This means that they can end up very wide as well as very long! To control how the information from a large spreadsheet is presented, you can select **File | Page Setup** (see Figure 19.27). From the Page Setup window, you can scale the printout to a percentage of normal—or even better, scale it to fit a specific number of pages in width and height.

Next select the **Sheet** tab, which contains some cool Excel-specific settings (see Figure 19.28). Here you can change the print area, and direct Excel to print gridlines or include the row and column headings (that is, the column headings such as A, B, C, and the row headings such as 1, 2, 3).

Figure 19.27: The Page Setup dialog box

On Second Thought, Things Look Great!

The Business Council is a non-profit group based in New York City whose 125 members are CEOs of major corporations. The group occasionally polls its members about the economy and releases the results to the press. On Monday, October 12, 2004, The Business Council reported that its members expected very little if any growth in the U.S. economy in 2005. This story was picked up and carried globally by the Reuters news organization.

The next day, The Business Council sent out a revised report saying that its members were actually expecting moderate to solid growth for 2005. What changed overnight? Someone at The Business Council had shifted one column of data, inadvertently causing the major chart for the spreadsheet to be out of whack. Always double-check your charts to make sure the results seem to match the data you entered—a little mistake can travel a long way!

Once you've created a chart or graph in Excel, you can copy and paste it into a Word document or a PowerPoint presentation. Give it a try!

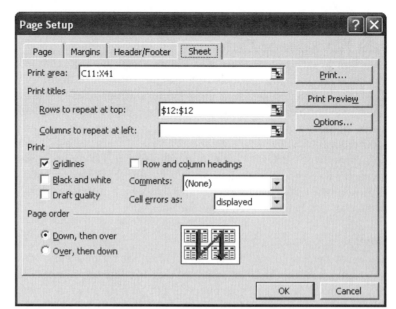

Figure 19.28: The Sheet tab on the Page Setup dialog box

The *Print titles* section is especially interesting. These two fields enable you to specify rows or columns to be repeated on every page. This is most helpful if you have a row of titles followed by many rows of data—or a column of titles followed by many columns of data. Setting **Rows to repeat at top** causes the selected row or rows to print at the top of each printed page, while setting **Columns to repeat at left** repeats the selected row or rows at the left of each printed page. In a document that is both extra wide and extra long, you can even specify whether the pages should print down and then over, or over and then down.

Here's one final printing trick, unique to printing spreadsheets, that you should know. When you set a print area and tell Excel how to scale to fit the desired number of pages, the pages may break in strange ways. You can easily control where your pages break by selecting **File | Print Preview** and then clicking **Page Break Preview** (see Figure 19.29).

Do you see the dotted line separating the two pages? You can click and drag this line to change what cells are printed on which page. This is very useful when a large spreadsheet has natural breaks in the data.

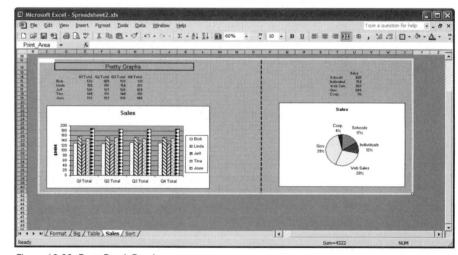

Figure 19.29: Page Break Preview

Sorting Worksheet Data

■ To sort data in a worksheet, highlight all the data and then select **Data | Sort**. In the Sort dialog box, you can choose to sort the data by any variable, or by multiple variables.

■ Any time you sort your data, you have the option of sort the numbers in either ascending or descending order.

What's Your Function? Working with Formulas and Functions

■ To create a basic formula in a cell, start with an equal sign (=), which indicates that a formula will follow. Then type the appropriate cell numbers, separated by the applicable function signs (+ - * / ^), to complete the formula.

■ To include a long series of adjacent cells in a formula, enter the starting and ending cell numbers separated by a colon (:).

■ In more complex formulas, you'll need to use parentheses to ensure that Excel performs the math operations in the order you intended.

■ Functions are pre-written formulas that can save you time and effort while helping ensure the accuracy of your spreadsheet's calculations. Commonly used functions include SUM, AVERAGE, MAX (finds the largest number within a range of cells), MIN (the opposite of MAX), and COUNT (determines how many cells in the range contain numbers).

■ To modify a formula or function entered in a cell, move the entry box to that cell, press **[F2]**, and edit the cell's contents.

■ The AutoSum feature can create functions such as SUM or AVERAGE automatically, based on which function you choose in the AutoSum drop-down list and a "best guess" on what cells you want to include. Drag the selection box surrounding the included cells to make the selection larger or smaller. The AutoSum button on the Standard toolbar displays the sigma character (Σ), and features a drop-down arrow which enables you to select a function other than SUM.

■ When you copy and paste formulas and functions, Excel changes the pasted copies so that they work properly in their new location. For most situations, this means that if a formula was pasted from a cell that contained the sum of the 10 cells to its left, the cell where that formula is pasted will contain not the original formula, but one that has been adjusted for the new cell's row number. This is known as a relative cell reference, because it has to do with handling cells based on their relationship to another cell. Cell references that don't ever change are known as absolute references.

■ Common spreadsheet errors include trying to do math on cells with only text; trying to use a formula cell's own contents to calculate its contents (a circular reference); and trying to divide by zero. These are all perfectly fixable problems!

The Aftermath of Math, or What to Do with Your Results

■ Spreadsheets are only as valuable as the information entered into them is accurate. It's important to review your table data and look for irregularities, in case you've made a mistake with data entry or a formula.

■ When reviewing a table prepared by someone else, judge for yourself whether the information is laid out in a way that is clear and logical, or potentially misleading. If the information seems incomplete or inaccurate, be careful about drawing conclusions from it.

■ To create a chart from your table data, highlight the cells you want to include and then click **Insert | Chart** to bring up the Chart Wizard. Here you'll select a chart type, enter a chart title and data labels, and specify whether to create the chart in the same worksheet or as a new worksheet. After you create a chart, you can always go back and change any of its characteristics, from chart type to the font used for the title. You can also change data and see the change reflected automatically in the chart.

■ Different chart types are suited to different types of information. A line chart is best to show trends over time; a bar chart works best for comparing information side by side; and a pie chart is best for showing percentage information.

■ Although you can often identify general trends from a chart, you should avoid making assumptions or drawing conclusions about data that is not included in the chart.

Printing in Excel

■ You can select a portion of a worksheet and select **File | Print Area | Set Print Area**. Then when you print, only those cells will print unless you set a new print area.

■ The Page Setup dialog box in Excel includes some specialized settings that affect printouts. You can scale your spreadsheet to fit on a certain number of pages, set rows or columns to repeat on each printed page, and control where each new printed page begins.

Key Terms

Absolute cell address

AutoSum

AVERAGE

Bar chart

COUNT

Formula

Function

Line chart

MAX

MIN

Pie chart

Print area

Relative cell address

Sort

SUM

Key Term Quiz

Use the Key Terms list to complete the following sentences. Not all the terms will be used.

1. The _____ function calculates how many numbers are in a selected group of cells.

2. To analyze trends over time, your best bet is usually a _____.

3. The _____ button automatically adds up a group of cells.

4. You can use a _____ to take the place of a longer formula in a cell.

5. The _____ function displays the smallest number from a selected group of cells.

6. When you copy a formula for use in other cells, you can use the dollar sign ($) to set part of the formula as a(n) _____.

7. To display the largest number from a selected group of cells, use the _____ function.

8. To analyze percentages, a _____ is usually best.

9. The _____ function adds together all the selected cells.

10. When you want to display numbers for comparison side by side, a _____ works best.

Multiple Choice Quiz

1. Which of the following functions adds up a group of cells and then divides by the number of cells in the group?
   A. AVERAGE
   B. MAX
   C. MIN
   D. COUNT

2. You asked 50 male and 50 female students in your school what they thought of several different TV shows. For each show, you recorded the number of boys and girls who liked that program. What chart type should you use to show the side-by-side comparison of the male and female responses for each show?
   A. Pie chart
   B. Line chart
   C. Area chart
   D. Column chart

3. What kind of cell address is adjusted for a change of location?
   A. Absolute
   B. Average
   C. Relative
   D. AutoSum

4. What button is represented by the Greek symbol sigma (Σ)?
   A. Average
   B. AutoSum
   C. Chart
   D. Print

5. Your local newspaper is celebrating its 50th anniversary, and your uncle (the paper's editor) has asked you to help him produce an attractive graph to run on the front page of the anniversary edition. He gives you the historical data on the number of newspaper subscriptions, which have grown almost each year for 50 years. Which type of chart should you use to show the growth of the paper over its lifetime?
   A. Pie chart
   B. Bar chart
   C. Line chart
   D. Column chart

6. Which function displays the largest number in the selected range of cells?
   A. AVERAGE
   B. MAX
   C. MIN
   D. COUNT

7. What kind of cell address is a copy that is identical to the original?
   A. Absolute
   B. Average
   C. Relative
   D. AutoSum

8. Which of these functions calculates how many numbers are in the selected range of cells?
   A. AVERAGE
   B. MAX
   C. MIN
   D. COUNT

9. You've selected **Data | Sort**, but in the Sort dialog box, you see Column A, Column B, and so on instead of your column titles. What's the most likely reason that your column titles aren't showing up?
   A. You forgot to include the column titles when you selected your table data.
   B. You chose **Descending** instead of **Ascending** for your sort order.
   C. You haven't formatted your first row of data as a column title row.
   D. You haven't selected **Header row** in the Sort dialog box.

10. You've conducted a poll at school to ask students which cafeteria special is their favorite. You found that 42% picked pizza, 26% chose spaghetti and meatballs, 17% preferred Caesar salad, 9% liked fish sticks, 4% went with Salisbury steak, and 2% were undecided. What chart type would be best for illustrating the breakdown of students' lunch preferences?
    A. Pie chart
    B. Bar chart
    C. Area chart
    D. Line chart

11. How do you specify which portion of your spreadsheet should be included in printouts?
    A. Select **File | Page Setup** and then select the pages you want to print.
    B. Select the cells you want to print before you click the **Print** button.
    C. Select the cells you want to print, then select **File | Print Area | Set Print Area**.
    D. Use the **Page Break Preview** feature, and select the pages you want to print.

12. Which of the following functions finds the smallest number in the selected group of cells?
    A. AVERAGE
    B. MAX
    C. MIN
    D. COUNT

13. You have a spreadsheet that's very wide. It has a large number of columns, spanning several pages, although it only has about a dozen rows. Which of these settings will come in handy when you print this spreadsheet?
    A. Page Break Preview
    B. Rows to repeat at top
    C. Columns to repeat at left
    D. Set Print Area

14. How many different sort criteria can you select at once using the Sort dialog box?
    A. One
    B. Two
    C. Three
    D. Four

15. Suppose you need to add together the values in cells B1 through E1, multiply the result by two, and then divide the whole thing by the value in cell F1. Which of the following formulas would correctly perform this calculation?
    A. =SUM(B1:E1)*2/F1
    B. =(SUM(B1:E1)*2)/F1
    C. =SUM(B1:E1)*(2/F1)
    D. =((SUM B1:E1)*2/F1)

Essay Questions

1. Describe three different types of charts you can create from a spreadsheet. Provide an example of a situation in which you would use each of these chart types.

2. Briefly discuss two different spreadsheet function terms. Why are functions sometimes better than formulas?

3. Describe two ways that you can modify formulas or functions in a cell. How does this differ from the ways that you can change a chart?

Projects

1. You've just been offered a job to move to Wall Street to be a stock market analyst. You'd better sharpen your skills! With your teacher's help, pick out an interesting stock that's listed on the New York Stock Exchange. Keep track of its value every day of the week for one week and list the daily values in a spreadsheet. At the end of the week, convert the results into a chart. If you had bought one share of this stock on Monday, would you have made or lost money by Friday?

2. Use a spreadsheet to analyze your test scores for this year. Ask your teacher for your last several test scores—at least four, if possible. Enter your test scores and dates into a spreadsheet and then convert the information into a chart. What chart type is best for analyzing a trend like test scores? Does your chart show a trend of improvement?

COMPUTER LITERACY: YOUR TICKET TO IC³ CERTIFICATION

Mastering the Art of Presentation

"Excrement! That's what I think of Mr. J. Evans Pritchard! We're not lighting a pipe! We're talking about poetry. How can you describe poetry like American Bandstand? 'I like Byron, I give him a 42 but I can't dance to it!'"

– John Keating, *Dead Poets Society*

This chapter covers the following IC³ exam objectives:

- IC³-2   4.1.1   Identify effective design principles for simple presentations

- IC³-2   4.1.2   Manage slides

- IC³-2   4.1.3   Add information to a slide

- IC³-2   4.1.4   Change slide view

- IC³-2   4.1.5   Change slide layout

- IC³-2   4.1.6   Modify a slide background

- IC³-2   4.1.7   Assign transitions to slides

- IC³-2   4.1.8   Change the order of slides in a presentation

- IC³-2   4.1.9   Create different output elements

- IC³-2   4.1.10   Preview the slide show presentation

- IC³-2   4.1.11   Navigate an on-screen slide show

In the 1950s and 1960s, before every house had a television set, people gathered in darkened living rooms for a ritual called the *slide show*—someone's photographs, usually from a recent vacation, projected one at a time onto a wall or screen. The slides were tiny squares of photo film, encased in little cardboard frames and placed into a slide projector (Figure 20.1). One person stood by the projector, explaining each slide and using a remote control to tell the projector when to display the next picture.

You can create a slide show presentation today using software like Microsoft PowerPoint, and, with a projector connected to a computer, turn a dusty presentation into a multimedia delight for your listeners. A modern slide show can display pictures, graphs, charts, explanatory text, and more. You can add visual effects to smooth the transition from one slide to the next. You can even add sound to a slide show. Nothing like adding the cannons from the "1812 Overture" to a presentation on a historic battle to make it vivid and more real for your audience! Finally, to make the maximum multimedia impact, you can even print copies of the slides as handouts for your audience.

This chapter teaches you the essentials of modern presentation software, using Microsoft PowerPoint as the primary example. You'll learn design basics—like what to do and what to avoid—and how to put together a basic slide show. The chapter shows you how to work with individual slides, to modify text and appearance and more. Finally, you'll work on presentation techniques, learning how to build transitions and movement. That's a lot of ground to cover in one short chapter, so let's get started!

Figure 20.1: A slide projector

Presentation Design

A presentation enables you to convey information to an audience. People use presentations in business meetings all the time. Many classroom teachers use presentations. You'll find them in use in church meetings, club gatherings, and more.

From a software perspective, a presentation is one or more slides created in a presentation application like PowerPoint. You hook the computer up to a large monitor or projector, thus enabling multiple people to view the show. You can design a presentation to run and inform viewers without a narrator or you can create a presentation to provide a visual component to go along with what you have to say.

A well-designed slide show helps people pay attention to and learn from a presentation. The visual cues keep them focused. In contrast, a poorly designed slide show can trash an otherwise good presentation, so pay attention to good design principles.

Good design follows two rules: clarity and simplicity. First, leave space on each slide so that a viewer can quickly grasp all the information presented. Second, put only necessary information on a slide with a minimum of clutter. You'll find as you get into presentation software that even the simplest program has the capability of doing all sorts of effects and stuff. You can easily over do it on a slide.

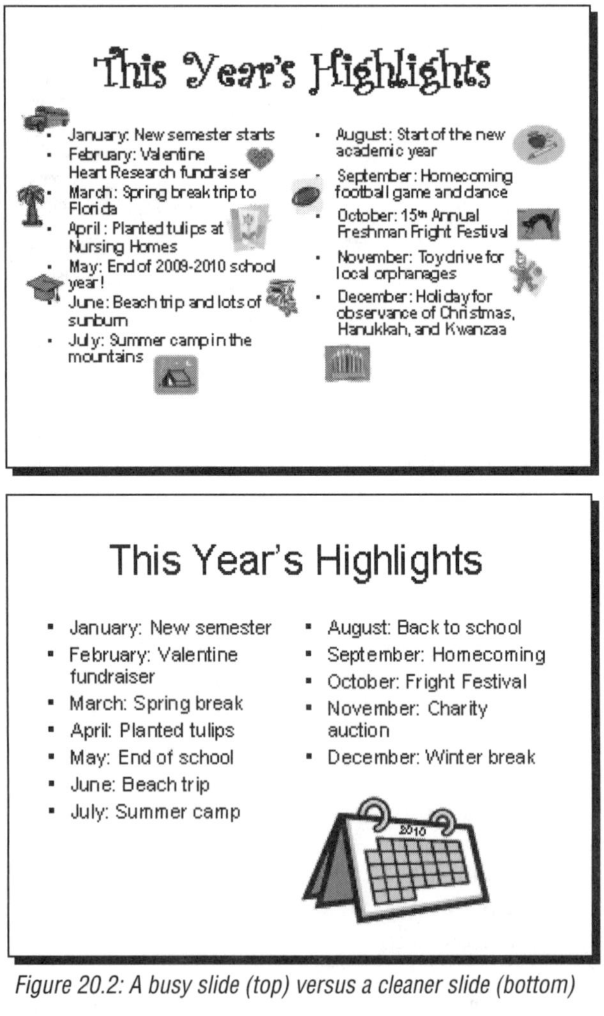

Some folks might enjoy all the blinking lights at a carnival, but that sort of thing is death for a slide show! A slide with too much going on at once is *busy* (Figure 20.2). Whenever possible, stick with a handful of important points on each slide—this makes for more slides, but your audience will thank you.

Listing to Starboard – Numbers and Bullets

Numbered and bulleted lists (see Figure 20.3) enable you to convey information in bite-sized chunks. Use numbered lists for things like instructions, when the order of the items matters. Use bulleted lists, on the other hand, for items that don't need to be in a specific order. More often than not, presenters use bullets to highlight points they make within a slide show, like an outline on screen. Most slide presentations use one or both list formats quite often.

Using Tables and Charts

Tables and charts enable you to present data in a visually friendly format. A set of numbers, such as sales figures for a month or quarter, would work great as a chart, but not so great as a list. Look at the two slides in Figures 20.4 and 20.5. The first shows a list of sales numbers. The second shows a chart using the same figures. Which format tells you more vividly that the company's sales need a serious boost? PowerPoint

---

This Year's Highlights

- January: New semester starts
- February: Valentine Heart Research fundraiser
- March: Spring break trip to Florida
- April: Planted tulips at Nursing Homes
- May: End of 2009-2010 school year!
- June: Beach trip and lots of sunburn
- July: Summer camp in the mountains

- August: Start of the new academic year
- September: Homecoming football game and dance
- October: 15th Annual Freshman Fright Festival
- November: Toy drive for local orphanages
- December: Holiday for observance of Christmas, Hanukkah, and Kwanzaa

---

This Year's Highlights

- January: New semester
- February: Valentine fundraiser
- March: Spring break
- April: Planted tulips
- May: End of school
- June: Beach trip
- July: Summer camp

- August: Back to school
- September: Homecoming
- October: Fright Festival
- November: Charity auction
- December: Winter break

Figure 20.2: A busy slide (top) versus a cleaner slide (bottom)

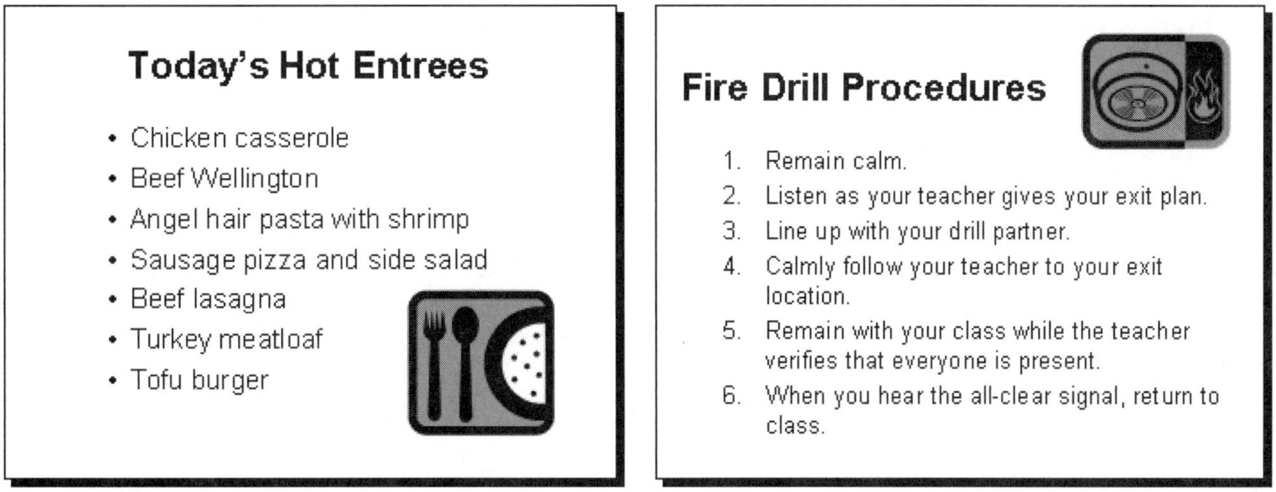

Today's Hot Entrees
• Chicken casserole
• Beef Wellington
• Angel hair pasta with shrimp
• Sausage pizza and side salad
• Beef lasagna
• Turkey meatloaf
• Tofu burger
Fire Drill Procedures
1. Remain calm.
2. Listen as your teacher gives your exit plan.
3. Line up with your drill partner.
4. Calmly follow your teacher to your exit location.
5. Remain with your class while the teacher verifies that everyone is present.
6. When you hear the all-clear signal, return to class.

Figure 20.3: A bulleted list (left) and a numbered list (right)

offers a variety of automated chart formats and table layouts so that you can concentrate on your data rather than worry about creating a table or chart from scratch.

Using Slide Masters for Consistency

You can give all of your slides a consistent, uniform look by using a *slide master*, which is a kind of blueprint for your slides. The slide master might contain your name, your company's name and logo, the title of the presentation, or other information. The text and graphics in the slide master appear in the same place on every slide in the presentation. Figure 20.6 shows a series of slides with slide master content at the top and bottom.

Creating Presentations

The process of creating a good presentation follows pretty typical steps. First, you make a new document or open an old one. Second, you insert slides and content. Third, you edit your slides for content, grammar, and typos. Fourth, you look at the whole slide show to see how well it flows. At some point, preferably before now, you save the document.

Making a New Presentation

You can create a new presentation in several ways. First, when you open PowerPoint, the application very thoughtfully starts up with a new, blank presentation already loaded. You can click the **New** button to create a blank presentation. Or, you can select **File | New** to open the New Presentation task pane and have a whole bunch of options (Figure 20.7). Clicking **Blank presentation** in the task pane creates a blank presentation (Figure 20.8).

Microsoft PowerPoint - [Sports Cars]
File Edit View Insert Format Tools Slide Show Window Help
Tahoma
Current Sales Figures
23,236
30,548
32,345
31,548
35,458
Slide 2 of 5
Blends

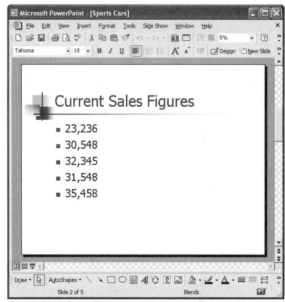

Figure 20.4: Sales figures as list

Microsoft PowerPoint - [Sports Cars]
File Edit View Insert Format Tools Slide Show Window Help
Tahoma
Sales Chart
40000
35000
30000
25000
20000
15000
10000
5000
0
1st Qtr
2nd Qtr
3rd Qtr
4th Qtr
5th Qtr
Sales
Slide 3 of 5
Blends

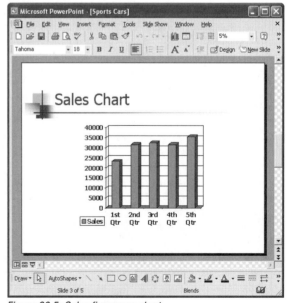

Figure 20.5: Sales figures as chart

Figure 20.6: Slide master content gives these slides a professional look.

Figure 20.7: The New Presentation task pane with various options

Abracadabra–Make a Presentation with the Wizard

*Create a new presentation in PowerPoint and run the AutoContent Wizard. Pick any style and any options you like, and give your presentation a fun title. After you click the **Finish** button, take a look at what you've created. It probably looks as good as (or better than) the presentations that many people in corporate America create every day!*

Use the AutoContent Wizard

If you don't want to build a presentation from scratch, the **From AutoContent Wizard** option on the New Presentation task pane enables you to put together a great-looking PowerPoint presentation in record time. When you click this option, the AutoContent Wizard starts (see Figure 20.9) and takes you through an easy three-step process to help you set up your entire presentation.

First, select a presentation type, as shown in Figure 20.10. This example uses Communicating Bad News, which would come in handy to report a drop in your company's sales—or maybe to tell your parents about a particularly bad report card. This screen offers options in different categories such as Corporate and Sales/Marketing.

Next, select a presentation style; most people use the default setting of On-screen presentation, but you could also tell the wizard to make a Web presentation, transparencies for an overhead projector, or even 35mm slides for an old-fashioned slide projector.

Finally, enter some information about your presentation: the title for the first slide, any text you'd like to appear in the footer at the bottom of each slide, and whether you want to include the date or slide number in the footer (see Figure 20.11).

When you complete the wizard and click **Finish**, the Wizard

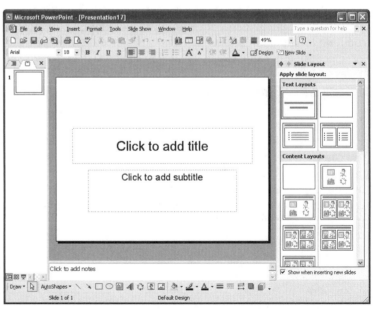

Figure 20.8: New blank presentation

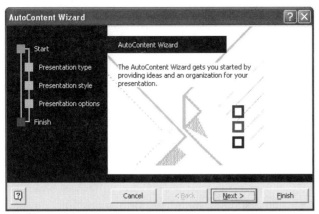

Figure 20.9: The starting screen of the AutoContent Wizard

Figure 20.10: Selecting a presentation type

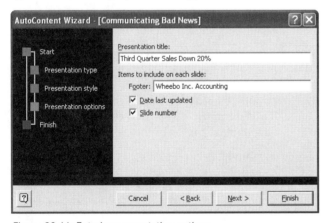

Figure 20.11: Entering presentation options

creates and displays the presentation, complete with pre-formatted slides, suggestions for each slide's content, and a background design for all the slides. Figure 20.12 shows the first slide in a bad news presentation called *Third Quarter Sales Down 20%*. From here, you simply add your own text on each slide; everything is laid out for you, so in many cases a presentation made with the AutoContent Wizard can be ready to go within minutes.

Creating, Opening, Closing, and Saving a PowerPoint Slide Presentation

In Chapter 12, "Working with Documents," you learned how to create, open, close, and save documents. How would you open an existing PowerPoint presentation from My Computer? From within the PowerPoint application window? What command would you use to save an existing presentation in a new location or to close a presentation after you've saved it? What file extension will a PowerPoint document normally have?

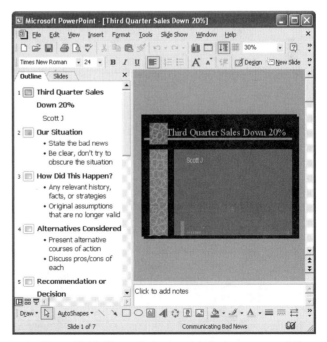

Figure 20.12: The ready-to-complete bad news presentation, including content suggestions

Apply a Design Template

If you like the idea of a pre-formatted presentation, but don't want the pre-formatted slide content that you get with the AutoContent Wizard, you can try using a *design template* instead. Design templates are professional-looking slide designs that you can use for your entire presentation, or just for specific slides in the presentation.

To use a design template, first select **Format | Slide Design** to open the Slide Design task pane (see Figure 20.13). Then scroll down through the available designs until you find the one you want to use. Click the template picture to select it—or just to get a slightly larger preview (see Figure 20.14). You can change to another template at any time, simply by coming back to this task pane and changing your selection.

Notice that in the Slide Design task pane, when you point your mouse at a template, a blue bar with a down arrow appears at the right edge of the template preview. Click this bar to view a list of options (see Figure 20.15) that includes **Apply to All Slides** and **Use for All New Presentations**.

Another way to select a design template is to click the **Browse** link at the bottom of the Slide Design task pane. This brings up the Apply Design Template dialog box, shown in Figure 20.16. Here, you can see all of your available design templates listed by name, and see larger previews than the ones shown on the Slide Design task pane. To apply a design template to your entire presentation, just select it and click **Apply**.

Managing Slides

Creating a presentation and making your first draft—just getting the information down on the slides—is about half the battle. More than likely, you'll want to make changes to your presentation as you go along. Here's how you manage and preview slides within your presentation.

Slide Views

As with Word and Excel, you can choose from different *views* in PowerPoint: *Normal, Slide Sorter, Slide Show,* or *Notes Page.* Most folks spend time in *Normal* view when making slides.

Normal view has three sections: the standard Task Pane on the right, a main work pane in the shape of a slide in the center, and two tabs on the left, Slides and Outlines. The two tabs enable you to organize and manage your

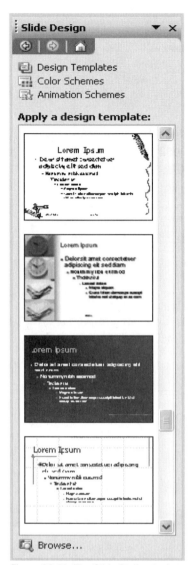

Figure 20.13: The Slide Design task pane

Figure 20.14: A blank slide showing the selected design template

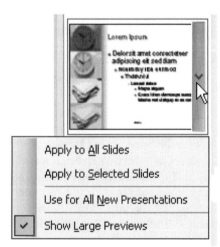

Figure 20.15: Slide Design task pane options

slide show. The *Slides tab* shows small numbered pictures of all the slides in the presentation (Figure 20.18). The *Outline tab* displays the outline of your presentation, as you can see in Figure 20.19. You'll learn more about both tabs later in the chapter.

The *Notes Page* view enables you to add notes for your own reference or for handouts. *Slide Sorter* view enables you to rearrange the order of your slides, and to do other things like cloning a whole series of slides to save time. When you're ready to see how your slides will look in the actual full-screen presentation, you use *v* view. To switch from one view to another, you can select an option at the top of the **View** menu, or use the handy little buttons at the lower left corner of the screen, as shown in Figure 20.17. Note that there is no button here for Notes Page view.

Create a New Slide

Each time you add a slide, you can choose from a large number of pre-formatted slide layouts. Start by selecting **Insert | New Slide**; this places a new slide in your presentation and opens the Slide Layout task pane, as shown in Figure 20.20. You can keep the default slide layout, or select a different one by clicking it in the task pane.

A slide layout defines where headings, talking points, and images go on a slide by default. A design template, in contrast, is more about background color, font styles, and so forth. Use layout and design together to create an excellent presentation.

Note that there are different kinds of slide layouts: Text Layouts and Content Layouts, which you see in Figure 20.20, plus Text and Content Layouts and a category called Other Layouts. Use text layout slides when your content will consist mainly of text, and content slides when you plan to include a table, chart, or other graphic element as the main focus of the slide. The other layout types consist of various combinations of items—you can scroll down the list to see them all for yourself.

While you can mix and match design templates, using different ones for different slides within the same presentation, it's best to pick one design template for your entire presentation and stick with it. Using a different template on each slide is a bad idea, as it's likely to distract the audience from your subject matter.

Figure 20.17: The view buttons

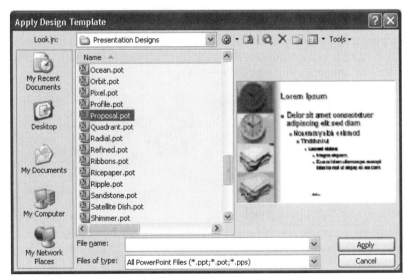

Figure 20.16: The Apply Design Template dialog box

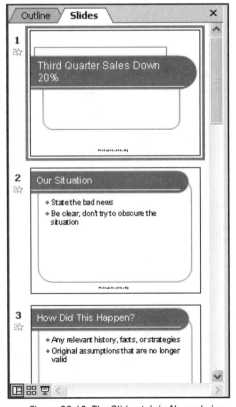

Figure 20.18: The Slides tab in Normal view

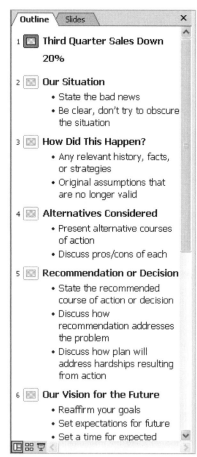

Figure 20.19: The Outline tab
in Normal view

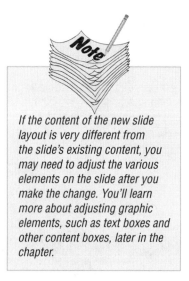

If the content of the new slide
layout is very different from
the slide's existing content, you
may need to adjust the various
elements on the slide after you
make the change. You'll learn
more about adjusting graphic
elements, such as text boxes and
other content boxes, later in the
chapter.

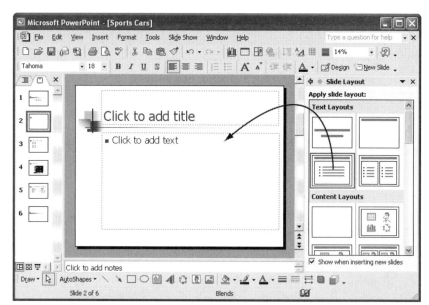

Figure 20.20: The Slide Layout task pane and a new slide with the default layout

Duplicate an Existing Slide

You can insert a duplicate slide and modify it, a quick way of adding to your presentation. For example, if you need Slide 4 to be almost the same as Slide 3, just find Slide 3 on the **Slides** tab and click to select it. Then select **Insert | Duplicate Slide** and watch what happens: Slide 4 appears, an exact duplicate of Slide 3. If there was already a Slide 4, it will now be Slide 5, and all following slides will also be renumbered. Just make whatever changes are necessary on Slide 4 (see Figure 20.21), and you've saved yourself some effort.

Delete a Slide

Deleting a slide is just as easy as duplicating one. To remove Slide 4 in your presentation, for example, simply select it on the Slides tab and press the **[Delete]** key on your keyboard. If you prefer to use the mouse, you can right-click Slide 4 in the Slides tab and select **Delete Slide** (see Figure 20.22). Either way, you'll see the slide formerly known as Slide 4 disappear; if there are slides after it, the former Slide 5 will become Slide 4, Slide 6 will become Slide 5, and so on.

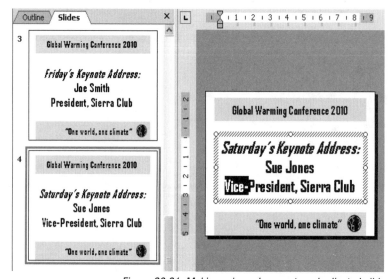

Figure 20.21: Making minor changes to a duplicated slide

Change the Order of Slides Using Slide Sorter View

When you're putting together a presentation, you may change your mind at some point about the order of your slides. Re-ordering slides in a PowerPoint presentation is easy, so you can swap slides around as much as you like.

Start by switching to Slide Sorter view, using either **View | Slide Sorter** or the **Slide Sorter View** button at the lower left corner of your screen. The Slide Sorter displays several slides on the screen at once—how many are visible depends on the size of your application window, as well as your current Zoom percentage setting.

To move a slide to a different position in the presentation, just click and drag it from its current position to a spot between two other slides. A vertical line will appear to show which slides will become the slide's new neighbors. For example, Figure 20.23 shows a close-up on the screen as Slide 7 moves to a new spot between Slide 4 and Slide 5. You know what this means—the former Slide 7 is about to become the new Slide 5! The old Slide 5 will become Slide 6, and all the rest of the slides will renumber accordingly.

You can sort slides using other methods as well. For instance, try holding down **[Shift]** while you click on one slide, then the following slide, and the slide after that—you can select as many adjoining slides as you want this way, and then drag them as a group to a new location within the presentation. You can also lasso a bunch of slides by clicking in the space between slides, and then dragging the mouse to select the slides you want; then drag them to their new home.

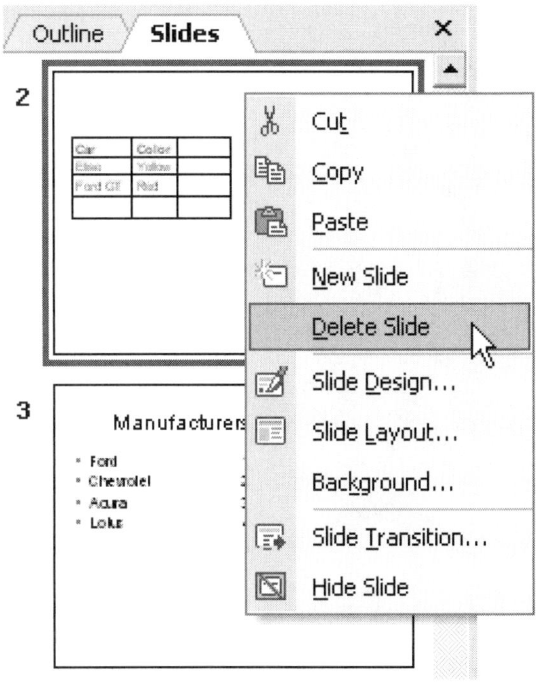

Figure 20.22: Deleting a slide using the right-click menu

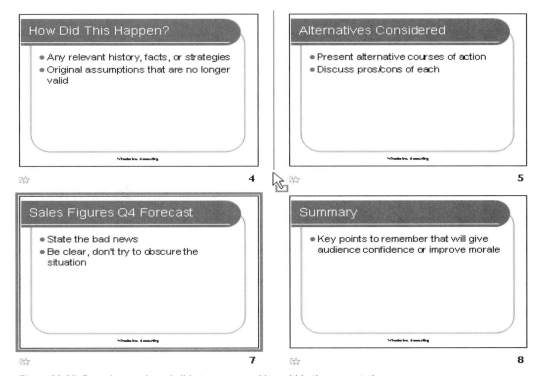

Figure 20.23: Dragging a selected slide to a new position within the presentation

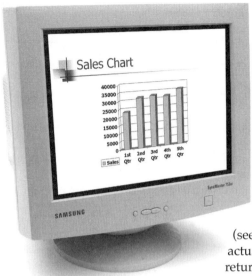

Figure 20.24: In Slide Show view, the slides take up your entire computer screen.

Preview the Presentation

When you've finished your slide presentation, or at any point while you're building it, you can take a look at what the presentation will look like without the menu, toolbars, ruler, and other application window elements. To do this, use the Slide Show view—the same view that you use to run the presentation when it's time for the real thing.

To view the presentation starting at Slide 1, select **View | Slide Show**. To view the presentation beginning with the slide you're currently viewing, click the **Slide Show from current slide** button at the lower left corner of your screen. Whichever method you choose, you'll see your entire screen suddenly taken over by a slide—your title bar, taskbar, clock, and application window will all take a back seat while you're in Slide Show view (see Figure 20.24). The slide displays exactly as it will appear in your actual presentation. If you find something here that you don't like, just return to Normal view and change the slide.

Unlike the other views, you can exit Slide Show view at any time by pressing the **[Esc]** key on your keyboard. When you do this, you'll return to the view you were using immediately before you switched to Slide Show view.

Modifying a Slide's Text and Appearance

Now that you know how to work on a presentation at the slide level, it's time to get down to the details of working with your actual slide content, starting with the main elements of text and background.

Adding and Changing Text

In most presentations, text plays a major part in getting your message across. Even on slides where the main focus is a chart, graph, or picture, you'll usually want to include a heading of some sort. Text is also the key to one of PowerPoint's most helpful features for organizing your presentation: the Outline tab.

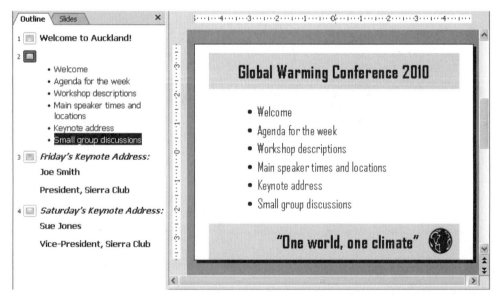

Figure 20.25: Deleting the highlighted text on the Outline tab will remove that text from the slide as well.

You've seen the Outline tab before—it's one of two display options for the left side of your work area in Normal view. While the Slides tab shows you pictures of your slides, the *Outline tab* shows you the text for each slide. You can actually type in new text, change existing text, or delete text in the Outline tab (see Figure 20.25), and watch the slide image in the main part of the work area change.

Of course, you can also work with text directly on your slides. Most new slides have "Click to add text" messages in various places, depending on your selected slide layout. You can type new text, paste text in from other applications, and format the text any way you want using familiar tools under the **Format** menu.

Apply Bullets and Numbering to Slide Text

To use bullets or numbering for text on a slide, you use the same buttons on the Formatting toolbar that you saw in Word. If you apply one of these features to a block of text that's made up of multiple paragraphs (that is, hard returns between the lines), you'll end up with one bullet or number per paragraph. Figure 20.27 shows what happens when you click the **Bullets** button with a block of text selected.

To change the bullet or numbering style for text in a slide, highlight the text and then select **Format | Bullets and Numbering**. Click either the **Bulleted** or **Numbered** tab, just as you learned to do in Word, then find a style you like and click to select it.

Change a Slide's Layout

You can change a slide's layout at any time. Just click on the slide you want to change and select **Format | Slide Layout**. This brings up the now familiar Side Layout task pane, where you can choose a new layout.

Modify a Slide's Background

One way to perk up boring slides is with a colorful or textured background. PowerPoint provides a number of background options, which you can access by selecting **Format | Background**.

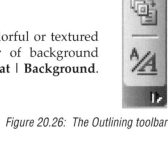

Figure 20.26: The Outlining toolbar

Outlining

If you prefer to type directly on your slides, the Outline tab is still helpful. For one thing, it can help you keep an eye on how the information is organized in your presentation. You can see at a glance the text on each slide, which is usually too small to read in the Slides tab. Also, if you have an existing outline (consisting of built-in headings such as Heading 1, Heading 2, and so on) in a program such as Word, you can select **Insert | Slides from Outline** to import those headings as a series of slides.

If your presentation includes a large amount of text, there's another advantage to working on the Outline tab: you can use the special Outlining toolbar, which works only when the Outline tab is selected. To turn on the Outlining toolbar, select **View | Toolbars | Outlining**; the toolbar appears along the left edge of the work area, next to the Outline and Slides tabs (see Figure 20.26).

This toolbar includes commands such as **Promote** and **Demote**, used to make an item more or less prominent on the slide; **Move Up** and **Move Down**, used to change the order of slides or items on a slide; and **Collapse** and **Expand**, used to display more or less of the slide's content in the Outline tab. It's a good idea to spend some time experimenting with this toolbar and its commands—they can save you serious amounts of time and effort on a lengthy PowerPoint presentation.

Figure 20.27: Before clicking the Bullets button (left), and after (right)

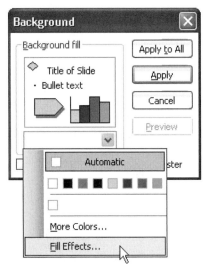

Figure 20.28: Selecting Fill Effects in the Background dialog box

In the Background dialog box, click the down arrow to see a list of color suggestions and other options. You can select **Fill Effects**, as shown in Figure 20.28, to view a list of gradients, textures, and patterns, or to select a picture to use for your background. Figure 20.29 shows how the addition of a simple granite texture can give a plain slide a quick facelift.

Add Slide Master Content

Earlier in the chapter, you saw how slide master content can give a presentation a nice uniform look. To access the slide master content for an existing presentation, or to set up some slide master content of your own, go to **View | Master | Slide Master**.

While you're in slide master view, you can select **Format | Slide Design** to see design template options for your slide master layout, just like with regular slides. You can change or add information here, such as your name, your school or company name, and the year or full date.

Figure 20.29: A plain slide (left) and the same slide with a textured background (right)

Using Graphic and Data Elements on a Slide

You can add nearly any type of graphic object (such as a picture or clip art) or data object (such as a table or chart) to a PowerPoint slide using various commands on the **Insert** menu. Many of the slide layouts that you can use to create new slides also include another quick way to add graphic elements—the *Content box* (see Figure 20.30).

The Content box is more than just a pretty icon! You can point at different parts of the box to choose which type of graphic or data element to insert: table, chart, clip art, picture, diagram or organizational chart, or media clip. When you click your selection, PowerPoint springs into action.

The **Insert Clip Art** and **Insert Picture** commands are already familiar to you—simply select an image from the dialog box and you're finished. The **Insert Table** command brings

Figure 20.30: The Content box in a slide layout

Click icon to add content

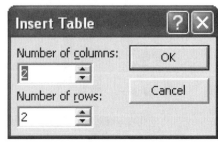

Figure 20.31: The Insert Table dialog box

up a dialog box (see Figure 20.31) where you can choose how many columns and rows your table will have; then just fill in and format your text as you would in a Word table.

When you click **Insert Chart**, the result is a bit more impressive. You get a pre-formatted sample chart, plus a datasheet where you can enter your own chart labels and values (see Figure 20.32). To create a different style of chart, right-click the chart and select **Chart Type**; the many choices here (see Figure 20.33) include just about any kind of chart you might want to use.

Inserting a Picture from Clip Art or a File

In Chapter 13, "Editing Documents," you learned how to insert a clip art image or a picture file stored on your hard drive into a document. Looking at your PowerPoint menus, do you see the familiar commands that enable you to include these kinds of images in your PowerPoint presentations? What are the steps you would take to look for an appropriate clip art image if you don't already have one in mind?

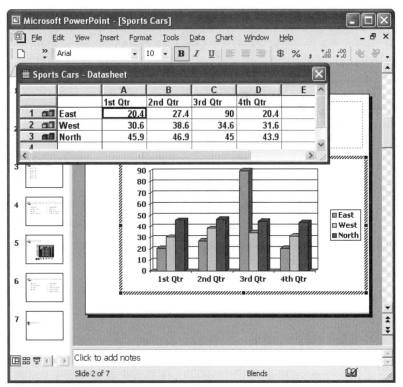

Figure 20.32: The result of clicking Insert Chart

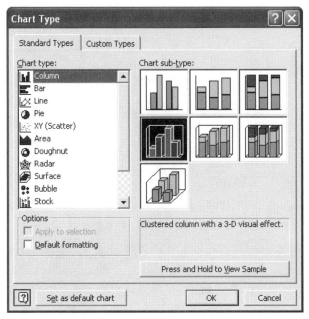

Figure 20.33: The Chart Type dialog box

Figure 20.34: The Text Box button on the Drawing toolbar

Figure 20.35: A new text box, with an insertion point ready for text

Figure 20.36: The border of a text box: during text editing (left) and with the box selected (right)

Drawn Objects

The Drawing toolbar in PowerPoint is the same one found in Word and Excel. As you learned back in Chapter 13, you can use the Drawing tools to create lines, rectangles, ovals, and other shapes; change the line or fill properties of an object; place an object in front of or behind another object; align objects with one another; and group or ungroup objects.

Text Boxes

When it comes to entering text on a slide, you aren't limited to using the pre-configured text boxes that are part of your slide's initial layout. You can create a *text box* anywhere on the slide, enter text in the box, and format both the text and the box however you like.

To add a text box, you can either select **Insert | Text Box** or click the **Text Box** button on the Drawing toolbar (see Figure 20.34). This changes your cursor to something that looks like a little pogo stick, or an insertion point with a small crossbar: ⊥. When you get that cursor, you're ready to place your new text box by clicking and dragging. Figure 20.35 shows an example of a newly created text box.

After you've typed some text in your text box, you can select the box to resize it, move it, or apply settings such as line or fill. Note that when you click a corner of the box, or anywhere on its edge, its border changes from one made of diagonal lines to one made of dots (see Figure 20.36). When you're working with the text inside a text box, the border will display as lines—but any time you want to apply a setting to the box itself, you should check the border to be sure you're seeing dots, not lines.

Adding Line and Fill to Slide Elements

You can use the Drawing toolbar to apply various line and fill colors and types to any graphic object, data object, or text box on a slide. Just select the item you want to outline or fill, then click the drop-down arrow next to the appropriate button on the Drawing toolbar—**Fill Color**, **Line Color**, **Line Style**, and so on. Borders and shading can help slide elements stand out and look better, as shown in Figure 20.37.

Today's Hot Entrees

- Chicken casserole
- Beef Wellington
- Angel hair pasta with shrimp
- Sausage pizza and side salad
- Beef lasagna
- Turkey meatloaf
- Tofu burger

Today's Hot Entrees

- Chicken casserole
- Beef Wellington
- Angel hair pasta with shrimp
- Sausage pizza and side salad
- Beef lasagna
- Turkey meatloaf
- Tofu burger

Figure 20.37: The added border and shading in the slide on the right make it more visually interesting.

Show Time! Presentation Techniques

Even after you've made and polished all the slides for your presentation, you're not yet ready for prime time! You still have some work to do, both to finish the presentation and to prepare yourself for presenting, before it's show time.

Assigning Transitions

When you put on a slide presentation, you need to keep the audience's attention—otherwise, all of your hard work is wasted. One way to add visual interest to your presentation is to use slide transitions.

The *transition* refers to the way PowerPoint changes the display from one slide to the next. By default, the transition for all your slides is very plain: one slide disappears, and another takes its place. You can make your transitions more interesting by using different kinds of transitions. To set up the transition for a particular slide, view the slide and then select **Slide Show | Slide Transition**. This brings up the Slide Transition task pane (see Figure 20.38), which shows you lots of different options for how this slide will transition to the next.

The default setting is **No Transition**; you can click on any other option here to see a demonstration of what that transition will look like when you give the presentation. (If this doesn't happen, check the **AutoPreview** box at the bottom of the task pane and then try again.) The best way to find a transition you like is to run through all of the choices until something catches your eye.

You can also set a transition speed, and select a sound to go along with the transition if you like. Note that near the bottom of the task pane, you can click **Apply to All Slides**, which is pretty self-explanatory. Consider using this option, if only to avoid the temptation to get carried away using all kinds of different transitions. Just like a busy slide, a presentation with too many fancy slide transitions can be distracting for your audience.

Figure 20.38: The Slide Transition task pane

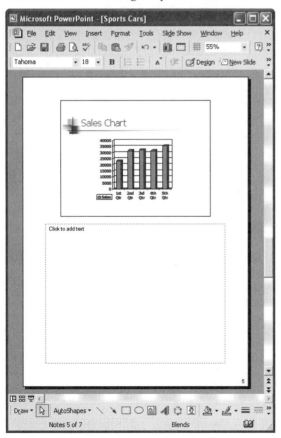

Figure 20.39: Notes Page view, before adding notes

Creating Speaker Notes and Handouts

Most presentations go substantially smoother when you have notes to go along with them. PowerPoint's *speaker notes* feature enables you to add notes for each slide. You access this feature by switching to the Notes Page view (Figure 20.39).

In the area beneath your slide, you can type additional text, either to read as you give the presentation or to give as handouts to your audience. Handouts are great for any presentation where the audience might want to follow along, make notes, or save the information for future reference.

Whether you use the Notes Page view to make speaker notes or handouts, you'll want to print them before giving your presentation or have a second computer handy to display them during your presentation. When you go to print, select **File | Print** instead of using the Print button, to bring up the Print dialog box. In the **Print what** drop-down box, select **Notes Pages** if you want to print out one slide with notes on each page—whether you're printing them out for your reference or as audience handouts.

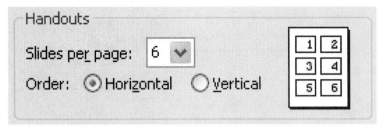

Figure 20.40: The Handouts area of the Print dialog box

You can select an option called **Handouts** here as well, but as you can see in Figure 20.40, this simply prints multiple slides on each page (you select how many slides per page), without notes. If your slides include a lot of text, this type of handout can be very useful for your audience.

Preview and Practice

This final step before giving your presentation is important for your success and peace of mind. Reviewing the entire presentation helps you spot errors, typos, slides out of order, or other glitches, so that you can fix them before the whole world sees them!

Practicing for a stand-up presentation prepares you for what you will say, and helps you notice any areas you may have left out. Also, if you've done a practice run-through, you're less likely to be nervous when the big moment comes.

To review your slides and practice your delivery, just switch your finished presentation to Slide Show view and use the following navigation methods.

Running the Presentation

You're finally ready to present your PowerPoint masterpiece! But wait—how do you drive this thing, anyway? Let's look at the hardware and controls that you use to navigate through a presentation in Slide Show view.

Hardware for Presenting

If you use a desktop PC, you'll probably use a regular mouse. Portable computers generally have different controls, such as a touch pad. You might be more comfortable adding a mouse to the laptop. You might even be lucky enough to have a wireless mouse or other remote-control device, so you can move around as you present. Whatever the case, try to practice with the controls you'll actually be using. Be sure to elevate your controls to a comfortable height if you'll be standing to present

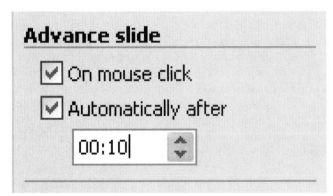

Figure 20.41: The Advance slide settings let you put the presentation on autopilot.

Navigating the Slide Show

Once you've started your slide presentation, the most common way to advance from one slide to the next by clicking the left mouse button. If you prefer, you can use the keyboard to advance to the next slide, by pressing either the down arrow or right arrow key. If you need to move backward, you can use the up arrow or left arrow key; you can also right-click and select **Previous** from the pop-up menu, but that's a much more distracting way to go back—the arrow keys are a better choice, if you have a keyboard handy.

If you'd prefer to have the slides advance automatically—for example, if you're using your presentation as part of a science fair display and want it to run by itself—you can go to the Slide Transition task pane and change the settings in the **Advance slide** area (see Figure 20.41). Just select the **Automatically after** box and then fill in the number of seconds or minutes that each slide should display before transitioning automatically.

Ending the Show

When you advance past the final slide of your presentation, you'll come to a black screen with white text at the top that tells you and the audience that the show is over (see Figure 20.42). This is a good time to stop if you're presenting, as one more click will show the entire room your application window—not the most attractive view. As soon as your audience has left the room or your projector is turned off, you can exit Slide Show view by advancing the show one more time. If you should ever need to end the show in the middle, just press **[Esc]** on your keyboard.

Figure 20.42: End of Slide Show screen

If you leave the **On mouse click** box checked as well, you'll have the option to advance to the next slide manually at any time.

Wheel Genius
If you use a mouse for your presentation, check to see whether it has a wheel control located between the left and right mouse buttons. With a wheel mouse, you can simply roll the wheel up (toward your fingertips) to advance, or down (toward your palm) to back up. If you choose this method, you may want to practice ahead of time—it takes only a slight twitch of your finger to move the wheel, so be careful not to get nervous and fast-forward unintentionally!

Presentation Design

- An effective PowerPoint presentation is as much about how you display the information as about the information itself.

- You should limit the amount of content you put on a single slide, as well as the number of flashy effects you use—if your slides that are too busy, they won't get your point across as well.

- On slides with lists of items, use numbers for lists where the order of the items matters (such as steps for instructions), and bullets for lists where the order doesn't matter.

- Tables and charts should be kept simple for best results.

- You can use slide masters to include your name, company name, logo, or other information in the same place on each slide automatically.

Creating Presentations

- You can use the AutoContent Wizard to create a presentation with a pre-formatted layout and suggestions for content. You can also create a blank presentation to custom-create your own look, or use a design template for professional-looking formatting without the content.

- In PowerPoint, you can select from four main views: **Normal**, **Slide Sorter**, **Slide Show**, and **Notes Page**. To switch views, use the **View** menu or click the appropriate button at the bottom left corner of the screen.

- To create a new slide, select **Insert | New Slide**, then select a layout from the Slide Layout task pane. Some layouts use only text, while others are designed for use with tables, charts, or graphics.

- To duplicate a slide, choose that slide on the Slides tab, then select **Insert | Duplicate Slide**. Change the new slide as needed; the other slides re-number themselves automatically.

- To delete a slide, select it and press the **[Delete]** key on your keyboard, or right-click it on the Slides tab and select **Delete Slide**.

- To change the order of your slides, switch to the Slide Sorter view, then click and drag slides to rearrange them.

- You can insert and edit text either in the slide or in the **Outline** tab at the left side of the work area. To change the slide's overall appearance, select **Format | Slide Layout** and select a new layout for the slide. To change the background color or texture, select **Format | Background**.

Show Time! Presentation Techniques

- It's smart to run through your presentation before your audience sees it—both to check for errors and to ensure that you're comfortable with the controls.

- You can select **Slide Show | Slide Transition** to choose a visually interesting way to move from one slide to the next—but don't go overboard with fancy transitions that overshadow your content.

- You can print out speaker notes or audience handouts to go with your presentation. To add notes for your slides, use the Notes Page view. To print either notes pages or handouts (multiple slide pictures on each page, without notes), use the Print dialog box.

- Switch to Slide Show view to run the presentation, then press the left mouse button to advance to the next slide. You can also use the down or right arrow key to advance, or the up or left arrow key to return to the previous slide. Press **[Esc]** at any time to end the presentation.

Key Terms

AutoContent Wizard

Clip Art

Handouts

Normal

Notes Page

Outline Tab

Slide Design

Slide Layout

Slide Master

Slide Projector

Slide Show

Slide Sorter

Slide Views

Slides Tab

Speaker Notes

Text Box

Transition

Key Term Quiz

Use the Key Terms list to complete the following sentences. Not all the terms will be used.

1. The _____ gives you a quick three-step process to create a presentation.

2. You can use a _____ to make the move from one slide to another look nicer.

3. You can add content in a _____ to make that content appear in the same place on every slide.

4. Use _____ view to preview your presentation.

5. Decades ago, before PowerPoint was available, you would have needed to use a _____ to show full-color pictures to a roomful of people.

6. The library of graphics that you can use in a PowerPoint presentation is called _____.

7. To change the way the information on a slide is arranged, you can make a selection in the _____ task pane.

8. You can easily rearrange individual slides or groups of slides using _____ view.

9. You can use Notes Page view to create _____, either for your own reference or to hand out to your audience.

10. A special toolbar that's available when you use the _____ makes it easy to organize and rearrange the text on your slides.

Multiple-Choice Quiz

1. What can you insert into a slide to put in lines or paragraphs of text?
   A. Text window
   B. Text slide
   C. Text Wizard
   D. Text box

2. What is the word used to describe the way the screen looks as you move from one slide to the next?
   A. Switch
   B. Zoom
   C. Transition
   D. Translation

3. Which view should you select to see what your presentation will look like?
   A. Slide Show
   B. Slide Layout
   C. AutoContent Wizard
   D. Slide Clip

4. What is the file extension for a normal PowerPoint presentation?
   A. .ppt
   B. .pwp
   C. .pot
   D. .pnt

5. If you don't want to use the AutoContent Wizard or a design template, what can you select to begin a new presentation?
   A. Blank presentation
   B. Begin presentation
   C. File presentation
   D. Layout presentation

6. Not counting the start and finish screens, how many steps are in the AutoContent Wizard?
   A. 2
   B. 3
   C. 4
   D. 5

7. What do you call text or graphics that you set up to appear on every slide?
   A. Slide Master content
   B. Slide Sorter content
   C. Slide Template content
   D. Transition content

8. Which of the following is a valid step in the AutoContent Wizard?
   A. Presentation Point
   B. Presentation Text
   C. Presentation Style
   D. Presentation Clip

9. What is PowerPoint's graphics library called?
   A. Clip Slides
   B. Clip Library
   C. Clip Layout
   D. Clip Art

10. On which task pane can you select a preformatted visual style for your slides?
    A. Slide Design
    B. Slide Layout
    C. Slide Master
    D. Slide Transition

11. Which toolbar includes the commands you can use to add borders and shading to items on a slide?
    A. Standard
    B. Outlining
    C. Drawing
    D. Elements

12. Which of the following will **not** advance to the next slide in Slide Show view?
    A. Down arrow key
    B. Right arrow key
    C. Left mouse button
    D. Right mouse button

13. If you needed to include a bar graph in your slide presentation, what command would you use to start?
    A. Insert | Graph
    B. Insert | Chart
    C. Insert | Table
    D. Insert | Picture | Clip Art

14. What must you do to make the Outlining toolbar available?
    A. In Normal view, click the **Outline** tab.
    B. In Notes Page view, click in the lower portion of the page.
    C. Select a slide layout that uses the outline format.
    D. Import an outline from a program such as Word.

15. Which printing option should you use if you want to print copies of your slide presentation for your audience, with six slides per page?
    A. Slides
    B. Handouts
    C. Notes Pages
    D. Outline View

Essay Questions

1. Your brother needs to make a PowerPoint Presentation and present it tomorrow at work, and he is 100% clueless. Describe to him the three-step process for using the AutoContent Wizard.

2. Your Uncle Bob is scheduled to give a lecture for a trade convention in a few weeks, and he plans to use an old-fashioned slide projector. Explain to him the advantages of using a PowerPoint presentation instead of a slide projector.

3. What are the different types of non-text content that you can put on a slide? How do you get these things into your slide presentation? How do you pick an appropriate slide layout that will include this type of content?

Projects

1. You are the new vice president of marketing for a huge video game company, and you've just come up with an idea for a cool new video game. Use the AutoContent Wizard to put together a presentation about what makes your game special. If you were the president of the company, would you be impressed with the presentation?

2. Go to http://www.google.com and in the search box type in ".ppt" and "presentation," plus one other word—a topic of your choice such as "football" or "horses." In the search results, find a PowerPoint presentation that someone else has done on your selected topic. How many pages are in the document? Do you recognize any of the PowerPoint features the author used? Did this person do a good job of communicating the message?

COMPUTER LITERACY: YOUR TICKET TO IC³ CERTIFICATION

Part 3:
Living Online

Network Basics

"Oh, so they have the Internet on computers now!"
— Homer Simpson, *The Simpsons*

This chapter covers the following IC³ exam objectives:

- IC3-3   1.1.1   Identify terminology relating to telecommunications, networks and the Internet, including server, client, node, electronic mail, modem, switch, hub, firewall, and wireless communication

- IC3-3   1.1.2   Identify types of networks, including local area network (LAN), wide area network (WAN), Internet, and intranet

- IC3-3   1.1.3   Identify how networks work, including the role of servers and clients, the types of computers used as servers, and how clients connect to a network

- IC3-3   1.1.4   Identify benefits of networked computing

- IC3-3   1.1.5   Identify the risks of networked computing

- IC3-3   1.1.6   Identify fundamental principles of security on a network

Imagine you just got a super-cool, brand-new computer, but you can't send e-mail, download music, or play games across the Internet with your friends. How boring would that be? Without the ability to connect with other computers, in today's world you might as well not have a computer at all. When you link computers together to share files and communicate and do all the things we like to do, you create a *network*. This chapter covers all the pieces that come together to make a network and the different types of networks available. You will also look at the benefits and risks of having a network, and how people called *network administrators* make networks safe from hackers, thieves, and other bad guys.

Servers and Clients

People use two types of computers in networks these days: servers and clients. In a nutshell, *servers* share things—such as files and printers—and *clients* enable you to access those shared things. Let's get one thing straight right off the bat. Almost any personal computer can act as a server or a client or both! A lot of it has to do with how you set the computer up.

Server computers come in all shapes and sizes, but they serve—if you'll pardon the pun—a similar purpose. Servers manage *network resources* (like printers, e-mail—all the stuff that makes a network valuable), provide central storage of files, and provide services for the users (like having the printer server tell the printer to print, or having the e-mail server send your e-mail).

Client computers enable you to access the shared resources and services on server machines (Figure 21.1). Most users access servers via clients, although there's no law that says you can't access a server from another server machine. The latter machine, in that case, would be *acting* as a client regardless of the firepower of the box! Let's look at the typical machines used for clients and servers.

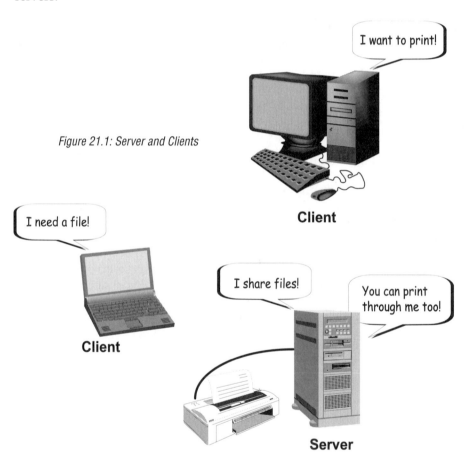

Figure 21.1: Server and Clients

Network Machines

Have you ever been driving down the street and seen an old car drive by and your parents or grandparents instantly knew what kind of car it was? They probably remember when that type of car first came out and what was cool about it back in the "good old days." But as the old saying goes, *they just don't make them like they used to* (Figure 21.2).

Just as modern automobiles only vaguely resemble the cars of yesteryear—sharing features such as engines, transmissions, and tires, but with a degree of sophistication and complexity unimaginable back then—modern computers only vaguely resemble ancient computers. The computers created in the 1940s, for example, could process hugely complex mathematical equations, but that was all they could do. Plus they were gigantic, the size of a whole building!

A modern Apple Macintosh mini, in contrast, can run circles around the old computers in raw number crunching prowess, and play the latest DVD movies in full color and stereo, plus enable you to play games, write a novel, and edit those pictures of your Aunt Betsy—all in a package barely larger than your hand (Figure 21.3)!

Clients

You know about client computers from the first two parts of this book, whether you remember the term "client" or not. Microcomputers running Windows, Macintosh, and the many varieties of Linux make up the vast majority of client computers (Figure 21.4). You'll also find other devices as clients, though, such as personal digital assistants (PDAs) like the Compaq iPAQ (Figure 21.5).

Servers

Server computers come in four basic types: supercomputers, mainframes, minicomputers, and microcomputers. The operating systems they use vary from type to type and within each type.

Supercomputers, Mainframes, and Minicomputers

The most powerful servers are supercomputers and mainframes. A *supercomputer* is an extremely fast computer dedicated to performing one task very well (Figure 21.6). From mapping human DNA to predicting the weather, supercomputers are used to do very complex math problems with unbelievably large numbers very quickly. *Mainframe* computers offer a similar level of firepower as supercomputers, but focus on enabling hundreds or thousands of people to work on many different programs simultaneously (Figure 21.7).

Figure 2: Old car, newer car (Photos courtesy of Campbell River Sales and BMW, respectively)

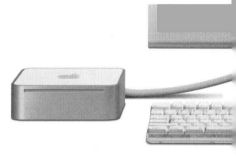

Figure 21.3: Mac mini (Courtesy of Apple)

Figure 21.4: Typical client computer (Photo courtesy of Dell)

Figure 21.5: iPAQ

Defined traditionally, a *minicomputer* enables many people to access a multitude of programs at a much lower price tag than mainframe computers. Think of minicomputers as scaled-down mainframes and you'll be pretty close. The term "mini" can be misleading with regard to the earliest versions of minicomputers. Though they were smaller than mainframes, they were closer in size to a car than to an average desktop computer today (Figure 21.8). These minicomputers were nevertheless an improvement over the building or room-sized mainframes they replaced.

Most companies today don't use the term "minicomputer" to describe their midrange server offerings. Perhaps "mini" makes the marketing departments cringe; regardless of the reason, most offer branded computers, such as IBM's iSeries and eSeries *midrange servers* (Figure 21.9).

> ### Clients
> *Chapter 1, "Field Guide to Identifying Computers in the Wild," covered client computers in some detail. Flip back to that chapter and see if you can answer these questions: What kind of components will you find inside a microcomputer? What are the key differences between the three primary types of microcomputer — Windows, Macintosh, and Linux?*

Figure 21.6: Cray X1E Supercomputer (Photo courtesy of Cray)

Figure 21.7: Mainframe

Microcomputer Servers

The vast majority of servers in use today run on microcomputer architecture, just like your typical client computers (Figure 21.10). Most have a lot more firepower than client computers, with more RAM, hard drive space, and processing power; they also run special server versions of Windows or Mac OS, or one of the many flavors of Linux or UNIX.

Figure 21.8: DEC VAX Minicomputer

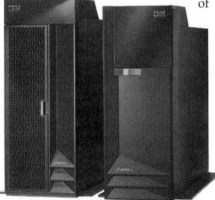

Figure 21.9: IBM eSeries i5 550 (Courtesy of International Business Machines Corporation. Unauthorized use not permitted.)

IBM PC-based Microcomputer Servers

The most common microcomputer, as you know from Part 1 of this book, is based on the original IBM x86 architecture. The servers in this family use Intel or AMD processors, sport gigabytes of DDR RAM, and have multiple hard drives to supply safety for your data if one of the drives fails. They're commonly referred to as *personal computers* (*PCs*). You'll find server PCs in two basic physical shapes: tower and rack-mounted.

Towers slip under a desk or hide in a closet somewhere, acting pretty much like a glorified client PC. Rack-mounted servers live in closets, generally affixed to a rack along side other rack-mounted servers (Figure 21.11).

Microsoft makes several versions of Windows designed to run on x86 server PCs (Figure 21.12). Each version offers support for multiple client computers, multiple CPUs, and gobs of RAM.

The primary differences are in scale: Windows Server 2003 works for small businesses, for example, whereas larger businesses would want to use Windows Server 2003 Enterprise Edition.

Figure 21.10: Typical server–
Hey! That looks like my PC!
(Photo courtesy of Dell)

Figure 21.11: Rack-mounted server
(Photo courtesy of General Technics)

Figure 21.12: Windows Server 2003

Apple Microcomputer Servers

Apple makes a version of its popular Macintosh hardware and operating system designed specifically for servers, called Xserve (Figure 21.13). Xserve servers use Motorola and IBM G5 CPUs and, like Windows servers, can have multiple processors, gobs of RAM, and tons of hard drive space. Apple Xserve server systems run a server-class version of Mac OS X called, appropriately, OS X Server. Apple Xserve servers support Macintosh, Windows, and Linux clients.

Linux on the Inside

Figure 21.13: Apple Xserve G5
(Photo courtesy of Apple)

Linux is the odd duck operating system, because you can run it on IBM-style PCs, Xserve G5 machines, and most mainframes! Linus Torvalds, a programmer from Finland, created the first version of Linux. Have you ever complained that you didn't like something, such as the dinner that one of your parents made for you, and they said, "Well, why don't you go make your own dinner?" Well, Linus didn't like any of the computer operating systems in use, so he made his own. He wrote the computer code for an operating system based on UNIX, posted it on the Internet, and told other programmers that if they could make it better, they were welcome to do so. Tens of thousands of programmers have made improvements, and Linux is one of the largest collaborative projects in the history of the world. Linux can run on just about any computer, plus it's free, so it has become very popular (Figure 21.14).

UNIX

The UNIX family of operating systems grew up in the heyday of mainframe and minicomputers, and continues to thrive on x86-based microcomputers. Dozens of versions of UNIX run on server computers, but the most popular (aside from Linux and Mac OS X, both of which are based on UNIX) are *BSD, IBM AIX, and Solaris (Figure 21.15). In look and feel, most versions of UNIX work like Linux, so most people today lump the two families together.

Linux can run on PCs and Macs alike.

Find Your OS

So, all this talk about network operating systems might have piqued your curiousity, so give into temptation! What operating system does your school or office network run on? Only one OS? What about the client PCs? How many servers can you find? Get up and find out!

Figure 21.14: Linux server

Figure 21.15: Sun Solaris 10

Creating Your Network

So now you've got a server and a couple of clients. What's next? I want to access the information on the server from one of the client computers. In short, I want a network! To create a network, you need to connect a client computer with a server in some way. Most often, you'll use a wire, but you could do it through radio waves to create a wireless connection. Let's look at two common types of networks, then turn to network hardware.

Network Types

Networks come in many sizes and vary a lot in the number of computers attached to them. Some people connect two computers in their house so that they can share files and play games together—the smallest network you can have. Some companies have thousands of employees in dozens of countries, in contrast, and need to network their computers together to get work done. Network folks put most networks into one of two categories: LANs and WANs.

A *local area network* (*LAN*) covers a small area and contains a modest number of computers (Figure 21.16). LANs are usually in a single building or group of nearby buildings. A typical home network and the network that your school runs on are considered LANs.

A *wide area network* (WAN) covers a large area and can have a substantial number of computers. Usually a WAN is composed of two or more LANs con-

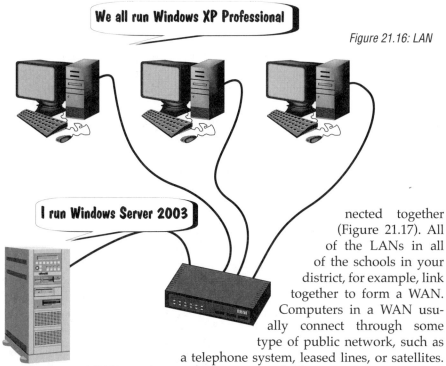

We all run Windows XP Professional

I run Windows Server 2003

Figure 21.16: LAN

nected together (Figure 21.17). All of the LANs in all of the schools in your district, for example, link together to form a WAN. Computers in a WAN usually connect through some type of public network, such as a telephone system, leased lines, or satellites.

The largest WAN in existence is the *Internet*, which is a worldwide network that connects millions of computers and networks. An *intranet*, in contrast, is essentially a private network that is a scaled-down version of the Internet for a very specific group of users.

Network Hardware

Whether you want to put together a LAN or connect a couple of LANs into a WAN, you've got to have connectivity between the PCs and a way to handle communication. Computers connect to a network in one of three ways: directly wired to a LAN via a cable from the computer to a LAN port; wirelessly to the LAN; and via a telephone line, what's called *dial-up networking*.

Wired Network

A typical network client has a network adapter or network interface card (NIC) that connects to a cable, connects to a central network box, called a hub or switch (Figure 21.18). (I'll explain the difference between them in a moment.)

To make this into a nicely configured network, add another network client. Throw in a server. Then just turn on network sharing and voilà! You have a network. Each machine attaches to a network cable that then connects at the other end to the hub or switch. Any machine attached to a network—client, server, printer, or whatnot—is called a *node*.

You might be wondering how you can tell what sort of cable to use for this network and how to determine the type of hub or switch required for a network. Networking means communicating; the computers need to be able to speak the same language and follow the same technology. If I started to write the

The Internet
The Internet ties together well over 100 countries to exchange news, data, and opinions.

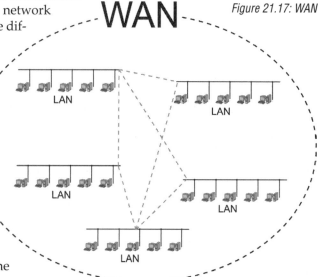

WAN

Figure 21.17: WAN

LAN

LAN

LAN

LAN

LAN

Figure 21.18: Wired network components

rest of this book in Esperanto, that might make it a little difficult for you to get much knowledge about the Internet, e-mail, and other topics we have to cover unless, of course, you read Esperanto!). By writing in English with Roman characters in a font that's legible, I make it possible for you to enjoy the information that I'm sharing. Networks require the same consistency of language and technology.

The *Ethernet* standard defines everything about modern network hardware, from the physical size and shape of the connector on the end of the network cable—called an *RJ-45*, if you're curious—to the electrical signaling that enables a NIC to break a message down into little pieces, send them across the cable, and have the receiving NIC reassemble the pieces into a useful message (Figure 21.19). If two machines do not have the same kind of networking technology—a common problem in the early days of computer networks—then they can't network together. I won't bore you with a list of all the networking technologies that have had a brief moment of glory and market share in the past. Suffice it to say that today, Ethernet is king.

Networking Process

Once you've assembled the pieces for a network, you can sit down at a client computer and access a file on a server. As cool as they may seem, networks aren't magic. A whole bunch of stuff happens in the background when you access network resources. Let's look at that process now.

Figure 21.19: Ethernet connection close-up

Johan has a slick new Windows XP laptop and wants to access an MP3 music file on his friend Maria's computer. Two things need to be in place before anything else happens. Both Johan and Maria's computers need to be connected to the same network, and Maria needs to share the folder that holds the MP3 file.

The connection part should be easy to implement. If both computers have Ethernet NICs, they can plug them into two ports on a switch or hub. Sharing requires Maria to share and set permissions on her share to allow Johan to access it. *Permissions* define what a user can do with a particular shared file or folder, such as read it, delete it, and so on. How you share and set permissions varies among the various operating systems. In Windows XP, for example, You would open My Computer, right-click on the folder containing her MP3 file, and select **Sharing and Security** to open the folder's Properties dialog box (Figure 21.20).

By default, nothing is shared, so Maria would need to select the **Share this folder** radio button and give it a share name, such as *Music* (Figure 1.21). The default permission on a new share in Windows XP gives what's called "Read" access to everyone who has access to the share. Click on the **Permissions** button to open the Permissions dialog box and you'll see what I mean (Figure 21.22).

Once connectivity, sharing, and permissions are taken care of, Johan can open up his My Network Places folder, navigate to Maria's PC, and double-click her shared Music folder to reveal the contents. A simple right-click and

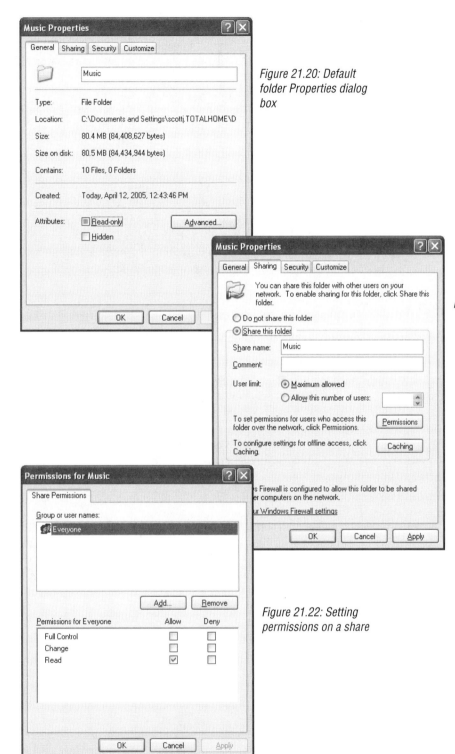

Figure 21.20: Default folder Properties dialog box

Figure 21.21: Creating a share

Figure 21.22: Setting permissions on a share

Sharing

You've seen sharing before, way back in Chapter 1, "Field Guide to Identifying Computers in the Wild." Glance back at that chapter and answer these questions: What can you share on a network? What is distributed computing and how does that compare with network sharing here? Would Johan and Maria's network benefit from clusters?

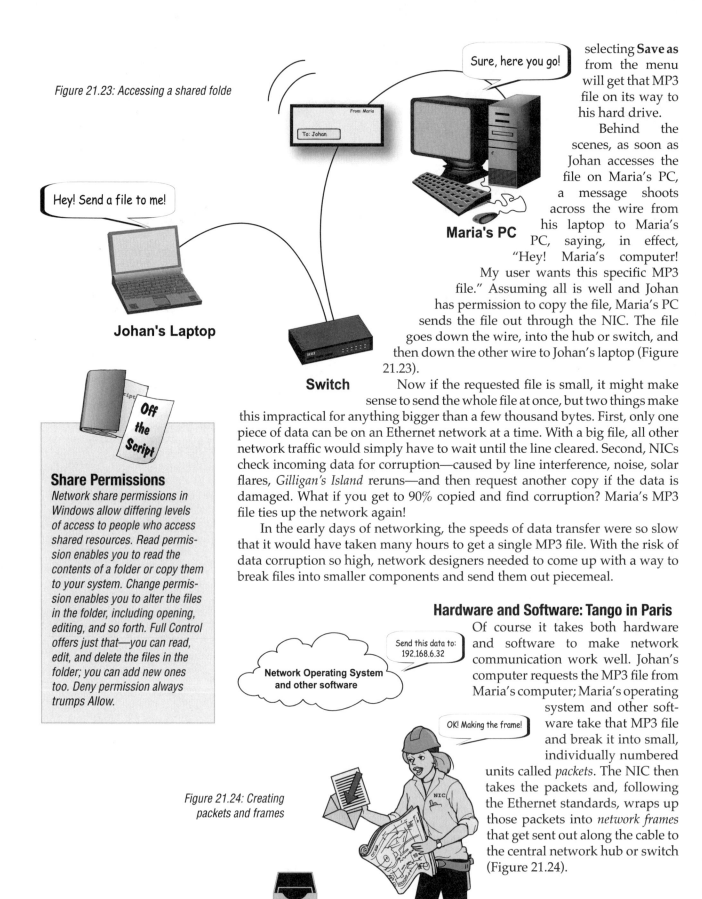

Figure 21.23: Accessing a shared folde

Sure, here you go!

From: Maria
To: Johan

Maria's PC

Hey! Send a file to me!

Johan's Laptop

Switch

selecting **Save as** from the menu will get that MP3 file on its way to his hard drive.

Behind the scenes, as soon as Johan accesses the file on Maria's PC, a message shoots across the wire from his laptop to Maria's PC, saying, in effect, "Hey! Maria's computer! My user wants this specific MP3 file." Assuming all is well and Johan has permission to copy the file, Maria's PC sends the file out through the NIC. The file goes down the wire, into the hub or switch, and then down the other wire to Johan's laptop (Figure 21.23).

Now if the requested file is small, it might make sense to send the whole file at once, but two things make this impractical for anything bigger than a few thousand bytes. First, only one piece of data can be on an Ethernet network at a time. With a big file, all other network traffic would simply have to wait until the line cleared. Second, NICs check incoming data for corruption—caused by line interference, noise, solar flares, *Gilligan's Island* reruns—and then request another copy if the data is damaged. What if you get to 90% copied and find corruption? Maria's MP3 file ties up the network again!

In the early days of networking, the speeds of data transfer were so slow that it would have taken many hours to get a single MP3 file. With the risk of data corruption so high, network designers needed to come up with a way to break files into smaller components and send them out piecemeal.

Hardware and Software: Tango in Paris

Of course it takes both hardware and software to make network communication work well. Johan's computer requests the MP3 file from Maria's computer; Maria's operating system and other software take that MP3 file and break it into small, individually numbered units called *packets*. The NIC then takes the packets and, following the Ethernet standards, wraps up those packets into *network frames* that get sent out along the cable to the central network hub or switch (Figure 21.24).

Send this data to: 192.168.6.32

Network Operating System and other software

OK! Making the frame!

Figure 21.24: Creating packets and frames

OUT

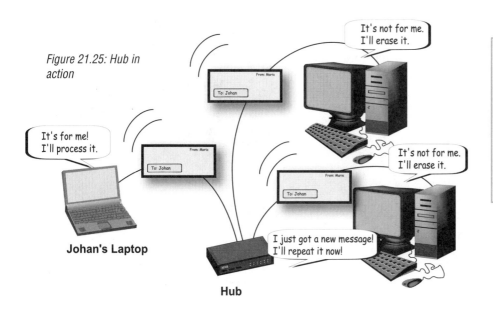

Figure 21.25: Hub in action

Johan's Laptop

Hub

Switch or Hub?
What sort of network boxes does your school or office use? How can you tell? (Hint: Switches and hubs look alike, so you'll have to do some checking of model numbers.)

HUB versus Switch

Hubs and switches function quite differently when they receive an Ethernet frame. A *hub* repeats the frame down every network cable connected, hoping one of the computers connected is the requesting machine, in this case Johan's laptop. A *switch*, in contrast, learns the network address of every machine connected to it, reads the recipient address on the frames, and sends them along only on the appropriate connection (Figure 21.26). The radically more efficient switches now dominate the marketplace, although you'll still see lots of hubs in service throughout the world.

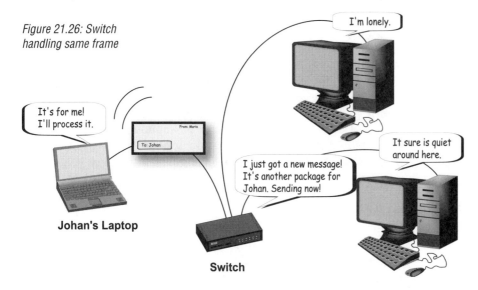

Figure 21.26: Switch handling same frame

Johan's Laptop

Switch

Wireless Components

It isn't always practical to string network cabling to every location where you need a network connection. Luckily, the bright boys and girls of networking engineering have come up with a variety of wireless methods to create the connection between devices on the network.

Older devices use a point-to-point connection with infrared light (Figure 21.27). You'll find this in communication between two PDAs, for example, and on some old laptops and printers.

Newer devices, such as Bluetooth and WiFi, use radio signals to send and receive information. Bluetooth can be used for networking, although you're more likely to see it used to connect peripherals like mice and keyboards wirelessly to a desktop computer (Figure 21.28).

Figure 21.27: Infrared

WiFi networks have invaded the United States! They're everywhere you look these days and almost every portable computer comes with some version of the technology for connecting wirelessly to LANs and WANs. The most common implementation of WiFi devices replaces the switch on the typical LAN with a combination of switch and *wireless access point* (*WAP*) (Figure 21.29). Landlocked devices continue to plug into Ethernet cables, but the switch/WAP also sends out a signal inviting WiFi-enabled devices to connect to the network as well (Figure 21.30).

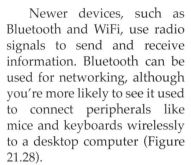

Figure 21.28: Bluetooth base device, keyboard, and mouse

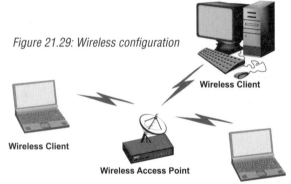

Figure 21.29: Wireless configuration

Wireless Client

Wireless Client

Wireless Access Point

Wireless Client

Figure 21.30: WiFi hardware

Modems and Dial-up

You can connect a computer to a network through a telephone line and a device called a *modem*, short for modulator/demodulator. Such a connection requires software, of course, and some kind of server on the other end to pick up the phone call. There's one issue that needs to be addressed and overcome before dial-up networking works: telephone lines use analog signals for the final connection to your house; computers use digital signals.

Analog Versus Digital

When you map a sound wave, you get an analog signal, meaning the wave goes up and down in a smooth flow, like a sine wave. With a digital signal, in contrast, you get hard 1s and 0s connected together into a pattern that makes sense to computers. Because the sound of your voice creates an analog sound wave, telephone technology naturally began with the intent to capture that wave and transfer it down a wire.

Stick a computer in place of a telephone, though, and you've got to have a device that can take the computer's digital signal and translate that into an analog signal to go over the phone line. On the other end, of course, you need a device that can read an analog signal and translate it into a digital signal. Modems handle the chore of translating (Figure 21.32). Software, such as Dial-up Networking in Windows, takes care of the interface between you and your modem (Figure 21.33).

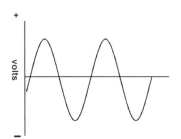

Figure 32: Modem modulating and demodulating fromdigital to analog and back again

Figure 21.31: Analog and digital signals

Perils of Pauline: Benefits, Risks, and Security

A network can enhance your computing experience greatly, but it can also invite risks to your data that would have been unimaginable in a non-networked computer. This section talks about benefits and risks, and what you—or a *network administrator*, someone in charge of configuring, maintaining, and defending the network——need to do to make a network secure.

Upside of Network Computing

Networks offer many benefits over standalone computing in several somewhat-overlapping categories:

- Enhanced communication and collaboration

- Easier sharing of files and resources

- Lower costs because of the sharing

- Easier management of machines in the network

Figure 21.33: DUN

Communication is pretty straightforward. You can e-mail your friends, family, and co-workers while sipping café au lait from a bistro in Paris, even if they live and work back home in Kansas (Figure 21.34). With the joys of Windows Messenger and other instant messaging programs your computer can alert you when your friends come online and you can send them a quick hello, any time of day or night.

Figure 21.34: Instant message

Communication leads to collaboration, enabling you to work and play with others over a network. Rather than simply e-mailing to say hello, you could send your next best-selling manuscript to your agent in Los Angeles from your secret hideaway in Tahiti. You can smack your best friend in an online game when he's 3000 miles away (Figure 21.35). You can work on a project with five other people, all of whom live in different cities. Only your imagination limits the possibilities here!

Networks enable you to share resources, such as files, folders, printers, and scanners. Plus you can access resources shared by

Figure 21.35: World of Warcraft online game

others. This leads to lower costs of operation in some ways. If you have ten people in your class, all of whom need to print something, you could share a single printer among all ten computers. Sure beats buying one for every desk!

Finally, grouping computers into a network enables centralized control over certain aspects of those computers. One computer can be designated as a file server, for example, or a print server. You can create a *workgroup* or domain for all the users and require proper passwords and login, thus enhancing security. This might immediately make you wonder: why security? Let's look at the downside of network computing.

Downside of Network Computing

Creating a computer network can add cost and cause security problems. The additional costs for servers, cables, and network cards can add up; you've also got a human cost—someone's got to handle the administration of network resources, and other folks need to maintain the network and fix problems. Network hardware or software failure is also a hazard that must be considered. If the network crashes, no one will be able to use it.

Finally, opening up a folder full of your data onto a network of any size creates a gaping security hole. Only your vigilance and forethought will stop a hacker or thief from grabbing or deleting your files. Just being on the Internet can create huge problems too, with the many viruses and evildoers out there running rampant.

Weighing the downside versus the upside in networking tips the balance in favor of networking, but you have to implement and maintain security. The life you save might be your computer's!

Security

In 1999 a person hacked into the networks of NASA and the Department of Defense at the Pentagon. The hacker downloaded $2 million worth of software that runs the International Space Station. He also got into the U.S. government's network, which monitors threats from nuclear and biological weapons all over the world. These networks had to be shut down for several weeks for repair—and just who had hacked into them? A 15-year-old boy in Florida was the culprit. He became the first juvenile to spend time in jail for computer crimes in the United States, and he also had to write a letter of apology to the Secretary of Defense. The Pentagon chief made him write "I will not hack the Pentagon" 500 times as well.

Security on a network is a key issue these days, but the term needs defining. *Security* refers to everything that can be done to make sure that data stored in a computer cannot be looked at, changed, or taken by anyone who shouldn't have access. Most security measures involve *data encryption* (when data is intentionally jumbled and unreadable without a mechanism to decode it) and *passwords* (private phrases or words that give a particular user a unique access to a particular program or network).

Servers enforce security by requiring users to enter a valid password, a process called *authentication*. Once they're on the network, different users will be able to access different parts of the network. *Authorization* is when a network administrator determines what level of access you have based on who you are. You and your teacher may both be able to get into your school's network, for example, but only your teacher can get to the screen where he or

Networking

I've touted some of the advantages to networking, but certainly haven't hit them all. What projects can you think of that could be enhanced by networking? What about collaboration on a project?

COMPUTER LITERACY: YOUR TICKET TO IC³ CERTIFICATION

she changes grades.

Authentication and authorization protect networks by making sure people get on the right way, but there are still lots of other threats. There are computer viruses, dangerous programs, and hackers. This is why firewalls are needed (Figure 21.36).

In the ancient days before computers, the term firewall applied only to walls in actual buildings and homes. Firewalls are fireproof walls that keep fires from spreading from one room to another. In the computer world, a *firewall* is a hardware device or software program that keeps bad stuff—such as viruses and identity theft software—from entering a network, then spreading from one computer to another (Figure 21.37).

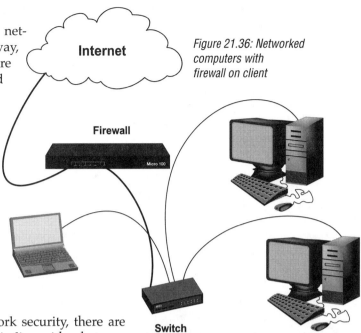

Figure 21.36: Networked computers with firewall on client

Principle of Least Access (PoLA)

Outside of the fundamental principles of network security, there are additional "layers" of network security that fall in line with what some have termed the *Principle of Least Access* (PoLA). This requires network administrators to take every measure possible to shut everyone out of all aspects of a network to which they shouldn't have access (Figure 21.38).

Let's look at an example of PoLA in action. Almost every item of software installed on a network originally has low security settings. Vendors set their software that way so people won't call them, accusing them of selling a broken application. It is dangerous for a network administrator to go with these low security settings and to try to gradually tighten access later. Users who have too much access never complain about it, but they certainly complain if you take away what they've gotten used to being able to do. Network administrators must make sure they optimize all of the security features of programs upon installation, before the users get into the mix.

The PoLA dictates having a sound network use policy (a set of network rules) that paves the way for educating and managing users. Organizations may not create a policy when they first start using a computer network, but circumstances almost always arise which make one necessary. If an employee at a company hacks the company Web site and damages it, for example, that company would have dif-

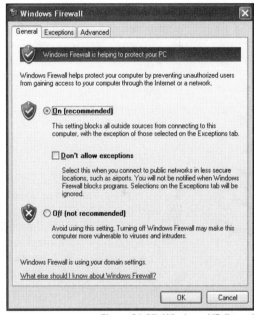

Figure 21.37: Windows XP firewall

ficulty investigating and prosecuting the employee if they didn't have a policy forbidding such activity.

The PoLA is not just about restricting your own users, but it is also about keeping bad programs out of your network. All networks have anti-virus software, but a network administrator can't just set it and forget it. Anti-virus software must be updated regularly to look out for new and more dangerous

Figure 21.38: Locking it down

Servers and Clients

■ You'll find two types of computers in most networks: servers and clients. Servers manage network resources (such as printers), provide central storage of files, and provide services for the users (such as having the e-mail server send your e-mail). Clients access those shared resources.

Network Machines

■ Clients on a network are generally microcomputers running Windows or Mac OS, although you'll run into Linux clients from time to time. Other devices, such as PDAs and mobile phones, can be clients as well.

■ Server computers come in quite a variety, from supercomputers, mainframes, and minicomputers all the way down to microcomputers. The operating systems vary for servers as well, with many companies making versions of Linux and UNIX; Microsoft has several server-specific versions of Windows, such as Windows Server 2003, and Apple has a version of the Mac OS dedicated to serving, the appropriately named Macintosh OS X Server.

Creating Your Network

■ Networks come in a couple of types. Local area networks (LANs) usually involve only a few computers, while wide area networks (WANs) are composed of multiple LANs. The Internet is the biggest WAN of them all.

■ Computers connect to a network in one of three ways: directly wired to a LAN via a cable from the computer to a LAN port; wirelessly to the LAN; and via a telephone line, what's called dial-up networking. A typical network client has a network interface card (NIC) that connects to an Ethernet cable that connects to a central switch.

■ The *Ethernet* standard defines everything about modern network hardware, from the physical size and shape of the RJ-45 connector on the end of the network cable to the electrical signaling that enables a NIC to break a message down into little pieces, send them across the cable, and have the receiving NIC reassemble the pieces into a useful message.

■ Wireless networks use infrared or radio waves to connect to a network. Most WiFi networks use a combination switch and wireless access point to enable connectivity.

■ Modems enable computers to use regular analog phone lines to call in and connect to a network. Modems take digital signals and transform them into analog signals; receiving modems do the same process in reverse.

Benefits, Risks, and Security

■ Networks offer a number of benefits over standalone computing, including communication, collaboration, sharing, cost, and centralized management. Networks enable you to exchange information via e-mail and to work remotely on projects with other people. You can share files and folders on networks, and lower costs by centralizing some machines, such as a shared server. Finally, central management of networked computers can enhance security.

■ Networking computers together certainly adds both cost and risks. Dedicated server machines, cabling, and other network hardware can set you back; There's also a human cost for administration, maintenance, and troubleshooting. Sharing opens the door for thieves and hackers; being on the Internet makes you more susceptible to viruses and hacking as well.

■ Security measures must be implemented on networks. You can encrypt data, require passwords and login, thus authenticating and authorizing a particular user to access specific things on the network. Applying the Principle of Least Access (PoLA) to all users makes a lot of sense. Give users only the access that they need and not a drop more.

Key Terms

Authentication

Authorization

Client

Data encryption

Ethernet

Firewall

Frame

Hub

Internet

Intranet

Local area network (LAN)

Mainframe

Minicomputer

Modem

Network

Network administrator

Network resources

Node

Packet

Principle of Least Access (PoLA)

RJ-45

Security

Server

Supercomputer

Switch

Wide area network (WAN)

Wireless access point (WAP)

Workgroup

Key Term Quiz

Use the Key Terms list to complete the following sentences. Not all terms will be used.

1. Two or more LANs combine to form a _____.

2. A _____ system enables you to access resources shared on a server.

3. A _____ is anything important that uses information in a network (like the client computer or a printer or a server).

4. Jill connects to her company network through a regular telephone line. Her computer must use a _____ to dial the server.

5. A _____ is usually in a single building or group of nearby buildings.

6. Most nodes on modern networks connect to a _____ using a cable, rather than to a hub or directly to each other.

7. When a network administrator determines what level of access you have based on who you are, this is _____.

8. A _____ manages network resources, provides central storage of files, and provides services for the users.

9. The _____ requires network administrators taking every measure possible to shut everyone out of all aspects of a network to which they shouldn't have access.

10. A _____ is a hardware device or software program that keeps bad stuff from entering a network.

Multiple Choice Quiz

1. Which job title best describes people who make networks safe from hackers, thieves, and other bad guys?
   A. Network administrator
   B. Network security chief
   C. Network server
   D. Network client

2. Which term below describes a network that can include multiple LANs?
   A. Client
   B. Mainframe
   C. WAN
   D. Universal

3. Linus Torvalds, a programmer from Finland, created which operating system?
   A. Macintosh
   B. Linux
   C. Windows
   D. UNIX

4. Jill wants to add a server computer to her network as a file server. Which of the following would work? (Select all that apply.)
   A. Apple Macintosh OS X Server running on an Xserve G5 microcomputer
   B. Microsoft Windows Server 2003 running on an x86 microcomputer
   C. Microsoft Windows Server 2003 running on an Xserve G5 microcomputer
   D. Apple Macintosh Windows Server 2005 running on an Xserve G5 microcomputer

5. Cinderella wants to get a file from her stepmother's computer and put it on her own computer. Both are logged into the same palace network and can access the Internet. What has to happen first for Cinderella to access the file across the network?
   A. Her stepmother needs to share the folder that contains the file.
   B. Her stepmother must open her Ethernet sharing port.
   C. Her stepmother must share her Internet connection.
   D. Her stepmother needs to connect to Cinderella's computer.

6. _____ describes how servers enforce security by requiring users to enter a valid password.
   A. Data encryption
   B. Authorization
   C. Authentication
   D. Administration

7. Which term refers to everything that can be done to make sure that data stored in a computer cannot be looked at, changed, or taken by anyone who shouldn't have access?
   A. Authentication
   B. Authorization
   C. Security
   D. Log

8. Jack has a new Windows XP laptop with an Ethernet port and WiFi built in. How can he connect to Jill's network? (Select all that apply.)
   A. Plug an Ethernet cable into his laptop and into her Ethernet switch.
   B. Plug a WiFi cable into his laptop and into her WiFi switch.
   C. Connect wirelessly through her switch/WAP combo device.
   D. He cannot connect to Jill's network without buying additional hardware.

9. Which is a powerful multi-user computer considered to be the largest and most powerful type of computer that is widely used?
   A. Macintosh
   B. WAN
   C. Supercomputer
   D. Mainframe

10. An _____ is a private network that is a scaled-down version of the Internet for a very specific group of users.
    A. Intranet
    B. Extranet
    C. Virtual Private Network
    D. WAN

11. Which of the terms below is used when data is intentionally jumbled and unreadable without a mechanism to decode it?
    A. Password
    B. Switch
    C. Authentication
    D. Data encryption

12. _____ are handheld devices that can be configured to connect wirelessly to a network.
    A. Personal computers
    B. Workstations
    C. Firewalls
    D. Personal digital assistants (PDAs)

13. What advantage does a switch have over a hub?
    A. A switch enables you to connect wirelessly.
    B. A switch learns the network address of every computer attached to it and sends data only to the appropriate computer.
    C. A switch repeats the data received down every network cable attached to it.
    D. None. Hubs are better than switches.

14. Janina has three computers that she wants to network together. What does she stand to gain from doing so?
    A. She will see a big increase in her productivity.
    B. She can share folders on the machines and move files over the network among them.
    C. She can enhance the security of all three computers by linking them to the Internet.
    D. Nothing. Networking computers together costs too much money.

15. Jim has four computers that he wants to network together, but Ramona points out some of the downsides of networking. Which of the following might she have argued? (Select all that apply.)
    A. Jim will see a big decrease in his productivity.
    B. Sharing folders leads to big security problems.
    C. Networking computers together costs money for cables, a switch, and network cards.
    D. Networking his computers together will restrict his ability to e-mail.

Essay Questions

1. Your boss is thinking about networking the office computers together. Write a short essay that outlines some of the benefits of networking.

2. In a two- to three-paragraph essay, explain why you need a switch or a hub in a network. What is the difference between a switch and a hub?

3. Your boss is a little confused with some networking terms. Write a memo that defines the relationship between a server and a client and how they can be connected.

Projects

1. Create a poster board drawing of a network, including two clients, a printer, and a server.

2. Go to http://www.google.com and type in "network security" (including the quotation marks). Research the subject and write a one-page summary on the latest techniques and software used in today's world.

Network Communication and the Internet

"Isn't it funny – you hear a phone ringing and it could be anybody. A ringing phone has to be answered . . . doesn't it?"

– The Caller, *Phone Booth*

This chapter covers the following IC³ exam objectives:

- IC³-3   1.1.1   Identify terminology relating to telecommunications networks and the Internet

- IC³-3   1.2.1   Identify the different ways the telephone system is used to transmit information

- IC³-3   1.2.2   Identify that telecommunication devices such as modems convert information from analog to digital and digital to analog formats

- IC³-3   1.2.3   Identify the units used to measure data transmission rates, including bits per second (bps) and kilobytes per second (kbps)

- IC³-3   1.2.4   Identify the Internet as a "super network" of smaller computer networks and that the computers connect to the Internet via the "onramp" of a smaller computer network

- IC³-3   1.2.5   Identify the hardware and software required to connect to the Internet

- IC³-3   1.2.6   Identify different types of Internet connections and the advantages and disadvantages of each connection type (such as connection speed, cost, and reliability)

- IC³-3   1.2.7   Identify the roles and responsibilities of an Internet Service Provider (ISP)

The Internet spans the globe like a giant copper and glass web, connecting countries and cities and people, from Rome to Rio, from Beijing to Marrakech. You know from earlier chapters that computing devices come in a vast variety of shapes and sizes and run with operating systems as diverse as Windows XP and PalmOS. Given that variety plus the inescapable fact that humans touched by the Internet speak a bewildering 5000 different languages, how can we communicate successfully?

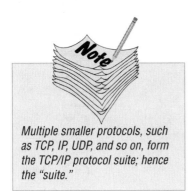

Multiple smaller protocols, such as TCP, IP, UDP, and so on, form the TCP/IP protocol suite; hence the "suite."

This chapter explores what it takes to connect and communicate over the Internet. We'll start with protocols and examine another global network—the telephone—and then look at the three types of Internet connections, dial-up, dedicated, and wireless. The chapter wraps up with a look at the programs that make all these connections—and communication—possible.

The Common Tongue

Computer networks have lots of pathways that send information back and forth. They can send it through the old-fashioned copper wires of telephone lines or through high-tech fiber optic lines that use tiny hairs of glass instead of copper. Computer networks can even send information to each other through radio waves and lasers.

The major issues for computer networks have never been which pathway you use to send information, but how you send the information so that it goes to the right place—and that it is readable by the network to which it is sent. These issues became a big problem for the U.S. military. The Navy bought their computer stuff from one company, and the Army from somebody else. They couldn't send information back and forth, since these different systems had different ways of treating information. The United States Department of Defense (DoD) solved these problems by developing a set of commands and controls for the networks to use, what's called the "TCP/IP protocol suite." That's quite a mouthful, no? Let's break the phrase down into its components.

In the mundane world of princes and presidents, *protocols* determine how the leaders and their staffs handle meetings. Who enters the room first, the prince or the president? Who stands up first and what sort of greeting should occur, a handshake or a hug? For that matter, what language should they speak? Following protocols ensures that both parties are comfortable, won't insult each other, and can focus on the important thing – communicating.

The *Transmission Control Protocol/Internet Protocol* (*TCP/IP*) protocol suite does the same thing for networks, providing a common set of rules and guidelines for electrical signals, packaging of information, and so on. The Internet uses TCP/IP, which makes the protocol suite the common tongue of the computer world.

As its name suggests, the Transmission Control Protocol (TCP) controls the sending and receiving of information. Two computers communicating use TCP to make a connection and handle the flow of data between them (Figure 22.1).

Computers use the Internet Protocol (IP) to determine packaging and labeling of data. When you send an e-mail to someone, it doesn't just go out in a big blob of information. Your e-mail is neatly cut up and packaged into bits of information that are all the same size. Your operating system uses IP to determine how to package

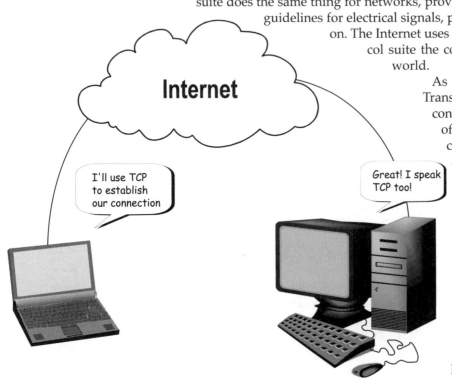

Figure 22.1: TCP at work

the e-mail, and the operating system on the receiving computer knows how to unpack the information (and how to put it back together) so it can be read like a normal e-mail because it too follows IP.

But how does your message know to go to the right place? Just like an old-fashioned letter will have the destination address and a return address on the envelope, your operating system uses IP to put a numerical destination and return address—called *IP addresses*—onto the packets of information that make up your e-mail (Figure 22.2).

IP addresses follow specific conventions. Most commonly, IP addresses have four sets of numbers ranging from 0-255, separated by periods, like this: 192.168.1.52. Part of the IP address defines your network—called the *network ID*, while the other part describes your *node*—the computer you use to access the Internet. That's called the *host ID*. No two machines on a network can share the same IP address, just like you wouldn't want two houses in the same city to share a street name and number.

Marco's school has 40 computers linked together into a network. His computer has the IP address of 192.168.7.23. All the other computers in the school have the same network ID—192.168.7—but have a different host ID, from 1-40. Network IDs become very important when you connect two or more networks, as you'll see shortly.

Telephone Systems

The (almost) worldwide telephone network provided the first method for computer communication. Although not ideal for computers, the fact that telephone wires ran all over the place gave inventors incentive to create a way for computers to talk, almost literally. To understand how computers use telephone lines to send information, you need an understanding of telephone systems.

Telephones work by translating the sound waves coming out of your mouth—"Hi Mom!"—into electrical signals that get sent along a copper wire. The receiving phone then makes those electrical signals into something resembling your voice. The recipient can then respond—"Hello, dear; need money again?"—and the process repeats. See Figure 22.3.

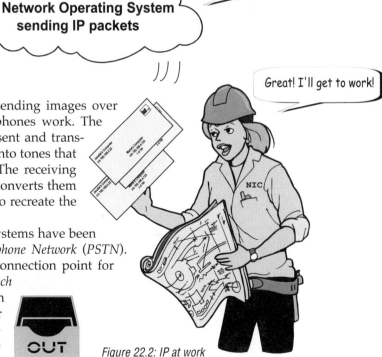

Interestingly, fax machines—used for sending images over telephone lines—work the same way telephones work. The sending fax machine scans the page to be sent and translates the black and white parts of the page into tones that then get translated into electrical signals. The receiving fax machine receives the electrical signals, converts them into tones, and then uses that information to recreate the image.

All of the world's different telephone systems have been linked together in the *Public Switched Telephone Network* (*PSTN*). Local telephone networks have a central connection point for local telephone lines. This *neighborhood switch* connects to a central city switch which in turn connects to other cities and eventually other countries. The worldwide telephone network is thus a collection of smaller telephone

Figure 22.2: IP at work

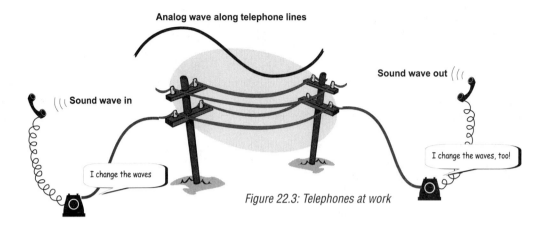

Figure 22.3: Telephones at work

networks (Figure 22.4). The PSTN sets telephone standards, so that your phone can send and receive calls to any country in the world—for all government owned phone networks as well as the private ones owned by companies.

Originally, all the telephone communication used the same technology. The electrical signals took the form of an *analog* wave, but this required a direct connection between two telephones. Old switchboard operators had to connect two phones together by literally plugging a cable between two telephone lines. Figure 22.5 shows an old switchboard, just like in an old Cary Grant movie.

Once telephone networks became more sophisticated, telephone companies started using digital signals for the connections between the switches. Using the same kind of 1s and 0s as computers to send signals created much more flexibility, because it removes the need for a direct connection.

Wrap your mind around this concept. If you call your mother on the other side of the country today, your voice gets broken into little digital packets at the neighborhood switch almost instantaneously, just as if you were sending an e-mail to her. They get reassembled at her neighborhood switch and she'll hear something hopefully resembling your voice when you say something (Figure 22.6). Pretty wild stuff!

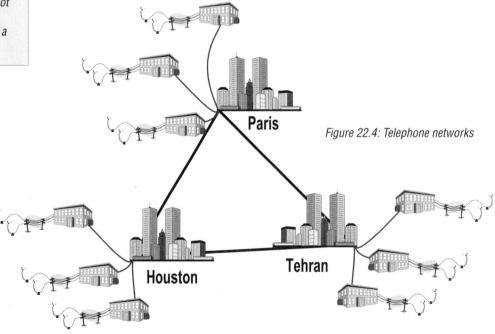

Figure 22.4: Telephone networks

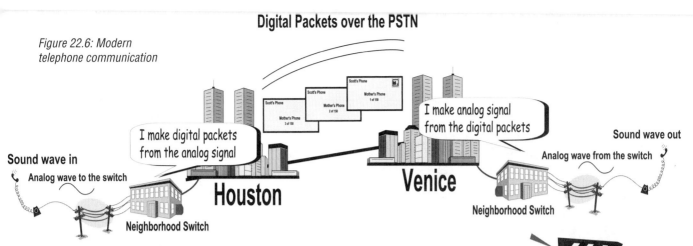

Figure 22.6: Modern telephone communication

Digital Packets over the PSTN

Types of Telephones

There are two types of telephones, standard and cellular (Figure 22.7). A standard telephone has a physical phone line that leads all the way back to the phone company. A cellular phone has no physical wire, but rather sends its messages in radio signals. Cell phones can communicate over a wide area because they have many clusters, or "cells," of transmitters and antennas in different geographical areas to pick up and relay phone signals. A cellular phone is really just a radio transmitter and receiver.

Throwing Computers into the Mix

You know from many earlier chapters in this book that computers use digital signals—strings of 1s and 0s—to do all processing. Inventors had to come up with some way to turn digital signals coming out of the PC into analog electrical signals like those used on the telephone lines. Thus was born the modem (Figure 22.8).

From its humble beginning as a tool to communicate from one end of Alexander Graham Bell's lab to the other, the world-wide telephone network developed into an amazing tool that enables you to send sound, pictures, and data nearly anywhere on the planet. But you want more, right? Let's turn back to the other worldwide network, the Internet.

The Internet

Hundreds of thousands of smaller networks connected together form the Internet. People often think of the Internet as some monolithic, centralized *thing*, but that perception couldn't be farther from the truth. Like the worldwide telephone network, the Internet is a "super network" of smaller networks.

The designers of the Internet wanted to make certain that nothing could stop the flow of communication, not even a nuclear attack, so they specified a highly *decentralized* network with multiple connections between the various computers. The central heart of the Internet—called the *backbone*—consists of many university, corporate, and government networks, connected together via thick bundles of glass filaments, called *fiber optic cables*. *Routers* provide the connection points between the networks and determine the route for a data packet to take from the source network to the destination network. Figure 22.9 illustrates the Internet backbone.

Modems

You know from Chapter 21, "Network Basics," that modems transform digital signals into analog signals and vice versa through a process called modulation and demodulation. Refer back to that chapter and see if you can answer these questions. What does an analog signal look like? Do modems need software to do their modem thing? If so, what's the name of one such software?

Figure 22.5: Ancient telephone switchboard

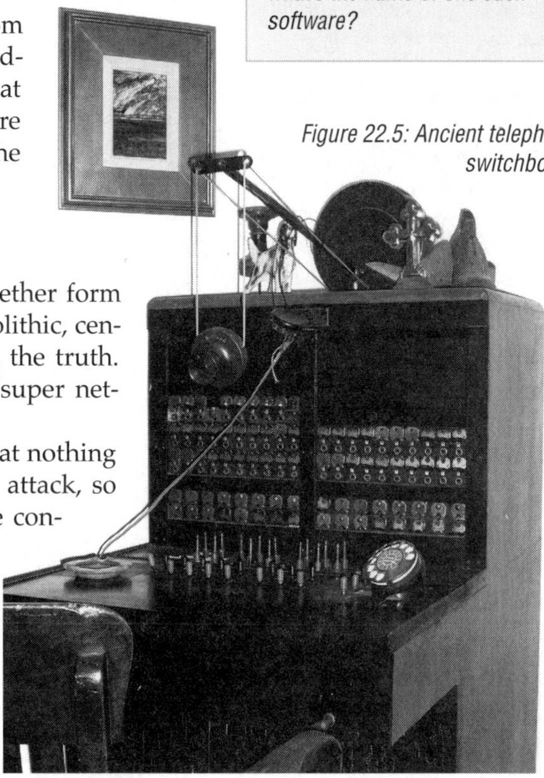

Figure 22.7: Standard and cellular telephones

Figure 22.8: Modem

Origins of the Internet

In 1962, a professor at MIT named J.C.R. Licklider wrote a series of memos trying to convince people to build a "galactic network" of computers where everyone could share files and programs. He went on to head DARPA (Defense Advanced Research Projects Agency), which is part of the United States Department of Defense. It took a little poking and prodding, but eventually his belief in the power of networking computers led to the Advanced Research Projects Agency, and thus to developing the first WAN (wide area network).

The ARPA connected its local area computers to the local computer networks of universities that assisted it in research projects, beginning with UCLA and Stanford. The WAN was appropriately called ARPANET and, as you might have guessed, it developed into the Internet we all know and love.

It is interesting that the vision of a mathematical genius in the early '60s has led to the ability of a villager in Malaysia to download Country & Western songs at three in the morning. One thing that is certain is that Professor Licklider would be thrilled to know that almost any computer, and most handheld devices, can be made to access the Internet with just some very simple software and hardware requirements.

Routers know the destination of packets of data because routers use TCP/IP, the common tongue of the Internet. They read the Network ID of each data packet and send the data packet by the shortest route they know about to its destination (Figure 22.10).

The multiple connections between the backbone networks offer great resiliency for the Internet in times of crisis. If one route goes down, the routers update their maps of the Internet and re-route traffic another way (Figure 22.11).

Making the Connection: ISP, Dial-up, Dedicated, Wireless, LAN

All of this wonderful technology doesn't do much for you if you're not on—or connected to—one of those university, corporate, or government computer networks. To get your computer to connect to the Internet requires some sort of intermediary network with a router you can tap into that in turn connects to the Internet. An *Internet Service Provider* (*ISP*) leases connections to the Internet

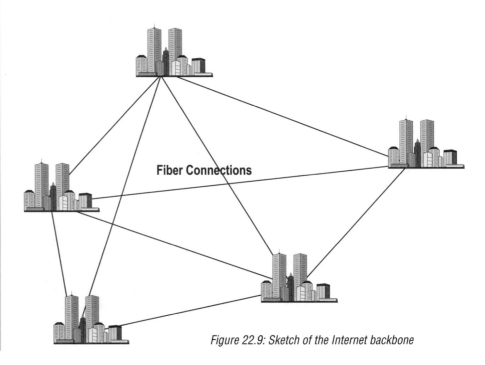

Fiber Connections

Figure 22.9: Sketch of the Internet backbone

from one of the backbone networks and in turn, rents a portion of those connections to you. An ISP acts as your *gateway* to the Internet (Figure 22.12).

Plus, you need the hardware, software, and connectivity technology to establish a link between your computer and the ISP. You've got to have some kind of network device on your computer, like a modem or network card; a cable or radio transmitter that enables that network device to access the world outside your door; and programs to make that hardware go, like Dial-up Networking in Windows and TCP/IP installed. Figure 22.13 shows a laptop with a wireless NIC and software running to facilitate the connection.

ISP Roles and Responsibilities

ISPs come in a variety of shapes and sizes and different companies offer different types of Internet connectivity for you. All ISPs enable you to connect to the Internet. Some offer only dial-up service, where you connect via a modem and then move slowly through the Internet. Others offer dedicated connections and blazingly fast Internet connectivity.

Figure 22.10: Router determines best route to server matching the Network ID of data packet

A router is usually a very specialized machine that just does routing, although you'll sometimes see high-end PCs functioning as routers by using routing software.

The Internet, like the telephone network, is actually a collection of smaller networks all communicating together because of standardized Internet guidelines and procedures.

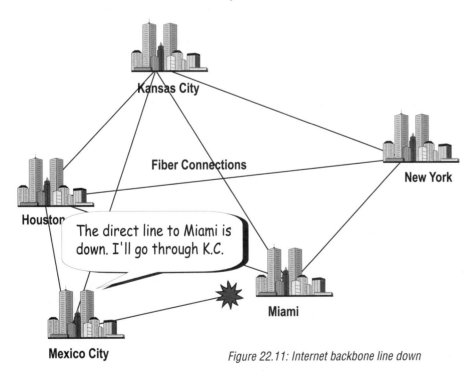

Figure 22.11: Internet backbone line down

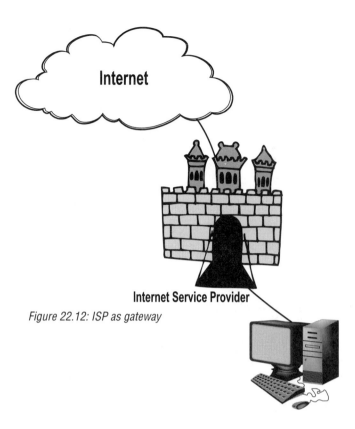

Figure 22.12: ISP as gateway

Figure 22.13: Essentials for connecting to the Internet

ISPs provide your onramp to the Internet, but they offer (or should offer) a lot more than that for your money. ISPs maintain the hardware and software that enables you to connect. The better ones provide superb technical support. This is true of both the big ISPs, such as NetZero, and the tiny ones. Finally, the ISP is responsible for protecting its portion of the Internet free from threats such as viruses and illegal activity. Note that this latter provision does not protect users from themselves. If you click on a Web site that dumps a ton of evil spyware on your computer, that's your own fault! What it means is that you can rest assured that the ISP won't sneak programs onto your computer or scan your drives for content.

Most markets provide you with many choices for ISPs, although when you get away from the cities your choices dwindle. In Houston, Texas, for example, you can find many ISPs, including local dial-up-only outfits to the big national companies, such as EarthLink, AOL, and NetZero. The picturesque San Miguel de Allende, in contrast, has only a couple and they're dial-up only. For the most part, price and package determine the choice of an ISP, so let's look at that next: dial-up, dedicated, and wireless, and then wrap up with a related discussion of LAN connectivity.

Dial-Up Connections

The most common network connection consists of three pieces: a modem, a working telephone line, and an ISP. The modem enables the computer to communicate via phone lines. The phone line provides the link between the modem and the computers at the ISP. The ISP computers connect to the Big Kahuna of all networks, the Internet (Figure 22.14). Properly installed and configured, the modem-telephone line-ISP connection enables you to surf, shop, and otherwise explore Web sites hosted by computers all over the world.

For this process to work, a great deal of setup is required. You have to

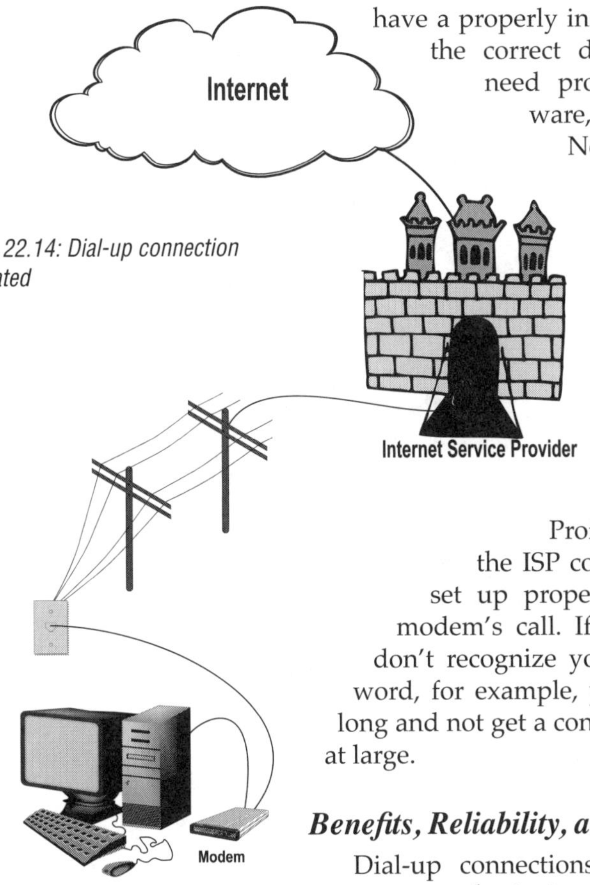

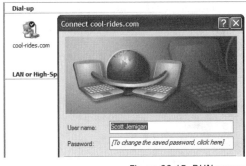

Figure 22.14: Dial-up connection illustrated

Internet

Internet Service Provider

Modem

have a properly installed modem with the correct drivers loaded. You need properly set up software, such as Dial-up Networking (DUN) in Windows. Your ISP gives you the configuration information, such as telephone number, user name, and password. Figure 22.15 shows the basic DUN configuration screen in Windows XP Professional. Of course, the ISP computers need to be set up properly to receive your modem's call. If the ISP computers don't recognize your name and password, for example, you can call all day long and not get a connection to the world at large.

Benefits, Reliability, and Disadvantages

Dial-up connections provide the least expensive method of getting your computer onto the Internet. Prices in the typical metropolitan area in the United States, for example, average $9.99 – $14.99 US per month. The technology has been around for a decade or more and works, smoothly and easily. So, what's the catch?

Dial-up connections also provide the *slowest* type of connection to the Internet, a bottleneck that continues to get worse as more Web sites incorporate multimedia content such as movies, Flash animations, and other things. How slow is slow? Let's turn to the numbers so this makes sense.

Data Transmission Rates

Modems send and receive information (data) across the Internet in measurements of bits per second (*bps*). For example, a 28.8 modem transfers data at up to 28,800 bits per second. One *Kbps* is 1,000 bits per second, so that same 28.8 modem would transfer data at up to 28.8 Kbps. One *Mbps* is 1,000,000 bits per second. You are going to see the terms bps, Kbps, and Mbps mentioned in the discussion of all of the different ways to access the Internet—with the larger numbers meaning faster data transmission rates.

Figure 22.15: DUN screen

Dial-up Rates

Numbers without context mean very little, right? Here's the scoop about dial-up. First, the fastest dial-up download speed you'll ever get is around 53 Kbps. More commonly, especially outside the big cities in the U.S., you'll get closer to 26 Kbps consistently. A glance at www.microsoft.com in the latter half of 2005 shows that it would take around 25 seconds at the fastest dial-up speed (at 56.6

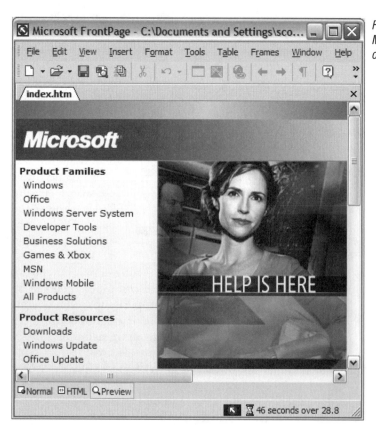

Figure 22.16: Microsoft homepage open in FrontPage

Kbps, the theoretical maximum dial-up speed) and a whopping **46 seconds** at 28.8 Kbps to open up the homepage (Figure 22.16).

Although dial-up speeds served us well in the 20th Century when the Web offered relatively simple pages of text and graphics, people use the Internet today for a variety of much more complex things, such as international phone calls, video conferencing, and multiplayer gaming. To make convenient use of some of these higher-end features and the rich, multimedia sites on the Web, you need a dedicated, high-speed connection.

Dedicated Connections

A dedicated connection gives your computer or network access to the Internet through a single high-speed connection. It's is always on, versus, say, a dial-up connection, where you have to sit and wait for the connection to go through. It's also much faster. Two technologies dominate the dedicated connection field: cable and DSL.

Both technologies require the same sorts of equipment on your PC: you need an Ethernet network interface card (NIC) installed with drivers loaded and software set up to make the connection between your computer and the ISP. Many motherboards come with an Ethernet connection built in; those that don't have a card that fits inside the computer case to provide network connectivity. Figure 22.17 shows a NIC installed in a PC.

Windows, Macintosh OS X, and the various versions of Linux come with software built in to support Internet connectivity. This means, as you probably have suspected already, that all three operating systems support TCP/IP natively; all speak the common language of the Internet. Figure 22.18 shows the Network Connections in a Windows XP PC with an Ethernet NIC installed. Figure 22.19 shows the configuration screen for that NIC, with TCP/IP installed.

Network Card

Figure 22.17: NIC

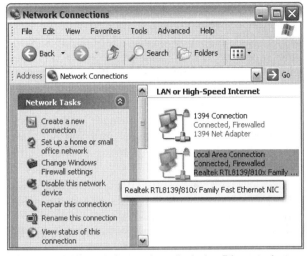

Figure 22.18: Network Connections displaying Ethernet adapter

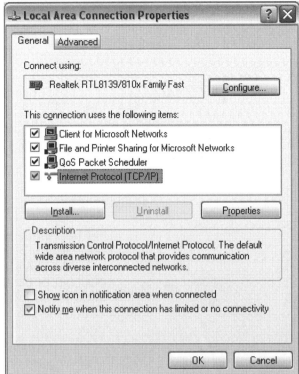

Figure 22.19: TCP/IP installed

Cable

Cable connections use regular cable TV cables to serve up lightning-fast speeds. Cable blows dial-up out the window, with upload speeds of around 384 Kbps and a phenomenal 2-5 Mbps download. That same Microsoft homepage on cable that took upwards of half a minute to download via dial-up? Almost instantaneous download!

The cable connects to a *cable modem* that then connects to a NIC in your PC via an Ethernet cable. Figure 22.20 shows a typical cable setup. The cable TV companies take advantage of the fact that their cable TV signals occupy only a fraction of the capacity of the cables running into your home. Cable modems aren't actually "modems" at all in the sense that the signals they send and receive are entirely digital, but because they perform a similar function, they go by the same name.

Cable and DSL collectively are called broadband connections, which refers to the fact that you can do more than one thing over the same wire or cable, like watch TV and surf the Internet.

DSL

Digital Subscriber Line (*DSL*) uses your telephone line as its pipeline, but it does so in a very clever way. The details are quite technical, but basically DSL exploits the fact that standard copper telephone lines can handle a much greater range of frequencies, or *bandwidth*, than what is needed to transmit your voice during phone calls. DSL uses this extra bandwidth capacity to send data over the telephone wires without disturbing

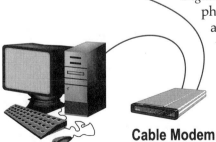

Figure 22.20: Cable connections

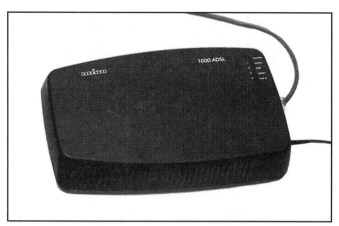

Figure 22.21: A DSL receiver

their ability to carry voice conversations. This enables you to use a single phone line for both normal voice communication as you've always done, and at the same time, for digital data transmission between your computer and your ISP or other computers on the Internet.

DSL connections to ISPs use a standard telephone line with special equipment on each end to create always-on Internet connections at blindingly fast speeds, especially when compared with analog dial-up connections.

Service levels vary around the U.S., but the typical upload speed is ~ 256 Kbps, while download speed comes in at a very sweet ~ .5-2 Mbps!

DSL requires very little setup from a user standpoint. A tech comes to the house to install a NIC in the Internet-bound PC and drop off a *DSL receiver* (often called a "DSL modem") (Figure 22.21). The receiver connects to the Ethernet NIC and to the telephone line; the telephone line goes to special hardware at the neighborhood telephone switch and from there to the Internet (Figure 22.22). The tech (or the user, if knowledgeable) then configures the TCP/IP protocol options for the NIC to match the settings demanded by the DSL provider, and that's about it! Within moments, you're surfing at blazing speeds. You don't need a second telephone line. You don't need to wear a special propeller hat or anything.

The only bad thing about DSL is that your house has to be within a fairly short distance from a main phone service switching center—the neighborhood switch you read about earlier in this chapter—something like 18,000 feet. This pretty much stops everybody but inner city dwellers from having access to DSL service.

Dial-up, Cable, or DSL?

At this point in the discussion, students often wonder which is better, cable or DSL. For that matter, why would you ever choose dial-up in an increasingly high-speed world? Three factors affect your choice. First, cable and DSL generally cost a lot more than dial-up. Cable is the most expensive at ~$50 US, but offers the highest download speeds. DSL sits in a nice sweet spot between cable and dial-up in both cost and

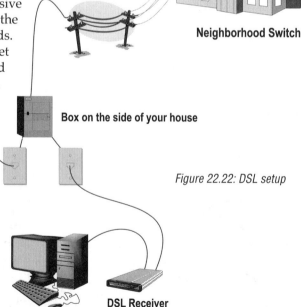

Figure 22.22: DSL setup

Line Filters

To use a DSL line and have voice communication that's not static-filled at the same time, you need to install a simple line filter to the voice-only telephone ports in your house. These come standard with most DSL packages, often in the same box as the DSL modem.

speed. Second, you can get cable in every metropolitan area (in the United States, at least), but it's not available in many rural settings. DSL coverage is even more limited, with availability limited even within cities. You can get dial-up almost anywhere. Third, cable and DSL offer extra inducements. If you have a TV tuner card in your PC, you can use the same cable connection (with a splitter) to watch TV on your PC. With DSL, on the other hand, you can use your existing phone lines and not worry about installing cable or any other equipment. Both DSL and cable modem

Internet connections can be used by two or more computers if they are part of a LAN, including those in a home.

Wireless Connection

Up to now, we have discussed ways of accessing the Internet through physical connections, but the latest trend is wireless technology, which has no physical connection at all. The term most often used to describe this is *WiFi*, short for Wireless Fidelity. When you hear the term *wireless*, you obviously get that there is no physical wire (like a telephone line), but beyond that, the signal is sent out between computers in radio waves. The term fidelity means that a piece of electronic equipment accurately produces the sound or image of its input signal.

For a computer to send or receive a wireless signal, it needs a WiFi card, which is a piece of hardware that fits into your computer. It takes the information you want to transmit and turns it into a signal, then sends it out to the world (similar to what a modem does to send a signal over telephone lines). Figure 22.13, earlier in the chapter, showed a typical wireless NIC plugged into a laptop. Figure 22.24 shows a USB wireless NIC that you would more commonly plug into a desktop computer.

The wireless signal connects to a WiFi router and from there goes to an ISP, just like a wired connection. In fact, current technology requires the router to connect via a wire, precisely alike a wired DSL receiver or cable modem connects. You'll most often find wireless and dedicated high-speed of some sort combined, as illustrated in Figure 22.25.

Just as with dial-up and dedicated connections, wireless connections require you to set up software on your computer to communicate properly with the devices (NIC and router) and with the ISP. This can get quite complicated, unfortunately, making wireless connectivity a hassle for a lot of folks. I have faith that as the industry matures, however, that wireless will sweep the marketplace.

Benefits of using WiFi

The number one benefit of WiFi technology is its increased mobility. If you have WiFi in your house, you could use your computer on the sofa, at the kitchen table, or in the garage. For companies with thousands of employees in one building who no longer have to cable everyone together, the time and cost savings can be massive.

T1

Many businesses use a dedicated connection called T1, because T1 offers an almost direct-to-the-Internet backbone connection. Plus, unlike cable and DSL, if you're willing to pay the price, any business can get T1 connectivity. No waiting around for us! A T1 line provides transmission at 1.544 Mbps, which is roughly 60 times more data than a typical residential modem. Figure 22.23 shows the Microsoft homepage shown previously, but set to download via T1—wow!

Expense is something to consider when deciding whether or not to get a T1. Its speed is guaranteed at any distance, but the farther you are the more expensive the T1. Generally speaking, the cost of a T1 ranges about $400 - $800 per month.

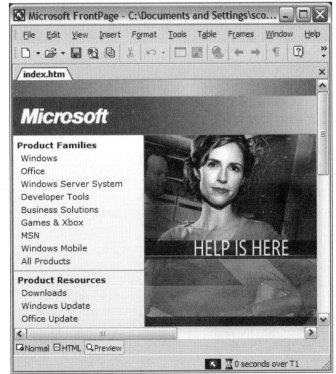

Figure 22.23: Microsoft homepage open in FrontPage

Figure 22.24: WiFi USB device

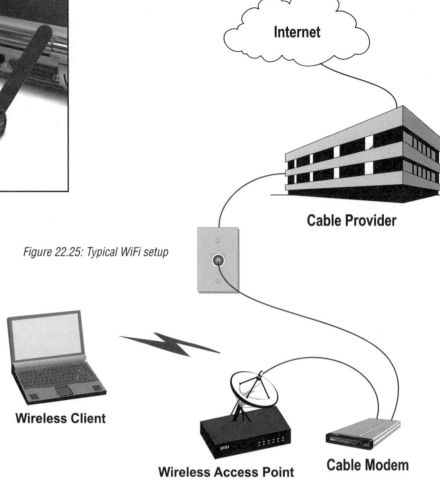

Figure 22.25: Typical WiFi setup

Internet

Cable Provider

Wireless Client

Wireless Access Point

Cable Modem

You can connect two WiFi-enabled computers directly and share information, a feature called ad hoc mode, which can be quite convenient in a pinch. Ad hoc mode does not get you onto the Internet, though; it's just for direct connections.

Finding Hotspots

Type http://www.wifi411.com/ in your Web browser, then type in your ZIP code or the ZIP code of the nearest big city to you. If you are outside the US, type in your country and city. How many wireless Internet hotspots are near where you live? Which one looks like the one you would most likely use if your had a laptop with a WiFi card? Why would you use that location?

Disadvantages of WiFi

- **Interference**
  Since WiFi equipment uses radio waves, it can be vulnerable to interference from household devices like microwaves and cordless phones. It is best to put some distance between these appliances and your WiFi equipment.

- **Updating your older computer**
  If your computer isn't equipped for WiFi, you will have to buy and install a WiFi card that works with your PC.

- **Privacy concerns**
  You may be wondering whether information you send wirelessly from your laptop can be intercepted. It can be, and it's also possible for hackers to use your access point to get on the Internet. For these reasons, all WiFi networks and devices include some way to encrypt data and provide a way to control access to your network. It is very important to be sure to configure these security measures when you set up your network.

PDAs and Mobile Phones

WiFi on a portable or desktop computer is not the only wireless game in town. Increasingly, people use cell phones and WiFi-enabled personal digital assistants (PDAs) to access the Internet. To make it work, you need both networking hardware and applications—built-in and preloaded or aftermarket add-ons—and an ISP. Many mobile phone companies offer Internet access for an extra fee. PDAs use the same sorts of ISPs as your regular desktop and laptop computers use. Figure 22.26 shows an e-mail application running on a Compaq iPaq PDA.

What's my Motivation?

LAN Connections

Thus far in this chapter you've read about individual connections to the Internet: dial-up with a modem, dedicated through cable or DSL, and wireless with WiFi. Increasingly, though, people have multiple computers at home or at the office, connected together into a local area network (LAN) via a switch or hub, and want all their computers to have Internet access (Figure 22.27). It would be wildly annoying to have to install multiple phone lines or cables and pay for multiple accounts with an ISP, so many folks have swapped their simple switch or hub for a combination switch and router.

Figure 22.26: Checking e-mail on a PDA

The hardware routers have two sections—a multiple-port switch for the LAN, and a single Ethernet port for the wide area network (WAN) connection—as in the big WAN, the Internet. You plug computers into the switch and then run the WAN connection to the cable or DSL modem. The vast majority of these multifunction boxes also add wireless connectivity—so a combined switch, router, and *wireless access point (WAP)* all rolled into one device. Sweet! Figure 22.28 shows a typical setup.

Making Your Wireless Network Secure?

So you just decided to get wireless Internet access at your house. It sure would be nice to use your computer anywhere you want. The funny thing is that the Access Point the Internet Service Provider gave you puts out a fairly strong signal. More than likely, it is strong enough for neighbors with a WiFi card to use it to get on the Internet. This is bad for a number of reasons. First, if they download a lot of large files, they will dramatically slow down your Internet service. Second, if they download something illegal and the government is monitoring their activity, it will appear as if it is you who is breaking the law. While this may seem like an un-neighborly thing to do, there are no current laws in the United States about using someone else's WiFi signal without their permission. The responsibility rests with you, having the access point, to keep the bad guys out by using all of your WiFi security features.

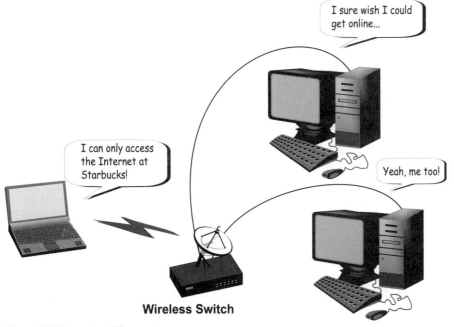

Wireless Switch

Figure 22.27: Lonely LAN computers

Internet Connection Sharing

Microsoft Windows comes with a feature called Internet Connection Sharing (ICS) that enables you to connect the computers in a LAN to the Internet without using a router machine. The PC running ICS has to have two network devices, such as modem and a NIC or two NICs; it uses one network device to connect to the Internet and the other to connect to the LAN. You set up each machine on the LAN to use the ICS-enabled PC as their gateway computer. It works well and, especially in dial-up settings, avoids the purchase of extra hardware.

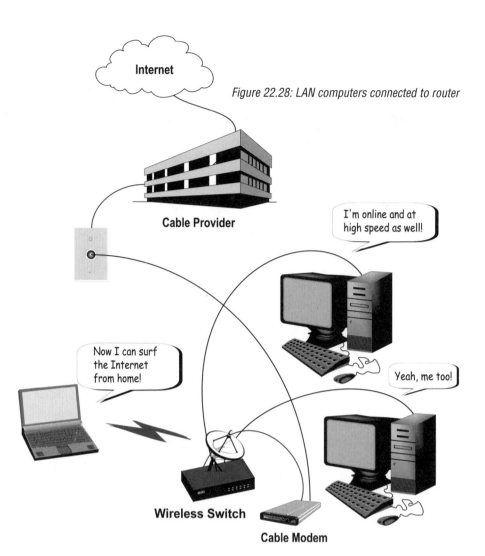

Figure 22.28: LAN computers connected to router

The Common Tongue

- The United States Department of Defense developed TCP/IP, a protocol suite for controlling information flow on the Internet. TCP handles the transmission of information between two computers. IP takes care of addressing packets so the packets sent get where they need to go and the computer on the other end can put them back together properly.

- IP addresses have four sets of numbers ranging from 0-255, separated by periods, like this: 192.168.1.52. Part of the IP address defines your network—called the *network ID*, while the other part describes your *node*—the computer you use to access the Internet. That's called the *host ID*.

Telephone Networks

- Telephones work by translating the sound waves coming out of your mouth into electrical signals that get sent along a copper wire. The receiving phone then makes those electrical signals into something resembling your voice. The recipient can then respond and the process repeats.

- Similarly to the telephone, a sending fax machine scans the page to be sent and translates the black and white parts of the page into tones that then get translated into electrical signals. The receiving fax machine receives the electrical signals, converts them into tones, and then uses that information to recreate the image.

- Modems transform digital signals into analog signals and *vice versa* through a process called modulation and demodulation. With a modem, a computer could use the phone line to send a message to another computer similarly equipped. The sending modem takes the digital signal, translates it to analog and sends it down the wire. The receiving modem reverses this process, taking the analog signal and turning it into a digital signal that the computer can understand.

CHAPTER 22: SUMMARY

Connecting to the Internet

- Hundreds of thousands of smaller networks connected together form the Internet. People often think of the Internet as some monolithic thing, but that perception couldn't be farther from the truth. Like the worldwide telephone network, the Internet is a "super network" of smaller networks.

- Routers provide the connection points between the networks and determine the route for a data packet to take from the source network to the destination network. Routers know the destination of packets of data because routers use TCP/IP, the common tongue of the Internet. They read the Network ID of each data packet and send the data packet by the shortest route they know about to its destination.

- An Internet Service Provider (ISP) leases connections to the Internet from one of the backbone networks and in turn, rents a portion of those connections to you. An ISP acts as your gateway to the Internet. ISPs maintain the hardware and software that enables you to connect, plus provide technical support. the ISP is responsible for protecting its portion of the Internet free from threats such as viruses and illegal activity.

- To connect to an ISP, you need some kind of network device on your computer, like a modem or network card; a cable or radio transmitter that enables that network device to access the world outside your door; and programs to make that hardware go, like Dial-up Networking in Windows and TCP/IP installed.

- The three most common connection types to the Internet are dial-up, cable, and DSL. Dial-up connections require a modem and ISP and offer the slowest and least expensive connection of the three. Cable uses a regular cable—like for your TV—connected to a cable modem, then to your computer's Ethernet NIC. DSL uses the extra bandwidth of your telephone cable to connect. Like with cable, DSL connections require a special DSL receiver that connects to your computer via Ethernet.

- Wireless connections use a WiFi card on your computer to connect to a WiFi router via radio waves; the router connects to your ISP usually through one of the high speed dedicated connections, DSL or cable. Many current cellular telephones and PDAs offer wireless connectivity as well. Cell phone companies act as ISPs, whereas PDAs usually connect via WiFi.

- Making a LAN connect to the Internet requires some sort of router/switch. The LAN computers connect to the switch; the router side connects to the ISP usually through one of the dedicated connections, DSL or cable.

Key Terms

Backbone

Bps

Cable modem

Digital Subscriber Line (DSL)

Dial-up connection

DSL receiver

Fiber optic cables

Host ID

Internet Protocol address (IP)

Internet Service Provider (ISP)

Integrated Services Digital Network (ISDN)

Kbps

Mbps

Neighborhood switch

Network ID

Node

Protocol

Public Switched Telephone Network (PSTN)

Router

TCP/IP

WiFi

Key Term Quiz

Use the Key Terms list to complete the following sentences. Not all terms will be used.

1. You can use a _____ connected to a cable TV line to provide a continuous, high-speed connection to the Internet.

2. A(n) _____ is a company that you pay to give you access to the Internet.

3. Of the three most common methods of connecting to the Internet, a _____ provides the slowest access.

4. The United States Department of Defense developed the _____ standard as a way for controlling information on the Internet.

5. The concept of an _____, though it never really developed on a massive scale, was to evolve into a completely digital telephone system, so that data would go faster through phone lines.

6. A _____ is a standard way of regulating data sent between computer networks.

7. Joe's computer has an IP address of 192.168.3.17; Mary's computer, which is on the same network, has an IP address of 192.168.3.44. This means that Joe's computer's _____ is 17, whereas Mary's is 44.

8. To connect to the Internet via _____, you need to be within 18,000 feet of a neighborhood switch.

9. In an effort to impress his friends, Eddie brags that his computer connects to the Internet via the _____; but you know that means he probably uses dial-up and a modem.

10. The most common wireless technology is called _____.

Multiple Choice Quiz

1. Which of the following protocols controls the sending and receiving connection between two computers on the Internet?
   A. TCP
   B. PHP
   C. UDP
   D. IP

2. What can you use the telephone network to send?
   A. Voice
   B. Pictures
   C. Data
   D. All of the above

3. John's modem connects to the Internet at 26,600. How fast can his modem send and receive data (assuming no errors)?
   A. 26.6 bps
   B. 26.6 Kbps
   C. 26.6 Mbps
   D. 26,600 Kbps

4. Elijah argues that the Internet consists of one big network that you get to tap into, but Maria claims the Internet is a super network of many smaller networks. Who's right?
   A. Only Elijah is right.
   B. Only Maria is right.
   C. Both Elijah and Maria are right.
   D. Neither Elijah nor Maria is right. The Internet consists of several backbone networks that you can access.

5. What protocol suite enables computers to communicate via the Internet?
   A. TCP/IP
   B. Apple/IBM
   C. Microsoft Windows
   D. DSL

6. If you live in a rural area, what is your most likely choice for Internet connectivity?
   A. Dial-up
   B. Cable
   C. DSL
   D. LAN

7. How do modems work?
   A. Modems take analog signals from computers and turn them into digital signals for transmission across telephone lines.
   B. Modems take electrical signals from computers and turn them into sound pulses for transmission across telephone lines.
   C. Modems take digital signals from computers and turn them into analog signals for transmission across telephone lines.
   D. Modems take digital signals from computers and turn them into sound pulses for transmission across cable lines.

8. What type of network connection enables you to stay connected to a network while moving from room to room?
   A. Cable
   B. WiFi
   C. DSL
   D. T1

9. Which of the following is a disadvantage of a wireless network connection?
   A. Other devices that use radio waves can interfere with wireless signals.
   B. Macintosh systems cannot use wireless connections.
   C. Wireless connections cannot be used in private homes.
   D. Wireless connections are much slower than dial-up connections.

10. Which of the following protocols puts a numerical destination and return address into the packets of information that make up your e-mail?
    A. TCP
    B. PGP
    C. UDP
    D. IP

11. Which of the following is an example of a valid IP address?
    A. 33FH
    B. 525.124.336
    C. 192.163.4.19
    D. www.irs.gov

12. What term describes the central part of the Internet, which is made up of fiber optic cables?
    A. The fibernet
    B. The Intranet
    C. The backbone
    D. The ISP

13. Which of these terms describes both DSL and cable Internet connections?
    A. Wireless
    B. Analog
    C. Broadband
    D. Dial-up

14. What piece of hardware must be installed on your laptop computer before it can access the wireless nework at your neighborhood coffee shop?
    A. Wireless NIC
    B. Wireless router
    C. Wireless access point
    D. Wireless power supply

15. Which of the following Internet connection methods is blazingly fast, but also by far the most expensive?
    A. Cable
    B. DSL
    C. T1
    D. TCP/IP

Essay Questions

1. Write a short essay (two to three paragraphs) on the advantages and disadvantages of wireless Internet connections.

2. Describe two types of dedicated connections for the Internet. Why are they better to use than dial-up connections through a phone line?

3. Your boss has decided that it's high time to connect your company's five computers into a network, but after doing some research, he's quite confused. Write an essay describing TCP/IP. Describe the role of the two major protocols that make up TCP/IP.

Projects

1. What would be a great network for your house or apartment? On a plain sheet of paper or using 3x5" cards, map out the locations of a switch, a wireless access point, and at least two wired computers. Where would you use a wireless device?

2. Do some research into the ISPs in your area. Put together a list of the top five that provide dial-up with a comparison of prices. Do the same thing for any that offer dedicated connections. If you have any dedicated connection choices other than cable or DSL, make note of these, especially how they compare with the standard dedicated connection technologies.

COMPUTER LITERACY: YOUR TICKET TO IC³ CERTIFICATION

Reach Out and Touch Someone – E-mail in the 21st Century

"If you want to receive e-mails about my upcoming shows, then please give me money so I can buy a computer."

– Phoebe, *Friends*

This chapter covers the following IC³ exam objectives:

- IC³-3   2.1.1   Identify how electronic mail works in a network and on the Internet
- IC³-3   2.1.2   Identify the components of an electronic mail mesage
- IC³-3   2.1.3   Identify the components of an electronic mail adress
- IC³-3   2.1.4   Identify when to use different electronic mail otions
- IC³-3   2.1.5   Identify different ways electronic mail is accessed
- IC³-3   2.1.6   Identify the difference between standard electronic mail and other forms of messaging
- IC³-3   2.2.1   Read and send electronic mail messages
- IC³-3   2.2.2   Identify ways to supplement a mail message with additional information
- IC³-3   2.2.3   Manage attachments
- IC³-3   2.2.5   Manage addresses

In 1971, Ray Tomlinson sent a message to himself—"Testing 1-2-3"—and the world changed forever. He sent the message from a computer over the ARPANET (the mother of the Internet), thus creating the first electronic mail (*e-mail*)—a document sent from one computer to another. Tomlinson went on to create the modern-day format of the e-mail address. It began as a user or mailbox name, the @ sign, and the machine's name, like scott@mailserver. E-mail has evolved into the most common use of the Internet today. For every single new page of Web content created per year, people generate 500 times more than that in e-mail content.

Figure 23.1: Outlook Express with mouse pointer over the Send button

This chapter delves deeply into e-mail, starting with how it works on internal networks and on the Internet, and the anatomy of an e-mail address. The second section covers accessing e-mail, including a discussion of e-mail software. The chapter finishes with two sections, one on sending mail and the second on handling incoming messages.

How E-mail Works

To send and receive e-mail, you have to have three things: e-mail software, an e-mail account, and access to a mail server. To send a message to your friend Betsy, for example, open your e-mail software (such as Outlook Express), put in her e-mail address, type a message, and press Send (Figure 23.1). The message zips out of your computer and goes to your mail server (Figure 23.2).

Your mail server reads Betsy's address on the message and then sends the message to her mail server. When your friend logs in to her mail server to check her mail, her computer downloads the message you sent. See Figure 23.3. The number of steps in the server to server communication part of this e-mail process differs radically depending on whether you send an e-mail over an internal network or over the Internet.

Internal Network Mail

On an internal network, both the sender and the recipient log into the same server. If you use a computer at school to send an e-mail to a friend in your school, the message goes from your computer to your e-mail server. Your friend logs into the same server and downloads her mail.

The message never leaves the network (Figure 23.4).

The mail server makes certain that nobody grabs the wrong e-mail because it *knows* everybody on the network—meaning that the server has a list of user names and passwords. This way, Bob Taylor (over in accounting) won't accidentally access Bob Galen's messages (you know, *that* Bob) if he tries to log in as bob**g** rather than bob**t**—easy enough to make the typo, but chances are good that the two Bobs don't share a password (Figure 23.5).

In such a simple network, e-mail accounts would be equally simple. If Bob T. wanted to send a message to Bob G., he would type **bobg** in the To: field of the message he wanted to send (Figure 23.6).

Okay, I've got it from here. Neither rain nor snow can stop the mail server!

Server, this e-mail is for Betsy. Make sure it gets there!

Figure 23.2: The first step in the e-mail process, mail from PC to mail server

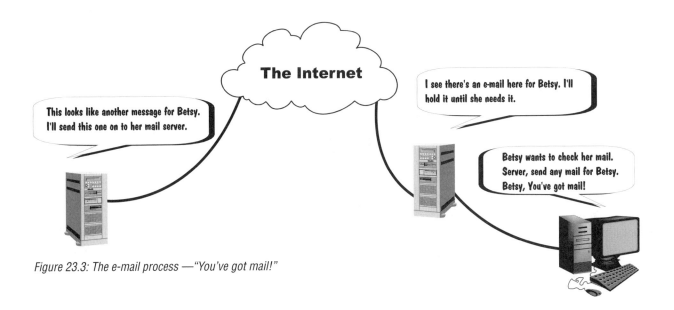

Figure 23.3: The e-mail process —"You've got mail!"

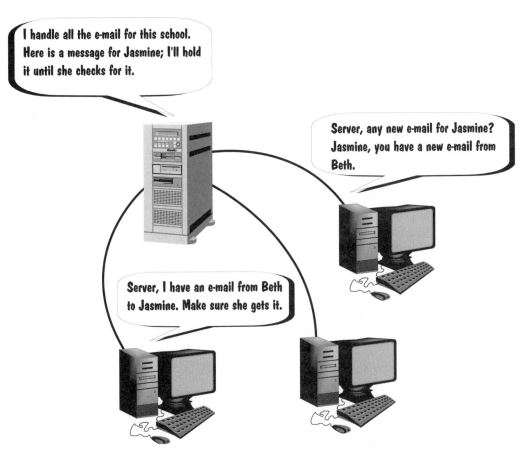

Figure 23.4: E-mail going from one computer to another within the same school.

Figure 23.5: Server refuses to accept bobt's password for bobg's account

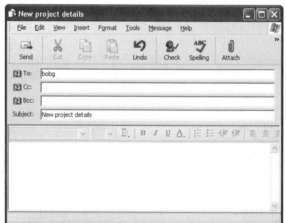

Figure 23.6: Internal mail addressed

E-mail over the Internet

Sending an e-mail message over the Internet requires a more complicated process than internal mail, because no single server in the world could handle all the e-mail addresses and traffic out there. Instead, as you know from earlier chapters, the Internet is a network of networks that include many thousands of servers. Each network must have a unique identity (name or domain), so that mail intended for a user on one network doesn't go to a user on another network. Each e-mail address likewise must be unique.

The mail servers on the Internet connect directly to one or more mail servers on different domains, creating an interwoven mesh of communication, but they don't connect directly to every other mail server (Figure 23.7). It's possible and even probable that an e-mail message from one domain to another might have to pass through many domains to reach its destination.

When you send an e-mail message to someone outside of your local network, your e-mail program connects to the mail server at your Internet service provider (ISP). The mail server looks at the address of the intended recipient and decides where to send the message (Figure 23.8). Each mail server has a list of known networks, plus knows where to send if it doesn't know the network.

The e-mail address provides the key component for sending and receiving e-mail and making this process make sense. Let's go there now.

Anatomy of an Internet E-mail Address

E-mail addresses have two key components, a *user name* and a *domain*, separated by the @ symbol, much like the original e-mail address format, such as **scott@totalsem.com**. While a user name can be pretty much anything—from **sjernigan** to **scott.jernigan** to **scottj**, for example—the domain consists of a computer or network name and a *domain code*. The name of the network in this example is **totalsem** and the domain code is **.com**.

COMPUTER LITERACY: YOUR TICKET TO IC³ CERTIFICATION

Domain names provide a great substitute for IP addresses, the numbers that make up the true "name" of a domain server, making it easier for you to remember someone's e-mail address. After all, which would stick in your mind better—**bill@microsoft.com** or **bill@207.46.130.108**?

The domain code, or *top-level domain*, in an e-mail address can tell you a lot about the person with that address, from business type to possible physical location. Domain codes get added periodically. Here's the list of the most frequently used types.

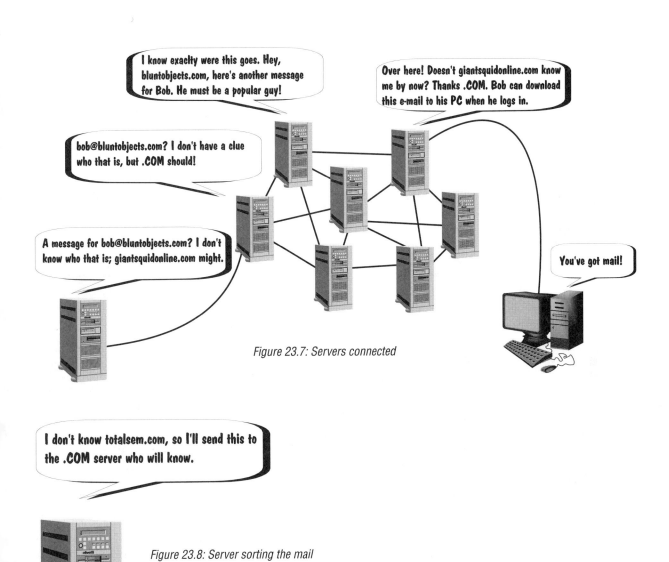

Figure 23.7: Servers connected

Figure 23.8: Server sorting the mail

.com

The *.com* domain code reigns as the main one for American for-profit companies, and many international companies and individuals use it too. Although originally intended to be short for *commercial*, you would do better to think of it as *common*, because most Web sites use .com.

.gov

Federal agencies and all aspects of the United States government except the military use the *.gov* top-level domain. There are *no* exceptions.

.mil

The United States military uses the *.mil* top-level domain. No one else uses this domain code.

.us

State government agencies in the U.S. use the particular state's two-letter postal abbreviation, in lowercase letters, followed by *.us* for their domain code. The e-mail address for the governor of Texas, for example, would be something like this: daGov@austin.tx.us.

.edu

All types of educational institutions can use the *.edu* domain code, although it's most commonly associated with universities in the U.S. This can lead to some funny moments if you're not careful, because early Internet-adopting universities snagged the shortest domain names, leaving the slightly less fleet-of-foot to use longer ones. An e-mail message to rpalmer@uh.edu, for example, would reach Prof. Bob Palmer of the History Department at the University of Houston, in Texas, not a Prof. Palmer at the University of Hawaii (Figure 23.9).

.org

The *.org* domain code was originally created for non-profit organizations and other non-commercial groups. Any group, individual, or company can now register a .org domain.

.net

Although originally envisioned to identify networks or organizations, such as Internet service providers, the *.net* has become the red-headed step-child of the original seven domains.

.info

The *.info* domain code is the first unrestricted top-level domain since .com, which began use in 1985. There are no restrictions on who may register .info names, since they were created for general use around the world. Why would this domain interest you? If you wanted a .com Web site and e-mail address and they weren't available, that domain would probably be available with a .info extension.

.biz

The business community uses the *.biz* domain exclusively. Anyone can register this domain name, as long as it is for a business or commercial use, such as exchanging goods or services. Just like .info, hard-to-find .com Web sites just might be available with a .biz extension instead.

International Domain codes

Domains in countries outside the United States usually end in a two-letter abbreviation for the country in which the e-mail server resides. E-mail addresses from the United Kingdom end in *.uk*, and *.de* is used for Germany (Germans call their homeland *Deutschland*).

Putting Together Clues

Like a 21st-Century Sherlock Holmes, you can sometimes learn a lot about someone who e-mails you just by knowing how to decipher his or her e-mail address. Look at the four addresses listed below, but don't look at the explanations below them yet. What can you guess about the four users?

- smith.john@harvard.edu
- jsmith@amazon.com
- john_smythe@amazon.co.uk
- smith.j@fbi.gov

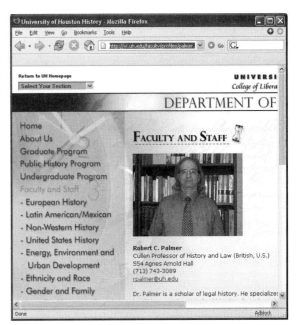

Figure 23.9: Prof. Palmer

Location? The first person has an e-mail address from Harvard University, which could place him in Cambridge, Massachusetts. The second user has a commercial address, possibly in the USA, in Seattle, Washington (the corporate headquarters of Amazon.com). The third user is from a British company, perhaps in Marston Gate, U.K., home of one of Amazon's European distribution centers. The fourth user is from the U.S. Federal Bureau of Investigation (FBI), possibly in Washington, D.C., although the folks in the dark blue suits are *everywhere*.

Occupation? The first user might be a student or professor or employee of the university. The second and third users are most likely employees of Amazon.com, and the fourth user is likely to be an FBI agent or employee.

TV-watching habits? Just kidding!

Accessing E-mail

Accessing e-mail requires having a valid account on a mail server, access to the Internet, and either a dedicated e-mail application, a Web browser, or some alternative device, like a cell phone. You can get a valid account in many ways, most commonly by contracting with an ISP or through your work or school. You can also get a free Web-based account from a number of sources, but these accounts do not come with Internet access. That you pay for separately.

Dedicated E-mail Software

Every computer operating system comes bundled with one or more dedicated e-mail applications, such as *Outlook Express* in Windows. Plus, you can download free or inexpensive programs from the Internet. *Thunderbird*, from www.mozilla.org, and *Eudora* (www.eudora.com) are two of the best e-mail

Mail Protocols

Dedicated e-mail programs use various protocols to communicate with e-mail servers. The two most common are Simple Mail Transfer Protocol (SMTP) *to send e-mail and* Post Office Protocol (POP) *to access mail. SMTP and POP are just Internet protocols like the ones you've seen before, such as TCP and IP. When you set up a new e-mail account in an e-mail program like Outlook, your ISP will tell you the name of your SMTP and POP servers—often the same server—so you can send and receive mail.*

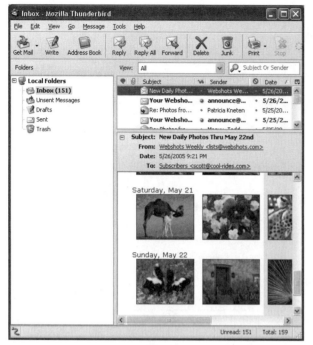

Figure 23.10: Mozilla Thunderbird

programs you can get, and one costs nothing; the second only ~$50 US. Figure 23.10 shows Thunderbird with the Inbox displayed.

Many businesses use applications that do e-mail and a lot of other features, such as keeping track of your daily calendar and handling many forms of messaging. Microsoft makes the most widely used software in *Outlook* (Figure 23.11). *Lotus Notes*, long a darling of industry but now fading away, provides an alternative.

To access e-mail in any of these dedicated programs, you simply connect to the Internet, make sure the software knows the name of your mail server, and go. Figure 23.12 shows the connection information in Eudora. Your ISP provides details such as the names of the outgoing and incoming mail servers.

When you access mail with a dedicated e-mail program, the program contacts the mail server and downloads any incoming messages into your computer. Most servers then erase your mail from their permanent memory, leaving the only copy of that message on yours (Figure 23.13). This works great for people who access mail from home or work and don't travel much. Web-based e-mail offers a wildly different solution that enables you to access your mail from any computer, from any location, anywhere in the world.

Figure 23.11: Microsoft Outlook

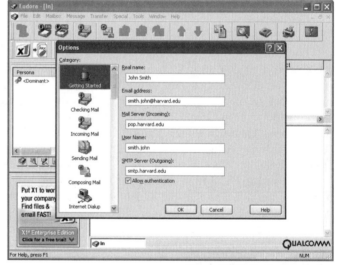

Figure 23.12: Qualcomm Eudora

Web-based E-mail

Many companies offer Web-based e-mail accounts that you access using, not a dedicated application, but with a Web browser, such as Internet Explorer. Most Web-based e-mail accounts cost you nothing, give you a certain amount of storage space on the Internet, and enable you to access your mail from many places. The search engine giant Google offers one of the slickest services, called *Gmail* (Figure 23.14). Microsoft offers *Hotmail* and Yahoo! has *Yahoo! Mail*.

Many of the Web-based mail services store your messages, so you can access them again and again, from many different locations. Such services prove invaluable to people on the move!

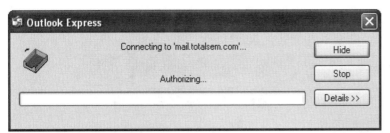

Figure 23.13: Downloading e-mail message

Sending E-mail

Sending an e-mail message takes a few steps. You must start a new message, fill in the fields, enhance the content by attaching a file or adding links to Web sites, and click the Send button. To start a new message, click the **new mail** link, called something unique in just about every e-mail program. It's called *Write* in Thunderbird, *New* in Outlook, *Create Mail* in Outlook Express, and *Compose Mail* in Gmail. Regardless, this opens a standard new message window.

Components of an E-mail Message

Virtually all e-mail programs use a similar window for composing an e-mail message. One of the first fields on the window is the *To:* field. To fill in this field, enter the e-mail address of the primary person (or people) you want to receive the e-mail. The next place on the window is the *Cc:* field. That's where you put the e-mail addresses of additional people you want to receive the message besides the main person. The primary recipient from the To: field will be able to see all of the people you list in the Cc: field.

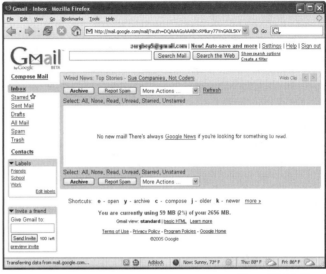

Figure 23.14: Gmail

Through a feature called *blind carbon copy* (*bcc*) you can send a copy of an e-mail message to people without the primary recipient knowing about it. Just add e-mail addresses to the Bcc: field. It's called *blind* carbon copy because the person from the To: field doesn't know who has been bcc'd. Figure 23.16 shows the header fields in Outlook Express.

After you have entered all of your e-mail addresses, enter a brief description of what your e-mail is about in the *Subject:* line field of the window. Although you could leave the subject line blank, you shouldn't do so. Many people will delete such blank e-mail messages without looking at them.

Below the subject line lies the largest field of the new message window, called the *message body*. This is where you type out your complete message. This is also where you attach any additional files such as pictures, sound, or video files. Attachments in most programs show up just below the Subject: line (Figure 23.17).

Most e-mail programs have additional features in the message body area such as Spell Check. They usually have a field where you can enter a *signature* that will automatically appear at the bottom of every e-mail message body you send. Signatures usually involve your name and contact information such as your phone number and your e-mail address. Some people like to jazz up their signatures to include small pictures or a funny slogan or catchy phrase (Figure 23.18).

The Odd Case of America Online

Possibly still the largest Internet service provider on the planet, America Online (AOL) offers a stark contrast to dedicated e-mail programs and offers Web-based access as well. To use AOL for anything but Web mail, you need to install AOL software—more than an e-mail program, the AOL software includes programs for dialing into the AOL world and accessing the Internet from there. AOL has long functioned like a gated community—part of the surrounding Internet community, but with special members-only content that you can only access using the AOL software (Figure 23.15).

Other Ways to Access Mail

Cell phones and personal digital assistants (PDAs) commonly have e-mail as one of their many features. Cell phones often get a unique e-mail address assigned by the cell phone provider to send and receive e-mail messages. PDAs usually sync up with a regular computer and send/receive e-mail via a dedicated e-mail program. The cool thing is that you can compose and read e-mail on your PDA, so you're not tied to a desktop or laptop computer..

Figure 23.15: AOL

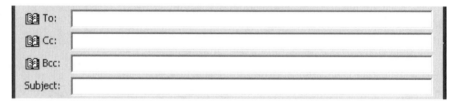

Figure 23.16: To:, Cc:, and Bcc: fields

What Does Cc: Mean?

As hard as it may be to imagine, business offices used to function without computers, copy machines, and faxes. When people wanted multiple copies of messages, they had sheets of paper that were connected together, and in between each sheet of paper was a sheet of carbon. All you had to do was to write on the top sheet and the imprint it would make on each sheet of carbon would copy all of your writing on the same place on every sheet of paper, thereby making exact copies of what you had just written. If Joe wanted to send a message to Paul, but he wanted copies to go to five other people, he would ask for the five other people to be carbon copied, or cc'd.

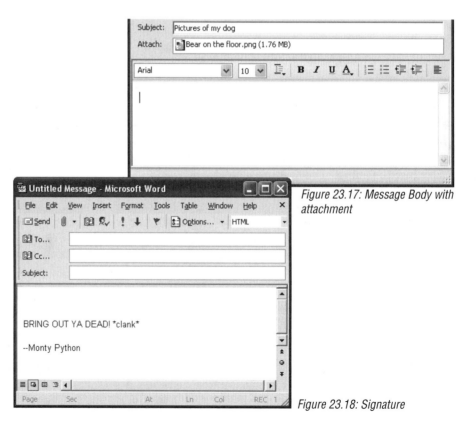

Figure 23.17: Message Body with attachment

Figure 23.18: Signature

Managing Addresses

Every e-mail program has an *address book* that enables you to collect and keep track of people you want to e-mail (Figure 23.19). The e-mail addresses in your address book are your *contacts*. You can use your address book to fill in entries in the recipient fields of the new e-mail window when you're composing an e-mail. Clicking on **To:** directly in Outlook Express, for example, opens your address book contacts list.

An address book functions just like an old-fashioned paper address book for telephone numbers, with a couple of advantages. Address books have a search function to look for e-mail addresses in a variety of ways (by name or e-mail address). Address books allow you to group different addresses together in a *distribution list* to send out the same e-mail to multiple people at the same time.

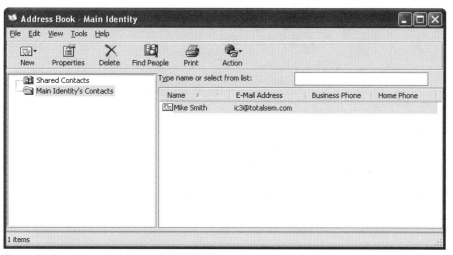

Figure 23.19: Address book

Adding Entries

Each e-mail program offers several ways to add a contact. You can open the address book (go to **Tools | Address Book**) and click on the **New Entry** button in Outlook (Figure 23.20), for example, or go to **File | New | Contact**. Fill in the details of name, e-mail address, and so on, and click **Save** and **Close** to save the new contact (Figure 23.21).

Editing and Deleting Contacts

To edit a contact entry, simply find it in your address book, double-click it, and the new message window will again open so you can make your changes. To delete a contact, select it in the address book and press **[Delete]** on your keyboard or click the **Delete** button in the address book. At the *Are you sure?* dialog box, click the **Yes** button and the contact is gone.

Enhancing E-mail Content

E-mail programs enable you to do more than send text. You can send links to Web sites so the recipient(s) of your message can get more information on topic, for example. You can attach photographs, movies, and other files. Links show up in the body of a message, like you can see in Figure 23.22, whereas attachments of any sort generally show up as a separate entry in a message.

To attach a file to an e-mail message, most programs enable you to click and drag the file from your desktop (or Explorer) and drop it into the message body of the e-mail.

What's my Motivation?

Contacts

It might seem like a lot of extra work at first to fill in all the little details on a contact, but the payoff can be great, especially in a business setting. Aside from the usual e-mail, phone, address, and business name, contact information can include details like nicknames, birthdates, kids' names, and more. What a powerful tool for a salesperson, for example, to make a call to a client from a year before and be able to say, with certainty, "Hey, I hear congratulations are in order—didn't you just have a birthday? How's little Johnnie? What is he, seven already?" Personal connections make sales.

Exploring the Address Book

*If you have a copy of Windows handy, open up Outlook Express (**Start | All Programs | Outlook Express**) and check out the Address Book. Fill out a contact entry for you that includes details that people should know, but nothing private, of course. What would be useful for a doctor to know? What about your lawyer? Save and close. You can delete it later.*

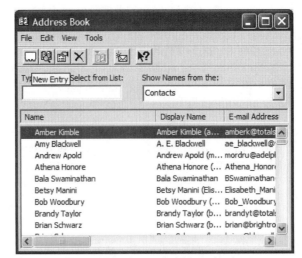

Figure 23.20: New Entry button in Address book

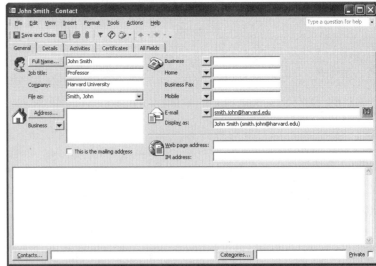

Figure 23.21: Adding a new contact in Outlook

URLs and Links

*Every Web site has a IP address that you can often use to open that site in a Web browser, such as Internet Explorer. Because most people find it hard to remember strings of numbers, Web sites get a name that corresponds to that IP address, called a **Uniform Resource Locator (URL)**, such as **www.microsoft.com**. Computer people refer to URLs placed in documents as links or hyperlinks.*

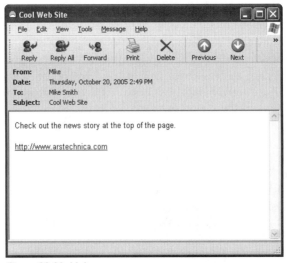

Figure 23.22: Link

Figure 23.23: Picture embedded (it shows as attached as well in this program)

Embed Multimedia

You can embed, rather than attach, pictures, sounds, or low-level animation into the body or signature of an e-mail in some e-mail programs. Figure 23.23 shows a picture embedded in a message in Outlook Express. To embed, don't drag and drop. Go to **Insert** and select **Image** or another option.

When you're done composing an e-mail, click the **Send** button to send it along to your mail server and even-tually to your reci-pient's mail server.

Handling Incoming E-mail

When you get an e-mail message in your Inbox, you can do quite a few things with it. You can view the contents of the message, open or save any attached files, or respond in some fashion. If you have a lot of e-mail in your Inbox, you can sort by sender or by subject, or run a full search for key words.

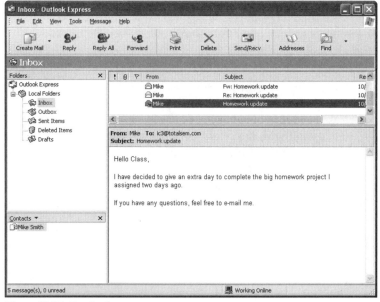

Figure 23.24: Previewing a message

View

Some e-mail programs open with the Inbox displayed and the latest unread message open in a Preview window, so you can start reading right away (Figure 23.24). Others require you to click on a button or link to open the Inbox. Still others show the Inbox as just a set of messages with no Preview. To open

You can change the default look and feel of most e-mail programs. If you don't want the summary page to open when you first open Outlook Express, for example, you can click on the little checkbox at the bottom of the page that says "When Outlook Express starts, go directly to my Inbox."

Caution

Attachments can be viruses or contain viruses, nasty computer programs that can erase files, crash your computer, or steal in-formation from you. Never open an attachment from an unknown source; don't open attachments from people you know that have file names ending in .exe or .com. This can make for a very bad day.

Other Responses
You can do more with your messages than the five typical options. You can print an e-mail, for example, by clicking the **Print** button in your software. You can flag the message to mark it as important. Chapter 24, "Effective E-mail," covers these and more options.

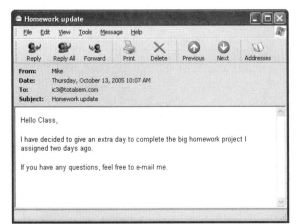

Figure 23.25: Message open

an e-mail message into its own window, just double-click the subject of the message (Figure 23.25).

Attachments

Once you have an e-mail open for viewing, you can open or save any attached files. The attached files show up at the top or bottom of the message, depending on the e-mail program. Double-click the attached file to open. Your operating system will select the proper program for the type of file—assuming it has that program installed, of course—and then open the file in that program. Figure 23.26 shows an attached Microsoft Word document—the icon looks just like the icon for Word.

To save e-mail attachments to your hard drive or to any other drive connected to your computer, right-click on the attachment in an open e-mail message and select **Save as.** A menu will pop up enabling you to choose where to save the file and what to name it.

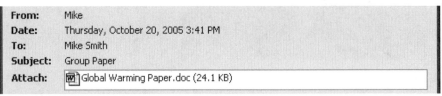

Figure 23.26: The icon tells you that Windows knows what program to use to open this file

Responding

Figure 23.27: Reply, Reply All, and Forward buttons in Outlook Express

You can respond to an e-mail in five basic ways: do nothing; press the **[Delete]** key on your keyboard to delete the file; reply to the sender; reply to the sender and all the recipients of the message; or forward the message and any attachments to someone else. The first two options seem pretty self-explanatory, but let's look at the other three typical responses: Reply, Reply All, and Forward (Figure 23.27). (Some programs use Reply to All rather than Reply All.)

Reply

If you want to send a reply message back to the sender of an e-mail, regardless of how many people the e-mail was sent to, click the *Reply* button. Most e-mail applications will create a new e-mail with the contents of the old one and with a space for you to type a response. Figure 23.28 shows a draft reply in Outlook, with the new text in blue and the original information noted and indented. The To: field of your draft will display the e-mail address of the person who sent the original e-mail to you.

Note that different software set off the original message in different ways. Thunderbird, for example, draws heavy blue lines around the original message. Regardless, when your recipient gets a reply, it'll have old and new messages and a subject line that begins with *RE:*.

Figure 23.28: Reply

Reply All

If an e-mail was sent to you and other people, and you would like to reply to it so that all of the original recipients and the sender can see your reply, click the *Reply All* button. A new e-mail will be created with the contents of the old one and with

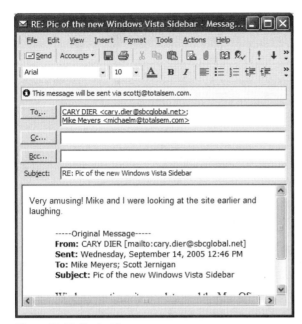

Figure 23.29: Reply All

a space for you to type a response. The To: field will be filled with all of the recipients of the original message and the e-mail address of the original sender. Figure 23.29 shows a draft reply with multiple addresses in the To: field.

Reply vs. Reply All

Use your best judgment when you get a message with multiple recipients on using **Reply** or **Reply All**. The most appropriate time to use **Reply All** is when you're working on some sort of project with other people. If everybody on the team needs to know a certain piece of information, then send it to everybody. If someone e-mailed a joke to 20 of his friends, on the other hand, don't click **Reply All** and spam all 20 people's inboxes with "Kewl joke, dude!"

Forward

You can forward an e-mail to someone by clicking the *Forward* button. This opens a draft copy of the message with an altered subject line—usually *FW:* is added—and a blank To: box. It will even say who sent it to you and when. The only difference is it will have a blank **To:** field for you to fill in the e-mail address of the person to whom you are forwarding the e-mail. The recipient of your forwarded e-mail will clearly see that you were the original recipient (Figure 23.30).

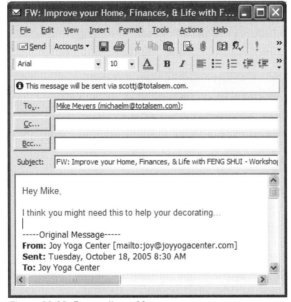

Figure 23.30: Forwarding a Message

E-mail is a very powerful tool and, like all powerful things, can cause problems if used incorrectly. Just because you *can* forward a message doesn't mean you *should* forward it. Use the Forward option when you receive an e-mail that has information someone else should know that wasn't given to you in confidence. If you have any doubts, reply to the original sender and ask permission to forward the message.

*Definitely never press **Reply to All** if you were bcc'd on a message. Because the cc'd people didn't know you got the message, replying to all of them would cause embarrassment to the original sender at the very least. Replying to all in such a situation is considered rude and a betrayal of confidence.*

Non-E-mail Electronic Communication

E-mail remains the most popular use for the Internet but there are other, non-e-mail and non-Internet related means of communication, such as paging and instant messaging. People with pagers, cell phones, and certain PDA devices can be paged. Paging sends a radio signal to their handheld device either instructing them to call in to their office to receive a message, or displaying a number they need to call.

Instant messaging enables you to use a cell phone or PDA to send a text message to a person who has a similar device. You type in the message using a key pad or a pen and send it to a phone number. The recipient can read it at his or her leisure. Just a word of caution: never try to text someone while driving (not that I've ever done that...).

How E-mail Works

- Electronic mail (e-mail) enables you to send and receive text and files generated on computers. You can use e-mail in an internal network or over the Internet.

- To send and receive e-mail, you have to have three things: e-mail software, an e-mail account, and access to a mail server.

- If you use a computer at school to send an e-mail to a friend in your school, the message goes from your computer to your e-mail server. The server has a list of all the users and passwords for mail. Your friend logs into the server with his e-mail software and downloads your message.

- The Internet is a network of networks, so each network must have unique identity (unique name or domain). Each user must have a unique identity and e-mail address, and the e-mail must contain information that enables many computers to get that message from origin to destination.

- When you send an e-mail message to someone outside of your local network, your e-mail program connects to your mail server. Your mail server reads the recipient's network and sends the message to that network or to the next server in line that can get to the network.

- Every valid e-mail address consists of two key components—a user name and a domain—separated by the @ symbol, for example **president@whitehouse.gov**. The domain has two parts: the network or computer name (**whitehouse**) and the domain code or top-level domain (**.gov**). The standard domain codes include .com, .gov, .mil, .edu, .org, and .net. Every country has a unique country code, such as .us for the United States, .fi for Finland, and .es for Spain.

Accessing E-mail

- Every computer operating system comes bundled with one or more dedicated e-mail applications, such as Outlook Express in Windows. Plus, you can download free or inexpensive programs from the Internet, such as Thunderbird and Eudora. Many businesses use complex programs that handle mail, scheduling, and more, such as Outlook and Lotus Notes. AOL offers special content if you use them for both ISP and as your e-mail software.

- One of the most popular methods of e-mail is Web-based e-mail. Various types include Hotmail, Yahoo! Mail, and Gmail.

- When you access mail with a dedicated e-mail program, the program contacts the mail server and downloads any incoming messages into your computer. Most servers then erase your mail from their permanent memory, leaving the only copy of that message on yours. Web-based e-mail, in contrast enables you to access your mail from any computer, from any location, anywhere in the world. Usually, those messages stay on your Web server.

Sending E-mail

- Sending an e-mail message takes a few steps. You must start a new message, fill in the fields, enhance the content by attaching a file or adding links to Web sites, and click the Send button. To start a new message, click the **new mail** link, such as **Create Mail** in Outlook Express. This opens a standard new message window.

- Typical fields of a new e-mail message include To:, Cc:, Bcc:, Subject:, message body, and signature. Use the To: field for your primary recipient and the Cc: field to send a copy of the message to other people. The Bcc: field enables you to send a copy to someone without any of the people in the To: or Cc: field knowing.

- E-mail programs have an address book that enables you to collect and keep track of people you want to e-mail, your *contacts*. You can add, edit or delete entries easily. Just open the contact and start typing. You can use your address book to fill in entries in the recipient fields of the new message window when you're composing an e-mail.

- You can enhance an e-mail message by embedding a link to a Web site. A simple drag and drop enables you to attach a document, picture, or other file to your message. You can also embed a picture directly into your e-mail using some e-mail software.

- When your e-mail is completed, simply click the **Send** button in your new message window to send the e-mail.

Handling Incoming E-mail

- You can view a new e-mail message in Preview mode or by opening it. You can also open any attached files by double-clicking them. Be cautious about opening attachments from people you don't know, though, because they can contain viruses. You can save attached files to your computer by right-clicking them and selecting **Save As** from the options.

- You can respond to an e-mail message in a variety of ways. Click **Reply** to reply directly to the person who sent the e-mail. Click **Reply to All** or **Reply All**, if appropriate, to send a response to everyone addressed in the original e-mail. Both methods create a new message with the original message inserted in the message body and Re: added to the subject line. Finally, you can click the **Forward** button to send the e-mail to another user, again, only when appropriate.

CHAPTER 23: SUMMARY

Key Terms

Address book	Forward	Paging
America Online (AOL)	.gov	Post Office Protocol (POP)
Attachment	Gmail	Reply
Bcc:	Hotmail	Reply All
Cc:	Instant messaging	Signature
.com	Lotus Notes	Simple Mail Transfer
Contacts	Mailbox	Protocol (SMTP)
Distribution list	Message body	Subject:
Domain	.mil	Thunderbird
Domain code	.net	Top-level domain
.edu	.org	.us
E-mail	Outlook	User name
Eudora	Outlook Express	Yahoo! Mail

Key Term Quiz

Use the Key Terms list to complete the following sentences. Not all the terms will be used.

1. Most e-mail addresses for U.S. university students, faculty, and staff end with _____.

2. A file sent along with an e-mail message is called a(n) _____.

3. With _____, a brief text message is sent from a hand-held device, like a cell phone, to another hand-held device.

4. _____ enables you to send someone a copy of an e-mail without the primary recipient knowing about it.

5. You can download the _____ e-mail program from Mozilla for free.

6. E-mail addresses for the U.S. Navy would end with _____.

7. The _____ is where you put the primary contents of your e-mail message.

8. A Web-based e-mail program offered by Yahoo! is called _____.

9. Every e-mail application has a _____ where you can save e-mail and other information about your friends, family, and co-workers.

10. If you _____ an e-mail message, you can send it to someone who was not part of the original e-mail sender or recipient, if that person has a need to know the information in the e-mail message.

Multiple Choice Quiz

1. Doug argues that e-mail sent from one computer on the Internet bounces through one or more servers and then winds up in the inbox of the recipient. Susan disagrees, saying that the e-mail most likely goes through many servers and then winds up in the mail server of the recipient. The recipient has to log into his or her mail server and download the e-mail. Who's right?
   A. Only Doug is right.
   B. Only Susan is right.
   C. Both Doug and Susan have it right.
   D. Neither Doug nor Susan has it right.

2. Mo picks up the argument, saying that Doug is right, but about internal networks. The mail server knows the addresses of every user and simply takes mail from one user and puts it in the inbox of the recipient. Susan disagrees, saying that the recipient still has to log in and download the e-mail, even on an internal network. Who's right?
   A. Only Mo is right.
   B. Only Susan is right.
   C. Both Mo and Susan have it right.
   D. Neither Mo nor Susan has it right.

3. Federal agencies of the United States use which top-level domain?
   A. .mil
   B. .info
   C. .eu
   D. .gov

4. In the e-mail address Alex.Smith@QRS.com, what term describes the Alex.Smith portion? (Select all that apply.)
   A. Address
   B. Domain name
   C. Mailbox
   D. User name

5. Google offers which Web-based e-mail service?
   A. Gmail
   B. Hotmail
   C. Yahoo! Mail
   D. POP

6. What is the part of an e-mail that that you can set up to display contact information or a catchy saying after the message body?
   A. Subject
   B. Preview
   C. POP
   D. Signature

7. Which of the following e-mail addresses would most likely come from someone in London, England?
   A. simon@bbc.co.uk
   B. simon@bbc.co.gb
   C. simon@bbc.london.en
   D. simon@bbc.london

8. Into which field in a new message window should you put an e-mail address for a person you want to receive your e-mail and show all other recipients that this person received the e-mail, but was not the primary recipient?
   A. To:
   B. Cc:
   C. Bcc:
   D. Forward:

9. Into which field in a new message window should you put an e-mail address for a person you want to receive your e-mail and show all other recipients that this person was the primary recipient of the e-mail?
   A. To:
   B. Cc:
   C. Bcc:
   D. Forward:

10. Which of the following is an e-mail program that comes with Windows?
    A. Eudora
    B. Outlook
    C. Outlook Express
    D. Thunderbird

11. How do you attach a photograph to an e-mail message in Windows?
    A. Drag and drop from My Computer or Explorer into the body of your e-mail message.
    B. Drag and drop from My Computer or Explorer into the To: field of your e-mail message.
    C. Drag and drop from My Computer or Explorer into the Cc: field of your e-mail message.
    D. You can't. You can only embed the picture.

12. How do you save a file attached to an e-mail message?
    A. Left-click and select **Save As** from the options.
    B. Right-click and select **Save As** from the options.
    C. Double-click the file.
    D. You can't. You can only open or delete attachments.

13. Joachim received an e-mail message by mistake, meant instead for his brother, Josiah, that had an attached picture. What's the best way for Joachim to send the e-mail to Josiah and include the attached picture?
    A. Click **Reply** and type Josiah's e-mail address in the Cc: field.
    B. Click **Reply All** and type Josiah's e-mail address in the Cc: field.
    C. Click **Forward** and type Josiah's e-mail address in the To: field.
    D. Create a new, blank e-mail message. Copy and paste the contents of the misdirected message into the new message. Copy and paste the attached picture into the new message. Put Josiah's e-mail address into the To: field.

14. What's the term for an entry in an address book?
    A. Address
    B. Contact
    C. Entry
    D. Person

15. You've received an e-mail message, but your name does not appear in either the To: or the Cc: field, although many other e-mail addresses do. You must have been in the Bcc: field of the sender's e-mail. The message asks for the recipients' opinion on an important matter, something you have strong feelings about. What should you do?
    A. Click **Reply** and give your opinion to the sender.
    B. Click **Reply All** and give your opinion to the sender and all other recipients.
    C. Click **Forward** and send to other interested parties.
    D. Delete this message.

Essay Questions

1. All of your relatives have been pestering your mother to get an e-mail account, so they can send lots of pictures back and forth. In a short essay, explain to her the advantages of Outlook and Hotmail and the fundamental differences between the two. Which one would be better for her to use and why?

2. Your group has decided to get an Internet domain name to promote what you all believe in passionately. They know the name they want to use, but don't know which top-level domain to use for the ending. Write a short essay explaining the differences among .com, .org, and .net, and make an argument for choosing one over the others. You can use one of these names for your organization or use one selected by your instructor:

   - Robotmonkeybutler
   - Giantsquidonline
   - Cool-rides

3. Your boss is trying to send a photograph of his wife, Ethel, to her mother in Milan. Write a short essay describing ways that he can get that photo from Newark to Milan electronically. Be sure to describe steps in whichever e-mail program you select.

Projects

1. If you have access to the Internet, go to http://www.hotmail.com and create an e-mail address. Share the address with your classmates or colleagues and send e-mail messages to each other. Send an attached file. Set up the address book to include one or more of your classmates or colleagues.

2. Do some research into dedicated e-mail programs. What makes Outlook Express better or worse than Thunderbird? Make a chart of the features that prove your point so that you can discuss this in class.

Effective E-mail

"Spam, Spam, Spam, Spam! Spam, Spam, Spam, Spam! Lovely Spam, wonderful Spam!"

– Vikings, *Monty Python's Flying Circus*

This chapter covers the following IC³ exam objectives:

- IC³-3   2.2.4   Identify how to manage mail

- IC³-3   2.2.6   Identify the purpose of frequently used mail configuration options

- IC³-3   2.3.1   Identify the advantages of electronic mail

- IC³-3   2.3.2   Identify common problems associated with electronic mail

- IC³-3   2.3.3   Identify the elements of professional and effective e-mails

- IC³-3   2.3.4   Identify when other forms of correspondence are more appropriate than e-mail

- IC³-3   2.3.5   Identify when to include information from an original e-mail message in a response as a method of tracking the "history" of e-mail communication

- IC³-3   2.3.6   Identify appropriate use of e-mail attachments and other supplementary information

- IC³-3   2.3.7   Identify issues regarding unsolicited e-mail ("spam") and how to minimize or control unsolicited mail

- IC³-3   2.3.8   Identify effective procedures for ensuring the safe and effective use of electronic mail

Effectively-used electronic mail (e-mail) offers numerous advantages over other forms of communication, electronic or otherwise. An e-mailed letter takes minutes to arrive, even on the other side of the globe, whereas a postal letter could take days or weeks. E-mail costs almost nothing, compared to carrying a physical letter somewhere. You can quickly and easily reply to an e-mail, even sending and receiving from your cell phone, to one or many recipients. Plus, you can reply when it's convenient for you. This makes doing a group project much easier than trying to use a telephone or snail mail (Figure 24.1).

Figure 24.1: E-mail at work, connecting the group

Because most e-mail applications keep track of e-mail you send as well as e-mail you receive, this creates an electronic trail of messages (a *paper trail* without killing any trees!). If you find you need to know something you or someone else said three months into a project, for example, you can simply open up your e-mail application and do a quick search. Try doing that with a traditional paper letter!

Chapter 23, "Reach Out," taught you the basics of how e-mail works. This chapter delves deeper into the process, covering the essentials of effective e-mail. You'll learn about techniques for communicating effectively, including style and structure tips. The second section of the chapter covers how to manage your e-mail to increase your organization and efficiency. The third section of the chapter gives you the troubleshooting tips and tools you need to survive e-mail in the 21st Century. Let's get started.

Creating the Message

Creating an effective e-mail message requires you to address many things, from the style and professionalism of the writing to the level of formality. You need to use a good subject line and know when to attach or embed files. If you're replying to an e-mail, should you quote the original message? E-mail presents a unique form of communication, a blend between a casual phone conversation and a formal paper letter. Sort of a "Hey Joe! What's going on?" and "Dear sir, I recently read your column . . . " mix that takes some thought to pull off.

Style

A well-crafted e-mail message should cover a topic directly and without excessive words. In Shakespeare's immortal words, "Brevity is the soul of wit." No one likes to read through hundreds of words of fluff to try to find the point in an e-mail. On the other hand, e-mail messages make your voice much flatter and toneless than your telephone voice, so you need to use enough words or your e-mail could seem terse or rude to the recipient.

Use a professional style, like in a formal letter, addressing people as Mr., Ms., and so on unless they specifically tell you to use their first name. Check your e-mail for spelling and grammatical errors. Don't use all capital letters in an e-mail message or subject line. That's considered SHOUTING and very rude. And definitely avoid the casual acronyms and e-mail-isms that you've probably seen, such as IMHO (for "in my humble opinion") and *smilies*, such as **:)** or **;-p** to indicate humor. Finally, avoid jokes. What's funny to you might be offensive to your recipient or to someone your recipient forwards your e-mail to, and your name will still be there as author.

Structure

Effective e-mail has a good subject line and proper use of attachments, embedded links, and embedded files. A good subject line offers a clear, short, direct statement of the purpose of your e-mail. If you write an e-mail message to enquire about a grade on a test, for example, just say so: "Inquiring about grade on test." Don't make it too short—"Inquiring"—too long (Figure 24.2), or off the wall, and never leave it blank.

Attached files can enhance an e-mail message. Your recipient can open a file or view a picture you send (Figure 24.3). Use good judgment about attached files, though, especially on size. As a general rule, don't send files larger than 1 MB to someone unless you know for sure that his or her e-mail server and connection can handle it.

Embedded files can cause problems with many e-mail servers and programs. Some e-mail programs, for example, simply won't download embedded files as a security measure against computer viruses. Embedded links are generally fine (Figure 24.4).

Response

When working on a project with other people and sometimes just in normal communication, you'll find that including portions of the original e-mail in your response helps everybody keep track of the discussion. This is especially true

Figure 24.2: Long subject line

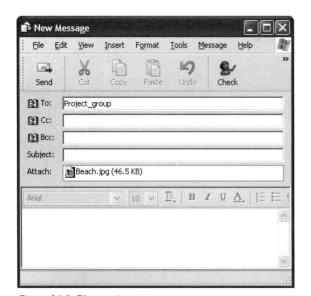

Figure 24.3: File attachment

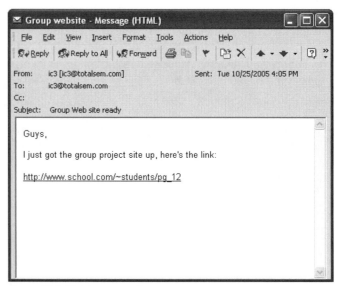

Figure 24.4: Link in an e-mail

when you reply and cc: multiple people (like with a Reply to All response). This enables you to keep a history of the conversation within the body of the e-mail. On the other hand, when an e-mail conversation has bounced back and forth through a couple of replies, you should delete some of the quoted material just for the sake of keeping your e-mail short and to the point.

When you decide what to keep of the original message, make sure you mark the text in some way so the recipient(s) can quickly see what part of your message is quoted. Most e-mail programs put angle brackets > in front of quoted text for you. You can also indent or separate threads with some kind of formatting, like the message in Figure 24.5.

Managing Your Mail

E-mail programs enable you to change basic settings, to save and sort your e-mail messages for fast retrieval, for example, and customize your account. You can even set a message on most programs to reply for you automatically when you're on vacation or simply unable to get to a computer for a few days.

You can, in essence, make your e-mail program into a post office customized to your needs.

Organizing E-mail with Folders

E-mail applications come with several standard folders for storing and sorting e-mail messages. By default, e-mail programs save all incoming e-mail messages in the *Inbox*. Outgoing messages go temporarily in the *Outbox* until they're sent, at which time you have a copy saved in the *Sent*

When E-Mail Won't Cut It

Sometimes e-mail is not the ideal way to send important documents. Legal documents, for instance, need an original signature, and thus should be sent through traditional delivery methods rather than electronically. (You can sometimes get away with faxing a signed document, but it depends on the circumstance.) The same goes for any document in which security is an issue.

Figure 24.5: Quoted text provides a history of the conversation so far.

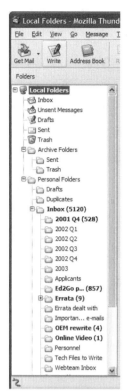

Figure 24.6: Messy Local Folders!

folder. E-mail messages you delete go to the *Deleted Items* or *Trash* folder; e-mail messages you start but don't send go to the *Drafts* folder.

Either periodically, or even with every message, you should move messages you have already read out of your Inbox. If they are no longer of any use to you, you should delete them to save space on your computer. If you want to hang on to them, file them in a different folder. Most e-mail programs enable you to create as many *local folders*—folders stored within the program but not visible in My Computer—as you like to sort your e-mail messages. You could create a folder for each of your friends and file e-mail messages that way, for example, or go for a more eclectic style (Figure 24.6).

You can accomplish any of the common housecleaning tasks—creating a new local folder, copying or moving a message from one folder to another, and deleting messages—with a couple of clicks of the mouse or keyboard. Go to **File | New | Folder** to create a folder. Left-click and drag a file to move it from one folder to another. You can also right-click and select **Move to Folder** or **Copy to Folder**. To delete, left-click to select a message and press the **[Delete]** key on your keyboard or right-click and select **Delete** from the menu. You can delete a local folder in the same ways.

You can also move or delete many messages all at once. If you have ten e-mail messages in your Inbox and you want to delete them all, click on the first message, then hold down the **[Shift]** key and click on the last message. This selects all the e-mail messages in between the two you initially selected as well. Right-click any highlighted message, and whatever you tell that message to do will be done by all of the highlighted messages.

If you want to pick and choose which messages to delete, hold down the **[Ctrl]** key. Click each message to select or deselect (it toggles selection on and off). Right-click on any of the highlighted messages and whatever you tell that message to do will be done to all of the highlighted messages (Figure 24.7).

You can recover items from your Deleted Items folder, just as you would from any other folder. The difference is that if you delete them from the Deleted Items folder, the e-mail messages are gone forever. Mail deleted from other folders just goes into the Deleted Items folder.

Microsoft calls the Sent folder Sent Items *in Outlook and Outlook Express.*

Hotmail Folders
Using the Hotmail account you created for one of the projects in Chapter 23, create one or two new folders and move or copy messages from your Inbox to the new folder(s). Create a new message and save it as a draft. What do the Tools options give you? (Hint: Think professional here.)

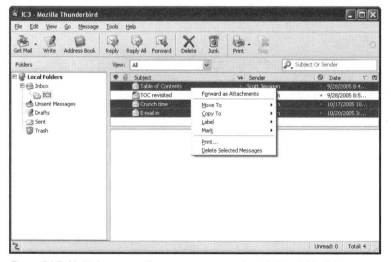

Figure 24.7: Multiple non-contiguous messages selected with right-click menu open

Flagging Mail

Most e-mail applications give you a way to mark e-mail, to *flag* it for viewing later, for example. You can mark mail as read or unread. Just about all the dedicated e-mail programs use a right-click menu for marking e-mail. Right-click a message in Outlook and select **Follow Up**, for example, to open the Flag for Follow Up dialog box (Figure 24.8). You can set all sorts of options here, such as the due date.

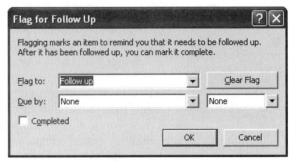

Figure 24.8: Flag for Follow Up dialog box

Thunderbird has a Mark menu that offers flagging and marking read or unread in one location. As a bonus, you can mark mail as junk mail here—more on that later in the chapter (Figure 24.9).

Most applications give you a way to mark outgoing e-mail—or change the *priority*—so you can quickly let your recipient know that an e-mail message is important or not important. In a new message or a reply in Outlook Express, for example, you can click the **Priority** button on the toolbar and change the priority from Normal to High or Low (Figure 24.10).

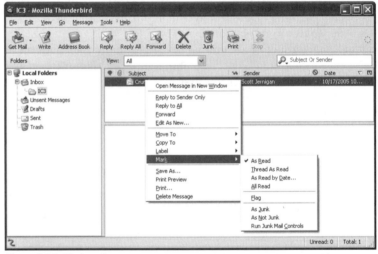

Figure 24.9: Mark options

Increasing Efficiency

E-mail software enables you to customize your mail so that certain behavior happens automatically. You know about signatures from Chapter 23, "Reach Out." You can have your program insert a tag line with each message so you can include your name, contact information, or some pithy slogan, all without typing. You can also automatically forward or redirect your e-mail from one account to another, or set a message that responds for you when you're away from your e-mail, although these settings need to be made on the mail server rather than in your e-mail application.

To set up a signature, go to **Tools | Options** in Outlook Express, for example, and click the **Signatures** tab. Click the **New** button and type what you want to include in the **Edit Signature** section (Figure 24.11). Click **OK** and you're done. Other programs work similarly.

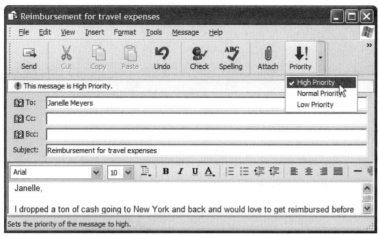

Figure 24.10: Changing priority

Figure 24.11: Signature

Auto-Forward

You can set up an e-mail account to *auto-forward* or *redirect* e-mail, so that mail goes from one account to another. You simply tell your mail server that when a message comes to account A, send it along to account B. Figure 24.12 shows a typical redirect screen set on an e-mail server.

Out-of-Office Reply

As a professional courtesy, you should always let customers and colleagues know when you're out of town on vacation and when you'll be back. That way they're not sitting around getting upset when you fail to respond to an important e-mail message in a timely fashion. An *out-of-office reply* automatically responds when someone e-mails you, sending a message to the sender. You can use this to direct the sender to a colleague who can help while you're away, as in Figure 24.13, or simply to let him or her know when you'll respond to the e-mail. Figure 24.13 shows a typical out-of-office reply, set on an e-mail server.

Troubleshooting

Just like anything in life, problems can arise that make e-mail fail to function properly. Some issues involve problems with e-mail servers and others with the configuration of your software. Some things you can fix, but others you can't. You can group typical problems in four categories: problems caused by the sender; server troubles; junk mail; and viruses and security threats.

What's my Motivation?

Dealing With Multiple Addresses

Many people use multiple e-mail addresses for different aspects of their lives, or sometimes just to help when someone mistypes an address. You can have an address at school, for example, a different one for work, and yet a third one for home. This helps you separate home life from work so you can forget about the former and relax. But when you're on vacation and the boss, sometimes it's helpful to stay in touch. Auto-forwarding your e-mail from one account to another can make this happen.

People also make mistakes on e-mail addresses, and redirection helps combat these mistakes and get mail delivered to where it's supposed to go. Mike Meyers (the best-selling author of computer books, not the Mike Myers of movie fame) gets e-mail from fans all over the world, but sometimes those fans don't quite get his primary address correct.

So, in addition to that address (michaelm@totalsem.com), he keeps other accounts such as mike@totalsem.com and mmeyers@totalsem.com, which redirect to his main account.

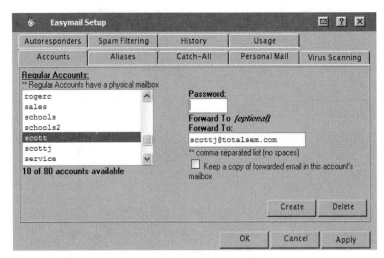

Figure 24.12: Forwarding from one address to another

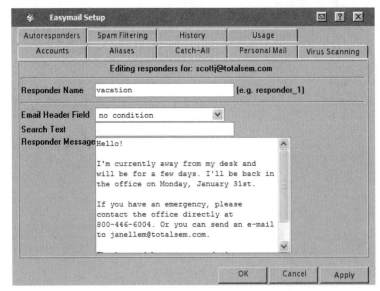

Figure 24.13: Out of Office message (here called an Autoresponder)

Sender Problems

Configuration problems and user errors cause a majority of problems for most users. These manifest as the failure of your e-mail program to send or receive e-mail; nasty replies to your messages; lost e-mail; and inability of your recipients to read your e-mail. You can fix all these things.

Failure to Send or Receive

When your e-mail software pops up with an error message saying it can't send or retrieve e-mail messages (Figure 24.14), this often points to either configuration issues (especially on new accounts) or connectivity issues. If you've just set up an account, check the settings to make sure you have the information about your mail server typed in properly. If it's an account that worked previously, check your cables. Anything unplugged or turned off?

If you receive mail properly, but don't get attached files, this points to your software automatically blocking certain attachments. Most e-mail programs enable you to turn this feature off. Microsoft Outlook is the notable exception.

Test Account Settings

Some errors occurred while processing the tests. Please review the list of errors below for more details. If the problem persist after taking the suggested actions, please contact your Internet Service Provider.

Stop

Close

Tasks | **Errors**

● Log onto incoming mail server (POP3): Unable to logon to the incoming mail server (POP3). Please verify the settings in the User Name, Password and E-mail fields.

Figure 24.14: Error message

Haste Makes Waste

People can't hear your voice when you send an e-mail message, which means they can't automatically tell when you're joking or asking an innocent question. This leads to frequent misunderstandings when people send and receive e-mail messages, especially when done in haste. People then get angry or hurt or both and say things that have no business being in an e-mail message! This problem is especially bad if you reply to an e-mail that you've been bcc:d on or do a Reply to All or Forward inappropriately.

Follow these simple rules to avoid the hasty or nasty e-mail message error. First, learn the policies at your work place or school regarding e-mail content, and then use the good manners you learned growing up. Lumped together, polices and manners form the basis of the unwritten set of rules governing e-mail conversations, called *netiquette*.

Second, most people who send e-mail to you do not mean to sound angry, scared, hurtful, or blunt. They simply don't necessarily communicate well with e-mail. Put yourself in their position and think about what they're asking or telling you before you start to respond.

Third, don't click **Send** in haste. Always take the time to review your e-mail. Make sure you haven't cc:d someone who shouldn't get the e-mail or done a Reply to All when you should do a simple reply.

Combined with the principles for writing effective e-mail covered earlier in the chapter, these three simple rules can make your e-mail experience a pleasant one. They can also make you a far more effective communicator.

Lost

Computers crash and files can go to binary heaven in a heartbeat. E-mail software is no different, except that it often contains messages you can't replace. You need to back up your e-mail messages and address book periodically. Most e-mail software enables you to *export*—save a copy someplace else—e-mail folders and your address book, although you sometimes have to jump through a hoop or two (Figure 24.15). If your computer crashes, you can rebuild or get a new one and then import your backed up mail files and address book.

Garbled E-mail

Every e-mail program can read simple text messages, but some can read and create highly formatted mail. If you send a message to a person formatted and his or her client can't decipher it, then it'll appear garbled.

Online message boards have this problem even more than e-mail, where seemingly simple or civil discussions can turn downright nasty. Everybody starts yelling or cursing and the discussion turns into a flame war. Avoid these like the plague!

Inappropriate Response
You learned about cc:, bcc:, reply, reply to all, and forwarding in Chapter 23, "Reach Out." Turn back there now and see if you can answer these questions. When should you not click **Reply to All**? What should you include when you reply to or forward a message?

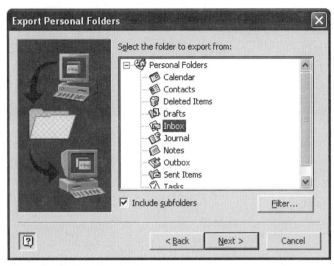

Figure 24.15: Exporting folders in Outlook

HyperText Markup Language (HTML) is a formatting language used in most Web sites on the Internet, enabling you to make text appear bold, for example, or italicized, among other things (Figure 24.16).

Outlook Express and other applications can enable you to do the same and thus make your e-mail more pleasing to your recipient, but you shouldn't use it unless you know he or she can read it. Figure 24.17 shows a new message with the Format menu down. See the Rich Text (HTML) and Plain Text options.

Server Problems

Problems on the server side range from full mail boxes to junk mail pouring into your Inbox. You can solve some of these problems.

The procedures for backing up messages and addresses vary widely among applications. Check inside the Address Book in some for the specific Address Book export feature.

You'll see the term archive *used* in place of backup or export on some exams.

Bounced Mail

Sometimes, messages you send may leave your e-mail server just fine, but are bounced back to you as undeliverable without getting to the recipient. This can happen if you have typed the recipient's e-mail address incorrectly, or if her e-mail server is not functioning properly, or if he has exceeded his own mailbox storage capacity on the server. You can fix your typo, but the other stuff is pretty much out of your hands. Try to send again an hour or a day later.

Spam

E-mail that comes into your Inbox from a source that's not a friend, family member, or colleague, and that you didn't ask for, can create huge problems for your computer and you. This unsolicited e-mail, called *spam*, accounts for a huge percentage of traffic on the Internet. Spam comes in many flavors, from legitimate businesses trying to sell you products to scammers who just want to take your money. Hoaxes, pornography, and get-rich-quick schemes pour into the inboxes of most e-mail users. They waste your time and can easily offend.

You can use several options to cope with the flood of spam. The first option is defense. Never post your e-mail address on the Internet. One study tested this theory and found that *over 97%* of the spam received during the study went to e-mail addresses they had posted on the public Internet.

Filters and filtering software can block spam at your mail server and at your computer. AOL implemented blocking schemes in 2004, for example, that dropped the average spam received by its subscribers by a large percentage, perhaps as much as 50%. You

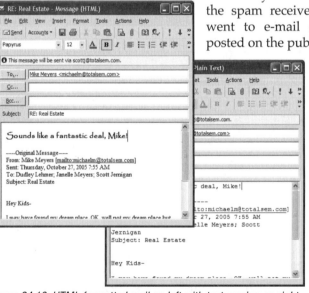

Figure 24.16: HTML formatted mail on left with text version on right

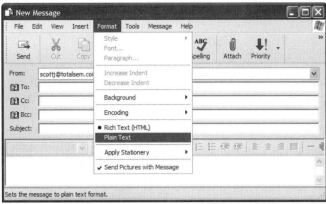

Figure 24.17: Switching from Rich Text (HTML) to Plain Text

can set most e-mail programs to block e-mail from specific people—good to use if someone is harassing you—or to a specific person. Some spammers use a bogus recipient and bcc: all the real addresses. Blocking the bogus recipient will block that spam. You can block by subject line or key words. Most people get a third-party anti-spam program instead of using the filters in their e-mail program.

Viruses and Security Threats

The wide-open nature of the Internet today makes it a dangerous place for your computer. Threats come from software designed to attack your computer to people who try to steal your personal information and use it to steal your money. You need to understand the threats and take the proper precautions.

Viruses

Viruses and other evil software can attack your computer, causing it to delete important files, damage your operating system, and even crash your computer completely. Common sense and anti-virus software can protect your computer. Don't open files attached to e-mail messages from unknown senders. Don't even open files from known senders that looks suspicious (the file, not the sender!). E-mail them back and ask about the attachment. If it's legitimate, they'll let you know and you can open it safely.

Theft

More and more people turn to the Internet to do common tasks, like paying bills, updating credit card information, and so on, that puts at risk very important information. A determined thief who gets hold of your credit card number or your banking password, for example, could do amazing amounts of damage to you. The thief could steal your money or run up a huge credit card bill. Worse, the thief could steal your identity and get credit cards issued to him or her and then run up a giant debt, trashing your credit rating forever.

Many e-mail users mask information in e-mail messages from prying eyes through the use of *encryption*, a technology that turns the contents of the message into a code. Only the recipient on the other end of the e-mail can decode the message and view the content. How to set up encryption goes well beyond the scope of basic e-mail use, but you can dive into it a little here: http://www.ciphertrust.com/resources/articles/articles/ssl.php

Fight Spam Right!
Spam filtering software that you purchase and put on your computer can help, but you have to do some research to see which ones offer the best performance. You want to avoid software that causes false positives—mislabeling acceptable e-mail as spam—because then you miss legitimate e-mail messages from family and friends. So, it's time to fire up your trusty Web browser and do some searching.

Start by going to Google and searching for **anti-spam software reviews**. One of the first sites that should come up takes you to PC Magazine's review list that they keep up-to-date. What's the current Editor's Choice? What other options do you have?

You read about anti-virus programs way back in Chapter 10, "The Good, the Bad, and the Ugly," so turn back now and see if you can answer these questions. What do anti-virus programs do? What are the two top programs? Why might you want to use Avast!?

Creating the Message

■ A well-crafted e-mail message should cover a topic directly and without excessive words. Use a professional style, like in a formal letter. Check your e-mail for spelling and grammatical errors. Don't use all capital letters in an e-mail message or subject line, because Internet users consider that shouting. Finally, avoid using emoticons or jokes.

■ A good subject line offers a clear, short, direct statement of the purpose of your e-mail. Attached files can enhance an e-mail message, but as a general rule, don't send files larger than 1 MB to someone unless you know for sure that his or her e-mail server and connection can handle it. Embedded files can cause problems with many e-mail servers and programs. Embedded links are generally fine.

■ When working on a project with other people and sometimes just in normal communication, you'll find that including portions of the original e-mail in your response helps everybody keep track of the discussion. This is especially true when you reply and cc: multiple people (like with a Reply to All response).

Managing Your Mail

■ E-mail applications come with several standard folders for storing and sorting e-mail messages. By default, e-mail programs save all incoming e-mail messages in the *Inbox*. Outgoing messages go temporarily in the *Outbox* until they're sent, at which time you have a copy saved in the *Sent* folder. You'll also see *Deleted Items* or Trash and Drafts. You can readily add more folders by going to **File | New | Folder** in most e-mail applications.

■ Use a simple drag and drop or right-click and go for menu options to manipulate your files and folders. You can move, copy, and delete with these options.

■ Most e-mail applications give you a way to mark e-mail, flagging it for viewing later, for example. You can mark mail as read or unread. You can change the priority of an outgoing e-mail to let your recipient(s) know that it's important.

■ You can increase your efficiency by customizing your e-mail program. You can add a signature, for example, that shows your contact information without you having to type it every time. *Auto-forwarding* or *redirecting* sends e-mail received in one account automatically to another account. An *out-of-office reply* sends an automatic message to people who send you e-mail so you can let them know when you'll be back in the office.

Troubleshooting

- You can fix some problems you'll find with e-mail through standard troubleshooting. Group typical problems in four categories: problems caused by the sender, server troubles, junk mail, and viruses and security threats.

- Configuration problems and user errors cause a majority of problems for most users. These manifest as failure of your e-mail program to send or receive e-mail, nasty replies to your messages, lost e-mail, and the inability of your recipients to read your e-mail. You can fix all these things.

- When your e-mail software can't send or retrieve e-mail messages, check configuration screens on new accounts and connectivity on formerly working accounts. If you receive mail properly, but don't get attached files, turn this feature off in your software.

- People can't hear your voice when you send an e-mail message, which can lead to misunderstandings, anger, and hurt feelings when people send and receive e-mail messages, especially when done in haste. Always take a moment to read your messages before you send them. Hesitate on the Send button!

- You need to back up your e-mail messages and address book periodically. Most e-mail software enables you to *export*—save a copy someplace else—e-mail folders and your address book.

- HyperText Markup Language (HTML) is a formatting language used in most Web sites on the Internet, enabling you to make text appear bold, for example, or italicized. You can use this to format your e-mail messages, but e-mail software that doesn't read HTML might show the message as garbled text.

- E-mail can bounce if your recipient's Inbox on the server is full.

- Spam—hoaxes, pornography, get-rich-quick schemes, and more—pour into the Inboxes of most e-mail users. You can combat spam using common sense and spam filters. Just don't post your e-mail address on a Web site or online forum.

- Viruses and thieves can compromise your computer's security and make things very bad for you. Viruses can destroy your files and crash your drive. Use common sense and anti-virus software to ward off viruses. Use encryption to stop thieves from being able to see your e-mail messages and get control over sensitive information, like passwords.

Key Terms

Archive

Auto-forward

Deleted Items

Drafts

Emoticons

Encryption

Export

Flag

Inbox

Local folders

Netiquette

Outbox

Out-of-office reply

Paper trail

Priority

Redirect

Sent

Sent Items

Smilies

Spam

Key Term Quiz

Use the Key Terms list to complete the following sentences. Not all the terms will be used.

1. Jon wanted to _____ his e-mail folders and address book so he could import them into his new computer.

2. When she went on vacation to Bermuda for a week and knew she wouldn't have access to e-mail, Valerie set a(n) _____ message on her e-mail so her clients would know to contact her business partner.

3. The proper term to describe smilies is _____.

4. By default, your e-mail downloads into the _____ folder.

5. When you send e-mail, it goes to the _____ first, then the Sent folder.

6. Unsolicited e-mail is _____.

7. Josiah changed the _____ on an e-mail sent to his boss from Normal to High, so his boss would know the message was important.

8. Ben accidentally deleted an important e-mail, but Sarah was not worried. She knew the e-mail would be in the _____ folder and not gone forever.

9. Maria set her work e-mail account to _____ or *redirect* messages to her Gmail account.

10. To mark an e-mail message so you'll remember to read it later, you can _____ it.

Multiple Choice Quiz

1. Which of the following describes an effective e-mail?
   A. Brief and professional
   B. Long and professional
   C. Brief and casual
   D. Long and casual

2. Jill set up her signature to include her name, e-mail address, a blond joke, and a winking smiley. When she e-mailed her boss, she got in trouble. What did she do wrong? (Select all that apply.)
   A. Included her name
   B. Included her e-mail address
   C. Included a blond joke
   D. Included a smiley

3. Which of the following describes an effective subject line in an e-mail message?
   A. Something catchy, to make it stand out from other e-mail
   B. Clear, short statement of the purpose of the e-mail
   C. A detailed statement of the purpose of the e-mail
   D. A blank subject line

4. What's a good maximum size for e-mail attachments?
   A. 1 KB
   B. 100 KB
   C. 1 MB
   D. 10 MB

5. Carolina is working on a project with two of her classmates, Bill and Janelle. She gets an e-mail from Bill addressed to both her and Janelle, asking about opinions on a particular topic. What's her best course of action here?
   A. Reply to Bill with a clean e-mail
   B. Reply to Bill with an e-mail that includes the original message
   C. Reply to all with a clean e-mail
   D. Reply to all with an e-mail that includes the original message

6. Marina has six folders in her e-mail program, including Inbox and Outbox. She wants to create a new folder called Answered Mail so she can move all the messages that she's responded to already out of her Inbox. Bill argues that she not only shouldn't do that, she can't do that. He says that e-mail programs come with six personal folders and that's all you get. Who's correct?
   A. Only Marina is correct. She can easily create a new folder and move her e-mail messages.
   B. Only Bill is correct. E-mail programs allow only the default folders.
   C. Neither Marina nor Bill is correct. Marina can't add a folder, but she can rename one of the default ones and move her messages into that folder.
   D. Neither Marina nor Bill is correct. Marina can easily add a folder, but she can only copy, not move, her messages from the Inbox.

7. How do you select multiple messages to delete?
   A. Click on the first one. Hold the **[Alt]** key down and then click on the last one.
   B. Click on the first one. Hold the **[Ctrl]** key down and then click on the last one.
   C. Click on the first one. Hold the **[Shift]** key down and then click on the last one.
   D. Click on the first one. Hold the **[Tab]** key down and then click on the last one.

8. How do you delete a message from your Inbox? (Select all that apply.)
   A. Select the message and press the **[Delete]** key.
   B. Select the message and go to **File** | **Delete**.
   C. Left-click the message and select **Delete**.
   D. Right-click the message and select **Delete**.

9. Ian set up a new e-mail account with the settings given to him from his ISP, but he can't send or receive e-mail. What's most likely the cause?
   A. He made a typo when entering the configuration information.
   B. He's not connected to the Internet.
   C. He didn't activate his account.
   D. The server is down.

10. Your friend, who's new to e-mail, sends you a brief message that reads, "HEY, WHAT'S UP? LET'S GO TO MALL TOMORROW." How should you respond?
    A. Immediately respond with a message informing your friend that you don't go to (the) mall with rude people who make typos.
    B. Spend some time crafting a response that says, "WHY THE HECK ARE YOU SHOUTING AT ME?"
    C. Spend some time crafting a response that addresses the question of going to the mall, and also mentions that typing in all capital letters is seen as the equivalent of shouting.
    D. Delete the message. True friends don't shout at each other.

11. Which of the following languages can you use in some e-mail programs to apply formatting to an e-mail message?
    A. Plain text
    B. HTML
    C. DOC
    D. Format text

12. What should you do to avoid losing saved e-mail messages and your address book in case of a computer crash?
    A. Export your local folders and address book periodically.
    B. Forward your local folders and address book periodically.
    C. Print them out.
    D. Delete them periodically.

13. Which of the following can cause a message to bounce from the recipient's mail server?
    A. Your computer is not connected to the Internet.
    B. You sent a message in rich text rather than plain text.
    C. Your mail server is down.
    D. Your recipient's mailbox is full.

14. What's the best way to avoid getting excessive unsolicited e-mail?
    A. Use anti-spam software.
    B. Use anti-virus software.
    C. Use America Online as your Internet service provider.
    D. Never post your e-mail address on the Internet.

15. Which method enables you to turn an e-mail message into code that only your recipient can decode?
    A. Encoding
    B. Encryption
    C. Babelfish
    D. You can't do this to an e-mail message.

Essay Questions

1. Your boss wants you to train new employees on how to use the company e-mail system. Put together a short essay that discusses netiquette, including at least five rules they should follow.

2. Write an e-mail message that describes what you want for your birthday. Follow the format outlined in this chapter for an e-mail message, including subject line, that's suitable for a professional environment.

3. Using information gathered from the "Fight Spam Right!" Action! sidebar earlier in this chapter, write a short essay about the best spam filter for your needs. Tell why you chose it over the others and explain how it fits with the way you use e-mail.

Projects

1. Put together a presentation that compares and contrasts features in three anti-virus programs.

2. Put together a presentation that compares and contrasts the features of two e-mail programs. These can be dedicated e-mail applications, Web-based e-mail, or a combination.

Information Sources on the Internet

Ted: "Here in Barcelona, everything was swept aside. The world was turned upside down and stayed there."
Fred: "Has it ever occurred to you that maybe the world was upside down before, and now it's right side up?"

– Ted and Fred Boynton, *Barcelona*

This chapter covers the following IC³ exam objectives:

- IC³-3   3.1.1   Identify terminology related to the Internet

- IC³-3   3.1.2   Identify the purpose of a browser in accessing information on the World Wide Web

- IC³-3   3.1.3   Identify different elements of a Web site

- IC³-3   3.1.4   Identify different types of Web sites by their extensions, and the purposes of different types of sites

- IC³-3   3.1.6   Identify different ways of communicating and corresponding via the Internet

- IC³-3   3.2.1   Identify the make-up of a Web address/Uniform Resource Locator (URL)

- IC³-3   3.2.2   Navigate the Web using a browser

- IC³-3   3.2.11   Identify settings that can be modified in a Web browser application

The Internet has changed the world like no invention before ever has. When radio was invented, it took 38 years before there were 50 million radio listeners. For television, it took 13 years before there were 50 million TV viewers. It took just 4 years for there to be 50 million Internet users—and now there are almost a billion. The vast majority of all businesses in the U.S. have Internet access. The most amazing thing is that the Internet is still growing!

The Internet offers a wealth of information in a variety of sources. Most folks think of the Internet as the *World Wide Web* (or simply, *the Web*), a set of servers that you interact with by clicking on things—text or pictures—with your mouse. In truth, though, the Web is but one portion of the Internet.

This chapter focuses on the different information sources on the Internet, starting with the Web and its army of Web sites and Web servers. You'll examine different types of Web pages and then go into detail about Web browsers, the software tools that enable you to view Web pages. The chapter wraps with a discussion about alternative information sources on the Internet that you won't find on the Web.

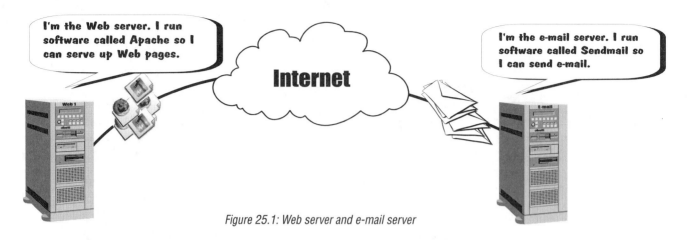

Figure 25.1: Web server and e-mail server

Web Sites and Web Pages

Web sites live on *Web servers*—computers that run Web site software. These servers are just like other servers you've seen in this book, like the e-mail servers in the last two chapters. They just run different (or additional) software (Figure 25.1). The Web has thousands of Web servers.

Each site contains one or more *Web pages*, text documents created using Hypertext Markup Language (HTML) or one of the fancier languages. You know from Chapter 24, "Effective E-mail," that HTML enables you to format an e-mail message in some e-mail programs, so you can add bold or italicized text, for example. HTML does the same thing for Web pages. Figure 25.2 shows you a Web page viewed through a *Web browser* program—an application specifically designed to display HTML—and the same page viewed as a text document so you can see the raw HTML coding turning things bold <b> or italicized <i>.

URLs

Every Web site that connects to the Internet must have a unique name, called a *uniform resource locator (URL)*, like www.google.com. The first portion of the URL is the *name* of the Web server, often www. The second portion of the name, as you probably suspect from earlier chapters, is the *domain*.

HTML

HTML enables you to format Web pages in a fairly logical way. It uses tags, simple codes that do one thing, like turn bold on or turn bold off. In almost every case, tags come in pairs, one to turn on a feature and the other to turn it off. So, if want to make a word boldface, you would put the <b> tag before the word and the </b> tag after the word. If you wanted to make a sentence boldface and italicized, you'd simply nest the tags, starting with these: <b><i> and ending the sentence with these: </i></b>. You can find one of the best tutorials on basic HTML at this site: http://archive.ncsa.uiuc.edu/General/Internet/WWW/HTMLPrimer.html

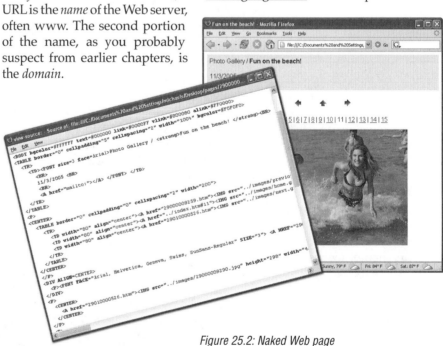

Figure 25.2: Naked Web page

Types of Web Sites

Web site domains, just like e-mail address domains, have two portions, the network name and the top-level domain (also called the domain code or *extension*—the two- or three-letter code at the end. Web sites can use any of the top-level domains, but the most common are .com, .edu, .org, .gov, and the international codes, like .us.

Just glancing at a Web site address can tell you a lot about a Web site before you even visit it. You can tell the *type* of Web site you check out by looking at the top-level domain.

Commercial (.com)

The .com Web extension was designed for commercial use, but all sorts of sites, commercial or otherwise, use it. The Web site for Alien Scooters in Austin, Texas, provides a good example of a .com site, at www.alienscooters.com (Figure 25.3). The Web site gives you information about electric bikes and scooters and tells you about the company. You can purchase electric bikes and scooters directly from the Web site as well, which makes the site an *e-commerce site*.

Figure 25.3: Alien Scooters

Academic (.edu)

Educational facilities—primarily universities—use the .edu extension. The Rice University site provides a good example (Figure 25.4). You can find information about programs, degrees, departments, faculty, research, admissions, and much more.

Organizational (.org)

Non-profit and political organizations use the .org extension. An example of a .org site is www.aclu.org for the American Civil Liberties Union (see Figure 25.5). You can learn about the organization in great detail here, including ongoing programs and fund-raising. You can donate but not purchase anything at this site, so it's not an e-commerce site at all.

Governmental (.gov)

Governmental agencies of the United States use the .gov extension. Figure 25.6 shows the Web site of the National Aeronautics and Space Administration (NASA), the fine folks who put a man on the moon. The site is chock full of information about space, the planets, the NASA missions, and more.

Funny Face

By convention but not by rule, most network people name Web servers www, short for World Wide Web, the official name of the Web. If you pay attention when you surf the Web, though, you might notice a lot of servers with other names. At this writing, for example, if you go to www. microsoft.com and click on the link for the Office home page, you'll open up a Web site named office.microsoft.com, which is definitely not the same server as www.microsoft.com.

*If you want a laugh, check out one of the first Web pages I ever made—it's still online, unchanged since 1996! Here's the URL: vi.uh.edu/pages/bizart.html. The name of the Web server? **vi**, not **www**.*

Although the technical name for the last section of the domain (such as .com) is top-level domain, the IC³ exam follows the convention used by many people, calling this the extension.

E-Mail and Web Addresses

You already know about the domain codes from Chapter 23, "Reach Out and Touch Someone." Turn back there now and see if you can answer these questions. What can the domain tell you about a particular e-mail user? Does this differ at all from what you might expect at a Web site with the same domain?

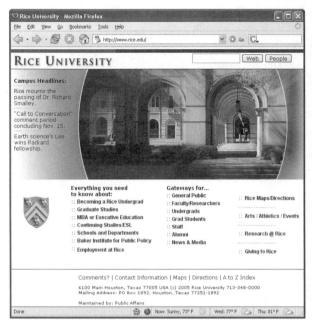

Figure 25.4: The Rice University Web site

Figure 25.5: The ACLU Web site

Figure 25.6: The NASA Web site

International (.uk, .jp, .de)

Many non-U.S. Web sites use the international extension for their home country. Web sites from the United Kingdom end in .uk, for example, while Web sites from Spain will end in .es (for España, which is how you say *Spain* in Spanish). Clicking on www.steamcar.co.uk will take you to the Web site of the British Steam Car Challenge, a group dedicated to making a steam-powered car that can go very fast (Figure 25.7).

Web Page Elements

Most Web pages use three elements to display their information, enable you to navigate to other places, and provide feedback: text, images, and interactive elements, such as links and forms. You know about text on a Web page. Text looks just like the words you're reading on paper in this book.

Images

The vast majority of files used as images on Web pages are GIF or JPEG files. A typical file name (if you had a picture of your family, for instance) would be family.gif or family.jpg. HTML codes embedded in the Web page tell the Web browser to display a particular graphic file and where to put it on the page.

Links

Links, or *hyperlinks*, make the magic of the Web happen, enabling you to click on something and go from one Web page to another. The new page can be on the same Web server as the link, or on another Web server altogether. Links can appear in many forms on Web pages, as text, graphics, buttons, menus, and lists.

A *text link* is an underlined word (or a connected group of words) usually in a different color from the rest of the surrounding text (Figure 25.8). Text links usually look different so that users will know that they can visit a different Web page just by clicking them. The Green Car Congress Web site provides a great example of text links, relying almost exclusively on them throughout the site so you can get to information about electric cars, engines, battery technology, and more very quickly. Note that the mouse pointer changes shape to a little hand when over a link.

Many Web sites use pictures as links, rather than words, or some combination of the two as *graphical links*. The always-amusing Altoids Web site, for example, takes this over the top in their Ad Gallery (Figure 25.9). More commonly, you'll see *buttons* of some sort that you can click or a *list* or *menu* of links. Figure 25.10 shows a typical drop-down menu.

Figure 25.7: The British Steam Car Challenge Web site

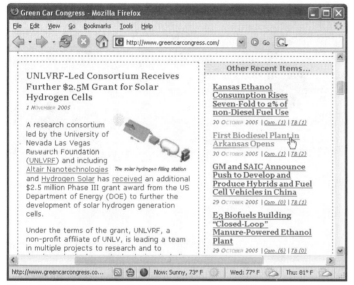

Figure 25.8: Text links on the Green Car Congress Web page (www.greencarcongress.com)

Forms

Forms enable you to interact with a Web page to send information to the Web site directly. You can provide feedback to the site owner, for example, or sign up for a mailing list. You use forms to buy things on the Web.

All forms have several interactive elements, such as text boxes, radio buttons, drop-down menus, check boxes, and buttons. Figure 25.11 shows a typical contact form. You can fill out the fields, select which department to send to, and then click the Submit button when you finish. Most likely, the result will be an e-mail to the site owners and an e-mail to you saying that they received your e-mail.

Accessing the Web

Web browsers enable you to view the Web. Here's how the process works. After you connect to the Internet, you open a Web browser and that browser immediately sends out a signal to the Web server that holds your *home page*—the page your browser goes to by default. That server responds and your

Picture This

You know from way back in Chapter 10, "The Good, the Bad, and the Ugly," that JPEG and GIF files offer two choices for images on the Web. Turn back to that chapter now and see if you can answer these questions. What is the third image format that can be used on the Web? What format would be best for printing, rather than viewing online? Why would you not want to use BMP files on the Web?

Figure 25.9: Ad Gallery featuring
graphical links

Figure 25.10: Drop-down menu selected

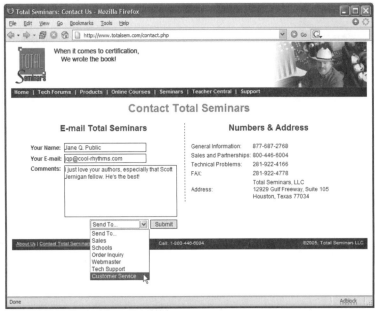

Figure 25.11: Typical form on a Web page

computer downloads information—text, pictures, forms, and so on—that the browser interprets and places on your screen (Figure 25.12). If that server is down, you'll get an error in the browser window, such as "The page cannot be displayed."

Web browsers and servers use the *Hypertext Transfer Protocol* (*HTTP*) to communicate. HTTP is another protocol like the many you've seen before, such as POP3 and SMTP for e-mail. It works with TCP/IP, the common tongue of the Internet, enabling Web browsers to request and download pages. A quick glance at the screen shots so far in this chapter, such as Figures 8 and 9, and you can see that the URLs all have http:// at the beginning. This means the browser tells the server that it's looking for a Web page, written with HTML.

Web Browser Interface

Although you can find many Web browsers out there, most share a fairly consistent look and feel. Figure 25.14 shows the most popular browser, Microsoft's Internet Explorer, with callouts for the items you should know: the menu bar, standard buttons toolbar, **Back** and **Forward** buttons, Address bar, Go button, main pane or window, and status bar.

Most of the changes made in Web browsers in the past ten years have occurred below the surface, where browsers can handle more sophisticated Web sites and servers. A glance at the NCSA Mosaic browser from 1997, for example, reveals a few layout differences, but pretty much the same features (Figure 25.15). Opening the same pages on the same high-end computer gives the tale of the tape, though. A page that opens in the 2005 version of Internet Explorer in a couple of seconds, for example, takes nearly four times that long in Mosaic.

Figure 25.12: Requesting a Web page from the Web server

Figure 25.13: Internet Options dialog box

Web Browser Variants

Every Web browser interprets Web pages differently—which might surprise folks. Browsers have to translate the HTML code on the page into (hopefully) well-organized pages, but have varying degrees of success.

Many companies make browsers, but two dominate the market: Internet Explorer and Firefox. Other browsers, like Opera and Safari, have a foothold because of innovative features or some lingering fan base.

Changing Your Home Page

You can (and arguably should) change the default home page of your browser. The default home page for Internet Explorer, for example, is www.msn.com, the Microsoft network. Although the site offers a lot of information and links to more, it also can take a long time to load, especially if you have a dial-up connection. Google offers a clean, quickly loading site that combines with the best search engine on the Web, so www.google.com makes a good alternative home page.

*To change your home page in Internet Explorer, go to **Tools | Internet Options** and select the **General** tab (Figure 25.13). Type in any Web address in the **Address:** field and click **OK** to make it your new home page. Alternatively, if you find a great site on the Internet, you can surf there, open the **Internet Options dialog box**, and click the **Use Current** button to make it your new home page.*

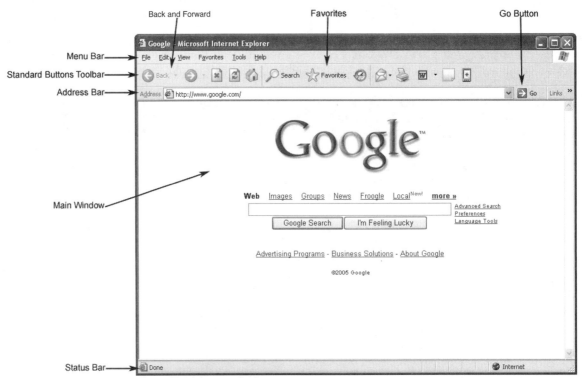

Back and Forward · Favorites · Go Button

Menu Bar

Standard Buttons Toolbar

Address Bar

Main Window

Status Bar

Figure 25.14: Internet Explorer

Figure 25.15: NCSA Mosaic, the browser that brought the Web to life

Internet Explorer

Microsoft bundles Internet Explorer with every copy of Windows, which means that nearly every computer on the planet uses Internet Explorer as the default browser (see Figure 25.16). Microsoft built proprietary features into the software—used to display active buttons, for example—and many Web site developers use those features in their sites. The market dominance combined with proprietary Web site features make Internet Explorer both the *de facto* standard for Web browsers and a pain for conscientious Web site developers, because a lot of users have switched to newer, more feature-rich browsers such as Firefox.

Firefox

The Mozilla Foundation—along with hundreds of volunteers—developed a free Web browser called Mozilla Firefox, that became an overnight success. It had over 25 million downloads in the 14 weeks after its release and stands as one of the most used free applications, because of its speediness and very good ability to stop pop-up ads. You can also have multiple pages open at the same time and flit from one to the other using tabs at the top of the document window (Figure 25.17). The only downside to Firefox is the fact that a small but meaningful percentage of Web pages only work properly in Internet Explorer.

Other Browsers

Browsers other than Internet Explorer and Firefox hold a tiny share of the market. Some offer advantages over the big two, while others survive because of nostalgia. Netscape Navigator once completely dominated all competition because it was both the first commercial browser and the most innovative, but it has virtually disappeared today.

Figure 25.16: Internet Explorer with default home page

Opera has a small *footprint*—meaning that it takes very little hard drive space to store, especially compared with monster programs like Internet Explorer—and displays Web pages quickly (Figure 25.18). Companies such as Adobe and Macromedia use its *engine*—the core programming code of the software, nicknamed "Presto"—in their Web-oriented products. Cell phone and PDA companies also have adopted Opera as the default browser in their products because of its Small Screen Rendering technology.

Figure 25.17: Firefox displaying a Web page with others open in tabs

Navigating the Web

The Address bar, Back and Forward buttons, the keyboard, and the mouse enable you to navigate the Web. The *Address bar* displays the URL of the site you're on or a URL you're about to access. The **Back** *button* enables you to navigate to a previously viewed site and the **Forward** *button* enables you to return.

Customizing Firefox
You can customize Firefox by adding free extensions—little programs written to do cool things. With Mouse Gestures, for example, you can hold down the right mouse button and use it to navigate or close a Web site with a flick of the wrist. Draw left and let go of the mouse key and poof! It's just like clicking the Back button. Once you've gotten hooked on extensions and tabbed browsing (discussed in the text), using another browser feels like you're forced to drive an old clunker rather than a sports car.

Grab Firefox by the Tail
If you have access to the Internet and permission to install software on your computer, surf on over to www.mozilla.org and download a copy of Firefox. After you install it, spend some time with the interface. Open up a Web page. Press [Ctrl + T] to open a new tab, then open a different Web site in that tab. Practice tabbing back and forth. What do you think?

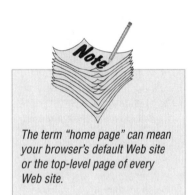

Figure 25.18: Opera displaying a Web page

To use the Address bar, type in a URL and press **[Enter]** or click the **Go** button. If you type a Web server's basic URL, the browser displays the *home page* of that server—usually a page called default.html, default.htm, index. html, or index.htm that the browser does not reveal in the Address Bar.

Once you open a Web page, you can use the links on that Web page to visit other pages within that same Web site or pages on other Web servers. Just click and go. To tell where a hypertext link will take you, hold your mouse pointer over the link and look in your browser's *Status bar*. The browser will display the URL associated with the link.

Your browser keeps track of pages you visit during a session, enabling you to go back to a previously viewed page with a click of the **Back** button. If you want to go two pages back, click **Back** twice. You can also use the little drop-down arrow to view all the pages you've visited during a session. You can return to any page by selecting it from the list (Figure 25.19). Finally, once you've gone back, you can use the **Forward** button to go to the page from which you returned.

Other Sources of Information on the Internet

Computers use many different protocols (languages) to communicate across the Internet. Web servers and browsers use HTTP, as you know from this chapter. You can access other sources of information on the Internet with FTP, mailing lists, newsgroups, chat rooms, and online conferencing.

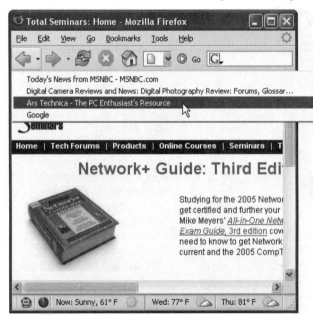

Figure 25.19: Selecting a previously viewed page to reopen

FTP

Outside of sending e-mails, downloading stuff has become one of the most popular use of the Internet. From games to music to videos, downloading off the Internet is a multi-billion dollar business that grows every day. The *File Transfer Protocol* (*FTP*) enables you to transfer files between computers much more efficiently than HTTP (although HTTP certainly works for transferring files). You can use a dedicated FTP program, such as CuteFTP, to access an FTP server directly (Figure 25.20). Some programs have FTP built-in, but invisible to the user. Many music-downloading sites and programs, for example, use FTP to enable you to download songs, but the FTP process just happens magically as far as the user is concerned.

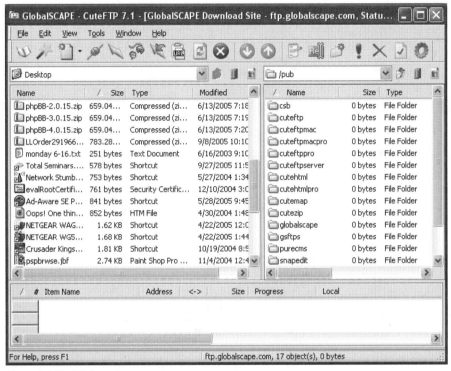

Figure 25.20: FTP in action

Mailing Lists

E-mail provides excellent sources of information through *mailing lists*, Internet communities that exchange information through mail that automatically goes to every member of the list. Many of the mailing lists use *LISTSERV*, software in continuous development since 1986, which means it works well! If some topic interests you and you'd like to correspond with other folks with similar interests, you can sign up and receive and send mail to all the other members of the list all at once. If you get on a mailing list that's too active for you, you can unsubscribe from it by sending a message via e-mail.

Newsgroups/Forums

Getting e-mail from a group that's into the same topics you're into can get overwhelming. When you get busy with other things or when some news hits that sets the list on fire, the simple volume of e-mail in your Inbox can become daunting. An alternative way to post and access the same information is to use a public *newsgroup* or forum. That way, you can access the newsgroup when you have time and not access when you don't.

Unmasking the Home Page

Because the home page of most Web sites is named "default" or "index" with the extension of ".html" or ".htm," you can quickly determine the name of the home page of a Web site by trying combinations of names and extensions. Open up a Web browser and surf over to the Internet Movie Database, www. imdb.com, the finest movie reference site on the planet. When you open the site, you should see http://www.imdb.com/ in the Address Bar, even if you didn't add the http:// manually. Now try in order these combinations: default.html, default.htm, index. html, and index.htm. Which one is the real home page? Try this with other sites too!

Finding Your List

It might take a little searching to find the right mailing list for your particular interests. If the topic is popular enough, you might have to choose among the many mailing lists available. Start with a search at Google or Yahoo!. The top link might not always be the best. A quick search for "mailing lists about electric vehicles" on Yahoo!, for example, turned up a dozen or more. Number 8 on the list was a LISTSERV list, the EV Electric Vehicle Discussion Mailing List. Try your luck!

The *USENET* is a collection of literally thousands of newsgroups that contain posts from individuals on every topic you can imagine, and probably quite a few that you didn't need to know about. You access USENET over the Internet using special newsreader software (Figure 25.21).

USENET can get you in trouble quickly in two ways. First, the USENET has unregulated content. People post everything from brilliant essays and poetry to seriously depraved photographs and movies—even things that will land you in jail if you download them. Be warned and stay away from things that might be offensive to you or illegal. If you think a post might contain something bad, it probably does, so don't even click on it.

Second, spammers use automated software to check all posts made in the USENET for e-mail addresses. The surest way to get your Inbox filled with spam is to post your valid e-mail address on USENET. Don't do it!

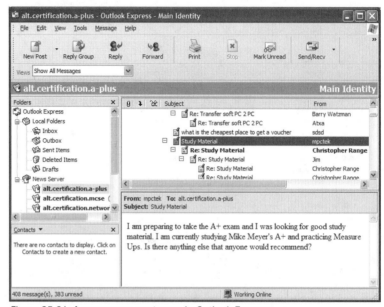

Figure 25.21: A newsgroup post open in Outlook Express

Chat Rooms

The Internet offers real-time communication with multiple people at the same time through various chat programs, the most famous of which is Internet Relay Chat (IRC). IRC servers can host *chat rooms*, virtual gatherings that act like mailing lists on steroids, where everyone can talk to everyone else (Figure 25.22). As you might suspect, you use an IRC client to connect to an IRC server, just like you use a newsreader to connect to a newsgroup server or an e-mail client to connect to an e-mail server. Chat rooms usually have a common theme or interest among their users, and the vast majority of people in chat rooms are there for genuine reasons.

Moderated Communication Forums

Some chat rooms, bulletin boards, newsgroups, and mailing lists have *moderators*, people who watch to ensure that certain messages are not broadcast because they do not conform to the standards set up by the operator of the service.

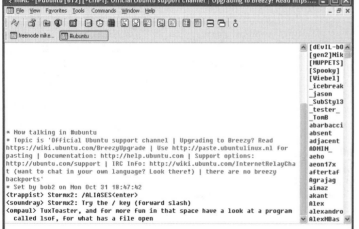

Figure 25.22: IRC chat room in action

They decide who can post messages and what messages everyone else can see, and may delete a message or ban a user if his or her discussion goes off the topic or becomes rude.

Online Conferencing

Online conferencing programs enable multiple people to communicate over the Internet, with voice and static or moving pictures. The better products enable the participants to share a whiteboard that anyone can write on and all can see. Many enable people to switch back and forth between camera feeds and the display of graphics (to show charts and graphs or other pictures) or even other pre-recorded video. Such programs make online conferencing a complete multimedia experience (Figure 25.23).

Figure 25.23: Online conferencing software in action

Bulletin Board Systems, the Early Internet

Before the explosion of the Web in the mid-1990s, the bulletin board system (BBS) provided the main source of online information. Some commercial BBSs were operated by computer hardware and software companies as a way for users to get the latest product news and download drivers and programs. Others were run by schools and community organizations. Still others were operated by individuals using their home computers. To access a bulletin board server, you dialed directly into that server using a modem. BBSs are relatively rare these days; the Web has taken over their duties.

Warning: *In forums lacking a moderator, you run the risk of exposing yourself to rude, hateful, and vile people. This is especially true in chat rooms. Because they think they're anonymous, some users (who might be perfectly civil in public) start swearing like sailors and attacking people online. Be careful if you use forums without moderators. Don't give out personal information to anyone, no matter how nice or harmless they seem.*

Web Sites and Web Pages

■ Web sites live on *Web servers*—computers that run Web site software. Each site contains one or more *Web pages*, text documents created using Hypertext Markup Language (HTML) or one of the fancier languages. Every Web site that connects to the Internet must have a unique name, called a URL, like www.gizmodo.com.

■ URLs can give you some clues about the content of a Web site. Commercial sites often end with .com, for example, and academic sites with .edu. Many non-profit and political organizations use the .org extension, whereas U.S. government sites use .gov. Each country has a country code, so you'll find sites in Finland often end in .fi and sites in Brazil in .br.

■ Web pages typically display three types of objects, text, images, and interactive elements, such as hyperlinks and forms. Images are generally in JPEG or GIF format. Hyperlinks can be text links or links attached to images, buttons, menus, or lists. Forms enable you to send feedback or submit information to a Web site directly. Forms have text boxes, radio buttons, and many other features.

Accessing the Web

■ Web browsers enable you to view the Web. Using HTTP to communicate with a Web server, the browser opens its home page by default. If the server is down or you can't connect for some reason, you'll get an error message telling you so.

■ Most browsers have similar interfaces. You'll find a menu bar, a standard buttons toolbar, **Back** and **Forward** buttons, A **Favorites** or **Bookmarks** button, an address bar, a **Go** button, a main pane or window, and a status bar.

■ Internet Explorer dominates the browser market, but Firefox has steadily gained on them since its release in 2005. Some Web sites use content that only works properly with Internet Explorer, which helps maintain

that browser's position in the market. Other browsers occupy niche markets, like Safari on Macintosh OS X and Opera.

■ The Address bar, **Back** and **Forward** buttons, the keyboard, and the mouse enable you to navigate the Web. To use the Address bar, type in a URL and press **[Enter]** or click the **Go** button. Use the links on a Web page to visit other pages within that same Web site or pages on other Web servers. Your browser keeps track of pages you visit during a session, enabling you to go back to a previously viewed page with a click of the **Back** button and then forward by clicking the **Forward** button.

Other Sources of Information on the Internet

■ You can access other sources of information on the Internet with FTP, mailing lists, newsgroups, chat rooms, and online conferencing software. FTP enables you to transfer files between computers much more efficiently than HTTP.

■ Mailing lists, like those using LISTSERV software, enable you to send a message to a list that goes to all members of that list. You receive posts from all the other members too.

■ Newsgroups, like the USENET, enable you to post to a public site and read all the posts others make. You can access the content on your own time rather than have your Inbox cluttered. But be very careful when using the USENET because much of it is not moderated.

■ Chat rooms enable multiple people to type messages to each other all at the same time. They often share a common theme. Online conferencing takes this a step further, adding voice and video into real-time communication.

Key Terms

Address bar	Hypertext Transfer Protocol (HTTP)
Back button	Hyperlink
Bulletin board system (BBS)	LISTSERV
Buttons	Mailing lists
Chat rooms	Moderator
E-commerce site	Newsgroup
Engine	Status bar
Extension	Text link
Form	Uniform resource locator (URL)
Forward button	USENET
File Transfer Protocol (FTP)	Web browser
Footprint	Web pages
Graphical link	Web servers
Home page	World Wide Web (the Web)

Key Term Quiz

Use the Key Terms list to complete the following sentences. Not all the terms will be used.

1. Web sites live on _____, computers running Web site software.

2. A _____ is a word or group of words on a Web page that can take you to a new page when clicked on.

3. The last element of a URL is the _____, which tells you the domain type.

4. When you open a Web site, the _____ area of your Web browser displays the Web site's URL.

5. A picture on a Web page that you can click on to go to another page is called a _____.

6. When your Web browser opens, it tries to load its _____.

7. You can send information directly to a Web site through a _____ on a Web page.

8. A Web site that sells goods or services is called a(n) _____.

9. Although it's not on the Web, you can post messages and read other posts in the newsgroups of the _____.

10. A person who watches over a chat room and bans users who misbehave is called a _____.

Multiple Choice Quiz

1. What can you use to format a Web page?
   A. DOC
   B. Format
   C. HTML
   D. HTTP

2. Mario tells you to check out something called www.commutercars.com. What kind of Web site should you expect?
   A. Academic
   B. Commercial
   C. Government
   D. Organizational

3. Mario then suggests that you look into www.austinev.org. What kind of Web site should you expect this time?
   A. Academic
   B. Commercial
   C. Government
   D. Organizational

4. Which of the following picture types would you most likely find on a Web page? (Select all that apply.)
   A. BMP
   B. GIF
   C. JPEG
   D. TIFF

5. Where would you go to change your home page in Internet Explorer?
   A. **File | New | Home Page**
   B. **View | Favorites | Home Page**
   C. **Favorites | Home Page**
   D. **Tools | Internet Options**

6. What protocol enables Web servers to transfer page information to your Web browser?
   A. FTP
   B. HTTP
   C. STP
   D. HTML

7. After you type a URL in your Web browser, what do you click or press to tell your browser to access that Web site? (Select all that apply.)
   A. Press **[Enter]**.
   B. Press **[Ctrl + Enter]**.
   C. Click the **Go** button.
   D. Click the **Send** button.

8. Joan surfed the Internet for a while, going through about four different Web sites before she realized the information she needed was on the first of the four sites. Bill says that the only way she can get that far back is to remember the URL and type it in. Margot disagrees, saying that Joan can use the Back button's drop-down arrow to go back quickly to the first site. Who's right?
   A. Only Bill is right.
   B. Only Margot is right.
   C. Both Bill and Margot are right.
   D. Neither Bill nor Margot is right.

9. Jake argues that the top-level page in a Web site is its home page, but Sandra disagrees. She says that a home page is the default page for a Web browser. Who's right?
   A. Only Jake is right.
   B. Only Sandra is right.
   C. Both Jake and Sandra are right.
   D. Neither Jake nor Sandra is right.

10. What browser comes with Windows?
    A. Firefox
    B. Internet Explorer
    C. Opera
    D. Safari

11. What protocol enables you to transfer files between computers on the Internet? Select all that apply.
    A. FTP
    B. HTTP
    C. STP
    D. HTML

12. Which of the following programs most likely would enable you to enter a chat room on the Internet?
    A. CHAT
    B. IRC
    C. LISTSERV
    D. USENET

13. What do you call it when group meetings and live presentations are handled over the Internet?
    A. Newsgroup
    B. Group meeting
    C. Encrypting
    D. Online conferencing

Projects

14. Which Internet service is designed to send e-mail to you about a particular topic automatically?
    A. Newsgroup
    B. Mailing list
    C. Chat room
    D. Text box

15. Which of the following is a potential danger in using a chat room on the Internet? (Select all that apply.)
    A. Rude people
    B. Offensive language
    C. Personal attacks
    D. None of the above, as chat rooms are all moderated

Essay Questions

1. Compare and contrast the features of Internet Explorer and another Web browser, such as Firefox, Safari, Opera, Netscape, or Mosaic. Write a short essay describing why you would choose to use one over the other. You can find information about the alternative browsers at the following Web sites, in order:

   - www.mozilla.org
   - www.apple.com
   - www.opera.com
   - www.netscape.com
   - archive.ncsa.uiuc.edu/SDG/Software/Mosaic/NCSAMosaicHome.html

2. You work for a small software company. You've been asked to set up an online forum to give your beta testers a way to offer feedback. Should you set up a newsgroup or a chat room? Should it be moderated or not? Give reasons for your choices.

3. You have a group of new employees who have never used a Web browser. Write a short essay describing the features of a Web browser and a typical Web page that make it possible to navigate the World Wide Web.

1. Analyze a couple of Web sites. You can choose from the list below or get URLs from your instructor Do the Web site's name and extension match the site (in other words, should a site that ends in .com use .edu or another extension instead)? How well does the site flow? What kind of links does it use? What about placement of graphics? Is it visually pleasing?

   - www.imdb.com
   - www.nasa.gov
   - www.altoids.com

2. Do some research on FTP. According to the Web site www.ftp-sites.org, how many anonymous FTP sites are available on the Internet? What countries have the most? If you're using Internet Explorer with its built-in FTP software, go ahead and click through to one of the FTP sites listed. What's there? How did your Address bar change?

COMPUTER LITERACY: YOUR TICKET TO IC³ CERTIFICATION

Web Essentials

"Go web. Fly. Up, up, and away web. Shazam. Go! Go! Go web go!
Tally ho."
             – Peter Parker (trying to learn how to shoot a web), *Spiderman*

This chapter covers the following IC³ exam objectives:

- ■ IC³-3   3.1.1   Identify terminology related to the Internet

- ■ IC³-3   3.1.5   Identify the difference between secure and unsecure (*sic*) Web sites (such as password-protected sites or sites secure for online transactions) and how to tell if a Web site is secure

- ■ IC³-3   3.2.3   Reload/refresh the view of a Web page

- ■ IC³-3   3.2.4   Show a history of recently visited Web sites and delete the list of recently visited Web sites

- ■ IC³-3   3.2.5   Find specific information on a Web site

- ■ IC³-3   3.2.6   Manage bookmarked sites/favorite sites

- ■ IC³-3   3.2.7   Save the content of a Web site for offline browsing

- ■ IC³-3   3.2.8   Copy elements of a Web site (including copying text or media to another application)

- ■ IC³-3   3.2.9   Print all or specified parts of a Web site

- ■ IC³-3   3.2.10   Download a file from a Web site to a specified location

- ■ IC³-3   3.2.11   Identify settings that can be modified in a Web browser application

- ■ IC³-3   3.2.12   Identify problems associated with using a Web browser

The Web offers great adventures once you know how to use a Web browser well, but has a dark side too. This chapter goes into depth about using your browser to get the most from a Web site. You'll learn about security issues, both with sites and what you can do with your browser settings. The chapter wraps with a bit of troubleshooting so you can handle the typical problems Web surfers face.

Working with Web Sites

Web site designers want you to have a great experience at their sites, so provide links of various sorts to help you navigate. Plus, your Web browser has many tools for working with the content of a Web site. You can save the Web site address so you can find it later. You can copy some or all of a Web page or even download an entire Web site. Finally, you have many options to print a page you like.

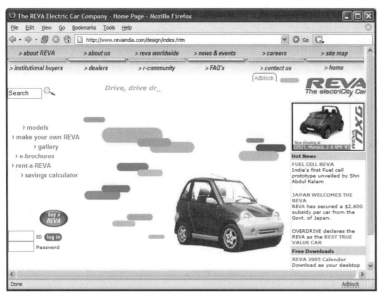

Figure 26.1: REVA showing an easy-to-navigate home page

Navigating a Web site

Using visual clues, you can go through a Web site and find the information you need. More often than not, the home page of the Web site does not contain critical information. You need to go deeper into the site, clicking through one or more pages to find your info, a process called *drilling down*. Nearly every Web page has some sort of link, like text links, graphical links, menus, or lists that you can click on to drill down into a Web site. The REVA Electric Car Company home page, for example, as you can see in Figure 26.1, has just about every feature you need.

A double row of text links at the top and the column of links on the left take you to various sections of the Web site. The *Search* box in the upper left of the main area, marked with a little magnifying glass icon, enables you to search through all the pages of site for *keywords*, words that would lead you to specific information on a page. If that's not enough, the very top right link takes you to a *site map*, a tree that lists every page in the site as if you were looking at Windows Explorer!

Managing Favorites/Bookmarks

Once you've discovered a site that you enjoy or want to explore later, you can use the *Favorites* or *Bookmarks* feature to store a copy of the Web site address so you can return to it easily. Every browser uses a similar process for saving a site address. With a Web page open—it doesn't have to be the site's home page—go to **Favorites | Add to Favorites** (in Internet Explorer) or **Bookmarks | Bookmark this Page** (in Firefox) to open the **Add Favorite** or **Add Bookmark** dialog box (Figure 26.2). You can accept the default name for the site or use your own naming system. Once you've added a favorite or bookmark, just go to the **Favorites** or **Bookmarks** menu and click on the site address to return to it.

If you're anything like most users, your Favorites/Bookmarks folder will quickly get out of control. All browsers give you a way to manage your saved sites. Figure 26.3 shows the Bookmarks Manager in Firefox. Internet Explorer calls the same dialog box the Organize Favorites. Note that you can readily add folders and dividers, and edit bookmarks here. Click and drag to move bookmarks between folders, just like you would in Windows Explorer.

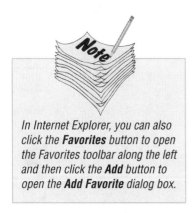

In Internet Explorer, you can also click the **Favorites** button to open the Favorites toolbar along the left and then click the **Add** button to open the **Add Favorite** dialog box.

Figure 26.2: Add Favorite / Add Bookmark

Saving and Copying Elements of a Web site

Web browsers enable you to save Web pages to your hard drive, copy text and images, and download specific files from Web sites. You can use those pages, text, and images in other documents, although you should not use them without getting permission or revealing your source.

Downloading to a Specific Location on Your Computer

Instead of saving a link to a Web page in your Favorites, you can save the entire content of a Web page onto your computer's hard drive. Go to **File | Save as…** and select a file name and location. You have the option in most browsers to save the complete page, just the underlying HTML code for the page (this gets all text, still formatted, but doesn't save the pictures), or as plain text (Figure 26.4).

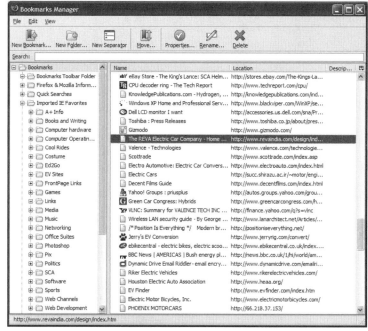

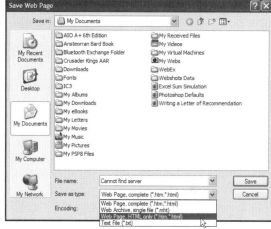

Figure 26.4: Saving options

Figure 26.3: Wow! Somebody needs to clean up!

Copy and Paste

You can copy the text and images on Web pages and paste them into other files and programs, such as Word documents or image-editing applications. To copy text, highlight the information you want to copy, right-click with the mouse, and choose **Copy** from the options. Open up your Microsoft Word document, right-click where you want the information to go, and select **Paste**. *Voilà!* The text from the Web page is now in your Word document (Figure 26.5). You can copy and paste almost anything from a Web page to a Word document using the same steps, including pictures, forms, links, and more!

To copy and paste a picture into an application for editing, follow similar steps. Right-click any image and select **Copy Image**, then open an image-editing application, such as Paint Shop Pro, right-click, and select **Paste as New Image** (Figure 26.6). Other applications require you to open a new, blank image and then paste the copied picture into the blank canvas. You can also paste a copied image into an existing picture or into documents, such as PowerPoint presentations.

Downloading Files

Downloading files from Web sites works similarly to saving Web pages or copying and pasting. Web designers can put links to non-Web content on their sites. When you click on such a link, your browser will prompt you about what you want to do, as you can see in Figure 26.7. If you click **Open**, your operating

Generating Web Pages

The option to save the HTML version of a Web page has two benefits. First, you retain the formatting of the text, so bold words stay in bold and text links stay underlined and functional. Double-clicking the saved page opens that page in a Web browser, even if you're not connected to the Internet.

Second, a good way to learn how to do Web site development is to see how other people do it. If you find a great looking or functioning page and want to do something like it, you can save it and open it in a Web-development program, like Microsoft FrontPage.

You can use the keyboard to copy and paste very quickly. When you have something selected on a Web page, press [Ctrl + C] to copy, then click in your target document or program and press [Ctrl + V] to paste.

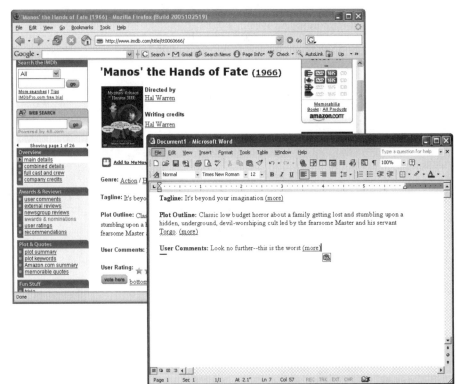

Figure 26.5: Word document with text copied from Web page open behind it

Figure 26.6: Pasting into Paint Shop Pro

system searches for the program associated with the type of file, opens that application, and then opens the file. Click **Save** to open the Save As dialog box that works just like it did for saving a Web page.

Alternatively, you can right-click a link and select **Save Target As** (in Internet Explorer) or **Save Link As** (in Firefox) to open the Save As dialog box. Select a file name and a file type, choose where you want to save the file on your drive or drives, and you're good to go (Figure 26.8).

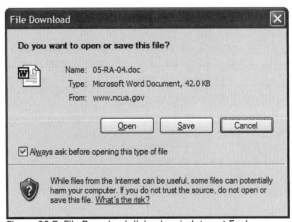

Figure 26.7: File Download dialog box in Internet Explorer

Figure 26.8: Save As dialog box

Offline Browsing

Internet Explorer enables you to download some or all of a Web site so you can look through the contents when you have time, even when not connected to the Internet. This option is great in cities that charge by the minute for dial-up, such as London and New York, or in cases where you're not sure you'll have Internet access later.

To download a site, go to **Favorites | Add to Favorites** to open the Add Favorite dialog box (Figure 26.9). Select the **Make available offline** check box and click **OK**. Internet Explorer will download the Web site to your computer.

You can set the amount of content that Internet Explorer downloads by clicking the **Customize** button in the Add Favorite dialog box. This opens the Offline Favorite Wizard. Click the **Next** button on the introduction page to get to the heart of the Wizard, shown in Figure 26.10. Clicking the **Yes** radio button enables you to select how deep into a site you want to go, getting linked pages up to three levels down. Following the Wizard's prompts you can set how often you want to *synchronize* with the site, to make your downloaded copy match the online copy of the Web site.

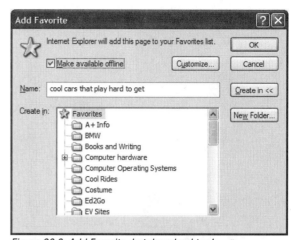

Figure 26.9: Add Favorite, but download too!

Printing a Web Page

All Web browsers enable you to print all or parts of a Web page. You can set printing options to change the orientation of the print. There are many options with printing, so that you can get just the information you want. To print a complete Web page, simply click the **Print** button, press **[Ctrl + P]** on your keyboard, or go to **File | Print**. Selecting and formatting require a bit more finesse.

Selecting What to Print

Print options differ among browsers, especially between Internet Explorer and Firefox, and also depending on what you select. If you want to print a select group of text or graphics in either browser, highlight the area and go to **File | Print** to open the Print dialog box. The Page Range area on the General dialog box gives you a choice of what to pick (Figure 26.11). If you leave the **All** radio button selected, clicking the **Print** button prints the whole page. You can click the **Selection** button to print only your selected text or graphics.

Internet Explorer enables you to print with a right-click, with the options changing according to what you select and where you click. If you select text or right-click on a non-picture part of a Web page and select **Print** from the options, you'll open the Print dialog box, just as before. If you right-click a picture or a link, you get the option to print the picture only or print the target, the page to which the link connects (Figure 26.12).

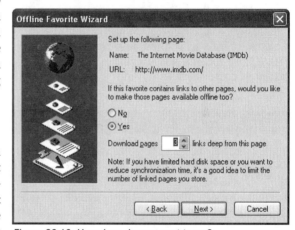

Figure 26.10: How deep do you want to go?

Setting Print Options

There are many ways to customize how your browser prints Web pages. To view what your printed pages will look like in advance, go to **File | Print Preview** (Figure 26.13). To exit the Print Preview window, click the **Close** button at the top center of the browser.

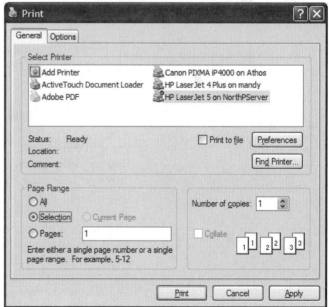

Figure 26.11: Printing a selection

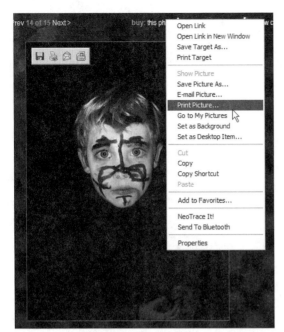

Figure 26.12: This picture is also a link, so you get both options

Figure 26.13: Web page in Print Preview

Figure 26.14: Page Setup dialog box

Page Options

You can change the orientation of the page on the paper and change the margins for a print. Normally, the page prints in portrait orientation, like a letter, with margins of .75" all the way around. To change to landscape orientation, so your print is wider than it is tall or to change the margins, go to **File | Page Setup**. This opens the Page Setup dialog box (Figure 26.14). Orientation and margin options are at the bottom.

Security On and Off

The Web offers an amazing variety of content, information, fun, and excitement, but it also poses risks to you and your computer. You need to secure your data both when you're online and when you're offline. You need to understand security on the Web and take steps to protect yourself from prying eyes.

Online

Web sites come in two main varieties: normal and secure. You know about normal Web sites from this and previous chapters—they run on Web servers that use Web site software and respond to requests from Web browsers using the Hypertext Transfer Protocol (HTTP). (Try to say *that* three times fast!) Secure Web sites use extra software and respond to *Hypertext Transfer Protocol over SSL* (*HTTPS*) commands. You'll recognize a secure Web page by two clues. First, the URL displayed in the Address bar begins with **https://** rather than **http://**. Second, a little lock icon appears somewhere on the screen, depending on what browser you're using; in Internet Explorer, the lock appears toward the right end of the Status bar (Figure 26.15).

You need secure sites because anything you type in a normal Web site form goes across the Internet in *clear text*, like what you're reading right now.

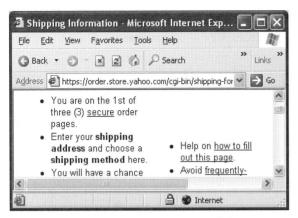

Figure 26.15: Secure site framed tightly to show both the https:// and the lock

Sophisticated programs, called *sniffers*, can monitor the communication between your computer and a Web server and pick up any plain text you send. If you type in valuable information, like a user name, password, credit card number, and so on, the person running the sniffer program can steal that information.

Secure Web sites use *encryption*—like a secret code—to scramble the words that you type. Only your computer and the secure server can unscramble the communication. Secure Web sites enable e-commerce to happen successfully, so you can buy stuff online and not have to worry about getting your credit card information stolen.

Offline

During the process of surfing the Web, several things happen behind the scenes that you need to deal with to protect your data and privacy. First, Web servers often have a little file called a *cookie* that your browser downloads along with the other Web page text and pictures. The cookie tracks what you do on that site to enable things like passwords to be stored in memory so you don't have to type one in each time you revisit a site. E-commerce sites can use cookies to keep track of items in your digital shopping cart, so you can continue to shop and add more items before you check out and give them money.

Second, your Web browser keeps track of all the Web sites you visit so you can return to those sites later. This list is called your *History*. The only problem with a History is that other people who access your computer can see precisely where you've gone on the Web, even the time you went there.

Third, your browser stores all those Web pages and pictures of the Web sites you visit in a spot on your hard drive called the *cache*. Like with your History, anyone who has access to your computer can get access to your cache.

You can deal with cookies, History, and cache by deleting temporary Internet files, clearing the cache, and modifying both security and privacy settings. All of these options you can adjust from within your browser, whether you're online or offline.

Cleaning House

Your first stop deals with the cookies, cache, and history files on your computer right now. In Internet Explorer, go to **Tools | Internet Options** (or just **Options** in Firefox) to open the Internet Options dialog box. The General tab enables you to get rid of all those files with a quick click of a few clearly-named buttons. Click **Delete Cookies**, **Delete Files**, and **Clear History** and you're set (Figure 26.16).

Figure 26.16: Internet Options, General tab

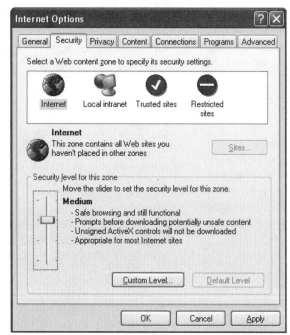

Figure 26.17: Security Tab in the Internet Options dialog box

Security Settings

You can adjust the overall security of your browser, like what pages you can access and how you download information, with the Internet Options dialog box. Click on the **Security** tab, then click on the **Custom Level** button to customize all of the security features of your browser (see Figure 26.17).

Privacy Settings

Your Web browser offers various levels of privacy that you can adjust, also in the Internet Options dialog box. Click on the **Privacy** tab (Figure 26.18). For the most part, the privacy settings revolve around the acceptance of cookies. Cookies can be used to track your activity on the Web, and if you don't want this to happen you can tell your browser not to accept cookies—although some Web sites will not allow you to access them if your browser won't accept their cookies.

Resolving Common Browsing Problems

Aside from dealing with the dangers of the Web, both online and off, people who use the Web run into a host of problems. Pages disappear or download slowly, even with fast connections. Web developers use fonts that you don't have or technologies that your browser can't support. Ads jump off the page at you, making your surfing experience not very nice. Dealing with such problems takes a little effort, but the payoff can be great.

Page Not Found (404) Errors

Web sites come and go and pages that link to those sites need to be updated. This doesn't happen everywhere, so you're bound to run into a dreaded *404 – File Not Found* error page (see Figure 26.19). The number is the HTTP code for an item (in this case, a Web page) not found. This can occur when you type a URL incorrectly, when a link is not working properly, or when a Web page no longer exists or is down.

Slow Pages

Some pages take forever to load. The slow pages can be the fault of your browser or network, but usually can be blamed on the host Web site's server having a lot more activity than it can handle.

Missing Fonts

A *font* is a specific size and style of type. Just about every Web page has text displayed in different ways, and these are all different fonts. It is possible for a Web page to use a new or different HTML code for a font that your browser will not recognize. Some browsers will automatically assign a regular font to this text while some will not display this text at all.

COMPUTER LITERACY: YOUR TICKET TO IC³ CERTIFICATION

Figure 26.18: Privacy Tab in the Internet Options dialog box

Figure 26.19: 404 – File Not Found

Foreign Characters

Browsers can have additional features not only for fonts, but also to display foreign language characters. If your browser doesn't have these features and it tries to read a Web page that is all or partially in a language that uses a different alphabet (such as Japanese or Russian), then your browser may end up displaying garbled text (see Figure 26.20).

Reloading/Refreshing Pages

You can fix some slow pages and even some broken pages by *reloading* or *refreshing* your browser. This tells the browser not to use the cached copy of a page, but to contact the Web server again and download the page content. You can manually tell your browser to go out and fetch the latest and greatest version of that Web page by clicking the **Refresh** button. Internet Explorer uses double green arrows for the button (Figure 26.21), whereas Firefox uses blue arrows.

Out-of-date Browser

Web developers push the limits of the Web by introducing new technologies to their sites. Not too long ago, for example, you couldn't play a movie directly on the Web. Programmers eventually came up with the Web server tools to display a movie, but you still have to have a Web browser that could handle the multimedia content. You might look at a Web site that appears partly broken, therefore, when the problem could be your browser.

Downloading a newer version of a browser and patching current browsers with little helper applications, called *plug-ins*, solve these problems. To get a new copy of a browser, go to one of these Web sites:

- update.microsoft.com
- www.mozilla.org
- www.opera.com

Image Display

*To make searches much, much faster, you can temporarily stop your browser from displaying any images from the Web—only the text. It is easy to adjust your browser so that it doesn't display images. In the Internet Options dialog box, select **Advanced**. You will see a list of options with a check box beside each one. Make sure the box in front of **Show Pictures** is empty, and no graphics will be displayed on your browser.*

Figure 26.20: Web browser trying to decipher foreign language text

Missing Browser Plug-ins

Plug-ins add features to your Web browser to support certain elements, such as sound, video, and 3-D animation files. Macromedia's Flash and Shockwave plug-ins enable Web pages to include multimedia objects like audio and video. You can find both here: www.macromedia.com.

If your browser tries to play a feature that requires a plug-in you don't have, you'll see an error message instead of whatever you're trying to load. Figure 26.22 shows a missing plug-in.

Pop-Up Ads

One of the most productive ways people have found to make money via the Internet is with advertising.

Pop-up ads are new windows that just "pop up" when you open a Web page, without your knowledge or choice (see Figure 26.23). Most browsers can stifle these annoyances, or you can purchase additional pop-up blocking software.

Figure 26.21: Refresh button

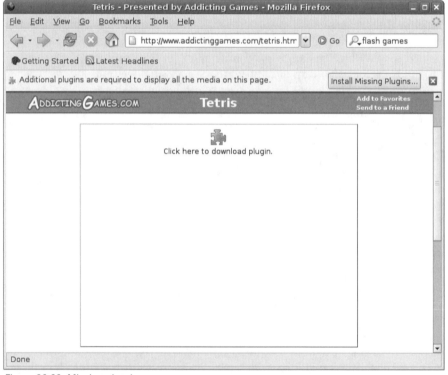

Figure 26.22: Missing plug-in

Figure 26.23: Firefox blocked pop-up

Working with Web Sites

■ Using visual clues, such as text or graphical links, menus, and lists, you drill down into a Web site and find the information you need. Some sites offer search functions; others have site maps.

■ You can add a Web site to your Favorites list or Bookmarks so you can return to the site again at a later time without having to remember the URL. With a Web page open—it doesn't have to be the site's home page—go to **Favorites | Add to Favorites** (in Internet Explorer) or **Bookmarks | Bookmark this Page** (in Firefox) to open the **Add Favorite** or **Add Bookmark** dialog box. Once you've decided on a name, you can access that link by clicking on the **Favorites** button, or by going to the **Favorites** or **Bookmarks** menu.

■ Instead of saving a link to a Web page in your Favorites, you can save the entire content of a Web page onto your computer's hard drive. Go to **File | Save as...** and select a file name and location.

■ You can copy the text and images on Web pages and paste them into other files and programs, such as Word documents or image-editing applications. You can also download files directly through your Web browser by right-clicking and selecting **Save Target As...** from the menu.

■ Internet Explorer enables you to download some or all of a Web site so you can look through the contents when you have time, even when not connected to the Internet. To download a site, go to **Favorites | Add to Favorites** to open the Add Favorite dialog box. Select the **Make available offline** check box and click **OK**.

■ All Web browsers enable you to print all or parts of a Web page. You can set printing options to change the orientation of the print. Click the **Print** button.

Security On and Off

■ Web sites come in two main varieties, normal and secure. Normal sites use HTTP, whereas secure sites use HTTPS. You'll recognize a secure server by the little lock icon in the lower right side of the Status Bar. Secure Web sites enable e-commerce to work safely by encrypting communication between your computer and the secure server.

■ You download more than just text and pictures when you access a Web site, getting cookies and gaining a History of your travels. Your browser saves files and pictures on the hard drive, its cache. You can and should flush all these files periodically. Go to **Tools | Internet Options** and click on **Delete Cookies**, **Delete Files**, and **Clear History** buttons.

■ You can adjust your Security and Privacy settings in the Internet Options dialog box. These change how various Web pages are handled, especially when dealing with cookies.

Resolving Common Browsing Problems

■ Some of the more common problems you'll run into while browsing include missing or down pages—that often generate a *404 – File Not Found* error message—and pages that load slowly. The latter can happen because of excess traffic to a popular site or server. Missing fonts and garbled pages go hand in hand. Reloading or refreshing a Web page can sometimes correct these problems.

■ New Web site technology comes out all the time and you need to keep your browser up to date to take advantage of the new stuff. Download a new version of your browser from Microsoft or Mozilla, or get plug-ins from a variety of sources, such as Macromedia. Updated browsers also stop many of the annoying pop-up ads.

Key Terms

404 – File Not Found

Bookmarks

Cache

Clear text

Cookie

Drilling down

Encryption

Favorites

History

Hypertext Transfer Protocol over SSL (HTTPS)

Plug-ins

Pop-up ads

Refreshing

Reloading

Search

Site map

Sniffers

Synchronize

Key Term Quiz

Use the Key Terms list to complete the following sentences. Not all the terms will be used.

1. _____ describes information that is not encrypted and is vulnerable to being stolen.

2. The _____ is the storage on your hard drive where previously viewed Web pages are stored.

3. _____ come(s) in handy when trying to find a specific term on a Web page.

4. A _____ error means your browser can't find a Web page you requested.

5. A _____ is a small text file Web sites store on your hard drive.

6. You can save a Web site URL in your _____ in Internet Explorer so you can return to the site without having to remember the URL.

7. Web pages that automatically load over other pages you want to load, trying to sell you something, are _____.

8. The collection of all of the sites you have visited is known as your _____.

9. Secure Web sites use the _____ rather than HTTP to communicate with a browser.

10. Small programs that enable a Web browser to use specific Web technology, such as Flash, are called _____.

Multiple Choice Quiz

1. Which of the following methods should Tammy use to find a page in a Web site? (Select all that apply.)
   A. Drill-down box
   B. Locate box
   C. Search box
   D. Site map

2. Joey uses Firefox and finds an outstanding site on the Internet that he wants to return to easily in the future. What should he do?
   A. Bookmark the site
   B. Add the site to his Favorites
   C. Write the URL down on a piece of paper
   D. White mark the site

3. Ellen has five sites in her Favorites that all deal with quilting, but one of the links no longer works. How can she get rid of the bad site entry?
   A. Delete the URL from My Computer
   B. Delete the URL from her History
   C. Delete the URL from the Organize Favorites dialog box
   D. Do nothing. All non-working links delete automatically.

4. Pippen finds a page full of great quotations on a Web page and wants to use one of them as a toast at his friend's wedding. How can he save the quotation he likes to a Word document so he can memorize it? (Select all that apply.)
   A. Select the text, then right-click and select **Copy**. Right-click the Word document and select **Paste**.
   B. Select the text, press **[Ctrl + C]**, then click on the Word document and press **[Ctrl + V]**
   C. Go to **File | Save As** and select **Web Page Complete** from the file options.
   D. Press **[Ctrl + A]** to select the current paragraph, then right-click and select **Copy**. Right-click the Word document and select **Paste**.

5. Which of the following can you copy from a Web page to a Word document? Select all that apply.
   A. Image
   B. Text
   C. Link
   D. Form

6. Why would someone want to browse a Web site offline? (Select all that apply.)
   A. The Web site changes constantly and they need to download the site to keep up.
   B. Many cities charge by the minute for dial-up. Browsing offline is cheaper than browsing online.
   C. They may not have Internet access later when they want to view the site.
   D. Why are you asking? You can't do that!

7. What are the proper steps to save a Web site for Offline Browsing in Internet Explorer?
   A. Go to **File | Save As** and select **Web Page complete** from the file types.
   B. Go to **Tools | Internet Options | Save Current Site**
   C. Go to **Favorites | Add to Favorites** and select the check box next to **Make available offline**.
   D. Go to **Tools | Save As** and select the check box next to **Make available offline**.

8. Aaron wants to print a Web page. What method can he use? (Select all that apply.)
   A. Press **[Ctrl + P]**.
   B. Press **[Ctrl + Prt Scr]**.
   C. Go to **File | Print**.
   D. Go to **Favorites | Print**.

9. Terrance wants to see how his Web page would look printed, but doesn't want to waste paper. How can he accomplish this goal?
   A. Press the **Print** button on the toolbar.
   B. Go to **File | Print Preview**.
   C. Go to **File | Print**.
   D. He can't. He needs to print it.

10. Martha wants to buy some new CDs online, but she's nervous about security. What should she look for to ensure that she's on a secure site? (Select two.)
    A. The RIAA logo in the top left of the Web site
    B. A small lock icon at the bottom of the browser window
    C. A URL that begins with *https://*
    D. A URL that begins with *htpps://*

11. What do secure Web sites use to scramble the words that you type?
    A. Clear text
    B. Cipher
    C. Encryption
    D. Passcode

12. Which buttton must Tiffany click to remove all record of the Web sites she's visited?
    A. **Delete Cookies**
    B. **Delete Files**
    C. **Delete Bookmarks**
    D. **Clear History**

13. Which button must Tiffany click to remove all record of what she's done on the Web sites she's visited?
    A. **Delete Cookies**
    B. **Delete Files**
    C. **Delete Bookmarks**
    D. **Clear History**

14. Why would you refresh a Web page? (Select all that apply.)
    A. To make sure you have the latest version of that page
    B. To fix a broken page
    C. To clear the page from your History
    D. To add the page to your Favorites

15. Margot opened a page at www.ifilm.com that should have played a movie trailer, but instead she got an error message. Why? (Select all that apply.)
    A. Her browser doesn't support that type of video.
    B. She's too young for that movie trailer.
    C. She forgot to disable pop-up ads.
    D. Her browser doesn't have the proper plug-in.

Essay Questions

1. You have two new employees and your boss has left it to you to explain the right and wrong of the Web. In a short essay, tell the new hires how to copy and paste information from a Web site to a Word document, but also explain the risk of plagiarism.

2. Write a short memo describing a logical way to organize your Favorites/Bookmarks. Hint: By subject? By region? By person? By interest? By date?

3. Your co-worker is really concerned about cookies. Write a brief essay that describes how cookies might be good or bad, or both.

Projects

1. The *404 – File Not Found* error is just one of many HTTP error messages. Do some research and list the top five HTTP error messages and their meanings.

2. You can view the files your browser puts in your cache. Find your cache and then explore it, but be prepared for the shocking discoveries you'll make!

   Hint: Try **Tools | Internet Options** in Internet Explorer.

Finding Information on the Internet

"The Internet has given everybody in America a voice. For some reason, everybody decides to use that voice to [complain] about movies."
— Holden, *Jay and Silent Bob Strike Back*

This chapter covers the following IC[3] exam objectives:

- IC[3]-3   3.3.1   Identify the ways a search engine classifies and looks for Web sites

- IC[3]-3   3.3.2   Identify other ways of searching for information on the Web

- IC[3]-3   3.3.3   Use a search engine to search for information based on specified keywords

- IC[3]-3   3.3.4   Search effectively

- IC[3]-3   3.3.5   Identify issues regarding the quality of information found on the Internet

- IC[3]-3   3.3.6   Identify how to evaluate the quality of information found on the Web

The World Wide Web is a staggeringly vast world filled with Web sites that cover every possible aspect of human knowledge. Most Web sites have multiple Web pages. While no one knows how many Web sites exist, a good guess is somewhere in the area of 11.5 billion! Somewhere on the Web there's a Web page containing the answers to any question you might conceive, if you know how to find that page.

This chapter teaches you how to find information on the Internet, starting with the tools that make it happen, search engines and directories. The second section dives into the arcane art of the search, examining effective keywords and ways to refine your searches. The chapter finishes with a look at what you need to know to evaluate the information you find on the Web. Let's go!

CHAPTER 27: FINDING INFORMATION ON THE INTERNET

Figure 27.1: Mars search results in Google

Tools for Searching the Web

Numerous Web sites give you tools for searching the Web, from the automated *search engine* sites to Web directories. Some sites have internal search capabilities and most have links to external sites that you can follow.

To use one of these search sites, such as *Google*, you simply go to that site and enter a word or words into the search line. If you want to look up information about the planet Mars, type **Mars** into the search line. Mars is your *keyword*—the word the search tool will look for in its database (see Figure 27.1). The search site will respond to your keyword and suggest a series of Web pages for you to review. If you want information about the movie *Mars Attacks*, on the other hand, you would search for both words.

Search Engines

Search engines are applications that comb the Internet, cataloging all the Web pages they find and storing the results in a searchable database that you can access from your browser. There are a number of major search engines to choose from, such as Google and Ask Jeeves (Figure 27.2).

Internet search engines use special programs that work their way from link to link across the Web, automatically downloading all the Web pages they find. This type of Web-searching program is commonly called a *spider*, *webbot*, or *crawler*.

A crawler looks for links in the pages it downloads and then walks or crawls down through a Web site. A crawler doesn't stop at the home page, but downloads multiple pages from the same Web site.

Most spiders used by search engines nowadays just download the Web

What is a Google?

"Googol" is a mathematical term for a 1 followed by 100 zeros. The term was created by Milton Sirotta, nephew of the American mathematician Edward Kasner, and was popularized in the book, Mathematics and the Imagination by Kasner and James Newman. Google.com uses the term to symbolize how much information is out on the Web to be indexed.

Figure 27.2: Mars Attacks search results in Ask Jeeves

pages they find and store them raw in a temporary database. Search engines use programs called *indexers* to organize the information into huge searchable databases. When an indexer processes a page, it strips out the HTML codes and so-called filter words—*the, and, for, is,* and so forth—and catalogs any hyperlinks it finds. Then it stores what's left of the page in the database for Web surfers to find.

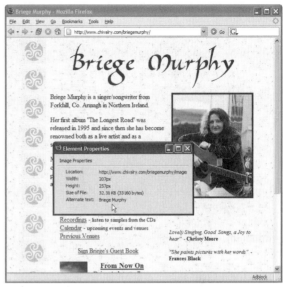

Figure 27.3: Repetition of keywords

How Search Engines Classify Web sites

All search engines use some form of Web crawling to build up massive indexes, but they differ greatly in what words they look for and how they index the information. This indexing may be done according to keywords in the visible text content of the page, or according to words hidden in the page's HTML code.

Automatic Indexing by Content Keywords

A Web page can have visible keywords in several places. The Web page title that you see in the title bar of every Web page, for example, is automatically a keyword or words. So is the text that shows up when you hold your mouse over an image, the *alternate text.* Words prominently featured on a page, using heading tags, can also tell the crawlers about a site.

Kate put together a Web site for Briege Murphy, the singer/songwriter from Ireland. To optimize the site for crawlers, she made the page title "Briege Murphy" and added alternate text to the photograph of the artist, also "Briege Murphy," as you can see in Figure 27.3. The link to her biography opens a page, not called simply "Biography," but "Briege Murphy – Biography." The subtle repetition of keywords helps optimize the site. Typing **briege murphy** in a search engine like Google turns up Briege's Web site as the very first hit (Figure 27.4).

Figure 27.4: Search success

Automatic Indexing by Hidden Meta tag Keywords

The developers of HTML wanted to make it easy to find information on the Web, so created invisible HTML tags, called *meta tags,* for Web page builders to use to describe their pages. There are actually half a dozen or so types of meta tags, but only two really matter in most cases: *description* and *keywords.* These two meta tags provide, respectively, a description of the page's content and keywords that the search engine can use to index the page in its database.

Although meta tags have fallen out of favor with some Web developers, you can still find them on many pages by viewing the HTML source. In your Web browser, simply

Optimized Sites

Kate Akers, the Web developer mentioned in this chapter, makes quite a few sites for various Irish and Scottish singer/songwriters; the UK folk genre of music is her passion. The question for you today, though, is how consistent has she been with optimization of her sites? Open up a Web browser and surf to www.andyirvine.com and www.andymstewart.com. Do the pages have proper titles? What about keywords applied to the alternate text for pictures? Finally, view the source of some of the pages and check for meta tags. Any luck?

Spamming Meta Tags

Unfortunately, many unethical Web site designers abuse meta tags in an attempt to increase their search rankings artificially. One common practice is putting often-searched words like sex in the meta tag keywords list, often multiple times, to fool the search engines into ranking a site as most relevant.

In response to tactics like these—called spamming in the search engine world—most search engines have altered the indexer algorithms so that not only do these techniques not help a Web developer, they actually hurt them. If a search engine detects common spammer tricks like too-often-repeated keywords, keyword text hidden by setting the font color to match the page background, or stop words like XXX or sex, it will put the site on a spammer list and block it from showing up in its results!

Figure 27.5: breige breege brege bridget briege cloghinne?

go to **View | Source** (in Internet Explorer) or **View | Page Source** (in Firefox) to see a naked Web page. Figure 27.5 shows the source for the Briege Murphy home page. Note that Kate wanted to make sure you could find the page, even if you misspelled the singer's name!

Directories

A *Web directory* offers a database of Web pages and Web sites similar to that of search engines, but people build the directory manually. Search engines use automated spiders to crawl about the Web; people submit Web sites to directories whose staff review the sites and categorize them in the database. *Yahoo!*, often referred to as a search engine, is technically a Web directory (Figure 27.6).

Web site owners can submit their sites to Yahoo! directly. Getting listed on Yahoo! used to be free to all, including businesses, but these days getting a business listed costs serious money. As of this writing, the *yearly* fee for a standard business listing is US $299!

Internal Search

Many Web sites offer tools for searching

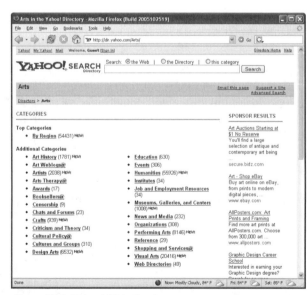

Figure 27.6: Yahoo! Web directory

within their site. Some use search tools provided by Google or other companies, such as the Chivalry Music site (Figure 27.7). Others have proprietary search boxes, such as the Internet Movie Database (Figure 27.8). Note that IMDB actually has both search options.

Large Web sites with extensive pages often offer a *site map*, a listing or *index* of all the sections of their Web site arranged by categories. A site map helps you search for what you need—or at least a general area—quickly. Figure 27.9 shows a site map for Dell Computers.

External Links

The power of the Web comes out when a person creating one Web site places links to other Web sites that he or she feels might be of interest to site visitors. These links might appear as a list on a dedicated page or they might just be links

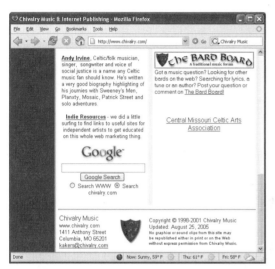

Figure 27.7: Search powered by Google

Figure 27.8: IMDB using both internal search and search powered by A9

set to the side of particular pages. Either way, the Web site makers find these links helpful and that's a strong clue that you might also find them relevant to your search.

Figure 27.11 shows the links for Green Car Congress, a Web site dedicated to alternative vehicles and environmentally-friendly technology. As you can see, the list of links includes biodiesel manufacturers, EV World (the premier site for electric vehicle news on the Web), hybrid car companies, and more. Just starting with the listed sites would provide with a ton of information on the subject alternative vehicles.

Optimizing Searches

Opening up a browser, going to Google, and typing in a keyword or two might work for some folks, but a few tricks and tips can turn your search from long and exhausting to short, sweet, and to the point. Effective keywords, Boolean

Most people use the term "search engine" generically to mean both classic search engines, like Google, and directories, like Yahoo! If you see the term on an exam, assume it's the generic use.

Engine vs. Directory: Fight!

So, which technology works better, automated search engines or manually constructed Web directories? Open up a browser and test them out.

Using Google or Ask Jeeves for your search engine and Yahoo! as your Web directory, run some searches for various subjects. Compare the results in a head to head competition between the two styles of search tool. Your instructor can give you a list of subjects or you can simply go off on your own. If you prefer, do a search for the following terms:

- Little Red Riding Hood
- ten best universities in the U.S.
- digital camera reviews
- Henry VII
- weird science experiments for kids

How relevant did you find the Sponsored Links in each search?

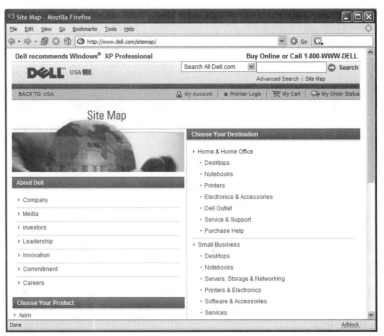

Figure 27.9: Site map

search techniques, and knowledge of how to refine a search offer the keys to searching success.

Effective Keywords

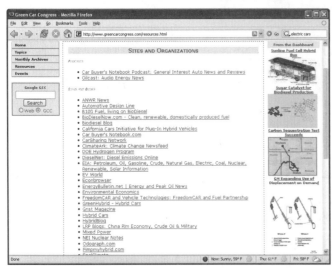

Figure 27.10: List of Links at www.greencarcongress.com

An effective keyword or set of keywords direct a search engine or directory to something specific and unique. Don't use general or broad keywords, because you'll get broad, general results. The goal is to provide the search engine or directory with words that can go precisely to the information you want and not give you a million other pages to sift through.

Ricardo wanted to learn more about an odd little two-seat car he saw on the streets of Seattle, called the Tango (Figure 27.11). It drove by him in near total silence, so Ricardo suspected that the Tango might be an electric or hybrid car.

Choosing the proper keywords for his search offers some challenges. The name of the car presents a problem, because *tango* is a popular dance that originated in Argentina. Searching for **tango** at Google returns a bunch of wonderful pages—about *dance*. Doing a context search likewise doesn't work well: **small two-seat car in Seattle** produces results ranging from the Honda Insight to private helicopters (Figure 27.12).

What works is a combination of keywords that seek for a unique quality of the item; searching for **Tango electric** on Google puts the Tango electric car at the top of the list (Figure 27.13). Another search that also produces 9/10 relevant results on the first page is **car tango**. If you have a specific word like **tango** that could be part of several categories—in this case, **car** and **dance**—it often works well to type in the general category of thing you're interested in first, like **car**, and then add your detail word, like **tango** or **electric** or better yet, both!

Just as an aside here, if you want a startling demonstration of the differ-

Figure 27.11: Tango (Photo courtesy of Commuter Cars Corp.)

ence between a search engine with links generated automatically and a Web directory where people decide what should go where and what keywords matter, the Tango provides a perfect example. Typing just the word **Tango** in Google produced dance sites, but the same single-word search in Yahoo! puts the Tango electric car as the number two link (Figure 27.14). Somebody at Yahoo! likes alternative vehicles!

Boolean Search Strings

Good keywords can handle most of your searching needs. For more difficult searches, though, you can make use of more advanced tools. What if, for example, Ricardo did not know the *name* of the small two-seat car that he saw in Seattle? That might make for a difficult search using only keywords.

Boolean search strings enable you to use terms such as *AND*, *OR*, and *NOT* to refine your search and produce that proverbial needle in a haystack. When you put AND between two words in a search, the search engine will return pages that include both words. You can use OR to search for related terms, and NOT to

Figure 27.12: Private helicopters?

Figure 27.13: That's a little more like it!

Figure 27.14: Tango near the top

tell the search engine not to include pages with specific terms.

Ricardo could go through these steps to refine his search and discover the delights of an electric commuter car.

1. Searching for **two-seat AND car** would return some results, but also a lot of sports cars. Because Ricardo wasn't sure about the drive train of the car, he could use OR to refine his search.

2. So, searching then for **two-seat AND car AND electric OR hybrid** should give a lot more precise results, although it'll pick up a lot of instances of the Honda Insight two-seat hybrid car and still have a bunch of sports cars. That's where NOT comes in handy.

3. With a final search for **two-seat AND car AND electric OR hybrid NOT Honda NOT sports**, his search might work just fine.

Search Reality

Most modern search engines and directories incorporate some or all Boolean search strings into their search functions. Google searches, for example, always include AND by default, although they drop common words from searches, such as "the" and "in." Most search engines enable you to use *Boolean operator equivalents*, such as + rather than AND or - rather than NOT, to refine a search quickly. So Ricardo could search for **car electric hybrid -insight** and skip all the references to the Honda Insight.

Most search engines and directories have an advanced search feature that enables you to refine your search (Figure 27.15). You can search for specific phrases, text strings, and keywords; even limit your searches by domain. Note in Figure 27.15 that Google Advanced Search picked up the Boolean operator equivalent of NOT and automatically put **insight** into the without *the words* text box.

Evaluating Web Information

You can find almost anything on the Web, from well-organized sites with detailed, trust-worthy information, to wild-eyed radical rantings of lunatics

Figure 27.15: Google Advanced Search

Figure 27.16: Fashion-Era.com

masquerading as informed sources. Anyone can publish anything on the Web, seriously. There's no policing, no quality control, no international law that can come down on someone for posting flat-out lies, misinformation, fake products, secret societies, or online games. The biggest hurdle in using the Internet for information, therefore, is evaluating the information you find.

Factors of Quality

You can determine the quality of information on a Web site by looking at five topics:

- **Relevance** of information to specified needs

- **Reliability** of information from a source that can be trusted to provide true and accurate content

- **Validity** of information when verified from more than one source

- **Bias**, whether commercial or political, of the site's owner or contributors

- **Sufficiency** of information for a specific purpose

Relevance

First, how relevant is the information on a site to the topic you're researching? If you're researching the history of jewelry and you find a site on the history of women's clothing, you might find it includes some information on the development of jewelry through history as well (Figure 27.16).

On the other hand, a site concerned with *modern* jewelry might have some useful facts that apply to jewelry in general, but it might not have much that helps with your history research (Figure 27.17). The more you already know about a topic, the easier it is to assess the relevance of a site's content to your search, so it can help if you get a basic grounding in your subject before you start poking around online.

Reliability

Second, how reliable is the source? Just because *everyone* thinks something is so doesn't necessarily mean you should believe it, but it does usually mean it's

International laws prohibit some behavior, such as theft, smuggling, and so on. The existence of the laws does not stop everyone, though, so you need to be on your toes!

Figure 27.17: Zales.com

worth considering. Likewise, no source of information is always going to be right, but it is good to start an information search by consulting sources with a record of putting out information that has proven over time to be correct.

The major national newspapers, for example, have reputations to protect, and they have internal checks and balances built into their organizations specifically to ensure that what they publish is accurate. Are they never wrong? Of course not, but information you get off the Web sites of the New York Times and the Wall Street Journal is much more likely to be reliable than a blog entry by somebody you've never heard of, or an article from an obscure site whose contributors are unknown to you (Figure 27.18).

A **blog** is a type of online journal or personal diary, where people often post whatever comes to mind.

Validity

When assessing the validity of information, it's a really good practice to see if you can find multiple sources that agree. The trick when compiling multiple sources is to be alert for the possibility that two sources that appear to validate each other are both just repeating information from the same third source. If you are looking for information in a field widely studied by professionals, like science or history, you can check for articles in peer-reviewed journals on your topic.

Bias

Before you trust information from a Web site, you should always ask the bias question: does this source have a motivation—making money, perhaps, or advancing a political or religious position—to slant their presentation in some way? Ask yourself what if anything the Web site's owners or contributors stand to gain by giving you this particular information in this particular way. Would they have something to gain by *not* telling you another side of the story, if there is one?

For example, you can guess that what you read

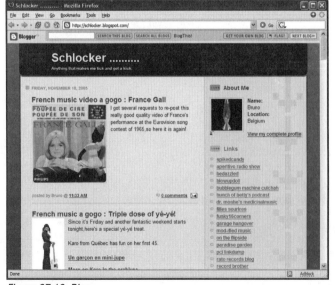

Figure 27.18: Blog

on a political candidate's Web site will cast his or her record and positions on issues in the best light possible, playing up the good stuff, and playing down or omitting entirely any inconvenient facts. Conversely, you would expect a negatively-biased account from an opponent's site (Figure 27.19).

Economics can be a powerful motivation as well. For years the tobacco companies put out studies and published information claiming that cigarettes were safe, did not increase your cancer risk, and weren't truly addictive.

The U.S. federal government is another source of information that many people don't know about. Part of the mission of all federal agencies is to share the results of their research and expertise with the public; they generate a huge number of printed reports and guides on almost every topic imaginable.

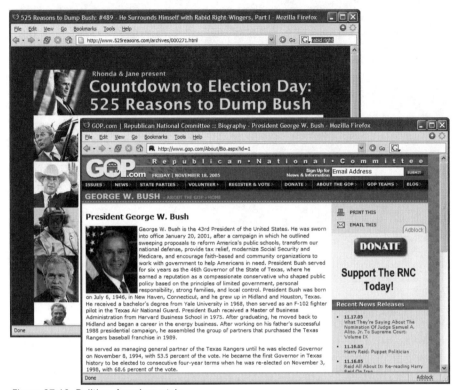

Figure 27.19: Politics, American style

Scientific evidence to the contrary piled up for years, and eventually it was proven that the tobacco companies had deliberately put out false information to protect their profits (Figure 27.20).

Sufficient Information

Finally, does the Web site contain enough information to serve your needs or do you need to go elsewhere for additional details? Some articles may just cover one part of an issue. Some may give you an overview but not go into all the details you need to know. For example, if you are researching the economy of the Hawaiian Islands, you might find an article on tourism on the state's official site, an article on Hawaii's famous Kona coffee on a site about coffee, and information on the macadamia nut industry on a commercial site (Figure 27.21).

Test of Fire

Each time you access a Web site in search of knowledge, put it to the test. Analyze the sources for the information. Test them for bias, commercial or otherwise. Evaluate the quality of the links within the site. If a site has a great argument and compelling story, but all the links in the site only post to places within the site, that's suspicious.

See if you can find reliable, printed sources that match what a Web site

Figure 27.20: Tobacco

says. That way, you have two sources for the same information when it comes to backing up your decision to use the information.

Evaluate Search Engine Ranking Results

Search engines list the Web sites that most closely match your keyword searches in order of relevance. The site on top will have the most, if not all, of your requested keyword terms, and it will have them used very closely together, if not in order. The further you go down the list of your search results, fewer of your keywords will be present or placed closely together on a page.

Contact the Site's Creator

One of the great things about the Internet is that it makes communication so easy. Just about every Web site says who produced the information it contains and provides some way of getting in touch with them (usually by e-mail), as in Figure 27.22. If you ever see a site with interesting but unproven facts, don't hesitate to e-mail the author and to politely ask him or her for sources or additional information.

Figure 27.21: Mauna Loa

Figure 27.22: Contact links for Electrifying Times

Figure 27.23: Electrifying Times

Tools for Searching the Web

■ To use a search site, simply go to that site and enter a keyword or keywords into the search line. Press **[Enter]** and the search engine or directory searches through its database of Web pages. Search engines are applications that comb the Internet, cataloging all the Web pages they find and storing the results in a searchable database that you can access from your browser.

■ Search engines use some form of Web crawling to build up massive indexes, but they differ greatly in what words they look for and how they index the information. Some search engines use visible keywords, such as the page title and alternate text of pictures to build their database. Others use meta tags, hidden HTML tags that provide a description of a Web page.

■ A Web directory offers a database of Web pages and Web sites similar to that of search engines, but people build the directory manually. Search engines use automated spiders to crawl about the Web; people submit Web sites to directories whose staff review the sites and categorize them in the database.

■ Many Web sites have search features built-in, so you can quickly find information within the site. These search features might be proprietary or based on technology from Google or other search sites. Some offer a site map, an index of categories for pages in the site.

■ Most sites have lists of links to related resources. These links can give you an excellent starting point to gain knowledge on a particular subject.

Optimizing Searches

■ Effective keywords, Boolean search techniques, and knowledge of how to refine a search offer the keys to searching success. An effective keyword or set of keywords direct a search engine or directory to something specific and unique.

■ Boolean search strings enable you to use terms such as AND, OR, and NOT to refine your search and produce results. Most search engines and directories use some of the Boolean terms by default—Google assumes AND with every search on multiple keywords—or can handle Boolean operator equivalents, such as +, -, and ^.

Evaluating Web Information

■ Because the Internet lacks censorship, the biggest hurdle in using the Internet for information is evaluating the information you find. You can evaluate the information on a Web site by looking at five topics: the relevance of what's there to what you need; the reliability of the source; the validity of the source; the bias of the source; and whether or not the information on the site has enough of what you need.

■ Each time you access a Web site in search of knowledge, put it to the test. Analyze the sources for the information. Test them for bias, commercial or otherwise. Evaluate the quality of the links within the site. If a site has a great argument and compelling story, but all the links in the site only post to places within the site, that's suspicious. See if you can find reliable, printed sources that match what a Web site says. That way, you have two sources for the same information when it comes to backing up your decision to use the information.

Key Terms

Alternate text

AND

Boolean operator equivalent

Boolean search string

Crawler

Google

Indexers

Keyword

Meta tag

NOT

OR

Search engine

Spamming

Spider

Webbot

Web directory

Yahoo!

Key Term Quiz

Use the Key Terms list to complete the following sentences. Not all the terms will be used.

1. You enter a _____ into a search engine to find relevant Web pages.

2. A _____ uses AND or OR or NOT to refine what you are looking for.

3. Google is a _____, automatically finding and indexing Web pages.

4. Yahoo! is an example of a _____, a search site that builds its database with people entering in Web pages manually.

5. _____ is a Boolean term used to exclude a certain word or words from a search.

6. Web developers can use _____ for a picture as keywords to enhance a Web page's hits in a search engine.

7. An invisible HTML tag that provides a description of a Web page is called a _____.

8. John runs a search on Google looking for a picture of his teacher that ends in a **-gif** tag to make sure GIF files don't show up. The - sign acts as a _____ for the NOT option.

9. When you do a search on Google with two terms, such as **electric car**, the Boolean term _____ is assumed by the search engine.

10. Unscrupulous Web designers put many hidden and repeated keywords into their Web pages, what's called _____.

Multiple Choice Quiz

1. Which of the following would most likely be the best set of keywords to find out information about the new Saturn sports car, the Sky?
   A. GM car saturn
   B. Car saturn new
   C. Car saturn
   D. Saturn sky

2. Joy says that automatic Web-searching programs used by search engines are called crawlers, but Dave disagrees, saying that they're called spiders. Who's right?
   A. Only Joy is correct.
   B. Only Dave is correct.
   C. Both Joy and Dave are right.
   D. Neither Joy nor Dave is right.

3. Which of the following meta tags provides a description of a Web page? (Select the best answer.)
   A. Content
   B. Description
   C. Keywords
   D. Title

4. How can you see meta tags on a Web page?
   A. **File | New | Web page**
   B. **View | HTML**
   C. **View | Source**
   D. **Tools | View Source**

5. Which of the following areas of a Web site would most likely provide additional related resources for you to search?
   A. About
   B. FAQ
   C. Links
   D. Title

6. When working with keywords, what's a good strategy?
   A. General descriptive words
   B. Specific and unique words
   C. Common words
   D. Foreign terms

7. You can trust everything published on the Web to be true and accurate.
   A. True
   B. False

8. Which of the following Web pages would probably offer the most *relevance* in a search for information about teeth whitening?
   A. American Dental Association home page
   B. Pearly Gates
   C. Teeth Through the Ages
   D. Whiter Teeth Now!

9. Which of the following Web sites would probably be the most *reliable* source for information about teeth whitening?
   A. www.ada.org (home of the American Dental Association)
   B. www.pearlygates.com
   C. www.TeeththroughtheAges.org
   D. www.WhiterTeethNow.com

10. Mario found three Web sites that talked about a new electric scooter that could go 200 miles on a single charge. When he excitedly told his friend Jane about the new product, she claimed that three sites weren't proof. Why would Jane not believe Mario? (Select all that apply.)
    A. The three Web sites might all use the same source.
    B. Mario didn't have a trusted, written source to verify the information.
    C. It takes at least four sites to agree to make something believable.
    D. Mario is a known liar.

11. Which of the following is a search engine rather than a Web directory? (Select all that apply.)
    A. Ask Jeeves
    B. Google
    C. Yahoo!
    D. Zoom

12. What sort of software do search engines use to compile their databases of Web pages?
    A. Arrangers
    B. Indexers
    C. Sorters
    D. Tree builders

13. All search engines enable you to use standard Boolean searches, such as OR or NOT.
    A. True
    B. False

14. When judging the quality of information on a Web site, which of the following should you test? (Select all that apply.)
    A. Check whether the site owner has a political bias.
    B. Check whether the site owner has a commercial interest in what they claim.
    C. Check whether the site owner runs other Web sites.
    D. Check whether the site owner offers other products.

15. Zelda read some interesting information on a Web site about zebras, including a breakthrough new way to tame them for riding. The problem is that the site talks about the process, but not enough for her to duplicate it on her zebra ranch. What might she do to find the information she needs? (Select all that apply.)
    A. Contact the site owner.
    B. Contact the local Center for Animal Control.
    C. Search reputable print journals for articles on the subject.
    D. Nothing. She should simply give it a try and ride a zebra.

Essay Questions

1. Your boss has hired two new assistants to do nothing but surf the Web, but they're both pretty clueless. Write up a memo describing how they might use various tools to aid in their searches.

2. Write a short essay comparing and contrasting the advanced search features available at Google and Yahoo!

3. The two new assistants have turned in reports that had some odd information. Write a short essay describing what sorts of bias they need to watch out for on Web sites.

Projects

1. On her television show, Oprah Winfrey once quoted a very powerful statistic: If every household in the United States replaced just *five* normal light bulbs with energy-efficient compact fluorescent bulbs, it would be the carbon-reducing equivalent of taking *eight million* cars off the road for a year. Using Google, Ask Jeeves, or Yahoo! (or all three if you want), do a search for sites that discuss common sense ways to go green at home and conserve electricity. Share your list of sites with your classmates so together you can compile an excellent set of resources. (Then switch out your light bulbs, too!)

2. Search the Web to discover five sites that are biased in their presentation of information. This doesn't have to be a bad thing, and the bias can be subtle or obvious. Try to find sites in more than one category, such as commercial, political, religious, and so on. Then share that list with your classmates to discuss how to look at sites with clear eyes.

COMPUTER LITERACY: YOUR TICKET TO IC³ CERTIFICATION

Computers in Homes, Schools, and Businesses

"What exactly are the commercial possibilities for flying sheep?"
— Voiceover, *Monty Python's Flying Circus*

This chapter covers the following IC³ exam objectives:

- ■ IC³-3 4.1.1 Identify how computers and the Internet are used

- ■ IC³-3 4.1.2 Identify the technology and processes involved with computers operating "behind the scenes" in everyday activities

- ■ IC³-3 4.1.3 Identify the impact of electronic commerce (e-commerce) on business, individuals and governments

- ■ IC³-3 4.1.4 Identify technologies that support or provide opportunities to the disabled and disadvantaged

Suppose the power went out in your home and stayed off for an entire day. Which would you miss most? Would it be creature comforts such as lights, air conditioning, and a working refrigerator—or would you miss your computer and Internet connection more?

In September of 2004, Yahoo! Inc., along with a leading media company, asked 1000 households to avoid using the Internet for two weeks as part of their Internet Deprivation Study. Regardless of their age, household income, or ethnic background, the overwhelming percentage of participants had feelings of loss, frustration, and disconnectedness when they were cut off from the online world.

Half of the participants said they simply could not continue as part of the study for another two weeks, and 47% said that they had at least one relationship (business or personal) that had been damaged by not getting on the Internet. Everyone said living without the Internet was much harder than they had expected (Figure 28.1).

The Dark Ages

The use of computers for school work has greatly changed how students produce their work, as well as how they look up information. Just a couple of decades ago, students turned in mostly handwritten homework assignments, either on notebook paper or on worksheets that were mimeographed or photocopied many times over.

When they needed a neatly typed document for an essay or paper, they hand-wrote their first drafts and then turned to a typewriter, stopping to correct mistakes with a tiny bottle of white paint. Research meant using encyclopedias, other books, and library resources, such as back issues of magazines, often stored on microfilm that required a large piece of specialized equipment to read.

Times have changed. In 1993, about 25% of all students used their home computers for schoolwork. In 2004, more than 75% used their computers for school (National Center for Education Statistics).

Figure 28.1: Give me back my Internet!

This chapter gives you a closer look at the role computers play in society as a whole, as well as in your personal life. You'll discover the many ways that computers and the Internet create powerful tools for you to use at home, school, and work. You'll then delve deeper into the many ways that computers work behind the scenes to power everything from cars to weather reports—and how the Internet in particular has changed the way many people do business and purchase goods. Finally, you'll see what computers can do for people whose physical challenges prevent them from using standard computer interface tools, such as the mouse and keyboard.

The Role of Computers in Modern Life

Since the 1980s, the culture of much of the world has moved from one that could take or leave computers—and had certainly never heard of the Internet—to one that can't properly function without them. Using a personal computer to send and receive e-mail and browse the Web is only one of the ways people rely on computers today. Most people who interact directly with computers do so either in a school setting, in their homes, or in their workplaces—and many people use computers in all of these settings.

Impact on Education

Educators across the developed world have embraced the personal computer as a useful learning tool. Teachers and administrators use computers to make record-keeping and lesson planning more efficient. In most schools, students learn to use computers, not only to do research and complete assignments, but also to help prepare for the workplace or college after they finish high school.

Students today have access to hard-copy encyclopedias, library books, and microfilm archives, as in the old days, but they also have the tremendous power of the Internet and the World Wide Web at their disposal. Facts that would once have required a trip to the library and an hour or more of searching are now available with a few clicks of a mouse.

Many school and university libraries have done away with their paper card catalog systems in favor of computer-based book inventories that track which books are currently available. This has freed up space for more computer terminals, which students can use for searching the library's resources or for doing research on the Web.

Instead of using typewriters, most of today's students have access to word-processing programs such as Microsoft Word, and presentation software such

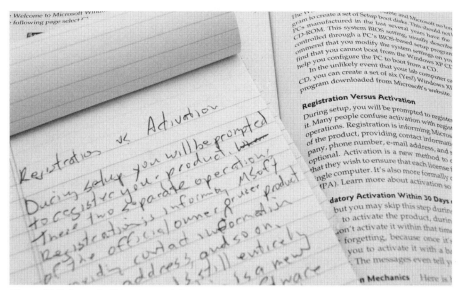

Figure 28.2: From draft to manuscript

as PowerPoint. While some students create handwritten first drafts, the later drafts and the final version are usually produced on a computer screen, not with a typewriter (Figure 28.2).

Handling Information

The real magic of modern computing happens when Internet content comes together with local computer programs to accomplish a goal.

As an example of this, consider Tiffany, who had a school assignment to write a research paper on the history of cosmetics. She began her research by using a search engine to collect information on the history of cosmetics (Figure 28.3). At one cosmetic manufacturer's Web site, she noticed the e-mail address of a public relations officer. Hey! Why not ask folks in the business for their opinions? She sent an e-mail to the company asking for information. The public relations person e-mailed her back with amazing facts and stories.

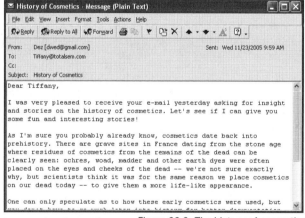

Figure 28.3: The history of cosmetics

Tiffany organized the data using a spreadsheet for statistics and a word-processing program for the outline. Now that she was organized, she could use other programs to evaluate the information. She used a Web browser to access the local library's card catalog to see what periodicals might cover similar content. She also used presentation software to create a set of slides about the topics she wanted to cover, and then assessed where she needed more information, or where her sources disagreed.

To turn in her final work, she eventually printed a copy, but prior to that the Internet enabled her to e-mail a rough draft to her teacher for comments. The teacher gave Tiffany some great ideas back by e-mail, so she incorporated those into the paper, again using Word. On the due date, she turned in the paper; her teacher loved it and gave her an A.

Tiffany then sent the paper to the makeup company and they gave her a free trip to New York City! Okay, so that last part is pretty improbable—but the rest of the example shows the common process for using the Internet along with applications on a computer to collect, organize, evaluate, and communicate information.

E-learning

E-learning can combine the Internet and local programs to facilitate learning both in and out of the classroom. You can use e-learning to access a virtual classroom from a Web browser and never have to leave your home. Everyone is doing e-learning these days. Half of all high schools in the U.S. provide online courses or are preparing to do so, and colleges and universities are teaming up with companies that provide distance learning.

Distance learning specifically refers to educational courses (either serious topics such as English literature, or more fun topics such as digital home video editing) where students aren't required to meet in a physical classroom. Teachers and professors can communicate with students through Web sites, e-mail messages, online message boards, and even printed material or audiovisual media sent through the mail (Figure 28.4).

Students submit their assignments (where applicable) using e-mail attachments or other digital means. Some courses require an in-person orientation, exam, or other meeting, but in many cases students have no face-to-face contact whatsoever with their teachers and fellow students. While this approach isn't for everyone, it does provide a flexible schedule, which is particularly important for working people who are learning in their spare time.

Another aspect of e-learning is the ability to participate in *collaborative projects*, which bring together students from all over the world. Students can use the power of communication technology to compare lifestyles, learn about their peers in other cultures, and make the world seem a little smaller. If a classroom in Illinois teams up with students in Shanghai to look at the latest advances in mathematics theory, the result is both an information exchange and a cultural exchange—not to mention the kind of educational opportunity that your grandparents never imagined.

Technically, e-learning refers to using a computer to learn a subject. It doesn't require the Internet. An interactive CD that teaches you Spanish, for example, and assesses your pronunciation when you speak into a microphone, is a great example of local e-learning.

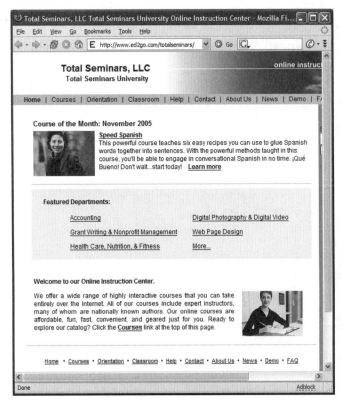

Figure 28.4: Online university

Impact on Home Life

The first big explosion of computer technology in homes was the Atari game system in the 1970s. This device, which used a simple one-button joystick and hooked up to a TV set, made its début with a little game called PONG (Figure 28.5). A few years later, a home version of a wildly popular video game called Space Invaders made the Atari console even more common in homes. Since then, the home video game business has grown by leaps and bounds—and with GameCube, PlayStation, and Xbox constantly striving to outdo one another, this trend won't slow down anytime soon (Figure 28.6).

The popularity of computer games extends beyond the realm of game consoles to personal computer-based games such as Civilization, the Sims, and Roller Coaster Tycoon. These games use a regular home computer as their platform, rather than a dedicated console and a television. Other microcomputer-based games, such as EverQuest and World of Warcraft, use the Internet to enable users to play with and against other people anywhere in the world in real time (Figure 28.7).

Computer games are only one type of entertainment that a home computer can provide. You can also use a computer to listen to music, view video clips, watch DVD movies, and edit and print pictures and home video. Of course, the computer is also your ticket to the entertaining world of the Internet—you can check out fun Web sites, watch animation or video clips, send and receive instant messages, download music, keep an online journal or *blog*, or read about your favorite entertainers on news sites (Figure 28.8).

Figure 28.5: Atari

Combining the Internet and local programs enables you to stay informed and can promote *critical thinking*—that is, the ability to look at ideas and opinions and form your own based on what you know. Surf to a site like Politics1 and explore the amazing variety of viewpoints on everything from local political races in your home district to over-arching themes that could affect you, your children, and their children as well (Figure 28.9): http://www.politics1.com/

You could use Word to write down your ideas or responses (so you can use the great spell-check and other features), and then post with a handle (like *Jack47* rather than your real name) in the message boards to see what others think about your ideas. When you get responses, think about them!

You might find that a lot of people think the way you do, or that you've got to expand or alter the way you think about an issue to take into account other ideas or information. Either way, you gain experience in critical thinking that will serve you the rest of your days.

Figure 28.6: Xbox 360

Home PCs do their share of work as well as play. With a computer at home, you can write business or personal letters, keep track of your household income and expenses, make signs for your garage sale, teach yourself a new language—the possibilities are almost endless! With your Internet connection, you can check the weather for your next business trip, get driving directions, keep tabs on current events, send messages to members of Congress, or

Figure 28.7: EverQuest

Figure 28.8: News site

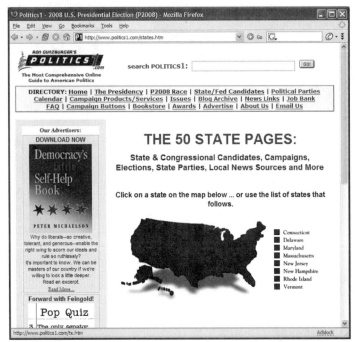

Figure 28.9: Politics1

even volunteer to maintain the Web site of a local charity (Figure 28.10).

Imagine that your friend Cheryl wants to buy a new car. She doesn't know much about new cars, but uses the Web to do some research and become a more informed consumer. She uses new car and consumer Web sites to learn about the car models that she likes, and then logs onto a newsgroup to post questions and get opinions about the car she eventually decides to purchase (Figure 28.11). If she finds a low-price dealer through the Web, Cheryl's hard-working computer might just pay for itself!

One of the most important functions of a household computer is commun-ication. The use of e-mail in the U.S. is more widespread than ever, with millions of messages being sent each day. E-mail on a home PC can help family members keep in touch with relatives, friends, work contacts—and sometimes each other! (See Figure 28.12.)

The impact of having an Internet-connected computer at home is significant. The computer saves time on everything from balancing a check-book to looking up movie times, leaving more time for other activities. The Internet makes a great homework helper, providing access to volumes of historical, scientific, and literary material. The computer can be a repository for the family's collection of digital photographs or home videos, and provide a way to share those resources with faraway relations (Figure 28.13).

Impact on the Workplace

Businesses have also seen their productivity increase because of the Internet and technology developments of the last few years. Networks, once only the domain of large corporations, are now present in even the smallest businesses, along with Internet access. Popular operating systems allow for virtually every operating function to interact immediately with the Internet. Files can be transmitted instantaneously, and e-mails outnumber paper memos 10 to 1 in corporate America, improving and speeding up communication.

Meet Jack. He works as a regional manager for a chain of music stores. As you might imagine, he uses computer programs and the Internet together to accomplish tasks and solve problems—such as a steady decline in sales due to music downloads.

To increase the productivity of his sales force, Jack first found sales statistics for other record stores on the Web (Figure 28.14). He then used PowerPoint to create a presentation to show to his salespeople. The vast resources of the Internet, combined with Jack's local software applications, helped to crank up the creative process.

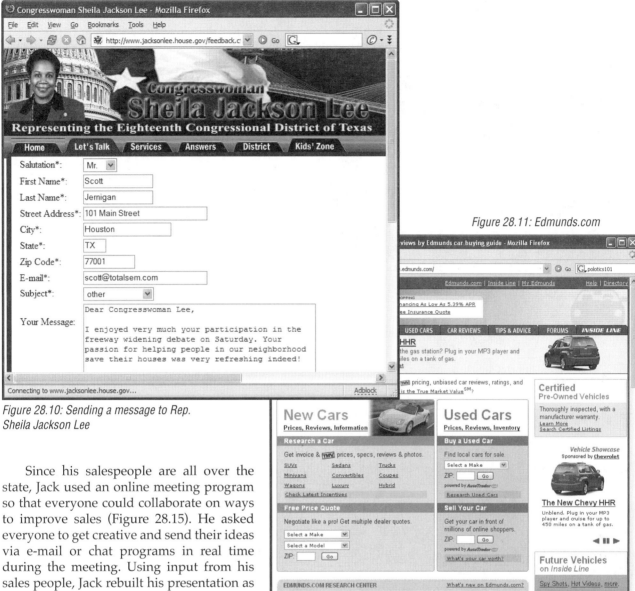

Figure 28.10: Sending a message to Rep.
Sheila Jackson Lee

Figure 28.11: Edmunds.com

Since his salespeople are all over the state, Jack used an online meeting program so that everyone could collaborate on ways to improve sales (Figure 28.15). He asked everyone to get creative and send their ideas via e-mail or chat programs in real time during the meeting. Using input from his sales people, Jack rebuilt his presentation as the ideas came rolling in; everyone contributed to the final document!

After completing the presentation, Jack pushed the sales force to increase sales by 20% in the next quarter. As an incentive, he offered a trip to Cozumel for the top salesperson at the end of the year. And just to cap off the connection between online options and local software, Jack used Excel to create a chart that tracked each salesperson's progress (Figure 28.16).

Computers behind the Scenes

Once upon a time, automobiles were purely mechanical beasts that anyone with a little engine grease and know-how could open up and fix. Today, however, the first thing a car repairman does when you bring your car in for repairs is hook up a computer to ask the car's internal microprocessor what's wrong.

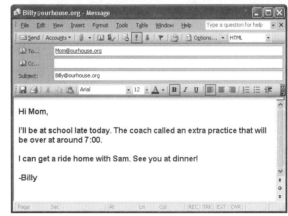

Figure 28.12: Using e-mail to stay in touch with someone who lives under the same roof

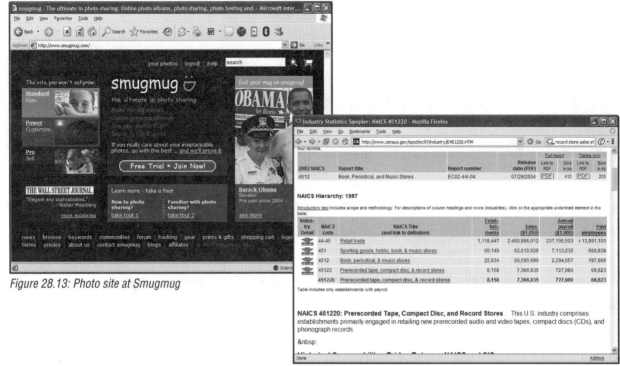

Figure 28.13: Photo site at Smugmug

Figure 28.14: Statistics online

Figure 28.15: smartMeeting in progress

Figure 28.16: Tracking salespeople

These days, computer chips are integrated into all of the car's major systems—they regulate the gasoline and oxygen mixture, sense the cabin and outside temperatures to adjust the air conditioning, determine how the car uses its brakes during bad weather, and even adjust the seat position automatically for different drivers.

The use of microchips in cars is just one example of how computers are involved in most every aspect of modern life. In fact, it's tough to think of behind the scenes processes that don't use computers! From banking to airlines, from manufacturing to department stores, computers make things happen.

ATMs

Imagine that it's Friday afternoon, you have the whole weekend ahead of you, and you decide to go to the movies. You need some cash for a ticket and popcorn, but banks have already closed for the night. This isn't a problem in today's world—you can hardly drive down the block in larger cities without spotting an *automated teller machine*, or *ATM* (see Figure 28.17).

Figure 28.17: A modern drive-up ATM

Can you imagine life without ATMs? Not so long ago, people who didn't remember to go by the bank to get some weekend cash before 5:00 PM on Friday were out of luck! Lines at banks on Fridays were huge—between people cashing their paychecks and people just withdrawing cash, you could easily spend more than an hour just waiting to reach a teller. The ATM has turned that picture on its ear. Now it's the drive-through ATM that may have several customers backed up, while the lobby of the bank is used more for people taking out loans, opening or closing accounts, or dealing with odd problems that the machines can't handle.

ATMs are really just data terminals that communicate with your bank's computer through a *host processor*—and unlike most other data terminals, dispense large sums of cash! The host processor is just like an Internet service provider, in that it acts as a gateway for you to communicate with an ATM network. Your ATM card has a magnetic stripe that identifies you, and this acts as your login ID. The ATM asks you for your *personal identification number (PIN)*, which works like a regular network password.

Doing Reservations

In today's world, it is hard to imagine that you would ever need a professional to help you get an airline flight. There seem to be a zillion Web sites that offer tickets on airlines and just as many that have hotel, cruise, and rental car listings. As hard as it is to imagine, back in the 1980s and early 1990s, people almost never booked their own travel. The nuances of dealing with airlines were thought to be too complicated, so people used travel agents to get flights.

As the Internet evolved in the mid- to late-1990s, the airlines realized they were missing the boat (so to speak), and decided to get rid of the middleman. They created databases of their collective flights. They let travel Web sites have access to these databases and codes so that they could all communicate together as in Figure 28.18.

What's my Motivation?

They're Everywhere!

Think you won't encounter a computer today? Even if you avoid sitting down at a PC at school, home, or work, you'll need to work hard to get anything accomplished without a computer figuring into the mix somewhere.

Did you drive or ride in a car? It needed microchips to run. Did you use a cell phone to talk with friends or send text messages? A microchip in the phone stores your numbers. Did you go to a sporting event or a movie? Your ticket was probably printed or read by a special computer. Did you just stop off at the corner store for a bottle of soda? The clerk most likely either scanned the bottle's barcode or typed the price into a computerized cash register. Even if all you did was go to the park and fly a kite, you probably checked out a weather forecast on the TV or radio (not www.weather.com, of course!) first, which your friendly neighborhood meteorologist compiled using computer projections.

The old saying goes: "If you can't beat 'em, join 'em!" Unless you move to a cabin in the woods—and don't buy any of your survival gear online!—you can't avoid dealing with computers. They're practically everywhere, and they provide career opportunities in all sectors of the economy. Learning to understand and use computers is a necessity in today's world, and learning specialized computer skills is a great way to get ahead.

Figure 28.18: Orbitz.com

Computers and the Internet made this work. In 2004, 70% of all travelers with online access booked their travel online, and another 25% looked up the information online and then called the airlines themselves. In 2004, people in the U.S. spent $54 billion in online travel, and that amount will be around $100 billion by 2009.

Automated Industrial Processes

The ISA (Instrumentation, Systems, and Automation Society) was created way back in 1945 so people could share ideas developed during the manufacturing peak of World War II. As the decades progressed, ISA members heard more and more about the advantages of computers and computer-controlled robots to perform complex and repetitive tasks resulting in fewer man hours needed and lower prices for all. Entire programming languages and networks were developed to teach robots how to do simple but time-consuming tasks.

Today, the ISA now has over 33,000 members around the world and sets the industry standards for automated business practices in many industries. Many automated systems now make many things you use, from video game systems to cars, some of which are hardly touched by human hands in the process (see Figure 28.19).

Figure 28.19: Computer-automated manufacturing robots

I, Robot

Check out www.isa.org to see how computer-controlled robots and other automated systems affect the world around you.

Point of Sale Systems

Let's face it: people love to buy stuff. Whether it's video games, books, or clothes, U.S. consumers are especially fond of spending money, even money they don't necessarily have! Today's stores, from small boutiques to huge supermarkets to clothing outlet stores, use computerized *point of sale* (*POS*) systems to process their retail transactions.

Figure 28.20: Barcode on toothpaste: a key to efficient commerce!

How do POS systems work? Well, suppose you pick up a few items at your local HugeMart; a POS system connects the register where you check out to HugeMart's distribution centers. When the cashier scans the barcode on a tube of toothpaste (Figure 28.20), the computer in the register tells the nearest distribution center that a tube of toothpaste has been sold. When enough tubes to make up a case have been sold, the distribution center automatically sends out a new case of toothpaste to that store.

These POS systems enable HugeMart's corporate executives to track which items are popular, how much the price of an item affects how well it sells, and other types of data used to make decisions and keep things running smoothly at the stores.

Weather Prediction and Reporting Systems

If you turn on the evening news, you'll see a weather reporter doing his or her best to predict what the weather will be like the next day. While weather forecasting is not an exact science, computers are the main reason that they can predict weather patterns as well as they do.

Computers store and process data well, which makes them perfect for computing the odds that the weather will be sunny or rainy, cold or warm. While people would eventually get sick of collecting every tiny detail of weather data, computers have limitless patience. They can transform years of collected weather data into fairly accurate predictions of what will happen next.

The computers used to examine hurricanes, tornadoes, and thunderstorms are far more accurate than they were a few decades ago, as their number-crunching power and speed have increased and programs have become more sophisticated. Also, because meteorologists all over the world can now network all of their weather observation equipment together, they can track storms and other weather patterns from one geographic region to another (see Figure 28.21).

Figure 28.21: Weather radar computer images

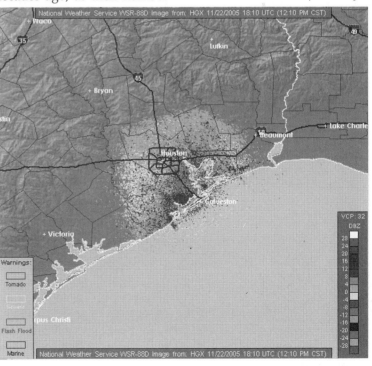

Embedded Computer Systems

If you look at an ATM or other system that uses a built-in computer, you don't see a monitor, keyboard, or mouse—these components are essential for a personal computer, but most systems that include a computer use an *embedded computer system*.

An embedded computer is very simple— it only needs to communicate with the traffic light, flight instrumentation, or whatever it's designed to operate. An embedded computer may need only a CPU, some RAM, and a way to input and output to a few special circuits.

As a result, an embedded computer doesn't look like much; often it's no more than a circuit board inside the machine (Figure 28.22).

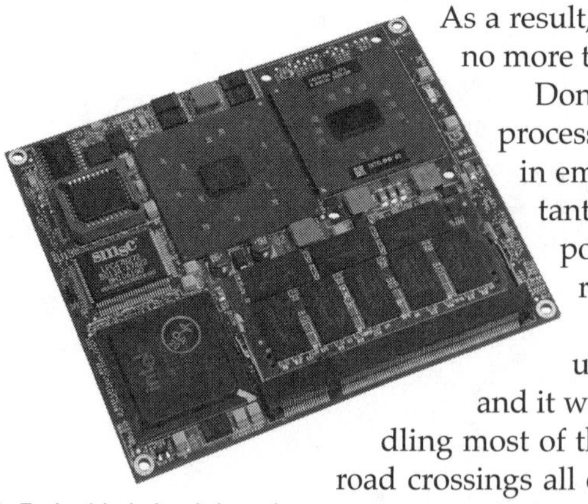

Don't let the simplicity of embedded systems fool you. Modern processors, designed to support a wide array of different devices in embedded systems, are the basis of some of the most important systems in the world. Embedded systems fly airplanes, run power grids, control traffic, and perform many other critical real-time functions.

Have you ever seen the screen an air traffic controller uses to direct planes? It is the ultimate in controlled chaos, and it would be an almost impossible task without computers handling most of the work. Computers and networks control trains and railroad crossings all over the United States. Computers manage home security systems and air conditioning units. Small, embedded computer systems are handling an ever greater number of the devices that make your life easier.

Figure 28.22: Embedded circuit board

Computers and Commerce

When people use electronic transmissions across the Internet to exchange money for goods and services, this is known as *e-commerce*, as you know from previous chapters. The use of e-commerce is so common today that customers visiting a Web site may assume that e-commerce will be available. Web sites that use older methods such as snail mail, fax, or phone ordering may lose business to competing sites that offer e-commerce.

Figure 28.23: Froogle

Shopping Without Leaving Your Home

There is nothing worse than driving all over town to track down a hard-to-find item. On the Internet, you can search for the same item in a fraction of the time with exponentially less effort. And you can do it all while still in your pajamas!

Comparing Prices

If you drive to a store to check out a new TV, odds are that the inconvenience of driving to another store, coupled with the excitement of being able to touch what you want, will keep you from driving elsewhere to see if they have the same TV at a better price. By shopping on the Internet, you can check out prices on the same TV from several different retailers without a salesperson putting pressure on you to buy it. There are even Web sites called *aggregators*—a fancy name for a computer program that checks multiple sources—that have done the comparison shopping for you and list out different stores' prices for the same item, as in Figure 28.23.

Finding Hard-To-Find Items

If you want to buy a baseball card of Barry Bonds from his rookie year, odds are that the sports store down the street doesn't have one. There may not even be one in your whole town. Fortunately, the Internet can easily tell you about one in Cleveland or Los Angeles. With *specialty shopping portals*—Web sites set up for buying very specific items—and search engines, even the most peculiar items can be found if someone wants to sell them (Figure 28.24).

Auctions

What is a Barry Bonds rookie year baseball card worth to you? If you are a huge fan, you might pay $100.00. If you hate baseball, you would probably not pay 25 cents. Since different items may have different levels of value to different consumers, the Internet has many *auction sites*—where you can bid against other people online to purchase something—to help establish the value of items. The leading auction site on the Internet is eBay (see Figure 28.25).

More than 100 million people have bought and sold things on eBay. Sellers upload a picture of their item and list a minimum price and buyers then have a set amount of time to bid on the items. Whoever the highest bidder is when the time expires pays with a credit card or an online account and has the item shipped to him or her by the seller.

Selling Products without Physical Stores

Some retailers have completely shifted their business to the Web and no longer have physical stores where you can shop. Amazon.com sold $7 billion worth of books, music, and other goods in 2004, without a single storefront—everything sold online (see Figure 28.26). No stores means fewer *overhead costs* (rent, utility bills, security, and so on), so they can offer lower prices to consumers.

Computers Helping the Disadvantaged and the Disabled

The Internet and computers have provided new realms of opportunity for people who are at a disadvantage in society, either economically or physically. Many public agencies provide helpful services for the disadvantaged, simply by offering free Internet access to those in need. Along with advances in other software and hardware technologies, the Internet has also opened new worlds for those with physical disabilities, such as paralysis, blindness, and speech difficulties.

If you have a computer in your home—maybe even in your own room—it's easy to forget that many families cannot afford the expense of a home computer. When you add up the cost of the computer, monitor, printer, software programs, and monthly Internet connection charges, owning a computer can be quite expensive. Fortunately, public spaces such as libraries, community centers, and work placement facilities often provide computers with Internet connections for use by people.

Public-use computers enable economically disadvantaged people to go online to do research for school, participate in e-learning, find and apply for jobs or public assistance, read news stories, and enjoy every other benefit of the Internet. With a free Web-based e-mail account from a source like Yahoo! Mail or Hotmail, someone with no computer at home can still send and receive messages by logging onto a public computer (Figure 28.27).

Figure 28.24: Specialty shopping portal

Figure 28.25: eBay

Businesses that have both Web-based and physical retail stores usually call the physical locations their brick and mortar stores.

Figure 28.26: Amazon.com

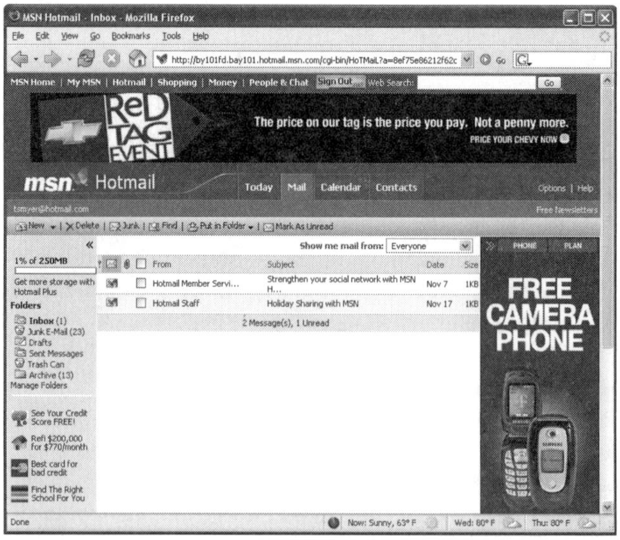

Figure 28.27: Web-based e-mail

Figure 28.28: Using Mouse Controls in Windows XP

The ability to stay in touch electronically with friends, family, educators, co-workers, and potential employers is one way to bridge the *digital divide,* which separates people who can afford technology from those who cannot.

Other types of difficulties face people with physical disabilities, for example: the inability to use a keyboard and mouse or to see the screen. With modern PC technology, however, people with disabilities can get more out of computers than ever before.

Every operating system provides support to individuals who have trouble with mice and keyboards. This support manifests as support for special keyboards and software that enables you to use the arrow keys on a keyboard as mouse controls (Figure 28.28).

Those who cannot use a keyboard may use *voice recognition software* to enter commands, create documents, and explore all aspects of the Web (Figure 28.29). Voice recognition software is an interface between the user's voice and the computer. The software converts the vocal commands into on-screen text and enables vocal commands to operate the software, such as Microsoft Office applications or a Web browser.

Advances in voice recognition technology have also helped non-disabled individuals in many ways. For example, people who type slowly or poorly can speed up their input and increase accuracy using voice recognition software.

Folks with vision problems may take advantage of a number of tools to make the image on the screen easier to read. High-contrast and magnified desktop themes are popular options you'll find on most computers (Figure 28.30). Users can adjust these settings to fit their personal needs.

People who are legally or completely blind can use a combination of voice recognition and *speech synthesis* technology to input commands vocally and hear the results instead of viewing them on a screen. Computer-synthesized speech has a somewhat mechanical sound—anyone who has heard acclaimed physicist Stephen Hawking give a lecture can attest to the distinctively flat tones of his speech synthesizer—but they open doors of opportunity. As with any software, the companies that offer them are constantly making improvements.

Using a combination of local programs and the Internet can empower you to accomplish all sorts of great things. The only true limitation to what you can do is your imagination.

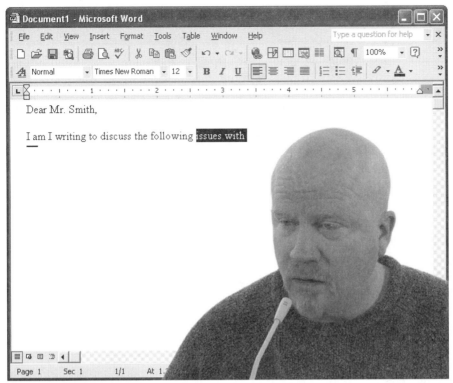

Figure 28.29: Voice recognition at work

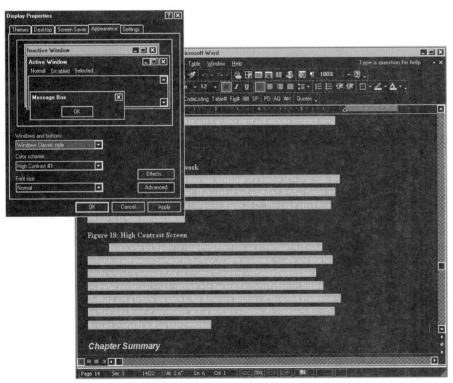

Figure 28.30: High-contrast screen

The Role of Computers in Modern Life

- Educators across the developed world have embraced the personal computer as a useful learning tool. Teachers and administrators use computers to make record-keeping and lesson planning more efficient.

- Students today have access to the tremendous power of the Internet and the World Wide Web. Facts that would once have required a trip to the library and an hour or more of searching are now available with a few clicks of a mouse.

- The real magic of modern computing happens when Internet content comes together with local computer programs to accomplish a goal. You can use Web searches, word processing programs, spreadsheet and presentation software, and e-mail to collect, organize, evaluate, and communicate information.

- *E-learning* combines the Internet and local programs to facilitate learning both in and out of the classroom. *Distance learning* specifically refers to educational courses where students aren't required to meet in a physical classroom. Teachers and professors can communicate with students through Web sites, e-mail messages, and online message boards.

- Combining the Internet and local programs enables you to stay informed and can promote critical thinking—that is, the ability to look at ideas and opinions and form your own based on what you know. You can use Word to write down your ideas or responses and then post with a handle in message boards to see what others think about your ideas.

- With your Internet connection, you can check the weather for your next business trip, get driving directions, keep tabs on current events, send messages to members of Congress, or even volunteer to maintain the Web site of a local charity.

- The impact of having an Internet-connected computer at home is significant. The computer saves time on everything from balancing a checkbook to looking up movie times, leaving more time for other activities. The Internet makes a great homework helper, providing access to volumes of historical, scientific, and literary material.

- Businesses have also seen their productivity increase because of the Internet and technology developments. You can use search engines to uncover statistics that you can compare to your company. The Web and online meeting and chat programs can make meetings turn into collaborations where people all over the world can share ideas in real time.

Computers behind the Scenes

- Many common items have computer chips built in. Cars use computers regulate the gasoline and oxygen mixture and sense the cabin and outside temperatures to adjust the air conditioning. Automated teller machines have computers that enable you to communicate with a central banking system and withdraw cash at any time (assuming you have some in your account, of course!).

- Airlines have databases of all their flights that you can access through travel reservation sites. You can book flights at any time, right over the Internet.

- Automation has greatly altered manufacturing processes. Cars, video game systems, and many other things use robotics to speed up manufacturing.

- Point of sale systems connected to distribution centers make it easier to control inventory, stock shelves, set prices, and more. Computers make all this happen.

- If you turn on the evening news, you'll see a weather reporter doing his or her best to predict what the weather will be like the next day. While weather forecasting is not an exact science, computers are the main reason that they can predict weather patterns as well as they do.

- Modern processors, designed to support a wide array of different devices in embedded systems, are the basis of some of the most important systems in the world. Embedded systems fly airplanes, run power grids, control traffic, and perform many other critical real-time functions.

Computers and Commerce

- On the Internet, you can search for the same item in a fraction of the time with exponentially less effort. And you can do it all while still in your pajamas! By shopping on the Internet, you can check out prices on an item from several different retailers without a salesperson putting pressure on you to buy it.

- Specialty shopping portals and search engines enable you to find even the most peculiar items. You can use auction sites like eBay to buy and sell almost anything. The price you pay or the price you get depends on what people think the product is worth.

- E-commerce enables retail stores to lower overhead costs—dropping rent, utility bills, security, and more—and passing those savings on to you.

Computers Helping the Disadvantaged and the Disabled

- The Internet and computers have provided new realms of opportunity for people who are at a disadvantage in society, either economically or physically. Many public agencies provide helpful services for the disadvantaged, simply by offering free Internet access to those in need.

- Public-use computers at libraries and community centers enable economically disadvantaged people to go online to do research for school, participate in e-learning, find and apply for jobs or public assistance, read news stories, and enjoy every other benefit of the Internet, including e-mail.

- Every operating system provides support to individuals who have trouble with mice and keyboards. This support manifests as support for special keyboards and software that enables you to use the arrow keys on a keyboard as mouse controls.

- Those who cannot use a keyboard may use *voice recognition software* to enter commands, create documents, and explore all aspects of the Web. Folks with vision problems may take advantage of a number of tools to make the image on the screen easier to read. High-contrast and magnified desktop themes are popular options you'll find on most computer.

- People who are legally or completely blind can use a combination of voice recognition and *speech synthesis* technology to input commands vocally and hear the results instead of viewing them on a screen.

Key Terms

Aggregators

Auction site

Automated teller machine (ATM)

Blog

Brick and mortar

Collaborative projects

Critical thinking

Digital divide

Distance learning

E-commerce

E-learning

Embedded computer system

Host processor

Overhead costs

PIN

Point of sale (POS)

Specialty shopping portal

Speech synthesis

Voice recognition software

Key Term Quiz

Use the Key Terms list to complete the following sentences. Not all the terms will be used.

1. _____ systems help retailers track what has been sold in their stores.

2. A(n) _____ is your password for an ATM network.

3. A(n) _____ is the equivalent of a server on an ATM network.

4. The difference in how easily people can access the Internet depending on their financial status is called the _____.

5. A classroom where students receive hands-on instruction combined with online course materials would be an example of _____.

6. Web sites that compare the prices of similar items for you are called _____.

7. An educational course in which the students and instructor never meet would be considered _____.

8. When people exchange money for goods and services across the Internet, this is called _____.

9. Programs that imitate the human voice to "read" text on the screen out loud use _____ technology.

10. A Web site that you can use to bid against others to purchase something is called a(n) _____

Multiple Choice Quiz

1. Which of the following has replaced paper card catalogs in many libraries?
   A. Books
   B. Computer terminals
   C. Microfilm
   D. Point of sale systems

2. Which of the following statements are true of distance learning? (Choose all that apply.)
   A. Students submit assignments digitally.
   B. Students must be in a classroom.
   C. It always involves e-books.
   D. It always involves the Internet.

3. What do we now call a traditional store where customers come to shop?
   A. Brick and mortar
   B. Fixed
   C. Overhead
   D. Portal

4. Which of these resides on an ATM card's magnetic strip and enables the user to access his or her bank account?
   A. The password
   B. The host processor
   C. The login ID
   D. The portal

5. Why was the ISA created?
   A. To define the formats of application document formats since the Apple II
   B. To improve worldwide communication after World War II
   C. To share ideas developed during the manufacturing peak of World War II
   D. To turn over older technologies to developing countries

6. Which of the following is the most obvious benefit of networking weather data from around the globe?
   A. Helping train weather researchers
   B. Improving highway design
   C. Predicting and tracking storms
   D. Verifying that weather equipment is working

7. When a school offers online classes, which of the following is it providing?
   A. E-commerce
   B. E-business
   C. E-learning
   D. eBay

8. Which of the following would be an advantage of online shopping over brick and mortar shopping?
   A. Ability to hold the item
   B. Cheaper shipping rates
   C. Ease of comparing prices from many vendors
   D. Supporting local businesses

9. What's the name of the most popular online auction site?
   A. eBay.com
   B. iVillage.com
   C. pets.com
   D. totalsem.com

10. Which term applies to the use of computer-controlled robots in manufacturing?
    A. Skynet
    B. Automation
    C. E-commerce
    D. Processing

Essay Questions

1. Imagine that you're a writer for *Time* magazine. Your first story is an introduction to online shopping for people who have never tried it before. Describe two advantages of shopping online. Can you think of any products that you haven't seen available online that you think should be sold that way?

2. You want to go out to your favorite restaurant, and suddenly realize that you have no cash, so you have to go to the nearest ATM. How does an ATM system work? How do you think people would react if ATMs suddenly stopped working?

3. Your uncle, who owns a chain of department stores, hires you to make his business more efficient. Explain to him why you need a POS system, and give him a high-level explanation of how a POS system works.

Projects

1. You have just been put in charge of e-learning for your school. Come up with a collaborative project for your class. What country will your partner students live in? What will you be doing together? What will your goals be?

2. Everyone has a "million dollar idea" that they've never been able to get off the ground. If you had an unlimited budget to design a Web site and to build your product, what would you sell on the Internet? On a large piece of paper, lay out what your main Web page would look like, and what screens you would need to carry out e-commerce.

Safety First – Protecting Computer Systems, Data, and Users

"Hi, folks. Mike Nelson here. Crow and Servo are about to help me with the annual Satellite of Love safety check. You guys ready?"

– Mike Nelson, *Mystery Science Theater 3000*

This chapter covers the following IC[3] exam objectives:

- ■ IC[3]-3 4.2.1 Identify how to maintain a safe working environment that complies with legal health and safety rules.

- ■ IC[3]-3 4.2.2 Identify injuries that can result from the use of computers for long periods of time.

- ■ IC[3]-3 4.2.3 Identify risks to personal and organizational data.

- ■ IC[3]-3 4.2.4 Identify software threats.

Nothing ruins the mood of your Half-Life shootout faster than your brother running into the room, tripping over the new subwoofer you forgot to move under the desk after you connected your new 5.1 stereo speakers, and cracking his head open on the extra computer case you were going to put back on the table just as soon as you finished your game. Making sure that your surroundings don't pose unnecessary risks isn't just a good idea because it protects your brother—or any other visitors to your Half-Life lair—from accidental injury. It protects you from the consequences of hurting yourself or someone else, having to replace your brand new speaker, or having to abandon a great sniper angle so you can explain why you hadn't gotten around to straightening up yet.

This chapter looks at safety issues, starting with steps to maintain a safe working environment. The second section covers some of the dangers involved with long-term computer use and what you need to do to keep healthy, wealthy, and wise. The chapter wraps with a discussion of ways to keep data safe – it's not just you at risk with your computer!

Maintaining a Safe Working Environment

Computers can be useful and entertaining, and at first glance they might seem pretty non-threatening, but in fact, both people and data can be at risk even from normal day-to-day computer use. Understanding the risks to people and data and knowing how to identify and guard against safety and security problems before they arise, will ensure that your computer use works.

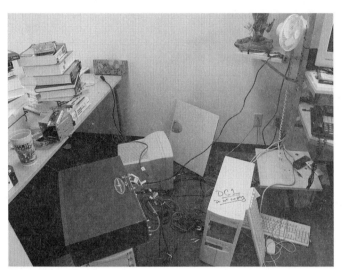

Figure 29.1: Mike's office

Set up Safely

Maintaining a safe work environment requires both knowledge and common sense. Think about safety when you set up your computer work area. As much as possible, for example, position your furniture and computer equipment to minimize the chance of accidental injury. Check to see if you are creating trip hazards, such as small pieces of equipment at low heights or chair legs that stick out into walkways.

Try to leave a clear pathway to and around your computer and nearby equipment, such as printers and bookshelves. Don't try to fit so much equipment on desks and shelves that you have to position things too close to the edges, or pile things on top of each other (Figure 29.1). Peripherals and floors make a bad combination.

It may seem funny that your computer and network equipment need to breathe, but in a way they do. Most computers have slots and openings that are designed to release warm air and to bring in cooler air so that internal components don't overheat and become ruined (Figure 29.2). Stacking equipment is not only a physical safety hazard, it can also block these openings so the equipment can't breathe, which means you could be buying new equipment all too soon. Overheated electronics die quickly.

What's my Motivation?

Offices Can Be Dangerous Places!

In 2003, according to the United States Bureau of Labor Statistics, 5,575 fatalities occurred while people were at work. Many of these fatalities occurred in obviously dangerous industries like manufacturing and coal mining, but a surprising number happened in regular offices and stores.

Connect Safely

Cords and cables should be out of sight and out of the way wherever possible. When you have to connect computers and peripherals, run cables through walls and ceilings if possible, or at least make sure they aren't laying on the floor where they pose a trip hazard. Most modern office furniture has specially designed slots and other places to run cords and cables through. Most importantly, make sure electrical cords aren't in danger of being pulled from their sockets accidentally.

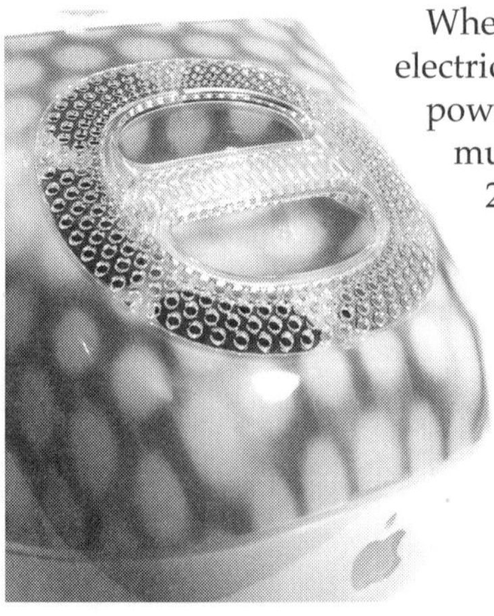

Figure 29.2: Ventilation holes

When you plug things in, be aware of potential electrical hazards you could create. Don't overload power outlets, for example, by daisy chaining multiple power strips on one socket (Figure 29.3). When too many extension cords and power strips pull power from one outlet, the *overloaded outlet* can cause a fire. And that, as techs say, is a *bad thing*.

Physical Injury – Risks and Remedies

Sitting at a computer eight hours a day may seem like a safe job, but it leads to

discomfort and poor health for many people. Until the modern era, pretty much everyone's daily activities involved moving around a great deal and doing lots of physical labor. Subtle, repetitive movements and long periods spent in sometimes awkward positions are common features of computer use that put potentially harmful stresses on many areas of our bodies.

Concern over the physical stresses of desk work is part of the reason for the field called ergonomics.

Ergonomics is the use of scientific information about the human body to design healthier work environments, including safer room designs, furniture, equipment, and tools. Ergonomics is responsible for advancements such as adjustable chairs, computer wrist rests, and easy-grip pens (Figure 29.4).

Sitting at a computer, staring at a monitor, typing and mousing for extended periods of time—all these can negatively affect the entire body, from top to bottom. Let's look at the most common computer-user ailments and see what the experts suggest to do to prevent them.

Proper ergonomic practices to avoid injuries include having a properly adjusted chair, properly arranged furniture and equipment, and properly positioned lighting. It also means using ergonomic aids like anti-glare screens on monitors and keyboard wrist pads (Figure 29.5).

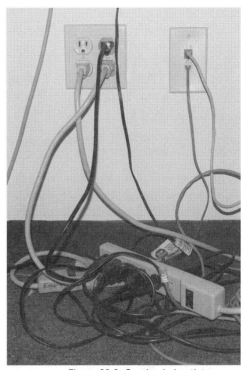

Figure 29.3: Overloaded outlet

Figure 29.4: Ergonomic Celle chair (Photo courtesy of Herman Miller)

Repetitive Motion Disorders

Repetitive motion disorders (*RMDs*) are muscular conditions that come from subtle but often repeated motions in the course of daily activities. Too many uninterrupted repetitions of these motions can strain muscles and joints and can cause a great deal of pain. The most common RMD affecting computer users is *carpal tunnel syndrome*. The main nerve running down your arm passes through a tunnel of bones and ligaments in your wrist—called the *carpal tunnel*—on its way to your hand. Overuse can cause your wrist to become inflamed, swell up, and compress or squeeze the nerve, which can hurt enough to make normal computer use impossible.

Electrical systems in the United States cause 40,000 fires every year, almost all of them preventable. One of the main causes of these fires is overloaded electrical outlets.

Figure 29.5: Wrist pad

To prevent carpel tunnel syndrome, people who use computers a great deal should make sure they avoid bad posture (see Figure 29.6), in particular check that the mouse is not too far from the keyboard, take frequent breaks to stretch and relax their wrists, and use ergonomic keyboards and wrist rests as needed.

Eye Strain

Visual problems, such as *eye strain*, are among the most frequently reported complaints by computer users. Eye strain can result from bad lighting conditions, glare from the screen, poor positioning of the screen itself, or copy material that is difficult to read (Figure 29.7).

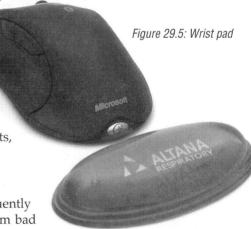

The contrast between a computer screen and a dark room can cause eye strain, and staring at a computer screen with a window or other bright light source directly behind it can cause serious eye damage. Finally, you should periodically look away from your computer screen to let your eyes relax and focus at a new distance.

Figure 29.6: Bad posture – Sit up!

Back Strain

Improper posture and placement of the computer can cause back, neck, and shoulder strain. Figure 29.8 shows the proper ergonomic position of a person working at a computer. The lower back should be supported, and the back should form a lazy S curve, the low back bowing slightly inward and the upper back slightly outward. The neck should be aligned above the spine, not pushed forward, and the head should be pointed directly forward, not turned to the side or craned upward.

The upper arms should hang vertically, not reaching forward toward the keyboard, and the elbows should be bent at more or less a

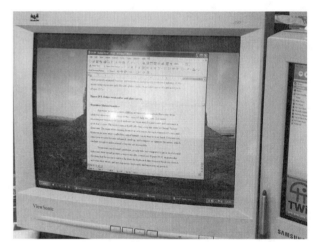

Figure 29.7: Bad screen glare

right angle. Finally, your seat and desk should be positioned so that your hips and knees bend at right angles, and your feet are firmly supported on the floor or a footrest.

Proper Ergonomic Position

Let's go over some ways you can make sure you are working in an ergonomically safe position, starting at the top. To keep your neck and head properly positioned, place your monitor and documents so that your eyes look straight ahead or downward no more than 45 degrees. Bring the monitor and any documents closer if you find yourself leaning forward to view them.

Figure 29.8: Much better!

You can use a document holder to keep papers in a comfortable viewing position. Raise or lower your monitor if you find yourself looking up or too far down at it. To ensure proper arm and wrist positioning, bring your keyboard and mouse close enough to your body to keep from extending your arms, place the mouse next to the keyboard, and use the keyboard's feet to raise its height if needed.

To make sure you have proper low back support, adjust your chair's backrest. If your chair isn't designed to allow proper support, consider using a lumbar pad to support your lower back. Adjust your chair height to make sure your leg position is correct, and remember that if your chair is too low for the desk it can affect the position of your arms as well.

Use a foot rest if the chair height prevents your feet from resting flat on the floor. Make sure you have enough room for your legs under the desk or table. Keep clutter out from under your desk, and if you need room for really long legs, try installing a keyboard tray so you can sit farther back.

Protecting Computer Data

A computer crash is all too often the wake-up call for computer users who never paid attention to protecting their data. Realizing you just lost the entire essay you had labored over all evening feels awful. Now, imagine you run a business with thousands of employees, and your tech comes in to tell you that your server crashed and all your payroll data went with it. Whatever the situation, *data loss* happens when you use computers, and it's important to understand the nature of the risks and what you can do to prevent the worst from happening to you.

Computer viruses are a much-publicized hazard, but they are only one piece of the puzzle when it comes to losing computer data. As of this writing, the biggest problem is hardware or system malfunctions, which are responsible for almost half of all data loss (Figure 29.9). The next most common cause (a third of all data loss) is the ever-popular human error.

Viruses, Worms, and Other Software Threats

Just like a biological virus gets passed from person to person, a computer *virus* is a piece of malicious software that gets passed from computer to computer (Figure 29.10). A computer virus is designed to attach itself to a program on your computer. It could be your e-mail program, your word processor, or even a game. Whenever you use the infected program, the virus goes into action and does whatever it was designed to do. It could wipe out your e-mail or even erase your entire hard drive! Viruses are also sometimes used to steal information or send spam e-mails to everyone in your address book.

Get Up
All these rules about proper ergonomic position of your back, arms, head, neck and legs mean nothing if you sit in front of a computer for too long without getting up. So get up. C'mon, do it now! Get in the habit of standing up and stretching every hour or so, just for a minute. Many people find this embarrassing at first, but that's a cultural oddity that needs to change. Your body will thank you, even if your co-workers look at you like you're crazy.

How Bad?
So, how bad are the computer work habits of people around you, in your office or school? Grab a note pad and writing implement—pen, pencil, crayon, quill—and take some notes on how people work. Pay attention to the legs, spine, and head level. Once you've gathered your data, go back and look at yourself when you work. How bad are your habits?

Figure 29.9: Eek! Flames!

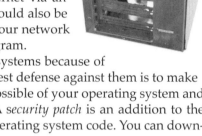

Publish from Home

Desktop publishing software, such as Adobe InDesign or Microsoft Publisher, can help you with layouts. They have pre-built templates designed for certain common tasks. All you have to do is think of what colors you like, and type in your personalized information—instant brochure, just add the details! If you have one of these applications, play around and discover how powerful they really are. If you have a business or hobby, this is perfect for you. You can create all your marketing and advertising documents in one application.

Most people lump worms together with similar threats like Trojan horses under the first and most common term for such infectious troublemakers, viruses. The IC³ exams, on the other hand, make a distinction between worms and regular viruses.

Unlike a virus, which is only a partial program, a *worm* is a complete program that travels from machine to machine, usually through computer networks. Most worms are designed to take advantage of security problems in operating systems and install themselves on vulnerable machines. They can copy themselves over and over again on infected networks, and can create so much activity that they can overload the network, in worst cases even bringing chunks of the entire Internet to a halt.

There are several things you can do to protect yourself and your data against these threats. First, make sure you are running up-to-date virus software, and especially if you connect to the Internet via an always-on broadband connection. You should also be protected by a firewall, either as part of your network hardware, or by means of a software program.

Since worms most commonly infect systems because of security flaws in operating systems, the best defense against them is to make sure you have the most current version possible of your operating system and to check regularly for security patches. A *security patch* is an addition to the operating system to patch a hole in the operating system code. You can download security patches from the software vendor's Web site (Figure 29.11).

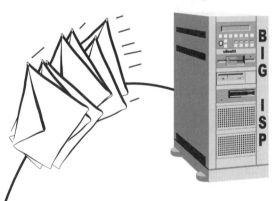

Figure 29.10: You've got mail!

A *spyware* program covertly collects information from your computer and can create significant problems for Internet users. Besides violating your privacy, spyware programs can secretly install themselves on your computer and use up large amounts of its resources, slowing your system to a crawl. Several programs, such as the widely-used Ad-Aware and Spybot Search & Destroy, will seek out and eliminate these threats (Figure 29.12).

E-mail is still a common source of viruses, and opening infected e-mails is a common way to get infected. If you view an e-mail in a preview window, that opens the e-mail message and exposes your computer to some viruses. Download files only from sites you know to be safe, and of course the less reputable corners of the Internet are the most likely places to pick up computer infections.

Chapter 30, "Safe and Legal Use of the Internet," goes into some detail on firewalls.

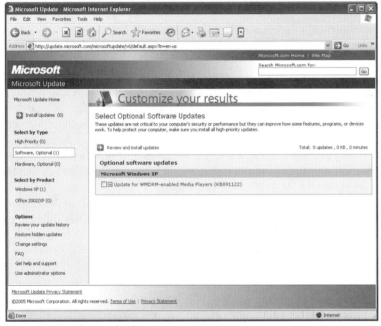

Figure 29.11: Windows Update

Spybot
If you haven't done this already, do it now. Go to www.spybot.info and download the latest copy of Spybot Search&Destroy. Install it on your computer and run it. Any spyware that slipped in past your defenses?

Because no prevention scheme is perfect, you should follow a regular procedure of identifying, isolating, and cleaning infected files. It is also a good idea to make regular visits to security Web sites that keep track of major viruses causing problems around the globe.

Figure 29.12: Spybot Search & Destroy

Unauthorized Computer and Network Use

Skilled computer programmers, called *hackers*, can take software and make it do something that the original programmer did not intend, what's called a *hack*. Most hackers create solutions to unforeseen problems or add additional capabilities to existing software. As such, hackers across the globe regularly save companies lots of money, protect jobs, and reap the benefits of good behavior.

In an evil twist on hacking, though, malicious programmers—called *black hats*—can use their skill to crack into a network or computer and steal money, information,

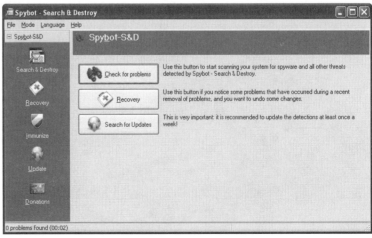

and identities. Black hats destroy Web sites, defame people, and do generally naughty things that should land them in jail for a very long time.

You need to protect yourself against black hats. Not surprisingly, banks are a major target of data thieves, as are online businesses of all sorts that store customer credit card information. Always make sure you use a secure Web page before you send any sensitive data out across the Internet.

A firewall filters incoming Internet traffic and blocks malicious programs and viruses that try to attack the network or computer it protects. Well-defended networks use firewalls, as you know from earlier chapters. Since some thieves will actually break into the premises to access a network, it is also important to keep business servers and equipment locked up in a secure room.

A third tool for thwarting thieves bent on stealing your data is to scramble it into secret code using encryption. Even if they steal it, encrypted data will just look like gibberish to anyone who doesn't have the secret key to decrypt it.

Data Backup

Storms, floods, hurricanes, and fires can destroy computers and servers in a heartbeat. Black hats can destroy or corrupt data without leaving a trace. Replacing the hardware is not what keeps system administrators up late, however; their big fear is a catastrophic loss of data. To protect against this disaster, most businesses and schools have a regular data backup procedure. Every several days, if not every day, network administrators copy all the information from their servers onto tapes or disks (Figure 29.13), which are often stored in a different location.

You can replace any kind of computer component, but you can't replace original data that goes down in a system crash. Even if you don't live in an area that's prone to natural disasters, that doesn't mean your data is safe from other threats, such as a laptop thief, a hard drive crash, a power surge, or even your little sister's spilled soda.

You should have a regular procedure for backing up anything on your computer that you aren't willing to lose. This can be as simple as copying important files to external media such as floppy disks, external drives, or CDs. In addition, there are programs built into the major operating systems, and readily available online or in stores at little or no cost, that will help you do a more organized job of backing up your data. These programs make sure you don't forget anything, and they keep track of what you've *already* saved so you don't waste time saving it twice!

Finally, don't wait until you've finished creating a document before you save it. Periodically saving your work will prevent you from losing hours of your valuable time retyping your masterpiece, or worse yet, recreating it from scratch. Most word processing programs will automatically save documents in progress at certain time intervals (such as every 10 minutes), and it is a good idea to make sure this feature is activated. A good general rule: if you've typed enough that you'll be unhappy if you have to redo your work, it's time to click the **Save** button (Figure 29.14)!

Passwords

The proper use of passwords is a simple but effective way to protect data, computers, and even networks. Proper use means always using passwords, using different passwords for different purposes, changing your passwords on a regular basis, and choosing passwords that are sufficiently complex and random that they aren't easy to

Exam Tip

People outside the computer industry often incorrectly use the term hacker to describe both good hackers and black hats. If you see the term used on an exam, assume the exam means black hat.

Secure Sites

You ran into secure Web sites back in Chapter 26, "Web Essentials," so turn back there now and see if you can answer these questions. How can you determine that a Web page resides on a secure server? What protocol do computers and servers use to handle secure connections?

Figure 29.13: Backup tapes

crack. Adhering to strict password rules can provide computers, data, and networks with an additional layer of protection from both deliberate and accidental exposure.

Weak passwords include anything that could be easy to guess, such as birthdays, phone numbers, or names of family members and pets; pretty much any standard dictionary word by itself; and strings of fewer than eight characters. *Strong passwords* are at least eight characters long; contain a mixture of uppercase and lowercase letters, numbers, and punctuation or symbol characters; and aren't proper names or common words, like Shakespeare or surfboard.

```
A problem has been detected and Windows has been shut down to prevent damage
to your computer.

PFN_LIST_CORRUPT

If this is the first time you've seen this error screen,
restart your computer. If this screen appears again, follow
these steps:

Check to make sure any new hardware or software is properly installed.
If this is a new installation, ask your hardware or software manufacturer
for any Windows updates you might need.

If problems continue, disable or remove any newly installed hardware
or software. Disable BIOS memory options such as caching or shadowing.
If you need to use Safe Mode to remove or disable components, restart
your computer, press F8 to select Advanced Startup Options, and then
select Safe Mode.

Technical information:

*** STOP: 0x0000004e (0x00000099, 0x00000000, 0x00000000, 0x00000000)

Beginning dump of physical memory
Physical memory dump complete.
Contact your system administrator or technical support group for further
assistance.
```

Figure 29.14: Crash!!!

What's my Motivation?

Some Facts About Why Data Loss Should Concern You
Somewhere in the U.S.:

■ *A hard drive crashes every 15 seconds.*

■ *2,000 laptops are stolen or lost every day.*

■ *32% of data loss is caused by human error.*

■ *31% of PC users have lost all of their PC files to events beyond their control.*

■ *25% of lost data is due to the failure of a portable drive.*

■ *1 in 5 computers suffers a fatal hard drive crash during its lifetime.*

Maintaining a Safe Working Environment

- Think about safety when you are setting up your computer work area. Position your furniture and computer equipment to minimize the chance of accidental injury. Make sure your equipment has room to breathe.

- Keep cords and cables out of sight and out of the way. Make sure electrical cords aren't in danger of being pulled from their sockets accidentally.

- Too many extension cords and power strips pulling power from one outlet can overload it and cause a fire.

Physical Injury – Risks and Remedies

- Ergonomics is the use of scientific information about the human body to design healthier work environments, including safer room designs, furniture, equipment and tools.

- Using ergonomic furniture and aids, maintaining a proper sitting posture when at the computer, and making sure you change position regularly can prevent repetitive motion injury and back strain.

- Repetitive motion disorders, or RMDs, are muscular conditions that come from subtle but heavily repeated motions. Carpal tunnel syndrome is a common RMD affecting the wrists of computer users.

- Back, neck and shoulder strain are usually caused by improper posture and placement of the computer. Assess and adjust your work environment to make sure you are working in an ergonomically safe position.

- Visual problems, such as eye strain, can be caused by bad lighting conditions, screen glare, and poor ergonomics. Avoid overly dark or bright lighting. Look away from your computer screen periodically to rest your eyes.

Protecting Computer Data

■ Data loss is a predictable risk of using computers. Hardware or system malfunctions are responsible for almost half of all data loss. The next most common cause is human error.

■ A computer virus is a piece of malicious software that gets passed from computer to computer. A WORM is a malicious program that spreads through networks, usually designed to take advantage of security problems in operating systems.

■ To protect yourself and your data against malicious software, run up-to-date virus software, install a firewall, and check regularly for operating system security patches. Guard against opening infected e-mail messages, and be cautious about downloading files from the Internet.

■ Programs that covertly collect information from your computer, called spyware, can steal your data and use up computer resources.

■ A black hat is a computer programmer who gains unauthorized access into computers and networks. Firewalls, passwords, encryption and secure Web sites are important protections against black hats. Note that many people use the term "hacker" to describe black hats.

■ Most businesses and schools have some form of data backup procedure to protect against theft, damage, or natural disaster. You should also have a regular procedure for backing up anything on your computer that you aren't willing to lose, by copying important files to external media, or by using a backup program. Periodically save your work in progress.

■ The proper use of passwords protects data, computers, and even networks. Always use passwords, use different passwords for different purposes, change your passwords on a regular basis, and choose passwords that are sufficiently complex and random that they aren't easy to crack.

■ Weak passwords include anything that could be easy to guess, and standard dictionary words. Strong passwords are at least eight characters long; contain a mixture of uppercase and lowercase letters, numbers, and punctuation or symbol characters; and aren't proper names or common words.

CHAPTER 29: SUMMARY

Key Terms

Black hat

Carpal tunnel syndrome

Data loss

Ergonomics

Eye strain

Firewall

Hacker

Overloaded outlet

Repetitive motion disorder (RMD)

Security patch

Spyware

Strong password

Virus

Weak password

Worm

Key Term Quiz

Use the Key Terms list to complete the following sentences. Not all the terms will be used.

1. The practice of using knowledge about the human body to make our working environment healthier is _____.

2. Using your birthday as your ATM code would be an example of a _____.

3. Keeping copies of your files on external media protects you from _____ if your hard drive crashes.

4. A(n) _____ is someone who tries to break into computer systems and networks.

5. Improper placement of your mouse and keyboard can cause inflammation in your wrist, which can lead to _____.

6. _____ are programs often designed to exploit weaknesses in operating systems.

7. A combination of nine random letters, numbers and symbol characters is a good example of a _____.

8. Programs that secretly install themselves on your computer and steal information about you are called _____.

9. The glare from a computer screen can cause _____.

10. A(n) _____ has too many electrical devices plugged into it, and can be a fire risk.

Multiple Choice Questions

1. Which of these is an example of a strong password?
   A. Jimmy
   B. 12345
   C. GGftV8Y7u
   D. telephone

2. What is carpal tunnel syndrome?
   A. Bad office design
   B. An overloaded electrical outlet
   C. A defective firewall
   D. A repetitive motion disorder

3. Which of the following can you protect against using a firewall?
   A. Power surges
   B. Black hat
   C. Repetitive motion disorders
   D. Encryption

4. Of the programs listed below, which attaches itself to the programs on your computer to do its evil deeds?
   A. A bug
   B. A virus
   C. A trojan
   D. A worm

5. To ensure this, adjust your chair's backrest, or consider using a lumbar pad.
   A. Proper low back support
   B. Proper leg room
   C. Proper wrist position
   D. Proper knee angle

6. How many computers suffer a fatal hard drive crash during their lifetimes?
   A. 50%
   B. 90%
   C. 1 in 5
   D. 1 in 100

7. Which of the following filters incoming Internet traffic to protect your network?
   A. Firewalls
   B. Modems
   C. Encryption programs
   D. Servers

8. Maintaining a proper sitting posture when at the computer and making sure you change position regularly will **not** help prevent this problem.
   A. Back strain
   B. RMDs
   C. Trip hazards
   D. Eye strain

9. A hardware or system malfunction can cause which of the following problems?
   A. Viruses
   B. Data loss
   C. RMDs
   D. Overloaded outlets

10. If you are a network administrator, what should you do with your server backup files?
    A. Store them securely in the office.
    B. Store them in a different location.
    C. Ventilate them.
    D. Delete them.

11. Why shouldn't you place a monitor in front of a window?
    A. It can cause back strain.
    B. It can cause carpal tunnel syndrome.
    C. It can cause trip hazards.
    D. It can cause eye strain.

12. Which of the following is **not** a proper use of passwords?
    A. Using different passwords for different accounts
    B. Choosing passwords with at least eight characters
    C. Always keeping the same password on an account
    D. Avoiding dictionary words when choosing a password

13. Your seat and desk should be positioned so that your hips and knees bend at which angle?
    A. 30°
    B. 45°
    C. 90°
    D. 120°

14. What can businesses do to protect their computer networks against black hats?
    A. Store their data on servers
    B. Keep their servers in locked rooms
    C. Send their data to servers
    D. Use spyware on their servers

15. Which of these ergonomic measures will **not** help prevent carpal tnnel syndrome?
    A. Anti-glare screen
    B. Wrist rest
    C. Split keyboard
    D. Frequent stretch breaks

Essay Questions

1. You are helping the school nurse give a lecture about the health effects of using computers. Write up a brief presentation explaining three health ailments that can affect computer users, offering at least two suggestions on how to prevent each of them.

2. Congratulations! You have just been put in charge of your school's computer network. Your first task is to draft a one-page memo to your users explaining the difference between strong and weak passwords, and offering five examples of each.

3. You are still in charge of your school's computer network. Your second task is to draft a memo to your principal explaining what measures you will be taking to protect your network from black hats.

Projects

1. The President just called, saying that she's made you the National Director for Ergonomics. She wants you to make a presentation in the Oval Office on the healthiest way to position yourself when sitting at a desk using a computer. Draw a picture of an ergonomically sound computer user. Make sure that your drawing includes a user in a chair, a keyboard and mouse, and a monitor.

2. You are a teaching assistant sharing an office with two other people. Each of you has a desk, an office chair, and a desktop computer setup, and the three of you share one printer that has its own table. The office is square, with a door in the south wall, and one power outlet on each of the other three walls. There is only one network connection, on the wall with the door. Draw a room layout that gives an example of how your office space could be set up safely. Include in your drawing the placement of your desks, chairs, computers, and printer, as well as where you would run the cords and cables connecting them to the power outlets and to each other.

Safe and Legal Use of the Internet

Peter Parker: "Spider-Man wasn't trying to attack the city, he was trying to save it. That's slander."
J. Jonah Jameson: "It is not. I resent that. Slander is spoken. In print, it's libel."

– Peter Parker and J. Jonah Jameson, *Spiderman*

This chapter covers the following IC³ exam objectives:

■ IC³-3 4.3.1 Identify reasons for restricting access to files, storage devices, computers, networks, the Internet or certain Internet sites.

■ IC³-3 4.3.2 Identify concepts related to intellectual property laws.

■ IC³-3 4.3.3 Identify the principles regarding when information can or cannot be considered personal.

■ IC³-3 4.3.4 Identify how to avoid hazards regarding electronic commerce.

■ IC³-3 4.3.5 Identify how to protect privacy and personal security online.

■ IC³-3 4.3.6 Identify how to find information about rules regarding the use of computers and the Internet.

■ IC³-3 4.3.7 Identify how to stay informed about changes and advancements in technology.

■ IC³-3 4.3.8 Identify how to be a responsible user of computers and the Internet.

The ease of sharing and moving information on the Internet has created massive challenges to personal privacy and copyright. It's way too easy to use copyrighted works (text, music, movies, or pictures) and to give out personal information in a dangerous and haphazard manner. You can easily expose yourself to fraud from those who steal your information or censure from teachers who find you using plagiarized works. In the worst cases, you might even get sued or arrested for stealing!

This chapter addresses the moral and legal issues you face in using the Internet. First, you'll learn about the rules protecting information that others own, defining the different types of intellectual property and your responsibilities when you use them. Next, the chapter looks at the some of the dangers of using personal information on the Internet and what you need to do to avoid people abusing your name, address, credit card, and bank account numbers. The chapter wraps with a discussion on the legal and moral issues relating to safe disposal of your old computers and what you should do to share the knowledge you've gained.

Plug-ins

You learned about plug-ins in Chapter 26, "Web Essentials," so turn there now and see if you can answer these questions. First, what's a plug-in do for you? How does a missing plug-in affect you? What's a common plug-in?

Libel

One thing that's always off limits, whether your school or work policies say so or not, is libel. When you post on a Web site or send in an e-mail something that is not true and causes harm to a person or organization, that's libel and totally against the law. You can call someone names or post a nasty message about a company—that's not libel, just meanness. In the U.S., posting "John is a big fat doo-doo head" is protected as free speech. If you post something like, "John hangs out on the street corner and steals candy from babies," and John is harmed by that statement, he can sue you and win.

Note that a statement is not libel if it's true. John really does hang out on the street corner.

Figure 30.1: Policies for Rice University

Rules of the Road

Although it might be true, as the (not so) old saying goes, that *information on the Internet wants to be free*, a lot of laws, rules, and regulations govern what you can and cannot do with computers. Every organization, big and small, has policies for computer use that you need to know. You also need to understand when something you create belongs to you or when it belongs to someone else. Finally, don't let the incredibly easy access to information on the Internet lull you into thinking that normal property rules don't apply. Let's take a look at these issues.

Policies on Internet Use

Businesses and schools almost invariably have rules restricting what you can do with their computers. Prohibitions can range from downloading and installing programs or plug-ins, to accessing questionable Web sites or sending e-mail that contains anything negative about the company or school.

Figure 30.1 shows the "Common Policy Questions and Answers" page for Rice University, displaying a typical set of restrictions. If you're a student at the school, for example, you can't let other people use your e-mail account, nor play games over the university network. Each student gets a Web page for personal use, but the university policy prohibits any commercial activity on those Web pages.

You are responsible for discovering and abiding by the rules and policies set forth by your work or school. In many cases, when you first enroll in a school or take a job, the information packets you receive have all the information you need to stay on the right side of the rules. If you don't get such a packet, *ask for one* or ask about the policies of the school or work place. No one wants you to get in trouble or break the rules, but it's up to you to protect yourself.

Personal and Not-So-Personal Information

You own anything you create by default, from research papers to short stories, from drawings to the essays you write in the course of working through this book. When you create and store something on your personal computer, that rule applies absolutely.

When you create and store something on a computer you don't own, such as a computer owned by your office or school, the rules of ownership get a lot murkier. Most employers require you to sign a document that in effect says, "What you develop while working for this company is the property of this company." That means that anything you create—during or even after business hours—on your employer's computer most likely belongs to the employer, not you.

There are exceptions to this, of course. If you have a company laptop and write a fictional short story while traveling on business, you own that story. But if it's a work-related document, your employer owns it.

The picture is even less clear with things you create on school-owned computers. Policies differ by school, so you need to read those policies and find out. It's important to know, after all, whether e-mail you write using a school computer belongs to you or to the school. You might be surprised by the answer!

Keep in mind you generally have more rights to stuff you create on your personal computer than on work or school computers.

What's Your Policy?

Now would be a great time to find out—if you don't already know—the rules governing computers at your workplace, school, or organization. Check online or through the personnel department. That's the most likely source for the rulebook, or at least a good place to start.

Intellectual Property

Considering how easy the Internet makes it to send files, pictures, and music from one computer to another, it often surprises folks to learn that *nothing* on the Internet is free for you to use without permission. Someone owns the rights to everything you see or hear. You need to understand copyrights, patents, and the concept of fair use to use Internet content properly. Let's look at the legal stuff first, and then see what you can do in the real world.

Copyrights and Trademarks

The act of creation gives the creator a copyright to what he or she has made. A *copyright* means exactly what it sounds like, that no one else has a right to copy the creation without the owner's permission. Copyrighted content you can find on the Web includes news articles, blogs, photos, cartoons, how-to articles, and the graphics that create the look of the Web sites themselves (Figure 30.2). Collectively, things people create are called *intellectual property*.

If you write a great short story to submit for publication and find a perfect picture on the

Figure 30.2: Look at all that copyrighted content!

Internet to illustrate a section, if you use that picture without permission from the artist then you break the law. If someone else comes along and takes your story to re-publish on his site without permission, he's violated your copyright to the story and joined you in violating the original artist's copyright to the picture you used to illustrate it!

A *trademark* refers to names, symbols, or other things that a person or company uses to identify a product or entity. No one else can use a trademark without getting permission to do so. Coca-Cola is a trademark, for example, that Pepsi-Cola can't use on a soda can. Trademarks are identified by icons, as shown in Figure 30.3.

Trademark™
Trademark©
Trademark®

Figure 30.3: Trademark Icons

Patents

Similarly to copyrights, an inventor or developer can get a *patent* on a product or process; patent protection lasts for a fixed number of years, during which you can't use the patented product or process without permission from the owner. In return, the inventor has to make public the details of the patented product or process, so that other inventors can use that information to help them in their own work. When you buy a product, the payment accepted grants permission to use it—that's not a legal definition, but one that works well enough in general use.

Fair Use

Suppose you write an article for an *online zine*—a Web-based magazine—where you analyze the characters in the Harry Potter books. Can you use quotes from the books to help make your points, or would that violate J.K. Rowling's copyright? Most countries abide by the concept of *fair use* to determine what you can and cannot do with content you find. Fair use means in some circumstances, including the use of limited excerpts from another author's work when you review or analyze it, you can use someone else's content without getting permission first (Figure 30.4).

The idea behind fair use is that copyrights should not be used to block discussion and analysis, especially if the context is educational or political. Limited copying by a student for academic work is protected by fair use, so including a photograph of a great horned owl you found online in a research paper about great horned owls, for example, is completely legal. The same is true about information from newspaper and magazine articles. You don't have to be using copyrighted material for commercial (money-making) purposes to be violating the law, but it definitely makes it more likely that the copyright holder will object!

Getting Permission

You can get permission to use things you find online in several ways. Many Web sites post their copyright information in an About page or something of that nature. Bigger companies have Press sections where you can read the permission statements and download and use high-quality images (Figure 30.5).

Finally, if you can't find permission granted or denied online, e-mail the site owner and ask (Figure 30.6). Most folks are happy to share for non-commercial purposes for free. For commercial purposes, they might ask for a copy of whatever you're making or at least recognition in the credits.

When you use things created by other people, even in a fair use situation, you must cite the source accurately by quoting and including the source (Figure 30.7). If you have permission to reprint a poem, for example, but then don't use the poet's name—and thus imply that you wrote the poem—you commit *plagiarism*. That's against the rules in any setting, academic or commercial, so don't do it!

Safe Surfing

The Internet is a bit like a giant city in cyberspace. Like any city, it has many different neighborhoods, some safer than others. Like in a city, you'll find every sort of person online as well, some helpful and nice and others who are looking to cheat and steal. Protecting yourself when living online is just part of being a citizen of cyberspace.

Dodging E-commerce Bullets

The ability to buy goods and services over the Internet—that is, *e-commerce*—makes the Web an amazingly powerful and useful tool. But with that capability comes the dark side. The chance to make money always attracts some people who want to take advantage of you, rip you off, or scam you.

It's up to you to protect yourself when you do business online, and there are a number of simple things you can do to thwart the bad guys. Start by double-checking the legitimacy of online offers. Remember, if it sounds too good to be true, it usually is (Figure 30.8).

Only give out your credit card information on secure sites. Be careful when you create and use IDs and passwords at pay sites. Never share your credit card or account information (logon and passwords) with anyone online outside of a verifiably secure Web site. Avoid e-commerce activities with companies you can't be pretty certain are legitimate. Finally, remember that companies out to scam you will try to make themselves look as much like the real thing as possible.

Ensuring Privacy and Security Online

Successfully protecting your *privacy* and personal security online includes understanding how Web sites track your activity using cookies and other behind-the-scenes systems; not sharing personal or family information with

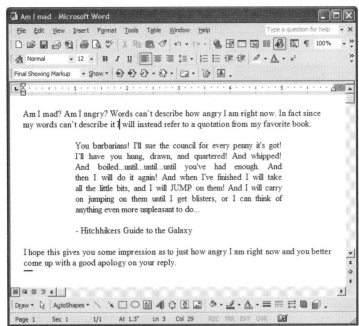

Figure 30.4: Quoting another work, in this case a block quote

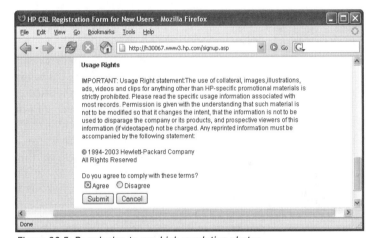

Figure 30.5: Permission to use high resolution photos

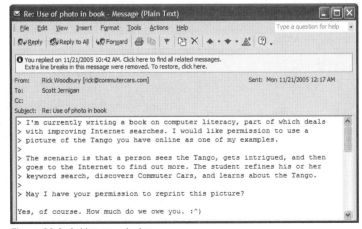

Figure 30.6: Asking permission

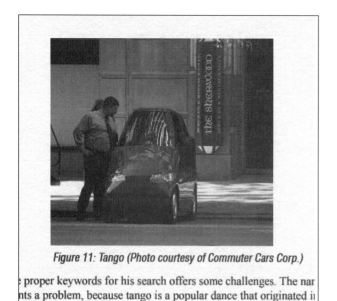

Figure 11: Tango (Photo courtesy of Commuter Cars Corp.)

proper keywords for his search offers some challenges. The nar
nts a problem, because tango is a popular dance that originated ii

Figure 30.7: Proper cite

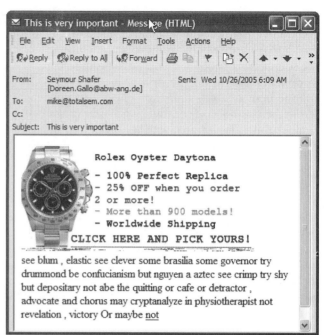

Figure 30.8: Too good to be true!

Derivative Works

If you take a picture off of someone else's Web page, change it slightly—or even a whole lot—and then claim it as yours you have just created a derivative work. Derivative works are just as illegal and immoral as plagiarized works! Don't do it!

unknown people or in public places; and using aliases when communicating in public forums.

You read about cookies in Chapter 26, but here's a quick refresher. A *cookie* is a small text file containing information about you. The data stored in cookies is used to authenticate or identify you as a registered user of a Web site, so it will remember you next time you access that Web site. Cookies are also used to keep track of the shopping basket of goods you select to buy from a site. Cookies enable sites to present different looks and content to different users, and to track your access to the site, including what products you look at, even if you don't buy them. Some browsers and browser add-ins can be set to partially or completely block cookies.

By not revealing personal or family information, and by using aliases when you join in public discussions online, you protect yourself against those who might want to impersonate you. Asking you to provide pieces of personal information, such as your mother's maiden name, is a standard method used by online merchants to authenticate you when you want to retrieve a password (Figure 30.9). A bad guy who knows that information could use it to gain access to your account. By protecting identifying personal information and using aliases, you can protect your identity from snooping bad guys.

Restricting Access

Not only is it important that *you* protect your personal information, organizations you deal with have reason to protect it too. Institutions like schools, hospitals, and government agencies store a great deal of personal and confidential information, which they must protect. Online businesses regularly gather sensitive information to which they restrict access, like credit card numbers from their customers (Figure 30.10).

Beyond the security issues, there are other reasons that some users will restrict access. Parents want to prevent their children from accessing Web sites with adult content, for example, and companies want their employees to avoid online shopping and other non-business-related sites while on the clock.

Figure 30.9: Password request form

You can use a variety of tools and strategies to restrict access to computer data, such as keeping restricted information on secure computers or behind firewalls, and establishing security procedures. Besides obvious strategies like personal supervision of computer users, technical solutions like specialized Internet blocking software and monitoring programs enable you to restrict access to Internet sites.

Firewalls

A firewall is anything—a piece of hardware on your network or a special program running on your computer—that tries to stop bad things from getting into your computer. There are three important words here: "bad things" and "tries." Anything or anyone you don't want on your computer is a *bad thing*. A black hat trying to take control of your system, an e-mail with a virus, or a user trying to download illegal music; all of these are bad things. The word "tries" is important, because no firewall stops every bad thing from entering your computer. Without a firewall, though, it's a 100% guarantee that bad things will get to your computer.

Every organization that connects to the Internet should have a *hardware firewall*—a special device that sits between your network and the Internet that acts as your first level of defense against bad things that come from the Internet (Figure 30.11). Professionally trained computer support people tell these firewalls what types of evilness to watch for and filter.

If you want more protection you need a personal firewall. A *personal firewall*, also called a software firewall, is a program that runs on your computer, watching for anything that your hardware firewall misses. Even a well-configured hardware firewall probably won't stop certain types of bad things. For example, very few hardware firewalls stop e-mail messages with a virus attached. Personal firewalls are inexpensive (most are free and most computers have one preinstalled) and do a great job at protecting your system. Figure 30.12 shows a typical personal firewall at work.

It's your job to install a personal firewall and to monitor it. If you're in an organization, talk to the computer people and ask them if they mind you installing one. If you're at home, then grab one and install it.

Who's Using Your Name
Try entering the name of the site as part of your name. For example, if Tammi Smith enters her name into a form at the www.abcfoo.com Web site, she would say her first name is "Tammiabcfoo." If she gets spam from another source addressed to "Dear Tammiabcfoo," she knows that the abcfoo people either sold or gave her information to someone else!

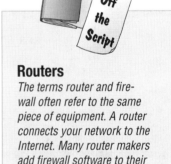

Routers
The terms router and firewall often refer to the same piece of equipment. A router connects your network to the Internet. Many router makers add firewall software to their routers, thus giving the routers two jobs.

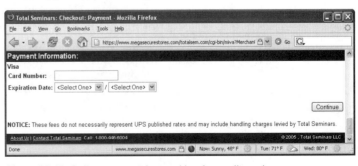

Figure 30.10: Online payment form asking for credit card

Blocking Software

Firewalls do a good job of keeping bad things out of your computer, but they do little to stop someone from going out and doing bad things such as looking at adult Web pages, chatting online when you should be doing your homework, or downloading illegal music. An *Internet blocker* is a piece of software or a hardware device that stops certain online activities. You can use Internet blocking software to save users from themselves. Figure 30.13 shows a typical Internet blocker in action.

Like firewalls, Internet blockers come in both hardware and software varieties. If you're in a school, there's a pretty high probability that you've got a hardware-based blocker. Those at home need to install their own blocker.

Unlike firewalls, good-quality Internet blockers rarely come with your computer, requiring you to research and then buy the one that works best for you. (Project #2 for this chapter has you doing that very research!) You can customize your Internet blocker to define exactly what you want to block and what you want to allow. Internet blockers not only block, but also keep a log of all attempts to access blocked areas so keep that in mind when you use a computer with an Internet blocker (Figure 30.14)!

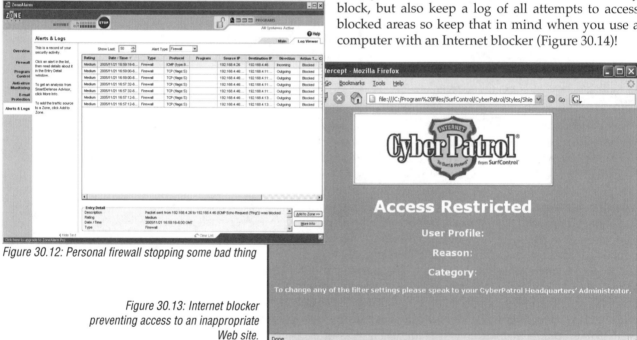

Figure 30.11: Typical hardware firewall

Figure 30.12: Personal firewall stopping some bad thing

Figure 30.13: Internet blocker preventing access to an inappropriate Web site.

Monitoring Software

Monitoring software doesn't stop users from doing any evil—it just tells someone else when a user does something against the rules. A supervisor or parent installs monitoring software on a computer and there is no way for the person using that computer to know the software is installed. The monitoring software records every e-mail, Web sites visited, and online chat performed on the system, and then shows the person who installed the program what was done (Figure 30.15). Good monitoring programs even watch for certain cue words and send the person who installed the program an e-mail to let him or her know that the user is going somewhere they shouldn't go.

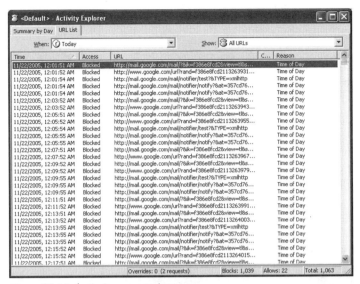

Figure 30.14: Analyzing your actions

Computer Citizenship

Being a responsible user of computers and the Internet involves more than just staying safe and not infringing on the rights of others. A responsible user of computers and the Internet keeps up with advances in technology, takes into account issues such as protecting the environment, and helps everyone get access to technology.

Keeping Up with Technology (so it doesn't freight-train you)

Internet bad guys don't rest when it comes to thinking up new ways to steal information and disrupt the lives of computer users, and as a user, you can't either. You should stay informed about the availability of product upgrades, and check for new virus threats. Regular checks for updated virus definitions and Windows security patches, for example, are critical to maintaining adequate protection against viruses and online baddies.

Many people stay current by reading trade magazines, like *PC Magazine* or *PC World*. If you find you love computers, then *Maximum PC* is the magazine for you (Figure 30.16).

Figure 30.15: Monitoring software at work

Figure 30.16: Maximum PC, the best computer magazine on the planet!

Old School Monitoring "Software"

If you need to monitor the computer activity of someone, but don't have access to fancy monitoring software, you can always fall back on the tried and true method of monitoring: stand over his or her shoulder and watch what happens. For some reason, most people don't break the rules when someone can see them do it!

Overlap

Firewalls, especially personal firewalls and Internet blockers often overlap in terms of what they do. Users need to try different programs until they come up with a combination that makes sense for what they need.

Recycling and Safe Disposal of Hazardous Materials

An important and relatively easy way to be an environmentally conscious computer user is to *recycle*. Recycling products such as paper and printer cartridges not only keeps them out of overcrowded landfills, it ensures that the more toxic products are disposed of in just the right way. Safely disposing of hardware containing hazardous materials, such as computer monitors, protects both people and the environment.

Paper

Printing makes a lot of trash so think before you print. Before you print, say to yourself: "Do I really need a paper copy?" Also, most applications that support printing come with a "print preview" feature that enables you get a good idea of what the print job will look like (Figure 30.17). Use it to prevent unnecessary reprints. Last, you should reuse the back sides of waste paper for those print jobs that don't need to be pretty.

Figure 30.17: Print Preview

The biggest source of waste paper accumulates right next to your printer due to bad quality prints or prints that weren't what was expected. Keep a recycle bin next to every printer to make sure all that waste paper makes it to the recycler (Figure 30.18). (It's also a great place to find scrap paper!)

Print Cartridges

Never throw your used printer cartridges in the trash! A lot of folks want those cartridges. All print cartridge makers provide a free recycle service: they send you the envelope and pay for the postage, and you just mail it to them. See if you can locate a local printer recycler—many of them will come and pick up your used cartridges for free, and a few pay you for them!

Computers

Anyone who's ever tried to sell a computer more than three or four years old learns a hard lesson: they're not worth much, if anything at all. It's a real temptation to take that old computer and just toss it in the garbage, but you should never do that!

First of all, many parts of your computer—such as your computer monitor—contain hazardous materials that pollute the environment. Luckily, thousands of companies now specialize in computer recycling and will gladly accept your old computer. If you have enough computers, they might even pick them up. If you can't find a recycler, call your local municipality's waste authority to see where to drop off your system.

An even better alternative for your old computer is donation. Many organizations actively look for old computers to refurbish and to donate to schools and other organizations. Just keep in mind that the computer can't be *too* old— not even a school wants a computer more than five or six years old.

Sharing

Sharing your knowledge and experience with others in your school, place of employment, and community is an important aspect of computer citizenship. By donating unused computer equipment to needy persons or organizations, you essentially recycle the material, while helping those in need.

You don't have to have computers to donate to be a good cyber-citizen. Everyone has some knowledge and experience to share. Volunteer at a non-profit organization. Helping others learn how to benefit from technology can be a rewarding way to share your interest in computers, and teaching others is the best way to learn something!

Figure 30.18: Recycle bin where it belongs

Maintaining a Safe Working Environment Rules of the Road

- Most organizations have written policies on how you use the Internet on their computers. If you're in an organization, read these policies to make sure you know what you may and may not do!

- Work you create on your own computer is your own intellectual property. Work created on computers you don't own at work or at home may or may not be yours.

- Everything on the Internet is someone's intellectual property and is subject to trade and copyright laws. You cannot copy anything from the Internet for your own use unless the creator has given you express permission.

- With the concept of fair use, you can use someone else's content without getting permission first in some circumstances, such as using limited excerpts from another author's work when you review or analyze it. The idea behind fair use is that copyrights should not be used to block discussion and analysis, especially if the context is educational or political.

- You can get permission to use things you find online by reading copyright information in an About page on a Web site, or checking the Press sections at larger companies. If you can't find permission granted or denied online, e-mail the site owner and ask.

Safe Surfing

- E-commerce makes the Web powerful and useful, but adds its own set of dangers. Protect yourself when you do business online by double-checking the legitimacy of online offers, and never giving out credit card or personal information to strangers or on non-secure sites.

- Keep your cookies under control. Don't give out family information, because scammers can use this to steal your identity, never a good thing.

- Use hardware and software firewalls to protect your computer and your data from black hats and other bad people who want to steal from you. Use Internet blocking software to stop certain online activity, like accessing questionable sites. This helps protects children from some of the seamier or dangerous sides of the Web. Finally, use monitoring software to track what users do on a computer.

Computer Citizenship

- Stay informed about the availability of product upgrades, and check for new virus threats. Read computer magazines, such as PC World, to keep up with developments in software and hardware. Knowing what's out there can help you protect yourself and others.

- Recycle products such as paper and printer cartridges to keep them out of overcrowded landfills. This also ensures that the more toxic products are disposed of in just the right way.

- Share your knowledge and experience with others. Donate your old computers. Donate your skills and your time to charitable causes. You have no idea how powerful a difference you can make in someone's life!

Key Terms

Cookie

Copyright

Derivative works

E-commerce

Fair use

Freeware

GNU General Public License (GPL)

Hardware firewall

Intellectual property

Internet blocker

Monitoring software

Patent

Personal firewall

Privacy

Plagiarism

Recycle

Trademark

Key Term Quiz

Use the Key Terms list to complete the following sentences. Not all the terms will be used.

1. Things you create on your own computer are your _____.

2. Taking an image from a site and changing it in some fashion creates a _____, which you cannot legally claim as your own work.

3. A program running on your machine that protects against bad things coming from the Internet is called a _____.

4. Always _____ paper and ink cartridges, instead of throwing them in the trash.

5. If you use someone else's words and don't cite the source, you commit _____.

6. Programmers can license _____ through the GNU GPL.

7. You own the _____ to things you create, so no one can copy them without your permission.

8. A symbol or distinctive name used by an organization or business is a _____, which can't be used by others without permission.

9. Software such as _____ programs can stop users from doing certain activities online, like accessing questionable Web sites.

10. A device that sits between your computer and the Internet and stops bad things from getting in is called a _____

Multiple Choice Questions

1. Which of the following would be viable computer-use polices for a business?
   A. No personal phone calls
   B. No personal surfing to questionable sites
   C. No personal items on monitor
   D. No personal use of fax machine

2. What term best describes posting untrue information on a Web site that harms someone?
   A. Dastardly
   B. Libel
   C. Plagiarism
   D. Slander

3. What's a good source for policies regarding computer use at a business?
   A. Lunch room
   B. Company president
   C. Personnel department
   D. Fellow employees

4. Who owns any work you do on a computer at school?
   A. You own it.
   B. The school owns it.
   C. Everyone owns it—information wants to be free.
   D. It's kind of murky.

5. What type of intellectual property protection can you get on a product you invent?
   A. Copyright
   B. Fair use
   C. Name
   D. Patent

6. John quoted part of *Moby Dick* in an essay on fish stories. Marie claimed he plagiarized by including it. What did John forget to do?
   A. Cite the source
   B. Underline the quotation
   C. Fairly use the quotation
   D. Nothing; you can't use stories written by other people.

7. Which of the following must you do when including content from another source under fair use principles?
   A. Indent both sides of the quotation an extra inch
   B. Italicize the quotation
   C. Use single quotation marks
   D. Cite the source

8. What can you do legally with software that's licensed under the GNU GPL? (Select all that apply.)
   A. Download the software
   B. Sell the software
   C. Change the software
   D. Claim it as yours

9. What do you call the process of buying and selling goods over the Internet?
   A. E-commerce
   B. E-mail
   C. E-buy
   D. E-bay

10. What should you never share with unknown people on the Internet?
    A. Credit card number
    B. Your name
    C. Your address
    D. All of the above

11. What type of software enables Web sites to track the contents of your shopping cart?
    A. Blockers
    B. Cookies
    C. Programs
    D. Trackers

12. True or false? Parents should restrict access to the Internet for young children.
    A. True
    B. False

13. What sort of software can tell you every Web site a user accesses?
    A. Application software
    B. Internet blocking software
    C. Software firewalls
    D. Monitoring software

14. What type of software can log attempts to access unauthorized Web sites?
    A. Application software
    B. Internet blocking software
    C. Software firewalls
    D. Monitoring software

15. Once you gain excellent computer skills, what can you do with them to benefit the community?
    A. Share your knowledge
    B. Teach others
    C. Volunteer at a non-profit organization
    D. All of the above

Essays

1. Write a short essay describing the computer-use policy you use (or should use) at home.

2. Why is plagiarism bad? So what if you copy other people's work? Where's the harm? Give your answer in a short essay.

3. Write an essay from the point of view of a person who has been ripped off in an e-commerce deal. Describe what happened and how it made you feel. What could you do differently, or suggest to others that they do to avoid the same problem?

Projects

1. Locate and install two personal firewall applications, such as Zone Alarm and Kaspersky Anti-Hacker. Work with the software and make an assessment. Which do you prefer? Note that you'll need to assess the programs one at a time because they don't play nicely together.

2. Do a Web search for Internet blocking software. Try searching on "internet blocker" or "internet blocking" in Google or Yahoo! What programs are highly rated? Can you find a review site? What can these programs do beyond blocking Web sites?

COMPUTER LITERACY: YOUR TICKET TO IC³ CERTIFICATION

Index

Symbols

COMPUTER LITERACY: YOUR TICKET TO IC³ CERTIFICATION

W

X

Y

Z

Simulations on CD-ROM

Part One – Computing Fundamentals

Section	Competency	Description

Chapter 6: Getting to Know You – Navigating and Managing Windows

Section	Competency	Description
IC³-1	3.2.2	Manipulate windows: maximize, minimize, resize, move, and close
IC³-1	3.2.3	Shut down, restart, log on and off the computer. Shut down non-responding applications.
IC³-1	3.2.4	Windows Start menu and taskbar: start programs, switch between programs, shortcuts on Start menu, online help, and version of Windows
IC³-1	3.2.5	Manipulate folders and icons: create, delete, move, rename, and display properties of folders and icons
IC³-1	3.2.6a	Windows Explorer/File Manager basics; start Explorer, file structure, folders, applications and documents, expand and collapse directory tree
IC³-1	3.2.6b	Folders in Windows Explorer; open folders, sort files, create, delete, copy and move folders
IC³-1	3.2.6c	Files in Windows Explorer; select, delete, copy, move and rename files, recover from Recycle bin, file properties
IC³-1	3.2.6d	Searching in Windows Explorer, use Find command, use * and ? search characters
IC³-1	3.2.6e	Formatting floppy diskettes

Chapter 7 – Taking Control of Windows

Section	Competency	Description
IC³-1	3.3.1 and 3.3.3	Windows Control Panel: date/time, display, audio, mouse and keyboard settings
IC³-1	3.3.4	Install Printers; display, add, and delete printers

Chapter 8 – Computer Applications

Section	Competency	Description
IC³-1	3.3.6	Install software: back up, install, and uninstall software; Add/Remove Programs; start applications

Part Two – Key Applications

Section	Competency	Description

Chapter 11 – Common Features of Windows Applications

IC³-2	1.1.1 and 1.1.2	Open and close applications: Word, Excel, and PowerPoint
IC³-2	1.1.4	Help files: software help, help search, and online help
IC³-2	1.2.2	Toolbars: display and hide toolbars
IC³-2	1.2.3	Multiple files; switch between open files
IC³-2	1.2.4 and 1.2.5	File views and magnification: Normal, Layout, Print Views, and Zoom

Chapter 12 – Working with Documents

IC³-2	1.2.6	Create files: create, use templates
IC³-2	1.2.7	Open files: open, file extensions and application associations
IC³-2	1.2.8 and 1.2.9	Save and close files; save, save as, file structure, save and close files

Chapter 13 – Editing Documents

IC³-2	1.3.1	Navigate open files: scroll bars, keyboard shortcuts, and Go To option
IC³-2	1.3.2 and 1.3.3	Simple editing: insert text and numbers, delete, backspace, insert/overtype, clear
IC³-2	1.3.4 through 1.3.7	Editing tools: undo, redo, repeat, find, replace, and spell check
IC³-2	1.3.8	Text formatting: fonts, bold, underline, italics, superscript, subscript, text alignment
IC³-2	1.3.9 and 1.3.10	Insert and manipulate graphics: insert pictures and clip art, resize, move, copy, crop, and delete graphics
IC³-2	1.3.11	Drawn objects: drawing tools, line, fill style, color, layering, grouping
IC³-2	2.1.2	Select text: word, line, paragraph, and document

Section	Competency	Description

Chapter 17 – Advanced Word Processing Skills

Section	Competency	Description
IC³-2	2.1.8 and 2.1.9	Date and time, comments: format and insert date and time in a document; insert, view, and print comments
IC³-2	2.1.13 and 2.1.14	Header, footer, and page numbers: create, modify, and format headers and footers; insert, modify, and format page numbers
IC³-2	2.2.15	Footnotes and endnotes: create, modify, and format footnotes and endnotes
IC³-2	2.1.20	Track changes: display and hide track changes; accept or reject changes

Chapter 18 – Basic Spreadsheet Skills

Section	Competency	Description
IC³-2	3.1.2 and 3.1.3	Selecting data in Excel: select cells, rows, columns, ranges, and worksheet
IC³-2	3.1.4	Excel structure: insert and delete cells, rows, columns and worksheets, row height, column width and AutoFit
IC³-2	3.18 through 3.1.8	Formatting Excel documents: number, currency, date/time and percent format, borders and shading, merge cells, wrap text, and AutoFormats

Chapter 19 – Advanced Spreadsheet Skills

Section	Competency	Description
IC³-2	3.2.1 and 3.2.3	Excel sort and formulas; one and two criteria sort, +, -, *, /, ^ and parentheses
IC³-2	3.2.4 through 3.2.7	Excel functions: SUM, AVERAGE, MAX, MIN, COUNT, worksheet functions, AutoSum
IC³-2	3.2.10	Excel charts: insert and modify charts; chart types; modify data, labels, legend, and titles

Chapter 20 – Slide Presentation Skills

Section	Competency	Description
IC³-2	4.1.2 and 4.1.3	Managing slides in PowerPoint: create, format, delete slides; outline view; apply bullets and numbering
IC³-2	4.1.3	Adding content in PowerPoint: insert and edit pictures and clip art; adding tables, charts, borders, and shading; using design templates
IC³-2	4.1.4 through 4.1.8	Modifying slides in PowerPoint: outline, slide layout, and slide master views; change slide layout; modify background; slide transitions and slide sorter
IC³-2	4.1.9 through 4.1.11	PowerPoint presentations: speaker notes, handouts, slide presentation navigation

Part Three – Living Online

Chapter 23 – E-mail in the 21st Century

Section	Competency	Description
IC³-3	2.2.1	Basic e-mail: read, create, send, view, reply, reply all, and forward e-mail; search and sort e-mail
IC³-3	2.2.3 and 2.2.5	E-mail addresses and attachments: attach, open, save, and delete attachments; create, modify and delete addresses in address book

Chapter 24 – Effective E-mail

Section	Competency	Description
IC³-3	2.2.4	Organize e-mail: Inbox, Outbox, and mail folders; mark and flag e-mail; select, save, delete, and back up e-mail

Section	Competency	Description

Chapter 26 – Web Essentials

Section	Competency	Description
IC³-3	3.2.2 and 3.2.3	Basic Web browsers: URLs, text and graphic links, forward and back buttons, browser home page, web site home page, reload and refresh
IC³-3	3.2.4 through 3.2.6	Browser history, links and bookmarks; add, edit, organize, and delete bookmarks
IC³-3	3.2.7	Save Web site content: save sites and HTML documents for offline browsing
IC³-3	3.2.8 and 3.2.9	Copy and print from Web sites: copy text and graphics; print all or part of Web site
IC³-3	3.2.10 and 3.2.11	Downloads and browser settings: downloading, browser security and privacy settings, cookies, and default browser home page

Chapter 27 – Finding Information on the Internet

Section	Competency	Description
IC³-3	3.3.3 and 3.3.4	Searching: search engines, Boolean searches

Notes:

COMPUTER LITERACY: YOUR TICKET TO IC³ CERTIFICATION

About the CD-ROM

The CD-ROM included with this book contains several useful resources that will help you learn the material and prepare for the IC3 Certification exams. The CD-ROM has a menu driven interface for accessing each of the resources. The interface opens automatically when you put the CD in your computer. If for any reason it does not open, go to My Computer and double-click your CD- or DVD-media drive. To open the interface, double-click the Launch. exe file. Below is a list of the resources and a brief description of each.

eBook

An electronic (eBook) version of the entire book is included on the CD-ROM. The eBook is for your reference and cannot be copied or printed. It is a violation of copyright law to distribute or give a copy of the eBook to anyone without express written permission from the publisher.

Simulations

The CD-ROM includes over 60 simulations to help you practice and learn the material. The simulations supplement the discussions in the book and give you visual step-by-step illustrations of how to perform various tasks. Not every chapter contains material that lends itself to simulations. A list of simulations, by chapter where applicable, is included after the Index.

The simulations enable you to learn to use Microsoft Word, PowerPoint, Excel, and other applications, even if you don't have those applications installed. All you need is Windows.

Chapter Review Questions

The CD-ROM contains chapter review questions. There are multiple choice questions, essay questions, and projects for each chapter. These files are printable and intended for your review. The answers to the questions are included in the Instructor materials that are available from ELKS Learning, a subsidiary of Total Seminars. For more information, contact sales@totalsem. com.

Exam Objectives

A complete listing of the IC3 exam objectives is included for your reference and to help you prepare for the exams.